W9-CGV-563

DOUBLES
Studies in Literary History

KARL MILLER

Oxford New York
OXFORD UNIVERSITY PRESS
1987

Oxford University Press, Walton Street, Oxford OX2 6DP
Oxford New York Toronto
Delhi Bombay Calcutta Madras Karachi
Petaling Jaya Singapore Hong Kong Tokyo
Nairobi Dar es Salaam Cape Town
Melbourne Auckland
and associated companies in
Beirut Berlin Ibadan Nicosia

Oxford is a trade mark of Oxford University Press

First published 1985
First issued (with corrections) as an
Oxford University Press paperback 1987

British Library Cataloguing in Publication Data
Miller, Karl
Doubles: studies in literary history.—(Oxford paperbacks)
1. Multiple personality in literature 2. American literature—19th century—History and criticism 3. American literature—20th century—History and criticism
4. Multiple personality in literature
I. Title
810.9'353 PS169.M8
ISBN 0-19-282047-8

Library of Congress Cataloging in Publication Data
Miller, Karl, 1931–
Doubles: studies in literary history.
Includes index.
1. English literature—History and criticism.
2. Doubles in literature. 3. Split self in literature.
4. American literature—History and criticism.
I. Title
PR409.D68M5 1987 820'.9'27 84-27207
ISBN 0-19-282047-8

Printed in Great Britain by
The Guernsey Press Co. Ltd.
Guernsey, Channel Islands

Family Life

I thought I saw my mother. There were snaps
Of someone else's children in her hand.
A picture that affected me. But then
I'd never been to see her very much.

Mother of my dreams, who knew the hand she held.
Tracked to her dingy room in some frail place,
Flat out in bed. And yet it was as if
I had to break the door down to get in.

James Darke

Look, this is my nose; a big one of the northern type, with a hard bone somewhat arched and the fleshy part tipped up and almost rectangular. And that is his nose, a perfect replica of mine. Here are the two sharply drawn furrows on both sides of my mouth with lips so thin as to seem licked away. He has got them, too. Here are the cheekbones—but this is a passport list of facial features meaning nothing; an absurd convention. Somebody told me once that I looked like Amundsen, the Polar explorer. Well, Felix, too, looked like Amundsen. But it is not every person that can recall Amundsen's face. I myself recall it but faintly, nor am I sure whether there had not been some mix-up with Nansen. No, I can explain nothing.

Vladimir Nabokov, *Despair*

PREFACE TO PAPERBACK EDITION

The present edition incorporates corrections. A few words have been changed, and a few added. Some of these further words are meant to bring out the dependence of nineteenth-century duality on the language of alchemy. The story mentioned here of David Hume's youthful owning-up was preceded by a similar, but different, story told by Launce in *Two Gentlemen of Verona*. This was a point which was noted when the book appeared, and it is one which would have been worth noting in a book on doubles. I don't think it shows that no such action can have been performed by Hume.

PREFACE

An aunt of mine lived, at the end of her days, in an old people's home, where the shoe pinched and she used to run away. She would then fall down, and be captured and brought back. I once stood reasoning with her. She whirled around dizzily before me, a little bird-like dervish, not altogether in touch with her whereabouts, or her visitor. 'If you keep running away, you'll fall on your nose again.' 'I recognize it,' she replied. 'But I'll do it. I'll be running away for the rest of my life. I'm two people rolled up into one.'

In former times she had never budged, had been staunch, and now and then severe: it was as if she had reserved the second nature of her departures for her second childhood, having been confronted by impulses which must, for the best part of eighty years, have been covered over and denied. She had come to experience the orphaning of the old. She lived in the past, and admitted to 'idiosyncrasies', and the law of her land had judged her an *incapax*. But she still possessed marvellous capacities. Her speech was a marvellous capacity. And her land was Scotland, where the sentiments I have quoted have often been heard. Her words belong to, and describe, the cultural heritage which is called in this book by the name of duality. Rolling up and running away are a long story, and I shall now try to tell it.

In seeking to demonstrate a continuity that proceeds from the Romantic period to the present, to lay stress on features of congruence, influence, movement, and arrest, I have referred to a wide variety of texts and occasions. But I can't claim that I am able to tell the whole story. Many features of the Continental experience are no more than adumbrated here; and I would have liked to write at greater length about certain contributors to the Anglo-American tradition—Twain, for instance, and Pater. No doubt the book is long enough as it is. It opens in the Romantic period with a cardinal text, James Hogg's *Confessions*, and goes on to matters of definition, to specimens of duality drawn from the romantic modern world of more recent times, and to the themes of isolation and escape, suffering and salvation. The idea of an after-life is treated, on the grounds that duality can appear to envisage for the individual a symbiosis which unites the injuring of a community with injuries which that community inflicts, and to dream of a heaven in which some part of the human totality survives these injuries. Thereafter the book advances chronologically from the Romantic period to the present day. It offers accounts of some latter-day living examples, by which I mean human beings who have testified to an experience of duality. Almost all of them are people I have known; all but one are now dead. A good deal is said about the last two decades of the nineteenth century—duality's heyday, as we currently suppose, though there have been two heydays at least in the course of the past two hundred years, and we may even be in the midst of a third. The subject has by no means been dropped.

The concern throughout is literary, rather than psychological or philosophical. I am writing about the dynamic metaphor of the second self, which was to conjure up, over these past two hundred years, the hallucinated double of ancient superstition, to generate, in popular and para-medical contexts, the hypothesis of a supervention, within the individual, of autonomous and adversary selves, and to transform the understanding and practice of literature. The double stands at the start of that cultivation of uncertainty by which the literature of the modern world has come to be distinguished, and has yet to be expelled from it. This is a large claim: but no larger than claims that could well be made for the importance of the subject in other spheres. Duality was to take part both in the Freudian and in the Russian revolutions: to the second of these it brought the dialectic of Hegel, with its progressive leaps and interplay of opposites, and it also brought the quasi-religious duo of exploiters and exploited, 'them' and 'us'. Marriage came to be conceived—by Yeats, for instance, and D. H. Lawrence—as a union of complementary opposites, and so did many other human arrangements.

'It is true all things have two faces, a light one and a dark': Thomas Carlyle opens the fourth chapter of *Past and Present* with a doubt which may be thought to wear the two faces of a truth and of a truism. It can never have been hard to believe, after a fashion, in faces, which is to say in doubles; to believe that every cloud has its silver lining, and every silver lining its cloud; to believe in the prevalence and primacy of choice, compromise and complication. But Carlyle lived at a time when it could often be devoutly held that all things are double and that there is an innate duality of man; and there was a time to come when an infinite contradiction, a boundless empire of irony and uncertainty, began to be credited. This book is sceptical about certain aspects of the historically-recurrent tendency to see the subject of duality as sovereign, to theorize it as such, and as such, as a basis for the treatment of madness and mental breakdown, to put it into clinical practice. But the book is not meant to be a work of literary history in which all theory is suspect, and the seventeenth chapter pays tribute to the psychology of Gardner Murphy for the truths it has to tell concerning the divided mind.

Reference is also made to theoretical writings of a more speculative order—in a work, however, which mainly consists of an attention to fictions, to the deliriums, impasses and impossibilities which are encountered in these fictions, and to the words—words like 'steal', 'strange', 'compound', 'inconsistency'—of which they are composed. More might have been said about such speculations than I have been able to say. At the end of the book, for instance, more might have been said about the simultaneous entertainment and overthrow of dualistic outlooks which can be ascribed to the arguments of Structuralism and Deconstruction. Lacan's writings are literally speculative in the sense that they have related the development of language capacity, and of the imagination of an ideal and integral self, to the child's dealings with mirrors. The image glimpsed there is thought to be perceived as the same as the child but different: and these are glimpses which reiterate the *alter idem*, the second self, of the many-mirrored, gleaming literature of romantic duality.

I feel it can be claimed that the writings of Lacan, and of Derrida, are intelligibly preceded by this literature, though there appear to be controversialists for whom the assimilation of the affairs of Deconstruction to the conscious concern with ambivalence exhibited in the nineteenth century counts as a vulgar error—for whom, as it were, the operations of 'intertextuality' pause or suspend themselves at this point. The error, if it *is* one, is committed in the present book, for which it cannot be accidental or trivial that a well-known modern theoretical dispute has been occasioned by a decipherment of the fiction of Edgar Allan Poe. In Poe's 'Purloined Letter' Lacan saw the truth of the Lacanian system—according to Derrida, who took the story to mean that there is no truth to be sought, beyond literature, by means of an understanding of literature's inherent ambivalence. In this dispute, the past is present. We have been told that Derrida's 'undecidable' is different from Hegelian contradiction, which is conscious, and impelled towards resolution, and the truth; we have been told that it is the unconscious of Hegelian contradiction. But if they are different, they are also the same. They are an example—as are the conscious and the unconscious mind—of a kind of duality in which these studies are interested.

In the light of Norman Mailer's latest novel, *Tough guys don't dance* (1984), I should try to avert the impression I may at one point be thought to give—that he has reneged on duality. Here once more in this whirling book is the vertiginous human being who can 'call upon two deep and divided halves of himself'. And since I shall be discussing the relationship between psychiatry's fugues and literature's flights, it may also be worth noting the emblematic fact that a fugue has lately been detected in the life of the far from whirling detective writer Agatha Christie. An entirely suitable element of mystery has been found to accompany it.

ACKNOWLEDGEMENTS

The book is dedicated to my daughter Georgia Miller, who helped me to write it—as did my wife Jane and my sons, one of whom, Sam Miller, compiled the index. I am grateful to Susannah Clapp, Mary-Kay Wilmers, Christopher Ricks, and Ian Hamilton for reading and discussing what I have written, to some of my students at University College London for various words of advice, to Kim Scott Walwyn of Oxford University Press for the care and consideration she has shown, and to Susan Oldacre and Hilary Clark for helping with the preparation of the manuscript and with items of research.

The author and publisher are grateful for permission to reprint the following copyright material.

Saul Bellow: from *The Victim* Copyright 1947 by Saul Bellow. Copyright © renewed 1974 by Saul Bellow. By permission of the publisher, Vanguard Press, Inc., and Laurence Pollinger Ltd. From, *Humboldt's Gift* (Secker/Viking, 1975). © Saul Bellow 1973, 1974, 1975, and from *The Dean's December* (Secker/Harper & Row, 1982). © Saul Bellow Limited 1982. By permission of A. M. Heath & Company Ltd., and Harriet Wasserman Literary Agency, Inc.

Anton Chekhov: from *Lady With Lapdog*, from Chekhov: *Lady With Lapdog & Other Stories*, trans. David Magarshack (Penguin Classics, 1964). Copyright © David Magarshack, 1964. Reprinted by permission of Penguin Books Ltd.

Fyodor Dostoevsky: from *The Insulted and Injured*, trans. Constance Garnett (Heinemann, 1915): from *The Double*, from Dostoevsky: *Notes from the Underground/The Double*, trans. Jessie Coulson (Penguin Classics, 1972). Copyright © Jessie Coulson, 1972: from *The Devils*, trans. David Magarshack (Penguin Classics. Revised edition 1971). Copyright © David Magarshack, 1953, 1971. Reprinted by permission of the publishers.

Robert Frost: extracts from 'Into My Own', 'An Equalizer', 'Away', 'To a Thinker In Office', 'The Road Not Taken',

'Build Soil'; and 'The Secret Sits' (complete), all from *The Poetry of Robert Frost*, edited by Edward Connery Lathem. Copyright 1916, 1934, © 1969 by Holt, Rinehart and Winston. Copyright 1936, 1942, 1944, © 1958, 1962 by Robert Frost. Copyright © 1964, 1970 by Lesley Frost Ballantine. Reprinted by permission of Jonathan Cape Ltd., on behalf of the editor and the Estate of Robert Frost, and Holt, Rinehart and Winston, Publishers.

Clive James: from *Unreliable Memoirs* (Jonathan Cape Ltd./Alfred A. Knopf, 1980). Copyright © 1980 by Clive James. Reprinted by permission of A. D. Peters & Co., Ltd., and Alfred A. Knopf, Inc.

Norman Mailer: from *Marilyn*, © 1973 by Norman Mailer; *Of Women and Their Elegance*, © 1980 by Norman Mailer; *The Executioner's Song,* © 1979 by Norman Mailer, Lawrence Schiller, and The New Ingot Company, Inc. Reprinted by permission of Scott Meredith Literary Agency Inc., New York.

Sylvia Plath: extracts from, *Letters Home Correspondence 1950–1963*, selected & edited by Aurelia Schober Plath (Harper & Row, 1975/Faber, n. e. 1978); and from 'The Moon and the Yew Tree', 'Edge' and 'Kindness' from *Ariel* (Faber 1965/Harper & Row 1966). © Ted Hughes 1965. Reprinted by permission of Olwyn Hughes.

Flora Rheta Schreiber: from *Sybil* (Penguin Books/Contemporary Books, Inc., 1975). Copyright © Flora Rheta Schreiber, 1973. Reprinted by permission of Contemporary Books Inc., and Penguin Books Ltd.

Every reasonable effort has been made to obtain permission to quote extracts still in copyright, where these extracts are in excess of the amount covered by 'fair dealing'.

CONTENTS

James Hogg by William Bewick
National Galleries of Scotland, Edinburgh

I. FLYING SCOTSMAN

The imaginative literature of duality speaks of the double, and of the orphan who may meet, or may be, that double. In 1824, in Scotland, a conjunction of the two appeared in James Hogg's *Confessions of a Justified Sinner*, which tells of the strange case of poor Robert Wringhim, who wishes to be a saint, to rise above the responsibilities of the human condition, and whose delusions of grandeur are turned, with the advent of a diabolical double, into the actions of a common criminal.[1] This is a protean book by a divided author. The James Hogg who wrote it is a flying Scotsman who shows a clean pair of heels, but he also has his feet on the ground. It has been romantically supposed an unaccountable work—and not to be by Hogg at all. It can in fact be accounted for in more ways than one, and in none that impugns Hogg's authorship. Even so, there is good reason to suppose it doubtful and indeterminate, and to suppose that the divided author effects an escape from criticism. What can't be done is described in a work which can never be fully known—a work which becomes the dilemma it reports. It is a work which may have been meant to be, and which has proved, a puzzle to the world.

Gothic precedents can be applied to it; it includes the international preoccupation with orphan and double which may be noticed in writings of the second decade of the nineteenth century; it alludes to the dualistic doctrine of Animal Magnetism. By now, the romantic novel, in its Radcliffian form, had been overtaken by the romantic lyric, in which the voice of the self-conscious grand exception can be heard; what the terror novel could do and what the lyric could do were done together in the 1820s, in works of autobiography and of autobiographical fiction. At the start of the decade, in Britain, stands Maturin's novel, *Melmoth*, in which a bad-tempered sympathetic demon attempts the souls of a cast of unfortunates. In De Quincey's *Confessions of an English Opium-Eater*, of 1822, an unfortunate takes geographical and chemical trips. Two years later came not only Hogg's *Confessions* but Scott's *Redgauntlet*, a specimen of the more innocently adventurous and sensational Gothic novel, in which he describes the double life of a bad-tempered sympathetic-Satanic Jacobite laird. Two years later still, the Scottish writer and doctor Robert Macnish published 'The Metempsychosis', a story in which an outcast turns into a delinquent, is offered a bargain which will restore his identity at the cost of his soul, and ends up a convinced Pythagorean, or metempsychosist, or reincarnationist.[2]

Both at this time and at times before, the Gothic writer was drawn to the conduct of the zealot, and to that of the hypocrite or whited sepulchre, such as 'Monk' Lewis's lascivious monk: piety and criminality were ambivalently regarded, and could be crossed and compounded in a single heart. Hogg's novel can be related to two earlier works of Gothic affinity where this theme is present. One of them is *Peregrinus Proteus* by the German poet Wieland.[3] The other is *The Devil's Elixir* by E. T. A. Hoffmann, the most influential of all the early Continental dualists. This was written in 1814, and translated by an Edinburgh friend of Hogg's at the time of the *Confessions*. Just as Hogg was later to write of a man 'turned into two men, acting on various and distinct principles',[4] Hoffmann writes of a world in which personality may be 'split into two hostile and contending powers'. His novel fashions the emblem of the knight, 'at variance' with himself, who fights with his double in a dark forest.[5] The theme of the two-faced is treated; the soul of man is attempted by the powers of darkness; duality and the outcast state are seen to be hereditary.

Some people have denied the importance for the novel of Hogg's knowledge of the Gothic mode, and have accounted for it instead in terms of the access enjoyed by 'the Ettrick Shepherd'—down in Edinburgh from his Border mountains, with the marks of a sheep-smearing 'legible', said Lockhart,[6] on his hands—to Scottish diablerie and other folklore. But there was no wall between the urban phenomenon of the Gothic novel and the superstitions of the countryside, and the one explanation does not exclude the other. Two confessions which stirred the city of Edinburgh when they were published there in the years that led up to the novel may also deserve to be taken into account. These are, or pretend to be, the very words of two great sinners and penitents, and in belonging, as they do, to the chapbook convention of the testament attributed to a malefactor under sentence of death, they may persuade us that part of Hogg's novel may be affecting a similar provenance.

A further edition of an old book, *The Confession of Nicol Muschet of Boghall*, was brought out in 1818. Muschet was executed for murdering his wife in 1721. The crime was committed in the valley below the hill of Arthur's Seat in Edinburgh, on the summit of which is located a crucial violence in Hogg's novel, and a cairn associated with the crime figures in Scott's *Heart of Midlothian*, which appeared soon after the new edition. Muschet claims to have been suborned, as Robert Wringhim is, by a devilish friend. James Campbell of Burnbank 'was the only viceregent of the devil to prompt me up to be guilty of all the following wickedness; which I greedily went on in, being so far inebriate with these wicked principles, which by degrees (after he understood how my natural temper was to be prevailed upon) he instilled into me'. This was 'the only person that ever tainted me with such hellish principles'. Muschet presently adds: 'I maliciously went on in many soul-destructive courses; and for my encouragement to do so, I wrested that place of Scripture concerning Manasseh, with many other instances wherein are held forth the riches of free grace and mercy, extended to great sinners.' But he still claims the benefit of those riches, and glories in God's 'catching me, Manasseh-like, in the thicket of affliction, opening my heart to repent, believe on his mercy'. Wringhim likewise wrests the Scriptural proofs for the Calvinist doctrine of election, of justification by faith, in order to find, in Bunyan's words, a grace abounding to the chief of sinners. Muschet's language corresponds to that of much of the Hogg text, which has the gift of tongues and employs both a vernacular Scots and an English which relies on the King James Bible, and on the eloquence of the pulpit and the Covenanter's, the martyr's, scaffold. In closing, Muschet alludes to Bunyan: 'And now I bid adieu to all earthly comforts and enjoyments; to this vain transitory world, the stage of sin and sorrow: and welcome heaven and eternal enjoyment of God and the Lamb, which, through faith in his blood, I, though the chief of sinners, hope to obtain.'[7] Wringhim's bitter end is that of a suicide. 'Farewell, world,' he writes, having lost all hope that he will be repaid in a better one.

A second recent publication which could well have appealed to Hogg is the picaresque *Life of David Haggart*, 'written by himself while under sentence of death', which came out in Edinburgh in 1821. His counsel was the historian Henry Cockburn, who left a holograph note in the copy now in the British Library:

> This youngster was my client when he was tried and convicted. He was a great villain. This life is almost all lies; and its chief curiosity consists in the strange spirit of lying, the indulgence of which formed his chief pleasure to the very last . . . .
>
> Being an eminent miscreant, the Phrenologists got hold of him, and made the notorious facts of his character into evidences of the truth of their system.
>
> He affected some decent piety just before he was hanged, and therefore the Saints took up his memory, and wrote monodies on him. His piety and the composition of the lies in this book broke out at the same time.

In his 'Phrenological Observations on the Cerebral Development of David Haggart', which were printed as an appendix to the first and second editions of the *Life*, the eminent George Combe found that the skull exhibited a 'great deficiency of conscientiousness', and he thought that two principles had been at war within this man: but Haggart's last state, according to his solicitor, was sufficiently Manasseh-like to give 'satisfaction to the respectable clergymen by whom he was attended'—Cockburn's Saints. In Hogg's novel, Wringhim's troubles are told twice: first by an editor and then by the sinner in person. This arrangement has been thought to derive from the alternating standpoints of the eighteenth-century epistolary novel. But it may also owe something to the many occasions in the past when a text, whether or not dubious or contentious, had been editorially presented. Haggart's *Life* is so presented—and Cockburn's notes could be called a further editorial intervention, which compounds the puzzle of what already existed in print by presenting the life as a pack of lies. Hogg's confession, and Haggart's, cry out for consideration by those currently interested in the enigma of the first-person narrative, and in the question of the responsibility of authors for their texts.

Antinomianism is a Christian code which had held that God's grace was sufficient not only to save such sinners as

Manasseh but to confer an immunity to the moral law. A possible awareness on Hogg's part of Antinomian controversies in the southern Scotland of the eighteenth century has been mooted.[8] But the ardours and vagaries of Scots religion were by no means a thing of the past. The old tempers—originating in the Reformation settlement and in the Covenanting initiatives—were still flying, had been rekindled, in Hogg's day. A sneering review of the novel—'His demon is no genius; nor is he'—complained that it had caricatured the opinions of 'the ultra-Calvinists of Scotland', opinions which were 'far from being obsolete'.[9] Quite apart from what was happening in the field of fine or fundamental theological contention, it was ultra-Calvinist to resent the intrusions of the state in the business of religion, and such resenters made up the 'Wild' party in the Church of Scotland—the Evangelical wing which flew off in 1843 to form the Free Kirk, thereby creating 'the Disruption'. The freedom they sought was not the freedom promised by a trust in God's grace, and a distrust of the criterion of conduct, or morals; it did not proclaim an adherence to the doctrine of justification by faith. It signified an escape from the institution of patronage, whereby livings were in the gift of landowners and subject to Erastian Court of Session control. But the two freedoms can't be kept severely apart. They were aspects of the same strain of fanaticism, the *perfervidum ingenium Scotorum* in matters of religion, which practised what it preached while preaching a hostility to practice, morality, and the state, and which, in the Romantic period, continued to draw the fire of the rationally enlightened. In other words, there were fanatics abroad in 1824 to whom Hogg's novel might have been felt to be addressing itself. Not many, however, appear to have been listening.

Some at least of Scotland's latter-day saints were justified sinners. Not long before the Disruption, in 1838, Henry Cockburn, historian and advocate and circuit judge, doomed such a saint to death in the Highlands. From the standpoint of an enlightened man who did not believe in ghosts, Cockburn tells the story of a fisherman, Malcolm McLean, whose attendant devil had induced him to perform the 'great deed' of stifling, 'Burking', his wife. 'Haunted' by his 'religious notions', McLean, from the island of Lewis, where the Free Kirk was to take strong root, was nevertheless, in other respects, a 'sound practical man'. At once practical and 'wild', McLean had suffered the ordeal of Hogg's justified sinner: 'He has got the better of the Devil at last, and is sure of defying him on the 11th of May.'[10] Thinking his notions mad, while also thinking him legally accountable for his actions, Cockburn writes of his ordeal with a balanced sympathy, and with mixed feelings. But his mixed feelings are very different from Hogg's. Hogg's sympathy is protean and orchestral. He could condemn enthusiasm and excess in matters of religion, and a wresting of the doctrine of justification by faith: but he could, as well, write tales favourable to the sufferings of the Covenanters, and there was a Hogg for whom religion was romantic and Wringhim's ordeal a great experience.

Hogg's divided mind is expressed by the division of his novel into, roughly speaking, two halves. The editor's narrative believes in reason and utility, sides with Robert Wringhim's enemies, and characterizes Wringhim's half-brother George Colwan as a generous-hearted, gentlemanlike 'spark'. Wringhim's narrative describes how his own wild ideas of freedom and election are confirmed for him by a distinguished stranger, Gil-Martin, who behaves like some foreign potentate but who turns out to be the Devil in disguise. Which of the two accounts is the right one? Those who disbelieve in ghosts and demons are unlikely to reject the editor's account out of hand: but *both* accounts could be right.

The Proteus we may find in the novel is far from simple. Gloomy Robert and his tempter Gil-Martin can sometimes be thought the same person: they are bound together by the cords, or chords, of a 'magnetic', Mesmeric sympathy, they ail in concert as the story proceeds, and both are hellishly unwell at the close. At the same time, Robert can also be thought the same person as George. When Robert senses that he is two persons, neither, as a rule, is '*myself*':[11] these persons tend to be George and Gil-Martin. And Gil-Martin has the knack of looking like both brothers. When the brothers fight on the top of Arthur's Seat, we may think of the knight in the dark forest, at variance with himself. When Robert follows George about in disapproval and is compared to his shadow, this shadowing makes us think that George is his own worst enemy.

Other aspects of this Proteus may be isolated. Robert's account tells of amnesias, in which he forgets his crimes: it is an attempt to account for this 'unaccountable' development. He speaks of what it may be to have 'two souls, which take possession of my bodily frame by turns, the one being all unconscious of what the other performs'. This accords with the tendency in modern psychology to define for multiple personality the requirement that there be states of amnesia, in which a central self is unable to remember what another self has done in a state of 'fugue'. The idea of 'lost time' is common both to Hogg's novel and to a modern 'true story' of multiple personality, *Sybil*:[12] 'one-half, or two-thirds of my time, seemed to me to be totally lost,' says the sinner. Modern psychology's fugues are related to Hogg's, and to romantic literature's, flights. His novel has fugues, and it has a final flight in which Robert seeks to escape his tormentor. As in the use of the words 'possession' and 'lost', the novel brings together the language of psychology, early and late, and the language of superstition.

Then again, in the manner of another novel of the time, Mary Shelley's *Frankenstein*, the narratives present Robert as an outcast and a monster, and a protean reading of the novel, a reading which joins Robert to a brace of ostensibly separate fictional selves, and distinguishes author from editor, has, I feel, to inquire into the origins of this monstrous misery—into the childhood of the justified sinner. A family situation, which is altered and partly effaced in the telling, and which partly corresponds to the one expounded for Frankenstein's monster, may seem to lie behind the novel, with Robert an imaginary orphan, the son of estranged parents who, having been rejected by his natural father, the laird, dreams for himself a resplendent 'real' father. The role of the preferred or imaginary father is successively played by the predestinarian divine, Wringhim, and by the friend Gil-Martin, who is therefore both Robert himself and the father he seeks, and seeks to escape. There are occasions in Robert's narrative when we hear the voice of the troubled child, and when we are given to understand how it is that the imaginary orphan may wish to fly, while also thinking himself expelled, from his 'native place'.[13] Robert's childhood contains a variety of troubles. He presents himself as having been the sort of clever boy who is liable to be jeered at, in Scotland, as a 'conceited gowk', but who is not clever enough to beat McGill in class. He takes his revenge on his rival by falsely denouncing him, and McGill's disturbing pre-eminence could be commemorated in the naming of his tormentor, Gil-Martin. A dislike of subordination, and of fathers, is widespread in the book, and is proteanly combined with a search for and a submission to authority.

Robert reports himself torn in adolescence between the lusts of the flesh and a hunger to be acknowledged one of the Elect: 'I went on sinning every hour, and all the while most strenuously warring against sin.' Soon afterwards, high and mighty, he is teaching a reprobate a lesson: the man is a worm, unable to grasp 'the opposing principles in the soul of man, correcting, modifying, and refining one another'. Hogg's *Confessions* may be regarded as having to do with a strenuous attempt to behave simultaneously as those opposites Robert and George. This does not affect its capacity to be read very differently: as the editor invites us to read it, or as a court might read it. It can, and should also, be read as the strange story of a lunatic, of an illegitimate son whose head is turned by his natural father's unnatural religious notions. In a later tale of Hogg's, firmly entitled the 'Strange Letter of a Lunatic', the hero is revealed as an alcoholic subject to autoscopic hallucinations, to the pesterings of a double, and the clinical, sceptical or reductive reading which this invites is equally possible for the *Confessions*. The novel is open to a multitude of readings, and the protean and reductive are compatible with one another, while also in some sense opposed.

Discussion of the dualistic character of the novel can be taken further by referring to its preoccupation with the word 'bound', a word that lends itself to puns. It is often used in the *Confessions*, which makes play with ideas of freedom and constraint: 'bound' can mean both these things. 'At one bound he was free': this is the language of adventure stories, which can be expected to avoid a pun which might advise us that we are all captive. Hogg, however, wants to write both about bounding or soaring free and about bounds in the sense of bonds or limits. Robert bounds free from the bonds of the flesh and of unregenerate society, he aspires to fall within the bounds of God's covenant with mankind: but he is also bound, 'as by magnetism', to his own, and mankind's, worst enemy. Hogg's interest in the subject of constraint can be called polyvalent: struck by his use of garters, John Carey[14] has considered the possibility of a deviant interest in 'bondage', but there is more to it than that.

The fanatics in the novel—the Wringhims, the possible natural father and his son—distinguish between two types of bond: there are 'the bonds of carnal nature' and 'the bonds and vows of the Lord'. The Wringhims hold that the bonds of carnal nature are no different from the 'bond of society on earth' which their adversary, the minister Blanchard, believes true religion to be—with the proviso that its principles should not be strained, in the manner of the Wringhims, 'beyond their due bounds'. The Wringhims and Blanchard are chalk and cheese, black and white. Hogg's names can be very expressive: for Blanchard, as for many readers of the novel, the Wringhims are wresters, wringers, of Reformation principles. Conversely, for Robert's reverend father, the 'earthly bonds and fellowships' believed in by Blanchard are 'absorbed and swallowed up in the holy community of the Reformed Church'. Wringhim then moves to the heart of the matter: 'To the wicked, all things are wicked; but to the just, all things are just and right.' These teachings impress and undo his son, who seeks to share 'the boundlessness of the true Christian's freedom', which is reserved for those 'born within the boundaries of the covenant of promise'. By interpreting the bounds of God's covenant as a perfect freedom, the fanatics in the novel are saying that the true Christian, who is one of a favoured few, is both sweetly bound and sweetly free, and they are joined by a demon who agrees with them.[15]

Gil-Martin completes Robert's corruption by developing his natural father's theme of the liberation of the Elect: Robert and Gil-Martin are knit together by 'an affection that has neither bounds nor interest', and this allegedly disinterested tempter assures Robert that his crimes are 'a specimen of that liberty by which the chosen and elected ones are made free'. Here, as elsewhere, the idea of freedom is coupled with the idea of rising, and of the risk of a fall: such crimes as his would have 'sunk an unregenerated person to perdition'. The boundless Christian, subject to the bonds and vows of the Lord, is able to raise himself above 'common nature' and 'common humanity'.

According to these ultra-Calvinists, the true Christian programme incorporates both bounding in the sense of soaring and the Medieval conception of an above and below, of nature and humanity as suspended between Heaven and Hell: a cosmology which ignores Copernicus and Galileo and from which few romantic people have been quite able to desist. Romantic people are great bounders, and so was Hogg, who participates in Robert's flights no less than he participates in the editorial caveats about the due bounds that religious soaring should observe. For Hogg, there was a flying religion and a comparatively earthbound religion of compassion and human solidarity, or bonding. In the *Confessions*, the two religions are run together dialectically, and a key occasion in the debate occurs when Robert, apprehensive about his flights, informs Gil-Martin that his friend's advice may render him 'a being either altogether above, or below the rest of my fellow creatures'. The dialectic is pervasive in romantic writing, and will frequently turn on the recognition that rises may be inseparable from falls. The romantic writer who endeavours to say goodbye to his fellow creatures may also be aware that the attempt to rise above humanity, while it may lead to some spiritually-privileged condition, to the condition of the saint, may just as well lead to an irrecoverable fall, to the condition of the outlaw, the monster or the beast.

The dialectic is apparent in the ironic praise awarded to romantic flight in Hogg's parody of Wordsworth: 'The Flying Tailor', a 'Further Extract from "The Recluse"'.[16] This mountain man is among the most sophisticated of parodists, and parodies are as natural as puns to the dualistic mode in literature. Their perpetrators see the funny side of a text to which they are likely to be sympathetically responsive; tempering the wind to their shorn lamb, they affirm, while also working against, what they imitate. Hogg here portrays the achievements of Hugh Thwaites, whose gymnastic 'bounds across the village green' are also the leaps of a fanciful, reclusive poet:

A pair
Of breeches to his philosophic eye

Were not what unto other folks they seem,
Mere simple breeches, but in them he saw
The symbol of the soul—mysterious, high
Hieroglyphics!

Conversely, Hogg's parody makes a pair of breeches of, let us say, the 'types and symbols of Eternity' glimpsed by Wordsworth as he crosses the Alps in Book Six of *The Prelude.* At the same time, we know from Hogg's other poems, which are rarely equal to the poetry of this parody, that he himself aspired to make imaginative leaps, to decipher the hieroglyphics of the ideal and the eternal. The mockery, and self-mockery, practised by him on this occasion—which ends with a premonition of the insulted and departed Keats of 'Adonais', in the shape of the prediction that the poet will one day be 'conspicuous like a star', and, for that matter, like Robert Wringhim, 'born an outcast' but destined to be 'conspicuous'—is no evidence to the contrary. At one point a philosophic eye picks out the principles of flight. We learn that sedentary people, like tailors, or indeed authors, must either jump or pine away, 'terminating in despair and death': but the passage also tells us that the 'excessive action' of flight 'tends unto repose'—a word which, in the meditative poetry of the eighteenth century, can suggest death. Both leaping and refraining, it seems, come to the same thing.

First, then, I would lay down this principle,
That all excessive action by the law
Of nature tends unto repose. This granted,
All action not excessive must partake
The nature of excessive action—so
That in all human beings who keep moving,
Unconscious cultivation of repose
Is going on in silence. Be it so.
Apply to men of sedentary lives
This leading principle, and we behold
That, active in their inactivity,
And unreposing in their long repose,
They are, in fact, the sole depositaries
Of all the energies by others wasted,
And come at last to teem with impulses

Of muscular motion, not to be withstood,
And either giving vent unto themselves
In numerous feats of wild agility,
Or terminating in despair and death.

Hogg must at this point have had especially in mind an extract, not from *The Recluse*, but from the third act of *The Borderers*—an extract favoured by Wordsworth himself, for he repeated it as an epigraph to 'The White Doe of Rylstone':

Action is transitory—a step, a blow,
The motion of a muscle—this way or that—
'Tis done, and in the after-vacancy
We wonder at ourselves like men betrayed:
Suffering is permanent, obscure and dark,
And shares the nature of infinity.

Action here is dualistically regarded: it can go either way. And it tends unto the repose of suffering.

The editorial Hogg of the *Confessions* does not refrain from the idea of a pre-Copernican heaven, but casts doubt on the space flights designed to reach it: 'the ways of heaven are altogether inscrutable, and soar as far above and beyond the works and the comprehensions of man, as the sun, flaming in majesty, is above the tiny boy's evening rocket.' The sinner deals with the same question of God's all but inaccessible remoteness in discoursing on the opposing principles in the hearts of men, and on the high heaven that overarches the earth. But the speech also holds out hope of access to heaven for a special category of human creature, sped by the infallible rocket of God's grace.

However abashed the editor may be by a sense, which even Robert shares at times, of God's mysterious remoteness, soaring is stoutly spoken for in the novel, and it can signify other things besides the hope of Heaven. The idea of a liberation from the state can hardly be thought to be exploited in the novel: but even Burns, for all his dislike of ultra-Calvinism, was capable of praising the Covenanters as freedom-fighters, and Hogg, who was able elsewhere to praise the Covenanters at length, would not have been ill at ease with the thought that there could be a Christian boundlessness which had in it a horror of state intrusion. Soaring certainly signifies, for Robert, a sense of social superiority, and a greed which he disowns but which feasts on his first father's estates. These help to make him, in the worst sense, a bounder. This outlaw craves the ordinary eminence which is widely mistaken for a species of spiritual elevation or exaltation. Robert's delusions include delusions of grandeur.

At the same time, he appeals to us because of the eminence of his misfortunes. Two decent, but also fallen, women—Mrs Logan, companion of George's father the laird, and the prostitute Bel Calvert—are determined to track down the criminal and bring him to justice. The two women are linked, as they go about their 'bounden duty', by Mrs Logan's 'unbounded generosity, and disinterestedness'. For them, as for the editor, Robert is a 'monster'. And yet he and Bel are alike. Bel's misfortunes are, as Robert's are, 'enough to stir up all the tender, as well as abhorrent feelings in the bosom of humanity'; both have been deceived by 'artful fiends', both have been abandoned.

George is another of the novel's cherished dupes and victims, and when Mrs Logan tends his body, arrayed in its wounds, in the coffin, it is the body of a suffering god. Afterwards, she seems to see the dead man arm-in-arm with his murderer, and the two women—by turns, magdalens and detectives—discuss this wonder. The thing is out of nature. Bel says: 'It is a phantasy of our disturbed imaginations.' But then Robert, too, is out of nature, being, as Mrs Logan puts it, an 'unnatural monster'. Where does nature end and fantasy begin? Romance is not averse to such perplexities. The word 'romance' is used slightingly in the book: but the book itself is a romance, and no less of one for incorporating a prudence on the subject of romances.

If Robert is called unnatural, so, by Bel, is George's father. Before the women have made friends, she refers to Mrs Logan's 'old unnatural master' the laird, and claims to have been acquainted with the laird and his son George—with 'the old and the young spark both'. This could suggest that the laird is Robert's father too; that Robert has been cast out by his true parent, and been forced to turn in fantasy towards—to adopt—the Revd Mr Wringhim; and that Robert and Bel have shared a betrayer.

Bound, bond, bounding, nature, fantasy—the theme that depends on the use of these words receives its most powerful expression in the central episode of the drama. Technically, the difficulties of managing the double, and in particular his arrival or début, are very daunting. The thing is both in and out of nature, both a wonder and not, both domestic and ideal. In this scene, the thing is done better than anywhere else in the literature of duality. In this scene, too, the theme of escape and that of the double are joined. As the victim rises from the ground, the double terrifically arrives.

Robert has received from his adoptive (or real) father the longed-for word of his election to the society of the just made perfect. He knows that he is God's own. Infallibility, boundlessness, lie before him. Up he jumps.

I wept for joy to be thus assured of my freedom from all sin, and of the impossibility of my ever again falling away from my new state. I bounded away into the fields and the woods, to pour out my spirit in prayer before the Almighty for his kindness to me: my whole frame seemed to be renewed; every nerve was buoyant with new life; I felt as if I could have flown in the air, or leaped over the tops of the trees. An exaltation of spirit lifted me, as it were, far above the earth, and the sinful creatures crawling on its surface; and I deemed myself as an eagle among the children of men, soaring on high, and looking down with pity and contempt on the grovelling creatures below.

As I thus wended my way, I beheld a young man of a mysterious appearance coming towards me. I tried to shun him, being bent on my own contemplations; but he cast himself in my way, so that I could not well avoid him; and more than that, I felt a sort of invisible power that drew me towards him, something like the force of enchantment, which I could not resist. As we approached each other, our eyes met, and I can never describe the strange sensations that thrilled through my whole frame at that impressive moment; a moment to me fraught with the most tremendous consequences; the beginning of a series of adventures which has puzzled myself, and will puzzle the world when I am no more in it. That time will now soon arrive, sooner than any one can devise who knows not the tumult of my thoughts, and the labour of my spirit; and when it hath come and passed over,—when my flesh and my bones are decayed, and my soul has passed to its everlasting home, then shall the sons of men ponder on the events of my life; wonder and tremble, and tremble and wonder how such things should be.[17]

Megalomania speaks here with the lilt of a psalm or of the pulpit; equally, this is what we might hear if we were to eavesdrop on the closet or the confessional. Robert predicts that his adventures will puzzle the world when he is no longer in it, and this has been the case. The passage is moving, and funny: the two are soon lifting their hats to each other in grave courtesy. 'What was my astonishment, on perceiving that he was the same being as myself!' He feels this must be his guardian. Gil-Martin explains that he is neither his brother nor his second self, but a sharer in his fierce opinions, come to sit at his feet. Robert is 'greatly elevated', but he informs the other that he will have nothing to do with him unless he has renounced all trust in the moral law, in the efficacy of good works. The other quickly tells him that he need not worry about that. We learn that this strange meeting took place 'on the 25th day of March 1704, when I had just entered the eighteenth year of my age'.

Time and again, the words employed for this crisis are the customary words of the Gothic. His strange visitor is 'this singular and unaccountable being', and the likeness between them is likewise 'unaccountable'. The word means out of nature, beyond the pale of certainty, and of the society which depends upon such certainties. Bel Calvert is deemed 'unaccountable' when she at first refuses to co-operate with Mrs Logan. This might seem a weak sense of the word, but it has the strength of its reminder that she is, like Robert, an outcast. Robert responds to Gil-Martin with the mixed feelings of the Gothic tradition, and of the novel as a whole: he is at once attracted and repelled. When his visitor leaves, he feels 'a deliverance, but at the same time a certain consciousness that I was not thus to get free of him'. The bounder bound. He is presently to fall into the condition of the monstrous outlaw, trussed and tangled in a weaver's loom at his journey's end. He is like Manasseh in the thicket of affliction. Unlike Manasseh, he is not to be shown God's mercy, not to be plucked from the burning. The wringer wrung. Or so one voice in the polyphony of the novel would have us think.

The boundlessness and hopefulness of infallibility are conferred by justification. The 'justified' of the title of the work refers to the great good luck of those perfect people who, from before birth, have been admitted by God to the society of the just, and are sure to be saved. It may be thought that such people existed before Calvinism did—we know, for instance, of the *parfaits* who crowned the Cathar communities of the Middle Ages in France—and perfection, election, dates back, in any case, indefinitely. And it is possible that Hogg intended the title to refer to all those who go too far, whatever the reasons or persuasions, and believe that they can do no wrong, or who believe that the end justifies the means. He may well have intended to refer to Machiavelli, who had not been entirely forgotten in the Scotland of his time, as well as to Calvin and Knox and Bunyan, who are never, in fact, named in the *Confessions*.

Hogg was rated at the time, by some, as illiterate in the period sense of uncultivated. He was a peasant, whose wraith, or so he said, come to carry off his soul, was once seen by an old woman. He was a peasant, however, who may be supposed to have known both about Muschet and about Machiavelli, who was a member of a cosmopolitan avant-garde, and the confederate of the Edinburgh journalists, Lockhart and Wilson. Gentlemen treated him as a liar and a joke. His autobiographical writings are charged with bucolic cunning and boasting—some of it quite McGonagall-like. And we must make what we can of the fact that he also wrote these profound *Confessions*. He was a singular and unaccountable fellow—singular and plural in the romantic style.

The experiences which followed the descent of the mountain man to the city were enough to make anyone a connoisseur of duality and division. He bragged that he could not read at the age of fifteen, and had access to no books beyond the Bible. He explained that he was introduced to poetry, on a hillside, by a 'half daft' wanderer who taught him 'Tam o' Shanter'.[18] He saw himself as a second self to Burns, as another of Nature's heaven-taught bards. Nature's bard had dirty hands, but was often to wash them before appearing in print, and to concede to Edinburgh gentility a heavy stress on purity and refinement. Taken up by the *Blackwood's* wits, he was also put down by them—tricked and derided and abandoned. A Hogg persona or parody figured in the symposium, *Noctes Ambrosianae*, serialized in the magazine. Hogg himself helped to write the Ettrick Shepherd's speeches there, but his involvement is known to have distressed him, may well have left him with feelings of division and possession, and of dispossession, and his protests on the subject draw near to the language of bedevilment produced in the *Confessions*. In later times, he was to be dispossessed of the novel by those who thought it too good for him to have written, and could inquire whether Lockhart might have written it instead. Kept down as he was during his lifetime, he nonetheless rose to fame in 'North Britain' and beyond. In 1832, the year of the Reform Bill, which Hogg the Tory condemned, he was hailed by a huge turn-out at a banquet in Holborn, and found to be a very different man from the Shepherd burlesqued in *Blackwood's*. It is plain from his career that duality and social mobility may go together.

The mystery of division which we respond to in Hogg's life deepens when we turn to his craft in the *Confessions*. He spoke of the Devil when he spoke of his fictions, and said that he neither planned nor revised: and Scott said that he should have spared more pains.[19] There are certainly times in the novel when we might be reading an author like the one, imagined by Borges, who 'composed his immortal work somewhat *à la diable*, carried along by the inertias of language and invention'.[20] Borne up, like Robert Wringhim, beyond the reach of earthly rules and pains. It might seem, therefore, that there is little to be gained by searching for clues with a view to discovering a plan or secret strategy. It might seem—and there is much in the book to suggest this—that Hogg was no encoder, that his novel is cryptic rather than cryptographic, and that an error in arithmetic is likely to be just an error in arithmetic, on the part of a man notoriously bad at keeping his accounts in daily life. The editorial epilogue has been worried over by detectives. In it, Hogg plays with the fact of his anonymity—he is known to have been keen that the novel should not be known '*as mine*', which would give him 'excellent and delightful scope and freedom'[21]—and he describes himself, by name, as refusing to join an expedition led by the editor and the editor's friend Lockhart to dig up the Sinner's remains on the top of Fall Law. The editor has been anxious to 'possess the skull'. The party uncovers the poor skull, damaged by a spade, together with limbs, garments, Highland bonnet, and it also lights upon a text, a title—*The Private Memoirs and Confessions of a Justified Sinner:*

Written by Himself—and an epigraph, *Fideli certa merces*: Hogg was the kind of peasant who had gathered that this meant 'a sure reward for the faithful'. The corpse has been preserved in the peat, but is the worse for their prying, and had already received rough handling from the Borderers who buried it: one of them had 'tramped down' the phrenologically uninteresting skull with his foot, uttering a curse. This grave-robbing appendix has a Tollund Man attraction, and it also appeals to the detective instinct. John Carey has argued, editorially, that it is meant to discredit the editorial narrative, and the behaviour of these gentlemanly vandals gives colour to such a reading.[22] The episode reads in the main like a ghoulish piece of magazine mystification. And yet the last sentence of all is both equivocal and crafty: 'in order to escape from an ideal'—an imaginary—'tormentor', the Sinner 'committed that act for which, according to the tenets he embraced, there was no remission, and which consigned his memory and his name to everlasting detestation'. While appearing to trample noisily on the Sinner, the sentence tramples harder on his doctrines, and this is apt for the novel as a whole, which cannot be said to detest Robert Wringhim.

There can be no doubt that Hogg can be both cryptic and crafty. He informed his editor and publisher, William Blackwood, according to Mrs Oliphant's book about the firm: 'I am writing for another Magazine, with all my birr, and intend having most excellent sport with it, as the editors will not understand what one sentence of my celebrated allegories mean till they bring the whole terror of Edinburgh aristocracy upon them.'[23] We may want to say that he is nevertheless no allegorist, just as he is no encoder, no cryptographer, no maker of 'elegant mysteries' and puzzles, like Borges' Chesterton.[24] But he is like Borges himself, in some respects. While he can't be thought to sail close to the Byzantium of that writer's fastidious imagination, each in his own way pursues the protean art of the hidden or ulterior or deferred meaning. And the art of Borges, with its passion for predecessors, can be taken to acknowledge the art of Hogg. In Hogg's autobiographical writings there's a Borgesian joke about a farmer upset by the present of a dictionary: 'I dinna ken, man. I have read it all through, but canna say that I understand it; it is the most confused book that ever I saw in my life!' And Borges has a story about a library which contains all books, and all of the world, and where people go, and go mad, in search of justifications.[25]

This allegory to enrage an aristocracy is not an allegory; it lacks the kind of secret which is accessible to the possessor of a key or code; but it is not a confused book. It resembles its hero when he is caught in the loom: it is caught, that is to say, in an arrangement of echo and allusion to which the play on the word 'bound' contributes an intentional and discoverable element. The play on this word is not a feature which vividly suggests inadvertence, or the devilish energy or 'birr' with which he said he wrote, or the *vis inertiae* of 'language and invention'. It suggests that the language and the invention were his, as well as those of a tradition, a fashion and a folk. It suggests an aim, if not a plan. The reader who takes from the book the sense that meaning itself is mobile and multiple and uncertain is apt to be aware of a collateral sense similar to one which was found objectionable in Hogg by Thomas Carlyle, who was himself well-versed in romantic multiplicity and authorial indirection. 'His morality', objected Carlyle, 'limits itself to the precept "be not angry."'[26] Hogg's novel is directed against 'the rage of fanaticism', but is kind to its fanatic, and is planned to show him as one of the many victims in the world. Hogg's character was as uncertain as his novel, so far as we can tell from the biographical record. The record is that of a romantic time. Contrast and change are picturesquely present. Shepherd, bard, buffoon, charlatan, monster, genius glide by, one after the other, as in some camera obscura; the confused, hard-up, 'half-fictitious' panjandrum of Mrs Oliphant's account of the time[27] moves in stealth towards the marvellous fiction of a justified sinner. But it is also true that this fiction, and the life of its author, can be awarded a single shape—that of a suffering and yet sportive response to the angers and terrors and chicaneries of a romantic and unromantic town, to an Edinburgh ruled by piety and by aristocracy, and by a literary élite or elect for whom Wordsworth was illegible[28] and Hogg illiterate.

Hogg was a man who could say of Scott: 'in all the common affairs of life he was unimpeachable. But after the thousands of *lees* [lies] that he told regarding the anonymous novels and even swore to them it is needless to bray [brag?] very much of his truth.' But he was also a man who could make to Lockhart the impeachable and immodest proposal 'that you will write Sir Walter's life in my name and in my manner,' on the grounds that 'it will give you ten times more freedom of expression both as a critic and a friend.' The present book is interested in each of these dissonant proposals. And it is interested in a tease of Scott's which was directed at an example of Hogg's literary manner, and was cheerfully reported by its victim: 'Well Hogg you appear to me just now like a man dancing on a rope or wire at a great height. If he is successful and finishes his dance he has accomplished no great matter but if he makes a slip he gets a devil of a fall.'[29] This tightrope delivers an intimation of duality, which has often exhibited the spectacle of great heights and devilish falls.

II. PROTEUS

'Duality' is a word which means that there are two of something, and which has also meant that some one thing or person is to be perceived as two. It is the second sense which matters to the present book, and it is in the speech of the last century, and in the literature which incorporates its speech, that this sense is chiefly to be located. Duality has said, of each of the pairs envisaged in its second sense, that the component parts may complete, resemble or repel one another. Such parts are partners, or enemies. But in most circumstances, whether of conflict or accord, part and counterpart are both perceived to be true. In the course of the last century it became customary to talk of such a truth, and to talk of it, every so often, as duality. This is a context in which duality is mutuality—just as it is a subject which delivers itself in rhymes and puns. One of the interesting males in *Villette* is portrayed by Charlotte Brontë as disinterestedly possessed, in exemplary style, of a public and a private self: 'Both portraits are correct.'[1] Duality also finds room, however, for the intrusive self which is perceived and portrayed as false.

There is a literature, and a magic, of duality, and they can be traced to antiquity. Dualistic lores and philosophies had been evolved long before the romantic literature of duality began to appear in the later eighteenth century. But Romanticism did much to secure for the subject an unexpired currency which can be located in the common speech and common knowledge, and in the literature, of the present time. This book is about the imagination of two minds or more for the human individual, and the term 'duality' is used to refer to facts and to fictions, principles and practice, to states of mind and of affairs, to a manner of speaking and a way of life, to an aspect and subject of the literatures of Europe and America from the Romantic period onwards. It refers to the double life, which can be treated as a matter of observation and record, and to the fictional double or *doppelgänger*. It refers to the clinical phenomenon of multiple identity, and to the cultural phenomenon of a multiple identity which opens itself to the world and to the experience of others, which both enhances and annihilates the self, and which became known to readers of John Keats as negative capability.

Psychic duplication and division, on the one hand, and the open mind, on the other, are conceptions which are kept apart by historians of Romanticism: but they were pursued at the same early point in its history, and they come together in writings of the later nineteenth century. These are conceptions which were to yield a conception of art: an author may be thought to lead a double life, or to achieve a second self, an alter ego, in the art he creates, and he may also be thought to lose himself there. They are conceptions which predict, and participate in, the young idea of the following century—the Modernist view of art's impersonality, of the artist's need to be absent from his creations. This is a view which has played a part in vehement theories of the last few years, where authors have been shown to be subdued by the medium and materials they employ. It should not be overlooked that they have been willing both to exalt and to subdue themselves, in theory, before now, and that impersonality has been an issue, and an aspect of the dualistic hypothesis, since the early days of Romanticism. A recent subverter of authorial intention, the Frenchman Derrida, has claimed for literary texts an uncertainty which derives from their employment of words with a double and undecidable meaning—words like Plato's *pharmakon*, which could mean either a poison or a cure.[2] Derrida's either/or' is a 'both', and it has its place in the long history of duality.

Duality's transformations, and long duration, direct enquirers to works which are widely spaced in time and ethos, and the same incongruities can be found among the profusion of works which has accumulated in the course of the past two hundred years. During this time, the subject has come and gone. The fictional double has been derided as a fraud, but has returned to haunt us. The hypothesis known to Victorians as the essential duality of man—to Conrad, for instance, as 'the duality of man's nature'[3]—has been deserted and neglected: it has also been remembered and re-invented.

To discuss the literature of the double is to discuss the literature of solitude—what may be called the annals of the orphan or singleton. The double life and the suffering or excluded single life are said in these literatures to steal, in the figurative sense of the word; to soar; and to be strange, in the sense of different, foreign or uncommon, and in the sense, too, of fey, 'fated', soon to die. Duality and romance can be studied in these convergent literatures as one and the same; they are among the strange compounds to which duality itself attends and of which it is constituted. Romance has often been equivocal, and the Romanticism of modern times has drawn on the dualistic outlook established in the ancient world in setting out its stories of the cleft stick, the tight corner, of domesticity and escape, of enlargements and enfranchisements. Stealing away has been seen both as beautiful and as reprehensible; romance reaches for an upper air, while describing plunges, prostrations. Such highs have lifted the hearts of the susceptible. Nerves, pulses, body and soul are tethered to an aspiration. Here below breathes the romantic sensorium, which a romantic succession, so to speak, has brought to us from the remote past. Such longings are romantic and, for all we know, genetic, a matter of endowment, like other constituents of the experience of duality. Looking-up, a propensity culturally enjoined from the remote past, and seeing double, in any one of a number of ways, may be innate. But if duality is a compulsion, it is also a recourse. It embodies a response to demands made by the environment—demands which are nevertheless equally intelligible as being of a kind to stigmatize duality as ominous and destructive, and to promote a belief in the biological necessity of the single self, of an experienced integrity.

Romance refers to an up and a down, an out and a back. It undertakes this or that departure and return. It intends, and refrains from, suicide. Its departures and adventures include marrying for love—a search for the outlandish partner—and the ambition to go to heaven; and they may try to reconcile these two ambitions. Many of its departures and adventures fail. Many end where they began. And some of them may seem to sympathize with the circumstances of family life, where beginnings end and leavers return. The literature of duality operates as a self-sustaining cultural preoccupation in which such circumstances are sometimes absent, or faint. But family life offers analogies and explanations for the choices, constraints, compulsions and discomforts which are presented in this literature. The family, like the human body—each an aggregation of pairs and opposites, replications and resemblances—has served to justify, as mirrors, pools, and shadows have, certain strains of dualistic conjecture. Man and wife are among the most compelling of all dualities—opposites of a sort, a pair who may become the parents of a pair of opposing subsidiary selves. The word 'familiar' has meant an attendant spirit or demon, and therefore a double, and there was once a synonym for it in 'fly'—which could also mean spy, can still mean mischievous, and is a word for what the literary orphan does.

To the idea of character, of a stable, impervious, monolithic human identity, the duality of modern times gave wings. It uses winged words. It speaks of volatility, versatility, variety, variance, vagary, vertigo. Character may come apart, for those who create and discuss it in the Romantic period and after; or it may appear to have passed into the diversity of momentariness and change. Duality may perceive a succession of moods and moments, or an internal contention of personalities. Contentious duality believes in a dynamic inconsistency, in a human nature which has its contraries, its collisions of intent, its incompatible aims and incitements. A man may belie himself, set eyes on himself, behave like two different people. The writers in question convey that duality is an endowment, that there is an innate dissociability. At the same time, mingling superstition with science, they convey that psychic division is, for the precious few, a doom, a disaster, a disability, and a distinction.

There is a popular duality which claims that there is no such thing as character, that human beings are a flux, and the sum of their changes, chances and contradictions. Such a view has been heard with reference to Eric Blair, alias George Orwell, a writer whose fictions and demeanour do not exclude themselves from the subject-matter of this book: Orwell's orphan *Nineteen Eighty-Four* visits on a world of the future the distresses of his lifetime and last days. A debate has occurred in which this stern and truthful, workmanlike chooser of a doleful pen-name has been called various and mutable; on more than one occasion in the past an alias or pseudonym has been used or construed as a dualistic signal, but friends have suggested here that although Orwell had two names, he should not be considered a divided man; and one of his biographers[4] has suggested that it is advisable not to interpret—to opinionate—this notably opinionated man. The biographer's opinion is supportive of an attitude commonly held in intellectual circles—that opinion is a violence. And this in turn supports the view that there is no such thing as a decision, or that decisions are irrational and accidental, that they are rarely more than the chances which are apt to conclude some stalemate. Duality, however, whether vulgar or advanced, should not dissuade us from believing that we are able to tell the difference between people and to anticipate what they do, or that the opinions we hold may affect and even determine the decisions we are able to take and to execute.

Dualistic fictions, in all their dream-like generic idiosyncrasy, continue to impart experiences of duplication, division, dispersal, abeyance. Many are at once alibis and apologies. They are works which can find themselves both innocent and guilty. Hostile actions are ascribed to some further or to some foreign self, are performed by proxy—a performance in which scribes, in which fiction itself, are deeply implicated. The actions can therefore be said to be both admitted and denied. Dualistic fictions may seem to say what it is for someone to do or to be two things at once, where these things are inimical or incompatible. This is a literature which does the impossible. It tells of the culture of escape which we inhabit and in which most of the escapes which matter must fail. Much of the literature and of the theory of modern times has taken flight—has engaged in a flight from history, and sense, and from the senses. Such a flight can never be completed this side of paradise: but it has been spoken of, and duality has ways of speaking of it. It is common knowledge, and a common knowledge of dualistic impossibility, that everyone tries to have their cake and eat it: explanations of the fictional, the impossible double, however, do not talk about cakes, do not suggest that the difficulty of the double, of understanding what it may mean, is the difficulty of literature in general and of life in general, of a general incidence of contradiction, hazard, and uncertainty. Explanations have tended to be esoteric and psychiatric. They include, and have perhaps been dominated by, the Freudian proposal that doubles attest to the fear of death, and to the possibility of a primitive and prehistoric narcissism, and of its counterpart in the incapacities of the modern neurotic.

The double life can sometimes be observed, while the double is imaginary. But the authenticity of both phenomena is hard to assess—by those, at any rate, who are inclined to place truth and fiction, truth and its invention by the individual human being, among the undecidable strange compounds of the romantic modern world. Another of these strange compounds is the poet Edward Thomas, who wrote these lines,[5] early in the present century, about an encounter with a double:

And now I dare not follow after
Too close. I try to keep in sight,
Dreading his frown and worse his laughter.
I steal out of the wood to light;
I see the swift shoot from the rafter
By the inn door: ere I alight
I wait and hear the starlings wheeze
And nibble like ducks: I wait his flight.
He goes: I follow: no release
Until he ceases. Then I shall also cease.

The poem which ends in this way, within sight of the poet's end, is called 'The Other', and it effects one of the genre's impossible or hypothetical schisms or severances, with a language which shimmers, as it were, accordingly: we may wonder which of the two persons in question is to be sighted in the second line. We are to imagine that some split poet is following himself, in the manner of a Georgian hiker or cyclist; that he is trying to pick himself up, as in some Platonic reassembly of the human halves. The enterprise is 'fortunate', though also fearful, 'queer' and 'sore'. There are 'moments of everlastingness': long before, for Henry Vaughan in his 'angel-infancy', there had been 'bright shoots of everlastingness'.[6] There is an urge to confess to the other. The poem's last lines assemble a steal, a flight, a wood, the emergence of a solitary from the wood, frowns and laughter—and they do so, we might mistakenly feel, for the first time ever. But these are features which had been in conjunction many times before.

The poet steals in the direction of light: his is a furtiveness which courts or desires disclosure. And he steals towards, rather than away—which would have been the more familiar move of the two in such a setting. Both are true, to and fro are true, of the human individual—at moments of crisis, among others: 'stealing away' was a move made, and reversed, at this time, in the poetry of Thomas's friend, Robert Frost. Here, however, the poet practises what might perhaps have been seen as a latter-day reversal of the usual dualistic relationship between pursuer and pursued: a malign social self is chased by a waif, a recluse, who may in his turn be thought to invite chasing as a sort of thief. It is as if Hogg's justified sinner were to set off in pursuit of his demon, rather than the other way round. Even so, these features tell an old story. This does not make the poem especially conventional, any more than it makes it, in a related sense, impersonal. We are likely to think that Thomas has something romantic to confess, and that this has to do with a struggle between the impulse to steal away from a society and the impulse to take part.

His poem may be compared with a true story of the double life—one which can be judged to derive both from literature and from the clinical record. Here once again is the mutuality, the duality, of truth and invention, candour and convention, earnest and play. The story has its teller in the imaginative neurologist Oliver Sacks. It is a strange case, and is called that by Sacks, who may be called an Anglo-American versed in the heritage of duality, and who has found an alter ego in the Soviet psychologist Luria. In 1981, Sacks published an essay on the fortunes of a patient of his, 'witty ticcy Ray', a victim of Tourette's disease.[7] Tourette's causes tics and convulsions, and is related to a primitive part of the brain—primitive both phylogenetically and in terms of individual development—which produces 'go' and 'drive'. The emotions, the passions, the nerves, are excited. The disease was named at the end of the last century, in the days, says Sacks, of a 'more spacious neurology', which was capable of joining body and soul, science and art: those were the days of an inventive psychology, when Freud was young and the American Weir Mitchell flourished—a man admired by Sacks—and they were days, too, when duality ruled the Anglo-American literary culture as never before or since.

Ray had learned to live with his ailments, to turn them to account, to affirm them. 'I consist of tics,' he could claim, and his frenzies were those of a talented jazz drummer, of a man capable of strokes of brilliance that were experienced as 'nervous' and 'frivolous'. Along came Doctor Sacks, with the drug haldol. A measure of cure was hoped for: but there was a cost to be counted. This haldol may be considered a match for the Platonic *pharmakon*, being both a cure and a poison. Ray stood to lose not only his tics but his spark and spunk, his old impudence and invention. A compromise, a middle way, a *tertium quid*, was devised. During the week, on the drug, he works in a Wall Street office. At weekends, ticcing, he reverts to his former self, and plays the drums. He remarks that he is, by turns, 'grave'—Dr Jekyll's word, in Robert Louis Stevenson's fable, for his own best behaviour—and gay.[8] 'So now, there are two Rays—on and off haldol. There is the sober citizen, the calm deliberator, from Monday to Friday; and there is "witty ticcy Ray", frivolous, frenetic, inspired, at weekends. It is a strange situation, as Ray is the first to admit . . .'. But this is not the first time that a strange situation of this kind has arisen. We have long enjoyed a common knowledge of the strange.

In developing a clinical account of the romantically unaccountable—of the current grave, gay tertian Ray—Oliver Sacks is necessarily committed to an account of the human condition, of the way people live. Many people are calm deliberators during the week, and at the weekend frivolous, frenetic, inspired. Many are introduced by drugs to a double life, or to experiences similar to those which are talked about by those who talk about dual personality. Ray's case reveals a dependence of talent upon trauma: this, too, is far from uncommon. And comparison of Sacks's case-history and the poem by Thomas reveals an area of common ground which trenches on the experiences of common life.

Each expresses the need to behave in two different ways, and to turn for that purpose into two different people, while also, we may feel, behaving as a third, an amalgam. In each of them, a solitary moves within himself towards, and away from, a social competence. Both of Ray's lives have a public element, but the life of the musician might be deemed reclusive—in part, and in a style which evokes the 'true self' of the Romantic era. Each work is from the heart of its author. For all that he is cultivating a genre, addressing a topos, adapting and inflecting, while also reversing, a traditional utterance, we may think that Thomas means what he says. What he says could never happen, though it could well be dreamt, and it had in some sense been said before by others: but we may think that in the manner of a lyric poet he means what he says and is speaking for himself. For all that he employs the methods of a neurophysiologist, we may think that Sacks, too, speaks for himself in this sense. In his essay Sacks the scientist waxes lyrical. Science and art are joined. Body and soul are joined.

It is human to try to do two things at once, and for there to be some third thing which holds out hope of a solution, and it is human to err in the attempt. In Ray's case, it seemed that a choice had to be made between the preservation of his talent and the avoidance of pain, and a decision was reached which took the form of a solution and an amalgamation. But the choice must surely have been experienced as comparable to such insoluble dilemmas as the one posed by Shakespeare in *Measure for Measure*, where Claudio mentions a human nature, human instincts, which cause us to be like rats eager for the poison which is their 'proper bane', to pursue 'a thirsty evil, and when we drink we die.'[9] Shakespeare's poison is a kind of cure—like Plato's ambivalent *pharmakon*, and Sacks's haldol—in the sense that human nature has to take it in order to slake a thirst.

Such dilemmas are connected with the drama of the double, with the tall tales of division and possession which belong to a nineteenth-century re-invention of ancient precept and argument, superstition and surmise. They are also connected with certain habits of speech, with the different names we use for the same thing (one of the cakes we have and eat in this country is alternatively known as passion cake and as carrot cake), and with the double meaning borne by some single word. What drama does, what duality's fables do, language can do. 'Let', for instance, is a word which has meant both to prevent and to permit, and the same story is told by the word 'deliver'. The two senses of such words may be said to tell the story of Hogg's *Confessions*, whose hero is at once bound and free: so that the duality of verbal ambiguity—which makes possible puns, prevarications, delphic profundities—can here be studied in close relation to the exploits of a *doppelgänger*. Again, as we shall see, the strangely twofold Robert Lowell was alive to such dilemmas when he created in his verse the magnificently problematic image of a cornered wasp and of its disastrous escape: in this image, a White Anglo-Saxon Protestant (and Catholic) confesses his double life. Lowell was an orphan prince of the romantic modern world to whom the old language of duality has been applied, at a time when we claim to have issued from an era of superstition and salvation: a wild man and a gentle, a leaver and a mutineer, the inhabitant of two countries who ended his days in suspension between two families (duality is a state which keeps crossing the Atlantic). An elderly, haughty London lady once greeted the delightful Robert Lowell at a party with an expression of her alarmed belief that the mad poet Robert Lowell had escaped from custody and was on his way to join them.

'Duality' can be awarded a meaning which encompasses all of these manifestations and alludes to a double and durable heritage, both ancient and comparatively recent. If the idea of dialectical progression was rare, was sporadic and scholastic, before the Renaissance, the idea of a necessary evil, as of the *tertium quid*, or the delphic utterance, is ancient, and has at most times been frequent. The same is true of the tragic contradiction, and of the fatal outcome which completes it. And there are other categories of dualistic thought which reveal an equally long history of acceptance: belief in the attraction of opposites, for example, or, for that matter, in the existence of a body and soul. Demonic possession and the transmigration of souls are dualistic categories which indicate that the subject has been due both to the dark ages and to the enlightenments of the past. The resemblance of sound and sense between 'double' and 'devil' has weathered the passage of the centuries, and is a specimen of the superstitions which have lent their forebodings to the common knowledge of the subject which is still about. In the dualistic encounters and crises which owe most—and all seem to owe something—to folklore, the note is both terminal and transcendent. The self is violated, invaded, destroyed, on such occasions: but it may also be saved. The loss of the self is supernaturally defied and averted. But there are many premonitions of its loss, as of its dispatch beyond nature to a regime of punishment. A contemporary of Edward Thomas's, Charlotte Mew, dreams in a poem of an ominous appointment with a second self which evokes the folkloric (and literary) appointment in Samarra where an orphan is welcomed home by the object of his fear, where death is at once avoided and encountered.[10] In this poem, as in the Thomas, the poet ends within sight of her death:

> The lamps just lighted down the long, dim street,
> No one for me—
> I think it is myself I go to meet:
> I do not care; some day I *shall* not think; I shall not *be*!

There is a Medieval duality—to be found, for instance, in the English Mystery plays. Equally, there is reason to suppose that, at the Renaissance, duality was revived with the revival of Classical learning. In the poetry of Spenser, where Una and Duessa play the parts, respectively, of truth and falsehood, purity and sorcery, both a Medieval and a Classical duality can be distinguished (and confused). Aristotle and the Greeks had a word for what became the Latin *alter ego*, or *alter idem*, which became the 'second self' of Shakespeare's Sonnets.[11] Shakespeare's language, and that of his contemporaries, mark a critical point in duality's long march from ancient to modern. In the stealing and soaring which occur in literary texts of the past three hundred years, Shakespeare can be discovered; in the literary thinking which concerns itself with paradox and tension, mixtures and opposites, a debt to Shakespeare, and to Donne, and to other poets and scholars of the Renaissance, was eventually incurred. Shakespearian duality has been pervasive, and Shakespeare is pervaded by duality. *Two Gentlemen of Verona* examines change of mind, flight, and stealth; in the manner of comedy, a perfidious Proteus is forgiven, and a double marriage is concluded—for perfidy and for constancy alike; a further comedy of duality elsewhere examines the errors occasioned by twinship, with Ephesus a town of sorcerers. And this is to look only on the comic side, and at examples which hold a special interest for the present book. In general, the alternative self of the Renaissance tends to suggest similarity, duplication, while the adversary duality of competing selves can in some measure be seen as a specialism of the future. But the latter is also apparent in alchemy—in the language of compounds and complexions, which was to be of service to the later duality.

'Duality' is a barely colloquial nineteenth-century word, and an unstable one. It is a word which refers both to the facts of a human instability and uncertainty, and to the uncertain comprehension of these facts, and which shifts and shimmers accordingly. It is used here mainly with reference to the canon of nineteenth-century narratives of the double: but the superventions of the double do not represent the compass of the subject. It is a subject which stretches beyond literature. At the same time, it is a subject which *is* literature, as a new body of theory has insisted: writers have been responsive from the first to contradictions, dilemmas, dialectic, ambiguity, puns, puzzles, conundrums, cruxes, corners, clefts, coalescences and coincidences, to the binariness of body and soul, to the two souls which may share a breast, to the tendency to run away which coincides with the tendency to remain. Contradictions may be thought both soluble and insoluble, tolerable and intolerable. And they can give the dizzy sense of an infinite uncertainty—a sense which itself appears to recede into an infinite past, puzzling the mind and the will, and to have been subject to transformation in successive cultures. In modern times, it has helped to produce the romantic impossibility which is composed in equal parts of the undoable and of the unknowable.

This is a book about romantic people and their words, and about their dreams of exclusion and escape. It pays attention to what common knowledge has long identified as the phenomenon of romantic escapism, to the image of the orphan, and of the orphan's flight, and of the double who may take part in, or precipitate, such flights: it wonders why people are shown to pursue themselves in this strange way, why orphans fly, why the excluded should seek to escape. These are the preoccupations of a parable by the Argentinian writer of the present day, Jorge Luis Borges. Entitled 'Borges and I',[12] the parable tells the story of his life, and turns it into a romance. It says that he is beside himself, that there are two of him. There is 'the one things happen to'—the public Borges, the professor, the eminent writer. And there is an 'I' who may be thought to stand for the true self of romanticism, who likes the prose of Robert

Louis Stevenson, and who accounts himself 'justified' by the writing Borges does, while recognizing himself less in Borges' books 'than in many others'. The true self seeks to be free of the other self, who keeps laying claim to his interests and themes: 'Thus my life is a flight . . .'. The parable ends with the sentence: 'I do not know which of us has written this page.' It is said[13] that, when accosted on the streets of Buenos Aires with the question, 'You are Borges, no?' the writer of this page replied: 'At times.'

'Borges and I' appears in the collection *Labyrinths*, a book which contains other books, as a man may contain another man—his rival or opposite, perhaps. There are books here by Kafka, and by Poe, and by Stevenson, and one by a Scotsman of an earlier time, the *Confessions of a Justified Sinner. Labyrinths* contains Cervantes, and causes *Don Quixote* to look—as it could look to some of the first romantics—like a romantic work. 'Borges and I' has in it two hundred years of the plural self, and of imaginary escape, and elsewhere in the collection we are conscious of other traditional preoccupations—captivity, misery, mystery, the fascination of the strange, of distant times and places. We are also conscious of the wonders of metempsychosis, of the transmigration of souls. *Labyrinths* is dualistic, and Gothic. It imagines an Aztec Frankenstein who dreams of a beating heart. It plays games with numbers, with pairs, with the literature and mathematics of multiplication and division, with chance, time and infinity, and with theology. It imagines the opinion that 'all men are two men and that the real one is the other, the one in heaven', and it imagines the delusion of a blacksmith who 'placed a huge iron sphere on the shoulders of his small son, so that his double might fly'.[14] Borges' wit touches the nerve of a literature in which sons are oppressed and may wholly or partly resist or run.

The romanticism which takes leave of the familiar, of the family, of rules and accords, of the senses, includes the behaviour of the man who is visible to passers-by on the streets of Buenos Aires, or of Stevenson's Edinburgh, while concealing the secrets of an inner life; the idea that the single self with which we are familiar may be experienced as two selves or a compendium, or as a continuum of times or moments—this idea can usually be assigned to the unhappiness which attempts to escape. Of the words favoured by the romantic people of the earlier nineteenth century, many refer to this unhappiness, and none has become obsolete, though there are those which have become old-fashioned, or been turned—'terrible!' 'horrid!'—into exclamations and expletives. The writers who use these words have distrusted talk of the perfection of a society, and have talked instead, though often equivocally, of the pangs and penalties of family life, duty, daily life, personality, publicity, and of the charm of incognitos, secrets and exits. For all his dark sayings, his sheltering in libraries, labyrinths and puzzles, Borges can present to the world a fairly cheerful face: but it seems clear that he has found his happiness in seclusion, in the familiar recourse of a flight from the familiar. Borges, Lowell . . . two of a kind, of a twofold kind of modern literary leaver and sufferer.

How do we tell the difference between contradiction and division, or defeat, or, in medical circumstances, breakdown? This is a question which neither the writer nor the doctor has been able to answer with ease: but their answers can sometimes be compared, and literary texts can sometimes be submitted to a modicum of medical examination. A definition established in 1947 by the American psychologist Gardner Murphy is not irrelevant to the notion that Borges is Borges only at times: 'Most cases of multiple personality appear essentially to represent the organism's efforts to live, at different times, in terms of different systems of values.'[15] Borges' approach is of course not clinical but confessional, and it is an artist's approach. At the same time, he can lead one to suppose that the good artist does not confess, or confesses only incomprehensibly or invisibly. He is among those artists of the modern world who suggest that the self which creates a work of art is capable of an abeyance of diffusion—of dispersing in sympathy with the selves and sensations which the work assembles and excites; any proffered authorial self is an illusion or an objection. We read about this aspect of modernity, and of duality, in *Labyrinths*—in 'Borges and I', and in the parable about Shakespeare which it precedes, 'Everything and Nothing'.

'No one has ever been so many men as this man who like the Egyptian Proteus could exhaust all the guises of reality. At times he would leave a confession hidden away in some corner of his work, certain that it would not be deciphered . . .'.[16] The Shakespeare of 'Everything and Nothing' is compared here to the Classical sea-god whose changing shapes—lion, panther, boar, running water, blossoming tree—are glimpsed in the *Odyssey*, and it is a comparison which dates from the early days of romantic duality. Proteus served as a prototype for the human inconsistency inherited, cherished, and bequeathed by the nineteenth century, for the powers of its most cherished artist, and for the strange new fictions of modern times. The Shakespeare of 'Everything and Nothing' is the Shakespeare of Hazlitt and of other writers of the first Romantic period in Germany and Britain. During these years the question arose whether Shakespeare was classical or romantic, objective or subjective, reserved or confessional, impersonal or 'interested'. For Coleridge, Shakespeare was a union of such opposites. He was a chameleon. *Einfühlung* enables him to 'draft himself forth' into 'all the forms of human character and passion'.[17] For Hazlitt, Shakespeare was 'the least of an egotist that it was possible to be. He was nothing in himself; but he was all that others were, or that they could become.' The 'striking peculiarity' of his mind was its 'generic quality'. In another place, Hazlitt writes: 'His genius consisted in the faculty of transforming himself at will into whatever he chose: his originality was the power of seeing every object from the exact point of view in which others would see it. He was the Proteus of human intellect.'[18] Lesser artists could also appear to transform themselves into the transformational Shakespeare, to partake of this faculty. Peacock's early poem 'Sir Proteus' has a dedication which smiles at Byron's alleged coat-turning, his 'protean consistency', and a footnote concerning the 'Anythingarians' of the modern world.[19]

Borges' anythingarian Shakespeare reproduces and contemplates the Shakespeare of the Romantics. He says in *Labyrinths* that 'Hazlitt's infinite Shakespeare' resembles 'all the men in the world', and that other writers do the same: such as Valéry, 'of whom we can say, as William Hazlitt did of Shakespeare, "he is nothing in himself"'; and (less plausibly, indeed a little unnervingly) Shaw.[20] Borges himself is Shakespearian in this sense: 'Borges and I' points out that he is scattered through many other books besides those publicly ascribed to his alter ego, and, in the poem 'Elegy' which follows these two parables, he exults in his diversity, in a destiny—'perhaps no stranger than your own'—which has meant that this inhabitant of Buenos Aires is also 'a part of Edinburgh'. God, too, like Borges and his peers, is Shakespearian: among his attributes is a multiple identity, an infinitely sympathetic and susceptible nothingness. *Labyrinths* takes pleasure in the everlastingness of romantic ideas. It testifies that the idea of a withdrawal from the world is not dead, and that the universal, generic, symbiotic, protean poet is not dead either. Such a poet may be expected to fight the violence of ideas, while submitting to the idea of his own diversity and absence, and to have submitted to it while tending the flame of English literature. Such a poet is alive and well, and living in Argentina.

He also lives in various other places. Romantic duality is, and has to be, charged with resemblances and coincidences, and it is in league with the supernatural: and the degree to which puns and happy chances have come its way, have been there for the gathering, can seem to border on the weird. Very much in the coincidental manner of romantic duality, Jorge Luis Borges has a namesake and counterpart in the pseudonymous English novelist Anthony Burgess, as well as a middle-namesake in Robert Louis Stevenson. Burgess is a romantic modernist whose novels aspire to the condition of music. In his 'biographical' fictions about Shakespeare, Keats, Christ, Napoleon, his subjects are musically and democratically rendered as types of humanity, and of Burgess. The great man stands for everyman, and for the darting, sympathetic artist. Character and opinion are drowned in sensation, and in the music of humanity. This is signalled in the Joycean title of his study of Joyce: *Here comes everybody*.

Joyce, too, may be called a romantic modernist. In *A Portrait of the Artist*, Stephen Dedalus teaches that God and the artist are 'indifferent' to their work and 'invisible' there: and yet this novel is a portrait of its artist. So is *Ulysses*. In *Ulysses*, Proteus and Shakespeare darkly participate, and so does Joyce. As so often, an author who is missing, presumed absent, can be detected, deciphered. The character of Bloom is as decipherable as it is protean, momentary, negatively capable. In the work of this author a progressive dispersal of personality takes place:

duality's march had reached the stage of Joyce's polymorphs, who include, in *Ulysses*, not only Bloom but the author of Bloom's being. The decipherment of Joyce's presence in the work must attend to a prodigious doubling, and to elements both of division and dispersal. Joyce is at no point indifferent; a new portrait of the artist has been composed whereby Stephen —the romantic star and autobiographical alter ego of the earlier novel—now alternates with Bloom, and with all Dublin.

In the modern world, Proteus has numbered among his portraits and disguises the activities of the actor, the author, and the adventurer. The Borges of 'Borges and I' is actor-like, and actors have given proof of the dualistic hypothesis since the earlier nineteenth century, when impersonation was once more seen to be important, when reality could be seen to be histrionic, when the madman and mesmeric subject could be suspected of putting on a show. Authors have also been evidence of duality, of an environment designed to be read in duplicate, and Proteus is the kind of author who is deemed impersonal by romantics. We have intermittently held that art owes more to humanity, in one form or another, than to the personality of the artist, that the artist's opinions and declared intentions, together with the interpretations of his biographer, should be suspected. We have believed that a novel is a multiple identity in which the novelist is dispersed and disguised and belied. We have been ready to believe that Joyce had a second self in Stephen Dedalus, and a third in Bloom—to believe, with Borges, that Valéry may have had a *doppelgänger* in his character Monsieur Teste. Proteus may be taken to stand for the human inconsistency of a certain time—as patron saint of the indecisive nineteenth century, with its looking alike and different, its looking-glasses and its looking-up, its new cult and compass of correspondences, opposites and counterfeits. At the same time, he has been felt to stand for the power that poets have, and Shakespeare and Keats became his leading incarnations. Hazlitt's protean Shakespeare and Keats's negative capability are aspects of duality which have been potent at times when the double was being hotly pursued: in the Nineties, as irony would have it, Mrs Oliphant thought to praise the versatility of Keats's scorpion critic, Lockhart, by calling him 'a very Proteus of literary capacity'.[21]

The changing shapes of a Jekyll and Hyde and the changing shapes of some Proteus or other are two different things. What distinguishes them is the existence, in the strange case of the first, of a break or separation, Proteus being seamless and continuous, momentary, while the split self is successive, and may even be amnesiac. They are different things, and can on occasion appear mutually hostile, if not antithetical. But they are also the same thing—in that they belong to the subject which is called here by its nineteenth-century name of duality. It is a subject which can be hailed as yet another case of multiple identity. It is compendious, inconsistent, and, at times, as doubtful and dizzy as any of the texts which sustain it. Duality includes both Hazlitt and Hogg, both negative capability and the duplicity of the double life. Its fictions suggest that a man may have two characters, or twelve, and that character is a chameleon or a chimera. It includes Dr Jekyll's guess that the individual would one day be known as 'a mere polity of multifarious, incongruous and independent denizens'.[22] And it may be taken to include some part of what happened in the eighteenth century when the mind was subjected to logical attack, and depicted in atomic terms as a succession of moments or sensations: to include Hume, as well as Hegel, and as well as *Tristram Shandy*, which refers to itself as *sui generis* in being 'at the same time' digressive and progressive, governed by 'two contrary motions', motions which are 'at variance' but which may be reconciled.[23] Two of the words I have just quoted count for something in a work which might on the face of it seem very different. But Hogg's *Confessions* and *Tristram Shandy* are alike in speaking a language which subdues and disperses the author, and in furnishing early and still unsurpassed examples of the epistemological, and of the modern self-referring, literary text.

III. FORLORN

Where the double is, the orphan is never far away, with secrecy and terror over all. To bring together the orphan and the double is to unite submission and aggression, freedom and impediment. Theirs is a proximity which is sometimes an identity, and it depicts the place of the individual in one or more of the environments which befall him.

In literature, and in the life of the feelings which learns from it, the orphan may serve as someone's double. Anne Frank, a girl who was not without a family, and whose short life was to terminate in secrecy and terror, 'used at times to have the feeling that I didn't belong to Mums, Pim, and Margot, and that I would always be a bit of an outsider. Sometimes I used to pretend I was an orphan, until I reproached and punished myself, telling myself it was all my own fault that I played this self-pitying role, when I was really so fortunate.'[1] She was fortunate enough to be sent to die in a concentration camp, for being Jewish. She can therefore be called an outcast, and her letter of 1944 allows us to say that a fantasy of misfortune was overtaken by the reality. It teaches the lesson that fictions of the imaginary orphan in which the uses of adversity are sweet are cultivated in a world which is not sweet, in which the innocent suffer, in which those who pretend to be unfortunate may have the worst of luck, in which everyone is an orphan, in the sense that there is no life to which the image does not speak.

In the literature and hearsay of the past two centuries, the orphan's plight is both literal and figurative. As in the remote past, misery has been made to appear magical, and has been rewarded with power and glory. We may reflect that the countries where the orphan is king are countries which have worshipped a miserable and compassionate god—in the words of a boy I know, 'that very sore man on two sticks'. But the orphan was also a king in ancient Japan. The homeless or defenceless person, the child whose parents are dead or gone, has been pitied, feared, envied, exalted and impersonated. And it would seem that this has been done, for the most part, by those with families who have been moved by the thought of what it is to be shut out and to run away, by the thought of the outcast and the stranger. For those with families, the white face at the window has signified both exclusion and escape.

In his capacity as author, and in the context of his life and work, the imaginary orphan presents himself as alone and not alone, as lost and found, bound and free. The result has been a literature of confinement which tells of escape and which also says that escape is futile and confining, which tells both of escape and of the determined and conditioned life, of the facts of life and the laws of physics, and of the claims which a community makes upon its members. Duality has thus taken up the impossible task of showing that the same person can be both at home and away.

These contradictions were digested in the romantic sensorium spoken of in the first half of the nineteenth century. The romantic person is driven, as other people are, by animal spirits, vital force, nervous energy, and his mind is a mixture, as theirs is, of associations and impulses. But he is not of common clay. His nerves are peculiarly susceptible. He is highly-strung. He is suspended between heaven and earth, torn between the two as he is between reason and imagination. He has his ups and downs, is neither here nor there. He is fastened to a body and a family and a society, but his soul, or some of it, longs to fly away. He is secretive and he is frank; his feelings are at once liberal and suspicious. He is sometimes called a 'feeler'. He is a specialist in contrasts and cross-purposes, and in misfortune.

I am mocking the romantic sensorium a little, keying my description to the reveries in *Villette*. The commitment to distress in this literature has been strong enough to mock itself, as duality has indeed obliged it to do, and to abide the mockery of others and the affectations of the sentimental, and to survive as a serious matter for the writings of subsequent times and of the present day. Among its emblems are the expressions of grief worn by the unfortunate and the austere, and by authors—the woebegone face of the pierrot, for instance, '*mort d'un chronique orphelinisme*'.[2] These are the words of the poet and ironist Laforgue, who is to be seen here, late in the century, moved by the sad clown he is mocking. In the course of the century, many had weighed the words of the 55th Psalm:

And I said, Oh that I had wings like a dove! for then would I fly away, and be at rest.
Lo, then would I wander far off, and remain in the wilderness. Selah.
I would hasten my escape from the windy storm and tempest.

More than one of these words became prominent in the language of distress: this is the storm from which the Victorian orphan was to seek shelter. The psalm was turned into a poem by William Bartholomew, was set to music by Mendelssohn, and went up to heaven with a sob and a shriek from the parlours of the respectable: the imagination of departure was responsible for a favourite song.

The orphan's troubles—as discussed in this book—are literary, and in some measure legendary; they appear to answer enduring imaginative needs. But his demographic vicissitudes may not be beside the point of the present discussion. During the lifetime of the first Romantic writers, industrialization took hold, and the population of Britain rose abruptly. The city of Edinburgh, which had few factories to attract migrants and their troubles, nevertheless doubled its numbers: and became a centre for the cult of the orphan. We may think that the time was ripe for a cultivation of privacy, secrecy, and the double life, for a preoccupation with isolation and the victim, with the ragamuffin and the motherless child, with the need for institutions to house them, for a literature in which they might be pitied and envied and feared. There does not seem to have been a rise in the proportion of real orphans in this country, then or later, as compared with the Early Modern Britain of the social historians. But there were more orphans in the world because there were more people, and a fear of the mob and of the masses would appear to have augmented the visibility of the orphan—as indeed of the double, in his capacity of intruder. The fears that were now abroad, in other words, were fears both of dispossession and of possession. And they were fears which produced an appetite for the prosecution and extension of established literary modes in which anxieties could be voiced and solitude extolled.

Early death is another demographic factor which needs to be acknowledged. A high mortality rate had persisted for a long time among the young—infants and parents alike. At the start of the nineteenth century, the rate had yet to turn down, and Lawrence Stone's book on Early Modern family life calculates that 'even in the 1840s the expectation of death next year for young adults in England was eight times greater than it is in America today.'[3] The image of the orphan has been full of death, and the literature of the orphan one which mourns and consoles, though also one which mutinies and perseveres. Despite the existence of a steadily rising illegitimacy rate from the seventeenth century to the present, this factor has never accounted for more than a low proportion of the parentally-deprived. In recent times, however, divorce and desertion have registered something of a challenge to the factors of early death and illegitimacy, and in Britain and America broken homes are now a matter of growing concern at the level of social welfare.

Stone's book traces the rise of 'affective individualism' in the eighteenth century. The term denotes the advent of a greater individual freedom, with the alleviation of kinship pressures which came about at that time, together with a more considerate child-rearing; these ensured a more tolerant attitude towards sexual behaviour and towards marriage for love. Women, children and the poor nevertheless remained inferiors, while the individualistic, and even the affectionate, father could be experienced as no less of a constraining force than his predecessors. Affective individualism, moreover, had soon to contend with the dictatorial ethic of Victorian family life. Stone's discussion uses the evidence of autobiography, but very little evidence from literature: it is as if they were different, and as if literature were skewed by the affective individualism of authors. But it seems quite clear that some of his stories are the same as those told by romantic fictioneers, that his calculations are not such as to suppress the excitements of a literary history which attributes to private lives of the later eighteenth century a 'gripping nostalgia for the nest', or the dualistic 'alternations of joy and fear caused by the Romantic Mother'.[4] It may seem that the authority of fathers was scarcely diminished in an age of filial independence, and that mothers were to gain a new power, as was the nuclear family itself, whose long supremacy in English life has lately been stressed by social historians. And it is probable that this was accompanied by some intensification of ambivalent attitudes towards parents, and that such attitudes had a part to play in the rise of romantic duality. If the family could be experienced as a haven in the nineteenth century, it could also be experienced as a prison, as a Newgate or Marshalsea, by children of the classes from which the literature of the orphan derived. Some of these children felt that they were like orphans.

Affective individualism may appear remote from the world of tribal magic, of mangers and bullrushes, where a divine sponsorship looks after outcasts and strangers, and moves in mysterious ways to award them power. We are by this time in a largely secular world, where kinship could eventually be thought to have contracted to the domain of the immediate family, where first events in the immediate family were eventually to be thought to determine the course of a life, and to be reproduced in adult encounters with members of the communities that surrounded the family. And yet the old stories and enchantments were not forgotten. Misfortune and its secrets still hold the promise of success, and even of divine aid. We notice that orphans (and the imaginary orphans who write books about them) become rich and famous. On the page, the unfortunate have tended to win. At the end of the day, the stricken deer sits down to dinner in a splendid mansion.

The literary tradition of Gothic strangeness has been the orphan's refuge. The mode rests upon imagined states of estrangement, and of advancement. Many of the early Terror novels, and many of their successors, comforted the public by finding prospects and heritages for the forlorn: once the mysteries of places like Udolpho were solved, estates and annuities came to light, and fainting Emily was revived by a sound marriage which was also a marriage for love—a medicinal compound of the time, and of later times. There was comfort in unhappy endings too, in recitals of affliction and extinction. On and off the page, and whether down and out and dead or saved and successful, orphans have been imitated, and sensibility, suffering, solitariness, darkness and mystery, envied.

The orphan has many shapes, and many names: outcast, outsider, stranger, changeling, foundling, bastard, lad, lamb, urchin, ragamuffin, waif, wraith, victim, outlaw, guerrilla, fugitive, refugee, escapee, evacuee, tramp, vagrant, vagabond, wanderer, maverick, clown, artist, writer, monster, misfit, queer. A further list can be compiled of words preferred in orphan narratives—in the earlier of these especially: independent, irregular, singular, unaccountable, curious, interesting, strange, fey, steal, soar, sore, sole, soul, solitude, imagination, fancy, flight, escape, dream, delirium, trance, confinement, captivity, contrariety, inconsistency, variance, whim, impulse, imbecile, victim, forlorn, sick. The earlier literature spoke of various mythical or archetypal figures: Proteus, Narcissus, Cain, Jonah, Judas, Satan, Don Juan and Don Quixote, the Flying Dutchman, the Wandering Jew. Other Jews have served as types of the outcast, and sentimental Englishmen of the epoch which brought the abolition of the slave trade held with Cowper that 'lambs and Negroes both are harmless things.' The 'coloured population of the globe' had become 'interesting', as Charlotte Brontë's *Shirley* makes clear, and was to remain so.[5]

A number of real people, some of them writers, have also served: Keats, the most notable of literature's and of nature's orphans, and the convivial Dickens, who was a famous performer in the role of outcast, and Kafka. Poe was a renowned isolate and wretch. Sir Charles Chaplin's Dickensian tramp won him a huge celebrity, and Marilyn Monroe's impersonation of Dickens's Little Nell met the same fate. Monstrous reputations in art and entertainment have been earned by orphans. And the incongruous sound of applause can be heard to blend, among the cells and sub-groups of distress, insult and injury, with a susurrus of mutual recognition. In the middle years of the present century a joke was current in which a homosexual murmured, to a fellow, an endearment which appears to have originated in the early exchanges of romantic duality: 'You interest me strangely.' They were doubles, that is to say—two of an exciting and excluded kind. The word 'queer' was used at this time for such doubles. It has now been replaced by 'gay', the dear old word for bachelors, which may suggest that, in coming out of the closet, homosexuals have come in out of the storm. Each of these words was favoured at an earlier point in the history of exclusion and of a dissident duality. Hamlet and Lear, both of them orphans of the storm which rages in this book, were 'gay', wrote Yeats, at a time when the word could sometimes mean immoral.

The names and attributes of the orphan warn that he is equivocal. So is his favourite activity of flight, and the word itself hovers between the activities of flying—in the sense of triumph or transcendence—and fleeing. The orphan has his double—the waif his wraith—in the sense that he is at once sole and several, singular and plural, weak and strong, small and large, soft and hard, silent and outspoken, a hero and a monster. Waifs will be wolves . . . This expresses what we think of the deprived, of those who have been badly treated, and it responds to a contradiction inherent in romantic preconception: the orphan has been worshipped by those for whom both privacy and publicity are attractive, by those who want both to quit the world and to control it. It also responds to a conception of family life which dwells on the choice faced by children who need both to fall in with it and to fall out. Family life has versions of the bind or predicament of the poisonous cure; it resembles the orphan it creates in having the double in it, and the devil. The ambivalence of family life is affirmed in the bisection of the orphan image, which is that of someone both at home and away, both benign and fierce.

Fictions of all sorts, from the first Gothic tales, have echoed to the blubbing and blabbing of the inscrutable child who appears to feel both excluded and imprisoned, locked out and locked in. In the words of Hogg's *Confessions*: 'if I had taken my measures to abscond and fly from my native place, in order to free myself of this tormenting, intolerant, and bloody reformer, he had likewise taken his to expel me, or throw me into the hands of justice.' To think about orphans can look like a way of thinking about the native place, where justice wears two faces, where human beings may be exposed to the orphan's double trouble of coercion and neglect. But the poisonous cures of family life have their counterparts in later, or other, life. The mutinous remaining and returning which runs in families is powerfully symbolic. Children who want both to stay and to go, to break and not to break with their parents, are sure to find that this dilemma of divided loyalties will be repeated. Early uncertainties can be deemed to recur, by those, for instance, who are persuaded that, while the notion of the double life has testified to marital ambivalence, the notion of the double has testified to the mixed feelings of the adolescent who wants both to supplant and to emulate the father he resembles.

The diversity of the literature of diversity is intimidating, but the images of orphan, double and flight intersect in most of the narratives which comprise this literature, and a scheme can be attempted for what sometimes happens when the hypothesis of duality is applied to the situation of the outcast and the activity of escape, for what happens when an outcast, who may be supposed to have nothing to lose, nevertheless quits or flits. Romance plots escapes from familiarity, and from the family—escapes which are then revealed to be ominous or impossible: in the context of duality, they may be recoils from some familiar and fatal spirit. Romance promises that bounds may be passed, bonds broken, that nature and society may be deserted, while also, on many occasions, retracting the promise. One of the functions of romantic duality is to secure that promise and that retraction. The scheme in question is fulfilled when an orphan, literal or figurative, distressed and oppressed, becomes aware of his double, who may perform, or incite the orphan to perform, misdemeanours and rebellious acts, and who will frequently prove an oppressor, one who may take his place in the world in which he has failed. The orphan may soar to heaven by way of escape, and sink back again to earth, or he may steal through life, and away from the community which death alone will permit him to escape. All three elements in the scheme aspire to secrecy—a tendency which is then dualistically reversed in terms of a habit of confesssion. The work in which such adventures are told is likely to be cast in confessional form. In gaining a double, the orphan duplicates the author of the work in which he figures: orphan and author collaborate in this confession. The confession corresponds to a course of action which has been attributed, in the present century, to family life—whereby someone seeks independence by imagining himself an orphan. This is what Anne Frank did, and Freud's 'family romance' is a name which has been given to the behaviour which resists a parent and invents for itself a glorious origin and the status of changeling.

The imagination of the double has been explained as an effort to deal with the existence of evil—an effort which leads to the assignment of destructive urges to another self, which may chase the subject as the spectre of his own disobedience. This interprets the fact that while the double may enable the orphan to attack his enemies, the double may also behave like an enemy, striking from outside—like an oppressor, a possessor, a tempter or devil, a tyrant or parent. Where the double reeks of aggression, revenge and deceit, these are aimed at the orphan: and yet they *are* the orphan. We are in a world of polymorphous hostility, from which he suffers and in which he is implicated. We are brought to feel that he is engaged in the impossible task of trying to escape from himself, or to separate himself from someone whom he can't help resembling or repeating.

Doubles are usually hostile or fatal to the first self, though some are virtuous and conscientious; when the second self is friendly, it tends to be called by that name, while the name 'alter ego' is usually neutral. According to the traditions available to the escape artists of Romanticism, doubleness was dishonesty, and doubles were bad omens, presaging death. The heritage depicts lost souls, their capture by the Devil, a traffic with darkness, and the subject has never shed the eeriness of its supernatural origins. Nor is it remote from the mentality of those many parts of the contemporary world where the stranger can still, in all seriousness, be seen as diabolical and hateful. Orphans are 'strange' for the literature that pursues them, as doubles and duplicity are, and 'strange' is a word which can mean both intrusion and death, which signals the existence of other people and of another world. Henry Cockburn, who spoke of a 'strange spirit of lying', also spoke of a strange spirit of dying. His last words were not Manasseh-like, but they can be considered romantic: 'This is death, and a strange feeling it is.'[6] In the literature of duality, strangeness steals. Strangeness, which does not belong, is seen to take what does not belong to it. Not to belong is, in this setting, to mean harm. We are, as I say, in a world of enemies—where the individual may be his own worst enemy, and may not belong to himself. Waifs will be wolves, and wolves will be waifs: where either is the case, the case is declared strange, and the hostility which it shows is recognized both as a liberation and as an intrusion, both as a deliverance and as deathly strange. It is both good and bad to be strange; the word is, as 'fly' is, equivocal. One of its German translations, *unheimlich*, in which *himmlisch*, or 'heavenly', is contentiously present, has been a 'both' word, and a celebrated crux, for Freud and for his interpreters. The equivocations of unhomeliness, uncanniness, and of flight, are a paramount feature of the romantic text. Romanticism has upheld the claims of the social groups from which its people are said to steal and to separate themselves; its enviable secrets and disguises and escapes are perceived as offences; the eagerness of romantic independence often comes to grief. All this invites the eeriness and strangeness of a melodramatic and moribund duality. Duplication has kept its ties with duplicity and damnation, with lying and dying.

Freud thought that the primordial double may have been the immortal soul, and that, having given promise of eternal life, the double later became deathly. Orphan, double and flight have certainly been expressions, in modern times, of an interest in avoiding and mitigating the fact of physical death: as the only complete escape from common life, death has been desired, disliked and equivocated. The secret orphan journey resembles and contains the fateful swoons and sicknesses of romantic writing in general: it can seem to be a flight-unto-death, after which a new life ensues, as it does, at journey's end, in *Jane Eyre*. Some of these journeys are no escape but a succession of escapades and wonders. Others are less picaresque than psychic: secret, solitary, conspiratorial, redemptive, suicidal, with all the danger and purported enlightenment of the modern 'trip'. There can be two places, the true and the false, just as there can be two such selves. The trip to the true place, where the falsities of common life cannot penetrate, is hard to complete, and the place is soon surrendered on arrival. The common knowledge of a true place to which an 'immortal part' is bound is still current, though no longer robust, and is quite as much a knowledge of duality as is the modern habit of invoking for marriage a Platonic 'better half'.

The primordial knowledge of the subject referred to by Freud is likely to have gone well beyond the exemption of the soul from common life. The human family and the human body are, after all, in one sense, proof positive of duality. Family resemblances and replications indicate that doubles exist in nature; and in art, doubles need be no more like the selves to which they correspond than a son may be like his father, or a character his author. As for the body, this is evidently a pair, and a bundle of binary forms. The brain is two brains, each with its own skills. The corpus callosum which joins the cerebral hemispheres can be severed in cases of injury, to produce what are reported to be two separate minds. In recent times, medical science has referred to 'dissociations of personality' caused by injury and disease, and to the 'divided personalities' that occur during fits of absent-mindedness.[7] The language employed here is not recent, and some part of the observations it conveys can be credited with a long history.

The story of the modern double starts with the magical science of the eighteenth century in Europe, when Mesmerists or Animal Magnetists went in for an experimental separation of the second self, and romantic writers went in for its cultural exploitation. Jean Paul Richter invented the term *doppelgänger*, and studied the notion of fellowship, of the friend as alter ego; Goethe, Tieck, Kleist, among other German writers of the time, sped the progress of the subject; Hoffmann identified the double with a part of the personality, with an element of internal threat, and portrayed himself in a character on whom he conferred a 'ghostly *Doppelgänger*, born of the heart's blood of his lacerated breast'. 'Romantic multiple man' had taken the stage, and this was the heyday of the Rosicrucian doctor, of Romanticism's scientific virtuoso or dilettante, of such men as G. H. Schubert and Hoffmann himself.[8] A craze for duality spread from Germany to the rest of Europe. The Gothic strain in the literature of nineteenth-century Scotland and England was to accommodate the lore and idiom of magic, and of the new pseudo-sciences, Magnetism and Phrenology. In relation to most manifestations of the dualistic epoch of the nineteenth century Magnetism and its successor, hypnotism, were to prove an enduring stimulus. Duality was, among other things, an abracadabra. It was a taste for spells, powders, draughts, elixirs, wizard's wands and doppelgänger-sticks. Literally, it took to the stage: the performer, the illusionist, became—together, eventually, with the spy—dualistic proofs and embodiments, and stock figures. We were to enter a world—a world of spectacle and sleight—in which dramas of deception, detection, and pursuit, of the double agent, would be an industry and a commerce. We may have come a long way from primitive apprehensions of the double, but ventriloquists and their dummies, whom they sometimes speak of as doubles, provide truly eerie instances of an objectification of the second self, in the likeness, very often, of a sinister and disobedient son. One English ventriloquist in current practice has as a dummy a weeping pierrot boy. The audience is informed that the tears are those of an orphan.

In the writer's closet, romantic multiple man created a theatre of the self, pored over the enigma of his own inconsistency, and nursed the sense that the mind could be a strange compound of this or that contending power. Hogg was 'a strange compound of genius and imbecility', according to Robert Macnish, who thought that Phrenology alone could 'account for' such a man, who was himself a strange compound of doctor and writer, and who said that he had made use of the pen-name 'James Hogg'. Thirty years later, in Bulwer-Lytton's novel *A Strange Story*, the wicked double was described as a 'strange compound of cynicism and credulity'.[9] These ideas appealed not only to writers of a sensational turn, but to many other writers too; they were not lodged only in the soft heads of the susceptible and in the hard heads of commerce. We now talk of the 'romantic novel', and not just of a romantic poetry quite separate from the underworld of the Gothic, and with little to show for itself in the way of an accompanying prose fiction. The romantic novel is no different from the Gothic novel of early and later times, and of the present time, and among its achievements are works which ardently use, even where they affect to disdain, the ideas in question, and the conjuring-tricks in question. Duality and conjuring were permitted for a while within the physicians' guilds where the orthodoxies of medical science were being built and defended, and it was only with anguish that they were driven out; it can be claimed that they have yet to be driven out of the modern semi-science of psychoanalysis. In the earlier part of the nineteenth century, literature and science could still be seen as aspects of a single knowledge: the writer and the doctor could be friends, and the sharers of a self. Dickens was a hypnotist as well as a novelist, and he was a friend of the leading exponent of clinical hypnotism, John Elliotson, who was made President of the London Phrenological Society in 1824, the year in which Hogg's magnetic *Confessions* was published, and was to be sent, in his eminence, beyond the pale of medical orthodoxy. In 1844, another doctor, A. L. Wigan, published *The Duality of the Mind*, in which the double was physiologically explained. He said that the hemispheres of the brain were 'capable' of separate and conflicting volitions, and that every man is conscious of these two wills, 'quite distinct from the government of the passions by the intellect'.[10]

Wigan's cerebral capability and Keats's negative capability are elements in the nineteenth-century consensus which believed in the duality of the mind, in a mental play of contending principles, and in a golden 'rule of contraries'. These contending principles tended both to promote and to prevent social integration, and they had a great deal to do with a conflict between good and bad, soul and body, with submission to impulse, and, despite Wigan's word on the point, with the government of the passions by the intellect. The black magic of doubles stood to one side of this consensus. Elsewhere, philosophers found ways of stating the rule of contraries, with Emerson, for instance, convinced of a universal binariness or twoship: 'An inevitable dualism bisects nature, so that each thing is a half, and suggests another thing to make it whole; as, spirit, matter; man, woman; odd, even; subjective, objective; in, out; upper, under; motion, rest; yea, nay.'[11] This may be contrasted with a statement of the eighteenth century, Bishop Butler's 'Everything is what it is, and not another thing', reaffirmed, well on in the history of duality, as an epigraph to G. E. Moore's *Principia Ethica*. Since Butler's statement, a principle of uncertainty had been affirmed. There had fallen the shadow of a doubt, the shimmer, shudder, teeter, tightrope and twilight, thrill and emancipation of a doubt. Everything was now another thing, and nothing was but what was not.

Orphan secrecy and flight, which may, or may not, summon up the double, are a feature of the modern world's experience of the romantic. Adults of the present time may be said to have attended a School of Night, where they were coached in the art of escape—while warned that romantic escapism was imbecility and immaturity. 'She united with Bellerophon in clandestine love': as a boy, I thought I saw these words in the Victorian translation of Homer by Butcher and Lang, and the image they gave was combined with another, that of the frontispiece to an edition of *Uncle Tom's Cabin* showing 'Eliza's Escape' from slavery. With her child in her arms, a child due to be stolen from her and sold down the river, she stole at dusk over the ice-floes of the Ohio. These have been our covert instructions, and they have afforded an education in secrecy. For the times of which I am writing, secrecy has been disobedient, wilful, truthful and delightful. Secrecy steals, and smiles. The impulse, whim or humour of escape has piled up a stock of secrets which relate to acts and shows of affective individualism, and to crimes. Many relate to Bellerophon's crime, and a few to that of Oedipus: romantic flight has been thought, as has duality, to disclose the strange return to a mother. It has often led to something less outlandish. There is a way out of the community which has led to membership of a community of the secretive, a family of the forlorn—to the readership, let us say, of that literature where secrets are kept, and confessed, and brandished, and where, in modern times, obscurity has served as a principle of expression. Secrecy is, as these developments may indicate, both social and anti-social, just as the secrets treated in this fiction are those both of solitude and of conspiratorial stealth.

The literature of duality is at once submissive and rebellious. But a male rebelliousness looms large. Comparatively few women are awarded doubles, or write about them, though many romantic heroines are orphans. One work in which a heroine rebels, or half-rebels, and is admitted to the discourse of duality is Charlotte Brontë's *Shirley*, a romance crowded with duplication, figurative theft, and a cistern-like physiology of sentiment. Hearts fill. Spirits rise and fall and flow. A secret thrill flows through the veins. Nerves are steeled, and are disordered. On every interesting and inconsistent brow and cheek falls the 'crimson shadow' of consciousness and susceptibility. There are two heroines and two heroes—which provides, for the novel's dualistic intents and purposes, little more than décor. At the centre of events Shirley Keeldar replaces Caroline Helstone, and Louis Moore his imperfectly distinguishable brother Robert. The orphan Caroline, who is destined to regain her mother, wishes to 'steal away' from the Whitsuntide festivities at a country school, but is steeled to attend by Shirley, who 'had no fear of her kind'. Shirley soon asks: 'Is it our double?' She is referring to the 'manifold wraith' of a rival procession of Nonconformist children which challenges the Anglican file in a lane, and is thrust into a ditch. The two orphans then witness, in secret, a night attack of machine-breakers on Robert Moore's mill. No one must know what these girls have been up to. They return to Caroline's rectory: 'We will steal in as we stole out.' They 'stole upstairs', breathes the opening sentence of the next chapter. Secrecy has been linked here with delinquency and with duality.[12]

Later, ladies are gathered in a drawing-room: 'their hostess'—Shirley—'had stolen from them to visit Henry's tutor', Louis Moore, who is shortly to tell the world in a major soliloquy: 'A strange, secret ecstasy steals through my veins at moments.' This is Romance, as opposed to Common Sense: Romance is enfeebling, but he has found that Shirley's scorn and perversity 'steel' his nerves. In the novel at large, the cold steel of male common sense corrects, and is corrected by, the stealth of the feeling female: this is among its dualistic reciprocities, and among the thrills which constitute what might be called its tutorial eroticism. The notion of the marital better half is hereby elaborated: the novel suggests that both halves are better. It is permissible for some, Louis reflects, to 'redden' and behave 'susceptibly' with Shirley, but not for him, not for a tutor, or a tenant farmer. She is queen and child: 'Both characters are in her nature.' 'Both portraits are correct'—we may recall the language of *Villette*. And we may say that if Shirley has no double, there are certainly two Shirleys—queen and child, or, alternatively, androgyne landowner and weak woman, free agent and captive. She is 'inconsistent', as she is then told to her face, *de haut en bas*, by the tutor, who addresses her in the inconsistent character of a proud subordinate. That face turns crimson as they talk: she is herself susceptible. And she informs him: 'I am nervous.'[13] In the course of these reflections and discussions, duality and delinquency have been placed together: just as one of these two Shirleys can elsewhere be seen to go through the motions of a thief. Late in the novel, when the manufacturer Robert Moore has been shot by a zealot and is subject to 'strange feelings' of being about to die, Caroline 'steals' to his bedside, burgling the house to get there, in the fullness of her heart. A double marriage, and an honoured place in the community for all four of these better halves, lie ahead. The rebellion of the lower orders has long since disappeared from the book. Within the ranks of their superiors, the rebellion of two nervous and poetic females has come to an end.

Much of the sentiment that invests the theme of the separate life is false, and no one knows this better than a latter-day defender of the spinster, of the 'excellent' single woman sequestered in an age which was to invent the singles' bar—the novelist Barbara Pym. 'Well, of course,' retorts Mildred in *Excellent Women* of 1952, 'a lot of people over thirty are orphans.'[14] This is what Byron says in the last canto of *Don Juan*, where the tendencies and proximities discussed in this chapter are addressed: 'The world is full of orphans.'[15] The poem retails the adventures of a nonentity, who commemorates the Byronic notoriety: but what matters is the self apparent in the vagaries of the poem, in the error of its ways, in the digressive play with ideas of fiction and affectation, contradiction and uncertainty. Preceded by a sexual 'stole' at the end of the previous canto, the unfinished Canto 17 opens by speaking of orphans—'mules', in an expressive Italian term. There are 'orphans of the heart' and 'orphans in effect'. The latter are the products of an education which 'transgresses the great bounds of love or awe'; 'only children' may thus remain children all their lives. 'The wealthiest orphans are to be more pitied'—like Byron himself, an orphan prince, and like his poem's Aurora Raby. The narrator then brings on the double. He moves to describe himself as a chameleon, while also sending up the topos of the chameleon:

> Changeable too, yet somehow *idem semper*;
> Patient, but not enamoured of endurance;
> Cheerful, but sometimes rather apt to whimper;
> Mild, but at times a sort of Hercules *furens*;
> So that I almost think that the same skin
> For one without has two or three within.

Shortly after this, the unfinished poem of an unfinished man rattles to a halt. The year of its suspension was 1823, when Hogg may be presumed to have been writing the *Confessions*.

Elsewhere in the poem,[16] Byron has said what others would say again about the truthfulness of the chameleon mode—of the unfinished—in art:

> But if a writer should be quite consistent,
> How could he possibly show things existent?

The poem has another name for the inconsistency of writers and others, and that name is mobility—defined by Byron as 'an excessive susceptibility of immediate impressions'. *Don Juan* leaves us with the thought that orphans are mobile, and that women are, and that 'actors, artists, and romancers' are, and that many of these people blush.[17]

IV. STEAL AND SOAR

In August 1833, a picnic was held in the Pentland Hills, a few miles to the south of Edinburgh. The same picnic took place every year, and every year the master of the revels was the prominent Whig, Henry Cockburn, who had helped to draft the Scottish equivalent of the great Reform Bill, carried only a few months before, and who was still in Ministerial office. In a letter to one of his daughters he gave news of the picnic of 1833. Extracts can be read in a volume of his correspondence, and the entire letter has lately passed into the keeping of the National Library of Scotland.[1]

Quitting their town houses and their country estates—the 'paradises' of which they liked to speak—the ladies and gentlemen of the picnic made their way to the 'pastoral, Classical valley', as it's described here, of Habbie's Howe. The spot was sacred to the memory of the poet Allan Ramsay, and was thought to have provided the setting for his play, *The Gentle Shepherd*: but a rival Habbie's Howe has since been conceded to have a better claim, so that Cockburn's worshipful picnic was mis-sited by some six miles. Their 'hermit fare' included cold veal pie, hot broiled salmon, tea, coffee, chocolate, drams of whisky. Puns and horseplay broke out. Somebody was very nearly pushed into the burn. But Cockburn's letter jokes about how he sat on a stone, apart, shunning the gluttons and buffoons, and yielding himself to the bliss of solitude. 'My soul was with the Gentle Shepherd.'

The reader of his published correspondence may feel that if this was a pastoral, classical occasion, a homage to 'the Scottish Theocritus', it was also, by virtue of the host's abstention and abstraction, a romantic occasion. And this impression would be enhanced by a passage that was deleted from the letter when it was prepared for publication. There Cockburn confesses: 'I steal a moment (as the romantic people say) to tell all this to you.'

His letter was written in fun, at a moment stolen from the discharge of his professional responsibilities: but its irony is not a scornful one, and it need not be refused admission to the history of romantic behaviour, whose deadly earnest has proved compatible with high spirits and a pursuit of the ridiculous. Cockburn's communion with Ramsay's shade was a kind of secret, but it was a secret that he was ready to tell, and the communion was publicly performed in nature's own theatre, and witnessed by an audience, however heedless and boisterous, of twenty-two persons. Time and again, romantic secrets must be seen to be secrets, and they are often divulged. Such secrets are as equivocal as any orphan.

Cockburn, the Pentlands' imaginary orphan, was right to think that romantic people steal—figuratively, and, as a rule, though not on this occasion, intransitively. The word is everywhere in the writing, and on the occasions, which we take to be romantic. It is a word for what the orphan does. Both the waif and the wraith who pursues him steal. The imaginary orphan has more to steal from than the literal orphan: both, however, can be found to perform the action, or go through the motion. Lovers do so too, and the double life is like the behaviour of a burglar. 'Steal' is a word which bears a double meaning. It is enthusiastic, and it is disgraceful. It may persuade those who hear it that romance is stealth, that romance is theft.

The French writer Jean Genet has been the arch-reinventor for modern times of the idea that thieves are romantic. His has been a career in which the literal and the figurative senses of the word nicely coincide. Genet was a real orphan who really stole. His works present him as a creature of romance, as an outlaw and a monster, thrilled by his treacheries, public and private. For this, he has been condemned, but has also become famous and respected. *The Thief's Journal* informs its readers: 'the greater my guilt in your eyes . . . the greater will be my freedom. The more perfect my solitude and uniqueness.' When this thief wanders into Nazi Germany, a 'strange force' prevents him from stealing: '"It's a race of thieves," I thought to myself. If I steal here, I perform no singular deed that might fulfil me. I obey the customary order; I do not destroy it.'[2] To be himself, to perfect his solitude and uniqueness, he must rob a community which is honest, and hates what he does. This is romantic of him.

Romance is stealth, and theft, and it is flight. If time flies, so does the thief, and in the Latin tongue the matter is given the appearance of a tautology: *fur fugit.* In English, 'steal' and 'fly' reveal an approximation in meaning to which the ambiguous relationship between 'fly' and 'flee' has contributed. The Latin verb *fugio*, I flee, stands close to *fur*, a thief, and can be translated into English verse by the figurative 'steal'. In French, the same word, *voler*, signifies both stealing and soaring. The Latin verb *volo* means both soaring and wishing: so that it may seem that fugitiveness became furtive in French. These semantic points call to mind the formidable power of communal life, and the possibility that to separate yourself from a community is to injure it. The Anglo-American poet and doctor, Alex Comfort, has written of some of the dissident, separate lives to be encountered in a context in which, at times, the injured injure.

> Lovers and visionaries and thieves
> pursue with such great stealth their assignations . . .[3]

'Steal' has its sonorous and ominous past definite. 'Stole' sounds the 'oh' of romantic misery, and the two words form part of a night music of endeavour and distress. Rises and falls, high roads and low, are whispered in the syllables of the past and present tenses, and in those of their cousins and cognates. Solemn and ecstatic, this music is composed of sibilants, echoes, rhymes, assonances, puns: 'soul', 'sole', 'dole', 'sore', 'soar', 'seal', 'still', 'forlorn' . . . The same tunes can be heard in German. In Thomas Mann's tale of 1903, Tonio Kröger is a Northern artist of burgher stock who flees to the South, who feels that artists are outcasts, sick and sensual, and believes that art demands from its practitioners an extinction of personality, but who ends in the hope that his own art will be saved by his weakness for ordinary persons like the boy and girl loved by him in his youth. This last condition is viewed as both healthy and stealthy. 'Thither he stole on soft feet; and his skin prickled with the thievish pleasure of standing unseen in the dark and spying on the dancers there in the brightly lighted room.' 'Stole on soft feet' translates, and sounds like, '*schlich auf leisen Sohlen*' (more literally, 'crept on soft soles', which may also be thought to carry the tune of the German original). Then, when Tonio declares that 'my deepest and most secret love belongs to the blonde and blue-eyed, the fair and living, the happy, lovely, and commonplace' at whom he has here been stealing a look, that 'most secret love' translates '*verstohlenste Liebe*'—an expression which suggests, together with its echoing of the '*Sohlen*' which precedes it, that secrecy is theft.[4] In 1854, the year of Henry Cockburn's strange death, his compatriot the Revd George Gilfillan suggested as much when he envisaged the castaway poet Cowper occupying a 'secret nook' and then 'watching the landscape, with the Thames stealing slowly through it like an incognito king, and the evening light betraying his splendid secret'.[5] 'Splendid secret' is a romantic oxymoron: Gilfillan's melodious conventionality gives us the sole self of the outcast attended by the two selves of a prince in disguise and casts an aspersion on the separate life.

The figurative and fugitive 'steal' has its cognates—in 'glide', for instance, and 'flit', which virtually coincides with the etymologically different 'flight'. This is a literature in which ghosts and interesting Victorian women glide, and in which poets flit to the Moon. In 'The Eve of St. Agnes', Porphyro is urged to 'flit like a ghost away', and when the time comes for the lovers to be 'fled away into the storm'—away from their families—they 'glide, like phantoms'—and like thieves. The suggestion of theft, for flight, for secrecy and separation, imputes, to the approved excitements and endeavours of romance, the character of transgression. The theft in question appears to be a theft from the family and its domicile, or from the community, which confers on the 'thief', as the family does, identity and obligation. To the importance for romantic people of the virtue of sincerity we may add the evidence supplied by the stealing metaphor, and by the language and music which surround it, to the effect that sincerity, too, has been experienced as theft, and romantic behaviour assessed in terms of property, in terms of a cost to other people, or to a community—to the bourgeoisies of Cockburn's Edinburgh or Mann's Lübeck. This is a judgement which Romanticism has passed upon itself by means of a vocabulary which is not all defiance, indifference, and complaint—a vocabulary dominated by the intransigent intransitive which might also be designated the apologetic verb to 'steal'. Like the cult of secrecy, and the interest taken in duplicity and duality, the judgement may evoke a time of rising populations and crowded cities when tribal and familial pieties could be felt to need reassertion, a time when an increasing social mobility co-existed with severe constraints and a determined insistence on differences of class, a time when appearance and reality were forced apart. It is a judgement which can be considered no less expressive of Shakespeare's London than of that of Keats.

Love and theft have looked alike at times; there are smiles which they share. This chapter comments on the figurative 'steal', and on related uses of the verb to 'soar', where separation and an anxious equivocation are also apparent. What goes up must come down, flight goes before a fall, while stealing is both beautiful and criminal. Romantic people, and romantic lovers in particular, have behaved both like birds and like thieves. The figurative 'steal' is important to, while pre-dating, the poetry of Shakespeare. 'By heaven! I'll steal away,' cries Bertram in *All's well that ends well*:

FIRST LORD: There's honour in the theft.
PAROLLES: Commit it, count.

Helena is later to say: 'For with the dark, poor thief, I'll steal away.'[6] Love and theft are at issue in this play: Bertram steals from an enforced marriage, but Helena, who has forced herself upon him, steals too. The play may be thought to force an unhappy marriage between their respective honours, and dishonours. The multiple Shakespeare of the Romantic movement included a poet who used this word for forbidden practices of a sexual kind. Shakespeare's plays can only have strengthened the customary notion of stolen loves, and the currency of the sexual 'steal' must often have depended thereafter on its capacity to bring to mind the purloining of someone's wife or daughter. The development of the term can perhaps be compared with that of the term 'irregular': having been a word for error and independence, for meteoric flights and strange old houses, it became a word for sexual offences and the clandestine union.

The Merchant of Venice uses the word 'steal' in a sexual sense, and in a way which predicts, while also contrasting with, the ways in which the word has served as a figure of speech since the eighteenth century:

LORENZO: In such a night
Did Jessica steal from the wealthy Jew,
And with an unthrift love did run from Venice,
As far as Belmont.
JESSICA: In such a night
Did young Lorenzo swear he lov'd her well,
Stealing her soul with many vows of faith,
And ne'er a true one.[7]

In these lines, the activity of romantic stealing is granted the splendid secrecy of a moonlit night, and is set to music, an intensely erotic music, that of a duet between Lorenzo and the teasing Jessica. At the same time, the lines allow us to criticize the activity. Jessica is the daughter of the Jew she has stolen from in performing her moonlight flit, and the language can hardly fail to remind the audience that she has literally stolen from Shylock in her 'flight' from his house. And if it comes to that, as I think it should, the audience has already been told[8] that Lorenzo has 'stolen' Shylock's daughter.

In the first of these two 'steals', a literal sense is more obtrusive, and easier to distinguish from the metaphorical sense, than it tends to be with comparable uses of the word in later times, and the literal sense recurs in the line 'Stealing her soul with many vows of faith', where it is fastened by a pun to the meaning 'nerve' or 'invigorate'. The word 'steal' is subjected in the passage to two successive puns, the first of which brings out the word's inherent duality on occasions of this kind. The claim made on its members by a watchful community, which is felt in later uses, is felt in the first pun, where it is represented by the suggestion that parents should not be robbed by their children. The suggestion may be accounted all but drowned, together with the memory of Shylock's ducats, in the music of the duet. But it is not beyond recognition. The music has the joy of those who marry for love; it celebrates a success for privilege, and for the law which serves it. But it does not hide the thought that romantic love, so far from being unthrifty, may represent a theft from parents.

In *A Midsummer Night's Dream* the figurative 'steal' is used continually, and is linked, as in *The Merchant of Venice*, to the word 'flight'. Lysander calls on Hermia to 'steal forth thy father's house' to a wood outside Athens. The lovers intend to elude the law of Athens, which requires a woman to marry according to her father's will. The following night, by moonlight,

> A time that lovers' flights doth still conceal,
> Through Athens' gates have we devis'd to
> steal.

In the wood, Lysander and Hermia mix themselves up with Demetrius and Helena; a chapter of accidents and substitutions carries the sense of a dark design both respectful and subversive of romantic love, and of the imagination. This is a strange place—equivocal, wholesome, homely, exotic, extravagant. The fairies rule it during the hours of darkness, and describe it:

> I know a bank whereon the wild thyme blows,
> Where oxlips and the nodding violet grows
> Quite over-canopied with luscious woodbine,
> With sweet musk-roses, and with eglantine . . .

Lysander and Hermia's consenting 'stealth unto this wood' is reviewed, late in the play,[9] by her father:

> They would have stol'n away; they would, Demetrius,
> Thereby to have defeated you and me;
> You of your wife, and me of my consent.

The four lovers then wonder what has been happening to them. 'Everything seems double,' says Hermia. And Demetrius says:

> Are you sure
> That we are awake? It seems to me
> That yet we sleep, we dream.

The play became popular in the Romantic period, and its language proved decisive in nineteenth-century romance. It is a play in which dreaming is both treacherous and fundamental, in which imagination is double, in which everything is double, and its changelings and equivocations must by then have seemed sufficient in themselves to warrant a rediscovery. Its lovers steal in disobedience towards happiness and play, and the sexual meaning of that word was to govern its nineteenth-century figurative use, as it was to govern the nineteenth-century conception of the double life which seeks its magic wood. The romantic Shakespeare of the early plays not only steals but soars: the poet's eye is rolled up to heaven, and, in his protean nothingness, he can make something out of nothing. Stealing and soaring are for the most part readily distinguishable double-dyed activities in this literature, with the latter more or less exempt from the self-reproach of the romantic thief. But they share a tendency to be figurative, imaginative, and to imagine a departure from the world. There came a time when a poet was to soar like a bird while stealing to a magic wood modelled on the one outside Shakespeare's Athens, and to ask himself in conclusion: 'Do I wake or sleep?'

Youthful and tuneful, this romantic Shakespeare was busy during the middle years of the 1590s, when *Romeo and Juliet*, and the last two plays I have been looking at, were all written. This is a soaring verse, and among its flights is the balcony scene of *Romeo and Juliet*. The play employs the human indeterminateness of the traditional imagination, the vicinity of human life to other modes of being and to strange places, its dualistic suspension between a lower state of beasts and monsters and an angelic higher state near enough to clamber to and touch, a travel of the mind from earth to heaven and from heaven to earth. Romeo is intent here on a heavenly leap. Below, he rolls up an eye to Juliet, who is forbidden him for family reasons, and who will be forced, as the Chorus has it, to 'steal love's sweet bait from fearful hooks'. She has appeared with a sigh on the balcony, in the likeness of a superior creature, a seraph. Romeo responds:

> O! speak again, bright angel; for thou art
> As glorious to this night, being o'er my head,
> As is a winged messenger of heaven
> Unto the white-upturned wond'ring eyes
> Of mortals, that fall back to gaze on him
> When he bestrides the lazy-pacing clouds,
> And sails upon the bosom of the air.

At the start of the play, still in love with Rosaline, Romeo has told Mercutio:

you have dancing shoes
With nimble soles; I have a soul of lead
So stakes me to the ground I cannot move.
MERCUTIO: You are a lover; borrow Cupid's wings
And soar with them above a common bound.
ROMEO: I am too sore enpierced with his shaft
To soar with his light feathers; and so bound
I cannot bound a pitch above dull woe.

In all of the three puns in this exchange, the element of constraint and detention in nineteenth-century duality is prefigured. In all of the three plays, constraint is identified with family life and soaring with resistance to parents. The braving of that storm takes place in what can be summarised as a twofold world answering to a twofold state of man—a *homo duplex* compounded of mortal and immortal parts, of familiarity and strangeness. The plays make us conscious of a future in which the repertoire of leaps and bounds would include marriage for love and respites from marriage.

A great occasion in the history of human ups and downs comes about in *Paradise Lost*. If there is this romantic Shakespeare, there is also a romantic Milton—the aspiring and defiant poet later claimed by romantic people in the course of their constructive 'misreadings' of the past. Eve is wooed as she sleeps by Satan, who calls her to an assignation, promising the Moon, and the love song of the nightingale. Darkness and light and love and truth and beauty are gathered into her dream. She assents, and ascends. Tasting the fruit of the tree of forbidden knowledge, this thief goes up like a bird or aeroplane:

Forthwith up to the clouds
With him I flew, and underneath beheld
The earth outstretched immense, a prospect wide
And various: wondering at my flight and change
To this high exaltation; suddenly
My guide was gone, and I, me thought, sunk down,
And fell asleep.[10]

Misreaders are entitled to say that Eve's rashness has been made beautiful, and her Icarian dream has been re-enacted in many a subsequent abortive escape, including her own: modern trips have been a drama of flight and fall, and the word 'Icarian' was to achieve a certain prominence with the coming of Romanticism.

In making its way from the occasions of Milton to those of the Romantics, English poetry stole and soared. A debt to society was paid, and was left unpaid. So far as it defaulted, this poetry turned towards nature, conceived of as teacher, mother, dispenser of sensations and of terminal sleeps, and as the opposite of urban life. The process can be studied with reference to a commonplace-book kept by Henry Cockburn and a few friends, lovers of rural leisure and of the Pentland Hills, between the years 1807 and 1809.[11] The manuscript consists of over two hundred pieces of verse, the choice of seven refugees from the city. These Edinburgh friends relocated themselves just outside the Athens of the North, like Lysander and company, or like Lorenzo and company: romantic secrecy, that is to say, is apt to run about as far as Belmont. They may be called Whig romantics. They felt for the poor and the miserable, while displaying a Whiggish indeterminacy, or hypocrisy, on that score; in the manner of a ruling class, they were both soft-hearted and hard-headed. They were romantics who would once have been held not to be, because of their connection with the supposedly anti-romantic *Edinburgh Review*, and because of the classical temper of Cockburn's histories. Their commonplace-book, however, points them out as classical romantics who were also Whig romantics.

The editor of the *Edinburgh Review*, Francis Jeffrey, Wordsworth's detractor and Cockburn's friend, belonged to this Whig *jeunesse* but did not contribute to their commonplace-book. He cared more about the controversial new poets than his reputation used to allege; the recently published *Lyrical Ballads* at one point 'enchanted' him.[12] As for his friends on the Pentlands, if they did not class themselves as romantic people, their choice of extracts, and Cockburn's own poems, offer a welcome to the worship of nature, and of childhood and solitude, which was being practised and enjoined by writers of the 'Lakeish' persuasion. At the same time, it is plain that if this was a new poetry, these were old themes. Chronologically, the anthology moves from copious amounts of Milton (there is no Shakespeare) on to Thomson, Akenside, Cowper, and to Wordsworth and Coleridge. Thematically, the anthology steals and soars into the arms of nature. It starts with two passages, in Cockburn's hand, from 'Tintern Abbey', and much of the poetry which follows these passages is the arterial poetry which led out of the eighteenth century into Romanticism. The anthology closes the rift which used to be set by romantic historians of literature between the Romantics and their precursors of the later eighteenth century—between, for instance, Wordsworth and Cowper.

The point can be enforced if we consult the cento or patchwork poem which was published by Wordsworth in 1835.[13] Three of his favourite pieces of eighteenth-century verse were collated to make a poem in which three other poets speak with one voice, as the one man of feeling, about solitude and communion with nature: Thomson, James Beattie and Akenside. From Akenside come the lines:

> What God in whispers from the wood
> Bids every thought be kind?

The notion of a 'Kind Nature' is widespread in eighteenth-century verse: formerly synonymous, the two words had parted, and optimists took pleasure in combining them. Wordsworth's cento, which talks of a god of shades and whispers, and which ends with Beattie's image of an owl winging its way as if to extinction, 'down' towards a 'more profound repose', gives the sense of a destination to which it would be appropriate to steal, and to sink, and to soar. The three constituent passages appear, separately, not only in the Pentlands anthology, itself a huge cento, but in David Nichol Smith's *Oxford Book of Eighteenth-Century Verse*, which called attention, in 1926, to the dependence of Wordsworth on immediate predecessors. The new poet was no enemy of the poetry of nature and romance which preceded him, and he was perhaps no more of a romantic than Cockburn and his friends, foregathering at 'Habbie's Howe' to worship nature in a land which was well-fitted for the purpose and which was already in business as a land of romance.

The idea of a soaring or stealing return to nature had already had a long and lively history when Wordsworth began to write, and none of his initiatives was such as to subvert it. The cento can't be considered a reactionary document of his later years. He had long been drawn to these lines: in 1819, the three passages appeared separately in a volume presented by him to Lady Lowther which included work by the seventeenth-century Countess of Winchilsea: 'Where is that World to which the fancy flies?'[14] Wordsworth did not slide back in middle age to admiring the capacity to ask questions about another world. He had already obtained his own answers from the world of nature.

The author of *The Prelude* is an orphan who steals, and whose stealing is the function of a multiple self—a 'strange rendezvous' of contradictory impulses.[15] The first 'stealth' in the poem is the borrowing of a boat, for which he is thunderously chased by a mountain: in retreat, I 'stole my way'. More ornamental 'steals' tell the story of the old soldier, discarded by his calling: in the 1805 version of the story, 'I steal along that silent road' at night, while in the version of 1850 it is a stream which goes 'stealing with silent lapse to join the brook'.[16] Then, in Book Nine, the story of Julia and Vaudracour is that of a stolen love, in which the poet's own lapse is remembered. One of the meanings of the poem concerns a search, among mountains, for a mother, on the part of a miscellaneous self which transgresses.

Over the interval of two hundred years, the two words 'steal' and 'soar' proceed towards their role in Romantic literature. No fundamental semantic change seems to have occurred. In each case, an erotic meaning and a pious meaning co-exist; in later times, both words have been frequent in devotional contexts. They are to be found together on an occasion copied for the Pentlands commonplace-book. 'O Nature!' exclaimed the Anglo-Scottish poet James Thomson, some fifty years before, at the end of 'Autumn', in *The Seasons*: 'Snatch me to heaven.' The anthologists picked a passage which falls a few lines earlier, concerning

> the man who, from the world escaped,
> In still retreats and flowery solitudes
> To Nature's voice attends from month to month,
> And day to day, through the revolving year.

And another passage, earlier again in 'Autumn':

Then is the time
For those whom wisdom and whom nature charm
To steal themselves from the degenerate crowd,
And soar above this little scene of things.[17]

Stealing and soaring are treated here as congruent or complementary; and the autumnal setting can be compared with others which are nocturnal or crepuscular. This 'steal' is unusual in being reflexive: we are told what it is that is being stolen from a society. But the turn to nature is wise because the society is corrupt. We might feel that a Shakespearian pun is being renewed—that this 'steal' carries an assertion, a steeling, of the will. This would add to the ambiguity which is there already in most figurative uses of the word, as it is in comparable uses of the word 'soar', and would alert us to a problem often raised by the language of withdrawal in the eighteenth century: how far is withdrawal an effort of will, a feat, and how far is it a fault, a fit, a lapsing or surrender? Thomson may be thought to correct any impression of laxity by stressing that nature teaches 'a moral song'

as I steal along the sunny wall,
Where Autumn basks, with fruit empurpled deep.[18]

The approach to nature and to heaven gathers effects of languor and ripeness which look like antecedents of Keats's ode to the same season. Thomson's 'Summer' has its 'steals' too, some of which are casual, ornamental and affected, and some of which are sexual:

Now from the world
Sacred to sweet retirement lovers steal . . .[19]

Sexual 'steals' tell the tale of Damon and Musidora. Damon watches Musidora bathing naked: according to Wordsworth, it was at this tale that worn copies of *The Seasons* were apt to betray most signs of perusal.

The road that leads in the anthology to the poetry of the Romantics is travelled, for the most part, in blank verse. But there is another metre which performs the journey, and it is that of Thomson's *The Castle of Indolence*, a work in Spenserian stanzas which appealed both to Wordsworth and to Keats. Thomsonian indolence is Spenserian indolence, in the sense—apparent in the anthology—that, for Thomson as for Beattie a little later on, something of Spenser's moods and décor was to accompany the revival of his stanza. In Thomson's poem, a state of sloth or stealth, a cultivation of the senses, is assailed by the active spirit which was making Britain, and Britannic industry and warfare, great. At the same time, sloth admits the pleasures of the imagination and the song of the nightingale: here again are the complexities which may enter into an abdication from the world. Thomson saw a point in the disgracefulness of bliss. He saw possibilities in 'thoughtless slumber', in stealth, stillness, and sensation, in estrangement and arrest. And Keats was soon to see Thomson's point, and to extend it. Thomsonian indolence was incorporated in his doctrine of negative capability, and in the language of his poetry. Keats's 'Ode on Indolence' is a tribute to the earlier poet, though it does not afford the extended view of the condition which we come across in others of the Odes, and in the letters.

An old indolence spoke to the romantic people of the early nineteenth century, among them the Whig romantics who copied from the poem ten years before Keats's odes to indolence and aspiration. Cockburn and his friends transcribed Thomson's question: 'What, what is virtue but repose of mind?' And they longed for 'the pleasing land of drowsyhed' displayed in his poem. In the very different country of Scotland, the equation of sloth and virtue may have seemed heady and exotic: but it was also a fanciful way of expressing the time-honoured preoccupation with rural leisure and holiday licence. For another Anglo-Scottish poet, Thomas Campbell, well-known to the Pentlands circle, Thomson's castle was a type of the paradisal country house. He hailed the Whig house of Althorp as a Thomsonian asylum for learned loungers while spending his time there slaving over proofs.[20]

At certain levels of Scottish life, indolence was practically an indictable offence. Cockburn was blamed for it in so many words, and he blamed himself, contrasting it with ambition, and with virtue. This man was a soarer and a success who was also slothful enough to fall into sore debt. His mixed feelings on the subject of idleness were uttered in the dualistic praise he was to assign to his friend the poet James Grahame, one of the compilers of the anthology, who became familiar with the inside of Thomson's castle. Grahame knew what it was to be indolent in the sense of drunk, as did Campbell, who also knew the equivocal pleasures of the leading opiate of the time—laudanum: for both men, drugs bore one of the double meanings of the new age. Cockburn claimed that Grahame had 'the softest of human hearts': he was angered by 'what he held to be oppression, especially of animals or the poor, both of whom he took under his special protection'. Cockburn and Grahame were alike in being acquainted with the soaring which sinks into sloth—to soar again another day. To Grahame, Cockburn writes, 'nothing was a luxury that excluded the etherial calm of indolence. Yet his virtue was by no means passive. He was roused into a new nature by abhorrence of cruelty, and could submit to anything in the cause of duty.'[21]

'Indolence' is used here as a volatile word, at once high and low, in that the motionlessness which it implies is felt to be capable of flight or compatible with it. Hatred of cruelty rouses, raises, Grahame, enables him to soar, and endows him with a second self. At the same time, the indolence of his original nature is called ethereal, soaring. If his virtue lay in a capacity for indignation, the encomium lets it be supposed that there was virtue in his inertia too. We think of the 'wise passiveness' which is commended in Wordsworth's poetry, and which was imparted to Keats's doctrine of the multiple mind. Passiveness is a quality in which a number of states and capacities are latent. There is feeling in it, and compassion, and weakness and suffering. *Per contra*, there is passion and imagination in it too, and the hyperactivity of flight. Cockburn's sentences paint the portrait of a Whig romantic, both sympathetic and paternally superior to animals and the poor, at times low and drunk, at other times high on philanthropy. They are equally a portrait of one of the protean personalities of the new age, in whom more than one nature could be comprehended.

Cockburn copied for the anthology a recent flight poem in which a traditional sense of the war between flesh and spirit is conveyed by a description of one of nature's amphibians. Tom

Moore's ode 'To the Flying-Fish' distinguishes between soaring and sinking. 'The soul may soar'—away from the contagion of the here below. But then it may sink back to earth: the ode affords, as Keats's 'Ode to a Nightingale' has been felt to do, an aerodynamics of flight and fall. In his lyrics Moore stands revealed as a superlative user of the figurative 'steal' ('Oft in the stilly night' would have had a 'steal' sung into its opening words) and as a great stealer of kisses. The volume in which the poem appears, and which came out at the time of the anthology,[22] contains languors and ardours and affectations, and a visit to America: written at Norfolk, Virginia, 'The Lake of the Dismal Swamp' commemorates, says Moore, a youth who 'lost his mind upon the death of a girl he loved', sought her in the swamp of that name, and there lost his life. The *Edinburgh Review* charged the book with immorality. This led to a farcical duel at Chalk Farm between Moore and his self-styled 'censor', Jeffrey, who admired in verse a 'soft and skyish' purity.[23] Grossness tangled with skyishness at Chalk Farm. But they also did so in the heart of Tom Moore. Having put away their pistols, these two small men made friends, and Moore went on to write hostile criticism for Jeffrey's journal.

In Moore's ode to the dualistic flying-fish, the stealth of romantic love is renounced in favour of a better world. The poem is a prayer in which flight is, as so often, a figure for the passage of the pure soul to its eternal reward. Moore ends by divorcing himself with élan from the little scene of ordinary mortals and boon companions:

Oh Virtue! when thy clime I seek,
Let not my spirit's flight be weak:
Let me not, like this feeble thing,
With brine still dropping from its wing,
Just sparkle in the solar glow,
And plunge again to depths below;
But, when I leave the grosser throng
With whom my soul has dwelt so long,
Let me, in that aspiring day,
Cast every lingering stain away,
And, panting for thy purer air,
Fly up at once and fix me there!

Cockburn was a passenger on this flight. We may imagine the transcriber breaking with a habit of indolence in prayerful aspiration towards virtue and the ether. For Cockburn, virtue and ambition were linked: worldly success might hope for supernatural and ethereal sanction. He transcribed another of Moore's soulful pieces, 'A beam of tranquillity smil'd in the West', in which passion, pleasure, luxury—a word of the time, and of John Keats, for indolence and sensual satisfaction—are again forsworn. But in transcribing it he altered some of the expressions and turned Moore's farewell to drawing-room amours into a poem about laziness, about a man who has been lost in a contemplation of his betters. Eros is lifted out of the text, and replaced by an envious idleness which has to be overcome.

In Cockburn's set, as elsewhere, pious flights of fancy could be provoked by landscapes, panoramas, old buildings. Thomas Campbell's heart leapt up in 1802 when he beheld Melrose Abbey,[24] and he invoked the Associationist aesthetics of his (and Cockburn's) teacher in such matters, Archibald Alison of Edinburgh, an Episcopalian clergyman, to explain how he felt. He also invoked the balcony scene of *Romeo and Juliet*: 'My associations, I confess, were picturesque and pleasant to a high degree in looking, with "a white, upturned, and wondering eye", to those relics of fallen grandeur.' Shakespeare's words—Romeo's 'bright angel'—may have encouraged the reference to Alison, in the same letter, as 'the angel of taste', and their soaring sense is applied to Campbell's comfortable awe at the sight of the abbey, by then a romantic resort. The right associations, in a 'high degree' of concentration, could project the beholder, like some flying fish, into a sky that held towers and mountaintops and angels and angelic women. Melrose, being both an abbey and the ruins of one, was a dizzy mixture of highs and lows, a proving-ground where the pulses of the man of feeling might beat to the knowledge that he inhabited two worlds, to the sense of an amphibious state.

Campbell was another amphibious classical romantic, and Whig romantic, and a Scotsman who came 'up', as Scotsmen then thought of it, to London around the turn of the century, and married. Matilda was a romantic name, and Campbell wrote in a letter: 'What more romance would you wish for?—a poet, a cottage, a fine name, and a fortuneless marriage.' But he also knew that 'a strong and virtuous motive to exertion is worth uncounted thousands, for encountering life with advantage,' and this poet was already famous. In London, in the wilds of Sydenham, he was to weed his speech of 'Caledonianisms' and get on with a cultivation of the romantic and the philomelic. Philomela was a romantic and a traditional name for that sweet singer and soarer the nightingale, and he relates that one night, at the time of the anthology, he stole from Matilda, a 'romantic listener', and, stationing himself a hundred yards away, 'began *whur, whurring*, and whistling in the true philomelic style'.[25]

A decade before, Campbell's double—his wraith, or fetch—had been glimpsed, just as James Hogg's was glimpsed, by an old woman. This was on the island of Mull:

> I observed the family looking on me with an expression of not angry, but scornful seriousness. It was to me unaccountable; but at last the old grandmother told me, with tears in her eyes, 'that I could not live long, for that my *wraith*, or apparition, had been seen!'—'And, pray, where—?' 'Oh leaping over the grave-stones, in the old burial-ground!' The good old lady was much relieved by hearing that it was not my *wraith*, but myself.[26]

Campbell was of Highland blood, and was here an interested if condescending witness of the survival of an old order of belief—of the survival of superstitions which Romanticism would be concerned both to deny and to accommodate. The visit to his ancestral Western Highlands and Islands moved him, in 1798, to write a poem, 'Epistle to Three Ladies', which he was never to print, and which may be said to bridge the gap between Cowper and Wordsworth. Two of these ladies were the admired Miss Hills of Edinburgh, co-compilers of the anthology, and maintainers of no less than six orphans. 'Oh, Nature—Nature!' cries Campbell, as Thomson had cried before him. 'Yes—I have found thy power pervade my mind': this is the language—and the year—of Wordsworth's contribution to the *Lyrical Ballads*. Nature 'warms' the heart, Campbell writes, and 'Romantic Nature in her wildest hue' inspired him to what may be his freshest utterance, and an 'arterial' utterance at that: the poems which were to make his name have come to seem coldly virtuous and ambitious. The Miss Hills and their cousin—James Grahame's sister Jean—are free spirits of a new age:

> Shall apish Art to Nature dictate rules?
> Shall critic hands to pathos set the seal,
> Or tell the heart to feel—or not to feel?

We may forget that Campbell was being taught to feel by the critic Alison.[27]

The poet Campbell moved with the times to play a romantic part: but he was also praised for helping to restore a classical polish. He wished to be seen as a genius whose bust might furnish an academy, the turner-up to a better world of a white and marble eye, his locks disposed in the likeness of a laurel wreath; and he can look like an ailing fellow who was always being, and imagining himself, robbed. He was both philomelic and philanthropic, caring about Negro slavery and about the freedom of Poland and Ireland. He was the bard of Hope, whose pleasures he recited, and of misfortune, and of Britannic valour. A whurring of humour can be heard with relief in his afflicted letters, and some of his afflictions were certainly authentic: his son went mad. His causes, moreover, were worth fighting for, and if it is true that he found a vocation in the role and service of the victim, it is also true that he did things, and that his philanthropy made a difference to the public life of his time. One of his flights produced the University of London, whose origins may be considered a translation from the German and an escape from religious constraints on university entry.

Philomelic soaring was a recognized poetic mode. Amply transcribed, like Campbell, for the anthology, Akenside wrote, as did Campbell, about the nightingale-attended Evening Star. Among his Odes are this poem and a poem 'To Sleep'. Both show a classical technique and a compassionate sturdiness: the nightingale's song directs the poet away from the sorrows of his own 'afflicted love', away from any Dismal Swamp, directs common sense to pity 'Nature's common cares'. Nevertheless, the thought of withdrawal is present in the poems too, and there are telling words which were to reappear in the romantic odes of Keats: the 'Lethaean rod' and 'opiate airs' of 'To Sleep' are effects resumed in the 'Ode to a Nightingale'.

Grave poems were now being written in praise of pleasure. Akenside, Rogers and Campbell dwelt respectively on the 'pleasures' of imagination, memory and hope. Akenside dwells, in his ode on the subject, on the pleasures of sleep, together with its well-known balmy and restorative powers. But sleep was important, as well as pleasant, in the poetry that runs from Thomson to the Romantic period, and progressively so. It was the drowsiness of rural leisure. But it was more. Sleep was the last word in sloth, a word for stillness, silence and seclusion, debility and imbecility: but out of these sweet nothings came forth strength, and it was also a word for sensation and imagination. It was a matter of life and death which can be placed among the dualities of the time: the age which was to invent a capable orphan was to find promise in the orphan weakness and negation of sleep. Dreams and daydreams were a surrender of reason, character and the single self in which a strange new power or faculty could be exerted, and in which art was deeply implicated. There were lotus-eaters who, in worshipping sleep, were worshipping the exertions of inertia, of absence of mind: they were worshipping a 'might half slumb'ring on its own right arm'. This is a definition of poetry which is offered in Keats's poem 'Sleep and Poetry', and the same might is assigned to his personified Autumn, in an ode in which achievement and exhaustion meet. Autumn is 'drowsed with the fume of poppies': these poppies recall, and transcend, Thomson's balm, the opium of indolence. It is Thomson rather than Akenside who is resumed in the Keats of such matters, as we are reminded by *The Philosophy of Sleep*, a treatise by Robert Macnish published in 1830: one chapter is headed by an extract from *The Castle of Indolence*, another by an extract from Keats's 'Ode to a Nightingale'.

Keats's ode shares a pattern, and a point, with Akenside's ode 'To the Evening Star'. In each poem, an afflicted lover thinks of his own and of common cares, and goes down rather than up in stationing himself to listen to the nightingale's song. Akenside's is a poem of instruction, character, and a debt to others, which is also a poem about darkness and stealth and death. There is more in it of solitude than of altitude. The Moon, the 'queen of heaven', has 'retired' with Endymion. Chased by an owl in the past, Philomela had 'fled her solemn shade': now, like Beattie's owl, she has regained a profound retreat, 'down' to which the poet follows her. The ode's allusions are Keats's allusions. The wood made magical by the bird's song has the hawthorn, mosses, beeches, and breeze which are there in the Keats, and in both poems the song is called 'plaintive'.

In the first of his eight stanzas, Keats writes that the song affects him as might some drug that brings sleep or death, a sinking 'Lethe-wards', and in what follows there is talk of another drug, of wine, and of an impulse to 'dissolve', to 'leave the world unseen' and 'fade away', as Thomson had once wanted to do at Norwood, and as Robert Frost would want to do in New England, 'into the forest dim'. In his book *Keats and Embarrassment*, which deals with the poet's alertness to blushes and flushes, Christopher Ricks examines the phrase, 'the true, the blushful Hippocrene'.[28] The Classical allusion turns the wine into water sacred to the Muses. We may add that a more mundane Classical allusion than those mentioned by Ricks—*in vino veritas*—can also be caught, and that Keats's scarlet was an established orphan attribute. The line refers to the truth that the body may blush to know, and to the truth of beauty, of art. The poet goes on to say that he will not fade in the indolence of drink, but will fly to the bird on the wings of song. He will not get drunk. He will not commit suicide—the ultimate in stealth. He will go on writing poetry. Poetry is flight.

But even in imagination—which the poem is later to impugn—he doesn't then fly to the bird. Night has fallen, but he does not ascend to the Queen-Moon and the stars. He is standing in a dim forest: 'I cannot see what flowers are at my feet.' These feet are on the ground. This is fading, not flying, stealth, not soaring—stealth being a feature of woods, propagated as such in *A Midsummer Night's Dream*. He is down, not up, down but not out—though there are hints ('fast fading', 'embalmed darkness') that one mode of escape has been succeeded by another, of which we have already been made ominously aware. There is a puzzle for this reading in a passage which seems to have induced fellow-feelers to believe that the poet does in some sense soar into the sky:

Already with thee! tender is the night
    And haply the Queen-Moon is on her throne . . .

The manuscript's faint exclamation-mark after 'thee' is slender evidence for this belief, and the word 'haply' might have prevented it.

The poet, it's true, has hoped to get up to the bird; art was to do it for him. Readers have read into the poem's successive states an attainment of the hereafter and the impossible, of a heavenly reward, and this is a meaning which can't completely be denied to the poem. In verse six, nevertheless, the poet listens 'darkling', fading, with his death-wish upon him once more—a state which has been hinted at in the description of the wood. At the same time, the description is largely that of a wood which is fresh and green—and literary. In this wood blooms the enchanted wood of *A Midsummer Night's Dream*: literature and fancy have transformed the poet's Hampstead garden. Shakespeare's play, with its moonshine, casement, its Philomel and mind-changing liquor, assisted Keats to write his poem. If part of the flora derives from Akenside, much is from the bank that Oberon knew of. Keats's eglantine and musk-rose were picked from the play, it would seem, and his hawthorn is mentioned there, as it is in the poem by Akenside, who may have been plucking at the same source. Keats's dark wood and imaginary journey take account of dark woods and imaginary journeys in the literature of the past, and account for others in the literature that lay ahead.

In verse eight, 'forlorn', the orphan's word above all others, moves the poet back to the world of domestic suffering, and to the 'sole self' which now attends to a merely 'plaintive' song. At this point we may remember *Endymion*:

> And thoughts of self came on, how crude and sore
> The journey homeward to habitual self![29]

'Sole' appears, in the ode, to mean solitary and single, and perhaps habitual and sore, and to imply that a second self has performed the flying and fading. This makes the ode a dualistic text, and helps one to tell the difference between this romantic poem and the poem by Akenside with which it shares a pattern.

If the poet is now back, he can only have been absent or away. We could suppose that an absence of mind, a reverie or dreaming fit, has occurred. But the poem has been widely read as more than that—as subsumed in verse four's rapturous or adventurous 'Away!' (which in fact harbours an ambivalence, in that it might half be taken to initiate the refusal to get drunk), as comparable to the modern psychic 'trip' which is performed on drugs, as subject to an aerodynamics of take-off, tolerance, temporariness, and a return to earth, and to the possibility of disaster. At the same time, its changing states are not such as to allow one to take for granted the value of this lively and deathly trip. 'Fled is that music:—Do I wake or sleep?' With this closing question, Demetrius's question, the reader has to make what he can of contrasting realities, ethereal and domestic. The question is no encouragement to think of the poem as escapist—bound for some true place compounded of sleep and poetry, art and immunity. But this is how it has been experienced, by way of collusion with the part of the poet which meant it to be, in the intentness upon the work which ensued in the later nineteenth century, among those intent on a higher order of reality.

It is better to think of it as a protean poem which sets to music a protean Keats. The poet inhabits a world of highs and lows, and a lower still which we glimpse when he speaks of sinking through the floor of consciousness and humanity. The 'high' of the poem belongs to a run of moods and sensations, which ends in a return to uncertainty, and which brings before us the blushing orphan of the period in all his suggestibility and impressibility, in all his erotic and artistic excitements, in his indolence and imagination, and in his loneliness and anguish.

If Keats refuses to come to a decision—one-sided, Akensided—about the moods, the Keatses, that transpire in the poem, this versatility and refusal can be related to his doctrine of negative capability, and to the claim I make that this is a dualistic doctrine. He had defined it two years earlier, in a letter of 1817:

> several things dovetailed in my mind, & at once it struck me, what quality went to form a Man of Achievement especially in Literature & which Shakespeare posessed so enormously—I mean *Negative Capability*, that is when man is capable of being in uncertainties, Mysteries, doubts, without any irritable reaching after fact & reason—Coleridge, for instance, would let go by a fine isolated verisimilitude caught from the Penetralium of mystery, from being incapable of remaining content with half knowledge.[30]

Elsewhere in the letters he says that negative capability is an affair of 'the poetical character' as this may be distinguished from the man of opinion who declares himself in Wordsworth's 'egotistical sublime'. The poetical character

> is every thing and nothing—It has no character—it enjoys light and shade; it lives in gusto, be it foul or fair, high or low, rich or poor, mean or elevated—It has as much delight in conceiving an Iago as an Imogen. What shocks the virtuous philosop[h]er, delights the camelion poet.[31]

Here is the Shakespeare of Hazlitt, and of Borges, and the rest—an artist who was 'nothing in himself'. And these are definitions which can be applied without discomfort to the 'Ode to a Nightingale'. The poem offers no opinion, and is a series of states; it is of a protean and poetical, indeed of an agnostic character; it is divided between heaven and earth, high and low, light and shade. It depends upon that 'knowledge of contrast, feeling for light and shade' which was vital to Keats's talent, and inimical, as his last days were to persuade him, to the recovery of the stomach.[32] It mediates between the sole self of everyday life and the self of someone's absences, abstentions and abstractions, when they may 'steal a moment' to be with the nightingale. Negative capability accommodates such contrasts; permits the poet to be up and down, away and back. And duality does the same: it is equipped to deal with the problems that arise from successive, or simultaneous, opposing states—with Keats's 'siege of contraries'. Negative capability can therefore be regarded as an aspect of duality, and it can also be regarded as an aspect of the divided self, the advent of which, in the modern world, was to coincide with the arrival of the anythingarian artist. The 'poetical character' of the romantics is no split personality, but it is not too much to say that the ethos which was to produce a Jekyll and Hyde had already produced—in its perception of the capacity to take an equal delight in the creation of both—an Iago and Imogen.

The fascination which the ode has held for later generations has served to cramp its multivalence, compressing it into an achieved departure from ordinary life tantamount to the departure of the soul from the body. There has also been a fascination with Keats's Odes and ideas which has helped to secure a taste both for romantic departure and for romantic multivalence among writers concerned to argue a hostility to Romanticism. I am referring to the practice and precept of Modernism, and to Eliot in particular. Eliot's hostility to Romanticism did not entail a hostility to Keats, and it has become possible to believe that it concealed, if not a devotion to the art of the Romantics, at any rate a fellow-feeling. It is no longer a strain to think of him as, hardly less than Yeats, an adept of romantic duality. The idea of a 'dissociation of sensibility', of a separation between thought and feeling, was advanced by Eliot at a point —around 1920—when dualistic approaches had been especially popular for over thirty years, and it is not remote from some other splits imagined in the past. The corollary or cure—the idea that there had been and could be again a poetry that would amalgamate thought and feeling—is not remote from those doctrines of the first Romantic period in which a horror of doctrine, and of authorial egotism, was expressed. The Modernist positions hark back to the dualistic and dialectical outlooks according to which the phenomenon of artistic multivalence was identified and explained with reference to the German notion of romantic irony and to the ensuing English notion of negative capability. The theory of the chameleon poet which was taken up and transmitted by a poet who wrote chameleon poems belongs to the chameleon history of duality, and plays an influential part in the development of a literary tradition which binds together the early Romantics and the Modernists who supposed themselves to be their opposites, but who were themselves more than willing to write chameleon poems.

Negative capability is present in the 'Ode to a Nightingale' by virtue of the presence there of a double poet who both confronts and deserts the world of his immediate anxieties, and who has the courage of his uncertainties. It is present in the Symbolist aesthetic by virtue of its capacity to say, as Eliot was to say, and Henry James, that a work of art has no author, and that opinion is a kind of violence. The rejection of character and opinion which we find in Eliot is to be found in Keats. Eliot's doctrine of artistic impersonality is a romantic text which piles, as its precursors do, diffusion on division. It rests on the ancient separation which distinguishes between soul and body, an above and a below, and which denigrates the life of the body, and of the community. For Eliot, poetry was 'an escape from personality'. Indeed, it was 'an escape from emotion'.[33] There can be no higher flight.

Eliot's art is no more exempt than his opinions are from the comparison with Keats, nor is its alleged approximation to the condition of music. In the course of the inquiries which have been made into the literary sources of *Four Quartets*, it has not been usual to make much of Keats. And yet the poetry of the *Quartets* resumes and resembles the poetry of the Odes, and in doing so it resembles music. Both poetries seek both to incorporate opinion and, as music does, to overthrow it. Both are musical: both appear to invite, and have been seen to submit to, the analogy with music. And Eliot's has that silent music which is entreated in the Odes: the 'ditties of no tone' audible to the spirit only. This is the higher music which escapes the ear, and in listening for it Eliot outsoared Keats. We think that over the centuries mankind has been grounded. But Eliot gets higher up than Keats does, or than Shakespeare and Thomson do, or than any poet has done since the Renaissance.

In the first of the *Quartets*, 'Burnt Norton', a bird is chosen as a conductor of insights, and to give advice. Keats's nightingale and Eliot's thrush tease their poets 'out of thought as doth eternity', and into thought as well; both poems belong to the same confessional-discursive chameleon mode. Each takes flight towards transcendence, while uttering different distrusts in the matter. 'Burnt Norton' has lines of warning about the tolerance of such flights:

> Go, go, go, said the bird: human kind
> Cannot bear very much reality.

Keats's poem conveys that it is the troubles of phenomenal life which have to be borne; he also conveys that there is a higher reality to be gained through art, while balancing this suggestion against others, and subduing it to the totality, and duality, of the poem's successive states. Eliot's higher reality was procured from religion. But in respect of the means employed to communicate the romantic idea of flight, there is no clear categorical difference between the poems. Within each one, description and discursive statement are joined, in roughly the same proportions, in order to tell about flight and the tolerance of flight.

Eliot remarked that he could not grasp what the 'Ode on a Grecian Urn' means by 'Beauty is truth, truth beauty': but there are statements in the *Quartets*, too, which are hard to grasp and which expire when lifted from their settings. On another occasion, he remarked that the 'Nightingale' Ode 'contains a number of feelings which have nothing particular to do with the nightingale, but which the nightingale, partly because of its attractive name, and partly because of its reputation, served to bring together'.[34] His own bird performs a similar service for a poetry which brings together, just as the Odes do, beauty and truth. In bringing the two together, Keats was doing what Eliot was to do, and he was also doing, at the level of statement, what Akenside had done before him in *The Pleasures of Imagination*:

> for Truth and Good are one,
> And Beauty dwells in them and they in her . . .[35]

Not only does 'Burnt Norton' take after Keats's Odes in this sense, it also alludes to them. The reader follows 'the deception of the thrush'—which recalls, in the 'Nightingale' Ode, fancy's 'deceiving elf'—and enters a garden which seems to be that of childhood ('our first world'), and yet to stand for an escape from time and nature. Upon its pool floats the romantic lotus—indolent, paradisal. There is an 'unheard music' hidden in its shrubbery, and we remember the 'unheard' music, the 'ditties of no tone', in the 'Ode on a Grecian Urn': a sweeter music than the one which has been canvassed for explanations of the title of Eliot's sequence of poems. We can conclude that he planned a departure from the world, to be achieved through contemplation and devotion, and was moved to assimilate this process to the process of romantic flight which his generation had despised. Mingling poetry and piety, he may have intended a sublime which would be different from what Romanticism could show. If so, English literature, and the language of Keats, frustrated him.

Yeats went on a journey which can also be related to that of Keats in the 'Nightingale' Ode. This is the journey which occurs in the poem 'Sailing to Byzantium'. There is now a third bird to consider: it is golden and artificial, and it furnishes a palace and paradise of art. To this true place Yeats is transported by a longing to be 'gathered' into the 'artifice of eternity'. Eternity is an artist, and its works are reminiscent of the 'cold pastoral' portrayed on Keats's Grecian urn. Yeats may have had that ode in mind: his bird is frozen in an attitude designed by 'Grecian goldsmiths'. But there is no sustained dependence on the language of the Odes. The poet wants to get 'out of nature', and, in the eternity of art, to assume this Attic shape—the form of this bird, Yeats writes, rather than that of 'any natural thing'. Its song will for ever be addressed to a 'drowsy' emperor, the inhabitant of a castle of indolence. 'Nature' is the love-making of 'dying generations'; elsewhere, it is 'the fury and the mire of human veins', which might be compared with Keats's 'the weariness, the fever and the fret'. If there is no sustained dependence on the language of the Odes, this poem is nonetheless conscious of the romantic escapes of the past, with its soaring art bird and its belief in the permanence of art.

'Sailing to Byzantium' has inspired the objection that its bird of paradise is no less a part of nature than the human body, than the living beauty from which, in growing old, Yeats could feel that he had become estranged. If we concede to that objection, we might have to think of Yeats's poem as one of the world's abortive escapes. The actions it proposes, and the orphan terms it disposes ('gather me'), speak of an attempt to leave the world for some everlasting safe place: but if religion allowed Eliot to believe that he would survive his death, it does not seem to have done as much for Yeats. For Eliot, the impersonality of the artist was no argument against the salvation of his soul. There is a poem to be imagined in which all three of these poems, and the differences between them, take part. That poem, that cento, would give something of the higher history of romantic escapism. It would not indicate that the commitment to it had ceased to hold out hope that souls may be saved.

Joyce's *A Portrait of the Artist* portrays a salvation, in the true colours, and with some of the soaring, of the religion it renounces; and Stephen Dedalus says that he means to steal from Ireland, into 'silence, exile and cunning'. A conformity, perhaps, with the long history of departure for strange places and a sullen celebrity? Soaring and stealing come together in the novel, and stand in dualistic relation to the sense it gives that an idea of salvation has indeed been renounced. The novel is a portrait of its artist, and that artist is the flyer whom the too-eloquent surname leads us to expect: this is a book in which romanticism is doubted, but which does not disappoint romantic expectations. Stephen is an artist, and he is an escape artist. He swoons and he soars. He falls when he is caught in the sensual snares deplored by Ireland's priests, when he submits to an ancient indolence revived by the Fin-de-Siècle: but after that, and in no more modern a way, he flies—out of bounds, past the snares of religion and race. Up he goes. 'His heart trembled in an ecstasy of fear and his soul was in flight.' Bous Stephaneforos has taken off like a Boeing 707. In *Stephen Hero*, the *Portrait* draft, Stephen is much less the hero of a romance, much more terrestrial, and we find him jeering at his mother's idea of the Ascension of Christ. 'Where did he go off?' he asks. 'Head first?' Off the hill of Howth? By balloon? In the *Portrait*, with Howth in the distance to the north, flight is not mocked. The writing has turned incantational, priest-like. 'His soul was soaring in an air beyond the world and the body he knew was purified in a breath and delivered of incertitude and made radiant and commingled with the element of the spirit. An ecstasy of flight made radiant his eyes and wild his breath and tremulous and wild and radiant his windswept limbs.' 'Strange fields' await the 'wanderer', and he there and then sees a strange sight on the seashore—a beautiful girl, with kilted skirts. 'A faint flame trembled on her cheek.' Stephen flushes back. His own cheek 'aflame', his limbs 'trembling', he blasphemes: 'Heavenly God!' He has lost his faith. He has lost his hope of Heaven. But he could well appear to be arriving at its gates. The old glory has not gone from his soul, just as the old flame of human susceptibility burns in his body. The girl is an 'envoy from the fair courts of life'. Joyce has mortal life in mind, but she is called an angel. The promise she brings is paradisal, and might lead us to think of the passage in *Stephen Hero* where Stephen taxes himself with enjoying a 'freedom which would dress the world anew in vestures and usages begotten of enslavement'.[36] The chapter ends with another of the book's swoons, in the languor of the Nineties.

V. COMIC TURNS

'Steal' and 'soar' are words which are still used for the many varieties of escape which offer themselves, but neither is fully idiomatic any more: like other escape words, such as 'elope', they can sound like poeticisms. For the pursuits in question, a new poetry of departure has grown up, which pays attention to the physical invasion of space and which travels out rather than up. For a long time now, much of the traditional language of sublimity has seemed ridiculous, and secrecy has been suspected: we have started to complain of it, and to think of restoring a balance between public and private, manifest and latent. All the same, secrecy and sublimity are still pursued, and the old vocabulary is not obsolete. In 1979 Leon Edel wrote philomelically about the economist Keynes. It was as if Keynes were Keats. 'Mankind plods along' while 'someone like Keynes leaps above it,' leaps above the irrational 'commonplace', as do other members of the fellowship whose early lives Edel is recounting in *Bloomsbury: A House of Lions.*[1] Virginia Woolf's conversation achieved 'vertiginous flights'. Roger Fry 'soared into the sublime'. Carrington was curiously 'flighty'. These lions lope about the Cambridge Backs, which whur to 'the soaring song of innumerable nightingales'. Some of the lions are said to have been 'dissociated', and some are spiritual voyagers. Edel's Bloomsbury contains a traditional duality and escape, and is presented—to unintentional comic effect—as romance.

His book communicates, as the poem itself does not, an escapist view of Keats's engagement with his nightingale. Projects of escape have a history which includes quests, picaresque wanderings, the exploits of adventurers, and in the course of the nineteenth century, the old idea of the exemplary journey was amended by new ideas in the field of duality, which encouraged writers to design journeys which both succeed and fail. We see something of this in Keats's ode, and in Yeats, whose voyage to Byzantium is that of a self-confessed dual personality, of a self and anti-self responsive to the rival claims of art and action. The imagination of two or more selves in one affirmed that the same person may soar and sink, budge and stay, be at large and at home, and the suitability of 'steal' and 'soar' in the context of emancipation is precisely that these are self-qualifying, self-retarding expressions, which carry suggestions of a debt to others and of a descent from heights. In the literature of duality, to be two is to be apart, or away. But it may also be to experience, for better or for worse, a return. This is a literature which mingles exclusion and rehabilitation, deliverance and death.

This nineteenth-century literature was rich in precedents; the equivocal had been richly acknowledged. It was already known that pleasure may be pain, drugs both a poison and a cure, that indolence may take off into the sublime. There had been an eighteenth-century concern with the necessity and the futility of flight, with the vanity and variety of human wishes. It lay with Romanticism to adjust the prevailing relationship between an avidity for escape and a suspicion of it by disclosing, as Keats did, the half-flights of the semi-self, to be interpreted as both permanent and ephemeral. The high-flyer has been perennially admired, and feared for:

> He flies through the air with the greatest of ease,
> The daring young man on the flying trapeze.

The story of this circus turn was now told with reference to a doctrine of human inconsistency and of the inconsistency of human doctrine.

There have been many forms of flight for human beings grounded by the failure of their religious hopes, and yet still hopeful, and, in due course, literally airborne. But the knowledge of a heliocentric Earth did not do away with the thought of a flight after death. This is what the word 'salvation' has chiefly meant: an accessible, though in due course a receding, heaven. It was to be a Victorian word for mere escapades, for a deliverance from straits and scrapes, and it is a word that Eliot can hardly ever have used. He nonetheless still hoped to be saved.

The dream of physical flight has, from antiquity, been strikingly important. We meet it now in sleep, when willing heels spring into the air; we meet it in the rise and fall, the register, of literary expression. A landscape poetry of views and panoramas arose with the Renaissance. Hills were climbed, balloons went up, aeroplanes roared, with flights of fancy, feats of poetry, fits of piety, pointing the way: Milton flew, before Montgolfier and Lunardi. In the Middle Ages, the Man in the Moon was rumoured to be there for gathering sticks on the Sabbath, and Sabbath-breakers, rebels, recluses, are among those who have wished or pretended to be this man. In 1638, Francis Godwin published *The Man in the Moone*, in which the author exercises 'a liberty of conceite', an imaginative freedom: 'Thou hast here an essay of Fancy, where Invention is shewed with Judgment.'[2] Not for the first time, or the last, literature and science flew together to the Moon. Eventually, they arrived. The astronauts of the present time are heroes of the state: but theirs is a sublime which can't be left out of the history of romantic escapism—from uplift to lift-off, moonshine to moonshot—and which can't have left unmoved those among whom suffering has tried to take leave, or to take leave of its senses.

Salvation, pastoral, privacy, travel, holidays, adulteries, incest, alcohol, laudanum, lunar modules—such are the latter-day escapes. On the eve of the modern mass tenderness for the temporary escape, for the trip, the stay, which was to emulate patrician and meditative leisure, Cockburn built himself a second home near the summit of a Pentland Hill: from Bonaly Tower, the seasonal absentee from the public life of Scotland stared down at the city of Edinburgh. He was fashioning his ivory tower at a time when Charles Maturin was writing *Melmoth the Wanderer*, a novel which harps on departure. But it is also a novel which says that wandering is futile, and that we are in God's hand: we are like the bird which, if it flies off into the bush, flies no further than a snare. Maturin conveys that we should stay where we are, with Dr Johnson's Rasselas—who comes back home, disenchanted. But Johnson's novel, that of an enemy of escapes, never tires of depicting them.

The Romantic period turned from Rasselas towards Shakespeare's Hamlet, whose family troubles made him wish that his body might 'resolve into a dew'. They made him both an avenger and a killer. They made him an equivocator, a chooser between art and action, to be and not to be. *Hamlet* is a dualistic work. But it would not be pointless to say the same of *Rasselas*, so far as it concerns itself with escape. Romantic writers can be charged with a revolutionary innocence and optimism more rarely than the looming of such elements in successive mass cultures induces us to suppose. These writers shared with their immediate predecessors a feeling both for flight and for the precariousness of flight—for wings of wax which melt at the apogee. They were the inheritors of a world which had begun to dream of the perfect prison, of an absolute captivity and surveillance, and which took an equal pleasure in dreaming of a Dedalus and an Icarus. Here as in other places the notion of the clean break is suspect. During the decades which surround the soaring and sorrowing of the vast Pentlands 'cento', if it was wonderful to get away, it was also eccentric, erratic, meteoric: romantic comets were brighter than before, but no less liable to burn out.

It has been wonderful to get away from your family. This is a form of escape which has long been inevitable, and the theme of sexual freedom was to matter more and more as the literature of duality took hold and the idea of a supernatural destination fell ill. Duality has imagined a relationship between home and heaven: these may meet, in one guise or another, and they may be put asunder. Not a few of its writers were to court the strange bride of a new country. Henry James and Joseph Conrad were émigrés and imaginary orphans who described their move to England as romance. In moving, they eluded, and failed to elude, their families. Theirs was an appointment in Samarra.

Where there is frustration and defeat we may expect to find humour, and if soaring goes before a fall, as we have seen, and as Romanticism saw, falls can be funny. There is a comedy of duality, and it is preoccupied with the abortive escape. From that day to this, there has been a protean fiction, and it has been apt to take a comic turn—to turn, for instance, in a manner prefigured by Shakespearian duality, into a comedy of errors and impostures.

For an early theoretical justification of this fiction, we can consult the writings of a believer in the duality of man, the German Friedrich Schlegel. These writings are among the attempts made by compatriots, at the beginning of the nineteenth century, to settle the question of the modern in literature—attempts which were to establish definitions of the romantic. For Schlegel, modern poetry was personal, rather than impersonal and disinterested; promiscuous, in its mingling of beauty and ugliness, tragedy and comedy; didactic and yet ironic. Irony was the apprehension of a paradoxical reality. In 1829, he spoke of 'our intrinsic dualism and duplicity':

so deeply is this dualism rooted in our consciousness, that even when we are, or at least think ourselves alone, we still think as two, and are constrained as it were to recognise our inmost profoundest being as essentially dramatic. This colloquy with self, or generally, this internal dialogue, is so perfectly the natural form of human thinking, that even the saintly solitaries of bygone centuries, who in the Egyptian deserts or the Alpine hermitages devoted a half-life to meditation on divine things and mysteries, were often not able otherwise to indicate the result of such meditations, to invest it in another dress, to bring it into any other form of exposition than that of a dialogue of the soul with God.

He went on to cite the irony of the Platonic dialogues, Socratic irony, as a 'form of disguise' which 'makes everything at once a joke and a serious matter', at once 'ingenuously open and deeply dissembled'.[3] The currency of the term 'romantic irony' emerged from these discriminations.

They were an endeavour to understand a literature which took account of the variety and inconsistency of the human individual; which favoured the dialogue form, among other recourses to the dramatic, in extra-theatrical contexts, thereby promoting a theatre and communion of the single mind; and which ran to irony, and to a coincidence of gravity and wit. Duality enabled people to tell the difference between modern literary practice and that of the Classical past, but it could do so in ways which complicate the issue as it may seem to be posed here by Schlegel. If we must be aware of an 'interested' writing in which the personality of the author is visible, we must be no less aware of a writing in which that personality is suspended or dispersed. In the literature of the new age, the interest of the author and the extinction of the author were both to be at issue. Both are embraced and explained by the doctrine of duality, and the role attributed by Schlegel to disguise and duplicity indicates how they may be combined in a particular work. The future was to hold particular works in which there would be few characters or none, in which drama and dialogue had become internalized within the individual, and in which, at a time when the opinions of authors were to matter as they had never done before, the opinions of the author would be problematical or invisible.

The recent literature on which Schlegel's discriminations rely had already made use of dialogue in this manner—we may call it the modern manner—and the dialogue form had already occasioned a literature of duality. Diderot's *Rameau's Nephew*, which may partly date from as early as 1761, but which was not publicly known until 1805, reports a conversation between two speakers: a staid and prudent Diderot and an acquaintance of his, a soaring artistic and instinctive rogue, Rameau's nephew, a brilliant impersonator and mime, a musician like his famous uncle. The authorial standpoint is implicitly contested between the two speakers, and it may be supposed to have been abolished or aborted in the process. I don't suppose so myself: but it is not difficult to feel that one Diderot is conversing with another, or that, as is sometimes deemed to happen with the appearances of the double in fiction, the repressed natural man is talking back to his civilized counterpart. The natural man tells him, for example, that education stops you from attacking your father and marrying your mother, while allowing you to pursue certain pleasures with impunity, including, perhaps, the imagination of these outrages. Diderot's part is to stimulate and to rebuke such talk, from this resenter of an uncle. *Rameau's Nephew* conforms to Schlegel's definition of the interested and ironic and divided modern work, and it is wide awake to the premiss of the divided self. Human greatness generally comes from 'a natural balance between several opposing qualities', while a man may be 'torn between two opposing forces and walk all crooked down life's road'. These are the views of Diderot's crooked interlocutor, whose duplicity and genius, when weighed against the reproofs they invite, may be thought to achieve a balance.[4]

If we can claim that *Rameau's Nephew* is a pioneering instance of the modern and romantic literature of duality, the same claim can be made for another dialogue of the period, in which Proteus is identified and comprehensively named. As with the Diderot, we witness the approach of a new writing, though hardly an unprecedented one, of which it can be said that orphan and double conspire to produce a subjective, a solipsistic fiction, where character is scarce, story is scarce, and drama, irony and humour flow from the affairs of the fissile and mutable self.

In the year 1791, the German poet Wieland published a novel called the *Private History of Peregrinus Proteus the Philosopher*. It was soon picked up in London: translations appeared there in 1796 and in 1804.[5] It is about a man who wants to 'soar above the ordinary pitch of human nature'—who wants, in the words of Thomson's *Seasons*, a poem well known to Wieland, both to soar off into the sky and to steal himself from the thievish crowd. *A Midsummer Night's Dream* was another English work well known to Wieland. He translated it. And, in a manner sympathetic to the concerns of the play, his novel alludes to flight, space and the Moon, to Icarianism, to the second self. Peregrine's travels suggest the picaresque tradition, and resemble the adventures of Smollett's rascal Peregrine Pickle, but they also belong to the start of the romantic literature of duality, with its enduring interest in chicanery and deception. And they look forward to the further confessions of a character in whom an ecstatic or extravagant piety is rated a sham, as if by exposure to the enlightened standards of the eighteenth century, and yet admired. Hogg's *Confessions*, alias *The Private Memoirs and Confessions of a Fanatic*, which is both a comedy, of errors, of mistaken identity, and a serious matter, of human suffering, may be judged to have a precedent in Wieland's 'extraordinary adventures and eccentricities' of a comical 'Fanatic'.

Wieland's book consists of a dialogue in Elysium between Peregrine—whose earthly life has been among the Early Christians and the sages and mages of that momentous time—and the celebrated Greek sceptic, ironist and dialogist Lucian, whose imagination flew to the Moon in the second century AD, and who was the author of an invective, 'Peregrinus Proteus', which commemorates, as little else does, a contemporary Cynic philosopher of that name: Wieland translated Lucian, and took part in the commemoration and emulation of the Lucianic which had begun with the Humanists of the Renaissance. The reader of his novel may wonder whether this Peregrine is a fool, a fraud, or what? The portrait shimmers with ambiguities, which the dialogue form helps to promote, as it does in *Rameau's Nephew*, where a philosopher may be felt to converse with his bad angel. People 'could not agree whether the fool or the profligate, the impostor or the fanatic, had the ascendant' in Peregrine's protean character. The same question was to arise with Edgar Allan Poe, among other romantics.

Eager for mystic transports and 'eudaemony', Peregrine falls into bed with a pair of worldly women: the little deaths of love-making are to subvert his intention to soar above human nature. Then he joins the Gnostics, whose heresies are subverting the Early Christian communities. He is persuaded to join by a deep Jew who is scheming for a world revolution, with precious few among the elect, and who informs Peregrine, in the accents of a Gothic tempter, that he is both the instrument of 'thy deliverance' and at the same time 'no more than thyself'.[6] When that scheme fails, Peregrine becomes a Cynic, but this very uncertain Diogenes can only secure his 'independence' of lust and common life by setting light to himself (as did, at the Olympic Games, the original philosopher to whom Lucian's invective refers). In the sparks of a 'voluntary exit', Peregrine's 'confession' ends.

Like other escape artists and revolutionaries, he is divorced from his earthly father, whom he is suspected of murdering. His search for spiritual fineness hits many reefs, but is wrecked largely by his dealings with women, who fail to supply him, we might think, with a mother, and whose power to seduce is, he thinks, that of a lower form of life. One way or another, he is for ever soaring and sinking. Lucian remarks that the Moon journeys in his own writings were performed only 'in sport', but Peregrine can appear to take such whims, trips, and 'presentiments' of the future, seriously. At the heart of the dialogue,[7] Lucian asserts: 'He that is born to be a man, neither should nor can be any thing nobler, greater, and better than a man.' And Peregrine replies:

> But, good Lucian, for the very reason that he may not become less than a man, he should be always striving to be more. It is undeniable that there is something daemoniacal in our nature; we are suspended between heaven and earth; on the father's side, so to speak, we are related to superior spiritual natures; on the side of our mother earth, we are related to the beasts of the field. If the spirit be not ever soaring upwards, the animal part will soon stagnate in the mire of the earth, and the man who does not strive to become a god, will find himself in the end transformed into a beast.

In responding, as he was eventually to do, to Lucian's position at this point—which does not misrepresent that of the historical Lucian—the poet Poe attributed it to Wieland, and was far from sharing Peregrine's view of how it is that we become beasts, become outlaws or monsters. 'In efforts to soar above our nature,' paraphrased Poe, 'we invariably fall below it.'[8] This highly traditional, not to say classical sentiment may seem out of character for Poe: a piece of his best behaviour, perhaps, which misrepresents his sympathy with the peregrines of this world. But then he was a man of more than one character, or of none. Peregrine Proteus Redivivus.

Peregrine concedes a good deal to Lucian's arguments in the course of their exchange, and, by virtue of his humorous falls and fiascos, he concedes a good deal more. He may be said to refute himself, in the manner of a protean character who inhabits a protean work, in which the two sides of a nature—mobile and stable, ingenuous and shrewd—and of an argument about the nature of human excellence, are simultaneously on show. *Peregrine Proteus* is prototypical, or at least prescient and forward-looking, in combining elements of confession and duality, fanaticism and farce: we learn here of a future in which the self-confessor and his medium can between them give a sense of the simultaneous selves which may be present in the one person, while establishing that fanatics may be farcical, or fraudulent, or at fault, and yet wonderful too. Wieland's novel indicates that satires on romance can be themselves romantic, and that humour, so far from being fatal or inimical to it, could accompany, in Schlegelian synthesis, the romantic surge of the 1790s. Schlegel explained that romance could criticise itself: humour and irony, and the modern mingling of genres, made this possible.

The novel won itself an English readership at a time when the modern romances of this country—in particular, the practice of Mrs Radcliffe, 'Monk' Lewis and the like—had become, together with the outlook and demeanour from which they sprang, a target for emulation and for censure: the satires of Peacock and Jane Austen were impending. Around 1797, Jane Austen began *Northanger Abbey*,[9] in which censure and a sort of emulation can both be observed. Catherine Morland, whose head has been turned by Radcliffian romance, goes to stay with 'the man of her choice', Henry Tilney, at Northanger Abbey, and experiences the house as an inventory of Gothic terrors. But then Henry's father, General Tilney, oppresses her in earnest on discovering the harsh fact that she is not an heiress. So Northanger has lived up to its name, and to the books with which she has been filling her head. 'I leave it to be settled, by whomsoever it may concern, whether the tendency of this work be altogether to recommend parental tyranny, or reward filial disobedience': these are the novel's ambivalent last words, and they suggest that its themes are the themes of the Gothic novel, which is ambivalent, too, in its concern with obedience and oppression. The tendency of this work is not altogether opposed, in the manner expected of satire, to that of some work by Mrs Radcliffe.

The first two chapters itemize the deportment of the romantic heroine, distinguishing between 'the common feelings of common life' and 'the refined susceptibilities, the tender emotions which the first separation of a heroine from her family ought always to excite'. Catherine's sister has started to lay modish claim to the possession of two natures; Catherine herself aspires to be a 'true-quality heroine', and has been in training for the role since the age of fifteen, for a future of storms, robbers, 'remote farmhouses' and 'desperate wretchedness', amid the 'general distress' of the work she inhabits. 'A strange, unaccountable character!' But Catherine does suffer authentically enough when she is expelled from Northanger, by which time the ironic condescension which has thought of her as 'our heroine' has had to think again.

Between the completion of this novel and its publication in 1818 came a work which was similar in tone and preconception: Eaton Stannard Barrett's burlesque of 1813, *The Heroine*. Here again is a tribute to the fascination of distress which is mediated by an attack on its romantic damsels, from a point of view which we may care to identify as classical. *The Heroine* contains an inventory and critique of the world of the Gothic and sentimental novels, of the deportments recommended there, of the language customary there, and of the literary themes and specialities which these inspired.

Barrett's book is a spoof which ridicules Gothic practice. At the same time, it is touched, as Jane Austen's is, by the seduction, and the conviction, inherent in that practice. In this respect, it resembles the romantic work which it criticizes—and which is often able to criticize itself. It also resembles Cervantes' *Don Quixote*: an exposure of romantic attitudes which is itself romantic, which thereby criticizes itself, and which was of interest to nineteenth-century readers, not all of whom can have been seeking disillusionment, criticism and correction. The Cervanticks performed by Sterne were resumed by Barrett, and, like *Don Quixote*, *The Heroine* can be read as both for and against romantic behaviour. So far from being authorially neutral or indeterminate, it is overtly polemical. But there are grounds for calling it a protean work, as there are for calling it—again in an early or pioneering sense—a dualistic one.

The Heroine's heroine, portrayed by her letters, is Cherry Wilkinson, another pretty head turned by the reading of romances. She rejects her honest farmer father, and imagines herself an orphan or changeling, faced with the prospect of a forced marriage. She takes flight from 'captivity', from 'the confinement of my father', and assumes the name of Cherubina de Willoughby: the surname is that of a suitor in Fanny Burney's *Evelina*, and of Marianne's stylish and disgraceful admirer in *Sense and Sensibility*, a work which could well have assisted Barrett's derision of romantic precept. The 'adventures of Cherubina'—the novel's subtitle—involve her escape from confinement into the clutches of predatory males, who encourage her delusions of misery and induce her to agree to the confinement of poor Wilkinson, her father, in a lunatic asylum.

The leading irony of the novel has to do with her principled ill-treatment of the father to whom she is deeply attached: 'Were a wretch going to the gallows, I could not help feeling for him. How much more, then, must I feel for a man, who, villain as he indisputably is, had acted as a parent towards me, during fifteen years of my life.'[10] Meanwhile she herself is ill-treated by the riff-raff with whom her principles cause her to mix. She is taught to see them in their true colours by Stuart, a reader of *Rasselas* who places in her hand a copy of *Don Quixote*. In its suspicions of romantic excess, those of a Canningite Tory and of an Irishman who died young, *The Heroine* claims the sanction of Cervantes' novel and is conscious, besides, of Sterne and of the harm done by *La Nouvelle Héloïse* and *Werther*. For much of the time, it proceeds through parody, with Mrs Radcliffe and Mrs Roche among the sources.

This is Cherry declaring her intention to set up as an orphan:

'Now, indeed, my wretchedness is complete. An orphan, or at least an outcast; robbed of my birthright, immured in a farmhouse—threatened with a husband of decent birth, parentage and education—my governess gone, my novels burnt, what is left to me but flight? Yes, I will roam through the wide world in search of my parents; I will ransack all the sliding pannels and tapestries of Italy; I will explore Il Castello Di Udolpho, and enter the convent of Ursulines, or Carmelites, or Santa della Pieta, or the Abbey of La Trappe. Here I meet with little better than smiling faces and honest hearts. No precious scoundrels are here, no horrors, or atrocities, worth recording. But abroad I shall encounter banditti, monks, daggers, racks—O ye celebrated terrors, when shall I taste of you?'

I then rose, and stole into Wilkinson's study, with the hope of finding, before my flight, some record or relic that might aid me in unravelling the mystery of my birth.[11]

Cherry's affected or deluded flight represents the kind of behaviour which we now know as that of the drop-out, and which we know to be, as often as not, ephemeral or provisional. The flight affected in the same novel by the actor Grundy is merely false. To ingratiate himself with the runaway, he tells the story of his life as that of a fellow romantic with a noble pedigree, who had once had the tremendous thought: 'Let me escape!' He goes on:

'I then contrived this ingenious mode of accomplishing my object. My chamber had a window: I opened it; and got out at it.

'During eighteen months afterwards, I wandered about the country, an itinerant beggar; as Napoleon had confiscated all my patrimony.'[12]

Cherry's flight fails, and she is returned to the arms and good books of her father and of the fatherly Stuart. She is the kind of orphan who has a family to reject. To be precise, she has a father to reject but no mother—a distress which Barrett refrains from adding to her store. She is a type of the imaginary, the vocational orphan who is exhibited in the literature derided by the novel. This orphan may or may not have parents, but must possess a certain style, a certain sensorium, a privileged access to affliction. According to Barrett, to be an orphan is to be an uncommon person obedient only to 'the common law of romance'. An orphan is a heroine or hero, just as 'a heroine is a young lady, rather taller than usual, and often an orphan; at all events, with the finest eyes in the world. She blushes to the tips of her fingers . . .'. Cherry executes a repertoire of positions or poses—which are sometimes termed classical and are a sculpture of the susceptibilities mentioned by Jane Austen. 'With an expression of sweet wildness and retiring consciousness, was observable a certain susceptibility too exquisite to admit of lasting peace.' She has lively feelings, and a body which shows them. Her blushes, like those of Keats, and of *Melmoth*'s child of nature, the rosy Immalee, no less susceptible for the intervention of these satirists, are the badge of her orphan state. She has trained herself to be a mistress of taste and effect who can make a décor of her troubles: 'a more elegant order of misfortune opens upon me.' Her glory is to be 'the most miserable creature that ever augmented a brook with tears' (Carlyle was to talk of Keats as a 'miserable creature, hungering after sweets which he can't get').[13]

Orphans are secretive, and Cherry 'steals' into her father's study, and into shrubbery. This is a prime posture or first position. She touches the actor for a loan, herself an actress, and then plays the part of one enchanted to be turned down: 'so graceful was his lamentation, so interesting his penury, that though the poet stole out of the room, for ten pounds, which he slipped into my hand, I preferred the refusal to the donation.' If her other friend the poet is dull enough to lend her money, at least he steals out to fetch it. 'Interest' is another of her parts or postures. Of some uncommon fellow who interests her strangely she exclaims: 'Interesting youth!' She shoots 'ineffable looks', and is given to recording that 'I never looked so lovely.' 'One glance from the corner of a villain's eye', she feels, 'is worth twenty straight-forward looks from an honest man.' But the eye of that villain her father is without charm. Looks matter in this world of taste, whose most becoming light is moonshine. Cherry is moonstruck till honesty reclaims her.[14]

This, too, may be numbered among the 'predestined events' in the life of a heroine. These events include: 'If of mysterious origin, her being first reduced to extremities; then her discovering her family, and lastly, her attaining riches, rank, and marriage'. It is said elsewhere of the heroine: 'For you be the mystic union, whose tie of bondage is passion, the wish the licence, and impulse the law.'[15] Yet conventional unions are apt to conclude 'romantic flights' and Barrett makes an honest woman of his heroine. At the same time, if Cherry's romantic flight is satirized and subverted, it is also made out to be interesting, and the novel reads at times like a manual of flightiness which could have influenced, as much as it could possibly have deterred, the separations and aloofness of the future. 'Moment of a pure and exquisite emotion,' cries a man transported by a kiss: 'Now to die were to die most blest!'[16] This is what Keats was soon to cry. Cherry addresses a poem to the Moon:

> The lonely nightingale shall pipe to thee,
> And I will moralise her minstrelsy.[17]

Six years later, Keats kept that promise.

The novel invents a journey for someone whose head has been turned. A turned head suggests a dual personality, and Cherry's adventures are like those of a robust second self to the comparatively inauthentic obedient and educable girl who marries and lives happily ever after, having redeemed her father from the asylum. She is a girl with two names and natures who is restored to a right relation with Tory and Augustan good sense, and to a perusal of *Rasselas* and *Don Quixote*. For the duration of her escape, we had witnessed the assertion of the new self proclaimed in her pseudonym. This is the opposite of any attempt to deny that Barrett's book is a derision, and that escape is ostensibly, and more than ostensibly, condemned there. *Cherry*, as it might be called, bears a resemblance to the American novel *Candy* of 1958, by Terry Southern (with Mason Hoffenberg), in which a pretty girl loses her head and goes about humping hunchbacks for derisory reasons of conscience. The Southern novel comes down on the sentimental humane—on radical chic. The Barrett comes down on its prototype—romantic chic. Both novels are in some measure sadistic, male-chauvinistic and politically conservative. But Cherry's adventures are told in such a way as to serve and transmit the outlook which the teller undoubtedly means to mock.

Cherry trenches, then, on the ground occupied by literary duality, and it raises questions about the relationship between literary duality and family life. The ambivalence it displays is, in part, the ambivalence which attends a widespread experience of families and of their repudiation. Cherry has a family, but behaves as if she hasn't; figuratively, she has locked herself out. Her adventures depict the personalities which may compete within a single human being when the time comes for him to leave his home, while also remaining in it, before going on to reconstitute it in marriage. With this picture, Barrett had moved into dualistic territory—where Hogg's eighteen-year-old, Robert Wringhim, would presently appear. For those who attempt to explain the double, the plight of Cherry Wilkinson is of interest. Other crises need to be considered besides those occasioned by the repudiation of parents; the double is more than the spectre of adolescence. But such repudiations could well be seen as a paradigm for many situations in which *homo duplex* endeavours both to go and to stay.

The literature of duality runs to comedy and to chicanery, to a fascination with tricks and hoaxes, and to a principled or accidental subversion of the author—of the kind of author who is deemed to create and control plot and character, to be separate from his characters, to be himself something of a character, and to hold, rather than administer or orchestrate, the opinions that go with a given work. The Wieland and the Barrett can be seen to adumbrate, if not indeed to fulfil, these conditions. When the conditions are fulfilled, then we have what can be called protean fiction, many of whose works approximate to the condition of the puzzle or the enigma. We may choose to say that it is the orphan and the double who devise such puzzles and lie hidden there. The works in question may proceed from the situation of an author who has come to know an adversary self or opposite number, as Barrett came to know the absconder Cherry Wilkinson.

Twenty years later, the Russian dualist, Gogol, began, in *Dead Souls*, on a panorama of national life which is also a state of mind. Living souls teem and swarm, and replicate themselves as clones or gnomes of the author. The leading character, Chichikov, is a comic orphan crook in the shape of an impostor and embezzler with a loveless family background. But he is hardly a character at all. He is a way of putting Gogol's experience of his huge country, and of Gogol. Five years after this picaresque work ended—appropriately enough, from a certain point of view—with the suicide of the author, Herman Melville produced an exercise in the suicidal-discursive picaresque: *The Confidence-Man.*

Protean features are present here on a basis of principle. The novel tastes both of solitude and of community. It is the work of an orphan, and it is the kind of work which other orphans had done and would do again. 'Post-Modern' theorists have recognized an early case of the self-referring fiction, but it also took, and knew, its place in an established tradition. The tradition is stated in the large number of literary references which the novel, spare and circumspect as it is, manages to make: it refers to the self-referring *Midsummer Night's Dream*, and to its protean author, to the irreligious Lucian, to Akenside's *Pleasures of Imagination*, to points of romantic etiquette and to the matter of romantic fraud. Because of this, and despite it, few fictions are more enigmatic, more peculiar. It was cast aside on publication, in the middle of the nineteenth century, and appears, with *Pierre*, to have put paid to Melville's own confidence and career, to have cast him out. In recent decades, an assiduous scholarship has rehabilitated it.

Down the Mississippi moves the steamboat *Fidèle*. It is a ship of fools, and of their deceivers. A plural Chichikov is on board, amid dead souls. The Confidence-Man of the title works the boat in a series of embodiments, which are hard to tell apart. The 'masquerade' of the subtitle means that each man is his opposite, that each of the virtues that are professed conceals its negation. *Fidèle*, faith, trust, joint-stock investment—the issue of confidence crops up in puns and in other guises. And we are asked to think about truth, as well as trust. What is a true book? Is the Bible true? Is the book we are reading true? The truth we eventually discover has to do with the fathoming, or savouring, of a bottomless error and imposture.

During the last of his hoaxes, the Confidence-Man holds up his face for shaving to the ship's barber: that face is 'like a flower'. We know him by now to be the snake who can quote Scripture, and can argue forcibly, as well as fulsomely. The barber is in the habit of refusing credit, and has hung up a sign:

'No trust!' The Confidence-Man reproves him for this: 'Don't you think consistency requires that you should either say, "I have confidence in all men," and take down your notification; or else say, "I suspect all men," and keep it up.'[18] The book addresses itself, not only to the issue of confidence, but to that of consistency, and the two issues are keenly related. Where consistency is lacking, confidence is shaken. But it also turns out that human beings are radically inconsistent.

We ask whether, in a distrust of false confidence and its prophets, Melville suspects all men. Is this 'Timonism'? In the course of one of the dialogues of which the novel is composed, mention is made of the romantic 'free development' of someone's 'inmost nature', and we then read: 'if some men knew what was their inmost natures, instead of coming out with it, they would try their best to keep it in.' Keep that in, and keep up the sign that advertises a general suspicion. The free development mentioned here is part of what Melville elsewhere calls 'the sweet dream of the impossible good'.[19] Where the novel seeks to be undeceiving, its effects can be trenchant enough to persuade the reader that they are authorial, 'straight', that this is what it means. So is there an authorial point of view? In attempting to elicit one, Elizabeth Foster's edition[20] shows how Melville's fellow writers figure in the masquerade. Emersonian optimism—doubly portrayed, and with the double face of 'moonshine' and Yankee hardness, flower and flint—is especially suspected. And Poe is present as a courtly 'shatter-brain': with its suggestion of the split, spread and scatter of the poetical character, the word may be taken as acknowledging a dualistic ambience for the masquerade.[21] Elizabeth Foster argues that the Melville of this time, delightfully portrayed by a friend as 'fresh from his mountain charged to the muzzle with his sailor metaphysics and jargon of things unknowable',[22] can be known as secretly agnostic, that a distrust of religion is both expressed and dissembled in the novel, and that once its latent meanings have been understood, it can be highly valued.

Marius Bewley is less optimistic about a book which is both boring and enthralling, both well and cruelly written.[23] He says that, in plumbing the secrets of the democratic American heart, it offers 'less a criticism' than a despairing 'denial of life': 'The one certain fact about the confidence man is that he does not exist. He is appearance drained of all reality. Lift any one of the masks that pass in succession before one: one encounters only vacancy.' There's no one 'there'. But then the Confidence-Man is not meant to be there. The novel has no characters, just as it has a plot that defies paraphrase. It is an earnest, indeed sombre and desperate, comic play of ideas in which the Melvillian unknowable is subject to the knowledge of human inconsistency and contrariness. The one certain fact about the Confidence-Man is the lesson he helps to teach—that the human being is, as the doctrinal Chapter 14 puts it,[24] like the flying-squirrel: 'incongruous in its parts'. Elsewhere Melville enquires: was 'the caterpillar one creature, and is the butterfly another?'[25]

Chapter 14, which follows on an ode of sorts to a protean easychair, employs an image, that of the flying-squirrel, which can be considered a version of Tom Moore's amphibian of fifty years before, the flying-fish. Both of the creatures in question hark back to the duality of the Ancient world, where Aristotle's biological taxonomy, and the folklore contemporary with it, took an interest in in-betweens, anomalies, 'dualisers', such as the bat, which was both bird and quadruped.[26] Both creatures are emblematic, besides, of the more familiar duality of spirit and flesh. But romantic duality may be said to have conquered when a belief in this traditional distinction can appear to have been corrected or completed by a feeling for the plurality of spirits entertained by the one flesh, and Chapter 14 is a sermon which celebrates such a victory—duality's *Te Deum*. It preaches the new gospel, and praises those authors whose characterization responds to it and incurs the charge of inconsistency. The word is that the flying-squirrel is like a character in a novel. 'That author who draws a character, even though to common view incongruous in its parts, as the flying-squirrel, and, at different periods, as much at variance with itself as the butterfly is with the caterpillar into which it changes, may yet, in so doing, be not false but faithful to facts.'

Simultaneously or sequentially, human beings are amphibian, anomalous, inconsistent. Authors are inconsistent, and their characters have to be too. God, the 'author of authors',[27] is inconsistent. The doctrine makes of the book a shadow-play of changing shapes, of 'phantoms which flit' and which flout themselves—genial misanthropes, humanitarian tricksters, grasping Transcendentalists who go to prove that one dualist may be inconsistent enough to bite another. All the world's a stage, a masquerade. A larynx may be usurped by some ventriloquist. Puns enforce the doctrine, as does a difficult, dualistic syntax. Where a character forms the subject of a sentence, the relevant part of speech may be lopped: '"With all my heart," and immediately stepping from the porch, gestured the cosmopolitan to a settee near by, on deck.'[28] It is as if identity, the subject, has ceased to matter. This is a sceptical view of human nature which severely restricts the amount that can be held to be known about it, and the vacancy which can sometimes be heard to echo in the literature of duality can certainly be heard here. No comedy is less funny. And yet Melville's repertoire of confidence tricks is at least as appealing as it is grimly denying. In its subversion of authors, the novel nevertheless leaves the reader with one. It leaves us with an author who wants to displease and deceive, and to undeceive and convert: to convert—to a doctrine of uncertain scope which is made to seem very forbidding—the readership he senses he has lost. It leaves us with the author of a work which is sited, somewhere between Timonism and Lucianism, on the very bleakest ground.

Protean comedy is a literary mode whose expressive range and historical development will become apparent later in this book. There is an American duality where Melville is followed by Mailer and by Bellow; the Irish Proteus is a part played by Barrett and by Beckett. Samuel Beckett does a little comic sum while dissecting a case of multiple identity in his novel of 1950, *Molloy*, in which a rancorous, humorous cripple crawls and crawls to join, and not to join, his mother, roosting in ditches and bushes like the outcast king of Medieval Irish poetry, or like Jane Eyre. The austere Beckett has not been above obeying the call, the cult, of the orphan, whose flight can be caught in the wanderings of his tramps. The orphan had long been peripatetic, peregrine: Beckett has moved with the years to make him immobile. In this early work, Molloy has a romantic pursuer in Moran, who may also be Molloy, whose pursuit comes to a halt, and who reckons 'there were three, no, four Molloys.' Then there are five. 'But let us leave it at that, if you don't mind, the party is big enough.'[29]

VI. SCOTT AND THE DEVIL

Secrecy and stealth are desired by romantic people: both serious secrecy and a semblance and parade of it on the part of those who are not thieves but who wish to steal through life, innocently and intransitively, and publicly. Then again, if romantic people are secretive, they may also be the reverse—impulsively or deliberately frank. Their confessions and soliloquies bring together a public self and the hidden self of the same person's solitudes and reveries. Secrecy is sincere and insincere, slippery and straight: it accommodates the true self while arranging for it to cheat. It finds room for self-consciousness and self-will. The object, or the show, is independence. But secrecy is concessive as well as disobedient; it defers to the opinion of others—just as the theme of double identity, and the practice or pretence of the double life, have been likely to appeal to the kind of person who wishes both to obey and to disobey. In this respect, it agrees with romantic estrangement in general—with its tendency both to love and to hate the world from which it purports to retire, and with its capacity to attempt to rule that world. Those romantic people who are important in a worldly way may be conscious of rejection, and behave as victims. Those who are victims may behave as if they were important, and may become so: the claims of megalomania are rewarded with acceptance, and confer standing. Every so often, it may appear that the secret of success—one of the secrets in which romantic people have certainly been interested—is failure.

A Scottish secrecy is no contradiction in terms, despite the ethos of plain speaking and single-minded austerity for which the North has been known. During the lifetimes of Henry Cockburn, and of his friend and political enemy Scott, and of the maverick Hogg, there came about what may be called the country's great age of secrecy. The modes and varieties of concealment which obtained then, in accordance, at times, with the spread of romantic principles, are a study in themselves. Cockburn was secretive, a sender up in smoke of private papers. He was also outspoken. And the journals he kept permitted him to be both. No less dualistically, he was a Whig romantic, and a classical romantic. This historian was a reader of Tacitus, and a resembler of Clarendon, and he concurred with reproofs directed at Romantic authors by the *Edinburgh Review*. On the other hand, he felt for the picturesque roughness of the Pentlands and Highlands, and the verse he wrote, somewhat secretly, about the Pentlands can appear to concur with Wordsworth. He did not hold with 'Germanism'. He did not care for the new impetus in philosophy, or for the Gothic Romanticism, which were delivered to, and derived from, Germany. But he could be intrigued by the latter, and was ready to use its expressions —its double talk. None of this makes him very different from Jane Austen, who was born four years earlier, and on certain subjects Cockburn's words were hers.

In *Northanger Abbey*, she distinguishes between 'the common feelings of common life' and those 'refined susceptibilities' and 'tender emotions' which she thought romantic: and Scott thought that her quiet way with 'common' life made her a very different novelist from himself. The young and at times tender Cockburn nonetheless felt that journals might attempt a 'minute fidelity to common nature'. In the middle of the eighteenth century, Horace Walpole set precedents for the Gothic strain in fiction by writing a novel which distinguished between surrender to the boundless power of fancy and 'a strict adherence to common life', and in the middle of the nineteenth Hawthorne was distinguishing between fancy and a 'very minute fidelity' to the 'probable and ordinary course of man's experience'. Fidelity, community, stood opposed to peculiarity and romance, and Jane Austen and Cockburn can often appear to be on the same side—that of a common life rooted in the 'actual soil', as Hawthorne put it, of a particular part of the world, some corner of Massachusetts, Midlothian or Hampshire.[1] The notions of 'sense', 'sensibility' and 'respectability', of the gentleman, and of the brutality which may be concealed by an 'amiable' and 'gentlemanlike' bearing, are active in the work of both Cockburn and Austen, and so is the notion of secrecy. One of Jane Austen's first pieces was a comic fragment about blabbing, entitled 'The Mystery'. She disapproves of a recourse to secrecy, and some of her most authoritative characters plead for candour (in the modern sense, which has moved towards 'frankness' and away from the prevailing Austen sense, a more communal one, of 'benevolence' or 'generosity'). But she also allows the recourse, and she knew that sealed lips were a serious business, not just in cities, but in small country communities where behaviour had to meet strict requirements of status and propriety, and where sensibility was spied on by respectability. She has a sharp eye for the difference between a real secret and an 'affected secret', or show of clandestinity.

In *Sense and Sensibility*, Marianne Dashwood is romantic, and as such she is open and outspoken, and yet secretive. On a sisterly walk, she 'steals away' towards the lanes, while the others make for the downs. 'No secrets among friends,' cries a hearty, prying matron, and we reflect that secrecy means not joining in, that this may be carried to excess as it is by Marianne, that it may be resorted to by the hostile and uncomplying, but that a person may have a right to it as a means of defending private concerns against gossip or coercion, or indeed Persuasion.

In *Mansfield Park*, Fanny Price is orphan-like. She is both admitted to and excluded from the grandeur of her relatives' establishment in Northamptonshire: in the end, in marrying her cousin, she takes possession. D. W. Harding has referred to Jane Austen's Cinderellas, or foundling princesses,[2] and Fanny is one of them. She is blamed by an interferer for having 'a little spirit of secrecy, and independence, and nonsense, about her'.[3] The point being made is that sense obeys, while secrecy does not. Fanny is a sensible girl, but there is sensibility there too, and exemplary suffering of the romantic sort: and readers now may feel that she does have a secret—in the shape of the tenderness for her cousin which must, for the modern reader, be steeling her decision to defy her uncle, Sir Thomas Bertram, by refusing to marry Henry Crawford. Sir Thomas is presented as a man of strong sense, which is what Henry Cockburn's father is called in his *Memorials*. Both writers commend the man of sense; both criticize him. The novel drily says that Sir Thomas lacks 'romantic delicacy'. He is not, however, above concealment. Nor is the unprincipled Crawford, of whom his sister says: 'As for secrecy, Henry is quite the hero of an old romance.'

The novel does not condone sham or subterfuge, or self-will, or giddiness. But Fanny's secret, such as it is, is associated with an exposure of the deficiencies of sense, and with a proper resistance to its demands, and it has something of a romantic colouring, which can be seen by the light of Harding's words about Jane Austen's fiction and the world it evokes: 'In so compact a civilised society, romantic love between individuals who freely choose each other for qualities not readily identified and categorised by those around them is a disruption.' The ideal is such as to 'express and support' a state well known to the literature of duality: 'the individual's partial nonconformity'. Harding goes on: 'This aspect of romantic love relates it closely to Jane Austen's concern with the survival of the sensitive and penetrating individual in a society of conforming mediocrity.'

As do others of her novels, *Mansfield Park* affords the spectacle of Cinderella's revenge and reward. In the novels in question, partial nonconformity, disobedience-and-obedience, has a habit of ending in upward mobility. This may reflect the wishes and frustrations of her personal life, though readers now may tend to think of her books as more impersonal, more anonymous, and less romantic, than that. There should be some agreement, at any rate, that they are far from pre-empted by an attack on sensibility. Her romantic people are egotistical, intransigent, wild, tender and apart. They are secretive and effusive. They call attention to the cruelties of kinship, and friendship, in that compact society. They cause trouble. But their absence from her fiction would be disastrous.

The secrecy of one of her romantics is upheld in a striking manner. The novel is *Emma*. None of her characters is more opposed to concealment than this heroine, once her own secrets have miscarried and she has been chastened into better sense: and the reader is not meant to be suspicious of this stance. Earlier, too, she had joined in the general abhorrence of the clandestine engagement in which the orphan Jane Fairfax had been involved. This act of disobedience, this rash attempt to elude her lover's odious and domineering aunt, could not be justified. And yet Emma is able to speak up for Jane's behaviour and bearing as a crypto-fiancée, and in doing so she uses words which few readers will be suspicious of. 'After what had happened to her . . .' is the thought, and Emma's words—with their quotation from *Romeo and Juliet*, the story of another justifiably secret engagement—are a troubled defence of the stealth to which suffering may feel compelled to stoop: 'If a woman can ever be excused for thinking only of herself, it is in a situation like Jane Fairfax's. Of such, one may almost say, that "the world is not theirs, nor the world's law."'[4]

This is to take no more than a flashlight to Austen's secrecies, whose purport and proportions are complex. They were not, however, and could not be, the cathedral, the kasbah, that concealment, what he called delitescency, was for Scott. By the end of Jane Austen's life the Wizard of the North had changed himself into a novelist. In that capacity, he was to prove a master of stealth, and it was to prove a stealthy capacity. Scott's spells were secrets of a kind, and it was a secret of a kind that Scott was the author of the Waverley novels. His anonymity mattered to him in a way that Austen's did not. His career as a novelist, moreover, was pursued at a time of secrets, the Scottish 1820s, when a series of *causes célèbres* in public life turned on issues of disclosure, when reaction and reform, reaction and revolution, came to grips, and the Whig cause grew in strength as it struck the momentum that led to the Reform Bill of 1832. At the start of the decade a case of secrecy came to light which allowed Edinburgh's gentlemen to play at soldiers: but there was more to it than the games that were played. The hardships suffered by the working class in the years that followed the Napoleonic Wars helped to stimulate Radical efforts and trade-union combination and subversion. It was rumoured that seditious oaths had been sworn, and a Government spy, Alexander Richmond, who had been befriended by the unsuspecting Cockburn and Jeffrey, set himself to observe and perhaps to administer the oaths. Presently, in 1820, at Bonnymuir, a handful of weavers took on a cavalry detachment. A farce, perhaps, or a fiasco: but a trial was held, with Jeffrey, and to a lesser extent Cockburn, enlisted for the defence, and three weavers were put to death. This was followed by a chapter of dirty infighting, between Whig and Tory, in the field of anonymous journalism: Scott played a part, as a trustee for one of the Tory papers, and Cockburn as an advocate in the opposing interest. A welter of squibs and smears, the work of 'latent enemies', threw up a duel, in which Boswell's wild son Alexander, a Tory defamer, was slain at Auchtertool.

For Cockburn, the anonymity of the *Edinburgh Review* was wholesome enough, but Tory secrecy—the publication of libels with covert Ministerial backing—was wicked. Subversion and its suppression had become a feature of Scottish life, and were to create a rich skein of mixed feelings on the part of progressives. Cockburn could claim that spying, like bankruptcy, had become a trade. But those on his side who were present at the critical Pantheon meeting of 1820 could behave as conspirators against entrenched political power: an 'old work' had been stealthily resumed. Whig romantics might volunteer to quell the insurrection which petered out at Bonnymuir (as at Peterloo), but they could also defend the rebels, and could be thought, and could think themselves, subversives. Chiefly evident in the spheres of politics, literature and the law, the subterfuge of the early 1820s may be accounted an efflorescence of practical duality. The modern Scotsman had gained an incognito.[5]

Another great event of this dark decade was the Burke and Hare trial. In the annals of Scottish crime the trial, like that of the double-liver Deacon Brodie in the 1780s, has exercised an abiding fascination. Two Irishmen made away with seventeen people—the poorest of the Edinburgh poor. Their method was smothering, which seems to have left no trace of violence for the forensic science of the day: a hand gripped the throat, the nostrils were pinched, and the assailant landed in an embrace on top of his victim. The body was then sold to the anatomist Robert Knox, who has been called the first British racist, and characterized as a social-Darwinist Frankenstein for whom Celts were disposable scum.[6] Hare turned King's evidence, and after a trial which ended on Christmas morning 1828, his confederate was hanged. The woman Burke lived with, Helen MacDougal, received a verdict of not proven. She had been ably defended by Cockburn, who noted Burke's reaction to Helen's escape, 'Well, thank God you're safe,' and said of him: 'Except that he murdered, Burke was a sensible, and what might be called a respectable, man.'[7] At the same time, Cockburn thought the incoming Irish—vagrant labourers and the like, some seven thousand strong in the Edinburgh region at this point—a seditious infestation.

Blackwood's Magazine made the affair out to be even worse than it was, adding atrocity to atrocity, in one of their series of imaginary conversations, the *Noctes Ambrosianae.* John Wilson ('Christopher North') appears to have been responsible for the inflammatory discussion of the subject there, and to have scripted contributions assigned to the Ettrick Shepherd. What did 'James Hogg'—a *nom de plume*, we may hope—think of 'the proceedings of these two Irish gentlemen'? 'That they were too monotonous to impress the imagination. First ae drunk auld wife, and then anither drunk auld wife—and then a third drunk auld wife—and then a drunk auld or sick man or twa. The confession got unco monotonous.' Still, the victims did include 'poor Peggy Paterson, that Unfortunate', and Daft Jamie. 'Hogg's' imagination took part in Burke's dying agonies, and pictured him being roasted by the Devil in Hell.[8] This Manasseh, we are meant to believe, did not repent. The more or less fictitious Hogg who contemplates his agonies—which are made to seem like those of a stifling or Burking—is both like and unlike the Hogg of the accredited fictions: some measure of continuity between these two specialists in pain and constraint can't be denied. The journalistic coverage of the affair abounded in scandalous lies, while the trial was enveloped in tactical complexities: these derived from the predilection for King's evidence deals on the part of the prosecuting authorities of the day (the Deacon Brodie case was an important precedent) and from the immunity that had to be bestowed on Hare; and from the antagonism between the formidable Whig defence teams and the Government-affected Bench. Burke's execution was watched by Scott, humanely aware of the life of the poor in Ireland and deeply hostile to Knox, and by 25,000 screaming citizens, reckoned to be the biggest crowd that had ever gathered in Edinburgh. 'Burke him!' they yelled. 'Hang Knox!' 'He's a noxious morsel!' No more noxious than the *Noctes Ambrosianae* on the subject of crime and punishment. Burke was given a handkerchief, which he spread beneath his knee on the scaffold. It carried a portrait of Burns, and some of his many lines about misfortune.[9]

Both the victims and their assailants have been treated as 'unfortunates'. Helen MacDougal, who was lucky to get off, disappeared, amid execration, after the trial, but there is a trace of her in a footnote which belongs to a book published a few months later—Macnish's *The Philosophy of Sleep*. It reveals how quick the affair was to pass into the condition of fairy-tale and romance, how soft hearts could feel from the first for one of the unfortunate assailants, and how victim and assailant can come together in the one person. It states that she had 'to steal away like a ghost' when a crowd had beaten her up. 'Often she besought pity as one willing to fly, if she only knew where.'[10]

The stealth of accessories after the fact, and of spies, and of hungry weavers, was not invariably remote from the stealing style favoured by romantic people, which might indeed at times approximate to delinquency as a jury of the day would have understood this term. Here and there—in the dawn brought by the French Revolution, and in the years to come—romantic rebelliousness caused or courted indictable offences. French sympathies were widely, and judicially, held to be criminal. The gentle shepherds of Edinburgh's Whig élite were nevertheless tainted: among the young, a spirit of independence declared itself. It impelled Cockburn to take to the hills for the consolations of the orphan and the imperfect solitariness of the Solicitor-General, and, in the fullness of time, to work for a prudently qualified Reform Bill. Two years after the Pentland picnic, in 1835, Jeffrey was resting in an Ayrshire paradise from his part in the Parliamentary struggle which had enfranchised the middle class and emancipated both the oligarchic Scottish burghs and the West Indian slaves. He summoned Cockburn to his side: 'You shall read Shelley, and allow a tame ferret called Susan to bite your fingers.' There is a note by Cockburn which refers to the summons, and to his friend's attitude to Shelley and Keats: 'He had always a foolish passion for these two.'[11] A foolish passion is a passion better hid: Jeffrey was willing to praise romantic writers in print, but he also appears to have felt that enthusiasms which would not please the men of wealth and sense to whom he had awarded the vote were better closeted and pursued in private. Such a man might steal a moment to peruse the obscure, the vulgar and the infantile. For Jeffrey, Shelley's revolutionary politics were of a kind that was better suppressed—perhaps of a kind to link him with Susan the ferret. So far as poetry was concerned, however—the poetry that was to be enjoyed in private or in paradise—Shelley's bite had brought a chronic infection.

Of the British secrecies of the period, few can have been more interesting, and yet more familiar, to romantic people of a literary turn than the phenomenon of anonymous journalism. It was written by such people, and for such people: but it was also written by their latent enemies, and could cause them to smart and pine. When *Mansfield Park* was published, itself unsigned, periodical journalism was, in general, anonymous. Journalists were not respectable—even the editorship of the *Edinburgh Review* lacked, at the outset, the status of an unequivocally gentlemanlike occupation—and it may have been felt that they did not deserve to be named: in any case, for purveyors of information, gossip and political spite—'intelligencers', to use a Victorian word—there were advantages in namelessness. Cockburn points out that, for the young Whig lawyers of an intolerant Edinburgh, 'concealed authorship was an irresistible vent.' Irresistibly, it paid, and could even pay well, while shielding them, to some degree, from retaliation. In the early years of the *Review*, with bar, bench and official preferment under Tory control, and with the local Whig leadership hostile to their claims, the young men in question were a confederacy, almost a conspiracy, and their incognitos mattered to them for that reason. But there was a further temptation which they failed to resist. The conspirators enjoyed their incognitos, which exercised, in this Watergate Scotland, a romantic appeal: Cockburn reports that his friends were shrouded in 'the anonymous mystery'. But he went on to add: 'which each is so apt to derive a second gratification by removing'.[12] The pleasures of anonymity would have been sadly diminished if it had spoilt the chance of building a reputation: in fact, the secret of who had written what was apt to leak, and Macaulay soon became famous as a result of his essay on Milton in Jeffrey's journal. In the field of journalism, the pleasures of secrecy could be dualistically indistinguishable from the pleasures of publicity.

Cockburn's circle of friends helped both to maintain and to abridge the history of anonymity. In 1820, the year of the conspiratorial Pantheon meeting in Edinburgh, the poet Thomas Campbell took over the editorship of the *New Monthly Review* in London on the understanding that it would have signatures, and indeed that it might benefit from his name. He believed that 'it is always a misfortune for a literary man to have recourse to anonymous writing—let his motives be never so innocent. And if there be any excuse more admissible than another, it is when his poverty and modesty conspire against him. But it lowers a man's genius to compose that for which his name is not to be answerable.'[13] Campbell's removal of the mask has been thought to have imparted a momentum to the process which led to a substantial revocation of anonymity in periodical journalism. It was not until the 1860s, however, that the tide appears to have turned. In 1867, in the *Fortnightly Review*,[14] John Morley attacked and abjured the traditional practice. 'Secrecy demoralises,' he wrote, meaning that it was bad for a man's character. Not only did it lower his genius. In the same editorial, Morley invoked the arguments against the secret ballot which stressed that citizens performing the public function of voting should do so publicly. The fact that these arguments did not succeed in preventing the adoption of the secret ballot hints that the case for disclosure, whatever the sphere, will seldom be self-evident or unobstructed. We can be certain that governments will continue to keep their official secrets.

In the early part of the nineteenth century, novelists, too, were often unnamed, and the most celebrated of all concealed authors was a novelist. At a theatrical fund dinner in 1827, the 'Great Unknown' shed his disguise and owned up to the Waverley novels, which may be considered a good deed in a Watergate world. Scott was encouraged to own up by the judge Lord Meadowbank, who was not above tugging at his domino, and who had earlier been unskilfully employed in detecting the weavers' subversive oaths. But if secrecy had found an opponent in Lord Meadowbank, his efforts on this occasion were superfluous, for the secret of the Waverley authorship had already been extracted by Scott's creditors and had long been an open one. For that matter, it had been said from the first: '*Aut Scotus aut Diabolus*'—either Scott or the Devil. This was the very time, of course, when duality was suggesting that it might be both—that Gil-Martin might have moved south, so to speak, to Abbotsford. Though the secret was out, Scott nevertheless affected, at this dinner, to be confessing to a crime, classing himself with such Scottish criminals as Macbeth (Macnish would have been nearer the mark), and explaining that his book was now buried, his wand broken. In referring to his original decision to obey the convention of anonymity, he could talk as if this had been an unconventional thing to do.[15] The words of another of Shakespeare's characters came to him in this connection—Shylock's 'It is my humour.' The comparison figures in Scott's discussion of 'my secret' in his General Preface to the 1829 edition of the novels: he says there that he shares what Phrenology might term the novelist's passion for 'delitescency' or concealment, and shows a lively feeling for the affectations which are liable to be found in the vicinity of this passion.[16] He was also to speak of the 'secret fountain' of gold accessible to him as a 'nameless romancer', whose '*nominis umbra*' was now gone for good: 'it would have been an idle piece of affectation to attempt getting up a new *incognito*, after his original visor had been thus dashed from his brow'—with the flying away of his gold. And he was to mention a certain harlequin who had been persuaded to remove his black vizard on the stage, and had then endured a flop: 'he had lost the audacity which a sense of incognito bestowed, and with it all the reckless play of raillery which gave vivacity to his original acting.'[17] This exposes a further justification for the practice of anonymity—one which agrees with the dualistic hypothesis. Anonymity liberates. It *raises* a man's genius, and may even make a new man of him. The wizard, in the shape of the delitescent novelist, would be advised to hold onto his vizard.

As his pantomime of criminality may be taken to imply, the Wizard of the North was in more than one mind about vizards and about multiple personality. When the French wizard, ventriloquist, and quick-change artist, Alexandre Vattermare, performed his tricks at Abbotsford, Scott gave thanks with a piece of verse, a parlour-game impromptu, which asserts, while also merrily superseding, an old view of the self:

> Of yore in old England, it was not thought good
> To carry two visages under one hood.

This Proteus had the night before shown them twenty faces, the 'arch deceiver'.

> Above all, are you one individual? I know
> You must be at least, Alexandre & Co.

Scott says that in his capacity as sheriff, he must read him the Riot Act, and disperse him. But then Scott himself was a man of many capacities. He was himself a company: not only a secret tradesman but the carrier of two visages at least.[18]

Novels were felt to be a risky venture when he chose to hide his identity, and it was a little unsuitable, he supposed, for a Clerk of Session to write them. His tradesmanlike connection with the Ballantyne brothers' firm could be kept dark by means of the incognito. But there was more to the decision, and certainly to his experience of its consequences, than this would suggest. Anonymity may not have been essential to him as a novelist: it can scarcely have amounted to his pound of flesh, as it were. But it may well have meant more to him than it did to the Edinburgh Reviewers.

At a point when he had accepted that his responsibility for the novels would become common knowledge because of his bankruptcy, he confided to his *Journal* that 'the magic wand of the Unknown is shivered in his grasp': he would now be 'the Too well Known'. The entry, for 18 December 1825, proceeds: 'The feast of fancy is over with the feeling of independence.' He then says, in effect, that he won't be able to go on with his bright fiction, which has enabled him to buy land, plant groves and create the picturesque: he might try history instead, but the public would like it less, or at least would dislike knowing, as it now would, that here was an author who had to write for money. Jane Austen's placing together of secrecy, independence and nonsense reappears in this passage, which conveys that the independence secured by the concealed authorship of fiction was both financial and other than financial: it was his humour to write works of fancy rather than fact, which brought him his plantations, and in doing so by stealth he felt independent of the public, who might not be able to know how the Laird of Abbotsford made, and had to make, his money.

He did, in fact, go on writing novels. For Scott, however, fancy was bound up with, and released by, clandestinity, and the loss of this distressed him. The Wizard of the North required not only his wand but his cloak of invisibility, tattered though it was. The Waverley authorship was both a secret and an affected secret. The hyperbole, and, in the modern sense, the humour, of his references to the matter should not mislead one into thinking that his clandestinity was just a pleasant charade. It was no picnic; it was something different from Cockburn's reclusive contribution to the Habbie's Howe festivities. It allowed him to write audacious novels, to play the magical or diabolical role of the concealed author, and to play the role of the laird who had nothing to hide and no novels to write. It forms part of the evidence which persuades us that the romantic people of the early nineteenth century may be identified by their capacity to play games and roles, and that these were a way of saying what their writings also say: that the self has a capacity for duplication and division. The secrecy deployed in his novels is deployed in many novels; many novels are like the old romances. Moreover, Scott was thought to be an honest and open-hearted man, and he may have kept no more secrets than most people do: the secret of Lady Scott's origins—still partly intact, as far as I know—was the kind that any man of sense would have kept. All the same, he must have felt that his life would have been incomplete without the roles which his mysteries enabled him to play, that the 'lees', as Hogg called them, which he was obliged to tell were necessary to him, and some of the cultural tendencies which he helped to foster did little to invite respect for the merits of an open-hearted simplicity and singleness.

His first novel, *Waverley*, begun in 1805 but then laid aside for several years, has qualities which answer to this account, and they are qualities which deliver the work to the incipient new literature of duality. Scott said[19] that his hero Edward was like a fairground dwarf, and that he was 'a sneaking piece of imbecility': if we suspect a missing 'but', a concealed adversative, in this soldierly disparagement, which corresponds to the second half of what Macnish had to say of Hogg, that 'strange compound of genius and imbecility', then the novel enables us to complete the description and assemble the duality. Edward is weak and ill and in error: but his condition may be called a version or prevision of negative capability. On these pulses are proved the claims of the barbaric Scotland of the Forty-five rebellion—claims which are succeeded and subdued by those of a Hanoverian commerce and common sense, capable of a British peace. Edward, the romantic youth from England, sneaks, as who should say steals, through Scott's 'romantic town' of Edinburgh, and through its Highland hinterland, which amounts to a foreign country. He takes flight to a Jacobite Beyond, whose conspiratorial politics can only have looked destructive and archaic to the novel's first readers, to Pittite and to Pantheon Whig alike: Cockburn's party may at times have resembled conspirators, but they were not rebels and they were not traitors. Having struck his silly, involuntary blow for the lost cause, Edward lays down his arms. Having fallen in love, he marries a suitable someone else. His flight has become an education, a ritual passage to maturity—and it was maturity which had taken up the novel again, several years after its false start, at a time when Keats was soon to write his letters, and which was to say of an Edward relieved of his illusions: 'The romance of his life was ended.' Secrecy here is the stealth of glamorous hereditary right, relished by Scott. It is Jacobite stealth, pictured at a time when Jacobin stealth was feared by Scott and others. It is not condoned. It is seen as sedition. But a sense of competing claims survives. *Waverley* offers strange sights and strange people: but Jeffrey was able to praise the 'fidelity'—to common life, we may chiefly take him to mean—of its characterization. This is not an impartial book; it has a lesson to teach. But it can also be classed among the strange compounds of the new era.[20]

It was Scott's humour to compare himself on one occasion to the poor wizard who has trouble in raising and in employing the Devil.[21] He was alluding to his secretary Laidlaw, but also, perhaps, to *Aut Scotus aut Diabolus*. The participation of the Devil in secret undertakings was an old work which was re-disclosed in the Gothic fiction of the Scottish nineteenth century. Hogg's *Confessions* of 1824 has its Devil and its double, and was itself a secret undertaking in that it was published anonymously. Hogg's authorship could still be regarded as doubtful late in the century, though his diabolical friends on *Blackwood's Magazine*, as he sometimes felt them to be, blew his cover after publication, for those who were attending. One way or another, the 1820s were Scotland's great age of secrecy. The Scotch spies and Scotch reviewers of the period may be thought to have prepared the ground for those decades of the later twentieth century in which, with reviewers mostly unmasked, the duality of espionage, the double life of spies, has attained the proportions of a cultural obsession.

In 1856, Cockburn played a posthumous part in a row about anonymity, which had for some time been subjected to intermittent challenge. His *Memorials* was published in that year. In August, the *Law Magazine and Law Review* poured anonymous contempt on the book, and on 3 September an editorial in the *Scotsman* reviewed the review, and, anonymously, unmasked its anonymous author. Harking back to the saying about Scott, the editorial asserts: '*Aut* Harry—*aut* Old Harry.' Old Harry is the Devil, and Harry was Henry Brougham, a former Whig co-conspirator of Cockburn's, Lord Chancellor in the Grey Administration of 1832. According to Cockburn, he was mad. According to Byron, 'a foolish clever fellow—*idem semper*'.[22] *Idem semper* is what Byron calls himself, ironically, in *Don Juan*: in the verse portrait quoted here, Brougham is seen as all too consistent, as the same old turncoat, bully, and coward (these are scarcely three different men), and, in Augustan style, as predictably unstable. He is a 'strange example', 'poor fellow', of what happens when law and a 'hasty temper' meet. But there is no sign of an *alter idem*. No double. Brougham's article denounces Harry Cockburn for making too much of the encroachments on civil liberty which took place in Scotland in the 1790s, when French principles had entered the country, and of the tribulations suffered by Whig lawyers in those days of Tory supremacy. It also denounces Cockburn for unfairness to the Tory hanging judge, Lord Braxfield. It might have been said that the author of the review had turned his coat, that the old Harry Brougham was very different from the new.

The *Scotsman* editorial begins:

To have a very peculiar mode of view and of expression is a considerable misfortune to anyone that desires to speak incognito, and to speak unpleasant and unfitting things. In some extreme instances, it is much the same case as that of a professional thief—or take perhaps a less offensive illustration, a professional thief-catcher—who squinted, and halted, and stuttered, and who could not look, nor move, nor speak, without everybody knowing who he was. And it would be much the same thing if the person seeking to disguise himself possessed, instead of such remarkable defects, some as remarkable beauties—if he had the eyes of an eagle, the gait of an antelope, and the utterance of a Brougham.

In years gone by, anonymity had been likened to the piece of crêpe worn on his face by a highwayman (Bulwer-Lytton's novel of 1830, *Paul Clifford*, traces the secret life of a hack who turns into a highwayman), and the *Scotsman*, too, links it with disguise and stealing. The theft, presumably, is of someone's reputation, his good name. The editorial goes on to say 'that if Lord Brougham had taken it into his ever-busy brain to review his old friend's book, it is just *so* that he would have reviewed it; and that if the review is not *his*, it must be the work of somebody that imitates to a marvel the walk and conversation of his pen.' The *Scotsman* is far from suggesting at this point that anonymities and pseudonyms, *noms de plume* and *de guerre*, may enable someone to play a role, and so liberate a devilish second self. The language of duality is ironized to suggest that there is only the one Brougham, and that the review could be by no one else. Speaking unfitting things from behind an ill-fitting vizard, this one Brougham has caused his old friend to stand and deliver.

The anti-German Cockburn, however, was once German enough to conceive that there might be two Broughams—Cockburn's and Sir James Mackintosh's—and you do not need to be especially vulnerable to the Gothic fables to ask whether, at times, anonymity and duality might not coincide. The review's revisionist account of an earlier Edinburgh could possibly be seen as a sweeping repudiation, by a new Brougham, of the old—possibly but implausibly: the new Brougham was nearly eighty, changes of mind and of coat are common in politics, and he was impugning, not his own political past, but that of the kind of old friend towards whom politicians are not always affectionately disposed. It could nevertheless be felt that his eerie boastfulness, his devotion to the public self of his achievements and reputation, the fabrication of a noble pedigree, the belief that he had spread the report of his death which enabled him to read his own obituary—that these features of his career help to explain why megalomania should be a condition which the language of duality is equipped to describe. The unsigned article, in which he could refer to himself in the third person, as he does here, but of which he could be recognized as the author, was a medium which obviously appealed to him, and there can be little doubt that fifty years before he had been one of Cockburn's gratified Edinburgh Reviewers—gratified both by the mystery and by the acclaim which the medium afforded.

Brougham's octogenarian critique does at least allow one to speculate about the pleasures of anonymity, and about the element of firsthand experience which we may wish to attribute to the Gothic fables. Those inclined to believe that duality took to writing the fiction of duality, and that such writers took to using false names or none, are likely to find the evidence intractable. But it is certainly true that two of the exponents of that fiction chose to conceal themselves at a time when the practice of concealment had started to fail—Hogg and Macnish; and that it is in the intensely dualistic literature of the modern world that we have become accustomed to the use of pen-names by leading writers. Some of these writers may have resembled Scott—if we can conclude that Scott chose to conceal himself in order to express a part of his nature that common life and other avocations might otherwise have suppressed. Modern Scotland's 'Hugh MacDiarmid' is surely a dualistic pen-name—one which proposes a warrior self, a clansman, in contrast with a sorrowful, Lowland-bucolic birth-certificate surname (Grieve). A clan of contrasts can indeed be found in MacDiarmid—a communist élitist, for and against a mass public, for and against a poetry that bore on practical concerns.

There is no reason to think that critical anonymity was set up on a basis of principle, but it was argued about on that basis when it was widely revoked in the middle of the nineteenth century, and again when the *Times Literary Supplement*, founded exactly a hundred years after the *Edinburgh Review* by means of a deed which insisted on anonymity, abandoned the practice in 1974. One may think that if signatures encourage writers to show off, so does concealment. A good deal of criticism is driven by aggression, and a malicious unsigned critique is just as unpleasant as an anonymous letter of the poisonous sort. It may be just as cowardly; by appearing in public, by appearing disinterested, and by appearing so, on occasion, even to the author attacked, it can do more harm. The *prestige de l'inconnu*, mentioned in the nineteenth-century discussions, has more to do with selling newspapers than with criticism. It is better, as a rule, to know who is addressing you, and to have no avoidable constraints on the attempt to know what he is saying and why he is saying it. Modern apologists for anonymity, however, seem to feel that to know about the person who has written something is no aid to knowing what he has written. It may be that Structuralism has tendered such an apology. Recent literary theory of this kind has been such as to license or legitimize a reversion to anonymity.

It would be hard to show that the practice of anonymity was maintained with the object of ensuring an impartial criticism. Can it be claimed that it nonetheless helped to ensure such a thing? In 1974, the skilful expounder of Structuralist and Deconstructionist ideas, Jonathan Culler, wrote to the *Times Literary Supplement* to protest at their change of policy: 'Anonymity is a stratagem designed to provoke intellectual inquiry rather than speculation about persons.' But apparently it did provoke speculation about persons, since Culler admitted that 'the game of guessing authors was fun.'[23]

The first romantic people were excited by secrecy and by anonymity. But they also went in for sincerity, openness, outspokenness, and for a worship of the artist and of the sensitive individual. In time, the cloak of invisibility became intolerable. The biography of the artist became beautiful, and the latter-day romantic has been known for his favourable attitude towards publicity. Later still, however, these attitudes in turn became intolerable. A number of writers, some of whom may be thought to have anticipated what might appear to be the Structuralist view of the matter, have acted to curtail the dependence on romantic conceptions by affirming the importance in literature of a principle of anonymity. In 1925, E. M. Forster stated that 'all literature tends towards a condition of anonymity,' and that 'the modern newspaper has taken advantage of this. It is a pernicious caricature of literature. It has usurped that divine tendency towards anonymity.'[24] But there also appears to be a tendency towards the identification of authors. To broadly the same effect as Forster, and at about the same time, T. S. Eliot was arguing, on behalf of an artistic impersonality, that a writer should try to separate his life—more specifically, and more romantically, his sufferings—from his art. Since then, it has been usual for critical theorists to insist that readers should try to separate their knowledge of a writer's life from their knowledge of what he has written.

Anonymity was shed in response to the mounting importance of the author, who was identified in order that he might be revered. One should also say that if romantic secretiveness took pleasure in anonymity, romantic candour helped to abolish the practice. Authors, artists, loomed large; without giving unlimited satisfaction in the role, they were treated as leaders. But the visibility of artists was not invented in the nineteenth century. It is ancient, and perhaps inherent. Shakespeare has long been identified, and intimately known, on the evidence of his plays and in the absence of a substantive biography. Such knowledge will not be lightly surrendered in exchange for an atavistic collectivism, and the new ideas of recent years would enable no one to predict that literature will revert to the condition of folklore.

VII. STRANGE CASES

Edmund Burke was thought in his own time to be a man who was always the same; and he himself, a respecter of bounds and bonds, checks and balances, admired 'consistency of character'. Now he can be seen as a storehouse of contradictions: as a man of dual nationality, an English constitutionalist and counter-revolutionary who nevertheless cared about the bondage of his Irish fellow-countrymen, as a denouncer of the French Terror who, as *cognoscente*, craved the terrors of infinity and obscurity.[1] Does the capacity so to re-imagine Burke suggest that human nature changed with Romanticism's assertion of belief in the changing mind of duality? Did the premise of a psychic mutability accompany a mutation, a leap: the arrival in the world of a divided or manifold mind, *homo duplex* or the *multiplex ingenium et tortuosum*, which managed to knot up the *perfervidum ingenium* of Scotland? *Homo duplex* was the invention of Buffon and the French eighteenth century. But the other Latin tag, which speaks of a *multiplex ingenium*, is from Cicero, who has also been associated with one of duality's oldest aphorisms, a saying from before Christ, about a gregarious solitude, a saying embraced by the pensiveness of the English eighteenth and nineteenth centuries: '*Numquam minus solum quam cum solus*.'[2] The Ciceronian commonplace was to interest romantics as an utterance of one of their most important paradoxes: that of an egotism—a self-cultivation, a self-creation—which is peculiarly exposed to other people and to the world.

Some of the cases so far discussed may have suggested that by the beginning of the nineteenth century the human mind had come apart or opened up—into the two minds that may respond to conflicting needs or incitements, into a foliage of moods and moments, highs and lows. It was held that minds might be entered, invaded. Indolence and elation and invention might meet. Such strange cases became the common occurrences of a diligent literature. But the protean personality had its exemplars in the ancient world too. Then and since, it has been viewed at times with disfavour, as indeed by the tortuous and exemplary Cicero himself: and the Romantic period ensued on a time when disfavour had been expressed. 'All mankind's epitome', a creature of 'ten thousand freaks', Dryden's Zimri, in 'Absalom and Achitophel', 'was everything by starts and nothing long'. Meanwhile that 'Amphibious Thing', Pope's Sporus, was

> Now High, now Low, now Master up, now Miss,
> And he himself one vile Antithesis.

Such amphibians, antitheses, epitomes, such Augustan fits and starts and freaks and flying fish, were vile, lunatic: but they were to become strangely interesting. There were to be occasions when it could seem that mankind had ceased to be always the same—had moved from an *idem semper* to an *alter idem*. A gregarious solitude was once again confessed, and was widely courted. There came about an imaginary human isolation which was thrown open to other men, in the shape of the second self, and, in the case, *par excellence*, of the hospitable impersonal artist, to all men. Romanticism proved amphibious enough both to affirm and to deny that the individual human being was single and separate. In 1794, three years after Wieland's *Peregrine Proteus* appeared in Germany, there appeared in England William Godwin's *The Adventures of Caleb Williams*, where political justice wears the face of a fearful domesticity, where hunter and hunted can be experienced as one and the same man, and a magnetic mutuality is put to the blush:

> The instant I had uttered these words, I felt what it was that I had done. There was a magnetical sympathy between me and my patron, so that their effect was not sooner produced upon him, than my own mind reproached me with the inhumanity of the allusion. Our confusion was mutual. The blood forsook at once the transparent complexion of Mr Falkland, and then rushed back again with rapidity and fierceness.[3]

Thirty years later, in Scotland, much the same equivocal, familial pursuit was staged by Hogg, in response, among others, to German precedents. Such are the accords by which the international duality of the nineteenth century was to proceed, and with which the present chapter is mainly concerned.

It can be said, then, that Cicero was followed, in a later world, by Chamisso—by Chamisso's *Peter Schlemihl*, which appeared in Germany in 1814, the year after Barrett's *The Heroine*. *Schlemihl* is a Yiddish word for the accident-prone, and the narrator of the tale has the bad luck to be persuaded by the Devil to exchange his shadow for the purse of Fortunatus. The deal is done during a garden party, from which the narrator 'steals away', only to succumb to his tempter, 'the man in gray'. Thereafter he is shadowless, and miserable, for all his wealth. He loses the woman he has wished to marry, whose family are worried by his detached state. He sets out on a seven-league journey round the world: botany, the feats of an Alexander von Humboldt, expiates the bad deal. Equally, the narrator is a type of the Wandering Jew: received in a hospital, 'I was called *Number Twelve*, and, from my long beard, was supposed to be a Jew, but was not the less carefully nursed on that account.'[4] Peter begins and ends as an outcast; by hazarding his soul for gain, he is barred from family life, from the happiness of marriage. The tale is marked by the superstitions of the past which had seen money as evil, shadow as soul, soul as forfeit to the enemy of mankind, and it draws on the dualistic apparatus of the past—twins, brothers, shadows, reflections, portraits. It is a tall tale of a cautionary kind. We may feel that Peter regains the quality he had lost—that there is soul in his scientific feats. And yet it would appear that avarice, succeeded by a penitential botany, has unfitted him for family life.

Shadow-play of this kind grew into a genre, the *Schauerroman*. Hans Christian Andersen was an admirer of Chamisso, and of Hoffmann, another shadow-romancer, and thirty years later *Peter Schlemihl* helped him to compose a touching dualistic fantasy. 'The Shadow'[5] tells how a shy Northern scholar visits a hot country, an Italy—just as Mann's Tonio Kröger does, in a story which resonates with the Andersen. This scholar, who writes 'books about what was true in the world and what was good and what was beautiful', sends his shadow to spy on a musical, muse-like girl across the street, and the shadow comes to life as his chilling supplanter—Chamisso's shadow remains inanimate, and uninteresting. The learned man and his marvellously thin companion—each as strange as the other, according to the latter—set off on a tour of European spas. The shadow is the master, and the master is the shadow. The shadow wins the affections of a princess, whose initial doubts, 'Does he have the necessary knowledge?' are allayed. It is the scholar who has the knowledge, but it is the shadow who gets the princess. The scholar is a poor fellow in a story which is about poor fellows, and unnecessary artists: 'What he said about the true and the good and the beautiful, that was for most people like casting roses at the feet of a cow.' But the story also belongs to a time when for most people, for the masses, impotence was important, and to be defended: at such a time, the princess knows that it is 'necessary to do away with him without fanfare'. And so, while she and the shadow marry, the scholar is quietly put to death. A friend of Andersen's wanted these words for the conclusion: 'People spoke about how the arm of justice had finally reached him, but no one knew what crime he had committed . . .'.[6] They are words which suit a story of innocence and self-incrimination, and of necessity, containing premonitions of Kafka. Kafka, too, was to write about crimes committed and uncommitted, and about a mysterious justice, and to predict the justice which was soon to turn innocent people into numbers—inscribing these numbers on their bodies—and to put them quietly to death. He was to be the author, moreover, of a metamorphosis in which a poor family fellow turns into an insect and breathes his last in that unfortunate capacity. Having shed him, his family is aware of a possible bright future.

Andersen's misfit suffers a metamorphosis. His lamb is shorn of its shadow. The light by which these adventures are disclosed is the romantic medium of moonshine, where shadows sprout and shoot and are shorn, where the misfit may meet his own worst enemy, but will always matter more than anyone else. Chamisso's story inhabits the same medium, but is closer to folklore. The Devil's seductions do not figure in Hans Andersen's fairy-tale, and it is easy to devise, in relation to what is represented there, domestic equivalents—to imagine some vocational task from which a man is distracted by other compulsions, losing his dearest hopes, let us say, in marriage and success. We are to think that it is only a writer's sordid self which can hope to please a woman, or a reader. Andersen's story, like Chamisso's and Mann's, deals with writers and with families, and suggests that writers must do without them. There is the further suggestion in this story of a defeat for fathers, and of a filial relationship between scholar and shadow, when the latter, newly independent, talks of a wish to marry: 'I can afford more than one family.' Andersen's scholar's shadow is no soul but a sinister thin philistine assassin who grows up and settles down and lives happily ever after. The story shows a war between types of fulfilment, and shows how a taste for truth and beauty may be defeated. It distinguishes between a rose and a cow, between the frail productions of writers and the preoccupations of the mass mind. At the same time, it seems that the mass mind may take an interest in the rose of human weakness, as Andersen himself did. Like his friend Dickens, he knew how to cast roses before cows. Both were poor fellows who made famous names for themselves by writing for, and about, poor fellows.

Between the Chamisso and the Andersen lies an interval which can be considered—as can the Fin-de-Siècle—a high point in the history of dualistic invention. The years that followed *Peter Schlemihl* brought a flurry of quick successions, and, in Hoffmann's *Devil's Elixir*, a work which was patently fabulous and patently familial, a work in which the family man could be like some fabulous knight, at variance with himself. The dualistic International—if the name can be applied to these accords, to duality's duplications, to the gospel that spoke to Europe and America of the freeing of a repressed or hidden self—owed much, as we have seen, to Hoffmann's 'ghostly *doppelgänger*'.[7] In 1818, two years after *The Devil's Elixir* had appeared, *Frankenstein* appeared. Mary Shelley's hero is an orphan who orphans the creature he has made, a creature who is then pitied as a monster capable of attacking his maker's bride. The work is valid as a fiction of family life, and was to spread the romantic word that monsters are unfortunate and that misfortune makes monsters. The tales of Hoffmann, and Mary Shelley's tale, were such as to arouse dark thoughts of a hereditary variance, and were themselves to prove strong transmitters of the language of this subject—a language which soon became routine. Its predictability, declamatoriness, formulaic woodenness, are the defects of a genre whose magic has spread and become mechanical. The formulas in question, verbal and dramatic, entered the mass magazines and melodramas of the industrial era: they also entered the minds of gifted and inventive writers whose every word was their own. The Gothic plights and spells were to repeat themselves, as falls the shadow, within particular works and over several generations, duality's *longue durée*. The time-and-again of romantic duality was to recite, for a lacerating world of delirium and hostility, a modern fairy-tale of variance, stealth and flight.

Not many months after *Frankenstein* came the Irishman Maturin's *Melmoth the Wanderer*. Maturin was—what the Hogg of certain writings, and the *faux*-Hogg of *Blackwood's*, can sometimes appear to be—a kind of sentimental Calvinist. Melmoth is a supernatural being who ranges the world for centuries on end, another *longue durée*, trying incompetently, as Poe for one perceived, to prevail on the hard-pressed to sell their souls to the Devil. Human beings are multiply captive. They are, say Melmoth and his maker, feeble, as feeble as birds: 'when thy hand, O Thou whom I dare not call Father, is on them, they scream and quiver, though the gentle pressure is intended only to convey the wanderer back to his cage—while, to shun the light fear that scares their senses, they rush into the snare that is spread in their sight, and where their captivity is hopeless!' At the same time, the novel thrills to the sweetness of escape, futile or fatal as it may prove. The escapee Monçada is 'an isolated being, rejected by father and mother'—who force him to be a monk. We are at this point in the incarcerating Inquisition Spain which has been imagined by English Protestants. Aided by a fellow monk who has murdered his father, Monçada embarks on an obstetric egress from the monastery.[8] Though conscious that 'all Spain is but one great monastery—I must be a prisoner every step that I take,' he has high hopes of the tunnelling project which is to conduct them through vaults, up into a garden and over a wall into his brother's arms. His companion explains: 'Our situation has happened to unite very opposite characters in the same adventure, but it is an union inevitable and *inseparable*. Your destiny is now bound to mine by a tie which no human force can break.' Monçada says of his inseparable companion: 'suffering without requital or consolation . . . arrays crime in the dazzling robe of magnanimity, and makes us admire the fallen spirit, with whom we dare not sympathize.' Theirs is a '*union of antipodes*'—Maturin's italics—

and of another such union, some four years later, Hogg's dazzling Gil-Martin was to say: 'sooner cause the shadow to relinquish the substance, than separate me from your side.' 'Stealing from my cell', 'panting for emancipation', Monçada is Siamesed with a parricide: 'driven to trust his life and liberation to hands that reeked with a father's blood'. This turns the monastery into a home, and turns the double into an incarnation of the semi-self which surfaces in rebellion.

'Anything for escape,' cries Monçada, and passes into the 'delirium'—Hogg's word, too, and Norman Mailer's—of a subterranean journey to the end of the night. Among the items in this 'noctuary of terror,—terror has no diary,' are the desperate straits of a narrow passage which reminds him of a traveller's tale about a man stuck in one of the Pyramids who frees himself with a spasm and then suffocates. Monçada is momentous, and momentary: he thinks of 'how we could, in such a moment, feed on a parent, to gnaw out our passage into life and liberty, as sufferers in a wreck have been known to gnaw their own flesh . . .'. In a vault they come to, a pair of illicit lovers, immured by the companion, had been driven to gnaw one another; illicit love is compared to incest; elsewhere the parricide mentions that half the world now wants to marry, defiantly, for love. The episode carries latent and patent and turbulent family meanings. The family and its constraints expand to swallow the whole of Spain, and contract to the contractions of birth. During the vicissitudes of the escape—delays, sleeps, winking lights, 'there was not a moment to be lost'—the companion retains the likeness of Gil-Martin. 'I dreaded him as a demon, yet I invoked him as a god,' says Monçada. And: 'Nothing but the iron link of necessity could have bound me to you even for a moment.' The companion tells Monçada: '*Emotions are my events.*' He represents those of Monçada's emotions which liberate and which betray him. He is an opposite and a duplicate self. They are one flesh, and they can be said to eat one another. They climb the wall—only for the companion to reveal himself in league with the monastery and to stab the rescuing brother. Monçada's escape delivers him into the hands of the Inquisition. In his new cell he is waited on by his false friend, who seeks, as Melmoth does, by a connoisseurship of suffering, to diminish his own, and who enquires: 'Which of us is the murderer?' Monçada's conduct has been the ruin of his kin. 'Your father and mother have separated.' But he refuses to surrender his soul to Melmoth.

A second escape is that of the castaway Immalee, who has never seen another human being until Melmoth lands on her desert island, and who falls for this fallen spirit. 'Vivid and susceptible', she is a responsive 'child of nature' who blushes, swoons, and is like to die. In Spain, odious parents command her to obey them in marriage—at a time when half the world wants to marry for love—but she tries to elope as the 'bride of perdition'. The difficulties which beset such attempts are underrated in romances, Maturin warns. 'Her mansion was a prison,' he writes of his heroine. 'Thus her escape was completely barred; and had every door in the house been thrown open, she would have felt like a bird on its first flight from the cage, without a spray that she dared to rest on. Such was her prospect, even if she could effect her escape—at home it was worse.'[9] And yet there is no place like home. We are betrayed when we try to get what we want. These castings-about on the subject of human fulfilment are an aspect of Maturin's belief in the paradox, in the heaven and hell, of human nature, in the union of opposites apparent in the story of the parricide's share in poor Monçada's flight. It is a story in which both Monçada and his own worst enemy are the enemies of parents: *Melmoth* is itself a romance. But it is no less the work of a clergyman, and a religious melodrama. For Maturin, duality was a novel which enlarges on the futility of escape while resounding with one version or another of the cry which would so often be heard among Victorians: 'O for the wings of a dove.'

Within the space of four years the cry was uttered in De Quincey's *Confessions* and in Hogg's. Both books are by 'amateurs in suffering', to use an expression of Maturin's,[10] connoisseurs of orphan flight, who fled to Edinburgh. Dualistic productions were becoming an established genre, indeed a mine of activity, in the literatures of Scotland, England and France, and in that of Russia, where the ores were especially rich, with Edinburgh and St. Petersburg the twin capital cities of the subject—the axis of international duality. They are the source and setting of two of its most impressive works: Hogg's novel and Dostoevsky's novel of 1846, *The Double*. The example of

Gogol assisted Dostoevsky to write a book which offers the divided mind, and which offers something of the dispersal known as negative capability. Russian duality was to practise both division and diffusion, with Gogol setting his adored precedents. These, however, are far from being the only precedents which matter in the case of *The Double*. A Russian critic[11] has spoken of 'a naturalistic transformation of the Romantic "doubles" of Russian Hoffmannism', while here as elsewhere in Dostoevsky we may recognize a debt to Mrs Radcliffe, whose romances were read to him by his parents in the course of long winter evenings, and to Dickens, who was also engaged in transformations of romance, and who was to inspire in Dostoevsky an ambition which brought a transformation of Dickens. There could be no debt to Hogg: but the two writers converge in the use to which they put the language of duality, and in their capacity to live out its hypotheses. Dostoevsky suffered fits and terrors which exposed an inner division, and his relationship with the salons of the Petersburg literary world, with the so-called Belinsky Pléiade, was a torment of ambivalence which duplicated Hogg's relationship with the *Blackwood's* set in Edinburgh. Each was a lion while also at times a butt and scapegoat, and Dostoevsky's bad times in this respect are present in the novel of 1846. Not long after its completion he woke one morning to the sight of a colonel clad in the light blue uniform of the secret police—with all the *éclat* of romantic clandestinity. Subversion cost him a Gothic captivity: a sentence of death was commuted—the news withheld until there was not a moment to be lost. Exile prevented a plan to revise the novel, but he did revise it in later years.

The transformer Dickens did not cease to be a romantic novelist: and Dostoevsky's novel is no transformation into anything other than a ripe spectacle of dualistic fantasy—with its insistent 'stranges', its glimpse in the mirror of the hero's counterfeit, its approximation to the form and ethos of the romantic 'diary of a madman'. In Gogol's story of that name, authority has a daughter who is desired by an office-worker mad enough to suppose that the Earth intends to land on the Moon. The story appeared twelve years before Dostoevsky's novel, and was followed by 'The Nose' and 'The Overcoat', which respectively concern a double and an outcast. In the first, a pompous minor official loses his nose and is mortified to find it looking down on him from the upper ranks of the hierarchy. He writes a letter to a woman whose daughter he suspects he is being forced to marry, and blames on her sorcery the loss of his nose—'its sudden departure from its place, its flight and masquerade . . . '. The nose is to the official what his shadow is to Andersen's scholar: the embodiment of an impossible social integration and success. The other story tells of a functionary who loses a treasured coat, dies, and returns to haunt the well-dressed. The three stories, and their paranoid-bureaucratic ambience, may be said to haunt *The Double*, where the hero's coat is prominent, along with his poor galoshes. It can also be said that with the work of Hogg, Gogol and Dostoevsky, among others, there had come about, within international duality and the Gothic mode, that special sympathy with the confessional and the maniacal which was to prove a steadfast feature of the literature of the modern world. The diary, and noctuary, of the madman is still being compiled.

In common with Belinsky and the Pléiade, Dostoevsky thought of *The Double*, originally subtitled 'The Adventures of Mr Golyadkin', as a work that ensued on the 'adventures of Chichikov' in *Dead Souls*, though the revision of later times was to cut some of the traces. Joseph Frank has spoken of an 'artistic endeavour', on the part of the young Dostoevsky, 'to penetrate into the psychology of Gogol's characters and depict them from within',[12] and has seen the one writer as preceding the other along the road of a naturalizing of romance. It is not arduous for the reader of Dostoevsky to think of one writer burgling another in the manner of a double. But then we can hardly help thinking of Chichikov as impenetrable, as the sum of his adventures. He has no more in the way of character than the artist has in the diffusionist or abolitionist version of that role which was written into the art of Modernism, and has rather less than a reader might look for in the doings of a crook who seeks to rise in the world by buying up the title deeds to dead serfs and putting them to work as security for bank loans. Chichikov is a poem. He is a response to multifarious Russia, and the instrument of a picaresque romance which includes a satire on provincial life. Golyadkin, too, is hospitable and instrumental in that sense: but he is more like a character in a novel, for all that the novel in question was to call itself a poem. He is indeed more like the kind of character whose psychology we think we may be able to understand.[13]

Dostoevsky calls his hero mad, and Golyadkin is haled off at the end by his German doctor; delirium has reduced him to the condition of a wet kitten. The story is that of an acute distress: yet we are often brought to regard him as strange and forlorn in the manner of a common humanity which calls people mad but which may itself go mad. He is at odds with his bureaucratic superiors in St. Petersburg, with the excellencies he must please, with the office Pléiade. State Councillor Olsufi Ivanovich Berendeyev, whom he treats as his patron and to whose daughter he aspires, has grown tired of him, if he was ever anything else. Chapter Four has him crashing a party at his patron's house: he takes up a position amidst the garbage, then joins the glad scene, feeling an 'utter insect', blushing, hoping to 'sidle stealthily'. The party expels him: he is fastened into his overcoat, his hat is pulled down over his eyes, he is in the courtyard. 'He tore himself away from the place where he had been standing as if rooted to the spot, and dashed headlong away, anywhere, into the fresh air and the open spaces, straight in front of him . . . .'.[14]

The next chapter describes a flight through the dark and drizzle of the Fontanka Embankment by the river.[15] One galosh drops off. He stumbles, 'and this caused the orphaning of his other shoe, when its galosh too abandoned it.' A wretched dog attaches itself. He has become aware of another human being on the Embankment, who interests him strangely. They go home together. The fatal hour of self-severance has struck. Dostoevsky's account of what happens next alludes to the titles of two of Gogol's tall tales.

The stranger appeared momentarily at the entrance of the staircase which led to Mr Golyadkin's flat. Mr Golyadkin hurried after him. The staircase was dark, damp, and dirty. Every landing was heaped with all sorts of tenants' rubbish, so that a stranger unused to the place, coming to this staircase in the dark, was obliged to spend half an hour climbing up it, at the risk of breaking a leg, while he cursed both the stairs and the friends who were so inconveniently housed. But Mr Golyadkin's fellow-traveller seemed to be at home there; he ran lightly up, without difficulty and with complete knowledge of the place. Mr Golyadkin almost managed to catch up with him; two or three times the tail of the stranger's overcoat even struck him on the nose. His heart sank. The mysterious personage stopped just outside Mr Golyadkin's own flat and knocked, and (what would at any other time have astonished Mr Golyadkin), Petrushka opened the door immediately, as though he had not gone to bed but had been waiting, and followed the newcomer in with a candle in his hand. Beside himself, the hero of our story flew into his flat; without waiting to take off his coat and hat he ran along the short passage and stopped thunderstruck at the door of his room. All Mr Golyadkin's forebodings had come true. Everything he had feared and foreseen had now become cold reality. It took his breath away and made his head whirl. The unknown, also still in hat and overcoat, was sitting before him, on his own bed, with a slight smile on his lips; narrowing his eyes a little, he gave him a friendly nod. Mr Golyadkin wanted to cry out but could not, to make some sort of protest but his strength failed him. His hair stood on end and he collapsed into a chair, insensible with horror. Mr Golyadkin had recognised his nocturnal acquaintance. Mr Golyadkin's nocturnal acquaintance was none other than himself, Mr Golyadkin himself, another Mr Golyadkin, but exactly the same as himself—in short, in every respect what is called his double.

Golyadkin is to connect his acquisition of a counterfeit, someone who is the same as himself but different, with humiliations visited on him by his enemies, before whom he has been grovelling. The morning after the arrival of his double he decides that this is the latest of his humiliations. 'Mr Golyadkin had known for a very long time that something was being prepared, that there was *somebody else* in reserve.' Office politics may be intent on replacing him: but we are soon to sense that he has been intent on replacing himself with a more resourcefully obsequious Golyadkin, and that the defence he has thus reserved for himself may prove his undoing. He is the son who wants to rebel and to keep his place: 'I accept the benevolent authorities as a father to me.' His real parents are absent from the book.

In an undergraduate thesis,[16] Sylvia Plath was to state her belief in 'the fundamental duality of man' and to point out that 'Golyadkin's reaction to his Double is paradoxical.' The reason for the 'relief' he is able to feel is that 'now Golyadkin's hitherto repressed and starved desires may be satisfied, even indirectly sanctioned. By creating a Double, the schizophrenic no longer needs to castigate himself or to feel guilty for harbouring these corrupt urges . . .'. At the same time, the double is taken to be a threat. Sylvia Plath deals with this paradox by citing Freud, who cites Otto Rank, whose essay of 1914 on this subject, that of an associate of Freud's who was later to quarrel with him, was expanded into a book, *The Double*. Freud is quoted as saying that the double

> was originally an insurance against destruction of the ego, an 'energetic denial of the power of death', as Rank says: and probably the 'immortal' soul was the first 'double' of the body . . . Such ideas, however, have sprung from the soil of unbounded self-love, from the primary narcissism which holds sway in the mind of the child as that of primitive man; and when this stage has been left behind the double takes on a different aspect. From having been an assurance of immortality, he becomes the ghastly harbinger of death.

Rank's book unites allusions to sundry Gothic texts with assertions concerning a prehistoric psychology, and employs the Freudian category of primary narcissism in order to claim that a condition of primitive man is resumed by the modern neurotic, who may then be rendered incapable of sexual fulfilment. The modern double spells a fear of death, and is a form of defence against that fear, while also being, or becoming, itself deathly. According to Freud, the course of human history and the individual's hazardous progress to maturity in the modern world are alike in exhibiting a transformation of the double from immortal self to bad omen. It is doubtful, however, whether these postulates have much bearing on Dostoevsky's novel, which has nothing memorable to say on the subject of immortality. Plath's paradox of Golyadkin's reaction to his double can't usefully be distinguished from the central paradox of there being two Golyadkins, which can be taken to mean that defence and relief may be indistinguishable from terror and destruction. This strange case of an official in distress has less to say about the fear of death than it has to say about a fear of the life that is shared with others, and about a fear of authority on the part of someone who seeks to embrace it. It can be said to show the organism's response to incompatible demands—and it can be said to show what happens when a young writer falls in, and out, with an élite. As in Andersen's 'The Shadow', one self generates another, which does what the first cannot do, which belongs and succeeds, and is able to mate. Both works were written at around the same time. Each justifies the outsider, and portrays essentially the same extremity and calamity. But Dostoevsky's novel is far less of a fairy-tale. His hero is declared insane, and a naturalistic approach is summoned to evoke the world inhabited and hallucinated by this madman.

The Brothers Karamazov is a romance in which we contemplate the thought that every man wants to murder his father.[17] The brothers have a murderable father who causes them to be like orphans. At one point Ivan speaks of a Swiss orphan prosecuted for murder who 'wrote to the court himself that he was a monster'. Soon Ivan says: 'I am a bug.' And at another point he says: 'I am a romantic.' He is visited by a lorgnetted Devil, shabby-genteel in the Gothic-diabolic fashion: but perhaps his true tempter is his bastard stepbrother and alter ego, Smerdyakov, who has made possible their father's death. Father and sons and doubles are like the slew of reciprocal identity which occurs in Hogg. The romance is sealed by Mitya's futile flight to the inn in the next town, where an interlude of truth and drink defers for a while the confessional outcome in court. Diffusion matters more to the novel than division does, the Karamazovshchina more than any single member of that family. Here is a book in which a multiple imaginary orphan, suspended between faith and reason in the manner of the modern world, achieves, and atones for, the parricide of his desire.

Dostoevsky and duality are virtually synonymous: he may be considered a living witness, and his engagement with the subject was lifelong. The engagement took stock of a struggle between fathers and sons, faith and reason, patriotism and socialism, country and cosmopolis, with the novelist fighting on both sides: meanwhile his ordeals and adventures were to make him a polemical Christian and Russian. E.H.Carr's study of his work, published in 1931, is that of a historian for whom modern readers had long since tired of 'fantastic fiction' and who thought that Dostoevsky grew out of it in the course of his career; this gives a welcome coolness to Carr's summaries of Dostoevskian duality, which is seen both as French and as obtained from Hoffmann and from Hegel. 'The Hegelian postulate of thesis and antithesis, to be resolved ultimately in a higher synthesis, was applied to psychology; and in the view of

Dostoevsky and others, the presence of the "lower" as well as the "higher" element was necessary in order to produce the synthesis by which alone humanity could achieve true unity and partake of the divine perfection.' Carr tells how Dostoevsky was thereby able to formulate the claims of an unconscious, and to write of a coincidence of love and hate, sin and salvation, pride and humiliation, and he traces the progress of this writer's commitment to the subject. Having started as a disease, duality became a duty—a duty, moreover, which his countrymen were fitted to perform. Duality turned into self-accountability, and the Russian soul was 'broad' enough to be a blend of good and evil. A native span and dichotomy might serve as a lesson to the West and to the world.[18]

Carr's anti-romantic account understates the richly traditional character of Dostoevsky's commitment, while also misconceiving the extent to which he meant, and suffered, what he found to say on the subject. What he said was not 'born of personal experience', according to Carr, who then goes on to quote from an early letter: 'it seems as if I were *split in two*.' As the equivocal dynamics of the Karamazovshchina attests, Dostoevsky experienced a struggle between faith and reason, and their surrogates, which did not cease with the conversion to a racist Christianity which has been dated from his Siberian exile. A crucial aspect of this struggle is the delirium of the antinomian individualist, of the superman who steals from his society and breaks its bounds, and who is finally restored to it and to the worship of its God. Here once more duality ensures and records the justification of a sinner. Once more, megalomania is proportioned to the dynamics of the divided self.

Karamazov was produced by a strategic conception—that of a sinful prince who capitulates to the Russian God—which had already produced, in 1871, *The Possessed* (alternatively, *The Devils*), where the part of the prince is played by Stavrogin in a style—that of some mysterious and outrageous man of feeling—which derives in part from Byron. His 'Confession', prudently omitted when the novel first appeared, gives content to his secrets and makes clear what, in the modern mode, is 'dichotomous' about him. Stavrogin has his counterparts, his other halves, among the radical chic of a provincial town—men who stand in awe of him and who reflect and complement him. We are aware, as in the later work, of a multiple consciousness, of an author stereophonically audible throughout his book.

Stavrogin is an orphan prince, and as such doubly aloof from the society from which he 'steals' by transgressing its codes and to which he comes to submit. What makes him a dualistic specimen, a strange case, is the conflict he feels between emancipation and submission, together with a context where emancipation is to submission what sin is to salvation, and where the antinomian hero is in some sense privileged to offend. His subversive friends are possessed by the demon of scepticism, rationalism, mockery, and so is he: such is 'the devil who took possession of that man'. Dichotomy is shown to require a kind of exorcism. But with Stavrogin's suicide we may be meant to suppose that the exorcism has failed. If we are, it would be as if his sins had failed to save him.

His 'Confession' is delivered to the monk Tikhon, an ailing orphan-like exorcist who suggests that Stavrogin become a novice. The orphan prince assures Tikhon that there is no resemblance between himself and his mother—'none whatever!' He says he has been thrilled by a sense of his own baseness and has committed crimes in order to savour it. The 'rule of my life', discerned after the worst of his crimes, has to do with the feeling of release occasioned by a refusal to acknowledge the categories of good and evil. At that worst point in his life, 'while we were all drinking tea', he realized 'that I neither know nor feel good or evil and that I have not only lost any sense of it, but that there is neither good nor evil (which pleased me), and that it is just a prejudice: that I can be free from any prejudice, but that once I attain that degree of freedom I am done for.' This part of his life has been spent in raptures: 'If I were to steal something, I should at the time of committing the theft have felt like dancing with pleasure at the thought of the depth of my villainy.' His delightful and terrible thefts, he now informs Tikhon, have to be understood as a way of seeking forgiveness.[19]

The 'Confession' also reveals a history of encounters with a sneering, sceptical double. The 'mysterious horror' of 'inward division' and the double had been endured—at an earlier period of his life, two years before he was sent to Siberia as a convicted subversive—by the author of the novel, who had at that time, moreover, 'a Mephistopheles of my own', in the person of a subversive friend. If we think that the plainly autobiographical narrator of the novel he wrote at a later time, *The Insulted and Injured*, is recollecting the nervous, giddy Dostoevsky of the 1840s, of the pre-Siberian literary and political tensions and plots, the young man who had begun to write and had suffered the mysterious murder of his father, we learn that Dostoevsky was visited then by a deathly presence which took shape 'as though in mockery of all the conclusions of reason'.[20] Stavrogin's is a double—later still—whose mockery and rationality may appear to be aimed at the conclusions of faith: a derision that would not have been out of place among the Petrashevsky conspirators joined by Dostoevsky in the 1840s. We can't assume that faith replaced reason as the target of successive apparitions in the course of Dostoevsky's life: but we can be sure that faith and reason continued to divide the writer who had received such visits, and that the creation of Stavrogin was a declaration of faith which was also an attempt to resolve a dilemma. Stavrogin explains to Tikhon

that he was subject, especially at nights, to some kind of hallucinations, that he sometimes saw or felt beside him the presence of some kind of malignant creature, mocking and 'rational', 'in all sorts of guises and in different characters, but it is the same, and it always makes me angry.'

These revelations were wild and confused, and really seemed to come from a madman. But at the same time Stavrogin spoke with such strange frankness, never seen in him before, with such simpleheartedness, which was so out of character as far as he was concerned, that one could not help feeling that his former self had suddenly and quite unaccountably completely disappeared.[21]

The apparition will only go away when Stavrogin manages to forgive himself: 'That is why I seek boundless suffering.'[22] His 'Confession' has pages which do indeed read like the romantic diary of a madman: but the Stavrogin of the novel as a whole, the Stavrogin who stands confessed there, is seldom measurably madder than its author. The two apparitions may differ in respect of what they can be taken to convey concerning the positivistic hopes of Dostoevsky's youth. But they are the same in being successively none other than Dostoevsky's, and in conveying the organism's effort to be at once scientific and religious. The epilepsies of such an organism are more than likely to be indistinguishable from epiphanies.

The strange case of Stavrogin is that of the outcast who turns into a monster. His rebelliousness sustains a team of revolutionaries who are willing to kill and maim for a new order, and whose organizer Peter Verkhovensky refers to Stavrogin as his 'better half'; Dostoevsky talked of the 'real monsters' among the Nechayevite political extremists who were his models here—an inferior species, he felt, to the Petrashevsky socialists of his own youthful adherence. Stavrogin's emancipation from the old order of morality, God-given, consists of acts which invite the constructions of political terror, blasphemy and sadism. They are acts of a kind to jeopardize—but also to ensure—the salvation of his soul. And they are acts which suggest that Hogg's *Confessions* is a predecessor of Stavrogin's 'Confession'. An antinomian 'boundlessness', of freedom and suffering, bombinates in both books, where the ordeal and delirium of a justified sinner bears a meaning which is at once religious and familial, sexual and political. Dostoevsky once observed that his fiction had shown as unsound those who supposed themselves sound: people with 'boundless confidence in their normalcy, and, *eo ipso*, they are infected with awful self-conceit, impossible narcissism, which sometimes reaches the level of the conviction of one's infallibility.'[23] Both Wringhim and Stavrogin are evoked by this description of the megalomania of everyday life. And the description does something to evoke their authors too. By these divided authors, Wringhim and Stavrogin are simultaneously justified and condemned.

Stavrogin's worst crime is committed in an unforgettable Petersburg slum—with its light-blue rooms, and the red spider on the geraniums. Here the aristocrat violates the innocence of an urchin girl, Matryosha. Proceeding to the seduction, Dostoevsky lets fall an old word for erotic and other transgression, which is thereby assimilated to the behaviour of a thief. Macbeth, about to kill Duncan, calls up an image of the murderer who

with his stealthy pace,
With Tarquin's ravishing strides, toward his design
Moves like a ghost.

Transgression is here awarded contradictory motions—stealing and striding: but the stealing may seem to win. Stavrogin's ravishing strides are those of a thief, and he himself is ravished by them.

> My heart began to pound. I got up and began stealing towards her. On their window-sill were many pots of geranium and the sun was shining very brightly. I sat down quietly on the floor beside her. She gave a start and at first looked terribly frightened and jumped up. I took her hand and kissed it quietly, forced her down on the bench again and began looking into her eyes. The fact that I kissed her hand suddenly amused her like a child, but only for one second, for she jumped up precipitately the next moment, this time looking so frightened that a spasm passed across her face. Her eyes were motionless with terror and her lips began to quiver as though she were on the verge of tears, but she did not scream all the same. I kissed her hand again and put her on my knee. Then she suddenly drew back and smiled as if ashamed, but with a kind of wry smile. Her face flushed with shame. I was whispering to her all the time, as though drunk. At last a most strange thing happened, something I shall never forget, something that quite amazed me: the little girl flung her arms round my neck and all of a sudden began to kiss me frenziedly. Her face expressed complete rapture. I nearly got up and went away, so shocked was I to find this sort of thing in a little creature for whom I suddenly felt pity.
>
> When all was over, she looked embarrassed. I did not try to reassure her and no longer caressed her.[24]

We do not need to believe the rumour which was heard at the time to persuade ourselves that all question of a difference between character and author has at this point lapsed, and that whether or not the passage approximates to some act of recollection, the author is speaking the truth. It is a truth which consorts, but only imperfectly, with Stavrogin's other appearances elsewhere in the novel. After her encounter with the orphan prince, Matryosha becomes convinced that she has killed God, and prepares to hang herself. Stavrogin awaits her death in a state of abstraction, studying a little red spider on the geraniums. Then, in a state of excitement, his heart pounding as before, he steals towards the scene, standing on the tips of his burglar's toes to peer through a chink at the corpse. As he peers, he recalls his state of abstraction, the red spider, his having thought how he would stand on tiptoe and peer. Throughout, he is excited, abstracted, divided, autoscopic. His 'Confession' claims that with this ability to see himself, and to anticipate what he was about to do, he was furnishing proof that he was sane, responsible for his actions. His actions indicate that boundlessness is elation and repose. It is the ecstasy which takes you out of yourself, which soars. At the same time, boundlessness creeps.

So the orphan prince, the justified sinner, can also be termed an elevated creep. If there is truth to life in the 'Confession', the Stavrogin at large in the novel is not lifelike. As a likeness, he cannot compare with the elder Verkhovensky, the liberal sponger, the singleton, whom Dostoevsky said that he loved. Dostoevsky does not love Stavrogin; he was not a man to dote upon his reflection in the pool. Nevertheless, Stavrogin's salvation, and the interesting outrages which promise to induce it, matter more to the author than do the fates of those characters whom this character condescends to, disdains, assists and attacks.

Stavrogin has in him the books of other authors, and the sources which helped to form him are an education in the literature of duality. These include not only Byron, and the Gothic practice which influenced Hogg, but Shakespeare and Dickens. He is the prince in *Henry IV*, and he is Hamlet, and there is a hinted resemblance to Dick Swiveller, the sentimental dandy in *The Old Curiosity Shop* who is 'magnanimous' enough to marry the waif known as the Marchioness. Megalomania breaks the rules of its society, while magnanimity respects them, and gives life to them. Stavrogin felt that 'magnanimous' was not a word that could be used of himself (even the word 'negative' would be too strong)[25]: and yet there seems to be some wish to present his 'Confession' as a great act of magnanimity. In marrying a demented and crippled girl, Stavrogin is like Dick, in Dickens's fable, when he marries the Marchioness, and Dostoevsky's interest in Dickens led him to repeat, in a dimension of candour, Dickens's interest in the fate of little girls. Matryosha's fate was worse than death—worse, therefore, than that of Dickens's Little Nell, who was exposed to the same dangers, and escaped them by dying young.

In *The Insulted and Injured* Dostoevsky dreamt up a double for *The Old Curiosity Shop*. The same but different, it contains the book of another author, and it contains an account of his own early days in literature. It tells how an orphan adopts another orphan. The narrator Vanya is a writer who is ill and 'going to die', who suffers the 'deceptive' sensations of such a man, and who is subject, as we have seen, to the visits of a double.[26] What Vanya records is the delirium of his love for a woman who awaits desertion by her protector, and who, herself one of the insulted, has insulted her father by taking up with the protector; and it is also the delirium of his own protection of little Nellie Valkonsky, who has in turn adopted her grandfather, an English curmudgeon who deems himself insulted. Out of all this there emerge the lineaments of a parable of forgiveness, as in the novel by Dickens. As in the Dickens, much is made of 'a strange story of the mysterious, hardly comprehensible relations of the crazy old man with the little grandchild who already understood him'. Like Vanya, Nellie is ill and like to die, and by the standards of nineteenth-century Romanticism, she may count as the complete orphan. Here she is as she comes stealing into Vanya's feverish life:

> At last softly and slowly she advanced two steps into the room and stood before me, still without uttering a word. I examined her more closely. She was a girl of twelve or thirteen, short, thin, and as pale as though she had just had some terrible illness, and this pallor showed up vividly her great, shining black eyes. With her left hand she held a tattered old shawl, and with it covered her chest, which was still shivering with the chill of evening. Her whole dress might be described as rags and tatters. Her thick black hair was matted and uncombed.

The following day, by daylight, she is more interesting than ever:

> And, indeed, it would have been difficult to have found a stranger or more original creature—in appearance, anyway. With her flashing black eyes, which looked somehow foreign, her thick, dishevelled, black hair, and her mute, fixed, enigmatic gaze, the little creature might well have attracted the notice of anyone who passed her in the street. The expression in her eyes was particularly striking. There was the light of intelligence in them, and at the same time an inquisitorial mistrust, even suspicion. Her dirty old frock looked even more hopelessly tattered by daylight. She seemed to me to be suffering from some wasting, chronic disease that was gradually and relentlessly destroying her. Her pale, thin face had an unnatural sallow, bilious

tinge. But in spite of all the ugliness of poverty and illness, she was positively pretty.

Nellie is vulnerable, susceptible. She is both friendly and hostile. Virginal, yet also sexual. She has the interest that attaches to an uncertain nationality, and she has the mute injurious look of a certain kind of film star.[27]

The novel is one in which orphan and double meet, and in which the idea of the orphan is joined to that of theft and to that of death. Meekness rules, but magnanimity must wrestle with the megalomania of the girl's secret father, a sinful and self-consciously rational prince. To the 'egoism of suffering' Nellie adds the eroticism of the innocent victim. She is constantly shown to blush and to steal, and may do the two things at once: 'the colour rushed to her face, her eyes grew moist. She stole a look at me . . .'. Such looks are sometimes tender: 'It is true I caught two or three glances stolen at me on the sly, and there was such tenderness in those glances.'[28] Nellie steals and is stolen. When Vanya discovers her in a brothel, the reader discovers there the geraniums of the seduction scene in *The Possessed*. Dostoevsky's preoccupation with the violation of innocence is in some measure Dickensian, but it means more to his fictions, and it is more systematic. Megalomania caresses the young; magnanimity cares for them. This, too, is Dostoevskian duality.

Both by himself and by others, Dostoevsky was in his own time thought to be deranged and delirious. And in due course the wholesome Chekhov had to respond to the suggestion that he was as mad as one of the strange cases diagnosed for literature, by this medical man, in one of his taller stories. Chekhov was interested in duality, and in the illness which attends it; in doubles and in the double life; and his writings bring together the duality of division and the duality of diffusion. The range of themes attempted in the nineteenth-century literature of the subject is reproduced in successive stories, and his books are no different from others of the time in appearing both to favour a withdrawal from common life and to stress the dangers of such a withdrawal, and of a manic self-importance.

'The Black Monk' is a traditional tale of the double which was written in 1893. Chekhov described it as 'a medical story, the case history of a disease. The subject is megalomania.' He denied that he had the disease himself. 'I believe myself to be sane. True, I'm not specially keen on living. Still, that doesn't yet rate as an illness in the true sense, but rather as a transitory and natural everyday condition.'[29] The story is about a fearful, ailing, possibly tubercular academic, with a sense of mediocrity and a tendency towards megalomania, whose life and marriage are undone when he starts having hallucinations. A black monk whizzes over the fields to gull him into delusions of grandeur. The monk tells him what Hogg's sinner had been told by his tempter double: 'You are one of those few justly called the Elect of God.' The monk also portrays the man as a version of Andersen's poor scholar, with talk of a dedication to 'the Rational and the Beautiful'.[30] We are firmly informed that this apparition is the symptom of a mental disorder. This is no epiphany. The man is mad.

'The Black Monk' can be compared with an earlier story in which a medical opinion of a kind is solicited from the reader. 'The Party' is collected in volume iv of the *Oxford Chekhov*: the stories in this volume were published over the interval of two years during which, having been pressed to be less copious and commercial, he first set himself to write for the 'Thick Journals' read by the intelligentsia. In 1888, at the age of 28, he began a long story destined for a Thick Journal—a thought which 'jogs my elbow as the devil jogged the monk's'. He wrote it nervously, 'slowly, as gourmets eat snipe', worried that 'my first pancake' might prove a 'dumpling'. The long story is called 'The Steppe', a work dualistically diffuse—indeed, as he recognized, encyclopedic—a work in which illness—a feature of all of the three stories in question—enables this diffusion to take place.[31]

'The Party' concerns a pregnant country gentlewoman, Olga, an heiress and graduate who, during a hard day's entertainment of the local worthies, grows sensitive about her dowry and feels a mounting dislike for her handsome husband: for his reactionary views, which dissemble a crisis of confidence, for his philanderings, his magistrate's airs, the awful back of his neck.

She decided to find her husband at once and have it out with him. It was downright disgusting, the way he attracted strange women, seeking their admiration as if it were the elixir of life. It was unfair and dishonourable of him to bestow on others what rightly belonged to her, his wife, and to hide his heart and conscience from her only to reveal them to the first pretty face. What harm had she done him? What had she done wrong?[32]

As the day wears on and the hospitality wears thin, a feverish darkness falls. Anxiety and hostility deepen, before we know it, into the drama of a miscarriage. The story ends with Olga's stillborn child, and with the reader's awareness of her love for her husband. There is a tension between the sense that her grievances may owe something to her physical condition and the sense that she could well, though ill, have her husband's number. Not many would finish the story thinking that its author was against higher education for women on the grounds that it turns them into viragos. At the same time, it expresses no views one way or the other on the vexed questions of this kind to which it refers. In the manner that we call Chekhovian, it floats. And it may appear that this buoyancy depends on its incorporation of a mind-changing illness. Illness admits a new mood, new truths, a new self: while also subjecting them to a principle of relativity.

With Chekhov, we are in the era when the word 'nerves' can mean something, can mean everything. Illness—with its viragos, vertigos, hallucinations and hysterias, its grievances, insights and intense perceptions—is both a theme and a pre-condition, not only of this story, but of half of the eight in the volume. 'A Nervous Breakdown' and 'An Awkward Affair' have the kind of interest in illness which assigns them to the 'clinical' vein familiarly distinguished in his work—what you might expect a doctor like Chekhov to supply, as it were. But his interest in the perceptions of the ill is more than medical. In these eight stories we discover that the perceptions they convey are those of the drowsy, the young, the distressed, that feeling and suffering, strength of feeling and bodily weakness, are potently related. In other words, we discover that Chekhov is a romantic writer.

No one could mistake 'The Steppe' for an example of his clinical vein. It is an example of his romantic vein. Its 'illness' is that of weakness, inexperience, innocence, which presently, to be sure, literally fall ill. A nine-year-old boy, Yegorushka, has lost his father, and is further orphaned by being packed off to school. On his way there, accompanied by his uncle and a priest, Yegorushka travels the prairies of Southern Russia, as Chekhov had lately done and as he had done before in his youth. The boy transfers for a while to a caravan of carters and perches on the loads. The birds and plants of the steppe are noted. A windmill looms. A thunderstorm inspires a purple passage. The steppe is a wild world where people are keenly conscious of one another, as the sailors of different ships used to be, though kept apart by long voyages and absences. The cowboy capitalist Varlamov is a ship that passes in the night. He knocks about this oceanic landscape: for ever over the horizon, inquired-of, reported—but at last the boy catches a glimpse of him at his masterful ploys. Yegorushka goes in for glimpses, for strange sights. He then catches a fever, sees the strange sights of its delirium, but gets to his destination in the city, where Chekhov forecast, for a projected sequel, that he would go to the bad. The story is not plotless, as its Oxford editor supposes, while serving as an occasion for odes, set-pieces, star turns, sub-stories. The gourmet remarked that the story 'describes the steppe—a romantic subject'. And it has a plot to match. This 'steppe story' follows in the footsteps of the romantic diffusionist Gogol in *Dead Souls*. 'I realise', said Chekhov, 'that Gogol will turn in his grave, being Russian literature's King of the Steppe. I've well-meaningly trespassed on his preserves, but I haven't half botched things.'[33] It is usual for Chekhov to take a poor view of his work, as of other matters too. And it is not unusual for critics of his work to take him at his word.

Yegorushka's journey reaches a high point at the country inn run by two Jewish brothers: Moses, a pantomime of servility, and proud, derisive Solomon, whose judgements on the society of the steppe are enough to darken the reader's impressions of the journey, whatever they may do—we are not told—for the boy's. This is what his innocent eye perceives:

In came Moses. He looked anxiously at Solomon and his guests, and again the loose skin on his face twitched nervously. Yegorushka shook his head and looked around him, catching a glimpse of Solomon's face just when it was turned three-quarters towards him and when the shadow of his long nose bisected his whole left cheek. The scornful smile half in shadow, the glittering, sneering eyes, the arrogant expression and the whole plucked hen's figure—doubling and dancing before Yegorushka's eyes, they made Solomon look less like a clown than some nightmare fantasy or evil spirit.

'What a devil of a fellow he is, Moses, God help him.' Father Christopher smiled. 'You'd better get him a job, find him a wife or something. He's not human.'

There are two of Solomon in the boy's bewildered vision, and Moses and Solomon, perhaps, are two faces of the Russian Jew, bisected here by a Russian writer for whom Jews were disturbingly exotic, and partly portrayable in medieval, demonic colours, as if not human, but for whom they were also human, and possessed of a vision of their own which deserved to be recorded, whose peritonitis had been treated with mustard plasters by just such a semi-repugnant 'Hebrew gentleman' as Moses. Moses apologises to his guests for his brother's offensiveness, saying that Varlamov had whipped them both for it in the past, and recalling how Solomon burned his share of the money left them by their father. He orders his brother out of the room, and adds some words in Yiddish. These strange words speak louder than his apologetic actions. Suddenly, as the guests are about to go:

Holding his broad-brimmed top hat, Father Christopher was bowing to someone and smiling—not softly and tenderly as was his wont, but in a respectful, strained fashion that ill suited him. Meanwhile Moses was doing a sort of balancing act as if his body had been broken in three parts and he was trying his best not to disintegrate. Only Solomon seemed unaffected, and stood in a corner, his arms folded, his grin as disdainful as ever.

'Your Ladyship must forgive the untidiness,' groaned Moses with an excruciatingly sweet smile.

A newcomer has entered the room, entered the boy's fantasy, in the lustrous image of a poplar he once saw, and in the image of the mother he must be missing. 'Was Varlamov here today?' a woman's voice asks—that of a fine, but kind lady.[34]

What scenes these are. Splendour and misery. Servitude and its transfiguration. We might say that Yegorushka is engaged on an entry into captivity which is also an escape. What constitutes this escape is his rapt experience of the steppe, and of the ladyship it bestows on him, and this escape in turn constitutes the plot that underlies, and is belied by, the desultoriness of Chekhov's '*Steppe Encyclopedia*'.

The consciousness of Gogol forms part of a ranging consciousness of the international Romanticism of the previous age. Yegorushka is a romantic imbecile or ingénu whose plight and plot are not remote from those of Scott's thistledown Edward Waverley, floating about the wild Scotland of the second Jacobite rebellion, and proving on his feverish, feminine pulses—with swoons, delirium, and all the rich rewards of physical impairment—the experience of a barbaric host and a divided nation. Yegorushka is likewise present in Chekhov's story for the sake of the susceptibility which literature had learnt to associate with suffering and limitation, with women and children and the unwell. He has little or no personality—barely enough for the reader to keep in mind that the boy is in a predicament. He is the people he meets, the sights he sees. We can trace here the extensive consequences of that belief in romantic duality which is lightly signalled in the boy's double vision of Solomon as at once clown and demon—of the belief that, for a variety of literary purposes, personality may be divided or diffused or dispersed. The competence of the boy's perceptions is ascribed to a powerless and characterless state—all Danaë to the steppe. He is more characterless than the story is plotless. The story *has* a plot, and it is one that is appropriate to a fecund absence of character, to a state of dispersal. Both in Scott's novel and in Chekhov's story a young man is put to bed with a case of negative capability.

One of the first professors of negative capability crosses the reader's mind when Yegorushka quits the inn, bemused by the sight of his motherly countess. There aren't any nightingales on the steppe at this time of year, but the bird is mentioned, and the boy's 'drowsy brain'—which 'utterly rejected mundane thoughts and became fuddled, retaining only such magical and fantastic images as have the advantage of somehow springing into the mind automatically without taxing the thinker'—is like that of Keats at the start of the 'Nightingale' Ode, Keats who could utterly reject all 'irritable reaching after fact and reason'. A flight from the world is mentioned too, as in Keats's poem, and the passage turns into an ode. 'On July evenings and nights . . . nightingales do not sing in wooded gullies . . . But the steppe is still picturesque and full of life.' The scent of hay, dry grass and late flowers is 'dense, sickly-sweet, voluptuous'. When the sun goes down, the prairie sighs, and its choir of sounds blends into a single boom. The 'boundlessness' of the sky is 'languorous and magnetic, but its embraces make you dizzy.' Chekhov's ode then declares: 'You long to fly above the steppe with the night bird.'

By now, for the time being, Yegorushka has been forgotten. Chekhov imagines that he hears from the steppe an anguished cry 'for a bard, a poet of her own'. He seems to have forgotten that she already has one in Gogol, 'King of the Steppe', but the passage itself has now furnished another, who knows not only about *Dead Souls* but about the philomelic mode in nineteenth-century verse.[35]

There is a story in volume iv which serves as an introduction to another aspect of this writer's transactions with duality—his treatment of the double life. It is a story which was not esteemed by Chekhov, and which is not esteemed by the Oxford editor, Ronald Hingley, whose lives of Chekhov often address the question of his didacticism, and of his tendency to disclaim it, and even to suggest that life has no meaning, and who refers to the story's 'moralistic thrust', to 'untypically "wet" characterization, the excess of hedgerow philosophy, and the lugubrious angle of vision from which some of the narrative suffers'.[36] The story is called 'Lights'. It deals with the seduction, by the engineer Ananyev, of a young woman, a former school friend of his now trapped in an unhappy marriage. Ananyev tells the narrator about her on a construction site, while imparting sententious reflections on how young heads may be turned by unearned ideas concerning the futility and uncertainty of life. After learning how Ananyev spent the night with Kitty in a hotel, deserted her, but then went back to the town to say he was sorry, the narrator rides off in gloom. The horizon seems to speak to him: 'No, indeed, nothing in this world makes sense.' Then the sun begins to rise, and with it, perhaps, the narrator's spirits. If there is anything wrong with 'Lights', it is not that Ananyev's philosophizings convict the author of a didactic crudity. And there is much that is right with it—chiefly, the delicacy with which Kitty is evoked. The philosophizings must in some degree be meant as a characterization of Ananyev, a fairly simple soul: as such, they can be accounted a feature of Russian literature. But there do appear to be faults in the design which ties them to the internal story of the seduction. They are indeed excessive, indelicate, and even, at times, irrelevant. At the same time, the internal story does have something to say about the futility of human life and about whether or not it makes sense.

In attempting to determine what that elusive something may be, and what sense may be made of the seduction and its aftermath, it is of some help to move on ten years, to a story of Chekhov's written in the last months of the nineteenth century. In 'The Lady with the Little Dog', a seduction occurs, but no desertion: the seducer enters into a liaison with the woman he has seduced, in which the futility of his life, well attested in the story, may be overcome. In withdrawing from the ordinary life of banks and clubs and marriage, Gurov effects an escape into secrecy.

This is a story about a married man and his mistress, who are 'very dear and near' to one another and who are also 'like thieves'.[37] The man comes to think that secrecy is truth, that secrecy is sense, and that civilization depends upon it. Far-fetched though it may sound in summary, this is an opinion which has been shared by many Europeans, for whom the most compelling of the solitudes of nineteenth-century Romanticism must often have been the solitude made for two. A cost to others is implied: but society, the community, common life, are valued by the hero only so far as they are able to sustain the true self in the secrecy it needs:

> He led a double life: one for all who were interested to see, full of conventional truth and conventional deception, exactly like the lives of his friends and acquaintances; and another which went on in secret. And by a kind of strange concatenation of circumstances, possibly quite by accident, everything that was important, interesting, essential, everything about which he was sincere and did not deceive himself, everything that made up the quintessence of his life, went on in secret, while everything that was a lie, everything that was merely the husk in which he hid himself to conceal the truth, like his work at the bank, for instance, his discussions at the club, his ideas of the lower breed, his going to anniversary functions with his wife—all that happened in the sight of all. He judged others by himself, did not believe what he saw, and was always of the opinion that every man's real and most interesting life went on in secret, under cover of night. The personal, private life of an individual was kept a secret, and

perhaps that was partly the reason why civilised man was so anxious that his personal secrets should be respected.[38]

The Chekhov, therefore, who at other times spoke against romantic love could also be for it; the Chekhov who was in favour of purposeful and collaborative action, directed at the public good and performed in the light of day, was also willing to fade into a sheltering privacy. All this is further evidence of his commitment to the dualistic outlook and methods of nineteenth-century literature. The double life, as practised by Gurov, is one aspect of romantic duality. Another is the device of the double. Yet another is the demeanour of a Yegorushka, in which fresh-eyed youth, together with its swoons and fever, signifies a suspension of personality, and of ideas, in submission to the sensory magic of the steppe. Yegorushka passes over at intervals into the condition of an ode-making poet, ceasing to be any kind of limited little boy on his reluctant way to school. He is nervously alert to the steppe, and to its human occasions, while also luxuriating in them. He wishes for a mother. And he wishes to fly up on the wings of a bird and away from the senseless world.

There is romantic duality, too, in Chekhov's shyness of ideas and messages, in his ambiguity and undecidability, in the place occupied by his writings in the history of ideas, to which he did not abstain from contributing, and which had come to include the big idea that ideas are a violence and should be avoided. His own avoidance and escape were explained by him with reference to 'The Party':

I am not a liberal. I am not a conservative. I am not an advocate of moderate reform. I am not a monk. Nor am I committed to non-commitment. I should like to be a free artist, that's all. . . . My Holy of Holies is the human body, health, intelligence, talent, inspiration and the most absolute freedom—freedom from violence and falsehood, wherever these two ingredients may be found.[39]

His words describe a romantic art which had taken to preparing the freedoms of the Modern and of the art of the future, and which had digested the dualistic interchange of a hundred years and more.

In the sequence of tales discussed in this chapter the orphan is celibate, ruined, defeated, cherished. It is the double—in the likeness of some other, the same but different—who is guilty of crimes. But then the orphan may turn out to share that guilt, and the two of them may share the likeness of the thief, the stranger, the monster. The tales express pity and self-pity, and they express a fear of other people. This fear is attributed to the orphan, and it is aroused by the spectacle of his persecution and invasion: but it does not exclude a desire for other people, for the community offended by the thefts and strangeness in which he is implicated. In these as in many such tales duality is both xenophile and xenophobe.

Here and elsewhere, strangeness steals, imbecility sneaks, and duality is a nervous breakdown. It is weakness, illness, and it is the powers they confer. It is division, and diffusion. It is the behaviour of authors, and it is the literature of the modern world. It is a way of writing in which character has been succeeded by consciousness, by an internal contention and inconstancy. The tales also tell that the modern world had come to know a megalomaniac, alias an antinomian, duality. Orphans could become supermen. Great deeds were done, with the help of the double. And magnanimity was to tender its regrets.

VIII. THE ADVENTURES OF PEREGRINE POE

Poe's poems and stories belonged, he felt, to different orders of experience. The stories are his better part, and his own preference for the poems reflects the enthusiasm of the time for the ideal, the eternal, the ethereally pure. Not that stories had to be earthbound, or ephemeral. Among the best of Poe's are two in which a wish to get out of the world is expressed, however equivocally. In 'William Wilson', a bad man meets his double and attempts an escape, only to find that he has 'fled in vain', while in 'The Unparalleled Adventures of One Hans Pfaall' a fellow escapes from financial miseries by building a contraption in which—not in vain, though perhaps in fun—he flies to the Moon.[1]

Each tale is the resumption of a standard concern, which is exhibited, respectively, in the image of the double and in that of the journey of escape. Double and flight are fates, fates that befall the outcast, and they are states, states of mind and motion: they belong both to an inner and outer space—an outer space which reaches as far as Outer Space itself, and the stars. A name had been devised for the unstable, for the mobile, volatile, labile, for those who change and move as Poe changed and moved. It was also a name for the adventurous, and it was devised in Germany—the Allemagne of the Gothic imagination. Poe was sure that his literary terrors were 'not of Germany, but of the soul'[2]: but he paid attention to foreign inventions, including this one—the name Peregrine Proteus.

I would like to study these two tales, and to propose that the images they use, and the tendencies in romantic literature to which the images direct us, may be seen as the one thing. That one thing has served to obscure, for some, the range and vigour of his professional activities, and to depict him as a failure whose purity and worth were only apparent to later generations. I accept that there are other things in Poe, and that if he was an unfortunate, whose exits and dismissals were notorious, he was also a success—not only posthumously, and not least as an editor and reviewer.

Thomas Mann regarded 'William Wilson' as the classical tale of its romantic kind. With an air of confidence, merit, and method, Poe's narrator tells the story of a submission, his own, to madness and magic. The air of confidence is familiar enough in Gothic practice, and does nothing to prevent a copious use of the vocabulary of distraction, delirium, clandestinity, and misfortune. In his sonnet on Poe's tomb, Mallarmé was to present him as an angel who gave '*un sens plus pur aux mots de la tribu*'. Mallarmé is evoking the romantic purity which flies to the Moon, and would not have permitted the suggestion that Poe used the language of a tribe which specialized in terror. Poe got the idea for his two William Wilsons from the story of a Spanish split sketched in an article by Washington Irving: Irving's story seems to have been based on an abandoned project of Byron's, drawn from the literature of Spain and suggested by Shelley,[3] and it passed on to Poe the comparatively unfamiliar feature of a good double. Wilson's woes begin at an English boarding-school, which has the deserted children of a ruling class quartered in the rambling irregularities of a Gothic mansion: to the same setting and system, a mainstay of the British Empire, the orphan Poe had been committed by his stepfather John Allan, a tobacco merchant, during a five-year visit to England. Wilson's authority among the other boys is rebuked by the arrival of a whispering sarcastic embodiment of his own conscience.

His 'singular namesake' inspires 'dim visions of my earliest infancy—wild, confused and thronging memories of a time when memory herself was yet unborn. I cannot better describe the sensation which oppressed me, than by saying that I could with difficulty shake off the belief of my having been acquainted with the being who stood before me, at some epoch very long ago—some point of the past even infinitely remote.' One night he relives that first acquaintance: 'I arose from bed, and, lamp in hand, stole through a wilderness of narrow passages from my own bedroom to that of my rival.' This rival might appear to incorporate a resented father; and so might the subsequent behaviour of the tale's superego second self. Poe's real father was not unlike the wicked William Wilson—who quits the academy that same night and engages in an escape which is a series of escapades, and which takes him to Eton, Oxford, Italy. His namesake dogs the debauchee, stops him cheating, and intervenes in Rome to prevent his seduction of a fine lady with a husband old enough to be her own and her seducer's father. Having attacked the intruder, he looks in a mirror and it is the intruder's face that he sees: he has murdered himself. It is the bad self which has tried to escape, and which has eliminated the rival, the good angel. But it is as if the good angel has lived to tell the tale: 'Have I not indeed been living in a dream? And am I not now dying a victim to the horror and the mystery of the wildest of all sublunary visions?'[4]

The facts in the case of Mr Poe, as these have been made known by a tribe of biographers, can be glimpsed, behind art's incognitos, both in this story and in 'Hans Pfaall': largely, they are facts he wished to escape. After his return from England in 1820, he dropped out of the University of Virginia, and out of West Point, and fell out with his stepfather. Having suffered under Peter Pendulum—his name for the methodical business mentality—he rose again as a writer: star of the *Southern Literary Messenger*, author of *Tales of the Grotesque and Arabesque*, in which 'Hans Pfaall' and 'William Wilson' appeared together. His poems soon gained a following. But to those on the watch he was always a falling star, his successes rewarded with the sack, and always, like his actor parents, a wanderer. He died, at the age of forty, in 1849. Two years earlier, after ten years of marriage—a long time, which no account of his short stays should overlook—his young wife had died of tuberculosis in their cottage at Fordham.

As for the notion or doctrine of duality, of the 'bi-part soul', as he referred to it,[5] we might ask how that relates to the biographical facts. It has nothing to do with any double life, in the colloquial sense. What does it have to do with the divisions which have been noticed in his work between madness and method, between 'Visionary Poe' and 'Logical Poe', as Julian Symons puts it,[6] between the Southern gentleman of old-fashioned sense and principle and the insensate life he has to confess, between the raving necrophile and the hoaxer, cryptographer and pure detective? He held that method was the madness of the businessman: but he, too, in his artist's way, was both methodical and mad.

Poe can be called 'an eccentric solitaire of the period': these words,[7] which refer to the human isolation of a hundred years before, can be revived for Poe. Like other singular fellows, he could behave as if he were plural. The doctrine of the bi-part soul involves an idea of variance or contrariety: a rivalry between soul parts and their associated styles. Romantic variance can be identified in 'the rule of contraries' by which, according to the Egyptological tale 'Some Words with a Mummy',[8] the spirit of the age proceeded, and it can also be identified in the contention between a wish to leave and a wish to remain or return, with mummies playing some occult role in that contention. The part of Poe which wanted to soar off into the ether was expressed in metonymies which take *that* part for the whole: 'My life has been *whim*—impulse—passion—a longing for solitude—a scorn of all things present, in an earnest desire for the future.'[9] We are to think that whim, contrariness, 'perversity', set him teetering on verges, and meditating or imagining murder or suicide. But romance is variance, as well as velocity and vertigo, and the soaring self vies with a self that stays, knowing that flights may fail.

It is difficult to establish limits, and an area of immunity, in relation to the effect on him of the romantic stereotypes and affectations to which he was drawn. They can be said to have claimed him, and to have involved a duality shaped by the awareness of Milton's Satan—outcast and outlaw, miserable and monstrous. This was certainly a part performed by Poe, who was given to shows of megalomaniac pride, while capable of deserting a church, in high emotion, when the preacher tactlessly referred to the 'man of sorrows'. And to the history of this particular bi-part Poe can be said to correspond the development of a bi-part reputation.

His early enemies made out that the true Poe was the fugitive and delinquent fellow disclosed in the tales. Remarkable among these enemies was the Scottish clergyman George Gilfillan, who felt for the ill-starred poets Burns and Cowper, but deplored Poe. Gilfillan's funeral was sung by the encomiastic poet William McGonagall, a teetotaller and self-styled suffering genius who was elsewhere to picture his friend

> Lecturing on the Garibaldi movement,
> As loud as he could bawl.

Poe was unable to keep his pledge to be 'temperate even to

rigour', in an age in which the deprived would be asked to abstain; his character went down badly in Dundee. Shortly after Poe's death Gilfillan bawled that he was a strange compound of the fiend, the brute and the genius.[10] Meanwhile Poe's supporters made out that he was someone quite different: a victim, often sober, an important writer betrayed by his editor, Griswold—a literary entrepreneur like Gilfillan. David Sinclair's biography defends Poe by arguing that he may have been diabetic, bound to die young, unable to drink a drop without poisoning himself and without disaster.[11] The same surmise has come from friends of Dylan Thomas, who have been struck by his poor tolerance of alcohol, his blackouts and sweet tooth.

Poe was a man who, whether or not he was bound to die young, was bound to yield to the idea of the dying poet, both in its terrific and its sentimental aspects, and if the reasons were medical, they were also cultural. The alternative to the evil genius which is usually preferred in recollections of him is no less of a romantic stereotype: this is the man of sensibility, the victim shut in his Fordham idyll with his cousin Virginia and her mother Maria Clemm—with a dying child bride and a second or surrogate mother. Orphan and outlaw were estrangements which were both true of Poe. But if he was the sum of the contraries projected by the scandalous legend and by its correctors, there is more to him than that: the record of his life contains more than two parts, more than a suffering delinquent, though it rarely loses touch with romantic convention.

While the idea of a true Poe is itself a matter of romantic convention, we do appear to come especially close to him in the scenes with these two women: in the letter to Mrs Clemm, for instance, where Virginia darns his trousers on their travels, and he talks of their cat. 'I wish you could have seen the eggs—and the great dishes of meat.' This condemned man 'ate the first hearty breakfast I have ever eaten since I left our little home'.[12] But perhaps, against these scenes, should be set, not so much the sulphurous self, the murderous reviewer, the plagiarist who hates plagiarists, the detective who commits his own crimes, as the Poe portrait which has been detected in Melville's *The Confidence-Man*: 'Nothing could exceed his look of picturesque Italian ruin and dethronement.' This is not exactly the portrait of a home-loving simpleton or singleton. 'In his tattered, single-breasted frock-coat, buttoned meagrely up to his chin, the shatter-brain made him a bow, which, for courtesy, would not have misbecome a viscount.' But he is also taken, by an 'invidious' observer, for 'a cunning vagabond, who picks up a vagabond living by adroitly playing the madman'.[13] It is enough to remind one of Poe's invidious words about the success of two of his most adroit productions: 'The bird beat the bug, though, all hollow.'[14] Melville's shatterbrain portrait may allude to the history of nineteenth-century duality, and it also carries a likeness, not only to William McGonagall, but to Harold Skimpole, the cunning sensitive and gregarious solitaire in *Bleak House.*

Does Poe belong, then, to the history of romantic chicanery? Does he belong with the charlatans portrayed in romantic fiction, who had their historical counterparts (in Skimpole's case, Leigh Hunt)? The problem is that Poe's conformity with period expectations was extensive and congenital, and it is to this conformity, rather than to the facts in the case, that contemporary witnesses often seem to be responding. The nerves that reportedly 'throbbed with pain at the slightest contact' could be taken as a symptom of diabetes, but they are also romance. So is the early insistence that he had no friends. Here was a real orphan, a changeling, bereaved of a heritage full of the patrician and picturesque South (both Scotland and the South having been won for romanticism by Walter Scott), and fostered out with a mere businessman. With such a birthright, a later life of throbbing pains and pleasures, passions and impressions, pit and pendulum, terror and retreat, would have been and was thought likely to follow, and did follow. The perception of him as deprived, and depraved, has been none the less intense for its conventionality. According to a sanctimonious account by Joseph Wood Krutch,[15] he must have been impotent, and his works 'have no place in the American literary tradition'. And that is not all. These works 'bear no conceivable relation, either external or internal, to the life of any people'. You can't be much more of an outcast than that.

Coincidences between his life and works, perfect fits and fitting ends, might almost suggest that he *was* what he imagined, and they sometimes appear to have survived his death. A Poe-like shadow has fallen on the activities of that large section of posterity which has been given over to the study and approval of his writings—with results very similar to those caused by the curse of the Pharaohs. A train leaves the track and shatters the gravestone that has been prepared for him. My namesake John Carl Miller, author of *Building Poe Biography*,[16] and of a monograph on the exhumation of the bodies of Poe, Virginia, and her mother, has recently exhumed the Englishman John Ingram, who undertook to clear Poe's name and build his biography, saw himself as a Poe redivivus, and altered the facts of the life for symmetry's sake. And so on.

Before the Apollo astronauts reached the Moon, this shatterbrain did. Poe has a story, that is to say, which coincides with, has found its fitting end in, the Moonstruck Norman Mailer's narrative of the Apollo 11 mission. In *A Fire on the Moon*, Mailer called himself Aquarius at a time when there was fanciful talk of an age of Aquarius, and his account is powered, as Poe's is, by ego, impulse, and imagination. It can be said that both writers, and that the Apollo crew, rode into the sky on the imagination of previous centuries, buoyed by the old dream of flight. 'The Unparalleled Adventures of One Hans Pfaall', published in 1835, may be awarded plenty of parallels. Hans was one of many, not least in being a one and only, and in the fullness of time he turned into Neil Armstrong.

The Apollo Moonshot, when it came, proved to be like a poem. 'Upon the night's starred face', and on television, were 'huge cloudy symbols of a high romance'. We watched a drama of flight and fall, a wonder in which birth and death converged. Diapered in their spacesuits, all brow and bum, the astronauts looked like babies. Inside the module, they bumbled and tumbled like babies in a bag. Walking in space, they were foetuses at the end of their tether. And yet they might never get back to Mother Earth. The thing could have been planned by the romantic imagination. It was not convincingly defended in terms of value for money, and seemed to hover somewhere between a joke and a serious matter. The Moonshot was science and sense and politics, but it was also sport and art and adventure. It could be read as an episode in the literature and culture of escape: in the language of the 1960s, as a magical mystery tour. It could be read as the repeat of a tale of mystery and imagination by Poe. Poe and Mailer float through space on the wings of a dove. Both perform mental leaps while rooted to the ground. Both summon, for their flights of fancy, the sense and science of their respective times, as others had done before them in the long history of imagined departures from the human condition which preceded the arrival of Science Fiction.

It may be said that Hans Pfaall stole to the Moon accompanied by Edgar Allan Poe, alias Peregrine Proteus. 'In efforts to soar above our nature, we invariably fall below it': Poe's Icarian reference to Wieland's novel belies both the novel itself and, as I have already said,[17] Poe's own peregrine tendencies. The Poe persona we are most conscious of is one that loves to soar, as another of his space flights, the didactic prose-poem 'Eureka', puts it, in 'regions of illimitable intuition'.[18] And yet this is a self which fears, from time to time, that it may fall. Poe's Icarian sentiment, and presentiment, are implied in the name he gives Pfaall, though Hans does not fall, and only offers to return to Earth. Romanticism shows us a sky tenanted by the fugitive parts of equivocal human creatures, each of whom has shed his sober side. But it also knows, and expounds in the doctrine of duality, that each of these creatures is both up in the air and down to earth. Poe, with one foot in Baltimore, and Wieland's Peregrine, in conversation with Lucian, to whose arguments he concedes a good deal, are specimens of the soaring and changeful self which is able to confess the risks it runs. From this point of view, Hans's adventure can be seen to be different from the companion trip undertaken in 'Eureka'. In the story, Poe both is and is not the crank who has cranked himself out of this world in a crazy machine of his own invention and imagination, whereas the Poe whom many have found in 'Eureka' is single, and singular, every inch a crank: in his every whim throbs the Heart Divine.

Hans's pflight and possible pfaall are several things at once: a hoax, a satirical joke, a Boy's Own adventure, a scientific experiment, and an exercise of poetic fancy. And if Poe is a Southern literary messenger who travels to the Moon, he is also a Dutch uncle. The story starts with a comic and sarcastic description of a bourgeois Rotterdam plunged into confusion by the arrival of a spacecraft in the shape of a fool's cap. In it is an earless Moon man, who resembles one of the devilish little old gentlemen who belong to the medium of Gothic terror and humour. He delivers Hans Pfaall's confession, and soars off. So much for Rotterdam's close encounter with another world.

Hans's confession introduces us to circumstances very like those endured by Poe and his two females: he is poor as a rat and chased by duns, with the trade of bellows-mending ruined by 'the effects of liberty, and long speeches, and radicalism'. Fires can be fanned by newspapers as well as bellows, he says, and we reflect that an old sort of literature, or long-windedness, has been ousted by another. Meanwhile treatises on astronomy and aerodynamics have applied a 'stimulus to imagination', with the result that this intender of suicide is soon behaving like the practical Benjamin Franklin and Neil Armstrong. He quits the scene of his miseries in a vehicle both ramshackle and precisely calibrated, burning to death three duns with the explosion of cannon powder that blasts him off.

The vehicle is a wickerwork basket which carries ample supplies of ballast and is towed by a balloon filled with special gas of a density '37.4 times *less than that of hydrogen*'. But the real gas is the long wind of literature, which can lift you from your troubles. The trip has plenty of fuss and contrivance, and yet it is also true that Hans flies through the air with the greatest of ease. He both frets and soars. It is right for a man who is defaulting on his debts to steal, as Hans does, to a safe place. The spectacle of Poe in the sky can seem at moments to amount to the homely sight of a clever, starving book-reviewer in a threadbare frockcoat, busying himself with pigeons, knots, and quantities of gum-elastic, dangling from the basket and pulling himself back on board—there was not a moment to be lost—with one last superhuman effort. Among the pigeons is a cat, which litters *en route* and lends to space a broad hint of the domestic happiness available, even to Poe, on Earth. And yet the trip foretells the future by being quite like the lay experience of the Apollo mission. At the end of it, 'the moon—the moon itself in all its glory—lay beneath me, and at my feet.'[19]

Hans finishes by speaking of his desire to return to his home and by soliciting a pardon for the deaths of his three creditors. But then the last paragraphs of the tale cast doubt on the exploit: there are those in Rotterdam who make fun of the city fathers, and Hans is called, as Poe was called, a 'drunken villain', whose absence from the city on some disgraceful trip and spree has not gone unnoticed. This could mean that Poe lacked the courage of his excursion, but it could also express a Lucian-like scepticism about excursions.

There is a passage where Hans presents reasons for getting away:

> In this state of mind, wishing to live, yet wearied with life, the treatise at the stall of the bookseller, backed by the opportune discovery of my cousin of Nantz, opened a resource to my imagination. I then finally made up my mind. I determined to depart, yet live—to leave the world, yet continue to exist—in short, to drop enigmas, I resolved, let what would ensue, to force a passage, if I could, *to the moon*.[20]

'Depart, yet live': the words might be thought to describe an impossibility, which is being measured in terms of the distance between the Earth and the Moon. This would have seemed a wildly long way, though the journey in question was one which Poe's story was romantic enough to predict, and which the astronauts performed. But if the words could therefore be taken to indicate a scepticism about escapes, about trips of whatever kind, they could also refer to a principle on which people act, on which romantic people act when they attempt their (often fatal) mock-suicides, and on which Poe is acting when he dreams to a woman friend of a cottage 'not *too* far secluded from the world'.[21]

It may be that two different persons can be heard in 'depart, yet live': someone restlessly hopeful, and someone very like the author of a story in which a man tries to escape from himself, and of various accounts of captivity. This is an author who can't have been unaware that the living never get away, and that liberty constrains and cheats, and who would have done well with the story, had he been able to write it, of what became of his mother-in-law after his death. In order to stay solvent, Maria Clemm sold copies of Griswold's edition of Poe, in which the poet was made out to be a drunken villain: her escape was at the expense of what survived of her dead Eddie's good name.

'William Wilson' was written around 1839; 'Hans Pfaall' four years earlier. The year before that, Poe's stepfather John Allan, had shaken his cane at him, and then when Allan died, he was ignored in the will. In 1835, there were drinking bouts and despondencies. The story was written in June, and a few weeks later Poe wrote to Mrs Clemm, in an extremity of feeling, to protest at the plan that Virginia, barely thirteen, should go to live with a cousin. In September, he took out a marriage licence.

Poe was a repertoire of Poes, and his life was a tissue of escapes and returns. He took trips, and invented them: among his tall stories is a visit to Russia. From the last of his trips he landed back, dying, in a Baltimore gutter, caught by politicians possibly, in that age of liberty and long speeches, and drugged or made drunk in order that he might be used to cast votes. The early death had come about. Posterity might proceed to adore the nerves of the runaway and shatterbrain.

I have tried to relate his moving from place to place, and, inwardly, from person to person, to a dependence on a set of ideas and accords whose motors were running, whose meteors were flashing through the sky, a good century before Poe himself flourished and flashed and crashed. While not in every respect surpassingly strange, Poe's flights are complex. He was both pursued and pursuing, both shut out and shut in: an anguish of exclusion is heard in his letters, but he also longed to be released. His journeys embody the search for a mother, and an effort to regain the mother he had lost, and his 'depart, yet live' may be matched with the tension in his writings between an impulse to guard against the horrors of premature burial and an impulse to be interred with the maternal remains. No one has given such point to the traditional joke about the romantic rhyme of 'womb' and 'tomb'. The romantic pun on 'mummy' which the visionary and the logical Poe collaborate to produce in certain of the stories has made sense to a readership of vast dimensions. Those for whom this makes him disreputably popular should be assured that what he does with his fantastic prose can be very like what Beckett was to do. 'The Spectacles' is a story which laughs like Lucian at the refusal to see the world in its true colours, while romantically suggesting that if you refuse to see an optician you may accidentally marry your great-great-grandmother. The story has much of the momentum of Poe's characteristic perversity, in which, as it declares itself in his most famous pieces, we think we recognize a crying need and desperate frustration.

This strange case was in some respects ordinary enough. It isn't surprising that someone whose life was so bitterly sad should have wanted 'some words with a mummy' and pursued, into the morbid and the esoteric, the sweets of an impossible consolation. He was having a terrible time, so he took comfort in the terrors of his imagination, and in the several women who wanted to look after him, and he relished the little homes which he was always leaving. He was no danger to his dangerous society, with its killing blasts of sentiment and censure, its diabolic theory of 'diabetes', or 'epilepsy'; and his masks, trips, desolate sprees, suffocating idylls, lies, and sadistic fantasies may well have been the best defence he could manage against illness, and against the calamities of his situation and temperament: a refuge from trouble which was itself a trouble.

Flight is sometimes held to be modern, and it is sometimes held to be American. It is certainly odd to think of the fugitive Poe as un-American. His was a time when American writers still took part in English literature, and his was a tradition in which nationality was among the conditions poets were expected to escape. But this does not mean that he had nothing in common with his fellow-countrymen, though it does help to explain why Englishmen have been fascinated by him. Quite a few of his biographers are English, and so was John Ingram, who started in the 1870s to expose Griswold's forgeries and distortions, and who, in correspondence with various confiders, built up a collection of reminiscences. Sensibility, the feeling for misfortune, sobbed and shuddered in the homes which received the writer in his later years. The ladies among Ingram's donors fell for Poe as a suffering poet who looked the part, but he stands occluded in their accounts, as if he weren't quite, or all, there. He was their dream. This, at any rate, is what Annie Richmond—the chief target for the terminal affections, and affectations, and expedients, of this *peregrinus moriturus*—felt him to be in the decades that followed. Her rival was the bluestocking Helen Whitman. Mrs Shew saw herself as 'a childish undeveloped loving woman', and she thought that Poe, whom she nursed, was 'as gentle as a child, and as tender as the most tender mother'. Others of the women were childish, but not Mrs Clemm—who felt able to predict a warm welcome for Poe in Heaven: '*now* he will be appreciated—God, who he is now with, understands him.' Maria Clemm, and her name, and her hard eye for the soft touch, are Dickensian: and Dickens was one of those who responded to her appeals.[22]

Julian Symons's recent English study is shaped by the conviction that in order to do justice to its miseries, he should 'separate' Poe's life 'as much as possible from the work'.[23] The idea of a separation between the artist as he is known to biography and the mind that we meet in his art is an aspect of Eliot's conviction that 'the man who suffers' should as far as possible be 'separate' from 'the mind which creates'. And there is every reason to think of these ideas as romantic. Distressed by his two natures, Stevenson's Dr Jekyll conceives the project of a 'separation of these elements', and he recalls it afterwards with the air of a man who had determined to force a passage to the Moon. With all that he hoped for from a 'classical' steadiness, Eliot was not free from a feeling for such projects. He was to tell the world what Poe had never doubted: that poetry is 'an escape from personality'. Eliot and Poe, Anglo-Americans, are partners in duality, whose writings may lead us to imagine that the subject has to do with pain and with relief from pain, and that protean and peregrine, double and flight, are the one thing.

IX. KEATSES

The most compelling of all orphans is Keats. Few famous poets have been more famous for their misfortunes—in his own expression, more 'mightily forlorn'. He was literally forlorn, and fairy-tale forlorn, and forlorn by fiat. Having lost both parents, he was exposed to the doles and narrow sympathies of a tradesman uncle. In his twenty-third year he witnessed the death of his brother from tuberculosis, and fell in love. The orphan's dream of flight and return which is recorded in the 'Ode to a Nightingale' belongs to the following year—a dream in which the word 'forlorn' tolls to summon him from freedom, fancy, and multiplicity back to his troubles, and to the 'sole', to the solitary and single, self which endured them. At the age of 26 he died of the same disease as his brother. Friends felt compelled to explain him as an orphan: Joseph Severn said that because he was an orphan he had always been unhappy. For some of his friends, his appearance was that of the poetical victim—that of a fainting girl, with ringlets and lustrous eyes. Other reports lay stress on a strong torso, short legs, the hands of an older man, and take care to show him as dauntless and nautical. He played cricket, fought a butcher's boy who was maltreating a kitten. But in one respect at least, he was the perfection of orphan insignificance: he was just under five feet tall, the size of a babe in the wood. Even in his own diminutive times, this mattered. And it mattered, too, that he was socially small and faint.

The dual Keats of the early reports[1] conveys something of the might, the magic, which has been assigned to marginality, and which was a familiar paradox of the age and of the heritage. The orphan was imagined as both large and small, strong and weak, angry and timid, effeminate and fierce. Charles Cowden Clarke, who praised Keats's 'terrier courage' in boyhood, spoke of 'a little body with a mighty heart', and noticed with approval that Richard Monckton Milnes's life of the poet had authorized the word 'magnanimity' for the description of Keats. This was a word often used by Keats, and of Keats by those who knew him. It was a quality which he displayed, which his goddess Moneta required of poets in 'The

Fall of Hyperion', but which he advised the poet Shelley to 'curb'.[2] For Keats, magnanimity was purposeful and communal. It was the enemy of egotism, and of the equivocal selflessness which he was sometimes to attribute to artists. He could use the word in a sense that appears opposed both to the selfishness and privateness, and to the impersonal open mind, of the artist—a sense which indicates that self is never easy to escape, that self-excluding negative capability will always be dualistically inseparable from the Keatsian categories of 'soul-making' and 'self-concentration'. But the word could also be used at this time to suggest a largeness of mind which lies open to the world, thereby trenching on the condition of the artist as Keats was sometimes to imagine him. It was also a common word of the time for courage, generosity, and public spirit.

If Hogg foresaw Keats's fate, Keats foresaw himself—foresaw the contrasts he would embody for others. His poems—rather than his letters—are conscious of the terms in which he would be revered, as his sonnet to Chatterton indicates. 'Dear child of sorrow—son of misery': the sonnet employs the language of the eighteenth-century poet Langhorne, who wrote of a 'child of misery'; and Chatterton's 'sad fate' can be read as, in Langhorne's words, a 'sad presage'—of Keats's own early death.[3] 'Genius mildly flash'd'—once more, the orphan oxymoron—from Chatterton's eye, and raised him 'above the ingrate world' and 'base detraction': now, 'thou art among the stars . . .'. Keats's detractors were mentioned after his death in a manner which improved the legend. Byron was a detractor in *Don Juan*, but the legend can hardly have been diminished by the rough handling of this 'poor fellow':

> 'Tis strange the mind, that very fiery particle,
> Should let itself be snuffed out by an article.

Shelley's 'Adonais' tells of a 'gentle child' and a 'mighty heart', who had bearded the forces of 'envy and calumny' and 'outsoared the shadow of our night'. In the Preface, a 'susceptible mind' has been violated by the article in the *Quarterly*. The elegy tells, moreover, of a meteor passing to its eclipse, of a 'Power/Girt round with weakness'. Adonais is like the Adonis of myth who dies young and rises again. Life is an abode of suffering, where we languish as under a glass bell, through which filters the white radiance of eternity. At the same time, the soul of Adonais is a fire which can be seen burning through the veils that cover the abode of the Eternal. Shelley writes of an elect whose being will take part in the eternal mind, but who may also shine, like so many Chattertons, as separate stars.

A recent historian has said of the nineteenth century's attention to Keats: 'Virtually the whole course of Keats criticism, directly until the 1840s, and indirectly until about 1900, was determined by two exceptional circumstances: his supposed death at the hands of the reviewers, and the early age at which he died.'[4] These exceptional circumstances are among the standard circumstances of romantic adversity—and Keats had predicted them. If he became the eternal exception, he was also—in the context of a cult of misfortune—the rule. There had been and there were to be many such exceptions, among whom and in deference to whom an Imitation of Keats has been pursued. With the approach of the Great War, the first of the modern massacres in which innocence was to meet the early death deplored in romance, Wilfred Owen's adolescent reading 'guided my groping hand right into the wound, and I touched, for one moment, the incandescent Heart of Keats.' Two of his fellow war poets, Graves and Sassoon, were, he felt, 'Keatses', and for Sassoon, Owen, too, was a Keats. Owen was a Keats who saw himself as 'always a mad comet'.[5]

The orphan of a hundred years before was the fiery particle which flies through the air with the greatest of ease, the meteor or comet which flashes to its doom, and he was the possessor of a set of feelings which stirred and dilated preternaturally: the orphan's might was to depend on a capacity to feel which both abbreviated his passage through the sky and fixed him there for ever. The romantic person bore the temperament of his predicament—a twofold temperament proper to a dualistic age and compounded of strength and weakness. He displayed negative capability, nervous magnanimity, meteoric impressibility, susceptible mobility. The 'sensorium' of the period was charged with sensations, impressions, passions, blushes, flushes; 'sensibility', another period term, embraced appetite, animal spirits, and their celebrated obverse—a shrinking concern with velleities and refinements. An excellence of the sick was detected here. Tuberculosis made you feel more, made you pale and wan, interestingly etiolated, but also rosily, rashly, hectically alive, made you at once impersonal and emotional. Medicine was to imagine a passionate consumptive. An emotional register of highs and lows, lively feelings, and several selves, inspired projects of escape from common life in the midst of a submission to its pleasures and pains. This was the world in which Keats discovered that while soul and body may be parted, and soul soar away on excursions, it is also the case that the soul is inseparable from the short-lived body, that poetry and physiology are one. To the interest of his time in the paradox of a powerful and preternatural debility he brought a meaning which is at once credulous and courageous, compliant and sceptical. It is the meaning of the 'Ode to a Nightingale'.

Meteoric impressibility, as exhibited by a contrastive Keats, was the phenomenon and faculty of an age in which error, and sensation, and comets, were revalued. In the seventeenth century, the comet's erratic course could serve as a warning to the sinful. In the mid-eighteenth century, in the poetry of Thomson, the comet could be beheld, by the 'enlightened few', as a 'glorious stranger'.[6] In Keats's day, too, the comet could be glorious as well as ominous, and he himself was a glorious stranger in the eyes of enlightened admirers: he was called the meteor of the age—and by John Sterling, an associate of Monckton Milnes, 'that fiery beautiful meteor'.[7] There were heavenly bodies which wandered and flashed and flushed, and the body of the gifted unfortunate resembled them strangely. Those who bore the 'impressible temperament of an orphan lad', as did one poetic Scots solicitor (who lived to the ripe old age of his profession),[8] were glorious and ominous, and their blushes proclaimed a meteoric career and a short life. Keats's blushes are, in part, those of the age he lived in. Maturin's innocent and suggestible Immalee, of the 'burning cheek', is mated with a grievous supernatural being who is put in charge of the comet's 'blazing and erratic orb'.[9] Children of nature, such as Immalee and Keats, are the red stars of the human condition—richly embarrassed virtuosos of feeling whose velocities soon cease. But then their fame may survive them. There is a fear of death which has ventured to suggest that sensations may make you a sensation, and that the impressions made by the impressionable do not burn out.

I want now to locate an imitation of Keats in a place where, so far as I know, it has not been suspected, and where a posture of mockery, on the part of the writer in question, might be thought to preclude it. It might be thought that Keats is not mocked, that no one would dare. But we are at an early point in the history of his reputation: he was not yet famous enough to be spared. In any case, mockery, like parody, may be a form of homage. This is not an account of the forlorn flush which is utterly derisive.

In Richard Monckton Milnes's *Life, Letters and Literary Remains of John Keats*, which appeared in 1848, the notion of an outcast genius was affirmed by a man of the world who was an expert on misfortune and on the doom that awaits promise and precocity. Milnes, eventually Lord Houghton, also produced an edition of the verse, which, when reissued in 1854, carried a digest of the biographical information which had been contained in the *Life*. He befriended Keats, posthumously, in much the same spirit as he befriended, in the flesh, the working-class poet Alexander Montgomery, who died young of tuberculosis, and he himself wrote poems of a miserable cast—such as 'The Lay of the Humble'. His work on Keats traced the stock trajectory which survives its crash and leaps from misery to the stars. For Milnes, Keats was what Wordsworth termed him—a 'youth of promise':[10] but Milnes's work was to persuade people to think of Keats in terms of achievement, while continuing to mourn his fate. Milnes was a person of rank and office who stooped to sympathize with the humble, and with talent, who frequented hospitals as well as Piccadilly breakfasts, who acquired a posthumous fame as a collector of erotica—a lord who was also a waif, and who was not alone as such in the century of the orphan prince and of the double life. There is a water-colour of him which shows a spruce balding head reflected in a drawing-room mirror: it may be that both heads were turned by Keats's sorrows, though one of them did remark that he could not 'expect any reputation' from 'the biography of a mere boy'.[11]

At the close of the 1867 *Life and Letters of John Keats* Milnes states 'the moral of the tale'. 'In the life,' he writes,

which here lies before us, as plainly as a child's, the action of the poetic faculty is most clearly visible: it long sustains in vigour and delight a temperament naturally melancholy, and which, under such adverse circumstances, might well have degenerated into angry discontent; it imparts a wise temper and a courageous hope to a physical constitution doomed to early decay, and it confines within manly affections and generous passion a nature so impressible that sensual pleasures and sentimental tenderness might easily have enervated and debased it. There is no defect in the picture which the exercise of this power does not go far to remedy, and no excellence which it does not elevate and extend.[12]

We are told here that his gift for poetry made a man of the child-like Keats, made him magnanimous. We are given the sadness of the outcast, the wrath of the outcast, and the ardours of the outcast. Until the bitter end, with the letters (unavailable to Milnes) which relate to his love for Fanny Brawne, Keats's correspondence has, in fact, few discharges of rage or grief: it could well be taken to reveal a temperament naturally cheerful. In Milnes's moral what we are looking at is the prevailing notion of the unfortunate—a notion to which Keats responded very much more in his poetry than there is any reason to think that he did in other capacities. The collector of erotica writes with a wince: 'It might have been expected that the impressible nature of Keats would incline him to erotic composition.'[13] Milnes portrays the salvation of this orphan as a little less than total and as a very close-run thing.

The verse is rich in sensation, suggestion, and sentiment, but we have sometimes been asked to consider that such tendencies had to be tamed or outgrown. The story goes that it is his early work which is suggestible and embarrassing—his own word for some of it was 'mawkish'—that, in the solitude of his condition, the orphan composed a poetry which was erotic if not, as Byron observed, auto-erotic, but that he moved to a verse which was manly, magnanimous, and public-spirited—in the revised 'Hyperion', above all. Hazlitt and De Quincey were sure that the early verse was effeminate, but about the time of Milnes's labours De Quincey was also ready to cast doubt on the public spirit mustered by the orphan at the end of his short span: 'As a man, and viewed in relation to social objects, Keats was nothing. It was as mere an affectation when he talked with apparent zeal of liberty, or human rights, or human progress, as is the hollow enthusiasm which many people profess for music, or most poets for external nature.'[14] Two recent critics,

John Bayley and Christopher Ricks, have been respectful of the early verse,[15] and Bayley comes near to reiterating De Quincey's doubts about the wisdom of Moneta in the revised 'Hyperion'. Both critics make us think tenderly of the orphan poetry of the apprenticeship, while Ricks's book makes it possible to think that the duality of the orphan—who is both this and that, so great and yet so small—is an aspect of that embarrassment in Keats which he is concerned to study, and which is by no means confined to the early verse. Embarrassment in Keats is a period attribute, and it is an affair both of his causing it and of his being free from it, just as a blush or a flush can signal both constraint and a deliverance from constraint: here as elsewhere, the orphan is at once bound and free. From this flow both the successes and the failures of the improvident first poems, where sensation takes risks, and liberties, and falls flat, where there's both a richness, and a fault, of embarrassment. The final phase—as in the wisdom of Moneta, magnanimity's enforcer—has its embarrassments too. These, however, are altogether less equivocal.

Milnes, at all events, was keen to represent the poet as at once effeminate and the master of his effeminacy, and there is reason to think that Charles Dickens paid attention to Milnes's efforts. In 1852, four years after the *Life* appeared, Dickens started to publish the instalments of *Bleak House*, and in 1856, a matter of months after Milnes's edition of the poems, bearing its memoir, Dickens started to publish *Little Dorrit*. Each of these novels is a collection of interlocking orphan predicaments, and among the predicaments which contribute to *Little Dorrit* we may perhaps make out an image of Keats: the image of an impressible, poetical, girlish, and manly nature, of a magnanimous waif, a great heart in a little body. The image is smiled at, and cherished, by a writer who was both for and against romance.

Within this writer was a little Dickens, with a great heart. 'Small Cain that I was, except that I had never done harm to anyone.' This small Cain was punished, expelled, by his parents. When, in 1847, he chose to confide in his biographer Forster, Dickens dwelt on the theme of rejection and on his consignment to the blacking factory: 'I never afterwards forgot, I never shall forget, I never can forget, that my mother was warm for my being sent back.' On this subject Dickens, too, is very warm. The father of Keats's friend Charles Wentworth Dilke met the small Cain in the blacking warehouse, where he had gone visiting with Dickens's father—handed him half a crown and received a low bow. Forster's mentioning this to Dickens prompted a confession, previously unspeakable, of these early sufferings, together with their locations—the warehouse, and the Marshalsea debtors' prison, where much of *Little Dorrit* is set.[16] Dickens and Keats were Cockneys, inhabitants of a teeming London which enrolled them in a cast of literati, theatre people, strollers, choice spirits, Byrons and Micawbers; and Dickens was acquainted with members of the Keats circle, as well as with Milnes. It is not far-fetched to propose that he must have listened to a good deal of moist and malicious talk about the poet's troubles, and that there must have been more of it than ever when the time came for Milnes to gather the materials for his life, and for his presentation of the poems, and to publish the results.

'Young John was small of stature, with rather weak legs and very weak light hair. One of his eyes (perhaps the eye that used to peep through the keyhole) was also weak, and looked larger than the other, as if it couldn't collect itself. Young John was gentle likewise. But he was great of soul. Poetical, expansive, faithful.'[17] This is not John Keats, but John Chivery of *Little Dorrit*, the 'sentimental son of a turnkey' at the Marshalsea prison, near the hospital where Keats had worked during his time as an apothecary's apprentice and medical student. Keats's first published poem was written at this point in his life:

> O Solitude! if I must with thee dwell,
> Let it not be among the jumbled heap
> Of murky buildings.

These murky buildings could well have included the Marshalsea. John Chivery 'turns crimson to the tips of his ears', and he has an eye not only for keyholes but for arbours and 'trelliswork'.[18] John Keats's poems are scarlet, and his 'Ode to Psyche' imagines an arbour and a kind of 'wreath'd trellis'. John Chivery's only ode is directed, as graffiti, at Amy Dorrit, whom he unrequitedly loves: 'Welcome sweet nursling of the Fairies.' John Keats was known during his lifetime for 'strange tales of the elf and the fay', as for 'blisses abounding in dark leafy bowers' (this is the language of George Mathew's poem 'To a Poetical Friend'). The 'chivalrous feeling' John Chivery has for Amy Dorrit makes him so 'respectable' that he does not demand the 'consideration' due to his weakness: a Goliath would have demanded less. John Keats became mightily forlorn. The two cases have much in common: more, I think, than can be attributed solely to the 'semblances'—Cowper's word in 'The Castaway'—which the conventions guyed here by Dickens bestowed on such cases. Dickens may also have been remembering—to the point of portrayal, parody, travesty—the story of Keats in particular.

Seen as a character in a work loaded with character which encompasses the all and sundry of a whole city and society, Amy Dorrit is what Keats was to De Quincey when seen 'as a man' and 'in relation to social objects': a nothing. Barely more, at times, than the sum of her submissions to duty and authority. And yet she is fundamental to the work which bears her name, and which says that littleness and lowness can work wonders where there is greatness of heart, and which turns society upside down to display the merit of its under-side and the shams and cruelties of success. This is a book which is biased in favour of misfortune, and which is as much sentimental as subversive; and Amy's greatness of heart is not without its defects. At the same time, her very nothingness serves to voice what the novel mainly means, and her plight enables the reader to keep track of many other plights: such semblances supply an organizing principle. The cast is a cast of orphans: Amy, her father, her family, the inmates of the Marshalsea, Arthur Clennam, with whom Amy is finally united, Clennam's parents, John Chivery, whom Amy refuses, Flora Finching, who has refused Arthur Clennam, Miss Rugg, who has been jilted, Tattycoram and her protectress Miss Wade, each of these two an illegitimate castaway, an outlaw, the angry opposite of a submissive nothing. That does not exhaust the list of those who are, or say they are, excluded, injured, and insulted, a list which contains the wife of the mighty capitalist Merdle, and Merdle himself, miming a captivity in the haplessness of bodily tics and contortions, 'creeping in with not much more appearance of arms in his sleeves than if he had been the twin brother of Miss Biffin'.[19]

Miss Biffin was the last word in unfortunates—a limbless circus freak mentioned in *The Old Curiosity Shop* and not forgotten fifteen years later. The Marshalsea is said by Dickens to be 'orphaned' by Mr Dorrit's accession to wealth. It is a prison, a sad place. But it is also an asylum for the orphans whom it incarcerates—an escape from the prison of English life.

The novel is determined by one species of loss far more than by any other. It tells several stories of the broken heart, of those who have been crossed in love. Another feature is its concern, in relation to suffering, with cases of false sensibility—a fault to which its broken hearts are not immune. Of the mysteries it makes, the most important originates in the ordeal of Clennam's father, forced to separate from his mother. In later times, Chivery is denied Little Dorrit, while Miss Rugg suffers a breach of promise, and is derided for taking legal action. Then there are Clennam's meetings with his childhood sweetheart, Flora Finching. These are known to have been influenced by Dickens's recent experience of embarrassed reacquaintance with an old flame from whom he had been parted by considerations of status, and who had turned up very much the worse, like poor Flora, for the intervening years. The comedy which the novel visits on the lovelorn is not visited on Clennam, and may be seen as somewhat vengeful, as a settlement of scores which enabled the writer to deal with his own successive orphanings, with his lifelong losses and reverses in love, and with the self-pity which is directly apparent in the unsmiling portrait of Clennam: 'In his youth he had ardently loved this woman, and had heaped upon her all the locked-up wealth of his affection and imagination.'[20] In this vale of tears, while Chivery can be thought to double for Keats, both Chivery and Clennam can be thought to double for Dickens—so that the laws of mathematics leave us with an imaginative equation between two great writers who are often kept apart. Here, to join the first Romantic age with its successor, are two Keatses.

High and low meet in this vale, and high may at times pretend to be low. Mrs Merdle, of the snowy bosom, the worldly wife of an unfortunate magnate, stretched on her ottoman with a parrot by her side, poses as a Little Dorrit, as the lowest of the low: power imitating poverty, and poetry, and sensibility, and magnanimity. Mrs Merdle squawks: 'I am very impressible myself, by nature. The weakest of creatures—my feelings are touched in a moment.' So are her son's. Impressibility, she explains, is 'not a misfortune in our natural state, I dare say, but we are not in a natural state.' She is a child, a 'child of nature', 'suppressed' by 'society'. Later we read that 'the Bosom flushed' and that this was 'one of her best effects'.[21] Amy Dorrit is no actress, is always pale, affected by misfortune: but she is sufficiently a child to have the stature of one, and Chivery extols her as a child of nature. Her affections are a theme for the affectations of sensibility, which the novel insults, and indulges. Amy is too much the good child to stand up to her father when he and her sister Fanny reproach her for being seen in the disgraceful company of an old pauper. 'I don't justify myself for having wounded your dear heart.' So saying, 'she clasped her hands in quite an agony of distress.' If Amy fails in magnanimity here, and may be felt to have suppressed, or to have lacked, the promptings of a justified self-will, Fanny is all self-will, and Dickens blames her for it without stint. But it is Fanny who stands up to the bullying Mrs General, an expert on deportment and false fronts—'I am not a child, and I am not Amy, and I must speak'—and when this happens, Dickens is able to give the girl her due, signalling that there are times when it is better to be a monster than a child, and administering a check to the glorification of humility that occurs in the novel.

This, then, is the setting to which is assigned the story of small John Chivery, of his having the greatness of soul to bear the rejection of his love for Little Dorrit, and to behave chivalrously—as his name leads one to expect—towards his rival. Clennam calls on the Chiverys and notices John—the would-be London dandy and man of feeling—moping and unkempt in the yard amid his mother's washing. The drying sheets and table-cloths are referred to as 'tuneless groves'.[22] Dickens was not an enthusiastic reader of poetry, but this novel makes it likely that he had read Keats's 'Ode to Psyche', which has the trelliswork fancied by Chivery, and which opens with 'tuneless numbers' offered to the goddess by a poet who volunteers to be her grove. Throughout the novel Chivery is associated, just as Keats could well be associated, with groves.

While still hopeful, the lovesick Chivery dreams of an epitaph for himself, and the inscription is periodically amended to suit

John's darkening fortunes as a lover, his sense of himself as dying 'of a broken heart'. One version is dated 1826, a time when the wording on Keats's gravestone in Rome, where episodes of *Little Dorrit* are set, had come to be contemplated by admirers. By the time Dickens was writing his novel, Keats's grave had long been a place of pilgrimage, and the drama surrounding his self-chosen epitaph was well known. Severn in Rome had eventually gone ahead with the following inscription for the grave in the English cemetery there—'the strangers' cemetery in Rome' where Amy Dorrit's father and uncle are laid to rest in the one tomb:

> This Grave contains all that was Mortal of a Young English Poet—who on his death-bed—in the bitterness of his heart—at the malicious power of his enemies—desired these words to be engraven on his 'Tomb-Stone'
> 'Here lies one whose name was writ in Water.'[23]

In one of its forms, Chivery's self-chosen epitaph reads:

STRANGER!
respect the tomb of
JOHN CHIVERY, Junior,
who died at an advanced age
not necessary to mention.
He encountered his rival in a distressed state,
and felt inclined
TO HAVE A ROUND WITH HIM;
but, for the sake of the loved one,
conquered those feelings of bitterness, and became
MAGNANIMOUS.

This wording lays a stress on bitterness which suggests an attention to Keats's epitaph, whose 'malicious' might seem to be answered by Chivery's 'magnanimous'; and it suggests a knowledge of the pugilistic feats recorded by Milnes. The allusion to Chivery's solicitor-like 'advanced age' may allude to the early deaths suffered by some others, while 'not necessary to mention' seems to echo both the 'incoherence' of Chivery's talk and the rambling disclaimers of Flora Finching's, and to supply a link, therefore, between Chivery's grief and that of Dickens.

Just before Chivery composes his epitaph in the form which has been quoted, a long comic scene takes place, in which he is snobbishly portrayed as rising above his tendency to be simple, sentimental, and effeminate, to be a 'great girl', or, for that matter, in Milnes's phrase, a 'mere boy'—to bask in indolence, to blush, and to indulge in the 'harmless luxury of a sob and a sniff'.[24] Here we are in touch with tendencies which Milnes praised Keats for overcoming. But did Keats have a broken heart to contend with? In writing about Chivery's heart, Dickens could well have been conscious of Keats's friendship with Fanny Brawne—and of a view of it which still obtained at the time the novel was written. Milnes is guarded on the subject in his Life, but there were those in the Keats circle who had given the impression that Fanny was unworthy of her lover, cold, and flighty, while the poet himself spoke of her at first, in a letter, as 'monstrous in her behaviour flying out in all directions': 'I was forced lately to make use of the term *Minx*.'[25] His feelings were soon to change, and eventually they were to darken. When his letters to Fanny were published, long after *Little Dorrit*, they were thought, even by the well-disposed, to be indecently susceptible, unmanly, and bitter: he had much to be bitter about, even if it must by then have been harder to think of him as a disappointed lover.

The Dickens who wrote in this novel about his own disappointments, whose own case is dispersed throughout its abundant images of loss, would not have flinched from writing about an unrequited Keats—while Finching from all mention of it—and from using him as a semblance of himself. Keats would then have been fair game for a mocking sympathy. He had not yet become a great writer: the piety which respects the dignity of great writers was still incipient for Keats, had yet to attain the proportions of a constraint that might have prevented Dickens, whose own reputation was then the greater of the two, from laughing at him. Further support for the hypothesis comes from the fact that Dickens was prone to satirical portraits, duly disguised, of writers of the age and of the previous age, and had introduced them into a novel which stands especially close to this one and was written not long before. The novel is *Bleak House*, whose Little Dorrit is Esther Summerson.

Sitting in church, Esther glimpses her childhood and her double, 'very strangely', on looking into the haughty features of her unknown mother: '*I—I*, little Esther Summerson, the child who lived a life apart and on whose birthday there was no rejoicing—seemed to arise before my own eyes.'[26] In this novel, wrote Dickens in his Preface of 1853, 'I have purposely dwelt upon the romantic side of familiar things.' As in the later novel, there comes to light a virtuous under-side of English life, and a variety of orphan states for the 'stranger's wilderness' of London. Chapter 6 has a romantic, formulaic evocation of Bleak House itself: compounded of chambers and cottages, of picturesque singularities and irregularities, of holes and corners and corridors, it might have served as the lair of some male usurper. But it belies its name and proves a sanctuary. It lives up to its encompassing prospects of 'green growth'. Likewise Mr Jarndyce's worrying philanthropy, and surname, do not fulfil the threat they may initially suggest.

Such is the setting to which two portraits of living writers are admitted. Both writers had connections with Keats. The angry Boythorn is a version of the poet Landor, who was a friend of Charles Brown, who was, as his tombstone affirmed, the 'Friend of Keats', and who was introduced by Landor to Milnes. Meek Harold Skimpole—said mutual friends of the author and of his original—was a travesty of Leigh Hunt, liked and then distrusted by Keats. A burlesque of Keats, for someone who had already travestied Landor and Leigh Hunt, would not then have been a matter of going further or too far. It may even seem to have been more of the same game. This game is the conjuring of orphan images, in all their ambivalence, from living examples. Boythorn and Skimpole inhabit a dualistic field polarized between rage and submission, and each of them belies himself. Despite appearances, the first is kind and the second predatory.

Immediately after the evocation of Bleak House, with its intimations of confinement and release, Jarndyce announces: 'There's no one here but the finest creature upon earth—a child.' This no one, this paragon, this paradox, is Harold Skimpole.

> 'I don't mean literally a child,' pursued Mr Jarndyce; 'not a child in years. He is grown up—he is at least as old as I am—but in

simplicity, and freshness, and enthusiasm, and a fine guileless inaptitude for all worldly affairs, he is a perfect child.'

We felt he must be very interesting.

'He knows Mrs Jellyby,' said Mr Jarndyce. 'He is a musical man, an amateur, but might have been a professional. He is an artist too, an amateur, but might have been a professional. He is a man of attainments and of captivating manners. He has been unfortunate in his affairs, and unfortunate in his pursuits, and unfortunate in his family; but he don't care—he's a child!'

When this creature appears, Esther relates that

there was a perfect charm in him. All he said was so free from effort and spontaneous and was said with such a captivating gaiety that it was fascinating to hear him talk. Being of a more slender figure than Mr Jarndyce and having a richer complexion, with browner hair, he looked younger. Indeed, he had more the appearance in all respects of a damaged young man than a well-preserved elderly one. There was an easy negligence in his manner and even in his dress (his hair carelessly disposed, and his neckkerchief loose and flowing, as I have seen artists paint their own portraits) which I could not separate from the idea of a romantic youth who had undergone some unique process of depreciation.

This interesting Skimpole spoke 'of himself as if he were not at all his own affair, as if Skimpole were a third person, as if he knew that Skimpole had his singularities but still had his claims too, which were the general business of the community and must not be slighted.' He has emancipated himself from 'the duties and accountabilities of life'.[27]

Misery and meekness, and their appearances, true and false, meant much to Dickens, to the artist who had painted his own portrait, and who had painted the portrait of other artists of his time. Skimpole is a child who is not a child. He is a self-made child, a self-made unfortunate, whose affecting alter ego is an alias for the exploitation of others, who speaks of himself as a little creature of great public consequence, and of the orphan as 'the child of the universe', which owes him a living. He belongs to Dickens's gallery of false or affected sensibilities, to the exposure there of the romantic person as cheat or sham or whited sepulchre. He has no idea of money but does what he can to get it. He is compact, Jarndyce says, of 'sentiment', 'susceptibility', 'sensibility', 'simplicity', and 'imagination', and conceives himself 'the victim of a combination on the part of mankind against an amiable child'.[28] Both of these novels oppose portraits of true feeling to portraits of a deceitful or self-deceiving simulation of such states, with Chivery's behaviour an embodiment of this opposition. They are portraits which proceed from an age in which the romantic concern with suffering touched many hearts, but in which tears and pleas—susceptible simplicity, impressible magnanimity—could be both admired and suspected. Dickens's suspicions of romantic excess were those of someone who was himself romantic and excessive: Charles Dickens was no less sentimental than John Chivery, and had some of the same tears to shed. Then again he was no less altruistic, no less susceptible of an unselfish fortitude. The fascination of misfortune was to diminish very little in later times, despite the onset of a more than Dickensian suspicion of sensibility—and of a suspicion of Dickens. By the closing years of the century the worship of Keats's misfortunes had reached a height which the novelist might not have thought possible.

It was the orphan Keats who was worshipped at first, together with the impressible, as opposed to the intellectual, content of his work. Then in the course of the present century there arose the notion of a progress to maturity not unlike the triumph predicated by Milnes, which enabled the poet to correct his faults and which arrived at a public-spirited writer not unlike the one who was nothing to De Quincey. Since then, in recent times, there has been the need to imagine a whole, sole Keats, sorely underrated in *Little Dorrit*, one might feel, whose importance for the history of ideas is that of a writer who shaped and transmitted the idea of a creative indolence and who wrote and enjoined a poetry in which the body thinks.

In his last days Keats said that 'the knowledge of contrast, feeling for light and shade, all that information (primitive sense) necessary for a poem are great enemies to the recovery of the stomach.'[29] Contrast is one of the faces of duality, and was a preoccupation of Keats's time, and of times to come, which remained responsive to contrasts of light and shade, rage and submission, true and false feeling, first and second selves. Here we have an account of the strange and contradictory orphan sensorium which can be taken very seriously and is in a sense subversive of any dualistic position. In an age possessed by the ideal and accustomed to denigrate the body, Keats knew that it was his body which had written his poems—'this warm scribe, my hand', and his other vulnerable organs. Here is a more terrible knowledge than the one taught by Moneta. It is a knowledge which makes everyone an orphan.

In portraying Chivery, Dickens may have been portraying Keats, and he was undoubtedly portraying himself—as another of the forlorn, the lovelorn, as a fellow unfortunate. The Keats who may be thought to double here for Dickens is an aspect of an abiding, of an abidingly self-implicated and autobiographical, concern with the theme of misfortune, on Dickens's part, and it is also an unfamiliar aspect of his concern with the second self. His last novel, the unfinished *Edwin Drood*, is an explicitly dualistic work, thronged with orphans and doubles. 'As, in some cases of drunkenness, and in others of animal magnetism, there are two states of consciousness which never clash, but each of which pursues its separate course as though it were continuous instead of broken (thus, if I hide my watch when I am drunk, I must be drunk again before I can remember where), so Miss Twinkleton has two distinct and separate phases of being': this might be the voice of the physician John Elliotson, Dickens's friend, as it might indeed be that of some subsequent investigator of multiple personality.[30] We may think here that a propositional matter is allowed to dwindle into a joke about Miss Twinkleton's blameless double life, but it is later apparent that these clinical tones have laid down a track which could have been meant to lead to that solution of the mystery which Dickens did not live to divulge—to the identification of a drug-taking murderer whose two faces are compounded by two states of consciousness. An early work, *The Old Curiosity Shop* of 1840, displays a less explicit but no less expressive duality. This is a Gothic novel, with a marked affinity to fairy-tale, and to pantomime, and to the two later novels I have been discussing. Little Nell precedes Little Dorrit. Dick Swiveller precedes John Chivery, who may also have been preceded by John Keats.

In later worlds, there continued to be Keatses. An Imitation of Keats ran high from the end of the last century until the Great War and its aftermath, and it ran together with a keen interest in the manufacture of doubles. In this unprecedented war innocence met a colossal early death. Lambs were led to the slaughter. And the writers who fought in the war were dualists for whom the consciousness of a century of exemplary suffering, and of Keats's fate in particular, prepared a response to the holocaust. The poet is present in Kipling's story 'Wireless', which appeared in a collection of 1904. The narrator spends the night in a chemist's shop where an experiment in wireless telegraphy is in progress, and where, by analogy, a consumptive apothecary drowses among the pastilles, unguents, and liquors, and receives messages from the infinite past. The rosy aromatic cave he inhabits is an olfactory equivalent of the feasts to be found in the poetry of the druggist Keats. He coughs up into a handkerchief the bright red 'arterial' blood self-diagnosed by his predecessor, is domineered over by an alluring ladyfriend, a whiff of Keats's unrequitedness having survived, and takes to writing and miswriting 'The Eve of St. Agnes'.

When the narrator witnesses this, it is as if 'my own soul' were 'considering my own soul', and the fearful encouragement he whispers is 'evidently to my other self'. He plays with the explanation that if the chemist has read Keats, then it's the Stevensonian chloric-ether he has drunk which is responsible for the poem, and that if he hasn't, then it's the tubercular bacillus, like some wireless wave, '*plus* Fanny Brand and the professional status which, in conjunction with the main-stream of subconscious thought common to all mankind, has thrown up temporarily an induced Keats'. It would then have been done by illness and by ill-starred love and by the chemist's calling and by the collective unconscious: whereupon the poor chemist proves indeed to have been ignorant of Keats's verse.[31] An earlier tale by Kipling is similarly metempsychotic, 'The Finest Story in the World'.[32] A frail vessel, a Cockney clerk with literary pretensions and with previous incarnations as a galley-slave, shows a capacity for recall which he barters to the alter-ego professional writer who tells the tale: but the deal breaks down when the clerk falls in love. In both stories love is an ill star. And both transmit the suggestion that the artist is as a wireless-set to unconscious powers of long duration in the world. Poems 'come' to people thus, inducing Keatses.

Metempsychosis has re-surfaced here as telegraphy, to provide a definition of literature tuned, as we might suppose, to some of the theoretical suggestions of later times.

Siegfried Sassoon took Wilfred Owen to be a Keats, though he is said to have been embarrassed by his lower-class accent, and Sassoon's earlier books of memoirs are comprehensively Keatsian, and dualistic. He 'loiters' there among his recollections of childhood and youth and war. The binariness of his imagination has been interpreted—properly enough, but also, for those intent on a longer term, restrictively—as, like Eliot's theory of psychic dissociation, a consequence of the war, of those 'four years of dichotomising', of that bisected Europe.[33] Sassoon's first words are: 'My childhood was a queer and not altogether happy one. Circumstances conspired to make me shy and solitary. My father and mother died before I was capable of remembering them.' This orphan and 'only child' is 'queerly touched' by the memory of his creation of another little boy—a 'dream friend' eventually to be replaced by a real one in the dour shape of a master of foxhounds. He looks like Esther Summerson at his 'small, long-vanished self with this other non-existent boy standing beside him', and remembers how he 'secretly stared at my small, white face' in a mirror, till 'the voice of my aunt speaking to one of the servants' caused him to steal away. At point-to-points, he feels 'extraneous and forlorn'. The fox-hunting man, and then the infantry officer, contain a romantic infant and imbecile, a waif adventuring in a harsh world. In the trenches, he encounters confusion and solitude, learns the 'Ode to a Nightingale'—'I cannot see what flowers are at my feet'—and tastes a 'little moment of magnanimity'. The soldiers on both sides are his 'fellow-victims'.[34] Owen saw them as that too, as his poem 'Strange Meeting' attests. The poem can be recognized as belonging to the same stage in the history of duality, and of retirement, as Edward Thomas's 'The Other'—a stage when the old lore was subjected to sophistications of treatment and to a new range of applications. It is written in the accents of Keats's Dantesque Moneta. Keats writes: '"None can usurp this height," return'd that shade . . .'. And Owen responds: '"None," said the other, "save the undone years. . ."'. Owen, the mad comet, foresaw himself here among the shades, where, queerly touched, he meets an enemy soldier, a fellow-victim—a 'strange friend' who is his lover and who is also none other than himself.

The imitation of Keats continues. In his novel *Abba Abba* of 1977, which describes the poet's last days, Anthony Burgess brings out the dualistic character of the doctrine of negative capability, suggests that the protean mode depends on this doctrine, and contributes, not only to the art of fiction, but to cultural history. Burgess's Keats is scarcely a character (for all that Keats himself was one). He is universal. He is the decapitated subject implied in the sentences of Melville's *Confidence-Man*. He is a Burgess, and an everybody, who is credited with the doctrine that we are all everybodies, all collective and collaborative. The Roman poet of the time, Belli, is contemplated in the novel by Keats and some Italian friends, one of whom explains that he 'is like two men always fighting each other': 'as he is torn between his soul and his lower instincts, so is he also torn between the language of Petrarch or Dante and the rough speech he hears all about him in Rome.' Keats responds with a statement which draws on his letters and on the inventive language of the surrounding novel ('dumpendebat' is a coinage for the life and self of the 'lower instincts') to claim that he

> could have counselled him to a way out of his guilt and unhappiness. The way out is the way out of the conception of ourselves as unified beings. We are, in fact, unities in name and appearance and voice and a set of habits only. We are nothing more, and to flesh ourselves with character we must identify ourselves, swiftly, temporarily, with one or other of our brothers and sisters of the universe. We have to dress up in the borrowed raiment of a comet, the moon, a pecking sparrow, a snowflake, boiling water, a billiard ball rolling towards a pocket. The dumpendebat self of our friend and the stabat mater self are but two among the many selves available.[35]

Keats is made to say that character is attained through the imitation of character—through the imitation of Keats among others. It is as much as to suggest that the sympathetic identifications of negative capability may heal the divided self. The therapeutic claim appears to be derived both from the ferment of Early Romantic duality and from the later history of the hypothesis, which was to coincide with an accumulation of Keatses.

X. MANKIND AND HEAVEN

Victorian sentimentality is a byword, and so is Victorian hypocrisy. These are slurs which were conceived and combined by enemies of the age long before the age was out. 'Sentiment' is a French word whose early employment by English-speakers could refer both to opinion and to sensation—a broad sense, active and passive, egotistical and negative, which can still be detected, and which can be detected in the Romantic period, when the body blushed and wept in accordance with sentiments which could accord with statements and decisions. For this word, moreover, as for certain cognates and derivatives, there had arisen in the course of the eighteenth century a specialized application in which the same broad sense of stigmas and stances is evident. Such words came to refer to feelings of sorrow, of sympathy with misfortune, to the imagination of release, to excitements in the presence of art and nature, and to the cultivation and exhibition of such feelings. The domain of sensibility, as opposed to sense, depended on fine feelings of this description—on what 'the man of feeling' might muster by way of credentials or a repertoire. In 1779 Dr Johnson wrote to Mrs Thrale of a female of the species: 'I can bear a feeler as well as you.'[1] His words are a portent of later resentments. By the end of that century 'sentimental' was a vogue word, as who should say 'a sentimental walk', and the vogue was for beautiful and terrible sights, for victims, and for the consideration of such things by the growing number of people who were willing to wear their hearts on their sleeves. Elms, and outlaws, and untimely death, were 'interesting': a word used by the considerate, and of the considerate. These interested parties were apt to display the self-assertiveness which they could be keen to disown.

Sentiment may bind the individual to a community of like minds—to a place, therefore, in the social order from which it promises a deliverance, while treating that deliverance as a form of theft. From the natural order there is no deliverance: but sentiment promises one. It promises boundlessness, weightlessness. It stokes sensation with the promise of an escape from it with impunity. The feeler stares up at a sky which holds out the hope of heaven, to which he may soar after death, or on the wings of song or of an adventurous sexuality. It is as if the heliocentric universe of the Renaissance had never happened. The romantic sky stoops low to human life. It is medieval, divine. It is as if you could jump up and touch it. It is 'as if there were no immensity of space between mankind and Heaven'. This is a sentiment which is expressed by the narrator of Dickens's *Our Mutual Friend.*[2]

Feeling placed its faith, or affected to do so, in possibilities of impunity and immunity from which there was by now, in Europe, clear evidence of alienation; it followed the older faiths in claiming access to a region set aside—according to James Thomson's 'Ode'—for the 'happy dead'. The hope of heaven became a sentiment and a hypocrisy which poisoned the wells of literary expression, from Thomson's time, for a hundred and fifty years. And yet the shams of feeling were recognized from the first for what they were: it was no secret that sense and sensibility, sentiment and sincerity, might not mix. The religion of sentiment passed into the Victorian age with its defects of condescension and pretence no less noticeable than before, and with its element of sexual escape more than ever deflected, as was later to be supposed, into a celebration of death. Charges of insincerity would continue to be averted in the context of a comedy of feeling in which shams and shamans could be found to coincide, in which, for the authors concerned, both were true.

A famous event in the history of nineteenth-century sentimentality is the 'Nellicide', as he called it, committed by Dickens in *The Old Curiosity Shop*. In time, the death of Little Nell became infamous: it was condemned as mawkish and false, with Wilde joking that only a heart of stone could read the scene without laughter. For another Victorian writer, Mrs Oliphant, Nell was 'a white smear'. For F. R. Leavis, in the present century, she was an incitement to self-approval and self-indulgence. As a character in a novel, he wrote, she was merer than mere: 'There's nothing there.' Which is what De Quincey said, not long after the novel appeared, about orphan magnanimity in the person of the public-spirited Keats. Aldous Huxley took the death scene as a prize example of 'vulgarity in literature', and made Dickens look like some cautionary instance from a Victorian account of masturbation: 'mentally drowned and blinded by the sticky overflowings of his heart'. But when chapters 71 and 72 were first read, in 1841, they caused widespread though not universal grief. Francis Jeffrey shed the tears of a Whig romantic and felt that there had been 'nothing so good as Nell since Cordelia'.[3]

Nell turns into an angel on her deathbed. The schoolmaster, in tears, refers to Heaven's justice on earth: 'Think what it is compared with the World to which her young spirit has winged its early flight, and say, if one deliberate wish expressed in solemn terms above this bed could call her back to life, which of us would utter it!'[4] Dickens conveys that it is good to be dead, that the bereaved may console themselves by believing in an abode of the happy dead no different from that of a century before. The message has been linked with his emotion at the death of his sister-in-law, which inspired reveries of a seraphic rebirth, and which may have appealed to a capacity for bereavement established early in life. It can also be linked with the frank suggestion in the novel that romance may be allowed to console in defiance of the facts. His literary practice in relation to loss has been seen in modern times, as by Huxley, in sexual terms, as a form of self-abuse. Sentimentality is solitary, narcissistic. Sentimentality is to grief what masturbation is to a loving sexuality. Dickensian pathos is an expense of spirit in a vale of tears. This may be the twentieth century's way of enlarging on what seems to be true enough: that love is outdone by loss as an occasion for feeling in the novel. It may even be thought that among the flights performed by Nell is a flight from sexuality.

The Old Curiosity Shop is a work built to soar and to steal. Nell's departure for Heaven, for the low-lying angelic skies of a surviving hope and new hypocrisy, is a continuation of other flights in the novel. She and her grandfather are presented as wanderers and adventurers, on the run from London and the schemes of a lustful dwarf, and they are so simplified and stylized as to seem like the creatures of a fairy-tale or pantomime, or of the fairground theatricals and waxwork shows discovered on their travels. Outcasts abound, and are set upon by outcasts: by the ogre Quilp, the sentimental bachelor Dick Swiveller, and the Brasses—the red-haired Sampson and his sister, who make sense, I think, as Jews and impart a xenophobic undertone to the conspiracy against innocence which spreads out from the London of the novel. It is a work suspended between city and country, and which suspensefully imagines, in time-honoured style, an intermediate mankind, hung between a high and a low. It points a period moral concerning the survival of the weakest, the magnifying of minuteness, the power of affliction: its 'little lady without legs or arms'[5]—the circus freak Miss Biffin, a precursor, as we shall see, of Robert Lowell's limbless wasps—might well, we may think, have been found to take flight had there been time to tell it. It tells a tale of two dwarfs and more, rather than one: Little Nell and Little Quilp argue a diminutive capability, but meet with very different ends. Quilp plummets into the Thames mud and is buried with a stake through his heart, while Nell is enskied.

Dick Swiveller also rises. He is one of Nell's pursuers at the start, but can then be numbered among her duplicates in the novel by virtue of his early protestations of distress, and of his marriage to the sharp little ragamuffin 'Marchioness', whose elevation from the lower depths, predicted by her nickname, ensures his salvation. At the start, he is a 'choice spirit' of the time who can be heard in his cups 'crying aloud that he was an unhappy orphan.'

> 'Left an infant by my parents, at an early age,' said Mr Swiveller, bewailing his hard lot, 'cast upon the world in my tenderest period, and thrown upon the mercies of a deluding dwarf, who can wonder at my weakness! Here's a miserable orphan for you. Here,' said Mr Swiveller, raising his voice to a high pitch, and looking sleepily round, 'is a miserable orphan!'
>
> 'Then,' said somebody hard by, 'let me be a father to you.'

This is Quilp's diabolical *basso profundo*, which strikes with a hint of leglessness here, and these are strong words. They are the words of a writer whose feeling for the fatherless was strong enough to be able to send itself up, and whose feeling for fathers could be one of dislike. 'You're *not* a choice spirit,' Dick goes on to inform Quilp. 'If you're any spirit at all, sir, you're an evil spirit.'[6]

Dick ceases to misbehave, and to be sent up. This change of character doesn't always suggest a salvation. It has suggested a change of mind on Dickens's part, and is occasionally awkward in the telling. But it is not incongruous with an intention which is fundamental to the novel, and which does have to do with the saving of souls. The manuscript has a cancelled passage which deals with the original, reprobate Dick's reaction to being jilted: he 'looked upon human nature in the abstract with the calm superiority of one who had raised himself far above its frailties, by the performance of some great and magnanimous action'.[7] But his affectation is to come true: it is just such an action that he performs when he stoops to marry his waif. The joke at his expense—which is like the joke that was to be directed at John Chivery, and that Chivery, too, was to bring to an end—is now over. In becoming capable of this action, Dick has lived up to and belied the instability of his sinister second name (which can be compared with that of Scott's charlatan Dousterswivel). As for his first name, this ties him to the author of the book, and it is possible to feel that the bohemian dandy, the quoter of Burns and Tom Moore, inhabits the London of the young Dickens, and of his disappointment in love, in which there persisted that of the chivalrous Keats. Dick's magnanimous action constitutes a triumph of the weak, and it is the most authentic of such triumphs in the novel: there must be others besides Chesterton who have felt that this is the most winning of the love affairs described by Dickens. Dick's adventures lend heart to the harsh city envisaged in Nell's escape, and they ease the strain of her progress to Heaven, which these adventures may be thought to imitate. This imitation, which can be called an imitation of Keats, was not lost, as we have seen, on Dostoevsky.

The novel has its diminutives and its duplicates; it can resemble a doll's house, a toy theatre. Magnanimity enables Dick to rise above himself, to be a different man, to grow, and to go to Heaven. He is a choice spirit who turns into one of the chosen few. Doubles and flight concur, therefore, in *The Old Curiosity Shop*. Duality is heavenly here, among these Flying Cockneys, as it so often is elsewhere. As so often, it is a matter of the immortal soul, of purity and impunity, and of an encroaching evil intent.

Nell's last flight takes her to the better place she deserves. Before that, she has fled from her pursuers, together with her grandfather, in a series of terrestrial escapes sited in the wholesome countryside. Chapter 24 is the most important escape of the series that precedes her departure to Heaven. This time she is avoiding the Vanity Fair of the races, and the not very menacing Punch and Judy men. Her grandfather imagines 'a crowd of persons stealing towards them beneath the cover of the bushes', and Nell magnanimously reassures him: 'her heart swelled within her, and animated her with new strength and fortitude.' He hears a noise. '"A bird," said the child, "flying into the wood, and leading the way for us to follow."' They follow, Nell in her lightness soaring and stealing through the wood.

> When they rose up from the ground, and took the shady track which led them through the wood, she bounded on before; printing her tiny footsteps in the moss, which rose elastic from so light a pressure and gave it back as mirrors throw off breath; and thus she lured the old man on, with many a backward look and merry beck, now pointing stealthily to some lone bird as it perched and twittered on a branch that strayed across their path, now stopping to listen to the songs that broke the happy silence, or watch the sun as it trembled through the leaves, and stealing in among the ivied trunks of stout old trees, opened long paths of light. As they passed onward, parting the boughs that clustered in their way, the serenity which the child had first assumed, stole into her breast in earnest . . .

Here is the wood, and the bird, which literature has used to speak of deliverances, and a language which might appear to be locked, as in a kind of stammer or paroxysm, in suggestions of soaring and stealing. There could hardly be a smaller stock of words for what Dickens says here at some length, flown—as on the wings of a dove—with a sense of what it has been customary to say. Soon after this, when the wanderers have witnessed the death of the schoolmaster's favourite pupil, Nell 'stole away to bed', and 'did not perhaps sufficiently consider to what a bright and happy existence those who die young are borne'.[8]

Nell's earthly escapes are carried out in secrecy, and the figurative sense of the verb to steal is used constantly. She steals over and over again from her enemies. But then, in a shocking scene, the old man, a compulsive gambler, steals literally from Nell.[9] One night she is lying awake in a 'strange place', a bleak house, rambling and suspicious. She has glimpsed someone 'stealing through the passage down stairs'. When, 'at last, sleep gradually stole upon her,' her dreams are of falling from towers. She wakes with a start.

> A figure was there. Yes, she had drawn up the blind to admit the light when it should dawn, and there, between the foot of the bed and the dark casement, it crouched and slunk along, groping its way with noiseless hands, and stealing round the bed. She had no voice to cry for help, no power to move, but lay still, watching it.
>
> On it came—on, silently and stealthily, to the bed's head. The breath so near her pillow, that she shrunk back into it, lest those wandering hands should light upon her face. Back again it stole to the window—then turned its head towards her.
>
> The dark form was a mere blot upon the lighter darkness of the room, but she saw the turning of the head, and felt and knew how the eyes looked and the ears listened. There it remained, motionless as she. At length, still keeping the face towards her, it busied its hands in something, and she heard the chink of money.
>
> Then, on it came again, silent and stealthy as before . . .

The figure replaces 'the garments it had taken' and crawls out. The wandering hands, which might seem like those of a seducer, have proved to be those of a thief, and the thief has proved to be her grandfather. His actions here have their effect on the figure of speech which has stammered out the sentiment of the book: the metaphor of stealth. We may think that these figures embrace. The previous accumulation of figurative 'steals', and their presence on this occasion, make the literal sense, as the occasion enacts it, even stranger than the fiction intends.

It is a fiction in which isolation, wandering, are pictured warmly but by no means unequivocally. Quilp's separation from mankind is evidently (though enjoyably) monstrous: but there is a taint of hostility in Nell's grandfather too, which shows itself when he is 'separated' from her in spirit by his compulsion. When the broken old man later implores Nell not to 'steal away alone'—something she has been in the habit of doing throughout the book—we may reflect that the same flight has produced separate and contrasting stealths. At no point are we ever likely to doubt that there existed a connection for Dickens between flight and stealth and theft. On another occasion, when 'the first idea that flashed upon her mind was flight, instant flight,' she 'stole to the room where the money was': not to steal the waxworks money, but to check that her grandfather had not stolen it.[10] And the hint of this connection which is whispered in the figurative use of 'steal' for romantic purposes may be thought to have come true when the old man lifts the 'little hoard' of the child who has been a mother to him. 'Steal' has been one of sentimentality's customary words, and such users of the word may be recognized by their unwillingness to acknowledge a literal sense. In this book, Dickens is willing. But he is also willing to talk, as sentimental writers do, of the higher plane of the consolatory heaven to which heroines steal away alone.

Nell has a sharp little sister in *Our Mutual Friend*, published at the end of Dickens's life in 1864. This is Jenny Wren, the crippled dolls' dressmaker. Each of these small females is enlarged and enskied: each is the leaver of a London of waifs and strays which is both baleful and vivacious. Lizzie, blamed by her brother for her 'romantic ideas', for 'giving herself up to the dressmaker', suffers the distress to which such ideas refer. Bella is taken from her estranged parents and farmed out to an affluence which threatens to betray her. The secretive man she marries is an orphan who inherits a fortune. The young die in their fortunate fashion, and there is an insulted elderly Jew: designed as a recompense for Fagin, Riah belongs to the chosen few of his religion while serving as mentor and mascot to the sentimental chosen few. Miss Podsnap is estranged from her parents, and is the victim of her father's view of what the 'young person' should be like. She must not be put to the blush by indelicacy, but is for ever bursting into blushes: 'There appeared to be no line of demarcation between the young person's excessive innocence and another person's guiltiest knowledge.' The pathos of Miss Podsnap has its funny side, but this is a humour of genius which does not mock her, and which creates an innocence which is neither excessive nor sentimental: 'it was not wonderful that now, when she was on most days solemnly tooled through the park by the side of her mother in a great tall custard-coloured phaeton, she showed above the apron of that vehicle like a dejected young person sitting up in bed to take a startled look at things in general, and very strongly desiring to get her head under the counterpane again.'[11]

Riah advises Lizzie that there are times when 'the most heroic bravery is flight,' and she flies to the country. Not every 'journey of escape' in the book makes as much sense. Betty Higden's makes romantic pathos instead, and is as much a departure from the world as a principled refusal of the poorhouse. The romantic ideas which are treated in the book refer to the deliverance from distress of those who go out of the world, and they also refer to those who go up in it. Here for once is an English novel in which the efforts of a schoolmaster and his favourite pupil, in which the aerodynamic power of education, are coldly pictured. So how are its characters to go up in the world? Inheritance is exposed, for some, as fairy gold, but for the virtuous it turns into solid coin. Critics who have made out in the novel the proposition that money and miserliness are the root of all evil overlook the large amounts which are donated to the right people. The bad faith to be discovered in romance, and in the cultivation of sentiment, is plain enough here.

Jenny Wren flies from the world by ascending to a roof-garden in London, in the City. She has seen visions of angelic children let down from Heaven like so many sunbeams, in slanting rows. The children would ask: 'Who is this in pain?' And Jenny would answer: 'Oh, my blessed children, it's poor me. Have pity on me. Take me up and make me light.' To be suspended up there in the garden is to levitate rather than soar: but the experience is heavenly. To be up there, she tells the crook Fledgeby, is to 'feel as if you were dead'. How does that feel? asks the crook. She holds up a 'transparent' hand.

> 'Oh, so tranquil!' cried the little creature, smiling. 'Oh, so peaceful and so thankful! And you hear the people who are alive, crying, and working, and calling to one another down in the close dark streets, and you seem to pity them so! And such a chain has fallen from you, and such a strange good sorrowful happiness comes upon you!'

Fledgeby is not among the sentimental chosen few. In the course of this scene—one of romance's most exotic and excessive set-pieces, and not the only one to be set in a kind of penthouse—he is rated 'not dead', and told to 'Get down to life!' When Riah mounts to the roof, the little creature, as good as glorified, calls to him: 'Come up and be dead!'[12]

When some sufferer fails to be magnanimous, Dickens can be severe. Virtuous John Harmon, alias Rokesmith, is allowed without reproof to beat up the one-legged Wegg for being greedy, on the glad occasion when the principal fortune in the book is redistributed among the deserving. Dickens feels for Jenny, but not for her alcoholic father, the semblance of his own father, and of Nell's grandfather—like him, the bad child of an escorting little creature. Much of the sentiment in the book adheres, but in contrasting ways, to relations between parents and children. A remarkable scene ensues when Bella is united with her lover Rokesmith, and with her father, during the lunch hour at her father's office in the City, not far from the roof-garden. Before Rokesmith arrives, Bella makes love, as she is given to doing, with her father, 'the Cherub': 'stealing her arm a little closer about him and at the same time sticking up his hair with an irresistible propensity to play with him . . .'. It is the Cherub, not her lover, who receives her more sensual caresses: 'Bella's hand stole gradually up his waistcoat to his neck.' A comparable wandering hand and erotic 'steal' appear elsewhere—when Eugene Wrayburn, desiring poor Lizzie but still unable to make up his mind to marry her, seeks to send his arm 'stealing round her waist'. She gives a look which troubles his 'better nature'.[13] At long last, rank is thrown down and he marries his oarswoman, but not before he has been injured by a rival and brought to death's door.

He is 'changed' by his marriage, and ends up 'not much disfigured' by the attack, and with a 'glow that shone upon him . . . as though he had never been mutilated'. He has risen above himself, and married beneath him, like the less exalted Swiveller; he has something of the same bachelor style and cultural formation, and is saved in the same way. They take part in love affairs which are among the few in Dickens which are moving. Each is, like John Chivery, a great-hearted London lover, and Wrayburn very nearly dies in the discharge of his act of magnanimity. Pathos is made palpably erotic by this narrow escape. There is an intimation here of that replacement of love by loss which has been ascribed to Dickens, and an approach to the romantic idea that love and death are dualistically interchangeable.

These are all transgressive 'steals'. As such, they are different from the 'steals' lavished in *The Old Curiosity Shop*, which don't excite more than the tremor of a sense of transgression or threat except when they occur in the context of the robbery. We may assume that, for Dickens, Wrayburn's caress has the character of an offence, and that the caresses which her father obtains from Bella do not: and yet Bella's matter more, and the same language of transgression is employed in both cases. 'Steal' is a word that is apt to appear sentimental where no offence can be intended. With Bella we may feel that there is something going on.

The restoration of a child to its parent drew more from Dickens than any of the loving exchanges which he describes between adults in a position to get married. Bella's marriage restores her to a second father, and she seems to recede from sexuality as a result, and indeed to shrink. All this has implications, though they are certainly obscure, for the *de haut en bas* of Dickensian hypergamy. It is almost as if marrying beneath could mean marrying a daughter too small to cause offence. Little Dorrit finds a father in Clennam, and could never have married anyone her own size—like Chivery. Little Nell behaves as a mother. But she has a heavenly father. And her narrowest escape from sexuality might seem to be impending when her grandfather steals into her bedroom.

Seldom had the young Henry James 'read a book so intensely *written*, so little seen, known, or felt' as *Our Mutual Friend*. Many now think that this is a book which *is* intensely seen, known and felt, and it is not too much to say that they stand in awe of it—of its Mississippi-like Thames, its imagination of money and waste, its powerfully invented and inventive human beings, whose energies serve, but also subdue, its escapist tendency. In 1865, when James reviewed the novel for the American journal, the *Nation*, its merits were invisible to him.[14] He thinks of it as tired and sentimental. The fantastic had been Dickens's 'great resource', but 'the fantastic, when the fancy is dead, is a very poor business.' James writes at moments like a tired businessman for whom Dickens's fancy, his poetry, has ceased to pay:

What do we get in return for accepting Miss Jenny Wren as a possible person? This young lady is the type of a certain class of characters of which Mr Dickens has made a speciality, and with which he has been accustomed to draw alternate smiles and tears, according as he pressed one spring or another. But this is very cheap merriment and very cheap pathos. Miss Jenny Wren is a poor little dwarf, afflicted, as she constantly reiterates, with a 'bad back' and 'queer legs', who makes dolls' dresses, and is for ever pricking at those with whom she converses, in the air, with her needle, and assuring them that she knows their 'tricks and their manners'. Like all Mr Dickens's pathetic characters, she is a little monster; she is deformed, unhealthy, unnatural; she belongs to the troop of hunchbacks, imbeciles, and precocious children who have carried on the sentimental business in all Mr Dickens's novels; the little Nells, the Smikes, the Paul Dombeys.

Here, half-way through the Victorian age, is a displeasure, that of an ambitious young writer, at Dickens's pathos, and his taste for the weak and the weird. (His precocious children are less fantastic than James thinks: common life has long been familiar with little adults—not all of them doomed.) Despite appearances, James is not really responding to the end or exhaustion of a talent, but to Dickens as he has been all along, to the writer whose sentimental business had from the first been a main feature of his work, and can't be said to have got worse, or to have changed profoundly, over the long interval between Nell and Jenny Wren. Since the start of the century, however, sentimentality itself had changed. If it had once been the mark of choice spirits at leisure, disposed in knots and nests about the upper slopes of financial security, it had now come to characterize the mass audiences of the modern world—those people, for instance, who went in droves to watch plays of a kind that James could not write, displeased as he was by such audiences, and fearful of them. Pathos could now be held, by writers who agreed with him, to be old-fashioned and cheap.

Thirty years later, at the very end of the century, James set to work on a novel, *The Wings of the Dove*, which has some of the same themes as *The Old Curiosity Shop* and *Our Mutual Friend*: sickness, suffering, death, innocence and conspiracy, love and money. By this time, it would appear, the old celestial sky had moved away. An immensity of space had rushed in. The 'boon of a contingent world'—James's words, in one of his stories—had lost much of its promise. But it would be wrong to say that there was now no trace of a feeling for victims, or for escape. James's title, with its words from the 55th Psalm, admits an interest in these matters.

His biographer, Leon Edel, has written that James was describing himself when he spoke of the compulsive travellers of modern times: according to Edel, James was someone 'in search of, in flight from, something or other'. James fled from America to England in search of romance, shaking with, that romantic thing, 'tenderness'. And it was James, not Dickens, who declared: 'To the young, the early dead, the baffled, the defeated, I don't think we can be tender enough.' In his story 'The Altar of the Dead', where we learn that there is no longer the 'boon of a contingent world', there nevertheless occurs an 'immense escape from the actual', experienced by someone 'bereft': and if we talk of a necrophile Dickens, we should not forget the worship of the dead, the withdrawal from the world, the candles and purity, to be wondered at in this work. We may take this as evidence that James was a romantic writer, at a time when romance could appear to have slipped down among the vulgar masses, and to the lower orders of literature. It was a time when it could be held that opinions were no business of the artist, and a violence to the mind, and James held that he held no opinions at all. But this is itself an opinion, and a romantic one, and it was not the only romantic opinion to which he was to yield. He held that *The Wings of the Dove* is 'a "love-story" of a romantic tinge'.[15]

Milly Theale is an orphan princess. That is to say, she is an American heiress, abroad and almost alone in Europe, who finds she is suffering from a fatal illness. She is said to commemorate a cousin of James's, Minny Temple, who died young of tuberculosis—as Nell's original is also said to have done. Milly makes friends with Kate Croy, who is secretly engaged to Merton Densher. Densher, another American, is depicted as poor, which means that he lacks a fortune and lives off his job as a London journalist. Kate leads him into a plot whereby he is to make friends with Milly, whom he likes, in order that the lovers may benefit financially. The plot miscarries. Milly dies and leaves money to Densher, but it is doubtful whether it will be accepted. There is no doubt that this outcome has estranged the lovers.

These girls are orphans (Kate's mother is dead, and she is rejected by her low father), and opposites. The bequest portrays Milly, though not very clearly, as sensitive and considerate in the mercy of her means: but it does not succeed in making her what the mischievous if not monstrous Kate has been throughout—interesting. Interest is assigned to Milly adjectivally, and as a matter of opinion; it is scarcely 'dramatized', in the sense approved by James's theory of fiction. The author teases and exploits, while seeming to share, her friend Mrs Stringham's sense of her as an orphan princess: Mrs Stringham is a romantic-sentimental New England novelist with a corner in perceptive heroines. Milly is exclaimed over as 'beautiful' and 'great', which may partly mean that she is a poor little rich girl, with the interest that attaches to her wealth and sad fate: her Christian name suggests the first of these attributes, and her surname the second, with its hints of 'feel', 'steal' and some stricken bird. She is the picture of innocence that we might come across in a fairy-tale or flight of fancy. As such, she need not perhaps be expected to prove an interesting character, of a kind we might hope for in a novel. And she is not. Of James's 'unspotted princess' Leavis says: 'she isn't there.' Of Nell, as we have seen, he says the same thing: 'there's nothing there.' According to Leavis, the fuss about Milly has 'the effect of an irritating sentimentality'.[16] Later readers, whether or not they share his disappointment and irritation, are unlikely to have lost the sense that the Nellicide of the one writer and the Millicide of the other are alike sentimental—an expense of spirit, a white smear.

James's Notebooks contain his thoughts about the novel he was planning in which Milly would figure.[17] She was to be 'pathetic in her doom' and 'tragic young despair'. This was a 'poor girl', a 'poor thing'. If Dickens's late fantastic and pathetic had been a poor business for James when he was young, the late James did not mind proposing to do what he could with pathos in *The Wings of the Dove.* At the same time, it is obvious from the Notebook entries that the novel was to have a further interest of a different sort. If there was to be pathos, there was also to be conspiracy. James's plot would be Kate's plot; the interest of the novel would be the interest attracted by stratagem and suspicion, and, one might add, by an art—James's art of fiction—which was equipped to make the most of such matters. Conspiratorial stealth forms part of the romance we find in the novel; with the single exception of the lovers' encounter in Venice, its principal scenes contribute very little to any love-story which brings together a living man and woman.

According to the entries, the outcome would be such that the exquisiteness of the dead girl would reveal to Densher 'how little exquisite' was the girl who had survived. James expresses the view that a young man who gets engaged ought to have 'means', and there is much in the book to suggest that this means private means, if not a fortune. We are told in the novel that Densher's conviction of a 'want of means' and prospects had been absolute, and we appear to be invited to take the view that it is not vulgar of the vulgar Mrs Lowder, Kate's aunt, to hold his poverty against him. When Densher is humiliated by his part in Kate's plot, James writes with some shade or other of irony: 'One had come to a queer pass when a servant's opinion mattered.'[18] Mrs Lowder's opinion matters in the novel, and it mattered to James, an author of means for whom serious poverty could not be among the very interesting misfortunes. The shabbiness of Selah Tarrant in *The Bostonians*, for all that his first name may recall the Psalms, is more odious than miserable, and almost as odious as his dishonesty. But James was certainly interested in the higher poverty, in stratagems of escape from it, and in Merton Densher, who is not shabby, and who incorporates a consciousness of Morton Fullerton, the lover of Edith Wharton, herself a poor little rich girl of a kind.

Kate imagines Milly as 'an angel with a thumping bank account'. She goes on: 'Her fortune's absolutely huge.' Mrs Lowder enjoys 'the perfection of the pathos' as she contemplates Milly's death: 'very much as a stout citizen's wife might have sat, during a play that made people cry, in the pit or the family-circle'. This is a reference to the type of play James could not write, and to sentimentality as a fault of large numbers of people. Mrs Lowder also responds to 'the mere *money* of her'—'as fairly giving poetry to the life Milly clung to'. Such a feeling for the poetry of money is not, however, confined to the mercenary Mrs Lowder: it is part of what must be meant to make Milly 'stupendous' for the reader, who can't always tell the difference between superlatives directed at Milly by the author and those directed at her in the novel by vulgar connoisseurs of pathos. She is praised to the skies in a book which can sometimes appear to be about the misfortunes of a fortune.

'Some ethereal creature, against whom powers of darkness

were plotting'—this is the humour of *Villette*,[19] an irony of its narrator, and it is a form of words which fits *The Wings of the Dove* quite as well as it fits *The Old Curiosity Shop*, which precedes *Villette* by a decade, and in which an assault on innocence and a stupendous early death, that of some ethereal and transparent creature, are no less important than they are in the James. These features are a stock-in-trade of Victorian fiction, and are far from absent from *Villette*. As a stock-in-trade, they were distressing to James: but they are present in *The Wings of the Dove*. This is a book about a plot, but it is also a book about the ethereal creature who is the victim of that plot, and who acts as a conductor of the pathos which James abhorred and which he set himself to achieve. It is a book by a writer of whom it is possible to say that he is conscious of a literature that precedes him, and that Dickens's fancy, when that fancy was alive, and the death of Little Nell, formed part of his resources. Nelly and Milly resemble one another, and for some twentieth-century critics of the nineteenth-century novel, they have both been nothings. Those who die young are unloved by such critics, for whom Nelly and Milly are not there, and for whom Heaven is not there either.

Milly's appearance on the great stage of Europe is studied at one point through the eyes of Mrs Stringham, who attends to her 'exceptionally red' hair and 'remarkably black' clothes (Milly is in mourning), thereby imparting—to a legend, or a lacuna—a flash of character and interest.

> It was New York mourning, it was New York hair, it was a New York history, confused as yet, but multitudinous, of the loss of parents, brothers, sisters, almost every human appendage, all on a scale and with a sweep that had required the greater stage; it was a New York legend of affecting, of romantic isolation, and, beyond everything, it was by most accounts, in respect to the mass of money so piled on the girl's back, a set of New York possibilities. She was alone, she was stricken, she was rich, and, in particular, she was strange—a combination in itself of a nature to engage Mrs Stringham's attention.[20]

Alone, stricken, rich, strange: Milly is these things for her sentimental companion. But Milly is these things for the writer as well. *His* attention is engaged by them. Mrs Stringham, for whom there is no orphan like an American orphan, is permitted to tinge with romance a work already imbued with it. James treats with condescension poor Mrs Stringham's idea of an orphan princess: but Mrs Stringham's romantic things were romantic for him too. For James, wealth was a romantic thing, and a golden bowl a supremely interesting thing. In *The Wings of the Dove* romance, like pathos, is both abhorred and achieved.

For the interval before Milly's death in Venice, she is lodged, as befits a romantic heroine on her way out of nature, at an elevation from the common ground. Here again, James is explicit concerning the romantic possibilities, and impossibilities, which can be imputed to Milly's fate. The weasel-like Lord Mark, bent on disclosing to her the secret engagement between Densher and Kate, has found her in a 'susceptible' mood, and she turns out to be susceptible to a romantic view of her own situation. James speaks of 'the perfection of the charm', a charm full of a certain poetry, and Milly speaks of 'the impossible romance'. The charm, the romance, of what? Of an idea which

> became an image of never going down, of remaining aloft in the divine, dustless air, where she would hear but the plash of the water against stone. The great floor on which they moved was at an altitude, and this promoted the rueful fancy. 'Ah, not to go down—never, never to go down!' she strangely sighed to her friend.[21]

Milly's 'never to go down' may be compared with Jenny Wren's 'come up and be dead': the London roof-garden and the Venetian *piano nobile* have the appearance of antechambers to the heaven in which James does not seem to have believed, and in which he does not here pretend to believe. But if he does not pretend to believe, the passage can nevertheless be judged to accommodate itself to what survived of the belief in the world to which his fictions were addressed. 'I stay up,' Milly says: this is her 'characteristic poetry', as identified on a previous occasion by Mrs Stringham, with reference to her friend's ethereal capacity to appear 'exalted' into a 'vague golden air that left irritation below' (and that would irritate F. R. Leavis). On this previous occasion, James suggests that the poetry is really Mrs Stringham's. But it is also his. It is seen as preferable to the financial poetry imputed by Mrs Lowder, in which, again, James may be thought to participate, but of which the novel does more to enable the reader to disapprove.

Recognizable in this scene, and in Milly's terminal state, is a Jamesian sublime which radiates an after-sense of the heaven that human beings had hoped to reach. And there is a Freudian sublime which, in this respect at least, can be recognized as contemporary with it. The Freudian sublime stood for the progress of mankind, for the upper storeys of the mind, for the ascents of a particular life from the sensual plane to that of the social and spiritual. Neither of these writers held out any hope of heaven, and Freud's work started a new scepticism about the progress of mankind towards a triumph of the top storey: his work had been confined, he said in old age, to 'the *parterre* and basement of the building'.[22] In the case of both writers, nevertheless, there survived an after-sense of the after-life in the form of a language and sentiment of the higher plane, and of a respect for virtues which had once given assurance of salvation. This isn't all they had in common. Neither of them held out very much hope that a servant's opinion might matter. Here, too, we may be aware of the imagination of the higher plane.

Early in James's novel, dining in luxury amid 'every English accessory', and accompanied by Mrs Stringham in the role, as he notes, of fairy godmother, this Cinderella scarcely 'knew where she was: the words marking her first full sense of a situation really romantic'. It could be said that, uncertain of her whereabouts, Milly has gone out of this world. It could also be said that she has gone up in the world. She has here acceded to the romance of uppity old England, with its golden bowls, which are always liable to reveal a fatal flaw. On the subject of Milly, Mrs Stringham reflects: 'One could never tell, with her, where romance would come in.' It comes in when Milly perceives that, as a possible marriage partner, Densher is disliked by Kate's unworthy sister, because of 'the state of his fortunes'. That is to say, 'he has no "private means".' The inverted commas may appear to attribute the thought to the sister, but it is one to which, as we have seen, the author could also be susceptible, in the 'privacy' of his Notebooks. It is a thought to which Milly is hostile, and to which romance is hostile. Here and elsewhere, the novel engages in a definition and critique of the romantic.

Milly's medical consultations are an instance of this, and of not much else. The great doctor whom she visits behaves in a fashion that makes the extolling of his powers read almost like sarcasm at the expense of his profession. His work has made him rich and tactful. 'Her only doubt, her only fear, was whether he wouldn't take advantage of her being a little romantic to treat her as romantic altogether.' We may say that the author of the book was no less unwilling to be treated in this fashion. Milly and Amy Dorrit have, and invite, feelings of a kind that might lead one to think of them as a little romantic. They are, indeed, little romantics. But both authors are at pains to keep their distance from certain stock romantic conceptions. Milly is aware of her 'queer little history' but doesn't want to be treated solely in such terms. And yet in James's treatment of her such terms recur: 'little', 'queer', 'odd', 'strange', 'unaccountable'. He can't be thought to have kept his distance from romantic magnanimity and the enlargement of minuteness.

The old idea of escape is brought into service for most of the novel's main characters. Densher wishes at the outset to 'escape': 'From everything.' He is at any rate inveigled into trying to escape from his poverty. Kate remarks in the same discussion that she has 'wished to escape Aunt Maud'—Mrs Lowder. Soon Mrs Stringham reflects that, 'for her princess', there could be no 'sharp or simple release from the human predicament. It wouldn't be for her a question of a flying leap and thereby of a quick escape.' She then likens her friend to a mine: 'The mine but needed working and would certainly yield a treasure.' James has to explain: 'She was not thinking, either, of Milly's gold.' Kate and Densher *are* thinking of it. Their escapes depend upon stealth and theft.[23]

The wings of the dove were a well-known emblem of romantic escape. But James uses it in such a way as to move it some distance from its customary meaning, and Leon Edel has noticed that the title of the novel refers not only to the 55th Psalm but to the 67th: 'yet shall ye be as the wings of a dove covered with silver, and her feathers with yellow gold.'[24] Early in the book, Kate tells Milly: 'you're a dove.' Later, Kate reiterates the praise—impressed, Densher feels, by that 'element of wealth' in Milly which was 'a great power, and which was dove-like only so far as one remembered that doves have wings and wondrous flights, have them as well as tender tints and soft sounds.'

Densher knows here that the wings of such a dove may be 'spread' for the protection of others; in the last scene of all, he knows that such wings may 'cover' people.[25]

'Our dear dove,' sighs Aunt Maud when the news of Milly's death reaches London, 'has folded her wonderful wings.' 'Unless it's more true,' she resumes, 'that she has spread them the wider.' Densher is pained by her words, one of which had once been his:

He again but formally assented, though, strangely enough, the words fitted an image deep in his own consciousness. 'Rather, yes—spread them the wider.'

'For a flight, I trust, to some happiness greater—'

'Exactly. Greater.' Densher broke in; but now with a look, he feared, that did, a little, warn her off.'[26]

He fears that he has a little warned her off suggesting that Milly, who had been a little romantic, is now a Little Nell. But he is, we may think, very much more afraid of the hint that Milly's cheque may cover him.

In the last scene, Kate and Densher face each other out over the cheque which their friend has bequeathed. The protective dove reappears on the page, with Kate recalling Densher's desire to 'escape everything'. Milly was, the two agree, 'stupendous'; and the cheque is unlikely to be meagre. Kate says: 'I used to call her, in my stupidity—for want of anything better—a dove. Well, she stretched out her wings, and it was to *that* they reached. They cover us.' But he doesn't want to be covered by the cheque. Densher declines it—and for Kate to accept it would be to decline Densher. She charges him with a worship of the dead, of his enfolding dove, and it is hard to feel that she is altogether wrong. The happy dead are not very far off. The heavens do not and cannot open up. But love and death are—for the length and the sake of an ending—one.

Ethereally present in the novel is a traditional language—the heavenly language of sensibility. The story of a conspiracy is thereby raised to the skies. *The Wings of the Dove* is the work of a specialist in refinements of feeling, and of dissembling, which concerns itself, however sceptically at times, with the old issues of romantic pathos and escape, and of romantic elevation, and enlargement, and diminution. The use to which it puts such words as 'poetry' and 'strange' argues for the presence in the novel of a certain conventionality of outlook: 'poetry' here can suggest purity and departure, and 'strange' can suggest—by way of an after-sense similar to that which still survives for the word 'fey'—the imminent and early death which is plotted by this author and plotted over in his novel. It is clear that we are not yet in that modern world where sensibility's traditional terms are widely distrusted, where 'imbecile', 'pathetic', and 'sentimental' are insults.

What there is of duality in the novel is an aspect and extension of the concerns embodied in this language, and has to do with the theft which the novel so insinuatingly evokes, with the two faces of the two thieves; and with the orphan antithesis constituted by Milly and Kate. The antithesis reflects a difference between the two nations to which the writer successively and dividedly belonged. The plot against Milly is Europe's plot against America. That the plotters are more interesting, and more romantic, than the little romantic who is their victim indicates a reason for James's flight from his native country. At the same time, the novel is pledged to that country, to an American innocence. On the subject of innocence and experience, as on the subject of pathos and of the tender tints of romance, James was in more than one mind. He was elsewhere to make more deliberate use of the conventions of duality, and on occasions when national differences count for even more than they do here.

Four years before, in 1895, James had written *The Spoils of Poynton*, where a virtuous orphan may at times be thought the accessory to a theft. Fleda Vetch is that traditional thing, the motherless girl who is more than 'a mere little flurried bundle of petticoats'. She deserves 'consideration', and receives it from an author whose sense of the action is hard to infer, and to distinguish from Fleda's. She is a 'free spirit', James was to point out—sensitive rather than practical.[27] She steals and she soars. Her flights are those of the imagination, and they allow her to glide from West Kensington to the great houses of Waterbath and Poynton and look down on the dramas enacted there. But then she has her 'sudden drops', in the form of setbacks which deposit her at 'the bottom of the heap': this is where the poor are sometimes said to be, and this is a work which calls them 'smelly' and 'smutty'. Fleda's flights are powered by her 'magnanimity'.[28]

James had found 'interesting' a story told him of a mother and son rowing over their works of art, their household gods. In the work of art which grew from this, Owen Gareth has rights to the spoils of Poynton—though James could privately suppose that such rights were an injustice to widows—and Owen's mother 'steals' the spoils. Fleda has fallen in love, and is to conspire, with Owen, who has become engaged to someone else. Mrs Gareth's burglary of Poynton causes Fleda to exclaim: 'You've operated with a quickness—and with a quietness!' Mrs Gareth echoes her friend's apparent praise for this specimen of what the friend knows to be a 'class of operations essentially involving the protection of darkness', and is elated by the manner of its carrying-off, with the aid of stalwarts from the Tottenham Court Road: 'as brilliant a stroke as any commemorated in the annals of published crime'. But Fleda is to strive for the restoration of the spoils. Her 'great flight', at the centre of the novel, is equated with the attempt, in 'magnanimity', to respect the interests of the philistine Mona, who won't marry Owen unless the spoils are restored. Fleda has wanted to help Owen 'live as a gentleman' by pursuing his engagement, and to 'reinstate him in his rights'. She comes to want Mona to renounce Owen, rather than the other way round. The things are returned to Poynton. According to Mrs Gareth, Mona has 'taken means', powerful and horrible means, to marry Owen. '"She knew how," said Mrs Gareth,' for whom Mona is 'a brute', and who tells Fleda: 'She did what you wouldn't!'[29] But it is more than possible that Owen has been taking means to marry Mona—means which are misjudged by a romantic heroine, a woman of feeling, whose secret love for the heir to an estate does not succeed. James can once more be seen as a critic and ironist, and as an exponent, of the language of sensibility.

XI. QUEER FELLOWS

During the Eighties and Nineties of the last century duality underwent a revival which carried the subject, together with its predicated psychic state, into the century that followed. During these years, which are sometimes mistaken for the inaugural years of the subject, a hunger for pseudonyms, masks, new identities, new conceptions of human nature, declared itself. Men became women. Women became men. Gender and country were put in doubt: the single life was found to harbour two sexes and two nations. Femaleness and the female writer broke free; the New Woman, and the Old, adventured into fiction, and might be found to hold hands there, as sisters. James's tale of 1894, 'The Death of the Lion', describes an age in which there seemed to be three sexes, an age tormented by genders and pronouns and pen-names, by the identity of authors, by the 'he' and the 'she' and the 'who' of it all. Proteus stole down the back streets of the Late Victorian Babylon, and his portrait came to life. Anglo-America, and well beyond, rang to the cry of Robert Louis Stevenson's Dr Jekyll: 'This, too, was myself.'[1]

A daring dualistic fellowship was convened among the writers of the time, and included Stevenson and his compatriot William Sharp, alias Fiona Macleod—Flying Scotsmen of the Fin-de-Siècle, virtuosos of the principled double life. Sharp's may have been the more radical self-severance. Stevenson was a divided man, and his *Strange Case of Dr Jekyll and Mr Hyde* was to prove a hugely influential book. The project of 'separation' which it celebrates was to be one of the wonders of the world. But perhaps it should be said that what Stevenson projected Sharp performed.

One day in 1889, some three years after the appearance of *Jekyll and Hyde*, a party of strangers was observed making its way along the main street of the port of Apia on the South Sea island of Samoa. Apia was known as 'the Hell of the Pacific', and this was the rainy season. The street looked out on a coral reef and a bay: access to the bay was blocked by the hulks of German and American naval craft, sunk by a hurricane. One of the party was a sallow male scarecrow of about forty, whose ailing look bore a kind of charm or promise. There was a woman in a straw hat, with a guitar, a young man with a ukulele who wore gold ear-rings and glasses tinted dark blue. Rovers? Beachcombers? Hopeful travellers? Holy drop-outs? An Anglican missionary guessed them to be a variety troupe, come from San Francisco to sing to whatever audience could be gleaned from the island's community of European masters and derelicts and Polynesian chiefs and estate workers. No. This was Stevenson, his American wife Fanny, and Fanny's son, Lloyd Osbourne.

Before long, the party presented a different aspect. At Vailima they set themselves up in a grand house—referred to by Stevenson as Abbotsford, after Walter Scott's grand house—on an estate with a pair of waterfalls. They took sides in the quarrels of the island's native patriciate, which were entangled with contentions between the interested colonial powers, and they were waited on by a household of native servants, the males handsome and colourfully skirted with bare brown torsos and loyal hearts. When Stevenson died five years later, his Samoans toiled with the corpse to the summit of a mountain and buried it there. A photograph shows a Swiss Family Robinson and the entourage of a governor-general at one of the further-flung outposts of empire. Stevenson was a drop-out who was also a chief, a wanderer who was able to live off his royalties and who ended his days as a landed proprietor. Having fought in his youth with his patriarchal father, he was to turn into a childless colonial paterfamilias. Travels with a donkey, adventures among the doxies of the Edinburgh underworld, did not keep him from serving as a lion of the Savile Club in London, or from joining a set of diners-out for whom the cultivation of Art and Style was a species of propriety, rather than the road to Reading Gaol. Henley wrote a poem about the aspects presented by his friend—who was Ariel but also the Shorter Catechist, and so on.

Stevenson's refusal of the ways of the Edinburgh bourgeoisie led him to behave not only as a pleasure-lover but as someone recognizably different—a man who could say that had he had his time over again he would have wanted to 'honour Sex more religiously'.[2] This was a time when such things were said. But there has never been a time when people have not been told that the pursuit of pleasure is reprehensible: the pleasure-lover's books make a point of saying this too, and can sound like a sermon. In the story 'Olalla' a Spanish woman drawn as the embodiment of a mind-melting sensuality is forsaken on the grounds that there is bad blood in her, and that she is the descendant of a line of hidalgos guilty of unspeakable cruelties. 'Olalla' preaches that 'pleasure is not an end, but an accident; that pain is the choice of the magnanimous; that it is best to suffer all things and do well.'[3] Sentiments which his father might have applauded. And yet this was a son who felt himself at one point to be murdering his father.

Henry Jekyll's 'Statement' or 'confession' explains that he had been torn between 'gaiety' and 'gravity', and tells how, by means of a magic medicinal compound, he has gleefully separated off that part of his nature—his 'original evil'—whose pleasures were shameful. When he first takes the powder, he shrinks to the stature of a child—and the very motions of Poe's William Wilson: 'I stole through the corridors, a stranger in my own house; and coming to my room, I saw for the first time the appearance of Edward Hyde.' Jekyll welcomes what he finds in the mirror. 'This, too, was myself.' Hyde then behaves like a schoolboy who attacks his father by destroying his portrait. The other exemplary acts performed in the ensuing delirium by the monster to whom Jekyll has given birth ('Jekyll had more than a father's interest; Hyde had more than a son's indifference') are acts of cruelty which look more like boorishness than sadism. But Dr Jekyll has taken 'pleasure' in releasing within himself a bad son whose only speakable pleasures have to do with the infliction of pain. Hyde's pleasures are not made in the least compelling. There is none of that compounding of pleasure and pain which was discovered for the period by Swinburne and others. Equally, we are very far from any honouring of Sex religiously.[4]

Most of the many readings to which the fable is prone are such as to yield the outlines of a filial ambivalence on Stevenson's part. This is true even of the recourse to phylogeny whereby Hyde is construed as an ape as well as a rebellious son, and an evolutionary Jekyll is seen to use chemistry in order to expel an animal nature. In another fable of the time,

Wells's Dr Moreau uses surgery on beasts in order to 'burn out' the animal in them. Such attempts are the backward looks of advanced writers. The superstitions of such writers are a feature of the romantic tradition, where hellfire casts a sunset glow—as on the burning, blushing sensorium of the early nineteenth century—and there is talk of pain and punishment and purification. D.H. Lawrence was eventually to use the buggery of women so that a 'burning-out' of shame might be achieved.

Jekyll's 'Statement' reads: 'It was on the moral side, and in my own person, that I learned to recognise the thorough and primitive duality of man; I saw that, of the two natures that contended in the field of my consciousness, even if I could rightly be said to be either, it was only because I was radically both.' Both natures were true. And Stevenson seems to have believed both that there were some fellows who were 'two fellows' and that, 'at times', 'every thinking creature' felt himself to be that.[5] 'Fellow' was a word of the age. It was the age of the fellow, and of the queer fellow.

Stevenson was not the only one of the queer fellows of the age to exhibit the two natures of the uncertain son—if this is what he can 'rightly be said' to have been, and if it is right to say that he seized on the fable of the double life, and on the implements of the dualistic Occult, in order to separate off the rebellious or parricidal wishes which originate, according to the modern world, in childhood. His break with his father was healed and not healed, and may have led to the celebration of the bad father in *Weir of Hermiston*, composed in the South Seas during the last months of his life. He grew up in Scotland at a high point in the history of authoritarian parenthood, at a time when middle-class life was gripped by strong rules and sanctions which only someone with a strong will might hope to defy. He admired his father to the end, but the resistance he offered when young to the Edinburgh of his father's self-will continued to recruit him. Equally, it continued to require amends, and a species of double life.

He has been considered remarkable for seeming to live out his fictions, for being Jekyll and Hyde in the form of the bourgeois drop-out who does not desert the fold, for camping on Treasure Island, and casting himself away there at the head of a Scots Family Stevenson. He is also remarkable for having been an eminent Victorian who was also an eminent bohemian. The debunking of the eminent is a branch of Gothic fiction, a matter of detecting the sexual agent within saint or sage, and Stevenson has been detected as the possessor of a strange sex life: homosexuality, impotence, a passionate feeling for his stepson, submission to a wilful and predatory wife—such charges have been pressed. Neither the facts of his life nor the fictions of his life—for all their appeal to the young, their avoidance of females and of sexual agents—make it possible to discuss with any confidence the Stevensonian secret life—if there *was* one. It is sufficient to say here that if his fictions are strange, they are strange largely in the sense of exotic and adventurous, and in the dualistic sense which has come to be emphasized in the present book: that is to say, they are images of disobedience dreamed by a loyal son. For all his rebellion, he can certainly be said to have been that. In his essays, 'style' meant playing the 'sedulous ape' to senior authors: a very different animal, or filial, from the one expelled by Jekyll. And there's obedience in the weave of *Weir of Hermiston* too, where style enables a contrite heart to pay an excessive homage to its hanging judge.

Stevenson's attentions to the theme of the double life ran to a play, written with Henley, which took a case from Scottish history and dressed it in the colours of romantic duality and adventure. *Deacon Brodie, or The Double Life* is, at the same time, an eminently respectable work: it defers to the ethos of his native town and sets its face against theft. It is worth comparing with what is otherwise known of the history it incorporates. William Brodie was hanged in 1788, at the age of 47, for his part in a gang robbery of the Excise building in Edinburgh. This burglar was a member of the Town Council, Deacon of the Wrights (joiners, cabinet-makers, coffin-makers), well-off and well-born, a descendant of Morayshire lairds—given, however, to cards and cock-fighting. In the Old Town there were two women with children by him. To the north, the New Town was going up in its grandeur—a windfall for wrights and deacons. The Town Council was both self-electing and self-employing: when the High Street was lowered in the Old Town, Brodie was entrusted with the supply of doors and locks for the shops that lined it. These were the bad old days of the

Scottish burghs, when the arch-exploiter of the municipal and Parliamentary system, the Tory potentate Henry Dundas, could say that 'it would be easier to reform Hell':[6] forty years were to pass before the Whigs attempted a harrowing. Brodie had accomplices (Smith, Brown, and Ainslie), and he had a sarcastic wit which he turned on the Kirk and which may have prompted the lifting of the University's mace. His various thefts may have been perceived as subversive or iconoclastic, and they must very soon have looked like inside jobs. When Brown informed on the gang, Brodie decamped to London, where he reported:

> My female gave me great uneasiness by introducing a flash man to me, but she assured me he was a true man, and he proved himself so, not withstanding the great reward, and was useful to me. I saw my picture six hours before exhibited to the public view, and my intelligence of what was doing at Bow Street was as good as ever I had in Edinburgh.[7]

These might themselves be the words of a flash man, or professional criminal.

Brodie acceded to folklore, though, as a kind of amateur, as an archetypal double-liver, and versions of the story published since Stevenson have maintained this approach—Forbes Bramble's *Strange Case of Deacon Brodie*, for instance, and John Gibson's *Deacon Brodie—Father to Jekyll and Hyde*.[8] These have also stressed the role of a resisted father. It is not difficult to tolerate an 'oedipal' interpretation which places *in loco parentis* a Town Council 'omnipotent, corrupt, impenetrable', in Cockburn's phrase.[9] From the standpoint of duality, however, Brodie may appear embarrassingly single—not so much oedipal as criminal. His concern for secrecy was not so much exquisite as deficient, and detrimental to his chances of remaining at large. His public character can hardly have been that of a town councillor whom few would suspect of being a thief. It was more like that of a town councillor with a known taste for low life and easy money. Arm in arm, he walked the streets with the shady-looking Smith, and can seldom have been mistaken for a Deacon Jekyll of the Wrights. He was a Dundasite, whose political mettle may possibly be gauged by the ability of his fellow citizens to believe that in taking a long time to make up his mind whether or not to support a renegade

Tory MP, Sir Laurence Dundas, he was holding out for a bribe. But when he and Smith stood trial, they were defended by Whigs—burgh reformers on the political plane, who hoped to curtail the privileges which Brodie had enjoyed. Influential friends secured as Brodie's counsel the Dean of the Faculty of Advocates, Henry Erskine: 'Now we've got the best cock that ever fought,' cried the sporting prisoner.[10] Flash to the last, a singer of songs from *The Beggar's Opera*, Brodie tried to cheat the gallows in Edinburgh—which he had helped to design—by means of a concealed steel collar and the services of a French surgeon.

Towards the close of his life, in 1894, Stevenson wrote: 'I am a fictitious article and have long known it. I am read by journalists, by my fellow-novelists, and by boys.' What genius he had was 'for hard work'.[11] Duality can itself be called a fictitious article, and yet Stevenson's own duality seldom seems blankly inauthentic. It expressed and comprised the 'feverish desire for consideration' ascribed by him to his childhood,[12] a repudiation of the father he loved and resembled, a dual nationality, pride in a masterful foreign wife, Markheim's evil genius, Jekyll's prediction that the human condition would one day be recognized as a 'mere polity of multifarious, incongruous and independent denizens'. It was a figment of his imagination. It was literary, stylish, fabulous. But it was more than that. This, too, was Stevenson. At the same time, the case may have been less strange than has been supposed. His experiences as a son, and his marriage, may have been more like those of 'every thinking creature' than has been supposed by thinking creatures with books and articles to write.

For over a hundred and fifty years Scotland had been compounded with England, and by now there were Scottish writers who passed in the course of their lives into a condition of dual nationality. Those who came to London did not cease to be Scottish, and they brought with them a native interest in the inventions which sustain the double life. Stevenson was not the only fictitious article to take flight from Scotland at this time. He was to be followed by another novelist, journalist, and romantic professional, who also acted out his books, books that avoid females and are read by boys, and who ended as a real governor-general. The later of these two fellows is Buchan. For the historian of duality, though, a different match must be made. Stevenson must be put with Sharp.

If there can be no certainty about Stevenson's sexual uncertainty or ambivalence, it is certain that this was the time for such a thing. Late Victorian duality may be identified with the dilemma, for males, of a choice between male and female roles, or of a possible union of such opposites. The Nineties School of Duality framed a dialect, and a dialectic, for the love that dared not speak its name—for the vexed question of homosexuality and bisexuality. Proteus became Narcissus, Ganymede, Danaë, and other still stranger citizens and denizens. Once upon a time there was a Flying Scotsman who became a hermaphrodite.

Sharp's practice in the matter of duality is a very strange story indeed, in which preoccupations of the past were to reawaken at a time of romantic revival, and the *Ossian* imposture was rivalled in what could well be pseudonymy's finest hour. The Anglo-Scottish writer William Sharp lit upon the presence within him of a female alter ego or true self, whom he christened Fiona Macleod and who proceeded in secret to write works of her own. It is a story which can be told to advantage with reference, not so much to the mists and twilight of Fiona's Celtic tales, as to the testimony of a douce Scots lady, Sharp's wife and cousin. Her memoir of her versatile husband was advertised by the publisher as a book about 'the dual personality which possessed the poet, William Sharp'.[13] This husband can be accounted one of the few people who have performed an act which many have been invited to perform. As his friend the poet Yeats recorded with appreciation, Sharp 'saw the sidereal body of Fiona enter the room as a beautiful young man, and became aware that he was a woman to the spiritual sight. She lay with him, he said, as a man with a woman, and for days afterwards his breasts swelled so that he had almost the physical likeness of a woman.'[14]

Sharp stood for a rebirth of Romanticism and of Celticism; and for paganism, druidism, medievalism, optimism, and sexuality ('passion'). To stand for these was to stand against Calvinism, Utilitarianism, and the modern world. But Sharp found room in that modern world for his imaginary Gaels. He looked forward to an Anglo-Celtic posterity, with no divorce from the British Empire. The day of the Gael was over; it was archaic; the Gael figures in Fiona's glooms and gloamings as a romantic waif. But this orphan had a part to play in a promising future. Sharp was opposed to the use of Celticism for racist purposes, and in the political sphere, as was happening in Ireland; and opposed to heavy talk of a 'renaissance'. Francis Hart has spoken of Sharp as moving on from Matthew Arnold's interest in Celticism towards the interest taken by Yeats. Sharp is a 'legendary moralist', rather than a 'romantic transcendentalist': 'legendary morality' is the crucial term, Hart says, for the work of Fiona. Nevertheless, it is clear that, whatever else Sharp was, he was very much the romantic transcendentalist of his day and age. He was also a romantic everyone, universally responsive, and as such a fit friend and admirer of the self-contradictory Whitman. He was a fellow who might have said as Whitman did that he was able to 'realize the meaning of that old fellow who said he was seldom less alone than when alone.' He came to look like a very eminent stage magician.[15]

A 'double strain', writes Mrs Sharp, a 'markedly dual nature', was apparent in her husband from the first; he was part Celt, part Viking; there were early wanderings in the West of Scotland, and Fiona has been thought the child of his storytelling Highland nurse and a Gaelic fisherman, Seumas Macleod. Sharp was a sailor and swimmer, but a swooner too, and ailing; he judged himself 'susceptible', and felt he had psychic powers. At school in Scotland there were 'stolen outings', and a running-away was recalled as 'my first flight for freedom'. Unable to bear a lawyer's office, he fled to London, where his two 'radical strains' were culturally accommodated. He joined the Pre-Raphaelites and wrote a life of Rossetti. According to his wife, 'rarely a day passed in which he did not try to imagine himself living the life of a woman, to see through her eyes, and feel and view life from her standpoint, and so vividly that "sometimes I forget I am not the woman I am trying to imagine."' Fiona was to enact 'the sensitive, delicate, feminine side of him'.[16] Meanwhile the other side made progress as a man of letters. In 1889, with the support of Browning, Meredith, and Pater, he considered putting in for the Chair of Literature at University College London—

now occupied by the present writer—but withdrew in distaste at the prospect of a steady job.

Fiona was not born until he had turned 38. The birth occurred in 1893, and the obstetrics may perhaps be related to a liberation experienced a few months before—to the excitements and enlargements of a second visit to Italy, commemorated in *Sospiri di Roma*, and of a friendship formed with the female dedicatee of that volume of free verse. *Pharais* was Fiona's first published work. In 1899, there occurred a further 'new birth'—that of an inner or third self, called Wilfion by Sharp's wife. Wilfion healed breaches which had opened up between Sharp and Fiona. Of, or as, his second self, Fiona, Sharp had this to say: 'I can write out of my heart in a way I could not do as William Sharp, and indeed I could not do so if I were the woman Fiona Macleod is supposed to be, unless veiled in scrupulous anonymity.' He then warmed to his confession: 'This rapt sense of oneness with nature, this *cosmic ecstasy* and elation, this wayfaring along the extreme verges of the common world, all this is so wrought up with the romance of life that I could not bring myself to expression by my outer self, insistent and tyrannical as that need is . . . My truest self, the self who is below all other selves, and my most intimate life and joys and sufferings, thoughts, emotions and dreams, *must* find expression, yet I cannot save in this hidden way.' In 1902, orphan and double, he told a close friend, a fellow lover of Italy, the Hon. Alexander Hood: 'Rightly or wrongly, I am conscious of something to be done—to be done by one side of me, by one half of me, by the true inward self as I believe—(apart from the overwhelmingly felt mystery of a dual self, and a reminiscent life, and a woman's life and nature within, concurring with and oftenest dominating the other)—and rightly or wrongly I believe that this, and the style so strangely born of this inward life, depend upon my aloofness and spiritual isolation as F.M.'[17]

His wife writes that Sharp 'seemed a different person when the Fiona mood was on him', though he could remember what Fiona had been up to—there were no amnesias. Fiona was the sum of certain moods or inclinations, which he valued above all others and set apart in secrecy and isolation—a secrecy and isolation that were, to be sure, culturally approved. In separating her off, he may have deemed himself an explorer, an astronaut of the senses, a new man, a new human specimen, a marvel of poetic engineering. What Stevenson had dreamed, Sharp, soon after, had done. If we can discount Wilfion as instrumental, as a binding or pacific element, we may want to accept Fiona as Sharp's true self: a tragic self, as has been proposed—that of a searcher in vain for a 'lost Eden'. Against this may be placed the view of the Irish mystic A.E., who declared in a letter to F.M.: 'The inner being is protean.'[18] These are rival interpretations which romantic duality had afforded for many years: the inner being as true self and as all-self. By Ernest Rhys in 1907, Sharp was invested with the Danaë-like all-self of Proteus the Poet. A romantic zealot, Rhys causes one to reflect that the proteans of the age—now you see them, now you don't—were contemporaries of the escape artist and magician Houdini. Sharp, Rhys enthused,

> was a romanticist, an illusionist . . . he had quite peculiar powers of assimilating to himself foreign associations . . . In Italy he became an Italian in spirit; in Algiers, an Arab . . .
>
> The same susceptibility marked his intercourse with his fellows. Their sensations and emotions, their whims, their very words, were apt to become his, and to be reproduced with an uncanny reality in his own immediate practice. It was natural, then, that he should be doubly sensitive to feminine intuitions.[19]

Fiona was Sharp's thrilling and enabling secret—a secret to be kept from his fellows, and yet obtained from his fellows as the outcome of a long history of clandestine practice and pretence. He pretended that she was, like his wife, a cousin of his, and that she was a recluse. His anonymity was 'scrupulous', by which this Scotsman may have meant that it was both careful and clean: but there were those who could see it as a repetition of the *Ossian* fraud, when James Macpherson had disguised himself in the robes of a Celtic bard. Anonymity had often in the past been sharp practice—it was an old recourse for duplicity, as for an affected sincerity: in this respect as in others, Sharp was an old-fashioned fissile, the product of his century's engagement with the divided mind and its manoeuvres. Most friends, including Yeats, were kept in the dark concerning the imposture, and received apologies from beyond the grave in a testamentary letter: but some were in the know, and newspapers guessed. The *Daily Chronicle* stated in 1902 that in the search for Fiona Macleod it was possible to turn to William Sharp 'and say with literal truth "Thou art beside thyself!"' It was more than the ageing George Meredith managed to say. Meredith, Fiona's 'Prince of Celtland', seems to have been a little smitten with her, and saw her as a writer of genius.[20]

Sharp dedicated and inscribed one of his books, *The Winged Destiny*, to himself—'To William Sharp from his comrade Fiona Macleod'—while continuing to publish under his own name. To stare at these handwritten words is to wonder what his game was. Did he play out a wholly inadvertent comedy of duality? Here was a virile biographer and book-reviewer who found himself—found contentment and a literary content—in the impersonation of a Gaelic female with a horror of publicity. In this impersonation there may be glimpsed, not just the search for a lost Eden, but a response to the painful difference between talent and its transcendence, between inspiration, mystery, and the professionalism of the books which he continued to write *in propria persona*. The Celtic Twilight, a movement which Fiona did much in her seclusion to promote, can be regarded as something of an adjunct to the School of Duality: this was a dusk in which ancient and modern, past and present, might meet, in which man and woman might meet within the individual, a dusk which held the half-light of the spiritual or sidereal hermaphrodite. Sharp was a decadent; he belonged to a time of indeterminate or dissident, furtive or fugitive sexuality, of adventures in London and Italy. He was a friend of the purposefully homosexual J. A. Symonds, and may himself have been bisexual, liberated. But this is a decadence which appears just as likely to have been platonic, poetic. It seems safer to say, in Sharp's strange case, that if the door to the closet now stood ajar, out slipped Narcissus. His is a case which shares an epoch with the theory of a primitive narcissism adduced by Freudians in order to explain the phenomena of the homosexual and of the double. Sharp's love-affair may chiefly have been with himself: his place in the history of self-love that of the rare bird who has been able to consummate that passion. He also has a place in the half-light of indeterminate nationality. He was a Scotsman who became a Pre-Raphaelite Englishman, a Celt, and a Mediterranean pagan who died near Mount Etna. These were changes and uncertainties suitable for embodiment in the dualistic calculus.

As situated and solicited in the Late Victorian metropolis of London, to which the adventurous were strangely and tenderly impelled, duality was an affair of expatriates. As constituted in the English-speaking world at large, the School in question was almost entirely composed of writers who knew what it was to reach decisions, or to experience difficulties, in the matter of the country to which they took themselves to belong, or in which they wished to settle: Stevenson, Sharp, Henry James, Wharton, Conrad, Wilde, Yeats. Frost, and then Eliot, whose early poetry and Modernism fall within the pale of duality, and, later still, Lowell, can be considered, in this context, their affiliates. In certain of these cases, national ambivalence and sexual ambivalence were one and the same: the change of country which came about was caused or conditioned by a search for the exotic partner, for a love that was domestically unspeakable. Romance, of course, had long ago licensed such a search. Queer fellows steal from their country of origin, and lovers do so too.

Such considerations are at any rate some guide to the more complex scene which duality had by now become: in it were Dr Jekyll's transcendental medicine, the spectacle of Sharp in Celtic drag, the Anglo-Irish mysticism of Yeats, the Anglo-American fantasies of the late James, the Anglo-Indian Kipling's metempsychoses, the ageing portrait of Dorian Gray, the Classical exoticism of Pater with its embellishment of romantic motifs, its Mediterranean Englishness, its stately talk of doubles or 'seconds'. Sensations, impressions, rained down by the moment on the aesthete's pained and privileged sensorium. A dogmatic duality was native to this bombardment, as were the themes of nationality and gender.

Yeats's double life and concern with the subject are an aspect less of the mature poetry than of the discursive prose dualistically produced by this enemy of the discursive. The subject was rehearsed in terms of the ingenuities of his magical system, while his concern appears to have been anterior to the creation of the system. His first poems strike the posture of the outcast, and are those of an adolescent, 'proud and solitary', who was to fall out with his wise and gifted father, and to treat him, so his father felt, like 'a black beetle'.[21] The parental agnosticism convinced Yeats that he could not live without religion, and he learnt to live with a religion of the Occult, and with the imagination of a Celtic, an archaic Ireland which conferred, on the grocerish reality and polity of his own time, a right of national self-determination. Despite this, he was a proud son of the Anglo-Irish Ascendancy, and loyal to the traditions of English literature. Yeats was both Ireland and its oppressor —a condition which may be thought to suit the quarrel with his father, which amounted to a 'half-revolt', as Richard Ellmann puts it, rather than a break. Ellmann's biography *The Man and the Masks* has this as the primary source for Yeats's double life, for the value he assigned to the anti-self, the mask, the perfection of a style, to the fashioning in art of a personality antithetical to the kind that preoccupies biographers: but Ellmann is aware that many other personal factors, and 'the spirit of the times', were also responsible for Yeats's programme. The marriage-bed, Yeats was to discover, could be accounted 'the symbol of the solved antinomy': but this did not dampen his ardour for antinomies. For all his half-revolt, he was not reluctant to perform grand gestures of repudiation: the paranoid oath sworn by him when he joined the hermetic Order of the Golden Dawn engaged him to 'keep secret all things connected with this Order and its secret knowledge from the whole world. . . . I further solemnly promise and swear that with the Divine permission I will from this day forward apply myself unto the GREAT WORK which is so to purify and exalt my spiritual nature that with the Divine Aid I may at length attain to be more than human. . .'. The authorization of such material has been fetched from the mists of antiquity: but it seems just as important to stress that the language and pretensions are those of the Gothic novel. Here, indeed, are the language and pretensions which are invoked and criticized in Hogg's *Confessions* and in *Peregrine Proteus*.[22]

Every man, wrote Yeats in his youth, has 'some one scene, some one adventure, some one picture that is the image of his secret life'.[23] His pursuit of contradiction and opposition and interpenetration contradicts, while also appearing to require, such claims. His pairs are plucked from a single tree, Yeats's Yggdrasil, in which are figured the integrity and paradisal self-sufficiency of the symbol, and of the Symbolist poem. Oneness can mean solitude and secrecy. It can mean the work of art which cannot and should not be violated by analysis and paraphrase. It can mean the unitary spectacle of the dance and of the tree—avatars of the work of art. But it can also mean a whole world of quarrels and convergences. Yeatsian duality serves to unite such opposites as art and life, science and suggestion, England and Ireland, father and son, and the two parts of the one nature. In his magical prose, a man has his masks, human life its parts and phases, human history its eras. The prose centres on a pair of diagrams. The first shows the Great Wheel, signifying the phases of the lunar month and the types of human personality. The second shows two interpenetrating gyres or cones, set within a circle which signifies a unified reality. The primary gyre is solar and signifies objectivity; the antithetical gyre is lunar and signifies subjectivity; and the phases of a life and of human history are expressed by the mingling of the gyres. Duality here impersonates the science which Yeats cites as a component of his system of contraries. But this is not science. The diagram is visionary, and hereditary. Some would call it that of the heir to a line of conjurors, an elaboration of the pentangles chalked on the floors of Gothic fiction—in Bulwer-Lytton's dualistic novel *A Strange Story*, for instance, published in 1862, and strangely prophetic of the Australian nuclear tests of modern times. Others would prefer to think of Yeats as a sorcerer. More than a few have sought guidance of various kinds from Yeatsian duality.[24] It is certainly easier to believe the strange story that symbols work wonders, that poetry is sorcery, if we hear it from a writer who is able to turn his own poems into spells.

Of all the oppositions cited or implied in Yeats's system, the quarrel between art and life means most to the reader of his poetry, as opposed to the respecter of his magic. Life could be shunned by him as chaotic and mean: but it could also give him metaphors for poetry. The spirits who spoke to him, with his wife as medium, promised that they would do the same—bring him metaphors: which enables the sceptic to think of these spirits as lifelike, and to say of the service they provided that this, too, was Yeats. In other words, art and life could meet, in the manner summarized by the mingling of the gyres. The earthly paradise suggested by the great house at Coole Park, and the heavenly city of the imagination which he called Byzantium, and to which he wanted to escape, can be found to intersect, just as Ireland and England can be found to intersect, and as the impulse to live can be found to intersect with the impulse to abstain. Duality in Yeats—which I have presented here with all the violence of a diagram—is the sum of such lively encounters. Perhaps it can be pictured as a hall of mirrors hung with a series of half-revolts commemorating a departure from his family which was never to be completed. Perhaps it is not too strange to say of the Yeats of the portraits and photographs that he has that orphan air which sometimes belongs to the mother's boy who is never to leave home.

Yeats and Kipling, Anglo-Irishman and Anglo-Indian, meet, and can be recognized as contemporaries, in appearing to subdue the question of nationality by summoning for duality the sense of a backward and abysm of time out of which come messages, transmissions. Kipling's metempsychoses correspond to the action of the Yeatsian 'great memory'. At the same time, in Kipling, duality is clearly designated as a family affair. In 'The Finest Story in the World' and in 'The Dream of Duncan Parrenness',[25] both of them work of the early Nineties, mothers and the love of women are decisive in relation to duplication. In the first tale, Charlie has a discouraging mother, and, as we have already seen, he has remote pasts, which are to be made available to the patronizing narrator: but the patron is baulked when Charlie falls in love. In the second, the memory of a 'sweet mother' encourages Duncan Parrenness: but Duncan is in eighteenth-century India, a drunken young sahib who has known a betraying young woman and a 'light' one, and who is now visited, when hung over, by a demonic older self, spotted with the guilts of the Warren Hastings fiefdom, and intent on a deal which delivers him to the prospect of a colonial success and a blighted maturity. His visitor looks like his dead father—and then 'I saw that his face was my very own, but marked and lined and scarred with the furrows of disease and much evil living.' In each of these stories someone, in effect, leaves home. Duncan's faith in men and, especially, in women will be 'stolen' from him by his demon. The hangover has 'burnt' away his boyhood; conscience is gone. Kipling contains East and West, and the orphan

Kim, contains a man who has lost his mother, and for whom, as for Blake, his writings are not his, are not so much written as received.

Another Anglo-Irish writer who engaged in dualistic practices was Wilde. *The Picture of Dorian Gray* was published five years after *Jekyll and Hyde* and in the year which beheld the blighted older ego of Duncan Parrenness—1891. It is a book about 'the terrible pleasure of a double life'. It is also a book about negative capability and its 'sensations'—those of its sensations which interested the chameleons of the Nineties. Wilde's wit proclaimed, in equal measure, as equal partners in duality, a fiction of the second self and a theory of multiple personality. The two, born of the same ferment, must often have seemed to stand apart in the course of the century and to go their separate ways—a high road and a low. Now they were boldly brought together. For Dorian Gray, terribly pleased with his double life, 'man was a being with myriad lives and myriad sensations, a complex multiform creature.'[26] The book is worked by this conjunction. The rest is melodrama, and décor.

This décor consists of the costumes and occasions of an elocutionary English upper class—a class exoticized, eroticized, by an outsider, who does for it something of what Disraeli had done before him. *Dorian Gray* is domestic and foreign—*Inglese e fantastico*, as the young Disraeli was said to be when seen about the Levant in Turkish dress.[27] Wilde lavishes a hectic civility on a London-that-never-was, done up in Latin lights and colours, and invents an English gentleman given over to conspicuousness, speech, preening, and slumming. There was indeed a preposterous London which Wilde inhabited and which he may be thought to be imitating here: and yet he is at such pains to fantasticate and tease that the note can seem like that of the burlesque practised by the queer fellows of a later time, can seem like a High Camp precursor. Even when he is being earnest, teases may be suspected. Covent Garden has 'huge carts filled with nodding lilies', and it has cherries handed free of charge to golden lads by white-smocked carters—cherries picked at midnight and penetrated by the cold light of the moon. Everything—not just the local greengrocers—is strange, and is so called. Strange contrasts play—of high and low life, youth and age, body and soul. Dorian's portrait grows old and bears the mark of his transgressions: 'the gold steals' from the hair of his likeness while he himself shines on unabated. This is one of the novel's plethora of secrets. The novel also suggests that the duplicate self and the multiform self have all along been secret sharers in duality.

Carts are filled with nodding lilies. And the first sentence of the novel reads: 'The studio was filled with the rich odour of roses.' Wildean repletion. *Largesse oblige*. But Dorian Gray—a dualistic name, like *Bleak House*, for a book which belies it by being filled with colour—may himself be a void. He is credited with a myriad lives: yet the life that is in him may be put there by Basil Hallward, the painter of his picture, and by Lord Henry. The question arises in the rose-red opening exchanges between Dorian's two friends, who discuss how much of the artist, and how much of his subject, may be present in a portrait. But the opening scene does not deliver the author's first words on questions of this kind. This aphoristic work is announced by a Preface which is filled with, wholly composed of, aphorisms: on the importance of being beautiful, and on art as morally indifferent or ambivalent. 'To reveal art and conceal the artist is art's aim.' This aphorism inverts the Horatian '*Ars est celare artem*,' and Hallward repeats the shocking new idea to Lord Henry in the course of the first scene: 'An artist should create beautiful things, but should put nothing of his own life into them. We live in an age when men treat art as if it were meant to be a form of autobiography.' But he has not long before said the opposite: 'every portrait that is painted with feeling is a portrait of the artist, not of the sitter. The sitter is merely the accident, the occasion. It is not he who is revealed by the painter; it is rather the painter who, on the coloured canvas, reveals himself.'

Hallward's shifting, multiple view of what art is made of is apparent elsewhere in the same scene. He wants to ascribe to his own work a content derived from Dorian—a content and a style, for Dorian, he thinks, has inspired him to create a new kind of art. And he adapts the Ciceronian dictum, '*Numquam minus solum quam cum solus*,' by remarking: 'He is never more present in my work than when no image of him is there.' But then he won't exhibit this new art of his, or Dorian's, because 'there is too much of myself in the thing, Harry.' In addition to all this, the Preface avers: 'It is the spectator, and not life, that art really mirrors.' So art is successively said to mirror the artist, the sitter, and the spectator. These turns and twists are appropriate to an age of multiplicity in which Narcissus flourished but in which, *per contra*, there also flourished detractors of Narcissus who were keen to deny that art was a form of autobiography. And this most sententious of melodramas can itself be described as a portrait of the artist which is also a portrait of the age. The gamut of contrasts to which Wildean duality attends includes contrasting views concerning the hero's plunge into libertinism and sensation. In these views the presence of a reader or spectator, and of the age, can certainly be glimpsed.

The Preface goes on being mirrored and amended. Much later, Hallward acknowledges the contradiction in his attitude to art, when he says in the same breath that the fateful picture was past exhibiting because 'I had put too much of myself into it,' but that, after all, 'art conceals the artist far more completely than it ever reveals him.' The novel has previously made us aware that this concealment may be the concealment of an absence or abstention. In such passages we recognize romantic ideas of the past, to the effect that the artist is a void, to be filled with his subject and with the world he experiences (Wildean repletion may be held to find its function here—a function poorly fulfilled, it has to be said, in the novel that is ours to read). It is all as if art can conceal the artist because there is very little to conceal. This point is made by a smiling Lord Henry with the aid of a quotation from Keats: 'Good artists exist simply in what they make, and consequently are perfectly uninteresting in what they are. A great poet, a really great poet, is the most unpoetical of all creatures.'[28] The artist is simultaneously voided and promoted. The novel uses the ideas of the past in order to effect a separation of the artist from his fellow human beings, of beauty from the beast, of high life from low. But it also reverses some of these ideas. Separation is pursued. But so is singleness.

Dorian Gray expounds the claims of a new spirituality, which looks like an old hedonism. The senses are to be spiritualized, while the spirit is to be made corporeal, even bestial. 'Was the soul a shadow seated in the house of sin? Or was the body really in the soul, as Giordano Bruno thought? The separation of spirit from matter was a mystery, and the union of spirit with matter was a mystery also.' Dr Jekyll had embarked on a project of separation: Dorian embarks on a project of union, in a work which strives, too, for separation. By joining body and soul, as by the exercise of insincerity, 'we can multiply our personalities.' Another way of doing this is to get married: according to Lord Henry, marriage makes some people 'more complex'—this may be Wilde's way of saying, with Yeats, that it solves their antinomies. Such people 'retain their egotism, and add to it many other egos. They are forced to have more than one life. They become more highly organised, and to be highly organised is, I should fancy, the object of man's existence.'[29] The preoccupation of a later literary criticism is foreshadowed here in what could almost be called a Darwinian prescription of adultery and bisexuality.

Elsewhere, the language of the novel pre-dates Darwin. Stock definitions of romance are issued and reissued. The habit of secrecy, thinks the clean-breasted Hallward, brings 'a great deal of romance into one's life'. Dorian searches for sensations which will possess the 'element of strangeness that is so essential to romance ('so essential', 'far more completely'—this is a pleonastic but not a beautifully-written book). He is an orphan, whose parentage is 'a strange almost modern romance'. His very resemblance to his mother, to say nothing of his animate portrait, is rated strange. And he is associated throughout with stealing. Traditional metaphors meet when he discovers the beguiling aphorist Lord Henry at a luncheon of stuffed shirts: 'a flush of pleasure stealing' into Dorian's cheek. This is a book which is all steals, and which is filled with transgressions —those of the Stevensonian kind especially, where pleasure and cruelty go together. The portrait acquires a hard look as a result of Dorian's experiments in the field of the new spirituality. As with Stevenson, these are accompanied by a sort of science, but are only very faintly specified.

As the hard look makes clear, Wilde wanted Dorian's misdeeds to be regarded as such; he did not want to be read as saying curtly or coarsely that people should have a good time. The new spirituality had to make its peace with an old censoriousness, and duality enabled this to happen. Duality ensured that the novel could be cited both by the prosecution and by the defence when legal proceedings were launched against him a few years later, and orphan youths assembled in court to speak of dinners and secret favours at Kettner's and the Savoy. One of these youths, by the name of Shelley, was a no less romantic specimen than Dorian Gray. Shelley had made himself 'ill with studying' when he knew Wilde, and had dwindled to a Gothic shadow. He told the highly-organized complex husband who had befriended him that he was 'nervous' and 'so thin, they think me strange'. He said he had once been mad enough to attack his father.[30]

In relation to contemporary attachments to the art and ideas of duality Henry James was not, as we know, inviolable. Jamesian duality displays, as Wilde's does, both an interest in psychic duplication and a commitment to the multiple personality of the protean artist. He took, moreover, a deep interest in flight —an interest which procured an indeterminate nationality, and which was by no means foreign to the work of his dualistic fellow artists in dictating for his fiction, and imputing to its persons, a consciousness, a sensibility, which proceed by indirections, and by leaps and bounds and descents.

James's story 'The Jolly Corner' appeared in 1908, seventeen years after *Dorian Gray*. Spencer Brydon has fled from America, and from its businessmen, to lead a life of cultivated leisure and pleasure in Europe. And he has done this 'almost in the teeth of my father's curse'. Living frivolously and as who should say scandalously, though hardly, one might feel, in the manner to which Dorian Gray became accustomed, he has wondered about the man he would have been had he stayed in New York and gone into business—about this 'strange *alter ego*'.[31] Now he has come back.

An old friend, Alice Staverton, a well-bred spinster, fragrant of Edith Wharton's Old New York, proposes, with his agreement, that the other self, had it bloomed, might have proved 'monstrous'; she also proposes that he is a narcissist. Amid the hard heads and hard looks of their compatriots, each is the possessor of a sensibility: these are the fine feelers of an *ancien régime*, whose opinions matter. Both can be found on the same page to 'flush'—she at his now managing to traffic skilfully in real estate, he at the 'wanton wonderment' of his frequenting, haunting, at night, his family's house, which stands empty, the shell of a Fifth Avenue palace. 'Impulse', 'humour', leads him a queer dance as he 'steals' from room to room on the tips of his evening shoes, monocled, and, we may imagine, portly. This queer dance is a *pas seul* of simultaneous flight and pursuit, a saraband performed to 'some rich music' of no tone, in the suspected presence of his might-have-been—the might-have-been which can on occasion construe the romantic second self.

These are the toes of a transgressor—though hardly of the Stavrogin who elsewhere lends his furtive steps to the nineteenth century's ballet of the divided mind. The mild Brydon 'prowls' in his patrician uniform about the house, prowls and 'creeps', or 'crapes'—Mrs Muldoon's pronunciation, that of a humble caretaker, is no less suited to the Gothic mode. He may be thought to be burgling himself, in that this may seem to be a sentimental journey into his own past, which disputes the common ground of his childhood with a phantom fellow squatter, and in burgling himself he lets himself go in an ecstasy of 'fine attentions'. If, as silly people had alleged, his former life had been 'a surrender to sensations', Europe had allowed him to taste no pleasure as fine as this. Or, for that matter, as strong: 'a preposterous secret thrill' is experienced. He has passed beyond the Edwardian pale—into the realm of the Irrational and Uncanny.

A *pas de deux* has now begun. He feels like a ghost who is formidable to other ghosts, or like 'some monstrous stealthy cat'. Hide-and-seek passes into big-game hunt, with his alter ego in the role of fierce animal, and when he senses that he has at bay the American business beast which is comprehended in his prey, there shoots through him 'a prodigious thrill, a thrill that represented sudden dismay, no doubt, but also represented, and with the selfsame throb, the strangest, the most joyous, possibly the next minute almost the proudest, duplication of consciousness'.[32]

At the top of the house, in the last room of all, behind a closed door, his prey appears to have been run to ground. Like the heroine of Mrs Radcliffe's *Udolpho*, he is aware that a door has been fastened by some unknown hand. Brydon had not closed the door: 'He *couldn't*, by any lapse, have blocked that aperture.' It is as if his adversary has done it. Brydon does not enter the room. 'He knew—yes, as he had never known anything—that *should* he see the door open, it would all too abjectly be the end of him.' The 'agent of his shame' would be left 'in general possession', and he himself would commit suicide. 'He stole back . . .'.[33] He retreats down the stairs: 'The closed door, blessedly remote now, was still closed—and he had only in short to reach that of the house.' On the street floor, the black and white marble flags which he remembers from the remoteness of childhood lead out into a vestibule, the door to which had been left shut, he thinks, but is now open. A figure is disclosed there—'as still as some image erect in a niche or as some black-vizored sentinel guarding a treasure'. Spencer Brydon may be about to learn the secret of the 'opposed projections' of himself by which he has been afflicted. Stevenson's friend Henry James's Henry Jekyll is about to encounter his Hyde. The friendship in question dated from the year in which Stevenson dreamt and transcribed his tale—so that James and the double came to him together, to be commemorated, for all we know, in a pair of initials and an approximation to the French word for James: the friendship was to give a great deal to the history of dualistic accords, and of their strong survival in the new century.

Resplendent in evening dress, like Brydon, but with a pince-nez instead of a monocle, the figure enacts a 'dark deprecation', shielding his face with his hands, from one of which two fingers are missing. When the hands are removed, Brydon reads the face as that of a spectral stranger, and he then swoons. When he comes to, he is in Alice's lap. 'You brought me literally to life.' He feels blissful, like the recipient of a boon: it is as if he has been away, and as if he has been born, or reborn. 'This brute's a black stranger,' he tells Alice, who has twice dreamt of the other Brydon, and has her own motherly views as to whether Brydon can know himself. 'It's not me,' he insists, while Alice seems to convey that if this is what he might have been it is not what he is now. He is able to hold her in a final, and perhaps also a first, embrace.

'The Jolly Corner' is a tall tale, and it is written in a willed and laborious manner which does not rise easily to balmy intimations of a release from mental constraints, an end to nerves and fear. It tells how an affectionate adult couple are made over into mother and child as a result of finding that a beastly, blighted businessman may be pitied and understood: Alice confesses that she '*could* have liked' the black stranger. It is a tall tale in the Gothic mode. It speaks the language of strangeness and distraction, and of sensibility, and it employs, or implies, appropriate conventions—those of the swoon, the exemplary journey, and the attainment of a mother. It locates itself in romance, speaking of its themes as more momentous than those of the old, chivalric romances.

It is more likely, however, to be read now as a tall tale in the Freudian mode, composed in the years immediately following Freud's *Interpretation of Dreams*. It has the momentum and preposterousness, and the violent fidelity to waking life, of a dream. It is a dream which is difficult to interpret, and which the tale refrains from interpreting. It is in that sense 'innocent'—rather as James has been thought innocent of the sexual meanings which have been disengaged from the figurative language of his earlier work, and prized as involuntary innuendoes, and which have their counterparts in pieces of the present text. Nevertheless, it would seem that he meant to write here, in later life, about the experience of birth and of union with a mother, and to apply it to a 'menopausal' drama of a kind. The story may be reckoned to belong to the era of sons and lovers. Lawrence's novel of that name lay five years ahead, and may well stand in much the same relationship to Freudian interpretation, to its advent and acknowledgement, and to its origins in the culture of romance. For Freudians, it is an oedipal story, and the romance which it contains is a family romance. For such interpreters, the hostile father whose curse has almost been defied is succeeded, and symbolized, by the deprecator caught or suspected on the other side of a door, and by the masked sentinel who guards a treasure, while the missing fingers—for the narrator, the story's 'special verity'—signify the displacements which occur in fantasy, and the transfer to a parent of the focus of a castration anxiety.

There is no record of any keen interest in Freud's doctrines on the part of William James's brother, but the story records what can only be a measure of sympathetic response to the cultural provenance of those doctrines: it may be that Henry James intended to show a dark father in the spectral American businessman, and to achieve a more poignant irony than meets the eye—the eye, at least, which is alerted only to what the story has to say about nationality and commerce—when Alice says of the brute at the threshold that she had pitied and accepted him, and that she '*could* have liked him'. There are two thresholds in the story, the one at the top of the house and the other at the level of the street, and it may be that James would have acknowledged that they were symbolic, and that they symbolize much the same thing. He does not always call a spade a spade in this story, which talks of a ladder as a 'vertiginous perpendicular': but it isn't just the Neo-classical stylist who chooses to say, with reference to a door, that 'he *couldn't*, by any lapse, have blocked that aperture.' This could as well relate to the descent from a mother as to the supplanting of the brute at the threshold, and as well relate to other things besides. Interpretation, paraphrase, in a case like this, is never prudent. But it is likely to be clear to many that this tall tale bears a sense—among others—which is reflected in the anxious italics which mediate its conditional moods, that this *could* and this *couldn't* are mutually dependent, that they help to tell the same story. We can be sure that the strange events which had come to be predicated of infancy, and of maturity, by the builders of the Freudian tradition, were visible to Henry James.

The house in 'The Jolly Corner' is—not to refuse a play on words—a house of birth, and of the body. And yet I do not think that many would feel that it is used to symbolize some outlandish fulfilment. This is a palace whose attics and mezzanine, whose vertiginous perpendiculars, do not ascend to heaven. It is enough that out of its closets should start a relatively mundane second self, who moves in a mysterious way to bring about the liberation of a middle-aged bachelor: as in other encounters with the double, a crisis of the middle of a life can be surmised. This top storey is a place from which you might fling yourself in despair, and the approach to the last room of all, at the top of the house, concludes with a discreet recoil. The tale has a happy, even a heavenly ending: but the emphasis is in large part terrestrial, and territorial. It can also be said to fall on nationality, and on family, and on convergences between the two. Here is a fiction which seeks both to accept and to reject America—the kind of thing which can't be done and which is done all the time, the kind of undertaking which causes Gothic literature to be preposterous and which enables it to be potent. James was stirred and troubled by the country on which romance had induced him to turn his back, and which he seems to have experienced as an aspect of his involvement with his family. The house, the story, are accordingly charged with a sense of family life, which biography can annotate. To the woman who accepts the American in Brydon James gave his sister's Christian name, and the boon Alice bestows is indeterminately that of a wife, a mother, and a sister; his father lost a leg in an accident; and it has been possible to detect in the story the rival presence of James's stay-at-home brother William. It may be that the mixed fortunes of family life are a reason to think of 'The Jolly Corner' as, like *Bleak House*, a dualistic title: James's jolly corner often proves bleak, while Bleak House proves a warren of jolly corners.

The Sense of the Past was begun in 1900, just before *The Wings of the Dove*; it was resumed but left unfinished around 1915, at the end of the author's life—some years after 'The Jolly Corner', to which it is something of a companion piece. For James's 'rare young man' in this work, the rich American Ralph Pendrel, London is 'within the pale of romance'. So is the text which he handsomely inhabits. The 'note of the strange' is sounded, in a prose which, again, is nothing if not strenuous. The accompanying notes, which are hardly less strenuous, sound the note of the artist at work, taking his delighted, difficult 'steps', driving home his exquisite 'silver nails', as he moves towards 'the climax of the romantic hocuspocus, of my sought total effect'.[34] In other words, James is once again turning the screw of the ghost story.

Ralph has had bequeathed to him, by a relative, an old mansion in a fashionable quarter of London, in recognition of his historian's, and more than historian's, passion for the past, and he jumps, more or less literally jumps—'there were moments, light as air, at which he proceeded by spasms of exhilaration,' on 'the tips of his toes'—at the chance of possessing the house in the manner of Spencer Brydon. He peers at and from it through the city's early, rainy dusks. London light is indistinguishable from London shade, and is so strange as to be at its finest when sinister: a perpetual English twilight is beautifully evoked, which beautifully serves a crepuscular dualistic tale. Ralph is especially intrigued by a portrait which hangs in a 'little innermost parlour'—for him, 'the most consecrated corner of the house'. The portrait is that of a youth, an ancestor, whose back is turned. But then, 'wonder of wonders', the portrait comes to life and faces him: and 'the face—miracle of miracles, yes—confounded him as his own.' Ralph has met his double, and has passed 'beyond sense'.[35]

Ralph is 'queer', in the sense of strange. He is a 'case'—of nerves, of breakdown. But he is also an 'adventurer', and, for the author who is writing about him, an object of love and a shining light. Back in New York, Aurora Coyne has loved him less than Henry James does: she has spoken of preferring a man of action, and, it may be, of business, and of committing poor Ralph to live in America. Since then, he has gone off to his mansion in London, where he has his surpassing adventure. Aurora Coyne is one of James's expressive names. It looks like a translation—into the splendour of an Edwardian poetic diction—of the words 'jolly corner', and the human body is present in both of these tales as an aggregation of holes and corners, and of innermost and topmost rooms: Aurora's name unites this with a sense of promise, and with the ring of cash.

As befits someone who, having exchanged identities with an alter ego, is relieved to be able to feel that he is 'still a gentleman, thank God', Ralph Pendrel runs for help to the ambassador of his country (a character derived from the poet and diplomat, Tennyson's frightful bore, James Russell Lowell). Ralph interests him strangely. Soon they are holding hands, and enacting one of duality's most diverting set-piece comic scenes. The notes explain that the Ambassador thinks his guest a 'curious and interesting case of dementia': the text shows him treating Ralph like a gentleman, if not a kinsman, and flirting with him as well, while urbanely sorting out the details of the case and plying himself with cigars. This flirtatious heavy smoker asks: 'You're sure that you know which of you is which?'[36] Ralph in reply invites the Ambassador to be gentle with him, and allow his flight a happy landing:

> 'It's a most extraordinary thing, you see, to have befallen a man, and I don't wonder at the queer figure I must make to you. But you'll see too for yourself in a moment how easily you'll wish to let me down.

It's the most extraordinary thing that ever happened in the world—but at the same time there's no danger,' he cheerfully declared, 'of my losing my way. I'm all here, or rather'—Ralph was gay about it—'*he* is.'

So Ralph can be 'gay' as well as 'queer'. These were favoured adjectives of the Fin-de-Siècle and after, which in the fullness of time were to become in succession the names which the English-speaking homosexual community has used to identify itself. James's use presages this, just as his tripping through empty houses—his notes, with their steps and silver nails, being the choreography for that ballet—may be accounted, like *Dorian Gray*, a form of early Camp.

The Ambassador puts a further apt question:

'I'm only puzzled by your not having spoken to me of your friend and yourself a moment ago as separate persons—but on the contrary of your having arrived, wasn't it? at some common identity or wonderful unity. You *are* the other fellow, you said, didn't you?—and the other fellow, by the same stroke, is you. So that when I wonder where the other fellow is,' he genially pursued, 'it would seem that I've only to suppose him here in this room with me, in your interesting person.'[37]

Ralph's lucidity is equal to the challenge: 'I didn't say, kindly understand, that we have *merged* personalities, but that we have definitely exchanged them—which is a different matter. Our duality is so far from diminished that it's only the greater—by some formulation, each to the other, of the so marked difference in our interest.' Where *is* the other fellow, then? 'Down at the door in the cab.' But when the two gentlemen descend they find the other fellow flown.

The Ambassador accompanies the interesting person of Ralph Pendrel to 9 Mansfield Square, where, with a rat-tat-tat at the front door, Ralph passes into the world of 1820. Inside the house he foregathers with a deputation of kinsfolk, gentry on the make, proud of their stock, up from the country to wait on their American visitor: Mrs Midmore of Drydown, her two daughters, with whom in turn Ralph falls in love, and her bucolic son. These country cousins are joined by a family friend, Sir Cantopher, a person of high though abrasive civility, an aesthete and man of the world, whom one might well imagine stealing a young man from an ambassador. What remains of the text brings the bombardment of Ralph's sensibility by impressions received as he parleys with his relatives in an atmosphere of nerves, flushes, glowing faces. His leaps and bounds as he carries off his adventure are overtaken by the malaise which he detects in his companions as they become aware of his queerness, and in which he shares.

The notes refer to the Ambassador, on one occasion, in obstetric style: Ralph hopes the Ambassador will be a mother to him for the duration of his adventure—in the dualistic sense that he will be the 'secured connection with the world he cuts himself loose from, dropping as from a balloon thousands of feet up in the air, and not really knowing what smash or what magically *soft* concussion awaits him . . .'.[38] Here to the life—tethered and free, leaping and bound—is the son disclosed in the literature of duality. The descent, or lapse, which is mentioned here is characterized by Ralph, in the text itself, as we have seen, as an exchange of identity with the young man of the portrait. But it is doubtful whether the text describes an exchange of identity. We are told of a 'double consciousness' in Ralph, which indeed appears to betray him to his kin as uncanny, and his double may not be enough of a participant in the tale for the reader to understand what Ralph means when he speaks of an undiminished duality. Ralph stays ignorant, we learn, of 'what his double's situation is in *his* sphere': yet he is to divine, according to the notes, that his double will feel injured when Ralph transfers his affections to the younger of the daughters.

It is plain from both text and notes that James had his work cut out in accommodating the art of the ghost story to the dictates of the novel of feeling, and in dealing plausibly with a time-warp and with all that is aerial and astronautical and obstetric in Ralph's experiences. The strain is terrific. Never has dream or delirium exacted so arduous a syntax, so many disobliging sentences, so many rereadings. But if James gives the impression of flogging himself through his leaps and bounds, of dancing in chains, it can't be because he had too little to say to exercise his great capacities. It is probable that he had more to say than the art of the ghost story and the convention of the double enabled him to express.

Since the young man of the portrait barely impinges, Ralph is left looking like a singleton. And yet there is, in the story, a duality of opposition—which is the usual sort of duality in literature. This opposition relates to a passion for the past which is contrasted with a commitment to the present and future, and it relates to the difference between England and America, between, in that sense, the old world and the new. Landed in 1820, Ralph after a while feels homesick for the time from which he has come. The notes record the thought—somewhat startling for the year of its utterance, 1915—that the modern world is an obvious improvement on what has preceded it. Given the extent to which the past is defined for the story as Europe, this is almost as much as to suggest that America is to be preferred. And perhaps we may go on to claim that the true duality of the tale resides in its contriving to say both this and the opposite—that the past is wondrous. The story, that is to say, is both bound to the past—securely connected—and free from it.

The story, then, is about whether Ralph will yield to the past—about whether he is, or will go, mad. According to the projected plot, the younger daughter would make the sacrifice of returning Ralph to the interesting future of which she stands deprived, while Aurora Coyne, having got into and 'passed through' what the notes call 'a "psychic" state', was to cause, or take part in, Ralph's recovery. His restoration to—or secured reconnection with—this hopeful Aurora, however, was to coincide with his restoration to that kindly, motherly Ambassador, and it is apparent that Aurora's interest in Ralph is less zealous than the Ambassador's, and inferior to it. It even looks in the notes as if James would have been pained by having to write further about the jolly corners, and bleakness, of Aurora Coyne. At one point he even contrives to forget her remarkable name.

The era of sons and lovers was an era which favoured restorations, as well as renunciations and sacrifice, which favoured homecomings and revisitings and mothers. In this romantic drama James played a part, and the part is played in *The Sense of the Past*. The work is a family romance in this sense, and in the sense that it is no less open than its companion to biographical annotation: we may reckon up the parental and dynastic ghosts who can be found to flit here. Fleetingly too, in each of these tales, a haunted house is wrought to an image of the human body to which human beings have been imagined as wishing to return. In each tale, psychic duplication is tied to intimations of such a return; the innermost or highest room in the house is in each case fateful. To haunt such a house is to plumb a past which is at once familial and ancestral and national. It may therefore be claimed that the common ground occupied by these stories is the holy ground of childhood, and that James's sense of the past embraced a sense of his childhood and native land. America and his family are experienced as one, and expressed by means of the leaps and bounds and involutions which were made possible by the conventions of literary duality. The difficult choice between America and Europe may never have been completed by James, just as the matter of his relations with his kin may never have been settled or sealed: it is no wonder that these stories should be hard to read.

James was a man for whom to talk profanely about your country was like talking profanely about your mother—and who was in the habit of talking a little profanely about America. When about to write *The Sense of the Past*, he pondered the fate of the American traveller 'in search of, in flight from, something or other', and his writings are moved to commemorate the experiences of those in search of, in flight from, some mother or other. Duality and nationality, and nationality and family, go together in his writings, and the conjunctions are as important as they are delicate. They are important both because they help to explain the inexplicable James and because they are far from unrepresentative. This novel, and 'The Jolly Corner', and *The Wings of the Dove*, are works which help to explain why it is that so many dualistic writers should have suffered the excitements and uncertainties of dual nationality. The tendency for a change of scene to be involved with changes and complications of heart, for expatriation to be involved with departures from family life, and indeed to take on the character of a destiny, is not in itself surprising, and is evident at earlier points in the history of this literature; we may think that Hogg's descent from his mountains was a destiny, and that it can only have encouraged him to cultivate the double.

But in the Nineties the tendency came to a head. Nearly all of the modern practitioners of duality, and nearly all of its modern masters, were affected by it.

No account of the Late Victorian dualistic scene should overlook James's tale 'The Private Life', in which, a few months after *Dorian Gray*, he produces, pat, a version of the established view that the true self shrinks from public display, and contributes to an ethos in which the double is expressly entrusted with the writing of books. Among grand friends in a Swiss hotel the narrator, an unsuccessful writer, stumbles upon a double duality. The friends include Clare Vawdrey, a writer who is famous but socially disappointing, and the stylish and ceremonious Lord Mellifont—names suggestive of Gothic melodrama. It turns out that Vawdrey has an 'alternative identity', an 'other self', while his Lordship has no self beyond the one so richly displayed in public. If Vawdrey is 'double', his Lordship is not even single, and vanishes when alone: in Cicero's sense, he is even less than *solus*. 'He was all public and had no corresponding private life, just as Clare Vawdrey was all private and had no corresponding public one.' Vawdrey is the more intriguing case. The narrator delights the actress he admires, Blanche Adney, by telling her that 'there are two of them'—two Vawdreys. 'One goes out, the other stays at home. One is the genius, the other's the bourgeois; and it's only the bourgeois whom we personally know.' If we have been accustomed to think that the true self leaves home in order to seek its freedom, we have also been accustomed to think, as the tale intimates, that such freedom can only be found at home. Abroad, Vawdrey is a bore, though a fine one: 'He's always splendid, as your morning bath is splendid, or a sirloin of beef, or the railway service to Brighton. But he's never rare.' What it comes to is that the 'real man' can 'gossip and dine by deputy', that the genius stays at home and writes his books. Multiple personality is a 'firm', whose members 'carry on the business', while assigned to their own offices.[39]

The narrator catches the real man at his holy work:

I stood there with my hand still on the knob of the door, overtaken by the oddest impression of my life. Vawdrey was at his table, writing, and it was a very natural place for him to be; but why was he writing in the dark, and why hadn't he answered me? I waited a few seconds for the sound of some movement, to see if he wouldn't rouse himself from his abstraction—a fit conceivable in a great writer—and call out: 'Oh, my dear fellow, is it you?'[40]

The tale carries a consciousness of the theatre of the time, which was unkind to James's offerings, and of which Mrs Adney seems intended to serve as a divine embodiment. This is a comedy of errors, of mistaken identity. And it is a comedy which has elements of the sheerly conventional and of the maladroit, as when the poet Browning—for Vawdrey was patterned on James's idea of Browning—is spoken of as a sirloin that is rare only in seclusion. We may find ourselves here imagining some deep freeze. The tale does not ask the reader to think twice, or for very long, about the anti-social rareness of the deep writer, who in the light of day is heard to talk distressingly about reviewers. There may also be an element of dubious faith. The listened-for 'my dear fellow' in this recognition scene is a nice touch which shows the desire of the lesser light for the star, and shows how duality may be used to measure the difference between genius and its obverse or opposite. But James himself was not only a genius but a star—who shone in company and whose art exploits the fact, while arranging, on this occasion, to obscure the fact.

He was a star who was willing to use the language of the 'queer occurrence' which had been assembled—by lesser lights among others—over the years. 'Odd', 'queer', 'dark', 'fit', 'nervous'—these are the bricks which had built the house of the double. James's double accompanies an orphan, and suggests escape, retreat, a balm, a bath, a lap, a happy death, a holiday, a hotel. The great good place, in the story of that name, is maternal, and the nervous writer who goes there for a while experiences a 'boon' which is for all the world like the boon of a contingent world, and which is attained by means of the discovery that 'every one is a little some one else.'[41] In expressing the tribulations of the successful and of the unsuccessful writer in what is taken to be the raging new era of star-worship and a mass public, Jamesian duality nevertheless gives a strong sense of the past, and of the literature of the past.

Over the last quarter of the nineteenth century literature and psychology—fiction and speculation—advanced together towards a new world based on conceptions of duality which were both old and new, the same but different. In Frederic Myers's essay 'Multiplex Personality', a remarkable piece of work which preceded by four years Max Dessoir's German treatise *The Double Ego*, we find, as in James's 'The Private Life', the notion of the human being as business enterprise, as factory or firm. Myers made his name as a literary critic and as a psychical researcher, an enquirer into the after-life; his essay appeared in 1886, in the *Nineteenth Century*.[42] He discusses, among others, the familiar case of Félida X, whose normal state was really her morbid state, in the sense that a second, 'somnambulic' self—to which, in terms of memory, her first self had no access—took command and proved successful. Myers writes: 'Let us picture the human brain as a vast manufactory, in which thousands of looms, of complex and differing patterns, are habitually at work.' Since the era of the ascidian (a marine invertebrate), in the course of the development of species, looms have been added. Some of the looms of 'my nearer ancestors', Myers goes on to say, 'have fallen to pieces unheeded; others have been kept in repair because they suited the style of order which the firm had at that time to meet. But the class of orders received has changed very rapidly during the last few hundred years. I have now to try to turn out altruistic emotions and intelligent reasoning with machinery adapted to self-preserving fierceness or manual toil.' Félida's looms had been jerked, jolted—violently but fortunately rearranged. 'Smaller changes' should now be attempted by the new firm—under scientific auspices, in the interests of evolution and 'moral progress'. And hypnotism is to serve this purpose. The refinements to which 'Mesmer's process' had been subjected promise 'a nascent art of self-modification'. There may now be 'pulleys' to 'disjoin and reconnect portions of our machinery'. By means of hypnotism Myers hopes to produce, for the life of the intellect, 'a state of insusceptibility to physical pain'. We are to fall asleep and be better people.

Myers can be placed among the discoverers of the unconscious. He held that the subliminal personality was both regressive and creative, and that its higher functions were explanatory of genius and might even permit necropathy—so to speak of that communication with the dead which was desired by the nineteenth century. It is plain that after an interval of a hundred years hypnotism and duality remained a pair, but that duality was now more deeply preoccupied with the consequences that appeared to flow from a detection of the second self of an unconscious mind. Mesmer's process, and its sequels, had given rise to two models of the mind: dipsychism and polypsychism—or the idea of a group of sub-personalities. The first of these raised the issue of whether the undermind was closed (dependent for its content on what came from its companion) or open (to the World Soul, to the Dead, to Everything). Dessoir was a dipsychist—and a bibliographer of modern hypnotism. *The Double Ego* argued that everyone has it in them to be double, and that the two egos consist, in turn, of complex chains of association. We catch sight of the underconsciousness in dreams and in cases of spontaneous somnambulism.[43] From these and other accounts of the subject we learn that this second self was now fit to challenge the first, and that its challenge was essential to the new era of complexity and self-modification which had dawned for the race, by the Nineties, in the higher thought of the period.

For William James, who respected Myers's work, and whose *Principles of Psychology* was published like the Dessoir in 1890, the higher functions of the hidden self might mediate between nature and a higher region, and reconcile religion and science. The divided mind produced by the criterion of consciousness argued, for many purposes, a different order of duality from the morbid states known to literature and to the earlier psychiatry: but there were important interconnections, and James for one was interested in both orders.[44] The *alter idem* of an unconscious mind served as a foundation for psychoanalysis, and made it, in the eyes of its founder, an exquisitely dualistic, not to say romantic system: for Freud, a more radical if less hopeful discoverer, the unconscious was one of two things in tandem, and was eventually judged as twofold in the further sense of harbouring a contention between life-principles and death-principles. The developing hypothesis displayed, and was fashioned to display, the beauty of duality. And it may be added that the psychology of Jung—with its extravert and introvert, its doctrine that each person is a cluster of personalities, its goal of a union of opposites to be attained by a kind of orphaning of the mature self, its sense of a shadow self or bad double, its collective unconscious—yields nothing to its rival in respect of an awareness of the romantic past.

In contemplating the formation of his system, Freud gave credit to the imaginative writers who had preceded him. And those who came after him gave credit to Freud for an investigation of the plural self which seemed destined to reconstitute all thought of meaning and intention. Both the antecedents and the consequences of the psychoanalytic rediscovery of the eminently rediscoverable dualistic hypothesis are perceptible in an event of 1930. In that year, William Empson 'invoked Freud' for the description of his seventh type of ambiguity, which identified the presence in some literary texts of opposites denoting a divided mind. Poems—to which the book in question had no need to confine its attention—were like Freudianism's dreams in bringing about a 'condensation' in respect of these opposites, which were defined in relation to desire, and to a context in which 'you want something different in another part of your mind.' Hopkins, Empson argued, wants different things in the 'Windhover' sonnet: both the free life of the bird and the self-denial of the religious recluse. The sonnet embodied 'a clear case of the Freudian use of opposites, where two things thought of as incompatible, but desired intensely by different systems of judgments, are spoken of simultaneously by words applying to both'. For *Seven Types of Ambiguity*, contradictory impulses could be held in equilibrium: religion, which fosters no such equilibrium in Hopkins's indecisive sacrificial sonnet, is found to do so in Herbert's poem on the Atonement, 'The Sacrifice'.[45]

Empson was mocked for his pile of ambiguities, and then widely believed. But it has generally been easier to believe that literature affords contradictions than that it achieves a balance. Literature's reconciliation of opposites, where this could be found to occur, may at certain times in the past have appeared to lend support to the belief in its supersession of religion. Such appearances are now wanting, and we have reached a point where it can be feared that literature has been superseded.

XII. GETTING AWAY

'The principal thing was to get away.' These words belong to Joseph Conrad's recurrent explanation, in his book *A Personal Record*,[1] of what it meant for him to go to sea when he was young. It meant leaving behind his Polish relatives, land-locked in continental Europe, and forsaking the perennial Polish struggle to get away from Russia and the Russian Empire—a struggle in which his father had played a part. And in the books he began to write when he left the sea there are signs that he feared he had been guilty of a desertion when he yielded to the romantic impulse to become an Englishman and a sailor. The thought of desertion helped to make him suspicious of romance, and it helped to make him a writer of it. The romantic Conrad has been undervalued in comparison with the achievements of the moralistic Conrad which are set out as canonical in Leavis's *Great Tradition*. If Conrad was suspicious of romance, he was also suspicious of morality, and the distinction is in any case, in its relation to his work, somewhat chimerical. There is a great fund of romance in the novels Leavis loves. In *Under Western Eyes*, for instance. This is a book about a betrayer who finds on one occasion that he has 'another self, an independent sharer of his mind'—a discovery which is framed by figurative 'steals'.[2]

Conrad's sense of guilt applies a steady pressure to *A Personal Record*. But the memoir has been rejected as guarded and uncommunicative, ruined by the gloomy Pole's or the Master Mariner's stiff upper lip. It appears to me to be faultlessly shaped by an intention to communicate the theme of romance, and its significance for Conrad in his capacity as son and kinsman. Much, including chronological sequence, is scanted and shut out, so that he can dwell on how he came to sow what he calls his 'wild oats' at sea, and on 'the somewhat exceptional psychology of my sea-going'—something, 'I fear', which Master Mariners might misunderstand, and which is linked to the exceptional psychology of his writing. The book shows him responding to the romance of the sea, and to the romance of England (and Scotland), and then discovering in himself an 'unaccountable' urge to write. Not a word about his wife, very few about his boys.

Many words, though, about romance. 'But then, you see, I have been called romantic. Well, that can't be helped.'[3] Being, or being called, romantic is something that is seen here as requiring help, and throughout his work he wanted to express the common knowledge that romance is illusion and desertion. At the same time, romance, for Conrad, was as plain as the nose on your face. And if romance was real, and wrong, it can also be said that he laid down his life for it—writing it, and about it, from first to last —and that it bore other meanings in his work besides those which, in the dualistic and romantic modern world, have made literary masters and Master Mariners contemptuous or suspicious. About romance, as about dreams, he was in two minds or more. A note of ambivalence and irony is frequent. He writes of his sea-going in the memoir:

> Alas! I have the conviction that there are men of unstained rectitude who are ready to murmur scornfully the word desertion. Thus the taste of innocent adventure may be made bitter to the palate. The part of the inexplicable should be allowed for in appraising the conduct of men in a world where no explanation is final. No charge of faithlessness ought to be lightly uttered. The appearances of this perishable life are deceptive like everything that falls under the judgment of our imperfect senses. The inner voice may remain true enough in its secret counsel. The fidelity to a special tradition may last through the events of an unrelated existence, following faithfully, too, the traced way of an inexplicable impulse.

Romance can make a man, indeed a faithful Master Mariner, of its deserters.

He is writing here about himself as he was at the age of 15, about his 'opening life',[4] and his fiction was often to create such openings, to stand at the brink of manhood and maturity, with its adventures and its rites of passage and its uncertainties. Soon after this, he introduces the figure of Cervantes' Don Quixote, whose charming frailty consisted of an attempt at defection occasioned by a surfeit of romances: 'he desired naively to escape with his very body from the intolerable reality of things.' At this point, too, Conrad is describing his exposure to the picturesque scenery of the Alps. In 1873, together with a tutor, he is at the head of the Furca Pass on his way to the Rhône Glacier. The St. Gotthard Tunnel is being built by British engineers, and in the dining-room of a hotel the boy catches a visionary glimpse of these enchanting creatures, breakfasting in the effulgence of their skills, and of the British Empire: 'the deliberate, bald-headed Scot with the coal-black beard appeared to my boyish eyes a very romantic and mysterious person.' He is further regaled with the glimpse of a British paterfamilias, marching across the mountains, with his servants and dear ones, in a twinkle of ivory calves as portentous as Don Quixote's wind-mills. But the drift of this account is ominous as well as humorous and uplifted, for the tutor is one of those known by the young Conrad to be troubled by the boy's submission to the romance of the sea, which was also, and now all the more, a submission to the glamour of the British who sailed that sea. There on the Furca Pass he is told by his estimable tutor: 'You are an incorrigible, hopeless Don Quixote.'

In learning English, Conrad learnt the English of Romanticism. The memoir makes use of the established vocabulary of wonder, terror, and escape: 'impulse', 'caprice', 'adventure', 'inexplicable', 'unaccountable'. This mystery-mongering has a dual purpose. It grants the appeal, and the folly, of the states to which the words refer, grants that, for all their worth, they may amount to no more, if not to something even worse, than a 'freak of affectation or perversity'.

He writes in the memoir about the imaginative person's sense of things—which is also the novelist's sense, as contrasted with that of the moralist Rousseau.[5] The novelist's 'conscience' is identified with an attention to the 'spectacle' of the imperfectly sensed phenomenal world. Conscience is seeing. Conrad may seem here to be invoking two opposite meanings which exist for the word in French—conscience and consciousness—and to be contrasting them, and his position looks almost like a way of meeting the charges which were to be brought against him by Forster and others: that his philosophy was a fraud, a fume. He does not want to be a philosopher, any more than he wants to be a moralist. He has an eye for action: not just for the action of adventurers or the exotic outdoors, but for all action, all appearance. The reality of things has to be seen to be believed. In his devotion to spectacle can be seen the workings of another great tradition of the English novel (to which Leavis was not indifferent—no friend of the cinema, he could mention, without losing his temper, Conrad's availability to the 'cinematographer'). Conrad claims here that 'the unwearied self-forgetful attention to every phase of the living universe reflected in our consciousness may be our appointed task on this earth. A task in which fate has perhaps engaged nothing of us except our conscience, gifted with a voice in order to bear true testimony to the visible wonder, the haunting terror, the infinite passion and the illimitable serenity; to the supreme law and the abiding mystery of the sublime spectacle.' These concluding expressions are used in the Gothic mode to evoke, and to revoke, escapes, to denote, and to doubt, the transcendence of limits. The memoir speaks of 'the limits traced by the reality of his time to the play of his invention'—limits which the novelist must exactly understand, rather than transcend—and it is reasonable to think that both the memoir and the mode oscillate between bounds and boundlessness, that they concur in this dual purpose. The man who attends to what he sees and tries to understand it can't be thought to be simply trying to escape it, just as the man who all his life remained loyal to the traditions of the Merchant Marine can't be thought, in any customary sense of the English word, to be without conscience. The memoir suggests a delight in the language of romance and a determination not to be defeated by it, a response to its attractions together with a sense of what there may be of weakness and delinquency in its incitements.

Romance is attached in Conrad's writings to the idea of getting away—and to the idea of the attraction which a man may feel to another race or nation. This idea is present in an electric sentence in the memoir—a sentence in which, we may think, the decision to leave Poland is fastened to Lord Jim's decision, in a novel written well before the *Personal Record*, to jump from the *Patna* and abandon its passengers to their fate. Conrad says in the memoir that he was a boy who took 'a, so to speak, standing jump out of his racial surroundings and associations'.[6] 'Jump', we may think, is used here with hidden reference to Lord Jim's departure from the *Patna*—and with reference to the memoir's mention of Don Quixote's naïve escape with his very body from the reality of things. With this word, Conrad speaks of his own guilt, and of the guilt which is in romance. Conrad's leaps tend to be debatable, even by the standards of romance. A standing jump sounds painful, if not impossible—it sounds like the injurious running jump of common speech, which someone may be invited to direct at himself. But Conrad did manage to leave his racial surroundings, and we tell ourselves here that Conrad jumped and that Jim jumped, that Conrad's departure from Poland rankled with him, and that romance was from then on both a compulsion and a sore subject.

Lord Jim was published in 1900, and was preceded by *Almayer's Folly* and *An Outcast of the Islands*, and by the sea story *The Nigger of the 'Narcissus'*. Having sown his wild oats at sea, he was now on dry land, and in a foreign country, and newly married. In the first three of these four texts, a disgraced man seeks refuge in a strange place, along with a woman. These preoccupations were to persist throughout the most fertile years of his writing life, which came to an end with the close of the second decade of the new century. 'Heart of Darkness' belongs to 1902; to the following years belong *Romance*, written with Ford Madox Ford, and 'Falk', a story in which the romantic secret of cannibalism is divulged. After this come the 'moralities'—*Nostromo, The Secret Agent*, and *Under Western Eyes*. To 1912 belong the dualistic tale 'The Secret Sharer', and *A Personal Record*. In 1915, in *Victory*, he took up once more the story of a *solitude à deux*. Two years later, in 'The Shadow-Line', he returned to the theme of the opening life, of desertion and maturity, of flight and the mariner's 'first command'.

Implicated as he may be in Jim's anti-social jump, Conrad is not to be mistaken for a coward, and Jim himself is by no means the absconder that Almayer is, or the outcast of the islands, Willems. For the narrator of *Lord Jim*, the professedly 'unexceptional' Marlow, Jim is both 'alone of his kind' and 'one of us': a romantic exception, that's to say, who is also bound by the associations and imperatives which surround an English gentleman who uses words like 'bally' and 'blooming', and whose very blushes are British. In Conrad, romance and race are closely connected, and the connection certainly matters in *Lord Jim*, which is both a romance and a discussion of the subject. Its adventurer is wreathed in the fumy speech of philosophers. When Jim dives from the *Patna*, leaving the pilgrims in the lurch, this is the action of a youth who had dreamt of how he would meet such colourful challenges. His failure to meet this challenge when it comes is therefore portentous—a fall in more ways than one. As the sententious Jewish trader Stein observes, 'it is not good for you to find you cannot make your dream come true.' In the retreating boat, Jim 'stole a furtive glance' back at the *Patna*. This is the customary language which calls escape a kind of theft, and Conrad was a habitual user of the verb 'to steal' in its figurative sense of desertion. Jim is not venal (though Willems is): but his theft is a defaulting on obligations to other people—to 'Poland', so to speak. After his original involuntary, dreamlike, somnambulistic act on board the *Patna*, he continues to jump: 'Strange, this fatality that would cast the complexion of a flight upon all his acts, of impulsive unreflecting desertion—of a jump into the unknown.'[7]

According to Marlow, Jim is 'excessively romantic' and has an 'exalted egotism'. Marlow's last glimpse of his friend prompts him to an epitaph-like statement: 'He was romantic, but none the less true.' One of us. At this point Marlow may remind the reader of Stein's dictum about immersing yourself in 'the destructive element' of dreams. Stein had said, in his broken English:

> A man that is born falls into a dream like a man who falls into the sea. If he tries to climb out into the air as inexperienced people endeavour to do, he drowns—*nicht war?* . . . No! I tell you! The way is to the destructive element submit yourself, and with the exertions of your hands and feet in the water make the deep, deep sea keep you up.

A man must learn to live with the dream he is born to. He must 'follow the dream'. While Stein's words could be taken to refer to the circumstances of Jim's jump, he is concerned to place romance in the light, not of a desertion, nor of a stealing or soaring, but of a form of commitment. He goes on to say that it is both 'very good' and 'very bad' to be a romantic, and, as the two philosophers 'steal' by candlelight about the mansion, it turns out that Stein himself is a romantic, but a very good romantic. His life has been rich 'in all the exalted elements of romance': it has been 'rich in generous enthusiasms, in friendship, love, war', and was 'begun in humble surroundings'. And he has followed his dream. Both the faithful and successful Stein and the fallen Jim are deemed 'exalted' in the novel.[8]

It is hard to tell whether Jim's alliterative retreat from the *Patna* to Patusan has the character of an ill-fated flight or of a submission to the destructive element which ensures a romantic salvation. His exertions against the pirates led by Gentleman Brown—sometimes accounted his bad double—are of a very bungling kind, and Conrad seems to admire him for it, and to admire what his woman (rightly) experiences as his desertion of her. His leadership of Patusan's lesser breeds may be meant to redeem whatever there is of flight in his retirement there, and whatever there is of failure in his pedalling movements in the destructive element. His muddles are felt to be interesting because they are romantic, and they are romantic partly because they are English. It is a doubly exotic book: set in the picturesque jungle and taking as its hero a chivalrous, phlegmatic, exalted English failure charged with the remorse and the romance of an expatriate author. The philosopher of fine sights delivers many fine sights and many interesting reflections.

Meanwhile he had also been at work, with Ford, on a different sort of romantic book. He hoped that *Romance* would 'hit the taste of the street', but sometimes took it more seriously. It was not a boy's book, he explained—of a book about the adventures of a boy who outgrows them. It reads like a Stevensonian frolic, and has what Jocelyn Baines describes, with a hint of understatement, as 'a particularly conventional and doltish hero'.[9] Conrad's dolts are, in general, evidence of a desire to treat the romantic critically, but there is very little of that in *Romance*: what there is is apt to occur in Part Three, which is reported to be mostly Conrad's, and in Part Four, which is reported to be almost wholly his. Conrad was responsible for the homely English seafaring characters and for nautical effects eloquent of flight and theft. He can be said here, in the words of Mrs Radcliffe, to hoist a 'stealing sail'.

John Kemp, a young Englishman of the Regency, grandson of an earl, grows up in a Kent infested by a Mafia of smugglers: an exotic doorstep, which he quits for foreign parts, in search of romance. He is kidnapped and borne to Cuba, where, in the palace of a Spanish grandee beside a settlement of smelly pirates, he falls in love with the heiress Seraphina, who is desired by an elderly Irish nationalist rapparee, O'Brien, who is hated for hating the English. The novel says that difference of race 'brings with it the feeling of romance or awakens hate'. The Spanish awaken both feelings: the difference in response is dictated by the class of the Spaniard in question, among other factors. England is romantic for the authors. Spain, with its Spanish lady, is romantic for their hero. Kemp and the lady nearly starve to death in a huge cave whose aperture is blocked by O'Brien and his pirates. The immured lovers escape —it is as if they were 'newly arisen from a tomb'—and make for a valley, with a waterfall and a stream. 'It was a wild scene, and the orifice of the cave appeared as an inaccessible black hole some ninety feet above our heads.' This wild scene is landscaped according to literary prescription, in the image of a mother's body, and O'Brien presides over it in the capacity of father-rival: 'this man whose passion had for so long hung over my life like a shadow'. When Kemp swoons from exhaustion, the idea of death and rebirth is revived.

It was delicious to die. I followed the floating shape of my love beyond the worlds of the universe. We soared together above pain, strife, cruelty, and pity. We had left death behind us and everything of life but our love, which threw a radiant halo around two flames which were ourselves—and immortality inclosed us in a great and soothing darkness.[10]

This is Conrad's work—the work of a man who had attempted suicide in his youth. The novel as a whole has the interest only of its display of, and presumption of a market for, hostile feelings, together with its voluble definitions of the romantic. At one level, it offers, to 'the street', a playful and condescending definition according to which romance is a 'mirage': a boy has his fling and regains respectability. The authors make it clear that they do not mean much of this—are only pretending to be off with those smugglers who have symbolized romantic stealth. They joke about romantic convention, as when 'poor Father Antonio' is heard to murmur 'Inscrutable, inscrutable'—words which Conrad himself can be heard to murmur in works where no parody can be intended. Empires are represented as the achievement of adventurers who get rich: this is a less playful definition of the romantic. Imperial Spain is praised: 'With what a fury of heroism and faith had this whole people flung itself upon the opulent mystery of the New World. Never had a nation clasped closer to its heart its dream of greatness, of glory, and of romance.' But if the Spanish and the British Empires are sometimes forgiven by Conrad for their fury and their grabbing, he never forgave the Russian Empire for grabbing Poland. He had mixed feelings about empire, and about race—and about outlaws. Kemp is a temporary outlaw who makes his true-blue English fortune by stealing away with an heiress. He is a higher species than the Cuban outlaws who chase him: 'cruel without hardihood, and greedy without courage'. These must be Conrad's words, for some of them are used, in 'Heart of Darkness', to characterize the unacceptable face of empire which is worn by an exploring expedition of mere exploiters, whose talk 'was the talk of sordid buccaneers: it was reckless without hardihood, greedy without audacity, and cruel without courage.'[11] British buccaneers are better than other buccaneers. But Seraphina is said to be 'above' Kemp. The more exalted female soul enables a man to fly up to heaven—for a while: Kemp and the lady, their love-death over, are then returned to common life and allowed to execute the street's idea of a happy ending.

Several years later, Conrad rekindled the notion of a love-death in his novel *Victory*. Axel Heyst is a romantic solitary who is the son of a romantic solitary: the novel makes us think that there can be a hereditary alienation. Heyst is also a living character, with winning ways, which elicit a light and supple narrative prose and a satisfying play of wit. The skipper Davidson remarks of this follower of a 'system of restless wandering': 'His father seems to have been a crank, and to have upset his head when he was young. He was a queer chap.' His fate was to have been, like his father's, 'a masterpiece of aloofness', his 'whim' solitude, his existence 'unaccountable' and 'strange'. The father's portrait makes him look 'both exiled and at home, out of place and masterful': outcasts can be masters, can be Poets Laureate and so on, but it is uncertain, when trouble comes, whether this son will follow in his father's footsteps and prove masterful, as well as out of place. Trouble comes when, having sought refuge like so many of Conrad's strangers in a nook of the South-East Asian archipelago, he steals, from her sleazy captors in a travelling orchestra, a second stranger in the person of the girl Lena. This abduction is termed 'the rescue of a distressed human being' by a 'romantic' human being who 'tinges' the world to the hue of his own temperament: so it is the act of a Don Quixote. It is also an act which admits him to a fresh, while compromising a first, seclusion. His new solitude is suspected of harbouring money, however, and three crooks, Jones and his henchmen, decide to burgle the paradise he has established on an island beside the derelict buildings of his coaling concern.

Heyst is called by Conrad a waif, a stray, a drifter, by Jones a man in the moon, and he is blamed for his 'independency' by another ill-wisher, who makes him out to be an impostor, a swindler. Nor is this the only countenance in the novel for the thought that he is a sort of thief. 'He stole away from the door, staggering . . .'. Heyst is said, and not by any ill-wisher, to have stolen the girl. A suggestion of theft may be located in his name, which perhaps incorporates 'heist' in the sense of lift or steal (a sense which had certainly become current in America by the end of the next decade), as well as 'hoist' in the sense of elevate or exalt: while 'Axel' may refer to the aloofness of Villiers de l'Isle Adam's aesthetic hero. But the only sense in which he is morally a thief is that which relates to his desertion of the human race.

Lena, too, is secret and solitary; she sleeps an 'enchanted' sleep which sends Heyst 'stealing' out of the living-room; she is delicately convincing in the part of waif or stray, and her flight from Surabaya affords some of Conrad's finest sights. 'She had come to him of her own free will, with her own soul yearning unlawfully': this may seem a little vapid, but Lena is not that, and her love-affair with Heyst, that of two strangers who are never to understand one another, is not that either. Such a success is unusual in Conrad, and would seem to rest on a form of ignorance. Women and foreigners were alike—unknown ground which might or might not bear fruit. He conceded that he didn't know the Malays he wrote about, and he doesn't know his Chinese: we read here, at any rate, about the 'Chinaman's mind' of Heyst's servant, which is without notions of 'romantic honour' and which moves in ways mysterious to his master. Nor does he always know the women he writes about. The otherness of certain women and of certain foreigners may or may not be romantic. Ignorance is bliss, or hate.

Heyst's alienation is doubled and distorted by that of Jones.

Jones, the brigand, perceives a sameness in his victim. He says that he himself is an outcast, 'almost an outlaw', a rebel, like the Devil, and he mentions Heyst's 'independence from common feelings'. This strain of duality in the novel lays stress on the weakness of Heyst's position as a thoughtful stray by disclosing an alter ego in whom the principle of desertion has been exacerbated into crime: the real thieves point up the degree of theft entailed by Heyst's aloofness. Jones and his partners are Gothically depicted as a ghost, a snake, and an ape: Heyst meets the challenge by mislaying his revolver and, with Lena dead, setting fire to himself. This could be called a love-death, a *Liebestod*, if not a suicide. Love and bungling hoist them to the stars.

'Ah, Davidson, woe to the man whose heart has not learned while young to hope, to love—and to put its trust in life!'[12] Baron Heyst the orphan prince has by now seen the error of his ways, of his solitude. Steal and soar, heist and hoist, are wrong. To trust in life is to trust in other people. Heyst steals from the world at the end of the book, and it is a book in which such a theft is both performed and condemned. It is a book which says, 'Leave the world,' and which also says: 'Stay.' Heyst invites us to put our trust in life while arranging to die: in a style which claims the sanction of Shakespearian tragedy and some kind of victory over death. I can't grasp, though Leavis can, how Heyst's dualistic Pyrrhic victory could encourage anyone to put their trust in life, but I can grasp how the contradictions which attend it may have helped Conrad to deal with the guilt which seems to have followed this jumper to his English Patusan.

Conrad's dualistic practice may be summarized as entailing a contest between suicide and survival, defection and community: his long stories, 'The Secret Sharer' of 1912 and 'The Shadow-Line' of 1917, are concerned with these matters, and each, but especially the former, has been reckoned a crucial text of the dualistic tradition. Duality in Conrad could well be thought inherent in the condition of undecidability enjoyed—as witness the profusion and variety of the critical accounts—by these two tales. They belong to that body of work in which he treats the circumstances of his first command in the Merchant Navy. 'The Shadow-Line' was provisionally entitled 'First

Command', and he explained that its main aim was to chart a passage from youth to maturity. Both stories describe the behaviour of a young man who might have defected, might indeed have destroyed himself, but who succeeds in taking command and in surviving among his kind.

The narrator of 'The Secret Sharer' is 'a stranger to the ship' of which he becomes captain, and which is stationed at the head of the Gulf of Siam, and he is 'a stranger to myself'. The tale is told in terms of 'my strangeness', and of the 'stealthiness' which the narrator embraces in his dealings with other sailors. It reveals how a second, guilty self goes free, while the first self to which it is joined, and which has survived to tell the tale, endures a test or ordeal which has to do with the liberation of its, as it were, Siamese companion. The second self, though guilty, had saved his former ship, while the first self risks his ship in order to pass the test.

What happens is that the renegade Leggatt swims up to the captain's ship, having accidentally killed an insubordinate negro in a storm, during which he had acted in such a way as to secure the vessel. His 'strung-up force which had given twenty-four men a chance, at least, for their lives, had, in a sort of recoil, crushed an unworthy mutinous existence'.[13] This involuntary and by no means unqualified guilt is not unlike that of Coleridge's Ancient Mariner. The runaway is welcomed on board by the narrator, and is turned into a stowaway. When Leggatt's old captain comes searching for him, the narrator receives this visitor with the hostile suspicion which has already marked his treatment of his own crew. Stowaway and narrator conspire to put the stowaway ashore: this is held to necessitate the dangerous manoeuvre of sailing in close to the island of Koh-ring, with its mountain, 'a towering black mass like the very gateway of Erebus', dropping Leggatt off to swim for it, and then veering out to sea, with not a moment to be lost, in the hope of cadging a breath of wind.

This drama of life and death maintains an unbroken suspense. It is a marvellous stroke to have the Captain's hat, lent to the swimmer, float on the water as a marker when the ship draws breathlessly away to sea. The bewhiskered Chief Mate has been frightened by this unaccountable hugging of the coast: 'Bless my soul! Do you mean, sir, in the dark amongst the lot of all them islands and reefs and shoals?' Leggatt is now 'gone from the ship, to be hidden forever from all friendly faces, to be a fugitive and vagabond on the earth'. He has earlier said that his fate, like Cain's, is to be off 'the face of the earth'. As a point of honour, of 'conscience', the Captain has helped him 'into the water to take his punishment as a free man, a proud swimmer striking out for a new destiny'. At the same time, we might reflect that, 'in the ignorance of my strangeness', the Captain is helping him overboard, and that this is the road taken, in some of Conrad's writings, by deserters and by suicides. And we might ask what captain would hazard his ship, with its twenty-four men or so, in order to give a stowaway a safer swim?

In the course of the story the stowaway becomes 'my secret self', is acknowledged by the Captain as his double. And this is a deserting double who resembles other deserters in Conrad's writings. Leggatt escapes from captivity, is no less hostile than his other self to those about him, carries an innocent sort of guilt, as a result of a more or less involuntary act which delivers him to a vulnerable sort of freedom: part of this applies to Jim. He jumps, as Jim does, and as the suicide Brierly does in *Lord Jim*. His father, like Jim's, and like the father of Jim's supposed original, is a country vicar. The Captain is conscious of the sensations of independence which go with command, and he domineers over his crew. But the reader has reason to feel that he will discover a dependence on his crew, and discover that he will do well to try to respect them. In this, he differs from Leggatt, who is on the run and on his own. It may be that the fable is about a single human being who experiences a wish to go and a wish to stay. But the wishes have scarcely produced separate selves. The self that stays is compromised by the other's departure—the Captain's feeling for his own transgressions causing him to hazard his ship, which is much the same, from a certain point of view, as jumping over its side. And the two selves are united at the close in an exercise of freedom which does not bode well—though Conrad seems to think differently—for the future of the ship.

In 'The Shadow-Line' a raw captain gains an 'undying regard' for his ship's company. The action is again located in the Gulf of Siam, with Koh-ring on the horizon. The narrator of the story jumps ship at the start of it: in a fit of despondency and uncertainty, of 'impulse' and 'caprice', he gives up a berth as mate and travels to Singapore, intending to return to England. 'Leaving the ship' has, for this man, who has a talent for feeling guilty and whose account is subtitled 'A Confession', the character 'almost of desertion'. He leaves 'inconsequentially', as 'a bird flies from a comfortable branch'. He feels independent and unearthly. The people at a naval officers' hostel, including the fatherly Captain Giles, provoke in him the irritable suspicions that belonged, for Conrad, to the threshold of maturity. The impulse to quit is overtaken by an impulse to take command, and both impulses are treated with reference to the language of flight. Giles sends him flying to a ship of his own. Once appointed, he 'floats along': 'I use that word rather than the word "flew", because I have a distinct impression that, though uplifted by my aroused youth, my movements were deliberate enough.' These movements may be like the exertions which are appropriate to Stein's destructive element. 'When a fully appointed gala coach is produced out of a pumpkin to take her to a ball Cinderella does not exclaim. She gets in quietly and drives away to her high fortune.' Literally an orphan, the narrator is behaving like one of the fortunate foundlings of romance, and one aspect of the becalmed voyage which is to ensue is that of an enchantment.

The new ship, which he joins in Bangkok, has a Chief Mate, Burns, who is sick, and who is possessed by a fear of the previous captain, an old man now dead, a hazarder of the ship with his caprices. Told that he is sitting where the old captain died, his successor has to repress 'a silly impulse to jump up'. The new captain insists on 'getting them away', and out of kindness the Mate is fetched on board as an invalid. There's no wind, though, to get them very far away. The narrator feels 'familiar' with the crew, 'and yet a little strange, like a long-lost wanderer among his kin'. Earlier, Burns has said that the bad old captain had 'meant to have gone wandering about the world': this Leggatt-like activity is elsewhere called 'acting the Flying Dutchman'. Flying, floating, wandering, drifting—Conrad is playing darkly with the old relation between planetary movements and human destinies. Flight is fate in the tale, as in *Lord Jim*. It is present both as desertion and as trajectory

—a fixed course to which 'impulse' may attest but which may be unconnected with the conscious will. When the wind fails, the new captain reflects: 'My command might have been a planet flying vertiginously on its appointed path in a space of infinite silence.' His appointment threatens to become a struggle between wandering off and the seaman's instinct and duty to protect his ship.[14]

So far from being a kind of independence, command becomes an experience in which, as he twice puts it, he is 'bound hand and foot'. The motionless ship is beset by fever, and he finds that his predecessor has sold their supply of quinine. 'The seed of everlasting remorse was sown in my breast.' Another trouble is Burns's anxiety that they are due to sail over the former captain's dead body in the Gulf. It is as if they are under an evil spell. 'I feel as if all my sins had found me out,' the Captain writes in his journal. 'No confessed criminal had ever been so oppressed by his sense of guilt.' He is the only well man on the ship, but his soul is sick. He is 'no good'.[15] A storm hangs over them. Then a wind starts up, and the ship feels like a runaway. But captain and crew have 'a jump or two' left in them, the suffering sailor Ransome plays the part of a redeemer, and with great difficulty these orphans of the storm get the ship to port. The captain's second flight has ceded to a solidarity with his fellow sailors. This he calls 'my education'.[16]

The story employs memories of Coleridge's poem, *The Ancient Mariner*. In both, there is a curse and a ghastly crew, seamen with fits, a boat with fits and starts, a world of impulse and arrest, and a loving reconciliation at the close. 'They passed under my eyes one after another—each of them an embodied reproach of the bitterest kind . . .'.[17] Coleridge's poem has:

> And every soul, it passed me by,
> Like the whizz of my cross-bow!

The bond between the two works is the curse that lies on the ship, and its relation to the involuntary guilt—the original sin, as it may appear—of a single sick soul. In one of the prose glosses to his poem Coleridge writes: 'But the curse liveth for him in the eyes of the dead men.' In the story a dead man, the old captain, has his eye on the crew. We may want to compare Burns's superstitious fear with the narrator's no less superstitious guilt, and to compare, as types of fatherhood, the two ancient mariners, Captain Giles and the wandering young captain's wandering predecessor. Such comparisons are typical of the various and equivocal literary text which we associate with the modern world. 'The Shadow-Line' can be called an adventure story, a ghost story, a god story, and a rite of passage. It can also be called an orphan narrative of departure and return.

At one stage there is an effect of 'inconceivable terror and inexpressible mystery'. But it can be said that, like Cinderella, Conrad does not exclaim here, as he does in some other places. With this convincing picture of trust and common action his critique of romantic separation and self-destruction was nearing its end. 'My education,' says the Captain. But then, in another work, *An Outcast of the Islands*, the dualistic Conrad speaks of 'our isolation'—the isolation of every human being, which not even the order, fidelity, and fellowship possible on board the good ship could hope to cure, and which is seen in that work to be an isolation constrained by 'warring impulses'.[18] Conrad's fork, so to speak, has caused Frederick Crews to say of 'the Conradian *Angst*' that 'it comforts us because it is shared, indeed it is built into the order of things, and we combat it with the fellowship of our orphanage. Underlying everything is the seductive, unmentionable thought that it is not so bad after one's fitful strivings to sink back into the maternal nothingness.'[19] This comes from an essay which has a striking analysis of 'Heart of Darkness', a work to which I would now like to turn in conclusion.

The orphan represents the human capacity for grief and fear, dualistically reversible into their antithesis and infliction, into the action of the aggressor, the monster and the thief. From the literature of the Romantic period we learn that it is good to get away, but good to get back, and that there is a bad self which steals from the community. In the literature of the later nineteenth century and of the Edwardian period this knowledge was preserved and extended. It is preserved and extended in the art and sophistication of Conrad and James, and in Modernism at large, with its protean artists and second-self narrators, its debt to the duality of the past. Much was made of the sayings and observances of the past, of its fictitious articles, its articles and vehicles of faith, its leaps and bounds, orphan and double, of departure as desertion and theft. There arose a new synthesis, which could be construed as a new age. The old knowledge is notably restored and reworked in 'Heart of Darkness', a tale of the double which was written at the same time as Chekhov's tale of the double life, 'The Lady with the Little Dog', in the last year of the nineteenth century, and which was quite soon to be followed by James's 'Jolly Corner'.

Conrad's tale may be thought to incorporate, or to portend, the revolutionary practices of Modernist fiction; and there is much that separates it from any tale of Chekhov's. But then Chekhov should not be buried in the nineteenth century, and both 'Heart of Darkness' and 'The Steppe' show a persistence with romantic themes and figuration: each tells of delirium and of an outcast's outlandish journey. Conrad's narrator Marlow, the sovereign sailor and clubman, recalls that at the outset of the adventure he chooses to recount, his sense of identity was shaken; in his 'sheer nervousness' he felt isolated, an impostor; he was all nerves and pulses; he was ill; and towards the end of the adventure he falls into what resembles a terminal swoon. The narrative he proceeds with, moreover, is tenebrous, preposterous, and absurd. James's wicked word for Conrad's alter-ego Master Mariner was 'preposterous'. But we may say that Conrad meant him to be, in a sense: 'preposterous' and 'absurd' were words for the Edwardian *outré* and its annals of estrangement, its journey out of nature into the realm of the supernatural. 'Heart of Darkness' is a self-conscious and sophisticated tall tale of the new age.

In the gathering dusk, Marlow tells distinguished hearers on a boat in the lower reaches of the Thames how as a young man he went searching in the jungle for the interesting thief Kurtz, an alleged genius who has built a store of ivory by taking it from the 'savages' who worship him. We discover that Kurtz is Marlow's secret sharer. 'I was anxious to deal with this shadow by myself alone':[20] Marlow's remark signals the presence of an orphan and a double, and of an engagement with the outlook and strange precedents of the Gothic tradition. A similar signal occurs just before the meeting with Kurtz, when Marlow's black steersman is speared and his life's blood soaks the adventurer's shoes, causing him to be 'morbidly anxious to change my shoes and socks'. He imparts to a bystander: 'I suppose Mr Kurtz is dead as well by this time.'

For the moment that was the dominant thought. There was a sense of extreme disappointment, as though I had found out I had been striving after something altogether without a substance. I couldn't have been more disgusted if I had travelled all this way for the sole purpose of talking with Mr Kurtz. Talking with . . . I flung one shoe overboard, and became aware that that was exactly what I had been looking forward to—a talk with Kurtz. I made the strange discovery that I had never imagined him as doing, you know, but as discoursing.

These shoes are dualistically expressive (and as such may seem to fit Golyadkin's galoshes in *The Double*). When they go overboard—where doubles and deserters go in Conrad—Marlow becomes strangely aware of what he has been seeking from Kurtz, and the reader may become strangely aware that Kurtz is Marlow's other shoe. Then again, the material pair in question is soaked with the helmsman's blood, which gives a sense of the 'remote' connection established in the tale between its narrator and the inhabitants of this prehistoric world in the stillness of its arrest. The steersman doubles for the sophisticate both in this and in a further respect: 'Perhaps you will think it passing strange this regret for a savage who was no more account than a grain of sand in a black Sahara. Well, don't you see, he had done something, he had steered; for months I had him at my back—a help—an instrument. It was a kind of partnership.' Kurtz, though, is Marlow's chief partner, or mate. He may be about to prove to be a talker rather than a doer, and to have yielded to the jungle, to an ancient horror: but it is with Kurtz that Marlow's main affinity lies.[21]

When both shoes have gone 'flying' into the river, Marlow is overcome by a feeling of savage desolation at the thought that he may not be able to talk with Kurtz. 'Absurd?' he asks his hearers in England. 'My dear boys, what can you expect from a man who out of sheer nervousness had just flung overboard a pair of new shoes!' If Marlow is nervous, Kurtz is 'high-strung'. And 'whatever he was, he was not common,' while whatever Marlow is, he is not as common as he calls himself in *Lord Jim*. 'I am Mr Kurtz's friend—in a way,' says Marlow. 'Mr Kurtz's reputation is safe with me.' Orphan and double talk together when Kurtz attempts to rejoin his worshippers: their disagreement registers as soliloquy or internal debate. Duality's most familiar face—talking to yourself—is shown. '"Do you know what you are doing?" I whispered. "Perfectly," he answered . . .'. '"You will be lost," I said—"utterly lost."' Earlier, Marlow has been 'lost'—in astonishment, and indeed in something worse.[22]

Then again, Kurtz is what Marlow is, in a way, and what Conrad is, since he turns out to be a writer, an artist, of a sort. He makes people 'see things': which is what, according to Conrad, novelists do. Both Kurtz and Marlow discourse in the dark, on their respective rivers. Kurtz has written a statement which boasts of bringing light to darkest Africa: 'a beautiful piece of writing'. The opening paragraph, with its airs and assumptions of romantic infallibility, is said by Marlow to impress him as 'ominous'. But it reads like a parody of Conrad's expansive or superlative vein.

> 'By the simple exercise of our will we can exert a power for good practically unbounded,' etc, etc. From that point he soared and took me with him. The peroration was magnificent, though difficult to remember, you know. It gave me the notion of an exotic Immensity ruled by an august Benevolence. It made me tingle with enthusiasm. This was the unbounded power of eloquence—of words—of burning noble words.

And a scrawl on the last page, which refers to Kurtz's Africans, reads like a piece of Late Victorian literature on the burning-out of the animal in human beings: 'Exterminate all the brutes.'[23] The bounder Kurtz is a writer, and he is another kind of artist besides—a musician, with someone in Belgium claiming to be an organist cousin of his. Kurtz can read like a portent or travesty of another artist, an inhabitant of the real world, who was also to go to Africa, not long after the tale was written, to exercise an authoritarian benevolence.

The tale belongs to a world which traces limits for its writer. At the same time, it is fashioned from correspondences and coincidences whose purport can appear boundless, vertiginous, preposterous. It can foretell the future, while containing aftermaths of the writer's childhood. It says, among other things, that the bad self steals. Kurtz steals from his savages, amassing a treasure. Meanwhile Conrad, who stole from Poland, created surrogates here which allowed him to speak of his own capacity for surrender and for resistance. The figurative theft which I have ascribed to his art is offered as an exemplary source, but as by no means the only source, for the anxiety and self-incrimination, for the fear of yielding, drifting, of going overboard, or too far, which form part of the dialectic of his fiction. It is a theft to which Conrad himself must have been more susceptible than the alter ego who narrates 'Heart of Darkness'. Marlow here is a resilient singleton, rather than a two-shoes or a forked creature. Conrad once fancied himself 'a Polish nobleman, cased in a British tar'.[24] But Marlow is a strange case for a depressive exile's experience of surrender and complicity. It is a tale which this British tar can only relate a little preposterously.

Ian Watt does not think this a tall story: there is 'really very little' in it which 'cannot be understood by a literal interpretation of what is said and done'.[25] Faced with Conrad's exclamatory Gothic adjectives, his sometimes self-mocking 'inscrutables' and 'inconceivables', it is natural for commentary to look for an adherence to 'the limits traced by the reality of his time to the play of his invention', and it is a search which is frequently rewarded. But it is clear that on this occasion Conrad wanted a figurative, far-fetched, unbounded work. Some readers perceive in it a Freudian family romance: a father figured in the ambience of Kurtz, with his treasure and his 'unspeakable' rites; and the recovery of a mother, such a mother being seen as an attribute of Kurtz's Intended, interviewed by Marlow at the end of the story. Frederick Crews's essay has in mind a Conrad who was at times nervous, passive, ill, and a courageous art which was subject to obstruction and arrest, and which can be subjected to psychoanalytic investigation. Concerning the 'dream' which shapes 'Heart of Darkness', Crews makes these observations, offering them as those of some psychoanalyst:

The dreamer is preoccupied with the primal scene, which he symbolically interrupts. The journey into the maternal body is both voyeuristic and incestuous, and the rescue of the father is more defiant and supplantive than tender and restitutive. The closing episode with the 'phantom' woman in a sarcophagal setting would be the dreamer-son's squaring of accounts with his dead mother. He 'knows' that parental sexuality is entirely the father's fault, and he has preserved the maternal image untarnished by imagining that the father's partner was not she but a savage woman, a personification of the distant country's 'colossal body of the fecund and mysterious life'. But given the anxiety generated by his fantasy of usurpation, he prefers to suppress the father's misdeeds. Such a tactic reduces the threat of punishment while re-establishing the 'pure' mother-son dyad. Only one complaint against the sainted mother is allowed to reach expression: the son tells her with devious truthfulness that the dying sinner's last word ('horror!') was 'your name'.[26]

Kurtz is an adversary self not unlike the possible former self imagined—as the guardian of a treasure—in James's 'Jolly Corner', and the resemblance does not impede the thought that Kurtz may be understood both as Marlow and as Marlow's father (however little of a son, for the most part, the Marlow of these adventures, or of their narration, may be experienced as being). It could well be thought that the story's correspondences and coincidences are grounded in the internal transactions of a single self, in hostile complicity with another human being, whose status as second self or imaginary father is a subordinate element; and that the family romance is glimpsed or approached, rather than constituted, in the text. But its presence there is not to be ignored, and the connections made by Crews are an aid to the comprehension of literary duality in general. Literal interpretation risks snuffing out the haze or halo, created by the 'spectral illumination of moonshine', which Marlow attaches, by way of 'meaning', to the tale he is about to tell. And we can take it that this is the kind of meaning which Conrad wanted to attach to the whole work, whose journey, he thought, was like something out of a fairy-tale. There is every reason to suppose that this believer in 'warring impulses' and 'the duality of man's nature' meant to bring out the division between a regressive self and a practical and even convivial self, set on doing its duty and on securing a future in which during 'discussions at the club'—Chekhov's phrase, of these same months, in 'The Lady with the Little Dog'—there might be harking-back to an old horror and malaise. In pursuit of this aim, Conrad gave himself to the kind of romance in which orphan and flight, orphan and double, meet, and in which, for spectral interpreters, for contenders with an illimitable haze, and for psychoanalysts, the same journey might reach to the ends of the earth and back to the beginnings of consciousness—that of the individual and that of the species.

Conrad experts—a community which can seem to grow larger by the week—have often seen him as more hostile to impulse and to romance than he is represented in this chapter. It is possible to see, for instance, in *Lord Jim*, a more sinister Stein than I am able to recognize, and a more atavistic Jim—whose jumps take him back, and down, to some sector of the heart of darkness, in accordance with scientific theories of evolution and of the unconscious.[27] There are those of us whom this might compel to make what we can of the outlandish thought that Conrad relates his expatriation to the degeneration of the species. Many thoughts, and many warring thoughts, have been expressed on the subject of his fictions, and the attempts that are now being made to determine his meaning are not about to come to an agreement. His is an art which is conditioned to sustain debate. Boundlessness and vertigo and moonshine are interminable, and in Conrad they are never more apparent than on this very subject of determination—of the fatal flight path, the traced way, the appointed course. This suggests, not that Conrad fails to make sense, but that he makes sense as a dualistic artist.

XIII. EDITH WHARTON'S SECRET

Just before the turn of the century, in her late thirties, the novelist Edith Wharton suffered a spell of nervous exhaustion—of asthma, nausea, and depression—in which a troubled childhood, and a distaste for her marriage to Teddy Wharton, can be perceived. She was treated in Philadelphia by the dualistic physician Weir Mitchell, who prescribed rest, food, fiction, and an isolation from family life. Confinement within an unhappy marriage formed part of her confinement within what survived, as much did, of Old New York—her name for the world of her childhood. She has described this as the world of the hereditary rich in that city, infiltrated by the new industrial fortunes, of matrons who believed in an undefiled and ceremonious past, of dry old male celibates, propped by the fireside like wooden Indians, who remembered and related such a past, and could speak of laxities condoned in the Faubourg Saint-Germain. Miss Edith Jones had an engagement knocked over by jealousies among the contending rich, and she was then let down by a man who went on to become a distinguished snob, and her dearest friend, Walter Berry. Then there was the eligible Teddy Wharton. From the confinements of wealth and caste, however, and of a suitable marriage, she was to imagine and to execute certain escapes.[1]

It was a liberation in itself that she emerged from her illness with the will to write unimpaired. In 1905, the year after James's *The Golden Bowl*, one of her finest novels appeared—*The House of Mirth*. Two years later she began an affair with the fatal Morton Fullerton—who was promiscuous and unreliable—and acquired an apartment in Paris, the city where, from then on, she was to be chiefly based. Around 1909, by which time the affair had about a year to run, she is thought to have learned of a rumour that she was the offspring of an affair between her mother and a young Englishman who had served as tutor to the family. In 1911, the story of the captive Ethan Frome was published by the former Edith Jones, and the following year she brought out *The Reef*, in which a stately woman agonizes over her love for a sexually compromised suitor, and in which, where others have hailed a resemblance to James, her friend since 1904, James hailed a resemblance to Racine.

Meanwhile Teddy's mental and physical health was breaking down, and she was shocked to discover that he'd been borrowing her money and splashing it on chorus girls. Divorce, by which Old New York had been affronted, overtook her in 1913—the year of *The Custom of the Country*. During the Great War, this refugee from the gilded, from the shocked and shocking, life of her native country set herself to work for the war's refugees, but she also managed to write a most eloquent book about a very different type of refuge—the novella *Summer*. Some months after the peace of 1918, it would seem, she composed the 'unpublishable' fragment, as she called it, of a story entitled 'Beatrice Palmato',[2] in which a father and daughter make love. Finally, in 1920, came *The Age of Innocence*, from which incest is absent, in which adultery is arrested, and in which, while continuing to find fault with its narrow-minded philistine devotion to kinship and routine, to ease and eating, terrapin and canvas-back duck, she signs an armistice with the world she had inherited and had hitherto resented. 'After all, there was good in the old ways.'[3] The canvas-back duck reveals a silver lining, if not a heart of gold.

The works which saw the light in the course of these fifteen eventful years carry a critique, in the mode of the novel of manners, of the society in which she was raised. But they are not all, or not unrelievedly, novels of manners: in some of them, satire is suspended, and a more frankly personal, even a confessional note is sounded. There are very few of them, moreover, in which she suspends her interest in questions of confinement and escape, and this has also been held to be true of her work as a whole. Blake Nevius has identified, as concerns prominent from 1905 onward, the mismating of a sensitive nature, and the degree of 'freedom or rebellion' which is to be permitted to such captives,[4] and in his *Portrait of Edith Wharton* of 1947 Percy Lubbock evokes her preoccupation with the themes of freedom and order. It is clear that her taste of freedom, and of the Great War, and of the far end of middle age, was to give her a new sense of the need for order. In her treatment of these themes, she drew on the worldly, sceptical capacities for which she is famous, but in yielding to the compulsions associated with such themes, she also drew on resources of quite another kind—on a language and outlook to which a statement from Lubbock's *Portrait* can be taken to guide us: 'wherever there is romance it is the proof that you are outside yourself and leaving yourself behind.'[5] The self lies in prison, and the prison is that of the family or community, or that of marriage. But you may move outside yourself and take flight. Or you may opt for a series of little flights—hops and skips, rather than leaps. Such efforts may succeed or fail, and the writer who uses this language is likely to appoint limits, to arrange for the traveller to return home. The possession of two or more selves may enable you to be both at home and away. American writers of the period as different as Wharton and Frost can concur in thinking it natural to talk of someone's being fuelled by the 'impulse to flight'. The old opposites, 'regular' and 'irregular', remained available to the Joneses to characterize the behaviour of outsiders and bohemians—such creatures as the 'drunken and demoralised Baltimorean', Poe[6]—and the irregular impulse to flight accounted for fits and feats of human waywardness and idiosyncrasy, for a practice of seclusion and for forms of theft. Wharton was an inveterate user of the figurative 'steal'.

The memoirs of her seventies, *A Backward Glance*, are interesting from this point of view. Her parents' set cared about language, and was on the watch for vernacular infection. All her life she thought that there was such a thing as 'insignificant people': her mother thought there was such a thing as common people, and that commonness was contagious. 'I still wince under my mother's ironic smile when I said that some visitor had stayed "quite a while", and her dry: "Where did you pick *that* up?"' The novelist of manners was born to a phobia about bad manners. Her first attempt to write, at 11, was a novel which began:

> '"Oh, how do you do, Mrs Brown?" said Mrs Tompkins. "If only I had known you were going to call I should have tidied up the drawing-room."' Timorously I submitted this to my mother, and never shall I forget the sudden drop of my creative frenzy when she returned it with the icy comment: 'Drawing-rooms are always tidy.'

We may remember Dickens's backward glance, his 'I never shall forget . . .'. Edith's drawing-room was to be her blacking factory. But she was to find a means of escape.

There was in me a secret retreat where I wished no one to intrude, or at least no one whom I had yet encountered. Words and cadences haunted it like song-birds in a magic wood, and I wanted to be able to steal away and listen when they called. When I was about fifteen or sixteen I tried to write an essay on English verse rhythms. I never got beyond the opening paragraph, but that came straight out of my secret wood. It ran: 'No one who cannot feel the enchantment of "Yet once more, O ye laurels, and once more", without knowing even the next line, or having any idea whatever of the context of the poem, has begun to understand the beauty of English poetry.' For the moment that was enough of ecstasy; but I wanted to be always free to steal away to it.

She read hungrily in her secret wood, and she does not seem to have missed the story of Keats's encounter with his nightingale, in another such wood.[7]

She was to gain the sense of leading 'two lives': her story-telling life took place 'in some secret region on the sheer edge of consciousness', though it was a region to which her critical faculties had access. This was a geography she could be doubtful of, and *The Reef* worries, on behalf of its heroine, that 'the secret excursions of her spirit' have returned her to 'the old vicious distinction between romance and reality'. But Wharton was to write, time and again, about there being these two regions.[8] Real life contained the unforgotten rigours and proprieties of her childhood, and the whole business of practical living. A philistine world. In the second region, dimly prefigured in its bohemian annexe, were art, heart, and the true self. A world that was esoteric, exotic and erotic. The boundaries and existential claims of the two rival species of reality were never to be exactly settled: the aesthete Walter Berry, who used to correct her writings, was more of an inhabitant of the first region than she supposed. But this geography stands in demonstrable relation to the successive faces which she could present to those who knew her, to the way in which the frightened Victorian waif, the Miss Dombey, who looks out from the lap of luxury in a photograph at the age of five was never really extinguished by the grand, smart, sharp, restless madame and martinet that she soon became—intelligent and competent, charitable to waifs but unkind to waiters, drawing herself up, putting down her pretty foot, and placing it to advantage in company, in its perfect shoe.

The victim, and her frightening obverse or alternate, both speak in Edith Wharton. If it was the orphan of the storm who used the romantic vocabulary of flight, then it is not hard to feel that the author of the satirical shafts and invectives had retained some of the old armed exclusiveness of her Manhattan faubourg. The name given to Charity Royall, *Summer*'s gruff waif, who is among the most intimately alive of her characters, is an inspiration which catches the spirit of these contradictions. Lubbock tries to catch them too, and resorts to what might now be seen as an old vicious distinction: 'she had a very feminine consciousness and a very masculine mind.' He concocts a 'mixture of the whimsical and the practical, the ribald and the romantic, in the mind of a boy'. Edith herself used to enjoy the joke that she was a 'self-made man'.[9]

It can be said that she escaped and did not escape from Old New York, but she was certainly bent on getting away. Lubbock mentions her 'flights', and that new luxury, the motor-car, was to serve, however convivially, the secret excursions of her spirit. One of her travel books is called *A Motor-Flight through France*. There they sit, the civilized 'Happy Few', as they and their friends chose to see themselves, in their open tourer. In the front, Teddy, with the chauffeur and an armful of Pekinese. In the back, a grave Henry James, beside Edith, whose face, swathed against the dust, makes them look like a pair of majestic bank robbers—the Bonnie and Clyde of an earlier age and ampler income. Setting out from favourite places, James's Lamb House at Rye, or Queen's Acre at Windsor, these tourists threaded the green lanes and white highways of half Europe, chasing the noble prospect that had divorced them from America. It was her humour to suggest that the English James had fled to the country to live there with his loot; and James, who was to advise her that her salvation lay in the creation of a double life, in the cultivation of a 'separate existence', and who was to be thrilled by the sight of aeroplanes, once complained that, in denying him time to pack for an escape from the American scene, she had not scrupled to 'project me in a naked flight across the Atlantic'.[10] For both of these formidable people, such jokes had point. Both, in the parlance of their time and class, had to fly their flight—a flight that may seem to hover somewhere between a fit and a fate.

In due course, she flew both the Atlantic and the coop: and Teddy was projected from the motor-car. She committed the adultery, and obtained the divorce, which Old New York had held in horror. The flight from America was powered, in part, by a breach with dynastic standards, and, in one sense, it was never to be revoked or returned from, for all that it landed her in a foreign country and left her, ageing anyway, with the problem of a receding subject-matter. In another sense, though, this flight, like other leaps that she made, ended where it began: such circularity is apparent in her coming to think that there was good, after all, in the old ways.

The ancient story of the inescapable, of that unfortunate appointment at Samarra, or Baghdad, is told in her memoirs. This 'strangely beautiful' story came to her from the blissful Cocteau. A youth informs his sultan that he must 'fly at once to Baghdad' because Death has threatened him. But Death explains: 'I only threw up my arms in surprise at seeing him here, because I have a tryst with him tonight in Baghdad.' There is another story in her memoirs which might seem to echo this. She and James have driven from Rye, gypsying through the Southern counties and getting lost, and James has stunned an elderly man with the virtuosity and elaboration of his request for directions:

> 'Oh, please,' I interrupted, feeling myself utterly unable to sit through another parenthesis, 'do ask him where the King's Road is.'
>
> 'Ah—? The King's Road? Just so! Quite right! Can you, as a matter of fact, my good man, tell us where, in relation to our present position, the King's Road exactly *is*?'
>
> 'Ye're in it,' said the aged face at the window.

The hopeful travellers have already arrived, at Windsor. But they are also back where they started from, in the sense that Lamb House and Queen's Acre are the same appointed haven—the same safe house of mirth and literature, from which one might want to take trips.[11]

The secret place disclosed in her fiction and recollections contained literature, and it contained love. To reach that place, some flight or leap had to be undertaken, and, where the love was extra-marital, any such undertaking was rendered all the more meaningful, and all the more difficult, by the mandates and fears which prevailed in her first environment. She recalled in her seventies that as a child she had been warned against adultery every week in church, and had believed that 'those who "committed" it were penalised by having to pay higher fares in travelling: a conclusion arrived at by my once seeing on a ferry-boat the sign: "Adults fifty cents; children twenty-five cents"!' But family censorship did not keep her from the Song of Solomon, *Phèdre* and *The Duchess of Malfi*, and when she wrote books they were such as to incur a rebuke from Charles Eliot Norton—a translator, as she points out, of Dante: 'No great work of the imagination has ever been based on illicit passion.' She heard that her own kin had suffered a Paolo and Francesca: 'The vision of poor featureless unknown Alfred and his siren, lurking in some cranny of my imagination, hinted at regions perilous, dark and yet lit with mysterious fires, just outside the world of copybook axioms, and the old obediences that were in my blood; and the hint was useful—for a novelist.'[12]

Adultery was theft, the theft of, or from, someone's spouse, just as certain other transgressions could be regarded as thefts from the community or the family. One of Edith Wharton's best-loved poems was Browning's 'Any Wife to Any Husband', in which a wife frets that, after her death, her husband may philander with women who appeal to him as images of herself. She says of these posthumous infidelities:

> So must I see, from where I sit and watch,
> My own self sell myself, my hand attach
> Its warrant to the very thefts from me.

In *The Custom of the Country*, a worldly bystander expresses a central concern of the novel, one which matches what James took to be a central concern of *The Bostonians*: the failure, in America, of 'the sentiment of sex', of what could be deemed the old chivalrous, passionate, and predatory relation between men and women. The passage runs:

Where does the real life of most American men lie? In some woman's drawing-room or in their offices? The answer's obvious, isn't it? The emotional centre of gravity's not the same in the two hemispheres. In the effete societies it's love, in our new one it's business. In America the real *crime passionnel* is a 'big steal'—there's more excitement in wrecking railways than homes.[13]

The custom of the country has reversed 'all the romantic values'. The big steal is the business coup, with women idle or ornamental in the domestic coop. The old, the European steal is adultery. And yet there are Americans, too, who commit adultery, and ponder it. Throughout her career, Edith was to use the word 'steal' to refer to a sexual disobedience. This was a woman who inhabited two countries, for whom travel was sexual, and who stole from America.

Love and money are painfully entangled, at the start of this period of years, in *The House of Mirth*, where the smart set of her youth is likened to the hellish house of mirth in the Book of Ecclesiastes. Lily Bart touches somebody's rich pig of a husband for a loan, he tries to touch her, and she perishes for want of a healing touch. This touch might have come from Lawrence Selden, whom she visits, yielding to a 'passing impulse' and having to pay for this 'least escape from routine' by being spied on and courted by the Jewish upstart, Rosedale. Selden lets her down, and he is one of a line of letters-down in Wharton's fiction—weak, amiable, cultivated bachelors with a bit of money. There are times in the novel when a rich and snobbish woman seems to be striking at the rich and snobbish, and when a clever woman seems to be putting down, putting to sleep, a vain and pretty girl. But the girl comes to life for the reader, on her way to destruction—a life in which the novelist shares. The novel is equal to the theme of Selden's irresponsibility, though there are lapses, and we are invited to sorrow over his loss and relish the 'moment of love' which he saves from the ruins.

In *The Custom of the Country*, New York's blue blood displays virtues, but its faults, those of a hidebound, exhausted mildness, are felt to excuse the selfish behaviour of the divorcing Undine Spragg, to whom Wharton awarded more than her own red hair, and with whose rebellious vigour there is some sisterly complicity. Nevertheless, the vigour of the book, and its retaliatory spite, are mainly directed against this unprincipled upstart. Undine steals off for solitude at one point, but is otherwise the reverse of romantic. The romantic language of the novel is generally bestowed on the dreams of her unfortunate well-bred husband, the Selden-like Ralph Marvell, whose 'inner world' is compared to the seaside cave he visited as a boy: 'a secret inaccessible place with glaucous lights, mysterious murmurs, and a single shaft of communication with the sky'. His inner world 'wove a secret curtain about him, and he came and went in it with the same joy of furtive possession' as he'd visited the cave.[14] But Ralph is betrayed by his dreams, and drifts, like Lily Bart, toward suicide.

Seven years later, in *The Age of Innocence*, the virtues of the past exert a stronger claim. The living death, as it has been thought, which overtakes the Selden-like Newland Archer when he surrenders to these virtues is offered as a triumph. Archer is engaged to May when he falls in love with the Countess Olenska, who has grown up in Old New York and is back from a bad marriage in Europe. Ellen Olenska consents to be let down—but not until several meetings have occurred in the enchanted land of secrecy. Both in this novel and in James's *Portrait of a Lady* an act of sexual forbearance or renunciation is praised. James is on record as advising someone that 'love was not the most necessary thing,'[15] and sooner or later both writers found reasons for causing their fictions to deny the reasons of the heart, and for refusing to condone unconventional sexual behaviour in public while accepting it privately among the fit few: Morton Fullerton was not only the lover of the one but the close friend of the other. For both writers, illicit passion was European, rather than American; for Wharton, it could also be Eastern, Levantine, Jewish. The Countess is European in her appeal to, and knowledge of, the heart and senses. But she is American enough, puritan enough, to tell Archer midway through the book, in words by which James might have been moved, and in which we can make out the image of the journey which takes you back where you came from: 'I can't love you unless I give you up.'[16]

Not long afterwards, though, we are told 'he had built up within himself a kind of sanctuary in which she throned among his secret thoughts and longings. Little by little it became the scene of his real life, of his only rational activities; thither he brought the books he read, the ideas and feelings which nourished him, his judgments and visions.'[17] This is not the only passage in Wharton's work where reference to a 'real life' might remind one of the language used by Chekhov to write about the double life, and in praise of the reality which may be attained through the lies and theft of an adulterous liaison.

The Age of Innocence is now poised in hesitation between the public place and the private. Archer has again met the conversable young French tutor who is thought by his wife to be 'dreadfully common', and who is thought by some critics to be a private allusion to Edith's presumptive father, or to the rumour on the subject. Then he has set out on a journey with Ellen Olenska, an embarkation from Boston to Cythera, where they are able to communicate 'in the blessed silence of their release and their isolation'. The paddle wheels turn, and the 'old familiar world of habit' recedes, just as her American subject-matter, dedicated to the same old familiar world, has been receding from the Franco-American author in her foreign fastness. The lovers 'were drifting forth into this unknown world, they seemed to have reached the kind of deeper nearness that a touch may sunder.' When he meets her at a further ferry, we may start to think of Charon, as well as Cythera. But Wharton's ferries are more amorous than ominous: Adults fifty cents. . . And yet, once again, he does not feel the need to touch her: 'A stolen kiss isn't what I want.' When they move towards a last flight, towards this stolen kiss, 'he saw a faint colour steal into her cheeks.' But stealing has just before been shown to be ominous enough: 'there stole over him the delicious sense of difficulties deferred and opportunities miraculously provided.'[18]

In the end, he resolves to make the best of his marriage to May: Archer's fate has lain in the hands of his two women throughout, and the wife's merits, claims, and strength of will are respectfully conveyed, as indeed they had to be if he was not to seem embarrassingly weak. Even after May's death he refuses to take up with Ellen—a refusal which may bring vivid memories of *The Portrait of a Lady*, whose Archer also becomes free to marry again. Cynthia Wolff's book on Wharton notes allusions to James's novel in *The Age of Innocence* and observes that the final scene in which Archer stands in the dusk staring up at Ellen's Paris window is like a scene from his own past once recounted by James: he, too, had stared up at 'the unapproachable face', which may possibly have been no more unapproachable than Ellen's now is.[19] Archer has missed 'the flower of life', Wharton writes. But he had been

> what was called a faithful husband; and when May had suddenly died —carried off by the infectious pneumonia through which she had nursed their youngest child—he had honestly mourned her. Their long years together had shown him that it did not so much matter if marriage was a dull duty, as long as it kept the dignity of a duty: lapsing from that, it became a mere battle of ugly appetites. Looking about him, he honoured his own past, and mourned for it. After all, there was good in the old ways.

One of the flights embarked on in Wharton's fiction belongs to her Gothic or ghostly vein, and is fastened to the idea of doubles. Around 1910, she wrote a couple of terror stories. In 'The Eyes' a figure resembling Walter Berry sees his double as two sneering disembodied eyes (James's 'Jolly Corner' had appeared a few months before), and he can only escape their gaze by letting someone down. In 'The Triumph of Night' the narrator, George Faxon, is a waif—'a stranger everywhere'—who makes friends with another waif in the person of Frank Rainer, who has an uncle, Lavington. The temperaments of these two poor fellows might suggest a measure of duplication, but it is Lavington who has the double—a spectre generated by his covert designs on the nephew's cash. Faxon yields to an 'impulse to fly', and the flight, shared with Rainer, is a flight unto death. Of the two, only the narrator survives: to recover from his ordeal, which may have relieved him of his weaker self, he flies east—to Conrad country.

The year after this, *Ethan Frome* was published, in which Wharton sees country life as worth escaping from. A mismated farmer, in a bleak and wintry New England, falls for his servant girl, Mattie. The heat of his tone 'made her colour mount', we read, 'like the reflection of a thought stealing slowly across her heart'. Mattie is expelled by the ailing wife, and 'an erratic impulse' prompts Ethan to take the girl on a last toboggan ride. And then another. It is a journey towards love, or towards death: 'it seemed to him that they were flying indeed, flying far up into the cloudy night, with Starkfield immeasurably below them, falling away like a speck in space . . .'.[20] Wharton talked of the delirium of finishing a novel as being like tobogganing, and there can't be any doubt that a good deal of Edith Jones was imparted to Ethan Frome. The tale is told by a Selden-like solitary, who witnesses the living death which has ensued, *à trois*, for Ethan and his women, and it was written in the aftermath of the friendship with Fullerton. Maybe it can be read as saying that suicide is the only escape, and that love can lead to fates that are worse. But then Ethan could always have got on a train to Florida.

If adultery is throned among the secrets of Wharton's sanctuary, we might ask what she does with illegitimacy. There are texts by her which attentively treat the subject, and that of mistaken parenthood. They do not confirm the rumour of her own illegitimacy, which the two principal books about her in recent times, by R. W. B. Lewis and Cynthia Wolff, do not accept. But it is by no means wholly implausible. The voice we hear when she is spoken of, on one of her motor-flights through England, as calling attention to the birthplace of her real father, and then remarking, 'I am not sure, and I don't care,' sounds like the voice of Edith Wharton.[21] It is also, of course, the case that she would very likely have been intrigued by the subject of illegitimacy, and by the conception of herself as illegitimate, even if she had flatly disbelieved the rumour—given the tendencies in her work which I've been examining. Illegitimacy does not complete her repertoire of secrets, and it is completed in a manner no less in keeping with the precedents of romantic literature. The main texts here are *Summer* and the 'Palmato' fragment.

She knew—and Conrad also knew—what she had achieved with *Summer*. Comparing 'Hot Ethan', as she nicknamed the tale, with her other work, she wrote at the close of her life: 'I do not remember ever visualising with more intensity the inner scene, or the creatures peopling it.'[22] Charity Royall lives in, and resents, a remote New England village, a sour and spiteful place, and she is primed with the 'impulse of flight'. She works in a library, which has on its shelves *The Lamplighter* by the American novelist Maria Susanna Cummins, published in 1854: a totally conventional orphan narrative—with its unruly little Gerty of the fine dark eyes, its stricken deer, its wings of a dove, its lost child restored—which is still being borrowed from the libraries of Britain. Charity is an orphan herself, having been fetched down in infancy from the community of outlaws on 'the Mountain' by Lawyer Royall. She gives herself to a Selden and conceives a child by him, but he lets her down and she lights out for the Mountain. The lawyer, though he has cursed her as a whore in drunken anger, comes to reclaim her from the outlaws, where she has been present at her mother's death. To the applause of literary critics, he then marries her, in her spent and desperate state. Not only is Royall *in loco parentis*, he could well have been her real father: his reasons for adopting her, and his role at the time, are somewhat obscure.

It is a strange union. And so is the one celebrated in the 'Beatrice Palmato' fragment. This is an erotic reverie, a self-exciting pillow piece, in which a suave, rich Levantine father makes sophisticated love with a willing daughter, who is due to be swallowed up in the doom of the Palmatos. The daughter has married a dull husband, whom her father believes himself to be effacing. Like James, Wharton could sometimes give expression to anti-semitic feelings in her books, and her imagination can sometimes appear to be assigning the sexuality forbidden in her youth to a cast or caste—Old New York's untouchables—of stealthy and desirable aliens and upstarts. Into this fragment she drops the most thrilling of her 'steals': 'As his hand stole higher she felt the secret bud of her body swelling, yearning, quivering hotly to burst into bloom.'

Cynthia Wolff suggests that the cold and hunger of an emotionally deprived childhood are remembered in the heat, and in the oral avidities, of the passage. It could also be thought to attest to the early bond with her father which is dwelt on in *A Backward Glance*, and which might have been revived by the discovery that he was not her real father. In her memoirs, Mr Jones is a romantic figure, who 'stole' to his Rhinelander fiancée in a makeshift sailboat. An early dependency of this kind, on Edith's part, might have helped to shape her emotional needs. Precisely how is indeterminable, since so much remains hidden. But those who, whether attached or estranged, are let down in childhood are not easily consoled in later life, and may go on being, and seeking to be, let down. And it may be that the disappointing bachelors of her satires and the attractive older men of her reveries are images or impacts of the same man. It is interesting that Berry was a combination of both species of male, while, in spirit, the Yankee Fullerton was straight out of the Whartonian Levant.

The passage also attests to the power which romantic preconception retained for the suffering woman who became one of America's leading novelists of manners, and one of its leading potentates. Romantic fantasy had long shown a fascination with incest. But the brute force of short-term literary precedent may also have mattered here. It is possible that the oedipal strain in *The Golden Bowl*, where one illicit passion is defeated by another, was, for Wharton, an incitement of this order, though she did not like the novel very much, and it is hard to picture the stolen kisses of Adam and Maggie Verver. There are signs that she did not like the contemporary researches of Freud very much either, but these, too, may have been an influence, and may have been experienced as romantic. It is likely, however, that the theme would have gripped her anyway, irrespective of what the culture was saying at the time. It may be that *Summer* and the 'Palmato' piece enable us to think that her secret journey took her back where she started, and took her back to her father. It is no harder to think this than it is to think, as some have done, that all her roads led to Rome, to the *Ave Crux Spes Unica* inscribed on her gravestone.

Cynthia Wolff's psycho-critical *A Feast of Words* describes a progress to maturity, a coming to terms with a regressive early self. Wharton is seen as a female victim, whose books affirm the injustice done to women by her society. But if Wharton was a victim, she was also, like some other victims, a master, who knew how to make other people smart and jump. *A Feast of Words* argues that *Ethan Frome* repudiates the impulse to flight, that *Summer* is a 'hymn to generativity and marriage'. Cynthia Wolff is struck by a word play in a public speech by Lawyer Royall, in which he urges that those who come back to his village of North Dormer, steadfastly presented as sleepy and unwelcoming, should come, in an intensive sense, 'for good'. Mrs Wolff writes: '*Summer* suggests that Wharton, too, was preparing to come back "for good".' She takes her to be urging, 'Order is necessary,' though with a less confident view than she had once held of its necessary element of repression. Charity Royall's return to North Dormer 'is no surrender and no regression'—it is 'the act of a mature adult'.[23] But Charity's acquaintance with generativity consists of being made pregnant by the man she has loved and been left by, and of having to marry someone else. It is true that the someone else has been shown to be attractive. It is also true, though less convenient, that there is a psycho-critical approach which might see him as symbiotic with the man she has been left by.

Wharton's progress is reckoned by Mrs Wolff to terminate in *The Age of Innocence*. It is 'a novel of maturity—acceptance and not submission—and it signals Wharton's truce with the spectres of childhood.' But, as she also informs us, the novelist spoke of it in *A Backward Glance* as a work in which she 'found a momentary escape in going back to my childish memories of a long-vanished America'.[24] In *Summer*, two types of refuge —the love affair, the outlaws—are succeeded by a third: I don't know why the work should not be considered regressive, and I don't know that it does any harm to enquire whether it tells the story of the writer's real or imaginary changeling state. It seems to me that we should be willing to tolerate the survival of an element of romantic regression in Wharton, and to recognize that 'maturity' might well furnish a portrait of her which is almost as tendentious as would be one which were to detect an account of her amid the wealth and stealth of *The Wings of the Dove*. It may be that something of her is foreseen in Milly's susceptibility to the tender tints of romance; and in the manner of the duality that subsisted between the two writers, James's novel managed to anticipate certain passages in his friend's dealings with Fullerton. Duality is prophecy, we may at times imagine. But Mrs Wharton was hardly a dove.

Percy Lubbock's *Portrait of Edith Wharton* is no hymn to maturity, and it is clear what he is getting at when, in his roundabout way, he refers to her adult life as exhibiting the persistence of a 'wound' or 'want'.[25] Lewis and Wolff do not think well of Lubbock's book, and impute a hostility towards its subject. But Lubbock acknowledges, and allows the reader to understand, his failures of sympathy: she was, on occasion, too public and brisk and orderly for this least happy, as he may seem, of the Happy Few. He had the advantage of knowing her, and of being a skilful writer, who creates a living woman. If he criticizes her too much, Lewis rarely criticizes her at all. She was 'not snobbish in the familiar American way', Lewis points out. 'When Berry saw a duchess, de Noailles has remarked, he saw two hundred years of duchesses. Edith did the same.'[26] Lubbock's is a mannered prose, its images drawn, in Jamesian style, from the treasure house of Edwardian loot. Edith is a '*faisan d'or*', 'a very Golden Bowl of a pheasant'—finely flawed, we gather. But against his 'gracilitys'—a word shared with James, who applied it to *The Reef*—we can set Cynthia Wolff's 'generativitys'.[27] This, too, is jargon of a kind.

XIV. ROBERT FROST CROSSES THE MISSOURI

Robert Frost's long life came to an end in 1963, and Lawrance Thompson's long life of Robert Frost—that of an authorized biographer, who was outlived by his labours, and whose third volume was completed by a colleague—came to an end in 1976. Frost's life rang with praise and applause, but he has so far been the subject of a disproportionately small amount of literary criticism. The oracles have been dumb, for the most part, and sometimes surly. Bernard DeVoto, who was one of the many friends with whom Frost quarrelled, told him that he was a good poet but a bad man, and the same impression can be gained from the Thompson biography.[1] Other Americans have preferred the still simpler view that he was both a bad poet and a bad man. His writings were judged with reference to the social divisions they tended to inflame: country against city, heartland against advanced urban opinion with an eye on Europe, patriotism against the anti-Americanism of the expatriate 'lost generation', piety against psychiatry.

The attacks that were made, in the Twenties and after, on native America and its favourite artists could be kind to Frost only to the extent of declaring him the wrong poet for the new time that had come, and he went on to irritate both the liberal imagination and the leftism of later times. *Partisan Review* has never been eager to write about him; nor has the *New York Review of Books*. For all his medals, prizes, honorary degrees, and visiting professorships, the universities have not been anything like as eager to study him as they have been to study Pound, Eliot, and Stevens. And yet, bad and wrong as he has been alleged to be, he is among the masters of American poetry.

Frost was more of a star than any other poet of the modern world has been, and stars do not cease to shine when they give a sense of the anomalous and the equivocal, or when they appear divided and divisive, or when they are seen to suffer. This is the story of the mastery of an art, and of a response to fear and pain. The comedy it yields is the high, black comedy of paranoid megalomania. Thompson's biography has plenty of such fun, and so has Nabokov's novel of 1962, *Pale Fire*, whose portrait of the mountain poet, curmudgeonly John Shade, contains pointed references to Frost, and is contained within the self-portrait of a devoted scholar. The biography tells of a series of terrible domestic misfortunes, and of a strain of insanity on Frost's side of the family. His father was wild and frightening, and punishing; tubercular and a drinker, he died young. His mother then worked as a schoolteacher, enduring hard times and hostility. When the doctor arrived to deliver Frost, the father greeted him with a revolver, to put him on his mettle, and Frost himself once waved a gun at his young daughter and his wife Elinor in the middle of the night, pressing the daughter to choose which of her parents should be the one to be gone by the morning. Feeling rejected and suicidal during his courtship of Elinor, he set off on a journey through the Dismal Swamp in Virginia: the very place appointed, as suitable for afflicted love, in a poem by Tom Moore mentioned earlier in this book —in Frost's day, one would think, a poem very little known. His sister entered a psychiatric institution. So did a daughter. Another daughter died in childbirth. A son committed suicide. Other children died in miscarriage or in infancy. On her deathbed in 1938, Elinor refused to let him in to see her. For the quarter of a century that followed, Frost was nourished by the care and friendship of Mrs Kathleen Morrison, who served as his secretary.

A gift for words became evident early in his distresses, but the fame to which it led was to prove as distressing to him, in certain respects, as any of his disasters. His distresses made him a star, and a monster. This victim was to show, as he himself confessed, an 'Indian vindictiveness'. This beautiful writer, 'scared', as he conceded, by his enemies, by the 'literary gangsters' who were out to get him, grew to have the face of a gangster or godfather.[2]

Here is the lovable, puritanical poet of popular acclaim in the act of procuring Bernard DeVoto to attack his enemies for him: 'I am going to have you strike that blow for me now if you still want to and if you can assure your wife and conscience you thought of it first and not I. The Benny-faction must be beyond suspicion of procurement on my part or I will have none of it.'

DeVoto's response to Frost's conscription of his friends was spirited—unlike that of Louis Untermeyer, who soldiered on for years and years. At one point, Untermeyer offended Frost by embarking on a divorce—always a sore subject with the poet. Not long afterwards, Untermeyer's son took his own life, and 'Frost, with typical austerity, viewed this death as a punishment the parents had brought on themselves through the self-pitying attempts of each' to win the son's sympathy. Here is Frost imagining a rebuke to Pound which invokes their relations with each other in the days when Pound helped to launch him in London, thereby saddling the Yankee with the embarrassment of a European début: 'My contribution was to witticisms: yours the shitticisms. Remember how you always used to carry toilet paper in your pocket instead of handkerchief or napkin to wipe your mouth with when you got through?'[3]

Thompson has a habit of seeming to hover at the edge of admitting the monstrous and comic nature of the incidents which fill his book, and, unlike Frost himself, he lacked the flair, and the sense of humour, to exploit them, to any pitch of vivacity, in the telling. You begin to wonder whether the strains and exasperations which befall the official biographer married to a procuring subject may not have issued in some suppression of Frost's kind actions and common humanity. The suspicion is not removed by an inspection of the list of 'topical sub-heads' which precedes the index to each volume. In the second volume, the topics include 'brute', 'charlatan', 'cowardice', 'enemies', 'escapist', 'fear', 'hate', 'insanity', 'jealousy', 'punishment', 'puritan', 'rage', 'rebel', 'revenge', 'spoiled child', 'vindictive', 'war'. That's almost half the list: it reads like a character assassination, and its most startling item is 'murderer'. But the really bleak thing about the book is that you eventually decide that its portrait of the artist in terms, so often, of his trophies, retaliations, and rigmarole of speaking engagements, must represent a more or less complete record. 'Check up on me some,' advised Frost, with reference to his own inventive accounts of his life. You decide that, in checking, Thompson has not been drawn to the atrocious, at the expense of other eligible topics. The book works well as a kind of Frost archive, though the scholarship can seem excessive. When Frost spoke of himself as a 'Scotch symbolist' (for

Untermeyer, he was a 'Yankee realist'), he can't have had in mind the three fifteenth-century Scottish poets whose dates, known and conjectured alike, are then furnished in the notes.[4]

The second volume is concerned with 'the years of triumph'. In the triumphant year of 1924, he left one of his academic posts as resident poet: resident but fugitive—these ambiguous arrangements were always coming to an end. His spells at Amherst were more difficult than the valedictories might suggest: President Meiklejohn, who had invited him there originally, in pursuit of a genuinely imaginative teaching programme, had been repudiated by Frost on the grounds that he was a liberal, and had subsequently been dismissed by the trustees. Another of Frost's sponsors, a witty Missourian, had also been repudiated by him, as a liberal and a homosexual: his sex life, Frost reckoned, gave grounds for dismissal. It was announced by the college in 1924 that Frost was to leave in order to persevere with his theory of 'detached education' at the University of Michigan, to which he'd been engaged for some while without informing Amherst. 'Detached education' meant greater freedom for students (and teachers), and an indifference to marks. His Michigan fellowship, 'for life', was to entail 'no obligations of teaching', and provide 'entire freedom to work and write'.

Frost was visited at this time by a reporter, who spoke of how dishevelled and forgetful this eminent man was, how he 'admitted' that Amherst colleagues disapproved of him for this, how keen he was that undergraduates who were 'poets on the sly' should be rallied by the poet-teacher.[5] 'As he stood on the step of his Amherst home bidding his guests farewell, the moon shone full upon him. His gray hair was tousled in the most grotesque manner, his hands were extended in a curious, generous gesture, and his voice carried across the yard a gentle invitation to come again.' The moon was shining on 'one of the friendliest spirits in the land, a spirit that refuses to attack, but refuses to conform'.

In fulfilment of his outstanding obligations to the college, Frost laid on the spectacle of that 'picturesque monster', the large and influential Amy Lowell. The visit passed off all right, despite her abrasive grandeur. Privately, though, Frost regarded her majesty as a fraud, and was nerving himself to expose her. Early the next year, what survived of his willingness to tolerate her pretensions was severely tested. He had agreed to be present at a party for her book on Keats, though, as the day approached, he felt tired out from a round of public appearances. But then Amy made it known that she would be too ill to attend a later birthday party for Frost himself. He chose, therefore, to be absent from the Lowell celebration. But then Amy chose to die, and Frost was left, in the words of his biographer, 'conscience-stricken'.

A telegram of condolence was sent, and he made a public statement in which exposure had to content itself with measured innuendoes: 'Amy Lowell was distinguished in a period of dilation when poetry, in the effort to include a larger material, stretched itself almost to the breaking of the verse.' Untermeyer seems to have been no less of a casualty than Frost in the battle of the canapés, and Frost wrote to him in such a way as to appear, by a characteristic sleight, to be palming off the wound he'd received himself onto his stricken friend.

I suspect that what lies at the bottom of your *Schmerz* is your own dereliction in not having gone to her Keats Eats just before Amy died. She got it on us rather by dying just at a moment when we could be made to feel that we had perhaps judged her too hardly. Ever since childhood I have wanted my death to come in as effectively and affectingly. It helps always any way it comes in a career of art.

His next notable public appearance consisted of a funeral oration for the president of the University of Michigan, who had freed Frost of 'all obligation' and who was praised for having ideas on education strikingly similar to those of the orator: 'detachment', 'magnanimous teaching', had suffered a loss. And so it all went on. These were among the laurels he gathered in middle life. This is what he did when he wasn't writing verse. And these episodes can be said to indicate that a pedagogic interest in detachment was allied to a more general interest in flight. One tenure was fled from into another. He was interested in flight, and he was also interested in threatening it, and in abstaining from it.

The collaborative third volume of the Thompson Life is entitled 'The Later Years', and one of these years was 1957, during which he travelled to England, together with his biographer, on a 'good-will' mission for the State Department, and drove to visit a friend, the merry old English writer Sir John Squire. Squire turned out to be 'a sight': 'He wore a baggy, loose-knit sweater, over a dirty white shirt that was open at the throat. He sat in a pair of worn and dirty gray corduroy trousers, with low sneakers on his sockless feet. What was worse, when he began to speak, his slurred voice suggested heavy drinking.' Worse still, perhaps, 'Martha appeared, with a beer keg for Thompson to sit on. Introduced by Sir John as his "secretary", she served drinks.' After an hour, their good will exhausted by this dubious secretary and by the discovery that Squire was a 'mere shadow' of his former self—a rather fraudulent self at the best of times, according to some—the delegation fled back to London. The following morning Frost affected a sore throat in order to escape a visit to the widow of his closest friend, the poet Edward Thomas, killed in the Great War. Decades before, Helen Thomas had disgusted him by 'saying too much in her autobiography about her sexual conduct with her husband before and after their marriage'.[6]

'When I am low,' Robert Frost remarks in a sonnet by Robert Lowell, 'I stray away.' The theme of flight, apparent in the biographical data, is equally apparent in Frost's writings. For Richard Poirier, the 'imagination of withdrawal' is of great importance in Frost, and his book about his verse, *Robert Frost: The Work of Knowing*, is preoccupied with it.[7] But if we are conscious of withdrawals in his work, we must also be conscious, as Poirier is, of their being both imagined and abandoned. The stray survived, after all—survived the Dismal Swamp and lived to a great age. These withdrawals need to be discussed with reference to Frost's participation in some of the forms of dualistic and dialectical thinking which were canvassed in the English and American literature consulted by him in his youth.

> It almost scares
> A man the way things come in pairs.[8]

But there was safety in pairs, too. Much of his verse was elicited by his fears, and much of his vindictiveness, and his fears could well have elicited his feeling for pairs, and for Emerson's feeling for pairs—Emerson, Thoreau, and William

James being the philosophic 'stays against confusion' that mattered to him, and began to do so in the days when he was seeking, and running from, a university education.

A note in the Thompson biography reads: 'Viewing truth as a continuing dialectic of opposites, he rarely took an extreme position except . . . for purposes of counterbalancing its equally extreme antithesis. Truth, for R.F., was always somewhere in the middle—and he would never presume to say exactly where.'[9] This information—together with the poem in which truth is a ghostly glimpse, impossible to say exactly of what, at the bottom of a well—allows one to reflect on the state of affairs whereby R.F. was alternately seen as a classical and as a romantic writer. But the notion of a never presumptuous Frost, of a middle Frost for Middle America, of a 'classical' stance of moderation, of a God-given instinctual golden mean between retreating and remaining, bound and free, may not be fully persuasive. His 'classical' traits were one of the opposites he kept on about, and are incorporated in a response to romantic duality; moderation is incorporated in mediation, so to speak, which is why he can sometimes appear so immoderate. The truth is that he was a romantic writer, and that it was romantic of him to be a pair of writers—realist and symbolist, domestic and wild—at a time when things came in pairs and pairs were romantic.

One of his pairs can be found in 'The Road Not Taken', where he writes about being in a wood and at a fork in the road he has been following. The poem says he is sorry there could be no course of action that would amount to a travelling, by the 'one traveller', of both of the roads before him, and it explores the moot point of which of them to take. One looks more worn than the other: then again, there is no real difference. But in time, he says, a difference will once more be apparent. He will think with regret of the decision he took, think of it as the strange decision of a stray, of a seeker of the less familiar.

> I took the one less travelled by,
> And that has made all the difference.

The poem contradicts itself, with too noticeable a cunning; it stands among the conundrums of romantic duality, and is said to have been a joke at the expense of a doubting Edward

Thomas, Frost's friend and fellow dualist. It is also a good poem about moot points, forks, and divergences, and about the uncertainty and fatality of choice. I like to think that it owes something to the seventh chapter of *Uncle Tom's Cabin*, where Lizzy steals from slavery towards the river, and a choice between two roads is debated: one of them is the 'least travelled' (but much the more imaginary). What is the 'balance of probabilities'? 'Gals' is 'made contrary', so who can tell which way she went?

For Frost, life was the knowledge of opposites, and the marriage of opposites. In 'Two Tramps in Mud Time', from the sequence 'Taken Doubly', he says that he wants to bring together love and need, work and play: 'As my two eyes make one in sight'. So he'll chop his own logs, and won't allow these out-of-work lumberjacks (he calls them 'strangers', and 'tramps') to do it for pay. The poem has a 'lurking frost' due to 'steal forth' at sunset: the tramps, too, are made to look like lurkers and thieves. Theft matters to this poetry, in which we find a lurking Frost who fears to be stolen from.

Such are the pairs and opposites of an 'Emersonian romantic'. Yvor Winters called Frost by this name, at a time when sophisticated people were apt to think of him as a classically sententious poet of country life with one eye on the city, as a sage sort of pastoral poet, and he did so in a powerful essay which reads at times like a vagrancy charge.[10] Winters complains that Frost has been thought classical because of his concern with the 'human average': the classical writer, Winters claims, is concerned with 'the norm of what humanity ought to be'. The complaint might cause one to feel that the romantic writer is likely to be concerned with the exception, with departure from the norm, or from the home, and that what annoys Winters is not so much Frost's glorification of the average, if that can be said to occur, as his glorification of the exception, and of impulse—which will often be the impulse to escape. Winters compiles a list of the views held by the 'spiritual drifter' on show in 'The Road Not Taken' and elsewhere, and it proves to be quite like Thompson's list of topical subheads: 'he believes that impulse is trustworthy and reason contemptible, that formative decisions should be made casually and passively, that the individual should retreat from co-operative action with his kind . . . that ideas of good and evil need not be taken very seriously.' We may feel, however, that the man who managed his affairs, and got others to help him, who enjoined, and even engaged in, co-operative action, who could resist the impulse to leave home, and who lived with his laurels to a great age, is missing from the list. So are the tensions and anomalies of Frost's life and art, and the middle ground—the mediation, marriage, and muddle—where much of his art is stationed. So is the dualistic Frost which largely enables us to think of him as an Emersonian romantic.

The dying David Hume is said to have repented his Scotticisms: Frost, on his deathbed, forgave Pound his shitticisms. He told Pound's daughter that Ezra was a 'great romantic', which looks like a way of saying that he himself was. 'Romantic love,' he went on, 'as in stories and poems. I tremble with it.'[11] But he was only now and then a love poet.

> We dance round in a ring and suppose,
> But the Secret sits in the middle and knows.

This, his least fortunate poem, tells us what many of his poems tell us—that he was interested in uncertainty. He was also interested in his own uncertain isolation. And he is a master of the language established, in the course of the last century, for the stories and poems of those who have pursued such interests. That is why he is a great romantic. 'Irregular', 'outlaw', 'fear', 'away', 'alone', 'bereft', 'strange', and 'steal'—the circumstances of his life were to require such words, some of which he chose as titles, and were to require the irony with which he was occasionally to use them. The language of romanticism points to a life-history ruled by the idea of withdrawal, and of the sad exception. The exceptional person will suffer, and will be like an orphan. His father may be such as to cause him to resemble one, or to imagine himself one. Sorrows, solitudes, and dangerous escapes will be in store, journeys through the Dismal Swamp, journeys from which he is able to return, since what he wants is to be both at home and away. At the same time, the orphan may turn out to be a master, a monster, a maltreater of orphans, a resembler of fathers. This is to describe a road well-travelled over the past two hundred years, and Frost's experience of life did not diverge from it in any important respect. His experience of life was certainly to teach the lesson that sorrows can make you sore.

The art of withdrawal, as practised by Frost, may seem to have been announced by his early journey of escape to the Dismal Swamp, an escape from which he returned but which did not rid him of the feeling that Elinor was rejecting him, and it may also seem to correspond to the behaviour of the person who pretends to be an orphan in order to break, and yet not to break, with family life. His victim or vagrant self was joined to a self which stayed at home, and to another which was aggressive and famous, and which flew to the Crimea to talk tough to Khrushchev, who then painfully embarrassed him by sending missiles to Cuba. He insisted that he preferred 'grief' to 'grievance', and yet his biography trembles with old scores. With more than his share of griefs, he could imagine he was being persecuted, and be a grief to others. In the romantic parlance of an earlier time, he was uncommon and unaccountable: the poet of common humanity can be found to lack it.

Such is the strange case of Robert Frost—seen in the context of the imaginative literature on which he relied for an account of his plight. He had his own way of being, and of having to be, this sort of creature, and his way was that of the inhabitant of a community which has admired its outlaws and been impatient with orphans: so that the political Frost (like the political Pound) was never the orphan's best friend. But then he also belonged to a world at large in which artists have often been hostile and afflicted human beings, anxious for power and sunk in a politics of hostility.

Frost resented the name 'escapist': 'a man may climb a tree and still not be an escapist. He may go up there to pick something.' But he was willing to describe himself as 'outside the law'. As a Harvard Overseer, he was invited to teach at the university as well, which would have been against the regulations. Remembering the rows and anomalies which had attended his Amherst and other academic stints, he wrote: 'I am prepared to hear you say next, as I am always hearing in this irregular life of mine, that an exception could probably be made in my case. But I am tired of living outside the law.' This particular multiple role—that of the outlaw overseer and seer—

was declined. But 'my impulse to flight', as he put it, had very nearly got him into the Harvard Latin Department.[12]

Frost's withdrawals enter his poems, as one would expect, at an early point. In one of his first poems, 'Into My Own', there's a vista of dark woods:

> I should not be withheld but that some day
> Into their vastness I should steal away,
> Fearless of every finding open land . . .

As for the loved ones left behind,

> They would not find me changed from him they knew—
> Only more sure of all I thought was true.

We may wonder about the truth which lies in the middle of those woods, and Frost cast a doubt in the first edition of his first volume of poems, *A Boy's Will*, where he provided a gloss on this poem, one of a collection of glosses with which he prepares the reader for the pattern of contradictory moods in the book: 'The youth is persuaded that he will be rather more than less himself for having forsworn the world.' Richard Poirier writes about the protective syntax of 'Into My Own', showing how the poem's imagination of withdrawal is modified by its conditional tenses, its 'shoulds' and 'woulds': 'The young man has actually forsworn nothing.'[13]

This is not the only Frost poem which fixes a doubtful eye on woods and other prospects. In the most acclaimed of his forsworn forswearings, 'Stopping by Woods', he decides not to enter his neighbour's woods because he has 'promises to keep'. A much later poem, 'Trespass', is about 'my woods', and some extravagant and 'unaccountable' stranger has been into them: a violation of property has taken place. The trespasser has been trespassed against, and this trespass is condemned.

Escape can be called 'stealing' by Frost, or 'stealing away'. The word turns up in a letter from Frost to Untermeyer of 1926. A few years before, he'd been in trouble over a tall story he'd been telling about how he'd compelled Joseph Warren Beach to make an honest woman of his research assistant. Beach had protested and Frost had been compelled to make amends. Now, to Untermeyer, he writes, not all that abashed:

> J.W. really seems to have been serious in that marriage. I made up my mind he should be as serious as lay in me to make him. He rather

played it on me the day he used me for a chaperone to sit in his Ford car for respectability while he stole off in whatever takes the place of alders in Minnesota. I could see he thought it was funny to be so romantic at my expense. So to be equally funny and romantic at his I went straight on from that moment and inside of two days had him sewed up in marriage for the rest of his life.[14]

His humour can be brutal and anxious; he thinks here that he has used it to cramp Beach's style; it can also be used to cramp his own. His young man 'forswearing the world' is funny in rather the same way that *Huckleberry Finn*'s 'poor prisoner, forsook by the world' is funny: the jokes are for safety's sake, and respectability's, but they are those of playful, truthful romantic books in each of which forsaking and forsook amount to the same thing and are not just a joke.[15]

Frost once used the word 'steal' to make a political point, scored off the welfare-state economist:

> 'Twas his idea that for the public health,
> So that the poor won't have to steal by stealth
> We now and then should take an equaliser.

In defence of property, he fudges up a tautology, as Thompson does in stressing the sly romantic character of Frost's poetic apprenticeship: 'Whenever he was in the mood for self-indulgence, he secretly and even furtively stole time for writing another poem.'[16] When Frost steals in a figurative sense, the claims of a community, and of a family, are both acknowledged and denied. The figure conveys, as in general it must, that solitariness is theft. And at other times in Frost the claims in question are acknowledged unequivocally:

> 'Men work together,' I told him from the heart,
> 'Whether they work together or apart.'[17]

In the course of his life, however, for all his capacity to utter such sentiments, he became convinced that poverty was theft, and that socialism was theft. A number of his actions and statements bear witness to an impulse of escape which was to lead to the solitariness of success, and to a narcissistic contempt for failure: 'God seems to be something which wants us to win.'[18] His fears made him famous, and they made him harsh. He is not endearing when he affects to balance the rival claims of mercy and justice, with the relevant secret suspended somewhere in the middle.

Near the end of his life, in the poem 'Away!' he was still threatening to steal off, some day, and die:

> Unless I'm wrong
> I but obey
> The urge of a song:
> 'I'm—bound—away!'

That song was a favourite with him, 'Shenandoah':

> Away I'm bound to go
> 'Cross the wide Missouri.

Frost's poem reverses the order of two of the words of this song and arranges them so as to obtain a pun on 'bound' and to summon up, for a double life, its supreme double meaning. 'Shenandoah' is about love and work, and the 'urge' Frost obeys is not an urge, in the song itself, but an obligation. Crossing the Missouri isn't the same—though it sounds it—as lighting out for the Territory, like Huck. This is the song of a slave. It supplied the title for Frost's poem, presumably: but the title could also call to mind a very different song—Keats's 'Ode to a Nightingale'.

In this poem by Frost, which anticipates an impending death in old age, his young man's preoccupation with an imaginary suicide, and with the people it 'would' leave behind, is resumed. The forsook forsaker reassures these people:

> There is no one I
> Am put out with
> Or put out by.

And in the last verse he is promising to come back from the dead:

> And I may return
> If dissatisfied
> With what I learn
> From having died.

The poem has a touch of the Spiritual, 'Steal away to Jesus', and a further poem[19] takes this as the text for a fireside chat:

Steal away,
The song says. Steal away and stay away.
Don't join too many gangs. Join few if any.
Join the United States and join the family—
But not much in between unless a college.

Be an orphan, he suggests. He then lists gangs you can join and omits the one you have to join in order to earn a living.

There is pathos in his stealing and staying at home, and a strength which sustains more than one of his best achievements. These urges are subtly incorporated in the contrast between the 'heavenward' and 'earthward' of two of his finest poems: 'The Silken Tent', a love poem, and 'To Earthward', the word-perfect poem of a romantic puritan, in which he hugs his griefs and hurts and punishments, and moves, from an old idea of pleasure in pain, into his own. And the same urges are present in another of his masterpieces, 'After Apple-Picking'. This poem about a farmer's surfeit of apples becomes a fading into woods, and a tribute to the most potent of romanticism's orphans and victims—Keats. Harvest, russets, stubble, cider—this might be his 'Ode to Autumn' if it weren't for its special closeness to the 'Nightingale' ode. Both of the odes, and the Frost poem, have drowsiness in them. Frost's drowsiness is like, and may allude to, the mood of the darkling Keats as he listens to the bird's song. Frost's 'I cannot rub the strangeness from my sight' is Keats's 'I cannot see what flowers are at my feet.'

Frost's poem says:

I am overtired
Of the great harvest I myself desired.

This is not a reference to a load of apples, and the sleep that comes on him is less like the hibernation he speaks of than like the last sleep of all. But it does not make light of the beginning of the poem, with its two-pointed orchard ladder striving 'toward heaven still'. Keats's heaven, in the 'Nightingale' ode, is an escape which has to do with works of art. 'Away! away! for I will fly to thee . . .'. Afterwards he falls earthward, back to the troubles of his daily life. Frost's heaven might almost be a heaven of hard work, which would include the hard 'work of knowing' investigated in Poirier's book, where it is seen as not only work but play.

The work of knowing—Poirier's is a striving phrase. It sets out to assemble, in the one activity, physical labour, love-making, and the making of poems and discoveries, and Poirier persuades you that the same work, and play, can be observed in the tightenings and relentings of Frost's 'The Silken Tent', which points heavenward too. The Jacob's ladder of the apple-picking poem stands, and strives, for a great deal; there is a great deal for the poet to lapse from. At the same time, Frost is someone for whom even work can have an aspect of withdrawal, as it has here, where it is meant to serve as withdrawal's opposite. He was a man who could believe that you were liable to be called an escapist if you climbed a tree to pick fruit. And even pain can have that aspect, as 'To Earthward' attests.

His stealing and staying can be encountered in his prosody. He promised, and performed, a dualistic metre, pledged to convention and to the vagaries of the speaking voice. His theory of 'the sound of sense' held that a sentence is 'a sound in itself on which other sounds called words may be strung', and that sentence sounds are 'gathered by the ear from the vernacular and brought into books'. He maintained that 'there are the very regular pre-established accent and measure of blank verse; and there are the very irregular accent and measure of speaking intonation. I am never more pleased than when I can get these into strained relation. I like to drag and break the intonation across the metre as waves first comb and then break stumbling on the shingle.'[20] The tension he hoped for, between freedom and form, is there in the poem about the tree at his window. 'Vague dream-head lifted out of the ground' is the vernacular at stumbling-point, and as a line about a tree it is monstrously good. He was able to prove the theory both on the page and on the platform: few poets can have read their poems so well, even though he tended to run for President in his words of introduction, compounding the blandishments of the weaker pieces.

His poem 'Design', about a spider and its prey, must have been a success in public, and it is possible to want to look for some theatrical—and theological—ploy in the question: 'What but design of darkness to appal?' But he meant it, I think, just as much as he meant to make a show of it. He can't have meant that the world is programmed to give people frights. But he believed in dark designs. He lived, he once said, in 'a world of suspicion'.[21] In the Twenties, he gave offence by boasting or joking that America, unlike Russia, had nothing terrible for writers to write about. You could not write like Dostoevsky about America. Well, it is true that while Middle America and more was sitting at Frost's feet, Russia, in the name of the community, was surrounding Mandelstam with gangsters, literary and political, and sending him on an orphan's flight which ended with his death in a prison camp. But then there can be no doubt that Frost suffered too—while stealing about and playing the part of the orphan. We may feel that terrible things happened in America, and that some of them happened to him, and that he did not write about them. There are sufferings of his, that is to say, which are rarely detectable in the confessional poetry of distress to which he gave his life. In Thompson's Life of Frost they are detected, and with a candour unusual in an authorized biographer. Mandelstam did not conspire against other poets, and this may be one of the reasons why you are often able to feel, in reading about him, that he was not afraid. Frost was.

XV. SOME NAMES FOR ROBERT LOWELL

Robert Lowell is not difficult to represent as the mad poet and justified sinner of the Romantic heritage. He is the dual personality who breaks the rules, kicks over the traces: he did this in the course of a series of manic highs which came and went from maturity, if not before, until the end of his life in 1977 at the age of 60. He goes up and he comes down. He was a man, as he said himself, of 'tumbles and leaps', a man of extremes, of moods and moments, and of the moment, of nerves, fresh starts, and escapes, whose illness and convulsive life gained access to, if they were not inseparable from, an art nerved to resist them. He was a bear, a bull, a threat to those who knew him. 'A born joiner,' said his second wife, but more of a born leaver, a disjoiner and divorcer. He was a maker of poems but also their unmaker and negator, falling into a habit of revision which became a compulsion: so that the scholarship of his verse bears an element of anguish, which sends its shadow before it into the twenty-first century.[1]

There is something Scottish, and something Russian, about this undoubtedly American poet. He is the justified sinner whom we meet in the fiction of James Hogg. And he is the superman, the Stavrogin, whom we meet in the fiction of Dostoevsky: the antinomian hero bent both on power and mischief and on the blessedness of the meek, so that he's Prince Myshkin too, and it's hardly surprising that he should have been a rereader of *The Idiot*. It is a mark of his poetry that it frets in all childishness, praising and blaming, over the actions and reputations of the great, while managing to make people feel that it is itself the work of a great man, however bashful, stumbling, and dishevelled. It is the work of a tyrannnicide subject, in Ian Hamilton's words, to 'tyrant delusions'.[2] Lowell was a pacifist who was able, at moments, to praise the ideology of the master race. Mischievously mad or mischievously sane, it was hard to tell which, he once urged companions to exercise a *sortes Hitlerianae* by opening at random a copy of *Mein Kampf*: 'There isn't a page that isn't well-written.' As chance would have it, the copy fell open at a shriek against the

Jews. At other time he laid claim to Jewish blood—tempering the true-blue Boston Brahmin birthright which conferred, as he sometimes felt, the first-class soul of the patrician. There isn't a line that isn't well-born.

Lowell's writings do not broadcast the conception I am describing, and it is one he would have been ready to mock. Such a rejection lay well within the compass of his ambivalence. He was modest and gentle, while also a terror, just as he was the best man in the world and the worst, the weakest and most marginal of creatures and yet a member of an élite who could serve as a leader in the crusade against the Vietnam War. A capacity for irony equipped him to suspect, while helping him to sustain, the worship of problematic heroes. He can be seen in other ways, moreover, besides the ambivalent, or antinomian. England has seen him as a High Catholic successor to Eliot on the Faber list, as another saintly poet; or as the New Englander who succeeded Robert Frost in the art of plain speaking in verse; or as a metropolitan radical, a Partisan Reviewer. No such construction as the one I am describing is entertained by Ian Hamilton in the *kampf* produced in 1982. There is no discussion of a dual personality, though the Lowell personality comes through very clearly. The poet is not seen as the orphan prince of the romantic novel. Nevertheless, in treating the seasons of his madness, the book provides testimony which brings out its susceptibility to romantic and dualistic interpretation.

Donald Davie has written: 'Great poetry is greatly sane, greatly lucid; and insanity is as much a calamity for poets and for poetry as for other human beings and other sorts of human business.'[3] These are impressive words. But of course many of the poets of the modern world, and of former worlds, and not the worst poets either, have 'speeded up' like Lowell, lighted out, taken off, fallen into despondency, and from bridges: and the primordial romantic tradition is unthinkable without reference to the subject, and to the proposition that this calamity may be favourable to the making of poetry. Davie's statement turns us towards Lowell with the thought that he may have been both mad and sane—a dual personality in this sense at least—and that his poetry may have been unaffected by his breakdowns. Advanced writers can appear to go further, and to suggest that his poetry, when it succeeds, is necessarily unaffected by his life. Such writers are latter-day romantics, who believe in their own way in splitting, in psychic variance and difference, and divide into two the poet and his poems. This poet, however, believed in a poetry which 'took the whole man', so that it is possible to propose that his poetry may have 'taken' the calamity of his breakdowns.

'My mind's not right,' Lowell writes in 'Skunk Hour'. And the doctors could not put it right. Lowell distrusted psychoanalysis, and psychoanalysts distrusted Lowell—as too severely ill to benefit from their services: he had therefore to rely on the trial and error of biochemical medication—on lithium salts and other drugs. Ian Hamilton does not attempt a diagnosis; he does not say what was wrong. What *happened*, however, is made vivid, and we have the sense of a hereditary disorder aggravated by a troubled childhood—as the unwanted son of a domineering mother caught in an unwanted marriage to a weak husband. The book is compassionate and sardonic in tracing the rises and falls, the grimness and the painful comedies, of Lowell's career. Lowell saw the joke himself, and was helped by seeing it: Hamilton sees it, but does not overdo it.

If we speculate about the cultural interpretations to which the life and work can be subjected, we might say that the idea of a destructive and suffering pre-eminence—accompanied by ordeal and delirium, and impugnable as megalomania—was joined to the idea of psychic division: Lowell appears to have been conscious of this connection. The idea was also joined to that of a licence to offend: an antinomian connection about which the Lowell of the writings was largely but not entirely silent. Such speculations put together the life and the work. They would not get far with those whose stress fell on a severance between the poet and his sufferings.

Against the assumption of a severance can be set a number of claims, which include the claim, challenged by experts but widely credited, that Lowell found himself as a poet when he found it possible to write poems about his life. They cannot include the claim that, on the evidence of this biography, and of the affinity which has been observed between books and breakdown in the life of the manic depressive author, it is easy to establish a correlation between the direction taken by his poetry and the incidence of his attacks. The relationship may be there, but it will have to be searched for, and it is unlikely to signal some triumph of literature over illness, any more than it will enable readers to infer without difficulty, from the pathology of the life, a pathology of the art. Meanwhile the features of his literary career are very strongly marked.

The first phase consists of the harvest of poems assembled under the dates 1938 to 1949 and published in this country in the following year. 'Mr Edwards and the Spider' takes the words of the famous Puritan divine and uses them to imitate a hellfire eloquence from the believing past. The eloquence of the collection which surrounds this poem is dark, strained, and intimidating, with a high rate of incoherence and collapse. Lowell was by now himself a believer, intent on election, salvation, and seclusion. 'The Quaker Graveyard in Nantucket' could be called Lowell's 'Lycidas': both this poem and Milton's are about the drowning of a man not especially close to the ambitious young mourner, whose grief is learned and elaborate. The Lowell elegy has almost as much, if a more rebarbative, music. It pursues a meditation on the ocean, and on Captain Ahab's mad encounter with his whale—a matter in which the poet did not lose interest and which was to colour his view of America's, and of his own, encounter with the world.

Hamilton prints a retrospective statement by Lowell which explains how poetry looked to him when he came to write it as a young man.[4] There were three choices.

One, which was hardly a choice, was the kind of poetry the public wanted, which was a rather watered-down imitation of 19th century poetry, that really had gone completely dead. The other was an *engagé* poetry, and the only kind that really seemed to inspire that kind of conviction was the Marxist, usually quite pro-Russian. And the third group, which I more or less belonged to, I think it derives somewhat from Yeats and from Eliot, and in this country friends of mine, Allen Tate and John Crowe Ransom. And a rather strange position was built up. There were great arguments that poetry was a form of knowledge, at least as valid as scientific knowledge, and in certain ways more so, because it didn't abstract from experience. We claimed any—the whole man would be represented in the poem. I think that was a sort of aggressive stance, that we felt at a disadvantage, and my friend and teacher John Crowe Ransom wrote a book of critical essays which might illustrate this, which he called, the book, *The World's Body*, that poetry was the world's body, it took the whole man. I don't think one would say that now exactly. And we believed in form, that was very important, and for some reason we were very much against the Romantics. We would say that the ideal poet is Shakespeare, who is not a poet of ideology but a poet of experience, and tragedy, and the sort of villains to us were people like Shelley—that he used too much ideology—and Whitman, the prophet, who also seemed formless.

This careful statement does not compel one to doubt that Lowell was a romantic artist; and it is not inimical to the middle period of his development, when his conception of what it was for poetry to be, in this sense, human was to undergo a change. Ian Hamilton reckons that 'The Mills of the Kavanaughs' (1951), fairly unfamiliar to Lowell's English readership, should be awarded a significant place in the transition to a more personal and more mobile verse. It is a long poem which owes more to Frost's long poems of country life and family torment than Hamilton indicates. ('Grin all to-whichways through your lower lip'—it even has the master's voice.) It jumbles childhood and marriage, just as Lowell was sometimes to jumble them in life. It is no less overcharged and ostentatious than some of the poems which precede it, but it is still a wonderful, and wonderfully liberating, piece of work.

There followed the collections *Life Studies, For the Union Dead* and *Near the Ocean*, in which he shortens his line and strikes his best vein. Here are poems which take the occasions of the writer's life, but which it would be inaccurate to call occasional, or confessional—though 'confessional' was to be a name for the new Lowell, and his school. They come from a time when his country had entered a crisis, *circa* 1968, and Lowell, agonistes, had become a public man. The public poems among them are private as well as public—to a degree which is not incompatible with the, for instance, Marvellian practice of the public poem, but which may not be compatible with the modes of ideology and prophecy mentioned in the retrospective statement and tried for, intermittently, here.

The third and last of these phases embodies collapse and recovery—I am speaking pathologically, of his art. The fourteen-liners of the *Notebook* sequence were recycled for subsequent volumes, rather in the way in which he started to recycle the poems of others in a series of translations and imitations. The sequence has in it the schoolboy who had seen, as Wordsworth himself saw, in Wordsworth's *Prelude*, ambition, genius, and the growth of the poet's mind: *Notebook* is to that slight degree *Prelude*-like, and it shares with Wordsworth's work a revolutionary crisis. But Wordsworth's crisis is summoned to the page as Lowell's is not, and 'growth' is not the word for what is recorded in the modern poem, which must be accounted—though it has its remissions—a nightmare. The last volumes of all, *Dolphin* and *Day by Day*, show signs of exhaustion, but also a return of his prodigious embattled energy and the regaining of his touch. The momentariness—as opposed to 'growth'?—which had emerged in his verse is carried over into these collections. 'We are designed for the moment,' he says. But there are moments here which communicate lifelong preoccupations: 'Fish break water with the wings of a bird to escape.' He also laments, or affects to lament, that 'Alas, I can only tell my own story,' while 'Epilogue' regrets and explores the display of souvenirs, 'snapshots', that his art had allegedly become.[5]

That *Notebook* fails may be an English opinion. Some Americans seem to feel that it is in the American grain, while there are those in England who think, as I do, that there's an avant-garde philistinism to the claim that it succeeds in being miscellaneous and random—by furnishing, in the vernacular, a native serendipity and rawness. I have no doubt that it is English to think that American criticism may be minded to secure Lowell for the empire by finding in these sonnets a sort of *sortes Americanae*. The possibilities here for mutual scorn and misconstruction are rich.

If the 'progress of his powers' as an artist—Wordsworth's words for what is recorded in *The Prelude*—may be thought to have taken these turns, the progress of Lowell's life brought hard work, fame, and an alternation of domesticity and escape. The breakdowns were for long intervals subdued and dispersed by drugs, but the escapes that accompanied them brought havoc, and farce. Having knocked his father down in adolescence, he smashed in a car accident, and then smashed all over again, the face of his first wife. Always the reviser. Such works were due for collection, not in any volume of poems, but in the biographies where the havoc and the farce would be retailed: there is a threshold of admittance to his art at which life can be found to pause. Perhaps the wildest of these works was his descent, on a government-sponsored trip, to Buenos Aires, where he ran amok, insulting generals and riding the equestrian statues. His second marriage, to Elizabeth Hardwick, was both interrupted and enduring, and her devotion and intelligence illuminate and support Hamilton's biography. Other women promised a new leaf, and eventually there was the romance of a departure for England: 'a new alliance', as he put it, 'and a new country'. This was not, he said, another of his 'manic crushes'.[6] What connections can be made between the two progresses in question, between the grand cycle of his writings and the epicycles of his manic onsets, and how do these connections relate to the difference between the times when he was crazy and the times when he was well? 'On my great days of sickness, I was God.'[7] Once a god, always a god? And yet always a reviser. On other days he can sound like Philip Larkin. Were there two Lowells, or only one?

Lowell employed the term 'dual personality', a term which belongs to literature, and which also belongs to nineteenth-century medicine. The meaning of the term has remained uncertain: but generations of writers have been moved by it, in their treatment of the subject of psychic division and of the phantasmagoric double, and it has also been used to treat the sick. It can be said that Robert Lowell addressed the subject of duality, and that the subject addressed him. He bore the two first names that might be deemed appropriate to a divided self: Robert and Cal (for Caligula, and perhaps Caliban). According to Elizabeth Hardwick, 'his fate was like a strange, almost mythical two-engined machine, one running to doom and the other to salvation.'[8] This is the language of the romantic tradition, and of a romantic religiosity: that it is employed by a shrewd wife may seem to authenticate its description of her husband. Lowell remarked of his generation of American poets, who were considered (as other poets have been considered) to be under a curse: Berryman 'in his mad way keeps talking about something evil stalking us poets. That's a bad way to talk, but there's truth in it.'[9] It's a diabolic and a dualistic way to talk. And it's a conventional way, as the poem 'To John Berryman' points out in passing. In one of his last poems,

'Home', he invokes the Devil in exhibiting a nostalgia for his former faith:

> The Queen of Heaven, I miss her,
> we were divorced. She never doubted
> the divided, stricken soul
> could call her Maria,
> and rob the devil with a word.

In 'Skunk Hour' he is in a state of possession, which includes possession by the Devil of *Paradise Lost*:

> I hear
> my ill-spirit sob in each blood cell,
> as if my hand were at its throat . . .
> I myself am hell,
> nobody's here . . .

And yet this poem is the more self-possessed of the two.

Frost wrote of a road not taken and of another that made all the difference. Hesitating in England between his second and third wives, before flying back to an appointment in Samarra and New York, Lowell appeared to himself to have taken both of the roads before him: 'I feel like a man walking on two ever more widely splitting roads at once, as if I were pulled apart and thinning into mist, or rather being torn apart and still preferring that state to making a decision.'[10]

The prose memoir of his childhood, in *Life Studies*, has this: 'Miss Manice, in her administration of the lower school, showed the inconsistency and euphoria of a dual personality.'[11] 'Inconsistency' dates, as does his image of the flying fish, from the dualistic literature of the Romantic period, and euphoric inconsistency can be taken to refer to the dual personality popularly associated with Lowell's illness of 'manic depression'. 'Dual personality' does not, to be sure, diagnose that illness, and can even appear to be clinically dissociated from it: it is best to say that it designates the cultural heritage to which he turned for guidance, and for metaphors, as he moved in and out of his mania's 'old perverse dark maze', with 'its hackneyed speech, its homicidal eye', its delusions of grandeur and infallibility.[12]

The serious duality in his work is mostly an affair of tight corners, cleft sticks, double binds, the 'choice of evils'[13] alluded to (along with Berryman's 'something evil') in his letters—of the inconsistency which responds successively or simultaneously to rival courses of action, which mists over on occasion and is torn in two. He is interested in the impossible escape, the disastrous rescue, the lighting-out which puts out its own light. This is the subject of his funniest and grimmest joke, which sounds like a limerick by Larkin:

> if we see a light at the end of the tunnel,
> it's the light of an oncoming train.[14]

'Waking Early Sunday Morning' is a poem, at once public and personal, which bends and breaks a Marvell metre in order to write about a variety of escapes, possible and impossible, and about President Johnson and war. It has the refrain: 'anywhere, but somewhere else.' Edward Hopper's superb American painting *Early Sunday Morning*—shop fronts, drawn blinds, heavy sleepers to be imagined behind them—is a there and nowhere else: Lowell wakes to a vista of elsewheres. 'O to break loose': the poem opens with a salmon making its leaps, nosing upstream to an 'impossible' destination, 'alive enough to spawn and die'. The middle of the poem has Lowell longing to be pure, unstained, to fly up to heaven on the wings of the soul.

> O that the spirit could remain
> tinged but untarnished by its strain!

Spirit flight is present in Marvell's poem about privacy, 'The Garden', which supplied Lowell's stanza form. And it is present in Tom Moore's ode 'To the Flying-Fish', which longs to 'cast every lingering stain away' and to climb to a 'purer air'. 'Let not my spirit's flight be weak,' pants Moore, known to the world as the poet of an amorous love. We discover that Lowell has tied himself to the four-stress line of the pious past. Whereupon the poem cuts amorously to

> O to break loose. All life's grandeur
> is something with a girl in summer . . .

This grandeur immediately becomes the elation of the President, 'girdled' by his cronies, and also both 'unbuttoned' and 'nude'. Lyndon Johnson plays the bear that Lowell would sometimes pretend to be: this potentate is the poet who is telling him off.

> Pity the planet, all joy gone
> from this sweet volcanic cone;
> peace to our children when they fall
> in small war on the heels of small
> war—until the end of time
> to police the earth, a ghost
> orbiting forever lost
> in our monotonous sublime.

These words were, and perhaps still are, politically effective. But they refer to another world as well as to the world we have, with its small wars. It takes a god to pity a planet (in certain of the poems, it is a god who goes with girls), and Lowell has turned into one. He has leapt up into the sky, and is looking down on the poor little policed earth, and on the *Pax Americana*. This apotheosis may count for some people as an impossible escape, but it does not do so for the poem in which it occurs. The poem does seem to be evoking a departure. Which way he flies is Heaven. There's a vertigo in getting as high as this, and there are qualms for the reader throughout the poem. It is as if it were being written by its words and by the resemblances between them, by its rhymes, by its 'stains' and 'strains': as if the writer's attention were at once fixed, intense—and wandering. But it is Lowell to the life, in all the majesty, and authority, of his distraction.

'Central Park' belongs to the same volume—*Near the Ocean*, completed in 1966—as 'Waking Early'. In this poem, flight and stealth are paired. The poor, who are also 'lovers', lie about in the park, sunning themselves.

> All wished to leave this drying crust,
> borne on the delicate wings of lust
> like bees . . .

A balloon, at dusk, is snagged in an elm, having been drawn up to the moon; kites are grounded, then seen to sail. At nightfall there arrives a threat to the rich, starving, after their fashion, in the surrounding towers. Flight does not seem a possibility for the people in the park: but theft does. It is the poor man's escape—in a poem of distant prospects, and of poor ones.

In the imagining of impossibilities, and in the hope of overcoming them, Lowell's tragic life received expression. It is expressed in a predicament which appears in one of the *Dolphin* sonnets, 'Fall Weekend at Milgate':

> The warm day brings out wasps to share our luck,
> suckers for sweets, pilots of evolution;
> dozens drop in the beercans, clamber, buzz,
> debating like us whether to stay and drown,
> or, by losing legs and wings, take flight.

The writer is by now in Kent, after his romantic flight to a new country. He is soon to return to his second wife in New York. And he is soon to die of a heart attack, carrying, for valuation, a painting of his third wife. The poem foresees what was to happen, in a way. This Wasp is one of his own wasps. The tight corners of the natural world appealed to Lowell, and spoke for him. He is the spawning salmon who leaps to his death, executing his negative escape. He is also a pilot of evolution.

There is a type of paradox, and predicament, which is peculiarly expressive of Lowell, and which is identified, for readers of Plato, and again in modern times for readers of Derrida, with the ancient Greek word *pharmakon*, a drug—a word, as we have seen, that could mean both a poison and a cure. And this is what drugs were for Lowell. They braked his euphorias, but demeaned him, tamed him with Miltown, poured their balm, but embalmed him there: Lowell must have felt with regret, though also with relief, that they had stopped him functioning as a god, and he must have feared that they might stop him functioning as a poet. Ian Hamilton explains[15] that the effect of lithium was 'to balance the sufferer between the two poles, as it were, of his affliction—between the extremes of elation and depression'. Lithium-users were not 'dazed' or 'sluggish', but might appear 'suspended', 'above the battle': nevertheless, for this sufferer, there was safety in lithium. Drugs are indeed, for everyone, equivocal. 'Each drug that numbs alerts another nerve to pain': Lowell was well-versed in the equivocal, and in the incurable.[16]

His conversance with duality ranged beyond what has been

said—to owning a double, for instance, in the bear-like poet Roethke, who proved, as doubles often must, an embarrassment. Nor was this the only such embarrassment. The joke attributed to Auden about Berryman's leap, from a bridge—a parting note is supposed to have read, 'Your move, Cal'—is about a further rivalry of the kind that prevailed with Roethke. As in the case of the Russian poet Akhmatova and her circle, there was a choice of clones available to Lowell among the *maudits* of his lost generation. In the poem which has his flying fish he hails a delightful 'double' in a soiled white horse. Here and there, the familiar language of the subject is used incidentally or ornamentally, as in the *Notebook* sonnet entitled 'Lunch Date', where 'double life' may refer to a friendship between black and white.

What duality meant to Lowell is one thing. What the language and outlook meant to those confronted with his behaviour is something else again—though not invariably. They assisted his friends, as they assisted him, to deal with the contrasts brought about by a vertiginous mutability, with occasions when the Old Lowell or 'real Cal' was felt to have been superseded, or to have become concealed—though capable, for some, of peering out from amid the mischief. He could seem like a man possessed by the devil, and a socialite girlfriend once came abruptly to grips with a vacancy: 'The person inside was not there. And I have marvellous guardian angels. I think that if I had struggled at the time I wouldn't be here.'[17] The person inside never seems to have liked her all that much, however, and it may be right to impute a change of mood on this occasion, rather than of personality. It may also be right to reflect that everyone suffers such changes, and that drink and drugs may cause them.

Most of his friends were sufficiently scientific in outlook to have thought it theatrical to talk of two Lowells, let alone of demonic possession. They would have been fairly sure that there was only the one. Those who stole with him to the pub down the street from Greenways nursing-home in St John's Wood, to be told on the way, in the weary, humble voice he was apt to use, of his descent from 'you know, Robert the Bruce and James Boswell', would have had no trouble in connecting this man with the man they knew at other times, when he was well. The two ancestors were an inspired choice—for all that accidents of language may have played a part in determining it. The reference to Boswell has the effect of seeming to gather together the various Lowells, on and off the page, into the one repertoire or register—a totality which ranges from James Boswell to 'Skunk Hour', and which is susceptible, as human beings tend to be, of dualistic interpretation. 'There's no disclaiming these outbursts—they are part of my character —me at moments.'[18]

'Designed for the moment': in the Confessions of Robert Lowell character and mood converge. Do we ever feel that the man inside is not there? The idea of the divided mind has been attended, since the Romantic period, by that of an openness to the world, and both conditions can be encountered in his writings. This openness has been a species of isolation, has communicated both presence and absence, an individual and a vacancy, and has not always excluded romantic egotism and delusions of grandeur. In Lowell, it communicates a mingling of innocence and experience, indifference and exposure, in relation to the planet's events, ideas, and people. Randall Jarrell —valued by Lowell for his ability to see the man in the poem— spoke early on of Lowell's lack of interest in people, and we need not think that the good poems about his parents, wives, and children, and about historical personages, dismiss this suggestion. But we do need to think that much of the poetry we have been accustomed to over the last two hundred years has lacked an interest in people. The paradox of innocence and experience is no copyright of Lowell's. This is what poetry has been like.

To history and to the great, to the 'great' Kennedy clan, for instance, he was both indifferent and acutely exposed. When he calls on the powerful to repent, while delighting in their power, it is of his own power, and of his Canossas, that we can be conscious: in the same way, the poems about his family, and the obituary pieces about other writers, can be poems about himself. This is a poetry in which public is private, and in which an immunity to people matches and explains an immunity to the politics to which he eagerly responds: these can be seen as the immunity of mutability. The conscientious objector who entered the tensions and uproars of the late Sixties, and marched on the Pentagon, has his dark double in the connoisseur of greatness and war. The left-wing Lowell of the admiration that accrued to a people's poet was no more left than right. In the late Forties he was caught up, miserably and madly, in what can only be termed an anti-Communist witch-hunt directed against the woman who ran the Yaddo retreat for writers. This was at a time when he was still a proclaimed and inflamed Catholic and ascetic, a visitor to Trappist as well as writers' retreats, half-inclined to the noviciate that was in mind for the great sinner Stavrogin, a pious poet even more tormented than Eliot—indeed, like the young Eliot, something of a Saint Narcissus. Christianity was on the march among the intelligentsia of the time. In his vulnerability and excitement, with religion locked into the recurrences of the manic cycle, he responded for several years: thereafter, not without misgivings, he stood divorced from the Queen of Heaven. To the move towards religion in the Forties, and to the move towards politics in the Sixties, he was in turn perceptively alive: and we may reflect that dual personality may be especially exposed to invasion by the environment.

This is not to deny that his swivelling made sense, for those interested in his opinions or in the times to which they bore witness. The same pendulum was on the move in the work of Norman Mailer, another diabolical dualist, another man of the Left whose sense of a stalking evil drew him to the right. Duality has done its bit to distract American socialism, and to instruct it. To a charge of complicity with the student protesters of the Sixties Lowell replied: 'they are only us younger, and the violence that has betrayed our desires will also betray theirs if they trust to it.'[19]

In the records of literary duality the great man and his terrible mistakes are inscribed. Dream, delirium, and the paranoid sublime plead on his behalf. The hypothesis of the divided mind and the double life is made over to fit the facts of idiosyncrasy and exaltation and error: such facts are thereby excused and disowned. The great man is made over into two men. Lowell cannot be said to pursue this defence in his writings: and I think that even if he had been a novelist, with a novelist's opportunities to 'disown', he would have refused it. But it may have been a reason why he became a historian and went into the past, where the tolerance of this defence, and of the great, is imagined to have been greater. He knew himself to be a strange case, knew what it was to have his own hands at his throat, and we have his word for it that he had functioned as a god and that he aspired to be saved, despite himself: who, he asked, 'can hope to enter heaven with clean hands?'[20] The ironies that can be assigned to such statements do not appear to be signalling a retraction. And the defence which he did not pursue may be thought to have helped to fashion his fame.

'My eyes have seen what my hand did': he took the blame for his mistakes, and he suffered for them, courageously. The 'monster' can therefore, in his own words once more, be 'pitied'.[21] But it is also the case that the literary culture, while fearing and disliking them, has admired such monsters. They are sacred. His double life is attested by the fact of his having been liked and loved by those familiar with his offences—some of whom may have divided him into sick and sane. Those less familiar may sometimes have seen him as single and as privileged to offend. Drunkenness, assault—no sin can be committed by someone in a state of grace, said the seventeenth-century Antinomian in his religious sect, and the same permission has been granted to poets. The poet Tom Paulin has suggested that Lowell's exploits in Argentina were a repudiation of the CIA, and that 'his madness' of this time was 'a form of extreme integrity'.[22] Not all of his antinomian exploits can as plausibly be defended in these terms: but attempts will be made.

Lowell can be placed with the authors and characters of a literature in which such justifications are offered, and in which art and life may appear to be indistinguishable. Boundless confidence and vanity, impossible escapes—these had been foresuffered by more than one of the writers to whom he is close. Frost and Mailer belong to the tradition. Hogg and Dostoevsky are novelists who tell their own story, in a manner to which we are more accustomed in poets, while telling the story of great deeds, and of monsters to be pitied: in both cases, an authorial duality is responsible for texts whose uncertainties are a matter of intent, and of doctrine, but may give glimpses of a void. 'Ahab's void'—such glimpses can be named by raiding the Lowell lexicon.

The tradition is one in which an author may come to power by conquering some literary world. This is not easy to do—as

Marvell wrote of Cromwell's return from Ireland,

> The same arts that did gain
> A power, must it maintain.

If the Irish joke about 'Famous Heaney' implies a practice of the necessary arts, the joke is misplaced: but Lowell was cannier in this respect than might have been looked for. He was willing to command and recruit audiences and disciples: the latter, their hour come, have assisted Ian Hamilton in his inquiries, and their thoughtful accounts are enclosed in his book. The literary persona, and the solitary's embrace and rejection of a literary world, were as important to Lowell as they were to the writers he resembles: not the least of their works is the impersonation of a writer who sets the world on fire. We may decide that this endeavour is integral to what they wrote—while complaining, if we wish, that Lowell was famous for being famous, and that the poet Elizabeth Bishop—whose excellence he unstintingly respected—has so far failed to be as famous, through failing to be famous. The autobiographical Hogg was a strangely boastful Hogg: and his celebrity, which was that of his duality, and an aspect of his subject-matter, was commensurate with his self-importance. Both were very great. Think of him, in his capacity as Ettrick Shepherd, as the people's poet from the mountains of the North, shining at a Holborn banquet, amid a cloud of English witnesses and worshippers. Then think of Lowell's persona and professional career, as exhibited by Hamilton, of his role as President of the Poets and King of the Cats.

For all Lowell's 'Lycidas', it is of Donne, rather than Milton, that we may think when we turn to link him with the remoter past. Donne was not only a dualist but a convert. And, according to some, a conformist: about his change of faith there hangs, according to Eliot, the 'shadow of the impure motive'.[23] We do not know whether he ceased to be the Catholic that we do not know whether Lowell became. We do know that he was forced into a contention with his God, and with himself. 'Lowell is distraught about religion,' wrote R. P. Blackmur: Rome and Boston quarrel in the early verse, and the conflict is not 'accepted', but 'hated', by the poet.[24]

Another partner in duality is Frost, to whom Lowell went in his youth with the air of a disciple—only to be patronized as such by a narcissist at the height of his fame and with long and bitter experience of the paranoid sublime. And yet Frost helped to form Lowell, by helping him to find a movement for his verse once the Hopkins and Dylan Thomas influences had subsided. Frost's dualistic prosody—with its tension between metrical regularity and the emphases of the speaking voice—was meant to secure for his poems 'the sound of sense'. This sound is heard again in Lowell. Meanwhile, in both poetries, the iamb was preserved through thick and thin, long lines and short.

The tradition of the bad self, of antinomian duality, with its fevers and remorses, great days and dumps, can be understood stylistically, but it has never been narrowly prescriptive in that respect, and it has left its imprint on verse that is very different from Lowell's. There are features of his poetry, moreover, which appear to depend on the tradition, but which are no different from what was expected of poetry—of the poetry, at any rate, which took the whole man—at the time when he undertook to be a great writer, in the Thirties. Some of these features, and some others, we may think we understand in relation to the history of his illness, in terms of its exhaustions and depletions. We do not suppose that the factor of rise and fall in his artistic development can be seen as a strategic counterpart of the manic cycle: can we suppose that many of the fourteen-liners fail as a mind might fail?

His first work is a poetry of the self which has yet to learn to tell his story: a poetry of churning energies, of turmoil and anathema, and of arrest. As Jarrell was to warn him, it piles up its best effects, its strong lines (the 'strong line' relished in Donne by his contemporaries, incidentally, had to do, among other aspects of his verse, with 'the sound of sense', with what Ben Jonson called not keeping the accent—Jonson who predicted that Donne would die out through not being understood). We should not assume that poets must take an interest in other people, but we should not assume that egotism always prevents this: it does seem that the early faults were corrected when Lowell became able to write about himself, and that this opened his poetry to the world in a way that was often fruitful, and unequivocal. Then came a poetry of imitation and imperfection. A dementia of sources and sayings, excerpts and extracts and occasions. An automatism of constant repair. So many of the sonnets an aggregation of strong lines, with a sententious or bombastic last line of all. Leaps and ellipses that can't be tracked. A conflation of this person with that, when persons put in an appearance. Arguments that start only to be dropped. A testimony in Hamilton's book tells of the reviser's habit by now of inserting 'not's' into his lines in order to improve them—so that there wouldn't be a line that wasn't well-written. This might look like some kind of dualistic exercise: seen in the context of a continual revision, however, it may appear to have rather less duality in it than derangement.

In an elegy for Lowell, 'North Haven', Elizabeth Bishop refers, in a somewhat different spirit, to what he did with, and to, his poems, refers to his 'derangements' and 're-arrangements', linking them with a power of nature, of the planet. 'Nature repeats herself, or almost does.' Nature insists: 'repeat, repeat, repeat; revise, revise, revise.' This is as much as to suggest that the courage shown in other areas of his life was also shown in his revisions, for all the harm they did (look at the harm nature does), and we can agree that there was a power there, as well as a pathos.

The peculiarities of his verse, moreover, can rarely have been experienced as severe, let alone as mad, by anyone widely read in modern poetry. They make us think of Pound, as well as nature, and they also make us think of many other very different poets, and of their undisputed soundness of mind. At the same time, none of these peculiarities is such as to exclude the thought of Lowell's sympathetic proximity to a literary tradition, and a prose fiction, which are in some sense mad, or half-mad. There are writings which do what they can with a series of elations, desolations, and depletions. There is a romance whose past masters have gone mad and which takes madness as its method and main region. Whole chapters, whole works, by Dostoevsky are spent in delirium, in fits and onsets. Myshkin 'wanted to be alone, so as to give himself up entirely and passively to this agonising feeling of insufferable strain, without seeking to escape it. He loathed the idea of trying to solve the problems that filled his mind and heart to overflowing. "Am I to blame for everything?" he muttered to himself, hardly realising what he was saying . . . He knew that at the time when he was expecting such an attack, he was extraordinarily absent-minded and often mixed up things and people, if he did not look at them with special, concentrated attention.'[25] We cannot say, however, in so many words, that this is Lowell. His poems are like this, and they are not like this. They do not contribute to the romantic diary of a madman which is still being compiled by writers, for a public confident that it can read it, but far from confident that it can distinguish between some of the insanities and some of its own states. There are times when his poems participate in the state described by Dostoevsky, or something like it, when they appear notably self-confined, when they commemorate, and may need to commemorate, the excitements from which, in life, he was glad to recover. But they can also be said to oppose the state. Opposing the state meant opposing himself, and expressing himself. It took heroism, as well as narcissism, to steer his talent into the storm, towards his own story.

The solitude of the modern poet is nothing new, nor are the violence and indifference which it may contain. But there is a reverence for hostility which may be peculiar to the modern world, and Lowell's writings, once he had found himself, rarely add to it.

XVI. WHO IS SYLVIA?

The American poet Sylvia Plath was a student and a further living embodiment of duality. Three very different books about her which appeared together after her death shed light, and darkness, on the lives she led: *Letters Home: Correspondence 1950–1963*, by Sylvia Plath, selected and edited by her mother Aurelia, a no-nonsense biography by Edward Butscher entitled *Sylvia Plath: Method and Madness*, and *Chapters in a Mythology: The Poetry of Sylvia Plath* by Judith Kroll.[1] Ms Kroll is opposed to the biographical approach to Plath's work, which is assimilated in her book to the status of myth, and seen to be swept up into a flight from biography, a bid for transcendence.

Sylvia Plath was born in Massachusetts in 1932, the daughter of Otto and Aurelia Plath, who were respectively of German and Austrian stock. If she was a 'second-generation achiever'—an expression Edward Butscher makes use of—then her parents were achievers too. Otto was a biologist and an expert on bumble-bees, which were later to buzz in his daughter's bonnet. Aurelia, who had been his pupil, went on to become a teacher herself. In *Letters Home*, she explains that her husband grew hypochondriacal, a brief-cased recluse, who declined to go to doctors, though ill and seeming to feel he had cancer. By the time diabetes was diagnosed it was too late to save him and in 1940, having lost a leg, he suffered a pulmonary embolism and died. When Sylvia was ten years old, the mother and her two children moved to Wellesley. What it cost her to enable the family to survive and prosper is something that Aurelia has perhaps found it difficult to assess, though it is clear that biographers will be ready to enlighten her. Sylvia loved it at Smith College—'as I always sit in the middle seat in the front row, it seems as if Mrs Kafka is talking directly to me'[2]—and she achieved a great deal there, including a holiday stint on *Mademoiselle* in New York, which she was to write about in her novel *The Bell Jar*, and from which she returned to perform a suicide attempt, in August 1953, taking pills and retreating to the shadows of a 'crawl space' under her mother's house. She was retrieved, hospitalized, and given electric-shock therapy. In England, at Cambridge, she met and married Ted Hughes, gloried in that marriage, had two children by him and lived with him, mostly in the West Country, for some six years. In 1962 she discovered that her husband had formed a friendship with Assia Gutman, and the marriage broke up. She was now in the phase during which practically all her important verse was written. These must have been months of the utmost strain. She took responsibility, not only for her poems, but for her children, and for a move to London, where on 11 February 1963 she ended her life. 'We have come so far, it is over,' she had recently written, in the poem 'Edge'. For a while, Aurelia was unable to believe, or at any rate to acknowledge, that her daughter had committed suicide.

This is a story which is told only very indistinctly in Sylvia Plath's letters and in her mother's commentary on those letters. Was she as agonizingly intent on prizes and places, as deeply captured by a fear of less than perfect marks, as this volume discloses, while also disclosing a bright, achieving, sugary domesticity? Her mother is apparent as 'Dame Kindness' in a poem which is as much about herself, and her own kindness, and about human kind, as it is about her mother. Were the tendings of Dame Kindness repaid in kind? In the poem they are feared—shown as an exasperation in the new sphere of domesticity which arrived for the poet when she married and gave birth.

No one would expect an absolute candour from anyone's letters home. Omissions are marked in the published text, moreover, and it seems that cuts were conceded (and refused) in response to objections. At the same time, we may not really need to bother about lacunae in examining the insufficiency of *Letters Home*. Aurelia Plath does not disguise her concern to sugar her daughter's strange history by producing her fond and normal letters. The commentary has it that she died of over-intensity, strain, and that the suicide attempt of 1953 had been caused, or conditioned, by disappointment at being denied a place in Frank O'Connor's creative-writing class. Aurelia says of her daughter's 'life-experience' that, in 1963, 'some darker day than usual had temporarily made it seem impossible to pursue.'[3]

Neither the commentary nor the letters enlarge on the poet's feelings about her dead father, which have been regarded as the source of her breakdowns, and of her double or multiple personality. Sylvia Plath could show herself to observers and readers as alternately benign and hostile, as Snow White and Old Yellow—to borrow terms from interpretations of her work—and as the possessor of true and false selves. And if we accept that there were several selves, we might also accept that only one of them is on show in her letters home. It might be said, therefore, that the letters are bent on withholding her 'true' condition. 'Starless and fatherless, a dark water': I remember seeing these lines from 'Sheep in Fog', and other late lines, in typescript, soon after they were written, and feeling that they spoke a frightening truth. But it is also possible to feel that she had chosen that orphan state, while also being chosen by it, and had invented that truth. These procedures may not have been made known to her mother, and Sylvia's conduct could often appear to disown them.

Plath saw herself as adoring and despising her father, whose death made her feel both bereaved and guilty. She may have imagined herself betrayed by his departure, which could have been experienced as suicidal, and may have needed to exorcize him, as she proceeds to do in her ritualistic poem 'Daddy'. Ambivalent feelings towards her mother, too, ensued, and she is awarded a hard time in the 'Dame Kindness' poem. Equally, emotions about her father could coincide with what she felt about her husband. As I say, this drama is excluded from the letters: here, wholly acceptable, is Miss Kindness, and Miss Success, who sets her heart on the women's magazines of the day: 'I will slave and slave until I break into those slicks.'[4] Success had to wear a smiling face, had to drink and offer cups of tea, and conspire with her mother to deny the existence of hostility: but it was always a momentous and perilous business. Kroll suggests that Sylvia worshipped, and was, the white goddess of poetry. Butscher suggests, with reference to the experience of women who seek to do well in a man's world, that she worshipped, and was, the bitch goddess of success. These might be regarded as rival forces in the Plath pantheon. Both worships, however, could be dissembled in domesticity.

'Dearest one,' she wrote to her mother on 3 March 1953,

. . . *The* dress is hanging up in my window in all its silvern glory, and there is a definite rosy cast to the skirt (no, it's *not* just my attitude!). Today I had my too-long hair trimmed just right for a smooth pageboy, and I got, for $12.95, the most classic pair of silver closed pumps . . . With my rhinestone earrings and necklace, I should look like a silver princess—or feel like one, anyway. I just hope I get to be a Junior Phi Bete this year so I can use it for my Phi Bete dress, too. (Do you realise that I got the ONLY A in the unit from Mr Patch!) . . . God, how I wish I could win the *Mlle* contest. This year would be so ideal while I'm still in touch with college. . . Bye for a while,

Your busy loving, silvershod Sivvy

What can there have been to excise from that particular letter? Later in the month she tells of receiving rejection slips: the self-styled 'rejected daughter' once said she had hundreds—'they show me I try.' She wants to 'hit' the *New Yorker* with her poems and the *Ladies' Home Journal* with her stories. She hears 'the great W.H. Auden' speak in chapel.[5] April is kinder: elected editor of the *Smith Review*. Then there's the text of a telegram, announcing her guest editorship at *Mademoiselle*. The excitements of her spell on the magazine are despised in *The Bell Jar*, and described there by means of a successful approximation to Salinger's wit and sophistication which no more resembles the self of her late poems than it does that of her letters home. In the letters, these excitements amount to glamorous fun. But they helped to thrust her into the crawl space.

Edward Butscher seems sure that, with more than one of her selves, she hated her 'dearest one'. In the words of *On the Waterfront*, a film of Sylvia's heyday, he declares that theirs was 'an unhealthy relationship'. He interviewed a large number of people who were willing to supply memories, so that his book abounds in dates, double dates, blind dates, necking, petting, sitting in cars, period pains, chilblains—an American graffiti. What friends have to say won't invariably be true or interesting: one of his informants is able at one point to offer only a 'vague memory' of something sexual, and the accuracy of his book has been impugned in Britain, where it has not in fact appeared.[6] He might well have removed a few memories to leave room for rather more of what Plath herself had to say in print. There might, for instance, have been some mention of a piece she wrote after her separation from Hughes: a review of *Lord Byron's Wife* by Malcolm Elwin. 'Mr Elwin begins, as might many a shrewd marriage counsellor, with a meticulous investigation of the bride's mother.' It is interesting to turn from the American graffiti, and from the silvershod Sivvy who slaved for the slicks, to the professional composure of her critical comments. 'How clearly one sees the killing dybbuk of self-righteousness in possession! And what better luck this cherished, sympathetic sister might have had as Byron's wife.'[7]

At Smith, a contest for supremacy occurred between a self-righteous Sylvia and Gloria Brown, a bohemian radical who drank rum. Sylvia threatened to inform the authorities of this habit. When Commencement Day arrived, Mrs Plath, suffering from an ulcer, had to be carried on a litter to watch her daughter being awarded her *summa cum laude* certificate, while her daughter was laid low by stomach cramps and had to borrow, for medicinal purposes, some of Gloria's rum. Sylvia wrote her enemy a note: 'Thank you for teaching me humility.' The episode is related in an excellent memoir of Plath by Nancy Hunter Steiner.[8]

The testimonies gathered by Butscher from those who knew the Hugheses at Cambridge University reveal the farcical side of one of those worlds of respectability and culture which Plath intended to penetrate, and which she has posthumously subdued. The Cambridge of 1956 could be idyllic: 'Dear Ted took me for a walk in the still, empty Clare gardens by the Cam, with the late gold and green and the dewy freshness of Eden.' Yet 'Eden is, in effect, helping murder the Hungarians.'[9] This other Eden was the prime minister, who, the Russians having invaded Hungary, had invaded Egypt. Cambridge could also seem cold, and its dons crass and inky. It is easy to see what she means when these dons testify: 'Ted, at that stage, was very definitely a provincial, while Sylvia had a very wide range of European culture and was totally civilised. She could have passed anywhere without putting a foot wrong, and I was quite sure Ted couldn't.'[10]

Judith Kroll is ingenious and determined. Many of her findings were checked with Ted Hughes, and the two of them were keen to move Plath's verse as far as possible beyond the reach of exploitative biographers and of those critics who treat it as 'confessional'. Plath was somewhat drawn to the confessional vein of her time, and said as much. But this book says that her poems are not autobiographical, not domestic. They express the vision of a 'mythic totality', writes Kroll, who can give the impression of studying the images and deciding that the only ones that count are those which can be related to the canon of books where the parent myths are expounded. Dictionaries, Classical concordances, are consulted. Though no one would think it an especially autobiographical poem, 'Totem' is dealt with here in a way which illustrates the governing impulse to get rid of autobiography: 'These and many other details from private life clearly do not enter into the meaning of "Totem". Instead, the personal level fuels the impersonal, providing concrete images which express the most universal themes, even as they are private emblems of what drives her to investigate such themes. The private is not the ultimate level of meaning but part of something extraneous to the poem which nevertheless helped make a successful poem possible.' The passage breaks down in struggling to convey that the poem uses private material which both is and is not extraneous. Ms Kroll's book states that the poems see a father and husband as surrogates for one another, and that a conflict between true and false selves is acted out in relation to the male. The male has subjected the true self to a death-in-life, and the true self longs to die and be reborn. The principal motifs of the poetry, therefore, are the male as god and devil, true and false selves, death and rebirth. 'The protagonist, rejected by her personal "god", characteristically attempts to resolve the resultant death-in-life by transforming him into (or exposing him as) a devil or similar figure as a basis for rejecting him.' Shortly afterwards she writes: 'Either the false self or the male (or both) must be killed to allow rebirth of the true self.'[11]

For all it has to say about the impersonal and the elemental and the eternal, this mythic scheme can look like the story of Sylvia Plath's life, as told by a female chauvinist. It is clear that Plath was impressed by these myths, and her use of them can be accounted part of the autobiography of a woman who could at times fear childbirth and feel hostile towards men, who could wish to escape from biography, a woman who kept cheerful but could also act the witch and bitch, and who, with plenty of dates, was something of a vestal virgin, as her first name might suggest. It suggests this to Ms Kroll, who is attentive to meaningful names: her story is rich in these, in the importance of possessing, for instance, some Welsh name for the anti-domestic White Goddess. Kroll's scheme is established on the basis of a comparison between the poems and certain books which the poet read: chiefly, Graves's *The White Goddess*, Frazer's *The Golden Bough* and the writings of Jung. So we hear about the art and magic consecrated to the White Goddess, about her votaries, about maenads, about the Moon-muse, and about Graves's Old Sow of Maenawr Penardd. We hear about the dying god, about the divine king killed in order to secure the future. We hear about ecstasy, and about its etymology. But that is not the end of Judith Kroll's contentions. She affirms that in her last days Plath passed beyond such conceptions of mythic rebirth by experiencing a religious crisis or conversion. Personal history was to be transcended in a more radical way than that implied in the previous doctrines. It is in this context, we are informed, that her suicide must be understood.

For many years she worked hard at prize and apprentice poems, as they could often seem, learning as she did so from Stevens, from Dylan Thomas. She then attained a poetry of a different order. The book argues that this is a poetry which carries the formidable subject-matter of a second severance from the divine male, and that she set herself to repeat, and to reconstitute, that severance by conducting a species of exorcism. For the purpose of such rituals, her parents and husband could be made baleful: but Kroll is aware that this is not all that they were to her, even at that late stage.

It may be that the new poetry can be found, coming into force, in 'The Moon and the Yew Tree':

> The moon is no door. It is a face in its own right,
> White as a knuckle and terribly upset.

The poem appears to have been written as an exercise in 1961, when the Hugheses were still together, but the words 'terribly upset', which are the words of speech to a degree that few of her earlier words ever were, signal a change. The '*Ach, du*' addressed to her Daddy in the fine poem of that name is speech too, intensely expressive speech, and it sends out the same signal. She is down off her stilts, off her *New Yorker* stool. The reader shares in the intimacy communicated by these words. A number of the late poems were written down at speed, like letters. She was released.

Judith Kroll's explanations—which pertain to a latter-day mythic model of multiple personality—help one to figure out poems that can prove as difficult as they are shapely and translucent. But she pushes these explanations into debatable ground. At an earlier stage in her life Sylvia declared that she did not believe in personal immortality, and I am left wondering what it is that she would have to have believed in in order to write and act as she is alleged to do here. Ted Hughes has testified that a religious crisis took place, but the question of how such a thing could validate an intentional suicide, if that is what we have to reckon with, is one that we could not hope to settle unless we came to know much more about her death than we do.

Some of Kroll's explanations seem arbitrary when placed beside the verse: they do not always manage to decode poems which, if her explanations are right, must hitherto have been perceived as cryptic, rather than merely difficult. According to the mythic scheme, the colour white can be both good and bad, and so can the influence of the Moon. Plath's moons are not easy to interpret, and the White Goddess lore is both useful and not useful. In 'The Moon and the Yew Tree', 'the moon is my mother,' who 'sees nothing' of her daughter's fall. To be content with this poem it would not be necessary to notice an attachment to the White Goddess. In 'Edge', written in the last week of her life, she looks down at her own dead body, that of a 'perfected' woman. Her children have been delivered back into that effigy.

> The moon has nothing to be sad about,
> Staring from her hood of bone.
>
> She is used to this sort of thing.
> Her blacks crackle and drag.

Here again, the Moon is indifferent to the spectacle below. That closing line is less cryptic if you learn that a cauldron is the emblem of the Moon Goddess: flames might crackle beneath such a pot. And the Moon's blacks might be said to drag from them the blood of menstruating women, or that of women poets. In another poem, perfection is linked to barrenness, and that thought may be present here too. Ms Kroll, however, has a footnote which observes: 'A description of the Moon card in a Tarot book owned by Plath might be compared with the import of the Moon in "Edge".' The description refers to sweet peace and voluptuous dreams. Sweet peace does not crackle and drag.[12]

Poetry is blood in the 'Dame Kindness' poem, which ends:

> The blood jet is poetry,
> There is no stopping it.
> You hand me two children, two roses.

This poem and 'Edge' combine to say that poetry abolishes domesticity, about which Sylvia had more than one view. In 1953 she wrote to her brother about what their mother had done for them: 'After extracting her life blood and care for 20 years, we should start bringing in big dividends of joy for her.'[13] This might be heard as the voice of her false self: but we should recognize that to call it that would be to attempt to abolish what her mother, who lived with her for twenty years, took her to be. Those who think that this self did not write poetry should consult the opening line of a birth poem: 'Love set you going like a fat gold watch.'

Is Aurelia Plath's kind account of her daughter's death less satisfactory than Judith Kroll's religious one? Mrs Plath's word needs to be compared with that of Nancy Steiner. This witness said that her friend, who had lived dangerously, shed her blood, for her poetry, was uttering a cry for help here, as she had done before, and was also uttering a threat. 'I do not believe that Sylvia meant to die.'[14] There is a strain of testimony concerning Sylvia Plath which suggests that other people did not care very much about her because, apart from her family, she did not care about other people: and this, to the extent that it was true, must surely have been an aspect of her final predicament. Almost alone, though still in touch with her husband, fighting for her children and for somewhere to live, spent from the haemorrhage that had gone into the poems that would make her name, twice bitten—or eaten, to use one of her own expressions—by the failure of a relationship central to her life—it is not surprising that at one point she should have lost hope and sought or risked her death.

During her adult life 'confessional' poetry was welcomed partly because it could appear to be a celebration of madness—like the Gothic literature of the nineteenth century, with which she was in sympathy. She knew about dybbuks. But she herself was not mad, and I do not think she believed, to the extent that Ms Kroll makes out, in the myths unfolded in that author's book, with their content of murders and curses. Nor do I think that she experienced an apotheosis. For most observers of her life the existence of such beliefs was altogether less obtrusive than it is for the posthumous Judith Kroll; and it may be that Plath entertained and employed them—in the sense that she did not so much believe them as believe them to belong, rather as laurels and hardships do, to the life of a poet. In her last days, despite the exorcisms and 'witchy' behaviour embraced in her verse, she could resolve to act generously towards her husband and to make new friends. Was this a false self or start? Connoisseurs of the deathliness of her true self would call it that. But it is also possible to think that there was a will to go on which failed her—temporarily, so to speak—and to think of her as dying of her poetry, of the greatest efforts of that poetry, of the exhaustion that followed them, of the troubles that filled them, of an anxious ambition and an incongruous selfhood.

We can't surmise that a divided self will show an indifference to others. But it seems clear that it does not prevent what others take to be egotism—the egotism, for instance, which has been thought to accompany the efforts of authors, and the greatness of authors. Her life can perhaps be seen in this light, and as a strange case of this kind. But did she really have a divided self? Mr Butscher presents her in such terms, and exhibits a series of colourful doubles and dybbuks—good girl and strumpet, and so on. They are terms which do not appear to be a travesty of the case, and which *are* the case since they are terms which she herself applied. A double bind of poetry and domesticity is beyond doubt here, and so is the importance of the tensions that prevailed for this daughter in her dealings with her parents. And it can surely be said of her that, at a time of crisis, the New Woman and the Old, among others, became mortal enemies. Those who may be sceptical as to whether she was divided in any sense that is not quite familiar do not, in my opinion, lack arguments. But these arguments could not include the suicide attempt which succeeded, whether or not it was meant to. Here is prima-facie evidence, and more, of duality.

Suicide comes when one self destroys another. It is a dualistic act, inescapably so, and it may indeed be duality's best proof: the plainest reason we can expect for believing that some of what this literature says is true. And it is in the nature of the strange case of suicide that we do not usually know whether the aggregate self meant to proceed to the bitter end. Acts of suicide are likely to be equivocal, unknowable, in just the way that Sylvia Plath's was.

XVII. SYBILLINE SELVES

If the literature of the nineteenth century was in love with duality, so was its psychology, and so, at times, was its physiology. Literature and science collaborated in spreading the gospel which enjoined the plurality of the mind. At the start of the century, moreover, they were themselves a duality—aspects of a single knowledge which could still be referred to as 'literature'. But a work of separation was soon to be pursued. They were set apart, and science was declared the domain of rational knowledge, with professions and institutions to secure the protection of standards. So we may be conscious of an early time when the lore of science and the lore of literature were mutually responsive, and of a later time when the interchange was proscribed, though still, at times, practised, when Eliot's idea of a seventeenth-century dissociation of sensibility—an idea which derives from romantic psychology and the nineteenth-century project of the multiple self—was never to be entertained as scientific. It was thought for a while, in Arts Faculties and in schools, to be true and historical. But it was nowhere thought to be science.

Henri Ellenberger's *The Discovery of the Unconscious* is distinguished, among modern histories of psychiatry, by an awareness of these old accords, and of their survival in an era of professional arrogations and rival understandings. He suggests that psychiatry began when Romanticism did, and that a 'first dynamic psychiatry', interested in Mesmerism, hypnotism, and hysteria, and fully persuaded of the joint existence of a conscious and unconscious mind, was succeeded by a 'new dynamic psychiatry' indebted to its predecessor and chiefly affirmed in the teachings of Freud. Both psychiatries rested on a devotion to multiple personality, and it is not rash to claim that both were a form of romance.[1]

The first romantics were inclined both to keep and to discard the proto-scientific Associationist model of the mind, which saw it as a blank on which impressions were inscribed, as a system of connections established in early childhood which generated a soul-like moral sense, and, in time, as a state susceptible to splitting. Among the first psychiatrists a struggle developed between associationists and organicists, who chose to talk of changes in the brain. Meanwhile Phrenology stressed externals, spying propensities in a skullscape of bumps and shallows. Here, too, division was a critical factor for the 'plurality of organs' which George Combe, for example, took to constitute the mind. The mid-century physician, A. L. Wigan, who could well be accounted a rather less antediluvian figure, for physiologists of the present day, than he was for their immediate predecessors, thought of the brain as two brains, the one subordinate to the other but with the ability to pull apart. These are conceptions directly related to inquiries pursued in this book: but of course there were other conceptions, and almost all the outlooks in question were affected by the varieties of religious experience. The old notion of spirit flight, of ascent to a higher sphere, was not gone. Long after the celestial had ceased to be accommodated in any scientific cosmos, romantic people went on looking up—went on thinking of a sky to which the soul, in contempt of the body, might climb. On all sides, in literature as in science, could be found the predicate of some fundamental division—in particular, body and soul, then, progressively, conscious and unconscious mind.

In the course of the nineteenth century, duality, as a paradigm of mental behaviour, was to give the impression of turning into multiple personality, dipsychism into polypsychism: but the duality of a conscious and unconscious mind was to remain a leading concern. It was a concern compatible with Romanticism's hidden self, which might be either closed or open: engaged with another self within the individual, or, in protean fashion, with a World Soul. The 'first dynamic psychiatry's' search for recognition from the flinty world of official medicine enjoyed a spell of success from the early Eighties, during which hypnotism was widely approved, and the sexual explanation of hysteria, and of the pathogenic secret deemed to operate in such cases, was united with theories of multiple personality. But around 1910, in medical circles, hypnotism fell from favour; a gaining sense of the role of histrionics in cases of hysteria, and in displays of psychic multiplicity and virtuosity, may have deepened the disfavour. Nevertheless, in the cultural life of Britain and America, the split mind held its place; and in recent years, as a cure for much else besides the split mind, hypnotism has come back into clinical practice.

In the 'new' psychiatry much of the 'old' was resumed, and Freud himself can look like a lineal descendant, and like a contributor to literature in the old, compendious sense. The new psychiatry followed on from the old in paying attention to hypnotism and hysteria. The old psychiatry had cultivated the idea of an unconscious mind, and of an incidence of sub-personalities within the individual: Freudianism did this too, and managed to persuade the world. Both psychiatries assigned autonomy to personality parts. The rapport between the magnetizer or hypnotist and his patient could be encountered in the analyst's consulting-room, and the Freudian doctrine of transference referred to feelings no different from those put to use by past healers, the makers of passes. Like the psychiatry which preceded it, with its infusions of romance, psychoanalysis sought the mysterious secret, the forgotten grief which might be restored to consciousness at a time of crisis. Freudianism spoke of a powerful mother, and of an imagined return to her protection, and of a 'family romance' based on the rebellious child's impersonation of a changeling and imagination of a glamorous parent: to speak in this way among others was to acknowledge a parentage for psychoanalysis in the precedents of Romanticism.

In the 1870s and 1880s two Frenchmen took up the subject of clinical duality: multiple personality was defined by Janet in terms of the malfunctioning of an associative system, while Charcot, specializing in hypnotism and hysteria, pursued a theory of the part played by amnesia in cases of hysteria. From these pursuits there emerged the name 'fugue'. A fugue was and is a state of dissociation marked by personality change and by wanderings from the immediate physical environment, by departures from home which may be accompanied by a forgetting of the past and be themselves later forgotten. Psychiatry's fugues are literature's flights. Such departures are like those performed by the self-imagined orphan. For the shatterbrain states and straits of earlier times clinical duality was to invent a set of often formidable technical terms: 'fugue', 'dementia praecox', 'schizophrenia'. The second has long been obsolete, while the third may be thought to have borne a charmed life.

In the English-speaking world of the later nineteenth century, professors of duality came to construe it, with reference to a fairly small number of famous instances, as an affair of amnesias, sleeps, and fugues, and several of the more prestigious of these professors worked together on the American East Coast: such men as William James, Morton Prince, and the neurologist and novelist Weir Mitchell, who wrote about Mary Reynolds, the so-called *dame de Macnish*, and who took care of the *grande dame* Edith Wharton in 1898. Mary Reynolds, whose wanderings date from 1811, James Hogg's contemporary Robert Macnish, who wrote about her earlier in the century, Weir Mitchell, Edith Wharton—here is an intriguing dualistic succession. America was hospitable to the subject of duality and some of the strange cases which comprise it are American—Mary Reynolds, Ansel Bourne, Miss Beauchamp. These cases bulk large in the literary-clinical record. There were cases which gradually inspired the thought that a factor of acting-out or up, a protean knack of impersonation, might be suspected. In most cases, moreover, an attempt at escape can be discerned. Most of these multiple persons were displeased with their environment, with their families or with dictatorial propriety, and their sleeps are apt to evoke the disappearing trick played by Washington Irving's Rip Van Winkle, who fled from a hostile wife, dozed for twenty years and awoke to find her dead.

In *The Principles of Psychology*, completed in 1890, William James addressed the grand question of human inconsistency.

The phenomenon of *alternating personality* in its simplest phases seems based on lapses of memory. Any man becomes, as we say, *inconsistent* with himself if he forgets his engagements, pledges, knowledges, and habits; and it is merely a question of degree at what point we shall say that his personality is changed. In the pathological cases known as those of double or alternate personality the lapse of memory is abrupt, and is usually preceded by a period of unconsciousness or syncope lasting a variable length of time. In the hypnotic trance we can easily produce an alternation of the personality, either by telling the subject to forget all that has happened to him since such or such a date, in which case he becomes (it may be) a child again, or by telling him he is another altogether imaginary personage, in which case all facts about himself seem for the time being to lapse from out his mind, and he throws himself into the new character with a vivacity proportionate to the amount of histrionic imagination which he possesses.[2]

James, who was sympathetic to Janet, said that the mind held sets of 'association-paths', and said that one such system might be 'thrown out of gear' with the others. Each of the resultant selves 'is due to a system of cerebral paths acting by itself'. Wigan's earlier theory of cerebral dissociation is declared crude. 'The consciousness of Self involves a stream of thought,' passing thoughts inherit past thoughts and form associations: inherent in this point of view is a whole modern literature. The identity of the thinker is rated a metaphysical question.[3] The brothers William and Henry James were a remarkable nineteenth-century American duo, with their sinister counterparts in the brothers James who were outlaws: here we have a more than ornamental double duality, supplied by the power of coincidence. William James was sufficiently respectful of religious experience to arrange for his wife and sceptical brother to place themselves in readiness, when he died, in case there should be a message from beyond the grave. None came.

Mary Reynolds fled from her kin, Ansel Bourne from Mrs Bourne, and Miss Beauchamp from the dictates of a New England conscience, jolted by a sexual shock, and sorrowing over the failure of her relationship with her mother. The Reynolds case is discussed in *Principles of Psychology*, where James draws on Weir Mitchell's version, which draws on the testimony of relatives and friends and on that of the prodigy herself. A dull and sober Pennsylvanian, Mary is thought by Ellenberger to have fallen under the spell of a brother-in-law, and in 1811 she fell into a deep and lengthy sleep, from which she awoke a different person. Mitchell quotes: 'Old things had passed away; all things had become new.' The new woman was cheerful, a 'perfect stranger', Mitchell says, a born-again romantic who looked on nature with the eye of the child in Wordsworth's 'Immortality' Ode, on a world 'apparelled in celestial light'. But—Mitchell is quoting from his witnesses once again—she 'never would acknowledge the ties of consanguinity, or scarcely those of friendship'. She showed no fear of wild animals, and drove off a grizzly with a stick, taking it to be a black hog. Presently she fell asleep again and awakened to her former self. 'Not a trace was left in her mind,' Mitchell writes. 'Her parents saw their child; her brothers and sisters saw their sister.' Whom, one may wonder, did her brother-in-law see? These alternations recurred over fifteen years until she was about 35. Her two selves then reached an accommodation: or it may be that a third, neither dull nor ecstatic, succeeded. She lived on in her community, a popular figure, and died at the age of 61.[4]

The Reverend Ansel Bourne also passed beyond the bounds of domesticity. Formerly a carpenter and village atheist, he had been converted to Christianity and became an itinerant preacher. In 1887, in New England, he drew money from the bank, boarded a horse-car, and, as 'A. J. Brown', turned up in Mary Reynolds's Pennsylvania, opening a candy store at Norristown. A nephew arrived to take him home—filled with a horror of the store. In 1890 William James hypnotized him and recalled the Brown self. Brown had heard of Bourne, a name preserved or secreted in his own. Faced with Mrs Bourne, however, he said he had 'never seen the woman before'. He also said: 'I'm all hedged in. I can't get out at either end.' The words could describe an Ansel Bourne uncomfortable both with his wife and with his faith. This traveller both returned and did not return from beyond the bourne. James sought by suggestion to 'run the two personalities into one', but 'Mr Bourne's skull today still covers two distinct selves.' James classed the case as 'one of spontaneous hypnotic trance', while considering the details 'all *compatible* with simulation'.[5]

Morton Prince got to know Miss Beauchamp in 1898. Twenty-three years old, this Radcliffe student was like the first Miss Reynolds—timid and dull, a runaway with an unhappy home life. In the course of hypnotic therapy, there surfaced a cluster of sub-personalities, some of them unknown to others, one of them ('Sally') a puckish player of tricks on the sober self of previous times, and another regressive ('the Idiot'). Eliciting these secondary selves, Prince discovered that his patient had had a fright at the age of 18: a male friend and preceptor, ascending a ladder, had peeped at her through a window. 'She saw his excited manner, and heard his voice between the peals of thunder.'[6] This is her visionary re-enactment of an experience which was reckoned of decisive importance to the history of her dissociation. It might have made a page in a Gothic novel: equally, Prince's accounts of the case made pages in later studies of multiple personality. The story of Miss Beauchamp, with its numbered personalities, BI, BII and so on, has been used to countenance later psychiatric attempts to repair the fractured self sustained by the casualty of family life. It helped to introduce the several selves—they may be called, for the purposes of this chapter, the sybilline selves—of latter-day duality. But it raises certain doubts. Are these multiple selves really moods, sides, phases of an individual life, and are we all multiple in that sense? How is the pathology of division to be defined? Miss Beauchamp was conscious of Prince—and Prince was conscious of himself—as a dualistic doctor: the likelihood of role-playing, in any psychotherapeutic context, must surely have been enhanced when doctor and patient were both, in different degrees, students of duality. Braving these questions, Prince embarked on a project which may seem to stand in a line of descent from Dr Jekyll's separation of the elements of human nature.

The project was to put Miss Beauchamp together again. To reconstruct her original personality. Despite the fact that it was the original personality which had broken down, or up, its reconstruction was to serve as the basis for an optimum personality of the future. Some of the sub-selves of her dispersal, some of the B's in her bonnet, were produced during hypnotic sessions which went brilliantly, and were able to subdue the mischievous Sally. Prince reckoned with a primary and a subliminal self, observed that the latter was not necessarily the same as the hypnotic self, and believed that an infinite number of selves was theoretically possible. Such selves need not be morbid or amnesiac. They were possible for everyone, and were cognate with the changes of heart and successions of mood spoken of in ordinary life.

Prince was a celebrated turn-of-the-century dualist who based experiments on those of Janet and relied on English physiological psychiatry. The essay on Miss Beauchamp from which I have quoted was read as a paper in 1900. In 1924 he said that cases of obvious abnormality were of interest because of the light they throw on 'the composite nature of man, and on the many little selves of which the mind is composed', and asked if we might not say that we all 'have as many selves as we have moods, or contrasting traits, or sides to our personalities', that Jekyll-like 'irreconcilable conflicts' were special cases which proved the rule of a general inconsistency.[7] Prince was estranged both from Freudian psychoanalysts and from the *enfants-terribles* Behaviourists. He was not estranged from literature, and referred freely to the Flying Scotsmen of the subject, Stevenson and William Sharp, alias Fiona Macleod. Stevenson's novel was an allegory of 'the two sidedness of human nature', produced at a time when 'real cases of double personality' were 'not known in actual life'. Of the Sharp duo he asked a question which was bound to force itself on the technicians who undertook to sew up the actual splits of the new age: was the primary self primary? Might not some rival self be that, and be the model for the work of reconstruction? In Sharp's case: 'Which was the real self? The masculine William or the feminine Fione?'[8] In a letter of 1910 to a friend of his and of William James, Prince seized Sharp's pen and flew beyond bound and bourne in the character of Fiona. It has been said[9] of this episode that 'he wanted to convey to his old friend, James Jackson Putnam, the depth of his affection for him as well as the depth of his anger and depression at the growth of a militant psychoanalytic movement. Prince felt that such extremes of feeling were outside the bounds of convention for himself, but that, as "Fiona Mac Prince", he could express them.' The debonair Prince had his 'sides', his fits of gloom, his female fits. He was himself a strange case. That of the Misses Beauchamp was soon turned into a Broadway play; his project of reconstruction captured the imagination and has been judged an exemplary success. It is worth noting, however, that William James warned him about such projects at an early stage, and urged him to be careful to distinguish between the spontaneous and the artificial in attending, and producing, the shows of the multiple personality.

In 1947, in his book *Personality*, the American psychologist Gardner Murphy braved these questions once again, and achieved a shrewd and persuasive account of the subject. Murphy deals with Prince's case: 'The imp Sally could not live in the same house with the staid Miss Beauchamp.' He goes on: 'a morbidly conscientious personality alternated with a free, vivid, and alert one . . . Whereas the conscientious personality knew the free one only by inference, the free personality was present all the time that the solemn one was present, knew her every thought and memory, was amused at her, and treated her like an odd stick that it would be convenient to eliminate if possible.' Murphy supposes that the case reveals an analogy with the charivari—the moods, sides, fits, and fluctuations—of universal experience, but that there is more to the rare cases of pathological dissociation—which are what we often mean when we talk of multiple personality—than the analogy can explain.

> Subtracting a little of the mystery, we may say that the case is suggestive of the normal alternation between states of narrow, self-reproving consciousness in which a person knows rather little of himself (because it would be disturbing to know more) and those breezier, more casual states in which he remembers the straitened self with amusement or scorn. In one state he can afford to remember; in the other he cannot. By this we do *not* mean that this analogy with the normal oscillation of moods provides all the necessary clues to the more unusual fluctations. For one thing, there appears to be in all these cases a deep dissociation, a capacity for cleavage which most of us lack. But perhaps the normal personality is more dissociable than we suspect, and the pathologically dissociated is a bit played up, dramatised by patient and doctor alike.

For Murphy, all behaviour in a social context has a histrionic quality, and in cases of dissociation where there is serious morbidity there may also be theatre. At the same time, 'the reality of the dualism in the self must be admitted' in such cases. 'The term "pose" is likely to assign to the associative systems a quality of voluntary control which they partially or altogether lack.'[10]

He states that since 1900 psychiatry had set itself to interpret dissociation by means of two rival explanations: Janet's idea of a failure in the associative system, and the idea of motivational conflict. And he tries to subtract a little of the mystery from the subject by proposing that the two explanations can be combined. Dissociation is fleetingly experienced in brown studies, or by the drowning man, and is a feature of many other modes of ordinary life: but the rare, strange cases indicate a factor of radical and congenital dissociability which assists in the creation of an autonomous alternative personality, a further ego. 'Such a fissure in the organic make-up can occur only when to constitutional dissociability there are added two or more warring impulses, so that a weak sense of unity gives way to two or more ego systems organised around different needs. Rarely indeed is this construction of forces found. Most cases of multiple personality appear essentially to represent the organism's efforts to live, at different times, in terms of different systems of values.'[11] It may be that Murphy was no less appreciative than Prince of the literary record in these matters: 'warring impulses' is an expression of Conrad's. Murphy comes to the conclusion that multiple personality may be both familiar and peculiar, that it may have both a weak sense and a strong or strange, and that in either sense it will require the existence of conflicting drives and rival demands. These are not rare, and the conclusion persuades us to see the subject as one of very wide interest and extent.

He is a rational guide to what can sometimes look like a specious subject, and he concedes no more to its famous mysteries than occasional talk of a 'driving-out' of the impish or unpleasant sub-personality. He suggests that multiple personality is likely to involve a conflict between a conformer and a guilty nonconformer, which may also be a conflict between a constricted, self-reproving personality and a blithe, free or mutinous spirit, with the former inhabiting a home from which the free spirit wishes to escape.[12] According to Murphy, amnesias may conceal from the bound personality actions performed and memories possessed by the free. Readers of the imaginative literature of this subject will be inclined to relate a clinical record which speaks of a main personality which is fashioned in constriction, and which may forget itself in flight, to the sleeps, swoons, and syncopes of romance, from which a new life may ensue.

Murphy accepts that, in cases of splitting, therapy should seek to obtain the integrity of a single personality: 'It would appear that the dissociations of most multiple personalities can be dispelled when appropriate motivation for renewed unity is supplied,' and that it is necessary to enquire into the motives which have made them need several selves rather than a 'single responsible self'.[13] He values an inclusive integrity: the wider the field of consciousness, the better. Knowing more is better, and he seems to think that blitheness knows more than solemnity. But the thought, which Murphy's book encourages, that all environments are constricting, that each person is a quandary, a quarrel, a confederacy, ranked somewhere on the spectrum that runs between singleness and fatal division, is not one which lends unqualified support to the belief in integrity, to the notion of a sole self to which the sufferer may be—whether by medical engineering or by magic—restored. In saying, moreover, that the capacious self harbours capacity, he does not say what might also appear to be worth saying: that the capacious self, which knows more, and has more to choose from, may be liable to crack or to split. Finally, the book suggests that human beings may embark on courses of action in the hope that conflicting aims may be achieved, reconciled, transcended or abolished, warring impulses conquered or compounded.

These, then, are renowned cases of nineteenth-century dissociation which have been of interest both to literature and to science: separate selves were taken to co-exist within the individual, and to stand in need of synthesis or exorcism, driving-out or engineering, with a view to the re-establishment of an integrity, and varieties of acting-out, or acting, were observed. They prepare the ground for some words concerning a well-known case of recent times in which literature and science can once again be caught in one another's arms. The case is recorded in *Sybil* by Flora Rheta Schreiber, published in America in 1973. The dualistic hypothesis has a long history, and it comprises intervals of rediscovery, when it can be declared as fresh as a daisy: this may be why the novelist Doris Lessing has said that *Sybil* 'forces you to look at yourself and the people around you in a new way'.[14] Flora Schreiber's book is subtitled 'the true story of a woman possessed by 16 separate personalities', raising hopes of exorcism and devils. The book reads like a novel, but is based on the data assembled during an 11-year psychoanalysis, to whose secrets the author was privy. The therapist had to prepare herself for this course of treatment by studying 'the relatively sparse literature about multiple personality',[15] about Mary Reynolds, Ansel Bourne, Christine Beauchamp, about the eight women and three men said to figure in that literature, and by studying the writings and hypnotic methods of Prince. Flora Schreiber claims that this was the first full psychoanalysis of a case of multiple personality, and that the case was unique by virtue of the presence of more alternating selves than ever before. Among the selves of the female in question were those of a pair of males. The names of the people have been changed for the book, and we learn that the real Sybil was known to its author.

Sybil Dorsett met the woman who was to become her analyst, Dr Wilbur, in Omaha, Nebraska in 1945, when Sybil was 22. The analysis was conducted in New York City, and lasted from 1954 till 1965, when she entered the 'promised land of integration'. She suffered at the outset from psychosomatic ailments which were rapidly thought to be 'not a psychosis but a hysterical condition' consistent with Charcot's *grande hystérie*.[16] She was unable to get on with her career as an advanced student. She showed a tendency to black-outs or blank spells, after which she could not remember what she had been doing for months on end, and during which she would be acknowledged by people whom she could not remember. She would wake up or come-to in strange cities. Sybil is described as a talented painter, and her talent seems to have been recognized in the community where she passed her childhood and youth—Willow Corners, in the remote Midwest. But Willow Corners is described as, in general, a bigoted and benighted place, a hysterical place indeed, all prohibitions and suspicions. Her parents, Willard and Hattie Dorsett, are portrayed as suitable and successful inhabitants of such a place: Willard, a master-builder, as well-intentioned but indifferent, Hattie as hysterical and hostile. Both are believers in a fundamentalist Christianity whose dinner-table talk is of the end of the world. When we are first aware of her, Sybil, reserved and withdrawn, speaks well of her parents. As the analysis proceeded, this attitude was to change, and the analyst felt that it had to do so.

Dr Wilbur established to her satisfaction that Sybil's first dissociation took place when she was two and a half, in 1926. She had taken a fancy to a male doctor in a hospital, at whose hands she had then fancied a snub. Sybil, it is said, did not return from that hospital. But two surrogates did: Vicky and Peggy Louisiana. These were the first of the 'independent' and 'autonomous' selves who were to 'steal time' from the main self, or what was left of it, who were responsible, as Dr Wilbur explained to her patient, for Sybil's fugues. At the time this discovery was made, Dr Wilbur drew up a family tree featuring the further selves that had descended—more were in store—

from the two newcomers. It was thought 'that Vicky's line consisted of Marcia, who had appeared in 1927, Mary (1933), Vanessa (1935), and Sybil Ann, the precise date of whose arrival is not known; that Peggy's line consisted of Peggy Ann, into whom the original Peggy had developed; Peggy Lou, who appeared in 1926; Sid, who arrived early in 1928, and Mike who made his entrance later that same year.' Vicky was to serve as the 'memory trace'—Gardner Murphy's term—for this plethora of selves. Owning more of the original Sybil than Sybil herself, Vicky had access to the collective memory.[17]

The original had been a busy, playful child, but had feared her mother. These fears had been repressed, and dissociation was understood to mean that the newcomers were the girl's defenders. The newcomers could do what Sybil could not—resent and reject her mother—but one consequence of this succour was an ailing and etiolated main self. Dr Wilbur had been on the look-out for trauma from the start, and trauma turns up in a manner—common in psychotherapy—which incriminates parents. At this stage in the analysis, the judgement was made that what was in question was not a single trauma but a series, in relation to which Hattie could be considered 'the taproot': Hattie's harmful influence was 'aided and abetted' by her husband's failure to notice the trouble and to intervene, and by their membership of a simple-minded social milieu which worshipped a punitive god and went in fear of devils.

In contact with the proliferating selves which served Sybil as a self-destructive defence, and which were also mutually destructive, the psychiatrist gathered that she had been subjected by her mother to systematic abuse. She may have been an unwanted child. At all events, Hattie, who had herself been subjected to an orphaning at her father's hands, treated her as such, according to the revelations which began to flow. Constant complaints and belittlings from her mother were accompanied by a ritual of violation, painful enemas were administered, her vagina was probed. The child also had to witness, night after night, for a long time, the 'primal scene'—intercourse between Willard and Hattie, who are meanwhile present in the record as sex-haters. Hattie came near to killing her daughter by exposing her to the risk of a fall from a hay-loft. This inventory of assault is presented as factual, but of course only a very little of it could be checked, and some of the selves who vouched for it are perceived in the book as liars. We are asked to believe that with the child in the room there were nightly copulations, and that, in the bushes by the river, Hattie took to organizing lesbian orgies—spied on by Sybil or a surrogate—with lower-class women.

Dr Wilbur saw it as part of her task to prevail on Sybil to hate her mother for what she had done to her, and she told Mike and Sid that they were right to think of Hattie as a 'dirty girl'. Sodium pentathol was administered, with a view to inducing hatred, but had to be stopped when the patient showed signs of becoming addicted. It was replaced by hypnotism, which dominated the later stages of the analysis. This seems to have worked well for the analyst, and may have helped to make Sybil the happy women she is eventually reported to be.

Willard was still alive during the analysis, though Hattie was not, and he was fetched to listen to information concerning atrocities he had failed to detect and investigate. Sybil, now in improved possession of the relevant facts and fables, herself confronts her father with them.

> Opening his eyes, he held up his hand in a gesture of entreaty, saying: 'Sybil, say no more. I'm an old man now. Spare me because of my years if for no other reason.'
>
> 'When I was very little, Dad,' Sybil persisted despite the entreaty, 'hideous things happened. You didn't stop them.'
>
> 'The wheat crib. The buttonhook,' Willard murmured. Then he looked directly at his daughter, imploring, 'Forgive me.'
>
> This time it was Sybil who rose to her feet, pacing. Forgive the lost time, the lost years? The anger that so newly seethed in her precluded forgiveness. 'Let the dead past remain buried,' was as close as she came to conciliation. She was ready to forget, not in the old sense of retreating from what she couldn't face but in the altogether new way of not making an issue of what had been done long ago.[18]

But then we may feel that the point has in fact been to make an issue of the past.

She explains to her father about the repertoire of Sybilline selves: Willard had not known about them, but neither, in full measure, had she, their landlady, until Dr Wilbur informed her. We are led to think that her analyst took a fair measure of responsibility for the distinguishing and naming of her constituent selves. Willard died shortly after this, and left Sybil, whom he had supported well into adult life, penniless. This confronts Sybil with a 'terrible truth, for which her dreams had already prepared her'. Dr Wilbur tells her 'consolingly': 'You have always had strong Oedipal feelings for your father, but you've also always hated him. The original Sybil hated both her mother and her father.' A few pages later we read that the therapist then considered 'doing away' with Sybil, the 'waking self', and vesting the purposed reintegration in Vicky. But she changed her mind. It was the waking or central self which had to be preserved for this purpose. 'This was pioneer work for Dr Wilbur.'[19]

Late in the analysis, while still prone to lapses and despairs, Sybil made friends with a South American accountant, who had grown up in poverty and studied in order to better himself—a goal with which she was in sympathy. Ramon took mathematical account of his erections: 'I measure. It's seven inches. Good?' This can't have been altogether reassuring to the multiply reserved and reluctant Sybil, but most of the wise and foolish virgins in her make-up warmed to Ramon. She was 'fond' of his sister's children, whom the couple were to look after when they were married, but whom she had never met: such fondness can be compared with her analyst's professed love for each and all of her sixteen selves. But she could not bring herself to say yes to Ramon, and moved instead to the shelter of an affectionate dependence on her analyst and on the author of the book. Ramon was 'superior to the mean gratification of hard feelings': this can be compared with Dr Wilbur's intention to elicit in Sybil hard feelings towards her parents.[20]

Soon afterwards, in the book, the analysis is rated a success. Eleven years have gone by, and sixteen personalities, and Sybil is now cured. Dr Wilbur notes on 2 September 1965: 'All personalities one.' This has the ring of 'All systems go,' and indeed the outcome is seen as some great technical feat like the Moonshot, with the fourth and final part of the book entitled 'Re-Entry'. The author mentions in 1972 that Sybil 'is climbing the professional ladder with alacrity', loved by her students, respected by her colleagues, and in a position to pay for her long course of treatment. She is leading 'the good life—a whole life'. She is the embodiment of a type of urban professional success—a way of life, as it were, which has no time to lose. It is held up throughout the book as a pattern superior to anything afforded by the hysterical, fissile, bigoted life of the Midwestern small town. Her ability to lead this life may have been affected by a new-found ability to accept and enjoy the friendship of women.[21]

In assessing this cure, the reader is at a disadvantage: he does not know Sybil as her analyst and author do—he only knows this book. But then Dr Wilbur and Flora Schreiber did not know some of the people who mattered to the case, and had to rely on Sybil's anguished recollections. No assessment can ignore a letter of 1959 in which Sybil disowns her several selves and two other letters of the same period in which she reaffirms them. On 17 August she wrote to Dr Wilbur:

> I do not have any multiple personalities. I don't even have a 'double' to help me out. I am all of them. I have been essentially lying in my pretence of them. The dissociations are not the problem because they do not actually exist, but there *is* something wrong or I would not resort to pretending to be like that. And you might ask me about my mother. The extreme things I told you about her are not true. My mother was more than a little nervous. At times she was flighty, clever, overanxious, but she did love me.

Having written this, Sybil underwent two days of lost time. When she came-to, she wrote to Dr Wilbur to deny that her multiple personalities were 'just put on'. Three weeks later she repeated the denial—to a nurse, Miss Updyke, whom she had known in her undergraduate days:

> When I had been in analysis for a few months, I wrote you that Dr Wilbur had explained to me about multiple personalities and that the 'blank spells', as I had always called them, were not blank in anything but my memory. I had been active, and another 'person' had taken over and said or done the things that I had not been able to do for some reason—whether fear of consequences, lack of confidence, lack of money, or for the reason of getting away from problems and pressures too great for me to face as 'myself'.
>
> The point I'm trying to make is really twofold: The 'blank spells' I have had since I was just under four were spells in which I, as another of the fifteen personalities that have emerged from time to time, did things to act out the problems or troubles of the past or the present. Many of these started with my mother, who was catatonic at times, at

other times laughing hysterically and joking very cleverly, dancing on the street or talking much too loudly in church or acting 'silly' at a party, sometimes cruel and sometimes entirely unreachable. We are trying to undo what has been done and what you, in your aversion to my mother, seemed to sense.

Reading this letter, Miss Updyke remembered a journey during which, 'chameleon-like, Sybil had revealed a swift succession of what had then been dismissed as moods. At one point Miss Updyke recalled that Sybil had put her head in her companion's lap, but Sybil had later insisted, "I'd never do a thing like that."' One possible comment on these epistolary events of the summer of 1959 is that what some might call moods, or times, since they could last for months on end, Sybil had been able, after a kind of lapse, to recognize—in Flora Schreiber's view, correctly—as persons.[22]

These letters are better-written than the book which is scrupulous enough to cite all three, and they impart a feeling for her own plight, and an understanding of it, which alternately exhibit and deny the instruction she is receiving. But they do not enable us to answer the question whether the several selves should be seen as moods or times or as persons. Who is Sybil? Is she—like the reader, her *semblable*—a succession, a chameleon: are we dealing with temporary and even fleeting sub-personalities which are functions of a main self, however precarious, of the 'Sybil' who is identified by the book as the author of all three letters? Or is she a walking compendium of sixteen or seventeen (I lost count) separate and independent selves? The idea of independence, of there being different persons in possession at times, is dear to this book. Let us look at one of the objective differences which are said to separate the selves.

The book makes a point of claiming that some of the selves have skills which others lack, and which Sybil lacks—such as arithmetic. This might suggest autonomy. But then it transpires that while Sybil paints best, other selves also paint, according to their lights, and that they may on occasion simultaneously paint the same picture: 'None of the paintings, of course, was Sybil's alone.' On one occasion, in an Omaha church, the pastor's words about the 'four great beasts' that came up from the sea were illustrated by Sybil, raised for the purpose on a scaffold. She was not alone up there. Most of the drawing was the work of Mike and Sid, and 'among the selves on that scaffold were five Dr Wilbur had not yet met: Marjorie, Helen, Sybil Ann, Clara, and Nancy Lou Ann.' But the congregation saw only the one artist, who is surely the sole claimant to any autonomy the episode might suggest. Sybil's experience as an artist—one that incorporates collaboration, orchestration —is what many artists might wish to report.[23]

'"Sybil," the doctor replied firmly, "I've told you again and again that none of the others go against your ethical code."'[24] Nineteenth-century hypnotists sometimes said this, though it must have seemed doubtful at the time, and was in due course experimentally disproved to the satisfaction of some of the interested parties. It does not seem true of Sybil's experience of duplication. Her other selves were out to achieve what was morally unacceptable to the self which could not admit that Hattie had done her daughter harm. There can be few cases of a heterogeneous selfhood quite free from any element of conflict between what Murphy calls 'systems of values'—from any element of the heterodox.

Mike and Sid, male chauvinists, are ethically different from Sybil. Mike coarsely exhorts: 'Doctor, it's time to wake up to the truth about Sybil Dorsett. She's a woman, and a woman can't wow the world.'[25] Histrionic words—of a kind rarely uttered off the stage and away from a book. Another of the voices which Dr Wilbur obtained from her patient is that of Blondie, Sybil's ideal girl. Blondie, too, talks like a book. Moreover, she inhabits a book. And its author, like other authors, must surely have dressed up the language of Blondie, Mike, Sid and so on in order to meet her own needs. It is also possible that Sybil, herself an author, as we have noticed, and a performer, and an expert on duality who had received instruction in its literature and history, dressed up the language she is found to use—and put it on. A complex histrionics may be on display. This does not mean that we should flatly disbelieve the performances that comprise it: but it should make us less than ready to think of the voices as autonomous. '*Not one of these selves had a single memory that Sybil did not also have*': this burst of italics refers to the selves that survived until late in the analysis, and it can only be an argument in favour of autonomy if we are able to believe that these selves had by then lost the memories that had separated them from Sybil.[26] It can't have been easy to establish this experimentally—given that everybody forgets things.

When Sybil asks, 'Then I'm like Dr Jekyll and Mr Hyde?' Dr Wilbur is affronted. The analyst

> slapped her hand in her fist. 'That's not a true story,' she said. 'It's pure fiction. You're not at all like Dr Jekyll and Mr Hyde. Stevenson wasn't a psychoanalyst. He created those two characters out of his literary imagination. As a writer he was concerned only with spinning a good yarn.'

A psychoanalyst *would* say this. Using the language of literary duality, Dr Wilbur tells Sybil on another occasion that she is 'not strange' (indeed, she is 'very likeable'), though multiple personality is here admitted to be a 'bizarre' phenomenon. For all the employment of the therapeutic fist, we may hesitate to decide how much truer *Sybil* is, how much less yarningly imaginative, than *Jekyll and Hyde*.[27]

To the 'classical' case-histories of multiple personality read up by Dr Wilbur the human imagination can be taken to have contributed, and the very names read like a book: William James's title 'The Strange Case of Silas Prong' suggests an almost exaggerated sense of literary fitness. At the same time, the case-histories were those of real people, whatever we may think of their also being in some measure consenters to the constructions placed upon their lives, and the same can be said of *Sybil*. The recognition, by the peruser of this material, of a collaboration between literature and science need not lead to a denial that the case-histories are true, and could well lead to a recognition that there is some truth in the strange fictions of the subject. *Sybil* predicates for multiple personality 'an initial milieu (the nuclear family) that is restrictive, naive, and hysterical'.[28] The strange fictions of the subject show that doubles may have to do with families and their constraints and discontents, with a search for relief and for freedom, with the agony of choice which dictates the ingenuity of trying to have it both ways: and there is much in Flora Schreiber's account which, where it cannot be simply imitative, may appear confirmatory of the old romances. It is striking, for example, that fire-breathing religion played a part—as of old and as in fiction—in promoting the disorders of division.

Sybil's letters are more intelligent than the speech given to her doubles. The doubles are said to have 'depleted' her, but they themselves look like depletions of the gender stereotypes thrown up by American life. And there are times when Sybil, and even one of her surrogates, can outdo, in discussion, her analyst and her author. It is plain that she brought courage and stamina to the long effort to achieve a cure. But Flora Schreiber admits that her book does not explain how this cure was achieved. The causes of multiple personality 'remain elusive', which may be thought to leave the matter more or less where William James left it when he said in discussing the 'proteiform individual' or 'alternate personality': 'Of course it is mere guesswork to speculate on what may be the cause of the amnesias which lie at the bottom of changes in the Self.'[29] Hypnotism, in its mysterious way, is reported to have made Sybil better—with the reporters insisting that autonomies which some readers may think chimerical were put down. But Dr Wilbur's sympathetic attentions were almost certainly as influential as the trances she produced in the undoing of what had been done to Sybil by parents who may indeed, as speculation has directed us to think, have been among the causes of her failures of control and of morale (we have no way of seeing the parents in any very different light, whatever our misgivings about her improved, and hostile, understanding of their responsibility for her sufferings). Gardner Murphy observes that dissociations can be cured when the right motivation is supplied, and it would seem that such motivation was supplied when opportunities for friendship became available to this woman, and as the relationship with her analyst and author progressed. There is nothing strange or exceptional about her need to depend in order to be independent, to join up in order to get away. As for the umpteen selves exposed in the Book of Sybil, it is safe to conclude that they are a manner of speaking, and of conjuring—that they are produced out of a hat in the manner of some strange fiction of duality, and by a trio of conjurors. Every life is made up, put on, imagined—including, *hypocrite lecteur*, yours. Sybil's life was made up by Sybil, by her doctor, when she became a case, and again, when she became a book, by her author. Sixteen selves were imagined. But it is not even entirely certain that there were as many as two.

XVIII. DUALITY IN AMERICA

America is an orphan of a kind. The ethos of the first European settlements spoke both of ostracism and of escape, of hardship and danger and of a new life. Then, at a later time, like some romantic person of that time, the country declared its independence, and the New World began in earnest. The New World began when romance began again in literature, and it entered upon a divided relationship with the Old, rejecting the past which it was nevertheless to resume and perpetuate. It became a haven for outcasts, but also their pursuer, a strange place of chases and journeys, which has been experienced as both virtuous and monstrous, has played its part in sustaining the idea of a virtuous and monstrous solitude, and has produced, among its most valued fictions, an outcast's dualistic account of an outcast's mad pursuit of a maverick whale. For such a place, the imagination of an Ishmael and of a plural self, of rebellion, hostility, and distress, of secrecy and mystery, adventure and escape, could not fail to make sense. These have indeed been imagined as the concerns of an American imagination, though they are no less characteristic of the literature of Romanticism.

Duality, then, has flourished in America. Americans have pioneered an imaginative dualistic psychiatry, have pursued the Gothic mode in literature, and have supplied keen exponents of its early history, as of its perpetuation in modern times: one such exponent is the outcast scholar and strange case, Leslie Fiedler, who has come to regard his excellent work of criticism, *Love and Death in the American Novel*, published in 1960, as a kind of Gothic novel. The tradition lives on among the country's living writers, fostering a shared interest in their compatriot the escapologist Houdini, and in the dancer Nijinsky. There is the sense of a surviving *entente*, and of its long duration. It is a tradition which brings together, as fellow practitioners of an art of moonshine, Hawthorne and Norman Mailer.

A recent American critic of Fiedlerian stamp is Paul Zweig, whose book *The Adventurer* holds that imprisonment and escape are 'the primary experience of most Gothic novels, of the *roman noir*, and of much popular literature since then', and that 'the

Gothic novel is a conduit for the mythology of modern times,' whose literature encompasses 'a deep thematic affinity with Gothic'.[1] The prose masters of the late nineteenth century—such as Conrad, with 'his relentless Gothic pessimism'—exhibit this affinity no less than popular writers do, and it is seen as hostile to the practice of realism, and to the great tradition of morals and manners, in the novel. Mr Zweig is sure that readers of the early Gothic novel had reason 'to acknowledge the tyranny of the castle and the darkness of the family drama', that its prisons bear witness to the confinements of the contemporary nuclear family. *The Castle of Otranto* is 'really about fathers and sons, mothers and daughters. Its crimes are incest, adultery, and infanticide; its virtue, filial obedience; its failure, a broken home.' Such novels are thought different from the plays of Shakespeare which Walpole tried to copy—though it is hardly clear that *Melmoth* is any more of a domestic drama than *Macbeth*. According to Zweig, in one of his rare moments of uncertainty, *Melmoth* is only a 'relative masterpiece', and he says that Gothic literary standards are usually low. Wondering how such bad books could prove so potent, while conscious that good books came of them, came of his 'deep thematic affinity', he argues that Gothic began not as literature but as entertainment, addressed to the new readership created by the spread of literacy and by the technical innovations which served it, and that it thereby resembled the oral arts embodied in the folk tradition. But Gothic literature has always been literature in every sense that counts—just as rock music, which can also manage to achieve high standards, is music as well as entertainment. Early and late, high and low, Gothic writers have contributed to art, and to knowledge. Had they not done so, their responsibility for the mythology of modern times would be as obscure as some of their own works.

Zweig considers that the modern world has blasphemously degraded the adventurer to the pages of pulp fiction and the annals of crime. But we may feel that there are still plenty of them about, such as America's astronauts; and high art still has its adventures. His own book adventures from Odysseus, via Nietzsche's Overman, to T. E. Lawrence, seen as the anguished adventurer of modern times: 'If Lawrence had a flaw as a military commander, it was his inclination to undertake unimportant but excruciatingly painful missions.' Casanova has 'perfect sex' with his hundreds of women, denies that all women are alike in the dark, but is fooled when a frump is slipped into his bed: this is 'the first crack in the pure youthfulness which Casanova kept so remarkably intact until he was an old man'. At this point it is the notion of Casanova's adventurous purity of intent which appears cracked. Both the adventurer and the orphan are seen to participate in the 'psychology of secrecy' attributed to the modern world by the adventurous André Malraux. Both are stealthy, mutinous, and meteoric. Both are escape artists. Zweig's account of the romantic is itself indigenously romantic and quixotic. He can seem ardently American.

Among the escape artists of modern times is the illusionist Erich Weiss, alias Harry Houdini, the American Jew whose vaudeville exploits, egresses from manacles, sacks, and strait-jackets, have been deemed the behaviour of a man constrained by a dependence on his mother. Other artists, high and low, have been fascinated by him. In the drafts of a letter which were written not long before his death Dylan Thomas described himself as 'a puny wheezy Houdini'. 'Why do I coil myself always into these imbecile grief-knots?' Some jottings of the same time implore: 'Come back, come back, Mother.' The letter contains tears, entreaties, imbecility and contortion, the foetal and the fatal:

> time and time again I cry to myself as I kick clear of the cling of my stunt-man's sacking, 'Oh, one time the last time will come and I'll never struggle, I'll sway down here forever, handcuffed and blindfold, sliding my wound-around music, my sack trailed in the slime, with all the rest of the self-destroyed escapologists in their cages, drowned in the sorrows they drown and in my piercing own, alone and one with the coarse and cosy damned seahorsey dead, weeping my tons.[2]

The drowner, downer, mother-seeker, and suicide gave proof of his existence, while improving the legend of that existence, by writing certain poems and by performing certain stunts, from the last of which, an alcoholic 'insult' to the brain, legend has it that he died. He died in 1953. In 1975, the narrator of Saul Bellow's novel *Humboldt's Gift* described himself as a Houdini, and as 'puny', while in the following year Houdini figured, 'wheezing', in *Ragtime*, where the novelist E. L. Doctorow claimed that fifty years after the escapologist's death 'the audience for escapes is even larger.'[3] Then, in 1979, Houdini was awarded the part, in Mailer's *The Executioner's Song*, of the hero's grandfather.

All these works mingle invention and historical truth in a manner that contributes to or prefigures the new 'factional' mode. All of them are knowing works, learned in the lore of Romanticism. Doctorow's knows about the turn-of-the-century dependence on traditional images and fetishes. Houdini is shown as 'passionately in love with his ancient mother'; a 'desire for his dead mother' is enacted in his feats. A reporter 'steals away' while Houdini kneels by the mother's grave. Soon afterwards Sigmund Freud steals from the Nazis into New York. A 'strange' boy shrinks from his father in 'independence of spirit' and 'discovers the mirror as a means of self-duplication'. A young woman leads a secret life and is infatuated with an urchin. *Ragtime* preserves a studious calm: the calm of an iconographic display, an oedipal museum. Here is a specimen of the anti-novel which Zweig identifies with the Gothic affinity.

Houdini can therefore be called a figure of importance in modern American romance, and for the mythology of modern times, which embodies concerns more ancient than the illusionist's mother and refers to the inner space of a desire for mothers. During the American Seventies a desire for the outer space of the physical universe, for the extraterrestrial, ran strong; and the natives of that country have made it to the Moon. The movie *Close Encounters of the Third Kind* conferred an American welcome on a craft from Outer Space, which was boarded by a man and woman who had united in clandestine love. The movie says that adulterers may see God, and has proved very popular. Meanwhile Kurt Vonnegut's novel *Slaughterhouse Five* said that the orphan who soars to another planet may be united there with a movie-star who combines the attributes of mother and whore. The benign prominence of the female prostitute in the records of American sentiment and of American falsehood may be felt to require the thought that whores in America are dual and oedipal. The expletive 'mother-fucker' is oedipal too, and its use has not been confined to those Americans who know about Freud and Romanticism. All this is very strange. These are deep waters. And they will seldom be investigated by any science which places its proscription on psychoanalysis and romance.

Bellow knows about both. His fictions put to use what can be recognized elsewhere in the mythology as fetish, fashion, and expletive. Like Doctorow, he puts to use the history of the recent and of the more remote past. Talking in 1982 about his youth in Chicago, he reaffirmed his feeling for Houdini, as a type of the ambitious Jew and of the Midwestern high-riser: 'We all thought in one way or another that the sky was the limit, that we were in a situation in which infinite expansion was possible.'[4] And it seems that he still romantically proposes-and-denies that infinite expansion is possible. In *Humboldt's Gift* Houdini's gift is ironized, and a comedy of duality is paramount. In *The Victim*, his second novel, which appeared in 1947, duality is sober and domestic. Between them, the two works offer a comprehensive response to the subject, and the difference between them is the difference between a diffusive and a divisive duality. The early novel is a fiction of the second self, the later a fiction of negative capability. Bellow's engagement with the subject is synoptic and complete, and is later simultaneous with a self-conscious confessional comedy of the paranoid response.

The engagement dates from his first novel of all, *Dangling Man*, published in Britain in 1946. Bellow's dangling man is an orphan who, while awaiting conscription, enters into a dialogue with another self on the subject of reason, alternatives, the possibility of 'changing existence' in one way or another, and of what it is to be a member of the human race. 'Joseph suffers from a feeling of strangeness, of not quite belonging to the world'—that of the child who 'feels that his parents are pretenders,' that of someone who lives under the shadow of a kind of conspiracy. This dialogue of his returns us to *Rameau's Nephew*: Diderot's dialogue takes part in this short and pithy text. The self with whom Joseph converses is called 'But on the Other Hand', or '*Tu As Raison Aussi*', Joseph having noted previously that Diderot describes Rameau's nephew as '*un (personnage) composé de hauteur et de bassesse, de bon sens et de déraison*'. The description is applied to a scapegrace friend here in Chicago—less shrewd than Rameau's nephew. Joseph has the good sense to see that, in an avid world, 'a man must accept limits and cannot give in to the wild desire to be everything and everyone and everything to everyone': so this married man's affair with Kitty must come to an end. He knows that 'thievery' can be committed, in one way or another, by those in avid pursuit of freedom, or of grace. But on the other hand we are aware that Joseph is drawn to boundlessness, to the changing of existence, that there is reason in that too.[5]

The Victim tells of the ordeal and release of a New York Jew, one sweltering summer. Asa Leventhal is grave, gruff, sore, brooding, impassive, indifferent, 'susceptible'—to the possibility, for instance, of madness in others. He is haunted by a brilliant, gruesome anti-semite, Kirby Allbee, who appears like some Gothic tempter to blame him for once having got Allbee the sack, and who causes him to feel that the charge is not wholly without foundation. His wife is away with her mother—an absence which may strike the reader as oddly protracted—and he has entered upon a time of trance and suspension, a dark time of 'nerves' during which he feels that he himself may be mad. Allbee's words, when he first accosts him, bear a double meaning which is capable of penetrating Leventhal's indifference: 'You're mad because you got caught.'[6] Calamities threaten, and one occurs: a sick nephew dies. At length Allbee leaves the scene, having been surprised with a woman in Leventhal's bed, and then in a suicide attempt in Leventhal's kitchen. Leventhal, who has been given to brooding over his grievances and his faults, now seems able to face up to these faults. He feels years younger. His wife conceives.

The two men are both victims and are in some ways alike. Leventhal is an orphan—with a hostile father, and a mother who died, possibly mad, when he was young. He had started work at a time—the Depression—when work was hard to find and needed constant applications and introductions, and he had drifted near to dereliction—'starved and thin', like Hans Andersen's Shadow. But one introduction did at last succeed. He would say to his wife: 'I was lucky. I got away with it.' With his bad start and mistakes, 'he had almost fallen in with that part of humanity of which he was frequently mindful (he never forgot the hotel on lower Broadway), the part that did not get away with it—the lost, the outcast, the overcome, the effaced, the ruined.' Allbee had not got away with it. He seems to belong to that part. And he may also belong to that part of Leventhal which had almost failed, which makes much of its injustices, and might have gone from brooding to worse. What Leventhal almost was, and may even be still, Allbee has become —a suspicious 'outsider'. They may be called secret sharers of the sack.[7]

Both victims, then, but mainly seen as two different men, the solid citizen opposed by a taunter, an actor, an impersonator, a cynical show-off, a lush. Leventhal is like Diderot in his wrangles with Rameau's nephew. Yet, as in the Diderot dialogue, it is possible to imagine that Leventhal and Allbee are at times the same. In later years, at the close of the novel, these victims meet again at a theatre, where a restored Allbee has arrived in a taxi as the escort of a movie actress, to inform Leventhal that at the time of their past involvement he, Allbee, had 'turned against himself': and perhaps at that time, too, Leventhal had turned against himself, and into Allbee, yielding to that degradation. 'You had to bring this woman into my bed,' he had told Allbee at that time, in the voice, one might suppose, of a man talking to himself.[8] An under-sense of the novel which is perceptible at this earlier point suggests that husbands play while their wives are away; that the adultery from which a good Jewish husband would normally flinch might be experienced by him as the action of his own worst enemy, some anti-semite; that Leventhal may harbour resentment against the wife whom he loves but who, during their courtship, had kept on for a while with a married lover. The two men are bound together in a fellowship which is only intermittently an identity, and the episode has only very faintly the character of a husband's nervous fling. But there are times when Leventhal is aware of Allbee as a double—as on this occasion, when he also senses in him 'an element of performance':

suddenly he had a strange, close consciousness of Allbee, of his face and body, a feeling of intimate nearness such as he had experienced in the zoo when he had imagined himself at Allbee's back, seeing with microscopic fineness the lines in his skin, and the smallest of his hairs, and breathing in his odor. The same sensations were repeated; he could nearly feel the weight of his body, and the contact of his clothes.

Even more, the actuality of his face, loose in the cheeks, firm in the forehead and jaws, struck him, the distinctness of it; and the look of recognition Allbee bent on him duplicated the look in his own. He was sure of that. Nevertheless he kept alive in his mind the thought that Allbee hated him.

Presently he has a dream from which he wakes to the conviction that 'everything, everything without exception, took place as if within a single soul or person': which assists the reader to experience Leventhal's shadowing by Allbee (whose name could be thought to allude to such convictions) as the internal drama of a receptive single self. We then read:

> He had a particularly vivid recollection of the explicit recognition in Allbee's eyes which he could not doubt was the double of something in his own. Where did it come from? 'Speak of black and white,' he mused. Black and white were Mr Schlossberg's words . . .[9]

Bellow is intent on using the old language and the old ideas of romantic duality in order to project Leventhal's at times regressive dealings with his precarious past, in the days before luck had allowed him to get away with it—days of error and offence, of rejection and the sack. Allbee's presence depends upon the absence of Leventhal's wife—unmarries Leventhal, therefore, while also seeming to plunge him into a vicarious infidelity. In the manner of the double in James's 'Jolly Corner', it signifies what he almost was, and may still have it in him to be. Bellow is using the language and ideas of duality with a difference—a difference glimpsed in his choosing to say, not 'someone's double', but 'the double of something'—and without falling into the conventional and the formulaic, without prejudice to a governing idiom which is utterly of the 1940s, supple and unforced, and which works as well for heightened speech as for the prevailing domesticity. Nevertheless, that the novel does, with a difference and in its own way, make use of a traditional approach can't be doubted. Leventhal is spellbound by nerves, imagination, and 'susceptibility'. Things are 'strange', 'queer', 'unaccountable'. 'Leventhal felt himself singularly drawn with a kind of affection' to Allbee: this is like the language of James Hogg in 1824, while also a fit language for 1946. Allbee the accoster 'grinned at him with an intimation of a shared secret': perhaps an allusion to Conrad's 'Secret

Sharer'. Late in the book Leventhal feels he is 'stealing away' from Allbee, whom he calls a counterfeit, meaning, perhaps, not only that he has been putting Leventhal on, but that he is another Leventhal: 'counterfeit' is a word that had been applied to doubles since the early nineteenth century.[10]

Duality is both courted and criticized. The critique comes from the wise journalist Schlossberg, who revives an ancient notion with 'it's bad to be less than human and it's bad to be more than human.' This is the notion expounded by Lucian in his dialogue with Peregrine Proteus, who wishes to soar above mankind; and it is not far from the ancient notion that it's bad to withdraw from the world, into solitude. Solitude favours the second self—'*Numquam minus solum* . . .'—and Schlossberg's humanism condemns a certain kind of duality, while being both for and against an infinite expansion. The wisdom of Schlossberg imparts new versions of the Classical *memento mori* and of the nineteenth-century idea of the self as business enterprise:

> Here I'm sitting here, and my mind can go around the world. Is there any limit to what I can think? But in another minute I can be dead, on this spot. There's a limit to me. But I have to be myself in full. Which is somebody who dies, isn't it? That's what I was from the beginning. I'm not three people, four people. I was born once and I will die once. You want to be two people? More than human? Maybe it's because you don't know how to be one. Everybody is busy. Every man turns himself into a whole corporation to handle the business. So one stockholder is riding in the elevator, and another one is on the roof looking through a telescope, one is eating candy, and one is in the movies looking at a pretty face. Who is left? And how can a corporation die?[11]

This sound advice is a return to the dualistic treatment of limits in *Dangling Man*, and it can be taken to imply a disapproval of the Gothic tendency to find glamour in that divided self which may be forced on the busy human being of the modern world. Leventhal is by no means glamorous. But he has turned against himself. He must manage to be one, to be himself in full.

He does in fact come out of it all—out of the 'suicide pact' with Allbee, and the rest of it—with a more hopeful sense of himself. He is less indifferent, less hostile, less drawn to a resentful solitude. He has turned, as never in the past, towards marriage and community. The opposite pulls of an internal division have relented, have disappeared as if by magic. This magic is as much a domestic as an exotic feature: we know that the depressed can become mysteriously buoyant, if only for a while. 'Something recalcitrant seemed to have left him.'[12] The guilty consciousness of having got away with it is gone. *The Victim* is about two different men, about a persecution which is equally a fellowship, and which conveys that there is more than one victim in the world, and that victims may be both good and bad. It is also about a divided life which moves towards a cure—a motion which may be rated unaccountable, but in relation to which the Schlossberg symposia and the exchanges between Leventhal and Allbee are co-ordinate occasions. The exchanges with Allbee are as enthralling as the intervening element of a comedy of manners is exquisite. This novel is among the masterpieces of literary duality, which is nowhere more moving than in the persons of Hogg's sinner, Andersen's scholar, Dostoevsky's clerk, and Bellow's victim.

Leventhal is someone other than the author who made him up, someone else, who is attended by a someone else again, who can also at times seem like another Leventhal. Leventhal can at times feel sure that everything takes place 'as if within a single soul or person': but in this novel we are usually aware of two different persons who are neither of them the author—of a division between these persons, for all that they are sometimes experienced as one. *Humboldt's Gift* is a different book, for all that the two books can sometimes be experienced as a pair. Here everything happens within the one head, Bellow's, and the two main persons of the book tend to converge. And this is only one of many mergers. Everyone tends at one point or other to slip into someone else. Division is overtaken by diffusion, though the book has both. Both books have both.

Romantic comedy, romantic irony, romantic chic are not dead. *Humboldt's Gift* was published in Britain in 1975. *Peregrine Proteus* was published in Britain in 1796. They are separated by nearly two centuries. And yet they are the same kind of book, and raise the same questions. Like Wieland's novel, Bellow's is a puzzle. Does he mean it? Does the narrator, Charles Citrine, speak for Bellow? Its deadly earnest is delivered in play, and is hard to isolate. The novel criticizes itself, turns against itself, turns and twists. Citrine's personality is protean, equivocal, universal: he appears to share the fate of some of the characters he talks about, and we slip continually from one to another of the times of his life. Citrine is an elderly Chicagoan whose life has entered a crisis, if it was ever out of one—a crisis which leads him to flit, on the mind's wings, between his present and his past, between the world of the present day and that of the nineteenth century. He is a comedian and a chameleon, if not an everything and everybody. He is a Wandering and a Flying Jew: a Jewish Keats, a lover of sensations and of elevation and of women, and a scholarly devotee of the romantic imagination, so that the novel is a compendium and flux of romantic attitudes and expressions. He displays negative capability. He worries about his 'true self' and what is to become of it. He is 'divided': either very rich or very poor, either a victim or a prestigious prize-winner in a philistine American city. In this last capacity he may be said to have stolen the laurels which his author was about to wear. The romantic self is not dead. It can, as this novel suggests, win the Pulitzer Prize and more. And it is the author of the plural self espoused by Modernism.

Citrine's chief relationships are with Humboldt, a *poète maudit*, who has talent, is a brilliant conversationalist, and suffers an early success, manic breakdowns, and an untimely death (and who has an original in Delmore Schwartz); with Renata, Citrine's colourful mistress, who is sceptical of his imaginative flights and humanitarian high-mindedness; and with Cantabile, a romantic misbehaver and would-be gangster who dogs Citrine and may perhaps think himself Rameau's nephew or Jean Genet. If 'Diderot' Citrine is compromised by his connection with this fellow Cantabile, he is also compromised by his dealings with Humboldt. Having lost his touch as a poet, Humboldt has become a juggler with big ideas, a traveller in romantic chic, in the poses and values highly rated on that New York cultural stock-exchange which is known to be obnoxious to Bellow. While posthumously willing to communicate to Citrine that he thinks him no good, Humboldt bequeaths his friend a copy of a movie script which they had once prepared in tandem, and which is then (implausibly) made into a hit, together with a further script about a blocked writer who retreats to an exotic paradise with a mistress (a part, he feels, for Marilyn Monroe). These constitute Humboldt's gift.

We have to ask whether Humboldt is Citrine's double. In the early novel, as we have observed, Leventhal and Allbee last meet at the theatre. Outside the theatre a taxi draws up: 'The door flung open and a woman was handed out.' The hand is Allbee's, the woman a movie star. In this novel, too, there is a theatre scene, when Citrine and Humboldt confront each other.[13] The play to be performed is by Citrine, and it is to make his name.

I swept out of the taxi with my lady friend and was caught on the sidewalk in the commotion. Police were controlling the crowd. His cronies were shouting and rioting and Humboldt carried his picket sign as though it were a cross. In streaming characters, mercurochrome on cotton, was written, 'The Author of this Play is a Traitor.' The demonstrators were pushed back by the police, and Humboldt and I did not meet face to face. Did I want him run in? the producer's assistant asked me.

'No,' I said, wounded, trembling. 'I used to be his protégé. We were pals, the crazy son of a bitch. Let him alone.'

'Close', a word applied to the relationship between Citrine and Humboldt, is a word applied, as we have seen, to Leventhal's consciousness of Allbee. With their common factor of a misdoubted or questionable success, their suggestion of the truth inherent in an abstention from society, these theatre scenes are duplicates, and they are an example of the way in which a finely functioning literary duality, in showing two different persons, may also show the internal tensions of the single life and the psychological vicissitudes of a lifetime. The moment of doubt experienced at times by the reader who has to decide whether there are two persons or only one on exhibition may seem to delineate his sense of the principal character's, and of the author's, uncertainties. We might be inclined to say here that these persons don't 'meet face to face' because they share a face. What does Humboldt say? About his pal's play he says: 'he did steal something from me—my personality. He built my personality into his hero.' In the world of 'castaways' dreamt of by Humboldt, Citrine dreams of Humboldt, whose name, in the literary world, is linked with his, and both of these citizens of the 'romantic country' of America, where, according to

Humboldt, 'mavericks' will 'try anything', are mavericks and castaways. Both are said to be 'peculiar'. 'I was peculiarly susceptible to his influence,' says Citrine. Citrine's criticisms of Humboldt can look like criticisms of Citrine, who has 'followed in Humboldt's footsteps', as we are informed on the occasion when Citrine is arrested in the vicinity of Dylan Thomas's White Horse Tavern, just as his friend had been during his last days of riot in the Village. If Humboldt is at times a charlatan, then we may suspect that his plagiarist is one too: at other times, however, Citrine is presented in the guise of a shaman.[14]

For Bellow, as for other writers, duality may be found to seek the stage, to be theatrical. In *The Adventures of Augie March* Mintouchian's interest in secrets is an interest in 'complications, lies . . . disguises, vaudevilles, multiple personalities'. Here, if Citrine has a double in Humboldt, he has another in Houdini, 'the great Jewish escape artist'. Both Citrine and Houdini were born in Appleton, Wisconsin. They are astral twins. Houdini's escapes are listed: he defies everything, including the grave. From each of his triumphs he would return home and make for the cemetery: 'He lay down on his mother's grave and on his belly through the grass he told her in whispers about his trips . . .' Houdini is dead, but that is nothing to the 'boundless' Citrine, who is equally engaged in a defiance of the grave. The novel ends on the knees of a Houdini—with a visit to a cemetery so that Citrine may re-inter his dead.[15]

Citrine's peculiar susceptibility is linked to a tubercular childhood: he has the 'sensibility' and the sensorium of such a sufferer (sensibility becomes glamorous during his lifetime, having been glamorous in the past). 'I sometimes felt, and still feel, poisoned by eagerness, a congestion of tender impulses together with fever and enthusiastic dizziness.' In adult life, excited by theft: 'I could feel the need to laugh rising, mounting, always a sign that my weakness for the sensational, my American, Chicagoan (as well as personal) craving for high stimuli, for incongruities and extremes, was aroused. I knew that fancy thieving was a big thing in Chicago. It was said that if you knew one of these high-rise super-rich Fagin-types you could obtain luxury goods at half the retail price.' Humboldt the 'great entertainer' and success shares in the 'soaring'. His idea was 'to go straight to the top. When he got there, this blemished spirit, the top saw the point. Humboldt met with interest and consideration'—which romantic writers have had the power to bestow on their castaways. Citrine is an escape artist who out-'sprints', out-steals, muggers: 'How was it that in my middle fifties I became inspired with flight and capable of great bursts of speed?' This Houdini can jump, cries Humboldt, 'like Nijinsky'. Charlie's rises are crowned by a trip to the top of a skyscraper—a trip which forms part of a punishment regime devised by Cantabile and enjoyed by his victim.[16]

But the supreme elevation or expansion is the one that takes the soul through the gates of death and enables it to look back at the world. This is a trip of which Citrine has premonitions: worries about being dead are dispelled by a sense of himself as 'sprinting through the star world',[17] and by an ability to believe in reincarnation, to believe, as Norman Mailer seems to, in the karma of rebirth. Citrine and (as we shall see) Mailer's Marilyn Monroe are high-risers who rise from the grave, and Rudolf Steiner's teachings have helped to make a metempsychosist of Citrine. It is marvellous that in the modern world of scientific Americans two leading novelists have been zealous for the immortality of the soul. At the same time, romantic irony ensures that Citrine's flights, worship of the dead, and devotion to the imagination, are criticized and sent up. For Renata, this is the behaviour of someone trying to 'dope his way out of the human condition'.[18] For some readers, it will be the behaviour of the man of feeling who has made real progress in that direction—who may talk of his children, for instance, but who hardly ever sees them.

Citrine's condition achieves its odes to the nightingale, then, and is rich in sensation, which is linked to suffering in the time-honoured way: the 'heart-wounded', like the tubercular, feel acutely and especially, and 'magnanimously'. Sloth is distinguished from sleep. The former is hyperactive, a bad state, while 'the true poise, that of contemplation or imagination, sits right on the border of sleep and dreaming.'[19] Can everyone sit there, or only some? Can we all benefit from the karma of rebirth? Of the people in the book, perhaps only Citrine—and Humboldt?—have sensibilities fit for the passage to another life, for a spirit sprint. Imagine Cantabile—who locks the narrator in a lavatory and stalls before his very eyes—endeavouring to soar. We don't doubt that at the day of judgement—whether as separate person or as symbiotic lower self—he will drop like a bomb. In this romantic book, as in others, there is word of a paranoid-narcissistic elect which lives for ever. Saul Bellow is a more conventionally peculiar writer, and a more peculiarly peculiar writer, than his reputation attests.

In his fiction, after *The Victim*, we encounter a passage from ordinary life; and we also encounter a move from heroes who do not closely resemble the author to heroes who do, and from a suspicion of eloquence to a high tolerance of it. Leventhal is none other than Leventhal. After that, the novels become a species of romantic poem in which the hero is the author and the author is the hero. Some reflections of Augie March signal the turn taken by this eloquent new author. 'Because you are powerless and unable to get anywhere,' Augie reflects,

> therefore in yourself you labour, you wage and combat, settle scores, remember insults, fight, reply, deny, blab, denounce, triumph, outwit, overcome, vindicate, cry, persist, absolve, die and rise again. All by yourself! Where is everybody? Inside your breast and skin, the entire cast.[20]

After the griefs and grievances of Leventhal, which Leventhal overcomes, there began the projection of a fissile, all-feeling fellow, of a multiple personality which suffers and enjoys the author's sense of threat, of insult and old scores, and of an encompassing meanness.

In 1963 Bellow suggested that the self-important single self of the romantic nineteenth century had been blown up by writers who hadn't anything—though they had, we may also feel, everything—to put in its place. Joyce turned away from the sovereign self, 'from the individualism of the romantics and the humanists', towards an 'everybody'. Modern writers are 'convinced that the jig of the Self is up.'[21] But the retrospective view of Romanticism which figures in *Humboldt's Gift* makes clear that the soaring self of its early days could be a self in dispersal; that its early writers were everybodies as well as individuals, were the nothing that could admit everything; that the mind which is powerful in its characterless, opinionless resembling sympathy with others did not have to wait for Joyce and

Eliot. At the same time, *Humboldt's Gift* would convince no one that the jig of the Self was up.

In this novel Proteus enjoys a joke, and it is fundamental to the high rises which occur and which the comic turns may appear to subvert. If there is a soulfulness which seeks a passage to another world, another life, there is a humour which can be read as preventing this, and as sealing the work in uncertainty. Flight is both affirmed and denied. This, one may add, is an uncertain work in which the author seems to contemplate his own fame: a portrait of the artist's engagement with, and estrangement from, the community which includes his public. Humboldt drops out. He is the poet, the Poe, who ends in the gutter, the dangling man who falls into the abyss. He loses his touch, and his readers. Citrine, for his part, yields to those readers at times, and can be considered a success. Here are two faces of the one self-sceptical and suffering writer.

In Bellow's latest novel a further change of approach has been discussed. The book is earnest, and its intention is to be 'direct'.[22] There is less in the way of humour, and of duality. *The Dean's December* is not narrated by its dean, and may occasionally appear to have reverted to what we have in *The Victim*, where author and hero are two different men, and duality does nothing to prevent this. Such appearances, however, are deceptive. Citrine was 'heart-wounded': the new hero, cordial Dean Corde, is 'heart-struck'.[23] He has to endure the collapse of civilization and the appalling plights of contemporary Chicago, and composes, on this subject, a literature of dismay, in the form of magazine articles which offend the complacently benighted inhabitants of that city. He is a Huguenot-Irish American of ancient lineage, but leaves no less Jewish an impression than previous protagonists; his catastrophic outlook—and some of the circumstances of his life—have been freely assigned, by readers, to his author. Narcissus has once again taken great care, and has shown his customary rare skill. From moment to moment, the Corde sensorium is sweetly and patiently rendered. He has his 'oddities', and his Gothic features—he is 'counter, spare and strange'.[24] This stranger, like many others, has a foreign wife, and here, as elsewhere, we may be conscious of a need to grasp what this means—conscious of a *cherchez la femme*. Minna is a famous astronomer, and her mother's fatal illness fetches the couple to a terminal Eastern Europe, so that Chicago and its madness and murders are recollected in Bucharest.

The Dean believes that '*something* deadly is happening to the world—something more than the lead poisoning feared by ecologists; he also has the author's established disposition to take revenge on tormentors. At the same time, the Dean and his opinions are criticized. He is matched, magnetically associated, with his chief critic and detractor among the people of the book: this is Spangler, a glib, egotistical columnist, superstar, and childhood friend, who charges him with 'abyssifying and catastrophising'. Corde sympathizes with the charges 'up to a point', but insists: 'It's all true.'[25] The novel is implicated in dualistic practice by virtue—as in earlier times—of its Siamesing of the hero with a charlatan: of negative capability with the egotistical sublime, if we accept that these romantic opposites are present, and convergent, here. The duality which it contains is less substantial than the amounts to be detected in earlier works, but there is enough of it to qualify the directness which the novelist intends, and to soften, a little, his warnings to the world. Yet it is difficult to suppose that he could have done without duality, and the indirections it brings. Corde is magnanimous, as his name implies, and nervously unwell: his is a traditional state, and it is a state which enfolds the novel which he does not narrate. Pulses and public spirit send messages which are valuable and unseizable. Corde's condition suffers and circumscribes the condition of Chicago. In Spangler he meets, and sympathizes with, his own egotistical opposite: and in his treatment of their relations Bellow may be thought to be treating once more with the spectre of his own celebrity. This is not what everyone would think of as a novel. It is what the condition of Chicago has, according to Bellow, extorted from Corde in his capacity as journalist. It is poetry.

Corde wants to put the spirit back into nature, while Spangler regards him as an intellectual 'in flight from the material realities of the present age'. The impulse to flight is plain enough, and the novel soars to its conclusion. Looking out over the lake, from his high-rise balcony in Chicago, and up into the sky, the Dean experiences a 'great expansion', passing 'very close to the borders of sense'. Then, ascending with his wife in a lift to the dome and telescope of the Mount Palomar Observatory in California, he stares into the starry heavens. If the motion of the lift were to go on, 'you would travel straight out. You would go up into the stars.' Mount Palomar is chilly, and Corde minds the cold that hits him. But the novel's last words are these: 'I almost think I mind coming down more.'[26] His ups and downs, his partial or arrested uplifts and expansions, are an aspect of the duality in the book, and are tied to the matter of how much has to be conceded to the outlook and behaviour of his adversary and crony. For all the novel's effects of sublimity, Corde gets away neither from the earth nor from the self. He can be considered flighty, like Citrine, and, like Spangler, egotistical—though his egotism is of that different order of magnitude which entitles him to be thought magnanimous. We feel that his senses embrace and are fit to outlast the book we are reading, and that his egotism is none the less egotistical for being that of the author of that book. But there is no discomfort in calling it by the ancient name of magnanimity, and in trusting its testimonies, trusting the senses which apprehend the material realities of the city. We believe that the horrors of its slums are horrors, and that his descriptions of them are true.

'It was his very disorder that made a hero of him.' The words are Saul Bellow's, and they are spoken by him, with an almost perfectly straight face, in the course of a movie. They refer to no hero of his own; nor do they refer to himself, or to the protean disorders of his more recent fictions. The hero in question is played by the woebegone Woody Allen, poet and pierrot, in his film *Zelig*, of 1983. *Zelig* is a comedy of duality in America, where the subject of multiple personality, and works like *Sybil*, have been accorded a respect unknown in other countries. The hero is a 'human chameleon' whose 'transformations' are caused by a desire to be liked. Bellow's arrival on the screen is eerie: it is as if Zelig has turned into Herzog. But it is also, of course, appropriate. It is right that Bellow, who has in recent times described himself as an early Romantic,[27] should have lent his proud shoulder to the wheel of a burlesque—which is equally a celebration—of the notion of the chameleon. Zelig is a hero of our ironic time. And so is Bellow. But it is also the case that they are both early Romantics.

If Bellow's work takes turns, so does Norman Mailer's. In his novel of 1965, *An American Dream*, he turns towards magic, demons, flight, passages, influences, lunar and magnetic fields. The romantic country of America has by now become for him 'Cancer Gulch', a wasteland from which escapes are in order, from which his writings and example promise a redemption. He is a writer of genius whose achievement is romantically unstable. In the course of his career he has turned from realism to romance, and become the exponent of a distinctly traditional, though still controversial, view of human life, in which duality is prominent. So far as he writes like anyone, he writes like Thomas Carlyle, in whom duality was prominent too. He is not an advanced writer, but a kind of *resartus*. By virtue of his interest in advances and escapes, among other matters, he can be reckoned a conservative writer whose secession from the political Left has gone with a growing commitment to the romantic past.

Genius, I think, crashes in *An American Dream*. Megalomania inflicts page after page of ugly and unruly talented prose, and the Gothic tradition abdicates from sense. Stephen Rojack is a Flying Jewish American who has a 'secret frightened romance with the phases of the moon'. By the light of the Moon he teeters on the brink of a skyscraper parapet, sure that if he took the plunge he would fly: 'I would rise, the part of me which spoke and thought and had its glimpses of the landscape of my Being, would soar, would rise, would leap the miles of darkness to that moon.'[28] From vertigo Rojack moves to a fine frenzy in which he strangles his wife (the author had stabbed his second wife shortly before). This creature of brinks and bounds and borders, uplifted by the experience of murder, descends to the maid's room to commit an exciting sodomy. 'The stroke which steals' enables him to feel 'like a thief, a great thief'.[29] A romantic transgression has once more been acknowledged as such in the language of its elation. The transgression is experienced both as a let-down, a fall to earth, and as a break-through. Boundlessness has had a busy night.

The man who was soon to do what Poe did and force a passage to the Moon, by celebrating the Apollo 11 space mission, was preceded by a surrogate who had made his romantic way up the rear of a rat-like German au-pair. Sodomy has at various times been invested by Mailer with a superstitious awe, the anus deemed a province of the Devil: this strange stuff can't be rated as incidental to the book, though it can also look like a bid to interject a Sixties or 'Aquarian' liberation. With these events a Gothic momentum takes hold of the novel. The bugger steals on his way at fever pitch, pursued by the police and involved with a woman who is the opposite of his demonic wife. At the end of the book he gets up on his parapet again, submitting himself to a form of magic test or ordeal, and walks swaying round the sides of a millionaire's balcony, buffeted by ill winds and very nearly blown into the gulf or gulch: 'the act of balance seemed less precarious . . . I took a step; and another step; and realised I had not taken a breath and now took one, and stole a look down the fall and pulled myself back from the impulse to go out like an aeroplane in a long glide.'[30] Verge, vertigo, the uncertain self, and the impulse to go out, are a conjunction long known to the culture of romance, but among modern writers Mailer and Bellow are perhaps especially insistent that duality is precarious: a balancing-act. Their gliders, bounders, buggers, brinkmen, dangling men share the same high wire. The drop—insanity's abyss, Skid Row, death—yawns at their feet. But Mailer's dizzy spells and teetering tread can also look like a high-flown moonlit version of machismo's wrist games: shows of courage to furnish a penthouse.

Five years later, in 1970, he advanced into space with the nation's astronauts, and flew back with *A Fire on the Moon*—a true romance and a book worthy of its subject which duplicates the Poe mission of long before. As does Poe's account, it rests one foot on the ground and, for that matter, in the grave. The 'Aquarius' who delivers Mailer's account calls himself a 'Nijinsky of ambivalence',[31] and is not expected to live for ever. The incoherence of Rojack's transactions with duality, with their alternations of love and murder, courage and cowardice, does not recur. Sense is restored. This permits the imagination of a way out of Cancer Gulch, while letting it be known that Mailer's astronauts were scarcely suicides, and that he himself is an earthbound, ambivalent writer—a writer, let us add, given to moonlighting as a man of action. What Poe said of his passage to the Moon can be said again: this work is a dualistic 'depart, yet live'.

There then ensued the attentions to the subject of duality which are to be found in Mailer's writings about the actress Marilyn Monroe—writings in which an idea of the double is explicitly linked to an idea of the orphan. The moonstruck Mailer had become Marilyn-struck. In 1972 he brought out a biography, *Marilyn*, which was succeeded by an essay for an album of photographs, *Of Women and their Elegance*, nine years later. The Norma Jean Baker who was to turn, at times, into the glittering Monroe was a real orphan who was also an imaginary one, and who played the part to perfection. She was illegitimate and parentally deprived, and saw the inside of an orphanage, and her adult life is thought by Mailer to accord with these facts. Her own sense of an outcast state may have helped to persuade her to join the Jews—to apply for conversion at the time of her marriage to Arthur Miller. This event accords with sympathies prevalent within the Anglo-American culture which emerged from the Second World War—whereby Jewishness became exemplary: the same application was made at this time in Bernard Malamud's novel *The Assistant*, where one of nature's victims ends as an honorary Jew. Mailer's biography is in tune with a time-honoured sentiment and with a settled philosemitism. It has the character of an imaginary biography of a romantic orphan who was also a real one. It is a reverie rather than a piece of research. What might seem to be advanced psychology of a speculative sort is mostly the eloquent resumption of an old order of feeling and surmise.

Marilyn is described as 'protean', and as having two selves, and more than two. Her multiplicity is presented both as a special case and as a specimen of the essential duality of human nature. Mailer says that 'exceptional' people, like Marilyn and the astronauts, have 'a way of living with opposites in themselves' which can 'only be called schizophrenic when it fails'. He goes on to say, 'One has to speak of transcendence,' and to speak of it without much reluctance as 'a mystical habit, not amenable to reason—it assumed that something in the shape of things respected any human who would force an impossible solution up out of the soup, as if the soup itself were sympathetic to the effort.'[32] This is the primeval soup of the biologist, where life began, and it is the daily travail of the orphan; and perhaps the leap here is both the beginning of a life and the 'Big

Out' of the American suicide. Elsewhere in the book transcendence is spoken of as having been attained by Norma Jean through her stardom.

Mailer is a metempsychosist. This version of duality includes the theory of rebirth which forms part of the Buddhist notion of karma: 'it could be time to look upon human behaviour as possessed of a double root. While the dominant trunk of our actions has to be influenced by the foreground of our one life here and now and living, the other root may be attached to some karmic virtue or debt some of us (or all of us) acquired by our courage or failure in lives we have already lived.' So some of us, or all of us, are dual because of a rebirth, while Marilyn was dual anyway, and perilously so, because of her orphan state. She could seem both tough and shy, shrewd and helpless:

> the answer is both, yes, both are true, and always both, she is the whole and double soul of every human alive. It is, if we would search for a model, as if an ambitious and sexual woman might not only be analogous in her particular ego and unconscious life to Madame Bovary, let us say, but rather is a woman with two personalities, each as complex and inconsistent as an individual. This woman, then, is better seen as Madame Bovary and Nana all in one, both in one, each with her own separate unconscious. Of course, that is a personality which is not seriously divided. One unconscious could almost serve for Nana and Bovary both. It is when Nana and Joan of Arc exist in the same flesh, or Boris Karloff and Bing Crosby, that the abysses of insanity are under the fog at every turn. And there is Monroe with pictures of Eleonora Duse and Abraham Lincoln on her wall, double Monroe, one hard and calculating computer of a cold and ambitious cunt (no other English word is near) and that other tender animal, an angel, a doe at large in blonde and lovely human form. Anyone else, man or woman, who contained such opposite personalities within his body would be ferociously mad. It is her transcendence of these opposites into a movie star that is her triumph . . .[33]

Mailer's 'both are true' echoes Henry Cockburn's period conclusion,[34] the period being 1829, as to whether trees or vines looked better in a landscape: 'both are best.' At this same point in his life Cockburn climbed a rock and, from the top, 'ventured to shout Napoleon and other doubtful sentiments'. Duality walked the parapet—two views of Napoleon were possible for a Scottish Whig. Meanwhile Mailer's Marilyn could be both Napoleon and Minnie Mouse. He holds that her orphan state made her multiple, protean, and that it made her a narcissist, with a taste for power, while causing her to lack confidence. She carried 'the devil of the orphanage in her eye', and the book carries a photograph of that devil. She is placed in the company of psychopaths, delinquents, mass killers, combat heroes, survivors (though her pathos, we might also think, is that of a failure to survive). This orphan is both inimical and angelic, deep-dyed in ambivalence:

> She is triumphant and crushed. She is a female Napoleon, but only for one pride. The other soul, more timid than ever, is a virus-ridden orphanage mouse. It is as if she has spent her life installing victories in all the psychic furnishings of one personality, while assigning all defeats to the other. So we are at the seat of complexity in such a view of her person. For if she is living with the full equivalent of two people within her, it is equal to saying that she will undertake many an action that benefits one at the cost of the other, and in turn like a frustrated general must retire from the action while her *other* mends. It is why so much of her life consists of stops and starts, and why so many of her affections are replaced by hate. Few are the activities she can perform where both of her selves can participate . . .[35]

Marilyn Monroe is presented as an orphan with a double, with a double life of power-seeking and retreat, and with a wish for transcendence which set her on a course of escape and poisoned her with barbiturates. Mailer's book incorporates formulaic claims which would probably have made sense to its subject had she lived to read it. She seems to have recognized in herself the mark of the orphan, an orphan misery and ambition. She is compared here, as were the unfortunates of the first Romanticism, to a comet, 'a comet of charisma', and a stricken deer. When transcendence takes her to heaven at the end of the turmoil, we feel that up there, out of the soup, she can't be far from Little Nell—and Mailer asks her to visit 'Mr Dickens' in the skies. 'For he, like many another literary man, is bound to adore you, fatherless child.'[36]

Marilyn is a book by a flamboyant literary man with a deadline to meet, money to make, and talent to burn. It exaggerates Monroe's talent for acting, though she was good at acting the orphan; it is excessively stirred by her Chaplin-like celebrity; it's as if one orphan heart were beating in homage to another,

Jew to Jew. Much of the analysis rests on a frank 'as if'—as if there were two of her, and so on—and few would claim that it was decisive. Nevertheless, as one of the many who think that they have been in a position to know something of this woman, I would say that the portrait is seldom unconvincing, and convincingly maintains that, where confidence has not been formed within the family, it may be formed outside it by means of the irresponsible, or monstrous, or flamboyant, exercise of power, by means of the exercise of talent or charisma, and through the magic of luck. For all its wild words and talk of witchcraft, the case Mailer makes has in it more than hypothesis, homage, and reverie. Here is a strong description of the interaction of opposing principles in categories of conduct and feeling, a strong imagination of the action of the double or several self. The following propositions, in which Robert Frost's two eyes—his analogy between conduct and vision—reappear, may be thought to evoke both Marilyn Monroe and Sylvia Plath:

> Two personalities within one human being may be better able to evaluate experience (even as two eyes gauge depth), provided the personalities are looking more or less in the same direction. A fragmented identity is the refusal of one personality within oneself to have any relations with the other. If such a notion has value, let us assume that the conditions of an orphanage are suited to creating too wan a psyche and too glamorous a one. Since the orphan's presence in the world is obliged to turn drab, the life of fantasy, in compensation, can become extreme.[37]

This account is compounded by the afterthoughts which Mailer expresses, in comic vein, in the evocation of Monroe which is contained in *Of Women and their Elegance*, where she is taught the lesson of duality at the doubtful hands of an incompetent acting teacher, and where the reader learns that duality can claim another order of proof. The acting teacher expounds, 'We don't have a single soul, but two,' and Marilyn, the narrator, obligingly responds:

> 'Two?'
>
> 'Two complete personalities inside us. We are made from two people, aren't we?'
>
> I remember we were drinking in the Beach-A-Tiki Bar out on Melrose Avenue, which they had decorated like a Tahiti slum—fake

old dirty palm trees and lots of grenadine in the drinks. I must have looked like I belonged in the circus (which deep down I do) for I was holding a red drink next to my extra-blond hair—it was extra-blond that day—and I was wearing sky-blue slacks with an electric-green blouse that, come to think of it, was as dirty as the fake old palm trees. Not only a weed am I, but a natural slob.

'Two people. You mean our father and our mother?' I asked.

'Precisely.' The spikes on his mustache were sharp enough to spear shrimp. It put a lot behind his theory. Precisely.

'I don't have a father and a mother,' I told him. 'I'm an orphan.'

The acting teacher makes short work of the objection, with Marilyn confessing: 'He was a Svengali, this man. My head felt like it was inside a magnet.'

'Two souls meet when a baby is conceived,' he told me. Afterward, for the rest of your life you had to contend, he explained, with those two different souls. Each became a separate person inside you. Both were receiving the same experience every day, but in different ways. It was like two naked actors in a closet who fought over each piece of clothing you handed in so one of them could get dressed for a role.[38]

This is a delightful scene, and it can be enjoyed as a joke—a joke which may appear to subvert the lesson in duality, and which has to do with the doubtful, the vaudeville character of the preceptor: 'He was a Svengali'—the magnetic Svengali being, like Houdini, a man of the theatre and a master of illusion. But then jokes, and subversive comic characters, are, after all, a dualistic recourse. Who could believe a man with a moustache like that? But this Trilby does, at times, believe him, and who could be certain that the magnetic Mailer—the real Svengali of the piece—does not? You might say of those opposites, doubting and believing, that both are appropriate here, and that the uncertainty which is inherent in humour teaches the lesson which it apparently subverts, and therefore furnishes a dualistic proof. We are left with a suggestion which bears thinking about: that the two parents who are required for each of the troubled lives we lead may help to bring about that double life which may be called schizophrenic only when it fails, to which the karmic cycle of rebirth may impart its quota of innate dissociability, and of which the orphanage or the orphan state may serve as an incubator. For the strange business of psychic division Mailer offers successive explanations. It seems that the multiple mind needs more than one.

In 1979 Mailer published his long book *The Executioner's Song* on the strange case of Gary Gilmore, the murderer who insisted on being put to death, insisted that the state keep its word. Rojack is supposed to have written a book by the name of *The Psychology of the Hangman*, but this is certainly not it. *The Executioner's Song* declares itself a 'factual account', and it abounds in researched particulars: but it is a factual account which joins the great tradition of Gothic strangeness. It practises the principle of division whereby someone may be two people, may even be a likeable assassin, and it practises the principle of diffusion whereby someone—some author, perhaps—may be more. The second principle confers on this most forward and presumptuous of authors a self-effacing capacity to see all sides of the Gilmore question. And Mailer's 'magnanimity' in this respect—a quality perceived in the book by Christopher Ricks,[39] who has also perceived it in the poems and letters of Keats—is a form of Romanticism's negative capability. In those words of Dickens which Eliot applied to *The Waste Land*, the book 'does' the 'different voices' of the paranoid people of working-class Utah—'they were all feeling pretty paranoid'—locked in a travail of love, hate, liquor, sticks of pot, split personality, the sight of *Sybil* on television, broken marriages, trailer camps, trucks, rental arrangements, lunatic asylums, prisons, guns. All this, and much else, may be adjudged romance. Research has discovered—or invented—a romantic grandfather for Gilmore in the person of Houdini, and Gilmore himself and others in Utah were found by the demonic, dualistic Mailer to share his interest in reincarnation, psychic division, evil spirits, vampires. Somebody jokes that Houdini should have taught Gary how to escape from jail. But Gilmore was above that—his aim more inscrutable than anything in the Houdiniad, his will steady. His was an escape which took the form of a refusal to escape.[40]

There is less here than there was in *Marilyn* of the internal presence of an adversary self—some loss of interest in that species of duality. But the adversary outlook which sets itself against its society is present in its true colours. Mailer has been drawn, over the years, to a myth of violence, which authorized the excitements of *An American Dream*, and had before that inspired the programme for 'hipsters' or 'adventurers', the double life for sensitive college graduates, laid out in 'The White Negro': 'the decision is to encourage the psychopath in oneself.'[41] The adventurer's courage may jail him: but then, the essay proclaims, America is already a cancerous jail. *The Executioner's Song* keeps its cool about the violence to which it refers, and articulates no such partly playful and patently harmful myth. But of course it is mythic in proportion as it is romantic, and Gilmore's true colours are unquestionably that. The evil spirits in the book are not innocent of myth. They are also those of a highly traditional artist, one who is willing to revert to the superstitions which accompanied the first phases of modern duality in the Romantic period.

There is an episode where Gilmore's girlfriend Nicole sees him, shortly before his killings, as very sinister. Not far from a lunatic asylum, they are making love.

> She had her legs wrapped around his waist, and her arms over his neck. With her eyes closed, she had the odd feeling of an evil presence near her that came from Gary. She found it kind of half agreeable. Said to herself, Well, if he is the devil, maybe I want to get closer.
>
> It wasn't a terrifying sensation so much as a strong and strange feeling, like Gary was a magnet and had brought down a lot of spirits on himself. Of course, those psychos behind all those screened windows could call up anything out of the night ground in back of the nuthouse.
>
> In the dark, she asked: 'Are you the devil?'

Gilmore the half-agreeable evil presence is eventually to write to Nicole: 'I'm not Beelzebub. And I know the devil can't feel love. But I might be further from God than I am from the devil.' This is no less superstitious, and it is no retraction, on Mailer's part, of the previous episode.[42] But that episode stays in the mind as something rather more than simply spooky or stagey, and the sense of Gilmore as possessed, and magnetic, is in one way neither strange nor odd nor supernatural: it is not at odds with other emphases which inform this factual account of the desperations of Utah. The Gilmore of the book is not Beelzebub, and he is no Melmoth the Wanderer. He is fully human.

In this connection, and in others, Mailer may be thought to be reverting to Dostoevsky. Few works show more affinity to this one than *Crime and Punishment* and *The Possessed*, otherwise called *The Devils*. In the latter, a character executes himself on grounds of principle, and Stavrogin's wife, demented and crippled, bears a resemblance to Nicole's sister April, who calls herself a split personality; and that novel's preoccupation with child-molesting recurs in the Mailer. But there is more to the affinity than the existence of common themes and elements. All three works are carried forward, as in a dream or in drink, on a tide of anxiety and fear and love: madness, or half-madness, and the half-agreeable, are debated and imputed, and seeing double is no big deal. The crimes to which the romantic novel will often confess are crimes of dementia and delirium: and yet it can suggest that madness is human and general—that everyone has it, at times. Even those writers, such as Bellow, who are opposed to any cult of the subject may leave their readers with the thought that paranoia is something more than an outlandish illness which doctors cannot cure or define, and which causes tactics and fiascos in court. It may seem strange, but it is not rare. It is all over Utah.

Perhaps it is all over Yorkshire. When it broke out there in the fashion that produced the 'Ripper' trial of 1981, those who knew Peter Sutcliffe talked the language of romantic duality, talked of a double life, while the psychiatrists who testified in support of an unsuccessful plea of diminished responsibility talked about paranoid schizophrenia. There were 'certain signs' by which the condition could be diagnosed. 'One was Sutcliffe's persistent and repeated looking up, on about 38 occasions, to the same spot—a light cluster about 10 feet above the judge's head.' Sutcliffe was himself acquainted with signs. He claimed to have been possessed, to have heard a voice in Bingley churchyard and been unsure whether it was God or the Devil. A German psychiatrist who was at the trial remarked: 'When you speak to God it's called praying; but when God speaks to you, it's called schizophrenia.'[43] In accommodating itself, as it appears to have done, to the notion of a high incidence of mental stress in the populations which have supplied its readership, Gothic fiction has employed a repertoire of signs no darker than that of Sutcliffe's numerate doctor. It may be that Sutcliffe, having revenged himself on prostitutes and other women, was aware of both repertoires, and was no saner for being so.

When Mailer was writing the Gilmore book, he received a letter from someone named Jack Abbott. This man had a lot in common with Gilmore. Both had spent a huge proportion of their lives in detention. Still in jail, Abbott went on to dispatch a series of letters which were meant to instruct Mailer in the ways of the American prison system. Mailer was impressed—for him, Abbott looked and sounded like Lenin—and the letters became a book, *In the Belly of the Beast*. Given Mailer's beliefs, it is possible to think of this as an incident in the history of his love-affair with duality, to think of Abbott as a deutero-Gilmore. 'The two men could not be more different,' Mailer protests in his Introduction: Abbott hates death, while, for Gilmore, 'a romantic and a mystic', who 'saw incarceration as a species of karma', death was 'a species of romantic solution'. Abbott is a thinker, and more of a writer, according to Mailer. But he then goes on to compare the two of them. Abbott tells him that he has 'completely identified himself with Gilmore', and that 'if you went into any prison that held Gilmore and me and asked for all of the prisoners with certain backgrounds . . . you will get a set of files, a list of names, and my file and name will always be handed you along with Gilmore's.'[44] This may mean that both were deemed to be trouble—hard-core convicts, subversives. Both men, moreover, had been in and out of the State of Utah.

Even if you were reluctant to accept more than a little of Abbott's information as wholly correct, it would be necessary to think that both men were victims of an atrocious prison system, which tortures and persecutes its inmates and sets them at each other's throats: convicts die violently, he says, at a rate of more than four a day. Half Irish and half Chinese, he was fostered out soon after birth, and his incarcerations and reincarcerations began at nine. At 18, he was sent for bouncing a cheque to Utah State Penitentiary, on a sentence of up to five years. Three years after that, he stabbed another prisoner to death in a fight. His book reaches eloquence when it treats the subject of the premeditated prison knifing, and makes it seem both like a matter of routine and like an act of love. In such murders we may detect the participation of the judge who sentences a youth to five years in jail for a small felony.

> Slowly he begins to struggle for his life. As he sinks, you have to kill him fast or get caught. He will say 'Why?' Or 'No!' Nothing else. You can feel his life trembling through the knife in your hand. It almost overcomes you, the gentleness of the feeling at the center of a coarse act of murder. You've pumped the knife in several times without even being aware of it. You go to the floor with him to finish him. It is like cutting hot butter, no resistance at all. They always whisper one thing at the end: 'Please.'[45]

From the age of 12 to that of 37, the writer of these words had been free for only nine and a half months.

He was now being considered for parole, and it appears that his parole was hastened by the intercession of Mailer—'it is certainly the time for him to get out'—and some associates. Soon after leaving prison on a work-release programme, in the summer of 1981, he took a knife to a waiter—reported to have been a 'promising actor and playwright'—and committed a coarse act of murder.[46] This event gave pleasure to opponents of liberal philanthropy and the literary Left—for which Mailer can still be taken to speak. Such events, and such pleasures, are quite common; and the feeling for victims, and for the moral superiority of prisoners, is both common and treacherous—it has its intricacies and declivities, its slips and its knives. In the same year, the London *Times* sympathized with Alan Reeve, a murderer on the run from Broadmoor, sent to approved school at the age of 13, a reader of Marx and Lenin in prison, like Abbott. Reeve told his interviewer about an unhappy childhood, and explained that a boy he killed 'died as a surrogate for all those I perceived as my enemies'.[47] While it was Reeve's misfortune to find himself in a world of enemies, this was the other boy's misfortune too, and that of the Dutch policeman shot dead by Reeve, in pursuit of a robbery, some time after the interview. But for all the hardness of heart that sentiment can display, it would be a mistake to make out that the prisoner's friend has always to be incapable of feeling sorry for those whom the hostile, in their misery, injure and destroy, or incapable of the knowledge that suffering creates suffering, and that suffering is not confined to those to whom the status of victim is accorded. And it may be that libertarians know more than their opponents of what it means to say, as Mailer does here of America: 'we won't get law and order without a revolution in the prison system.'[48]

Abbott's Confessions are those of a man who has passed most of his life in prison, who denounces America's penal practices, and who came in the course of his ordeals to admire the torturers and imprisoners Stalin and Castro. Mailer doubts his political opinions, but makes out that there's a chance he may prove to be a great writer. But his letters are seldom those even of a good writer. They are very sententious—Notebook material which excessively relies on aphorism and assertive abstraction. Gilmore deals, by contrast, in particulars, as Mailer points out, and, as Mailer omits to point out, in plain speaking. Abbott is nothing like the writer that Gilmore is, when roused, during his last days, in his letters to Nicole:

> I'm so used to bullshit and hostility, deceit and pettiness, evil and hatred. Those things are my natural habitat. They have shaped me. I look at the world through eyes that suspect, doubt, fear, hate, cheat, mock, are selfish and vain.

Gilmore's natural habitat can be regarded as familiar ground in romance. Later, though, in the same letter he writes: 'What do I do, rot in prison? growing old and bitter and eventually work this around in my mind to where it reads that I'm the one who's getting fucked around, that I'm just an innocent victim of society's bullshit?'[49] Gilmore is here resisting one of Abbott's compulsions, and one of the principal compulsions of romance.

Some of the faults of Abbott's book are the consequence of hardship unimaginable to most readers: the drive to get even, the advocacy of a punitive Communism; the talk of how his IQ jumped with the study of Marx and Lenin—as measured by the prison psychologist he presumably despises; the bookishness, the dropping of the austere names of Carnap and Quine. There is also the sense that what he says in one place denies or weakens what he says in another. The book describes a body of convicts who are always at each other's throats and who are always backing each other up. 'No one', he writes (to Mailer, who has 'come the closest'), 'has ever held out a hand to help me to be a better man.'[50] But the book opens with an Acknowledgement of the gratitude he feels to the sister who 'saw me through everything described in this book'.

On the subject of hostility, however, he can be challenging and acute, with something of Gilmore's grasp of what his habitat has done to shape him. If everyone is paranoid, prison is bound to make you worse.

When I'm forced by circumstances to be in a crowd of prisoners, it's all I can do to refrain from attack. I feel such hostility, such hatred, I can't help this anger. All these years I have felt it. Paranoid.

It occurs to him, he writes while reading Stendhal, 'that, in this existential age, the last vestiges of romanticism appear to us today (in social intercourse) as *paranoia*.' His own relation to romanticism is deceptive. He seems at this point in the book to be denying a connection, and it may indeed be right to think of him as a philosopher, doping up among the hard cases, gaining the respect of the other prisoners with his punitive Communism, and as very different from a romantic like Gilmore, the death-seeker and reincarnationist. At the same time, he is a target for romantic feelings—including his own. He is an outcast coldly pleading for 'justice', and for 'consideration'. He is the kind of outcast whose behaviour has been made monstrous by monstrous ill-treatment. He rounds off the story of an ex-cop persecuted in prison, and driven to suicide, with the remark: 'This pig was so typical a dirty pig, he could have passed for the Georgian highway patrolman in the car commercial.' And he is the kind of outcast who dreams of a grand freedom—of an absolute liberation of the will. He says of the murders that have to be undertaken among prisoners: 'If you can kill like that, you can do anything.' He stands beyond good and evil in the antinomian-paranoid posture of Stavrogin.[51]

'My heart is pounding,' Abbott writes of an early and hopeless bid to escape.[52] Stavrogin's heart 'begins to pound' as he steals towards his innocent girl. Mailer's and Abbott's America may be known by elations which are vividly predicted in the literature of the past and for which Dostoevsky is the source of sources. It is understandable that he should be among the important writers mentioned in Abbott's book—Dostoevsky the prisoner, the sufferer, the creator of Stavrogin. But it is equally understandable that he should be misrepresented there. Dostoevsky is seen as conveying that sinners, shits, 'are *all* capable of dying for a just cause, a "beautiful idea", a *principle*'.

After a while the Russian terrorist Nechayev is mentioned too, without a word about the fact that Nechayev's activities helped to generate the hostility to revolutionary terrorism, and to radical chic, which possesses *The Possessed.*[53] Retribution's aphorisms may need to bring in Dostoevsky: but they may also need to keep a part of him out. The difficulty is one that reproduces the duality which was perceived by Dostoevsky in the revenger's tragedy of his own day, and which can be perceived in the revenger's tragedy of Shakespeare's day, and of any day.

XIX. ANGLO-AMERICAN

Marius Bewley was born in St. Louis in 1916, and there is a photograph of the class with which he went to school in Missouri: a few rows of sturdy tow-haired country boys in dungarees. Their clothes are now the fashion with middle-class children in London: yet all but one looks as if he might have gone to school with Mark Twain, and would grow up to be like Whitman's Missourian who 'crosses the plains toting his wares and his cattle'.[1] All but one, for at the end of a row stands a shy brunette, who looks and is dressed less like Tom Sawyer than the young Chopin. This is Eugene Augustine Marius Bewley, never to be known as Gene, who grew up to be embarrassed and excited by the photograph, allowing it to be shown only on special occasions, as if it belonged to some hoard of erotica.

I first met Marius in Cambridge, England, in 1951, just before he withdrew for good to his native America after a second period of years spent in Cambridge as the pupil, colleague, and friend of F.R. Leavis. He and his clothes were to leave behind them a vivid memory. We were to recall, and write about, sponge-bag trousers, fancy waistcoats, and a dark broad-brimmed hat which might have passed, in that critical town, that seat of judgement, for a sombrero. These were garments which he was in the habit of going out to buy when he needed lifting from a depression, and one or two of them, for all the general air of decorum, might have wakened the dead. His manner was understood to combine the rhetoric of W.C. Fields and the suavity of the Hollywood-English movie-actor George Arliss, though late at night there could be screams of rage over God's treatment of cats. The manner paid tribute to the life and works of Henry James: this was interesting, but we were equally interested to learn that, as a baby, he had sat on the knee of the widow of Frank James the outlaw, brother of Jesse, and that he had served not only as Tennessee Williams's secretary but as a social worker on a Red Indian reservation.

We liked to think that in Marius a Jamesian civility and a Jamesian licence met. The Wild West, the Frontier, had sent to Downing College, Cambridge, where Leavis wore the open-necked shirts and plunging necklines of the disdainer of elocution, a literary critic with the wardrobe, wit, and panache of a man of letters, but one that was capable of falling into ditches, and of being haunted on the Chesterton Road by the Devil in the shape of a black dwarf. He lived in the imagination of his friends as a repertoire of stories and sallies, delivered in an Anglo-American accent of rare device, and, when feelings ran high, in the manner of Edith Evans's Lady Bracknell. His stories, and the stories told about him, made him seem theatrically urbane, a little licentious, prone to the accidents that happen to a grand manner and an exotic accent: at the same time, he was thoroughly kind and true, and the best of friends. A pigeon once bombed his coiffure as he waited outside the Senate House, having arrived, very early and very uneasy, to sit a Tripos examination. Fortunately he had brought along several spare clean handkerchiefs.

He was the complete Anglophile. He was both an American and an Englishman. It could be alleged of him that, like the author of *Huckleberry Finn*, whose works he neglected, he practised the magic art of duality, that the dreaming-up of a deutero-Bewley, of an English self, turned him into a Marius Twain. This is a romantic hypothesis, and his theory of American literature can also be called dualistic and romantic. He held that the major nineteenth-century American writers were conscious of, and wished to close, a split in American experience. This is not the only area of concurrence between Marius's theory and subject-matter and the theory and subject-matter of Romanticism, and it is not the only reason for thinking that he was, as he eventually acknowledged himself, a romantic.

His first book, *The Complex Fate*, was published in 1952. Its chapters, which are mainly devoted to Hawthorne and Henry James and to showing that they shared distinctively American concerns, had appeared as articles in Leavis's journal *Scrutiny*. Leavis himself is present in the book, expressing dissents, and by those familiar with his performance in dispute, the lesser asperity of his interventions on this occasion may be taken to denote the forbearance due to a warm collaborative relationship. The book has an epigraph from James: 'It's a complex fate, being an American, and one of the responsibilities it entails is fighting against a superstitious valuation of Europe.' Was Marius's valuation of Europe superstitious? I want to discuss the complex fate of his possession of two nationalities, one of them adoptive or preferential, and perhaps also provisional.

His love of England was sometimes thought to be quaint and idiosyncratic, and to embody a contradiction. If he loved it so much, why did he not settle there? Why, after he'd left, did he never return, despite the attempts that were made to fetch him back by those who felt that he was sick of America and sick with nostalgia for England? But there is nothing very extraordinary about this. Not every Jacobite would have been entirely pleased to witness the restoration, from over the water, of the Stuart dynasty in the person of its bonny prince. The exiled English self of Marius's later years belonged to an inhabitant of America; he was then, I think, in no state of internal emigration, though he could appear to be. In earlier times the Englishman's friend was closer to impersonating, and to being mistaken for, an Englishman of a certain kind, and may possibly have come close to emigrating.

People who appear to like another country better than their own, who look abroad for the land of the free, can be heard to object to the patriotic claims and national prejudice of their native country. But they themselves will exhibit the faults of patriots and nationalists if they overwork or invent factors of national difference, in order to insist on a general superiority. One might want to say that if Leavis thinks too highly of England, E.M. Forster thinks too highly of Italy and India. And this puts one in sight of a further consideration. A vicarious or next-door nationalist is likely to be more intent on his native country than on the preferred alternative: the preference may carry or conceal an element of retaliation—against parents, neighbours, teachers, authorities, and other such offenders. The note can be detected in Forster's maxim about its being better to betray your country than your friend. As for Marius, he would probably have taken it for granted that nationalistic claims are nearly always implausible and ill-natured, though they could be tolerated and even desired in a context of irony or play. The England he praised was not a place whose virtues and advantages could easily be tested. In part, his England was an imaginary place, fashioned for his own instruction and delight. Then again, the English outlook to which he was attracted stood in an adversary relationship to much that went on in the England of the day. When Marius was young, one England was attacking another—not for the first time, or the last. For the man of two nationalities, England was itself two nations. Leavis and those who agreed with him were contemptuous of 'the London literary world', of the tastes and interests which were seen to reside in the quality press, the BBC and the universities. It has been suggested that it makes sense to think of this episode as a renewal of the old war between Roundheads and Cavaliers. If so, then, in Marius's case, a Cavalier had enlisted on the side of Cromwell.

The intelligence, and earnestness, and energy, and pain, which animated Leavis's attack on his enemies were such that few of those who came to him as students found themselves resisting or questioning his strategies. Against this must be set an observation of Ian Hamilton's: the trouble with his call-to-arms is that he won't let anyone join up. But Marius, for one, *did* join up, and he was promoted to *Scrutiny*, and to the confidence of its chief editor, which few associates were able to retain. Leavis attempted to turn literary (or practical) criticism into a self-sufficient yet responsive discipline at the heart of the humanities. This attempt gave more support to the subject of English studies, as it had been secured for the universities and pursued in literary worlds of the past, than the awareness of his militancy, and of the increasing reluctance of this collaborator to collaborate, of this responder to respond, permitted readers to recognize during his lifetime: since his death, however, literary controversialists of the Left have moved to make good this omission. Here we come to the matter of Leavis's 'élitism'. A relentless depreciation of popular taste—of mass civilization—was attended and projected by a civility of address which none of his acerbities was ever quite able to curb, which kept referring, even in anger, to Mr Eliot and Dr Tillyard. These were the misters and doctors of a minority culture whose values were to serve as an example and a rebuke. It was never really all that odd or scandalous, therefore, that one of his pupils should have looked more like some man of letters, about town in the 1890s, than any kind of soldier or devotee of the open air. None of this is meant to make light of the importance, and indeed the influential novelty, of the Leavisian militancy—of the quasi-political cutting edge of his work, and of its tendency to live by the sword. One of his last titles declares that he has wielded one. We can accept that he set himself to build a heavenly city in his native country, and we can also accept that it is no longer thought to be under construction.

Leavis's appeal to standards and to authority appealed to Marius, and so did his tendency to inquire into lines of descent, into the tradition which the individual talent inherits and transmits, and which contained the 'great tradition' of the nineteenth-century English novel, and into the national heritage of morals and manners, which had to be in a good state, which had to be a rich soil, if talents were to come to anything and traditions to be of value. Leavis would have felt, as Marius did, that Texas could never have produced Shakespeare—rather as Twain and Van Wyck Brooks had felt that Dahomey could never have produced Edison.[2] Marius followed Leavis's lead here by undertaking in successive books, *The Complex Fate* and *The Eccentric Design*,[3] to characterize a great tradition of the nineteenth-century American novel. The talents were those of Cooper, Hawthorne, Melville, and James, with Missouri's Mark Twain neglected. Twain's absence from Marius's great tradition can be compared with Dickens's absence, at first, from Leavis's, and it can also be compared with the coolness shown towards Whitman in *The Complex Fate*. Twain and Whitman were artists who spoke for his own early environment, and who spoke to some part of his own nature, and it may be that his imagination had lit out from Missouri, leaving those artists behind, as the result of a recoil from that environment: and yet we have to bear in mind that it was that of his mother, who was always very important to him. It is possible to suppose that his early environment remained so important to him that there were times when he had to keep it secret.

His chosen writers are Palefaces rather than Redskins, as the saying used to go, and they are Anglo-American in that they took themselves to be contributing to English literature. For Marius, American literature had yet to declare its independence. For him, as for Henry James, England was at once romantic and in certain essential respects symbiotic with

America. While such a sensibility has become residual or eccentric in America now, and was never that of Uncle Sam himself, it can be said to have originated in a general conviction among Americans that the two nations were one: a faith that moved mountains, and opened a path across a waste of seas. Leavis could often imply that England was different from and superior to America, and yet his tradition, as well as Marius's, is a testimony to that faith. Their traditions can appear to coincide, to collaborate in the production of talent which is simultaneously American and English. For Marius, James was both American and English. He was not French, or cosmopolitan. His independence of the French novel is firmly and polemically declared in *The Complex Fate*.

The alliance with Leavis proved liberating for Marius, but it could also prove confining. Leavis was a critic who knew where to jab, as another ally once remarked, with feeling. Marius was not like that. He was tender and generous—never very interested in the jugular. However, something of Leavis's severity and suspicion, which were not without reason, which were not without suffering, and which were not without tenderness and generosity and wit, was imparted to Marius's earlier writings—a little awkwardly imparted at times. We can't be absolutely sure how concerned he is when he refers to plots, when he recalls that 'the most distinguished American critics appeared to enter a conspiracy for the purpose of establishing Lowell's'—Robert Lowell's—'literary reputation on as sound a base in as short a time as possible.'[4] The opinions expressed, however, were his own. Differences of view that developed between them were publicly explored, with Leavis summoning his lesser asperity. Marius made up for Leavis's disparagement of Scott Fitzgerald, while Leavis made up for Marius's gingerly and 'secretive' treatment of Twain.

Bewley's commentaries on Hawthorne's fiction may be thought co-ordinate with Leavis's approach. They take up the question of the novelist's exposure to what we have been taught to describe as the bare, mannerless, inhospitable world of the America in which he lived. It is James who has done much of the teaching: these descriptions are evidence of the power, the pressure, exerted by his sense of his own situation, by his snobberies and romantic excitements, which have helped us to see the American artist 'in all the terrible deprivation of his stark American condition'. The words might be James's. They are Marius's, together with the faint falsetto note of alarm at 'stark', a word constantly used—as a synonym for 'naked', or for something worse?—in the course of his inculcation of the point in *The Eccentric Design*.[5] In his first book he compares *The Blithedale Romance* with James's *Bostonians*, and calls attention to one of the ways in which Hawthorne's society may be reckoned to have failed him in the practice of his art. He deals with the comedy furnished, in James's novel, by Selah Tarrant's progressive enthusiasms, and states that 'a darker kind of life' enters the comedy with the reference to Selah's having once belonged to the Cayuga community, where, as in the historical Oneida community or commune, there were no husbands or wives. Marius finds Selah 'an actively sordid presence', beside which that of Hawthorne's wicked mesmerist Westervelt seems pale, undernourished, a piece of Gothic conventionality.[6]

Leavis would have approved of this analysis. He would have approved of what it implies about Cayuga. It is unlikely that Marius set great store by a strict adherence to the conventions of marriage, but here he gives the impression of doing so. I remember the tales he used to tell about commuters embracing each other on the evening run of the Staten Island Ferry. Had the persons on that 'raft' of his been rumoured to call each other 'honey', he would not have minded, or uttered the smallest shriek: but he was offended when Leslie Fiedler used these expressions in discussing the friendship between Huck and Jim, Fiedler's 'anti-family of two', just as he was offended by the anti-family goings-on at Cayuga. On this as on other occasions in *The Complex Fate* Marius the Epicurean can be found to yield to the outlook of Leavis's Cambridge, with its rigour and *pudeur*. At the same time, the pleasure-lover is never invisible for long. He reasserts himself, for instance, in a consenting account[7] of James Laughlin's patriotic Whitmanesque poem about America's male comradeship and courtesy, 'Go West Young Man':

> Yessir they're all named
> either Ken or Stan or Don
> every one of them . . .

Ferries have been romantic in America, and Whitman's wonderful poem about the Brooklyn Ferry was called to mind by Marius's tales. In the course of the poem Whitman's ability to see that he is like everyone else enables him to see that he is, as they are, divided: he is one with the fellows on the Brooklyn Ferry, and each of them is two fellows. In saying so, he brings together terms which have been singled out for attention in this book. Cunningly compounded, here once again are the dualities of division and of diffusion. Not for the first time, multiple personality blushes, and confesses, and embezzles.

> Nor is it you alone who know what it is to be evil,
> I am he who knew what it was to be evil,
> I too knotted the old knot of contrariety,
> Blabb'd, blush'd, resented, lied, stole, grudg'd,
> Had guile, anger, lust, hot wishes I dared not speak,
> Was wayward, vain, greedy, shallow, sly, cowardly,
>   malignant,
> The wolf, the snake, the hog, not wanting in me,
> The cheating look, the frivolous word, the adulterous
>   wish, not wanting,
> Refusals, hates, postponements, meanness, laziness,
>   none of these wanting,
> Was one with the rest, the days and haps of the rest,
> Was call'd by my nighest name by clear loud voices of
>   young men as they saw me approaching or passing,
> Felt their arms on my neck as I stood, or the negligent
>   leaning of their flesh against me as I sat,
> Saw many I loved in the street or ferry-boat or public
>   assembly, yet never told them a word . . .

It is striking that, for all his adoption of a dualistic critical method, and for all his double life, Marius kept as silent as he did about the dualistic heritage of his own country. He wrote about James Hogg, but not about two of nineteenth-century America's foremost multiple men, Whitman and Twain. Some part of this abstention must surely have been due to the suspicion of Romanticism prevalent, certainly in Cambridge, at the outset of his career.[8]

He regrets that Hawthorne thought of his fictions as romances rather than novels, saying that the word 'romance' does not do them justice. He relates this liking for romance, as he relates a certain immaturity which he senses in Hawthorne, to a gap between morals and manners in New England, and to the poverty of its manners. But romance is not only what Hawthorne thought he was writing: it is what he wrote, and what writers in other countries wrote, countries far from conspicuous for their lack of manners. Nineteenth-century American life was not as bare and raw and recent as commentators have alleged, and its romantic proclivities are no argument to the contrary.

I accept that it was a complex fate, being an American, but only on the margins of the society can it have been an ordeal of cultural deprivation. When Mark Twain went West, he went to Carson City and Virginia City, Nevada, the second of which had more theatres than the city of Edinburgh has today, and after that he moved to San Francisco, where a French landlady complained about him for firing pistols and drinking beer in his room. In a letter of 1864 he insinuated—falsely, it seems—that some at least of her charges were true: 'What in the hell is the use of wearing away a lifetime in building up a good name, if it is to be blown away at a breath by an ignorant foreigner who is ignorant of the pleasant little customs that adorn and beautify a high state of civilisation?'[9] It could be said that he is boasting about the West's lack of decorum, commenting on the absence of a society there. But it could equally be said that in that breezy, crafty sentence of his there is a society and a civilization. Not that these have been fully perceptible to critics for whom no civilization deserves the name unless it has reached a high state, and who have blamed Twain for his immaturity, sexual repression, inability to resemble Henry James, and for submitting to the demands of an unsatisfactory milieu.

Those who delete, from the nineteenth-century American environment, the operations of a literary culture shared with Britain, who ignore such enrichments, can then agonize over lacks and limitations: but some of these limitations have more to do with the Anglo-American heritage than with the setting in which they have often been presented—that of the difficulties which may afflict a new society. While intending to trace a difficult if not afflicted separate development, Fiedler nevertheless brings out how much the two literatures, and the two societies, had in common, and assigns to American sexuality features of attenuation and displacement which are hardly less descriptive of the English experience. Superstitiously low valuations of the American cultural background do not restrict themselves to the nineteenth-century position, one may add. Hannah Arendt has spoken (barbarously) of a 'relatively traditionless America'. To the James who stressed the 'thin and impalpable' deposit left by history there, the 'thinness' of Hawthorne's circumstances, to the James whose 'foremost feeling is that of compassion for a romancer looking for subjects in such a field'—to the James of this impoverishment has succeeded the writer whom I recall remarking, not long ago, in the Europhile *New York Review of Books*, on the 'thinness of the cultural humus' in America.[10] The rich soil of Europe has long been a superstition in America, and in Europe.

Classic American literature is a rich achievement, which some have interpreted in terms of the poverty of its social context and in terms of its response to a surrounding philistinism. It is worth more than the literature contemporary with it in Scotland—a country where people had come to feel an American remoteness from the centre of things, and to ponder enigmas of psychic division, and a country which drew on a tradition of mind and manners several centuries old. Hawthorne's achievement is a rich achievement in itself. No doubt he was partly a recluse, and his art suffered for that reason. But the claims of privacy are subtly concerted there with those of community, and there could be considerable doubt as to how much of his isolation was native to, and attributable to, America. There was isolation elsewhere in the world, and there was a world literature of isolation, which had often conveyed (and denied) that societies were deficient and hostile, and to which Hawthorne's art can also be attributed. The strangeness, the anti-social ideality, the flight from manners, and from sexuality, the notorious 'duplicity', of the classic American fiction discussed by Bewley, and Fiedler, invite interpretation as distinctively American, and as a response to difficulty: but they also invite interpretation as distinctively romantic, and as a response to difficulties no different from those experienced in other places.

The model made by Marius for the work of these writers takes account of difficulties which it is right to think peculiar to his native country. To the extent that it is dualistic and romantic, however, the model can also be understood to refer to difficulties and tendencies of wider incidence. It employs the idea of a tension which may be discovered in American history and art, and which the major writers attempted to solve. In *The Eccentric Design* he argues that

this tension was the result of a struggle to close the split in American experience, to discover a unity that, for the artist especially, almost sensibly *was not there*. The nature of the division that supported this conflict was partly determined by those deprivations in American society I have discussed above: deprivations of which the practising American novelist was deeply aware, for they confronted him with a society in which the abstract idea and the concrete fact could find little common ground for creative interaction. From a more positive point of view the division took on many different forms concurrently: it was an opposition between tradition and progress, between democratic faith and disillusion, between the past and the present and future; between Europe and America, liberalism and conservatism, aggressive acquisitive economics and benevolent wealth. These same divisions existed in Europe also, but there they were ballasted by a denser social medium, a richer sense of the past, a more inhibited sense of material possibilities.[11]

In speaking of a tension between the 'faith' and the 'fears' of the novelists in question, concerning the progress of democracy in America, he was over-impressed by their fears, and by the rich soil of Europe, its 'denser social medium'. He was nevertheless able to show, with the utmost elegance and clarity, with a marshalling firmness of touch and with the flourishes of a kind of critical *bel canto*, that the important writers shared important and interesting preoccupations, and that these were the preoccupations of Americans—though some could also be the preoccupations of foreigners, with the 'same divisions' and their own complex fate to worry about. None of them is obsolete—locked away in its period.

Marius exaggerates the element of difficulty and of stark division. This does not mean that his scheme—or that Fiedler's, to which it bears a resemblance in this respect—is obsolete. But it does reveal him as a man of his time, as a graduate of that twentieth-century School of Duality for which Eliot's 'dissociation of sensibility' has served as an instrument of investigation. In the above passage, with its perception of an American duality, of a division determined by a deprivation, we can perceive a consciousness of, and an approximation to, Eliot's concept. They are evident in the words about 'a society in which the abstract idea and the concrete fact could find little ground for creative interaction'. The soil, as it were, was too thin for the single mind. Leavis, together with other critics of his time, had looked in literary texts for a reconciliation of opposites—a study which has its origins, or most of them, in the Romantic period: and now here was Marius Bewley arguing that this reconciliation could not have taken place in America. But where has it ever taken place? Where, at least, has it ever taken place in any fashion that would enable one to think of the nineteenth-century American as especially divided? Reconciliation has always been hard to find: the search for it has often had to turn to religion, and has now been rated chimerical by the sceptics of Deconstruction. For all that, it has gone on for a long time, and been directed, in many places, at a wide variety of evidence: and it was carried from Europe to America, where Marius Bewley was eventually to become aware of it. The Ambassador to the Red Man may therefore be said to have spoken with the forked tongue of Anglo-American duality. But there is something more that could be said. It may be that Bewley's writings evoke an Anglo-American common culture with which his conception of an American dividedness does not agree.

Marius himself was divided into an American and an Englishman. Why did he not go on living in England if he thought it such a good place? Why did he not keep up the collaboration with Leavis? These questions can be jointly answered, and the answers may tell us what kind of life he made for himself in America on his return, and what his politics were like. In losing touch with Leavis, who was later to be flown to America in an academic aeroplane, at the height of his fame, in order to give lectures, he seems to have wished to go his own way in criticism, and to have lost some shade of his old respect for an ethos of high standards and moral disapproval which had few blessings to bestow on the honeymoon of the Staten Island Ferry; on the romantic lightness of heart which could allow the author of *Masks and Mirrors* to sit at dinner in a Marilyn Monroe mask; or indeed on much that he lived for in his native land.[12] Leavis was for certain students and adherents the severe father who could be loved: but the truth is that this student was attracted to both of the Englands of the time. Marius was a homosexual—an 'Athenian', as he liked to express it—whose loyalties were divided in his youth between Leavis's Downing College and another very different Cambridge which co-existed with it. It is also true that he preferred America to England, and that his keen interest in England was in part an expression of his feelings about America, which were those of a patriot.

Mark Twain fell treasonably in love with England when, locking up his pistols, he visited it in 1872, and the words used of Twain by his biographer Justin Kaplan could be used of Marius Bewley. Twain 'adored the English because their way of life offered him for the first time a baseline by which he could measure his discontent with his own country'. Kaplan writes that Twain saw about him in England 'stability, government by a responsible élite, the acceptance of a gentleman's code'.[13] Marius saw these and other good things about him in England, and when the evidence failed him he was willing to pretend. He was aware, I think, that he was reconstituting the country in order to deal with his feelings about America. He adored a certain kind of America more than he adored a certain kind, which was two kinds, of England, while feeling that his America stood in need of the English lessons he had devised for it. The America he adored was an America of eccentric designs, lived in by Ken and Stan, and by older women of character such as the picturesque and peculiar Peggy Guggenheim. It was not inhabited, or inhibited, by Eisenhower, Nixon, or Cardinal Spellman. It was open to experience and pleasure in a way that no amount of make-believe could represent as universal in the England of the 1950s, or as familiar in the Cambridge that was ruled by the critical comment.

In the mid-Fifties he was teaching at the Catholic University of Washington, and he invited me to talk to his students. 'You'll lecture on *Heart of Midlothian*? That would be charming.' Delivered to an audience of priests, my lecture on Scott's Protestant work was to have the charm of the exotic, and the audience was exotic too, for some of them were holding hands. On the day of my arrival Marius held a party. But the

Buick which I owned, which was driven that day by the English critic speedy Alvarez, and in which, when driven by me, Marius had sensed the wingbeat of the Angel of Death, was becalmed for a while on the parkway, so that the party had been swinging for a long time before we came in to cast an English blight. There were Ken and Stan and other young persons, in a state of euphoria, whirling around the apartment. I lit a pipe and sat down in an armchair, wrapped in clouds of rank blue smoke. Marius approached, beaming like a harvest moon through my signals of embarrassment and retreat, and said: 'I've never seen a briar do such sterling work.' That ironic sentence, with its English words and associations, set its crown on an occasion which was, in a way, like a scene from a Dracula film—from the one Marius used to describe, telling how an innocent young Englishman abroad, 'of the best kind', was exposed to an unnerving hospitality. The sentence about my phlegmatic briar was an approval of English reserve which was nonetheless a hint that he would rather be in that Washington apartment than back among the embarrassable Englishry.

A taste for England on the part of Americans can go with conservative political attitudes, with a taste for responsible government by gentlemen. But it would be wrong to be expansive about such traits in Marius's case. He was a liberal to the marrow, to the last miaow of his cat Zenobia. He was an American patriot whose political stance was that of an Anglophile Democrat, and his favourite politician was Adlai Stevenson—Anglophilia itself. But he never had much time for the Labour Government which ruled Britain from 1945 to 1951, and changed it to meet new standards of public responsibility. The only British politician he was friendly with was the extravagant Norman St. John Stevas—a philosopher and panjandrum of the Conservative Party, a Catholic who favours the canonization of Princess Grace of Monaco, his hobby taxidermy, his style that of a diminished latter-day Disraeli. Marius was working on the fiction of Disraeli towards the end of his life. Here we'd be faced with the picture of a Cromwellian fancying a Cavalier if we refused to accept that Marius had changed. He *had* changed. He had overcome his early disapproval of romance. But he never was and did not become a conservative, though it is true that some of the fears he responded to as a literary historian were among those which have impelled the politics of conservatism in the English-speaking world.

His concerns were sometimes to cross those of another Anglophile American critic, Lionel Trilling, whose lifelong interest in England produced lengthy stays in London and in Oxford. During the Sixties Trilling was out of sympathy with the student activism in America which was directed against the Vietnam War and against the universities, and towards the end of his life he gave his mind to the theme of 'establishment'. This was his word for a type of prosperity and security: it does not refer to the social security intended by a welfare state. His book *Sincerity and Authenticity* discusses the 'qualities of affluent decorum' praised in the work of Shakespeare, Ben Jonson, Marvell, and Yeats, and dreamt of by certain novelists:

> The best of the novelists of the 19th century and of the beginning of our own epoch were anything but confident that the old vision of the noble life could be realised. But in the degree to which Balzac, Stendhal, Dickens, Trollope, Flaubert, and Henry James were aware of the probability of its defeat in actuality, they cherished and celebrated the lovely dream. The young James Joyce gave it a name, one that suggests both its anachronism and its allure—he spoke of his desire to enter 'the fair courts of life'. In that phrase, nostalgically recalling the vanished noble dispensation, he expressed all that the world in the time of his youth might still be fancied to offer in the way of order, peace, honour, and beauty. The credence that could formerly be given to material and social establishment and the happiness which followed from it was the very ground of the moral life as the novelists once represented it—the moral career began with the desire to enter the fair courts of life; how one conducted oneself in that enterprise was what morality was about.

You might well be taken aback by this if you had supposed that it was art, and, to be sure, fame, which interested Joyce, and that he made up his mind to steal from his society into exile. If the aim of his youth was to achieve an affluent decorum—the aim of the nineteenth century's bourgeois patrician or *aristocrat roturier*—then he failed painfully. The fair courts of life spoken of by Trilling somehow suggest Trinity College, Dublin, characterized by one American visitor as 'something of a mudhole, but in the very best way, as Marius would say', and little frequented by Joyce. The fair courts of life spoken of by Stephen Dedalus are an image for his response to the sight of a girl, for his leap at the chance of love and marriage. Family life can be foreseen in this utterance of the young Joyce. But affluence has nothing to do with it.

Lionel Trilling has more to say about this matter. He rightly observes that modern literature treats the goal of an affluent decorum as open to the reproach of philistinism, but that in our capacity as householders, and parents, rather than writers and readers, we are less inclined to admit that the reproach is deserved. Having said that, however, he reverts to his unqualified ascription of the goal to eminent writers of the past. 'Shakespeare unabashedly uses material and social establishment and what it is presumed to assure in the way of order, peace, honour, and beauty as emblems of the spiritual life, as criteria by which the sufficiency of the inner condition may be assessed.' Bewley was never to think that virtue can be measured in terms of wealth. He was radical enough to think that it will often be its own reward.[14]

On New Year's Eve, 1972, when he had only a few more days to live, he wrote me a letter. He was now 56. The democracy had returned Richard Nixon to power, and he had gained his accommodation with Communist China. The Christmas bombing of Hanoi had just taken place, the Watergate disclosures were still to come. There are those, who, had they read the letter at the time that it was written, would have thought it wild and histrionic: after Watergate, a more receptive reading might have been expected. This is the letter of someone whose fears about democracy were a democrat's fears, and who knew what Nixon was long before it had become common knowledge. Some of the letter is in his briar vein of romantic hyperbole, or High Camp; some of it is written by Marius the Epicurean in the role of Dracula, among others. He is nevertheless in earnest. This is the letter of someone who has been through a serious illness, and who was never to recover his health.

I can't explain why it has been virtually impossible for me to write letters at all for a couple of years. It takes more and more energy just to perform the act of living in this God-blasted country which, by the hour, falls deeper and deeper into darkness. I have really become convinced that under the horrible shadow of Nixonian crime this country has passed the point beyond which any return to moral light and air is impossible, not only today, but forever. You have no idea how paralysing, how ghastly, it is to live in such a situation, and one which can never be redeemed. I wish the British would invade.

I think I heard from you last when I had just got out of the hospital. That was a long time ago now. The whole ordeal changed me very much. I'm no longer carefree and giddy as I was once, but drag a long shadow behind me that withers the greenery as I pass. I can't drink at all any more, and in fact haven't even had a sip of wine for nearly two years. I don't miss the drinking itself, but psychologically the blow has been pretty awful. I've improved a bit in appearance, since I no longer look like an educated pig, but I never go to parties and have become pretty much of a recluse. I'm enclosing a couple of very recent snapshots that show my new Leavisian countenance since you must recognise me next time we meet, which, pray God, may happen some day. Garry, as you see, is much as ever. The little dog—Beppo—I've had for several years, and he is all my hope and joy. He's a little Italian greyhound—bred by Tolstoi's niece: and he sustains in me the conviction that decency and goodness have not yet vanished from the earth. He possesses all the virtues except courage and fortitude.

Under Dick's good shepherding Rutgers remains one of the spots still wooed by a pure moral air. If it weren't for Rutgers I'd be ordering straitjackets from my tailor. But I fear that no academic fastness will prove impenetrable at last to the reeking miasma breathed out from the Nixonian lungs, which covers the whole land like a fog filled with evil things. I'm always hoping to see you and Jane over here, but how could anybody want to fall into this Blakean Ulro?

Could this have come from someone deeply attached to America? No other person could have written it. Not many care as much as he did, in his own wild way, about politics and public life.

The letter mentions an anthology he did of Romantic verse, and his 'brand of romanticism'. He must long since have stopped regretting Hawthorne's weakness for romance, and was drawn in particular to brands of romanticism—Byron, Disraeli—that could be called both classical and romantic, public and private. The letter tells of his dismay that Nixon—prompted, he suspects, by Daniel Moynihan—should have likened himself to Disraeli. The use of the word 'moral' in the passage I have quoted is suggestive of much—of Jacobean literature, of James, of Leavis, of Trilling's talk of honour. It suggests that his first loyalties as a writer and teacher were not forgotten. It had never been the case with Marius that *rigor Leavis* set in, despite a joke of George Barker's to that effect: but there was an *amor Leavis* which never left him. At the same time, some kind of victory of temperament over training was gradually completed, which brought him ease. His literary tastes, formed during a period when brands of romanticism were widely rejected, were to settle down in terms of a commitment to romantic modes—a commitment far from deaf to the siren sounds of the great tradition and of the classical; the generous and affirmative impulses which fill his criticism were to find fresh play. In the expression given to such impulses, elements of his Christian training—and, it may be, of Christian belief—seemed to have survived his lapse from the Roman Catholic communion into the 'Athenian persuasion'. Their survival can be studied in *The Eccentric Design*—in Marius's vision of Melville's vision of the mother whales and their babies.[15]

Moby Dick describes a host of sperm whales circling round an inner stillness, round 'that enchanted calm which they say lurks in the heart of every commotion'. Marius writes: 'Now the question is, what did the *Pequod*'s whaling boat, when it broke through the living circles into the enchanted calm, find there?' Melville reveals what was found: 'suspended in those watery vaults, floated the forms of the nursing mothers of the whales, and those that by their enormous girth seemed shortly to become mothers.' As Marius shows, Melville's vision appears to be based on the vision of Heaven in *The Divine Comedy*—of that centre of intense light round which, in concentric circles, revolve the angelic intelligences. Beatrice explains to Dante: 'From that point doth hang heaven and all nature.' Melville and Marius believed that Leviathan is the image of a suffering God, and it could be said that this is Marius's best argument for the belief. His feeling for animals, and for mothers, ran deep, and it affected his criticism. He made room in his house for cats and dogs, and for a Gothic iguana that looked more like the Castle of Otranto than any beast known to zoos. I spent my honeymoon in his Staten Island castle-cathouse, and can vouch for a hospitality that was never unnerving.

In the field of Anglo-American literary relations, it would appear that the initiative, the action, is currently thought by many to have gone over to the American side of the water. Since the start of the Second World War, sensitive souls have been running to New York, as to the centre of things. They are off to a land 'richer in incident and opportunity': these, if I remember them right, are among the many words which have expressed Cyril Connolly's fascination with 'the flight of Auden and Isherwood'. It is a land where English stars may seek refuge from their fans. A land where there may be more money, and where there may be love. There is also the sense that the movement of writers and others from the periphery to the centre of the world-wide English-speaking community—a centre located first in Britain and then in America—has been driven by a doctrine of provincialism: by the damaging idea that there is a centre, and that angelic intelligences must revolve round it or else fade away into the freezing darkness. The failings of the old American Anglophilia were related to this doctrine, to the sentiment it spreads, and the same sentiment has now sent the British hurrying to America.

The self-made exile expects too much, and too much is made of the deprived state of provinces and peripheries. No matter how little there may be to work with at the worst, it can be made to go a long way, and there are times when centres can seem less important than the single talent, no matter how reclusive or remote that talent may be. The contemptuous talk of patriots about the worthlessness of a foreign literature, or of vicarious patriots about the worthlessness of their own, may well be the expression of a private resentment, but there may also be found here a tribute paid by the periphery to the centre, and a consequence of 'literary imperialism', in Marius's phrase. There are many kinds of literary imperialism. Its highest pretensions have been patterned on the support given by literature to the ancient empires, and these pretensions are part of what we mean when we talk about the Classical tradition, and about a classic, and about a civilization. They are part, too, of what it has meant to condemn Mark Twain. He could not be thought a classic—either of the

English literature which served the British Empire, or in relation to Eliot's great tradition of Roman and Roman Catholic civility. There is no line which runs from Virgil to Virginia City. Marius, who shared a birthplace with Eliot, also shared in his traditions and superstitions. St. Louis, and Mantua, made them both. But he was hostile and resentful only, and only at times, on Athenian and on animal matters, or late at night, in drink, when a bitter shrillness would rage out, a second self never otherwise apparent. His notional preference for England over America was only apparently imperialistic, while the American pride which it was sometimes to obscure was not of the kind that wishes to invade. He made you feel that there could be some merit in being a patriot, though you weren't always sure which country he was in favour of.

A culture is, among other things, the voices you hear, and hold in your head, and the stories you hear. I shall hear his voice till the end of my life. There was something heavenly about him, and while I doubt whether he hoped to go to heaven, I do not find it very hard to think of him there: a heaven with Gothic murals by his friend Garry Mackenzie, where God has relaxed his ruling against cats and granted them souls. I shall hear him, Marius the Athenian, tell a Wellesley feminist, 'I have always thought that I was something of a suffragette myself,' and tell me in my Buick with a smile: 'I have always thought that Leavis was something of an Athenian at heart.'

XX. TWINS

During 1980 and 1981 there were reports in the British papers concerning identical twins, Freda and Greta Chaplin, who had been had up at York for making a nuisance of themselves, and who seemed like creatures in a fairy-tale. Infatuation with a lorry-driver had turned to hostility, and Hansel and Gretel had been hitting him with their handbags. These siblings were sent to jail for a month: the defence found them inexplicable, and the magistrate found that 'there is no other way of dealing with you.' In and out of court, they were given to speaking in unison: 'We won't go, we won't be separated.'

This story was much displayed in the press, which dearly loves a twin, and it can't have escaped the eye of Bruce Chatwin, an expert on strange places and strange people, and on strange words, who has published three notable books. *In Patagonia* told of a trip to Latin America's Ultima Thule. *The Viceroy of Ouidah* was no less exotic—a work of the imagination which was based on, and which supplanted, historical research on Dahomey in the era of the slave trade. His third theme is encoded in his surname. Chatwin's twins in *On the Black Hill*, which came out in 1982, are hill farmers from the wild Welsh Marches, Lewis and Benjamin Jones. They are identical, monozygotic, and are capable of telepathic communion. They won't be separated: Benjamin feels 'inseparable—even in death'.[1] They are victims. Unlike Freda and Greta, however, they are not hostile. They are a no less heavenly pair than Castor and Pollux, duly mentioned in the text, and a familiar pathos helps to make them so.

There is a knowledge of twins which purports to be scientific but which does not seem quite secure, and which may at times seem on fire to prove that two can be one. The *Sunday Times* has carried accounts of research which describes what happens to twins who are reared apart from and in ignorance of each other: such people have been discovered to call their children by the same names, to have the same tastes and talents, to be linked in ways that elude the long arm of coincidence (which can be held to have conferred the name Chatwin on the author of this book). Then again there is a literature and fairy-tale of twins, and it is to this category that *On the Black Hill* belongs. In this category, too, we meet with an outlandish mutuality. The Chatwinshire we read about in the novel is apt to look apocryphal, like some Kamchatka—Russia's Patagonia, which figured, during the Romantic period, in the inventory of the remote, as part of the fairyland of the traveller's tale. This exoticism is no accident, no coincidence. This is the strangeness of the traveller's tale and of the fairy-tale, and of a mode of writing to which Mr Chatwin has always been drawn. In Patagonia, in and around pre-Falklands Comodoro Rivadavia, he lit on the wonders that travellers come home with and are charged with making up—the traveller in question being a self-effacing romantic singleton. Now we have the wonders of the near-at-hand, located in and around the Black Mountains of Radnor.

Mr Chatwin's strange new place accommodates the lore of twinship in the manner of a romantic work which is also, in some degree, a religious one. An established theme is thereby embellished. With this novel, that of a gifted writer with access to an admiring public, the long career of romantic duality proceeds into the future. The joint life of Lewis and Benjamin Jones can call to mind a certain 'double singleness' of long before—that of Charles Lamb and his sister Mary.[2] These too are apt names, and they enable us to say here that nearly two hundred years later, but in much the same cruel world, Lewis is Benjamin's little lamb. Benjamin must look after his more practical but more vulnerable brother, and stop him from getting hurt, and from sleeping with anyone. The halves of this harmless pair are alike rather than different. Such differences as they do exhibit (Benjamin is effeminate and has a connubial feeling for his brother) do not call to mind the antagonism which has been ascribed to the traditional double—and to the type of folkloric twin to which the traditional double can be thought to correspond.

Locked in a seclusion which they share with their well-born, kind mother and oafish father, the two simple-minded farmers are at the mercy of the Britain of modern times. They retire from it, and seldom venture beyond the confines of their farm, 'The Vision', named after a supernatural visitation of the distant past. A neighbouring farm is named 'The Rock'; and the landscape has its holy innocents, ragged saints, Franciscan animal-lovers. One of these is Meg, and another her friend Theo. Such names, such circumstances, are no coincidence, and may make this a Christian romance—the *exemplum* without the sermon, so to speak. The Joneses have the interest—and no other—of the significance which can be read into their reclusiveness, and that significance may be as much religious as romantic. Had there been a sermon, it might have pointed to the Christianity of Romanticism. Romantic duality, dualistic twinship—whether of doubles or of twins—takes its meaning from a concern with isolation. To be two is to be apart from the world, or to leave. The Joneses 'steal' away from the world in all directions, and the book reaches a blissful climax in flight. Lewis has a passion for the air (and for crashes), and the brothers' eightieth birthday is celebrated with a spin in a plane. The poor old souls are whirled into the sky and look down in wonder at 'The Vision'.

'You might have some difficulty with the words.' Strange places deserve strange words, and Bruce Chatwin is keen on these. Here a minister is warning the hippy Theo that he may have trouble when he reads in Chapel from the Book of Revelation—where there are words like 'chrysoprase', 'chalcedony'. Theo replies, 'I know the stones of New Jerusalem,' and reads word-perfect and superbly.[3] Mr Chatwin seems to count on his readers to be Theos. Difficult words may be bricks to build a New Jerusalem, and are certainly exit visas from the here and now of modern Britain.

The Chatwin lexicon is large, and Dahomey enlarged it—a country whose fruit bats and 'vague smell of guavas and stale urine' are among its more mundane features: 'Their skin cracked in the harmattan; then the rains came and tambourined on their caladiums and splashed dados of red mud up the walls of their houses.' *The Viceroy of Ouidah* abounds in banquets, which incorporate word feasts:

> Pigs' heads were anointed with gumbos and ginger. Black beans were frosted with cassava flour. Silver fish glittered in a sauce of malaguetta pepper. There was a ragout of guinea-fowl and seri-flowers, which were reputed to have aphrodisiac properties. There

were mounds of fried cockscombs, salads of carrot and papaya, and pastes of shrimp, cashew nuts and coco-flesh.

The names of Brazilian dishes were on everyone's lips: *xinxin de galinha, vatapa, sarapatel, muqueca, molocoto.* There were phallic sweetmeats of tamarind and tapioca, ambrosias, bolos, babas and piles of golden patisseries.[4]

This is the jewelled prose of the upper-class English traveller, carried to the threshold of burlesque—and maybe across it, to produce a variety of Camp and a latter-day Wildean largesse.

On the Black Hill has its feasts too: 'There were rolls of spiced beef, a cold roast turkey, polonies, brawns, pork pies and three Wye salmon, each one resting on its bed of lettuce hearts, with a glissando of cucumber slices running down its side.' Humble fare is enchanted here, so far as Welsh larders will allow. On every page, moreover, old or odd words appear: 'blennies', 'whinchat', 'costrel', 'domett'. Some of them are enough to strain the dictionary. Perhaps 'heliotrope' is a rare word now: in this context, it looks like the living vernacular. Cornucopias of fruit and vegetables disgorge within a general herbaceousness. An ancient lady 'yanked at some convolvulus that threatened to smother the phlox'. Indoors, 'potted pelargoniums shed their yellowing leaves over the piles of pamphlets and *Country Lifes*. A budgie clawed at the bars of its cage; demijohns of home-made wine were busy fermenting under the console, while, dotted here and there over the carpet, were the urine stains of generations of incontinent pugs.'[5]

In keeping with the prevailing purple of its verbal and vegetable life, the weather in the novel is weird and obtrusive. It is as if human heads were in the clouds. Bits of sky detach themselves: 'patches of blue flew low over their heads.' A little earlier: 'The wind was whipping the surface of the pond. Meg was indoors, up to her elbows in a bucket of dogfeed.' Deaths, murders, squalors, and derelictions are the order of the day, and Meg turns into a tramp and a tree-stump in the style of the Irish saint whose piety and frenzy drove him to roost in a thorn bush. But this is by no means the worst, and may be the best, of the human world which is disclosed. This world is contemptible. Lewis is subjected to the tortures and persecutions which were practised by soldiers and patriots on malingerers and the simple during the Great War: its flags and feasts and hysteria are condemned. The landed gentry gets the worst of the Chatwin words; a one-legged privileged survivor of the war is shown to be lustful and weak. It all adds up to the poor look-out portrayed by romanticism: here is a world from which it is right to retire.

There is an absurdity which can't be coincidental, but which can't be altogether intentional, in this hectic vision of Chatwin-shire or Kamchatka, and at least a trace of Cold Comfort Farm: 'them do say as she's a witch.' And of Flann O'Brien. Convolvulus continually threatens to smother the phlox. Simpletons, saints, and grotesques face a ubiquitous aggression and duplicity—and it is a welcome stroke when the worthless nephew to whom the brothers plan to bequeath their farm is revealed as less odious than the others who are battering at the gate. There are several funny scenes when hippies arrive, to prove for the most part crooks—together with a few middle-class cheats. Among these strangers is a vile antique-dealer who rooks the Joneses of their bric-à-brac, and an arty, leggy, lipsticked urban sophisticate, who brings to unlikely fulfilment what has been anxiously awaited throughout and relieves Lewis of his virginity, beneath an ancient pine. 'Very romantic!' she tells her husband. 'Rather damp!' For this relief neither Chatwin nor the twin is at all thankful to the urban sophisticate, who can't be said to have caused Lewis to suffer, though it must indeed have been uncomfortable, and who could even be said to have been taking a kind of interest: she drops from the narrative like a stone which is neither chrysoprase nor chalcedony, or like a witch. Them do say as she came from Lunnon, and she and her husband had 'kicked around the Mediterranean', drinking gin. The country is better than the town, the novel seems to convey: but the country is terrible. Where, if not in heaven, are we to live? This is a more accomplished and decorative book than it is an interesting one. It is a *tour de force* of doorstep exoticism which, so far as it can be accounted Meg-magical or Theo-centric, fails. It appears, however, to have been well received by sophisticated readers—by a readership which has lost its faith in God, but which has not lost its faith in literature, which is experiencing a world in many ways worse than it has been for a long time, and which has remained attentive to romantic religion, to anti-social romance, and to the charms of duality.

Strange to relate, a similar novel was published, by the same publisher, Cape, twenty years earlier. In some respects, Patrick White's *The Solid Mandala*, of 1966, can be considered an *alter idem*.[6] This, too, is a novel about twins who curl up together in a cruel world. Here, too, innocents meet, orphan and double meet. The resemblances between the two works might suggest that the river of duality has not been flowing fast. There are occasions now when the relevant accords and replications can look like the ripples on a still water: but it is fair to add that there are occasions, too, when this stillness can appear to form part of a great calm which has prevailed since Diderot. In White's novel, a limited duality gives a basis for the evocation, not so much of some internal division, as of a marriage of males. This does not separate it from *On the Black Hill*. Both works reveal a double singleness which is used to commend a variety—a visionary variety—of religious experience; each surrounds its simpletons with an exotic language.

In *The Solid Mandala* one nuzzling hermaphroditic twin succeeds the other as the focus for a narrative of the same events. Arthur and Waldo Brown live out their peculiar lives down a lonely road beyond White's imaginary Sydney suburb of Sarsaparilla. Beyond the house stretches an immediate hinterland of lost, inchoate countryside and an interior of sheep stations which it would take, you feel, thinking of White's adventurous nineteenth-century hero, a Voss to penetrate. Arthur is simple, a monster in the eyes of the monstrous Australian populace which figures in the book: 'people', in this book, are great ones for laughing at you, and worse. But Arthur is also an oracle, and inspiringly kind to certain of his neighbours. Respectable Waldo is sustained by Arthur, whom he thinks of himself as sustaining, and whom he sometimes hates and envies, irked by his foolish chocolate eyes. They are opposites, but they are also, in their seclusion, the same. Their symbiosis is more of a marriage than a relationship of siblings. They are Darby and Joan, with the lid off. Their parents are from 'Home'—from Britain: a limping dad and a mother of grand stock. The grand mother, who may perhaps be accounted an oedipal feature, is a feature of both of these novels.

The Solid Mandala movingly describes the shifts and succours of this pair, the snail's pace of their lives, which are nevertheless very quickly over. In a sense, these are the persons in any society who scarcely ever stir outside the house, who are indeed affronted, if not contemptuous, when asked to do so; these are the captive wives, the keepers of secrets, of pets and elderly parents, the sharp critics of their unshunnable partners. You don't need to be a freak or a cissy to be like this, let alone a rather extravagant 'narcissyist' like Waldo. White's use of freaks recalls the Gothic novels of the American South, where sensitive individuals make what they can of some brutal White Protestant environment. It is as if only the afflicted and their friends can be borne. White is at pains to show his suburbs in a horrible light: the very place-names are grotesque. 'Mrs Poulter was one of the 57 things and persons Waldo hated'—White himself would score a lot higher. Arthur is Christ-like, but he saves only a precious few, and it is possible to resent the way the novel treats the remainder, the rejected, the multitude. The rumbling of a belly is a thunderous token of mediocrity. False teeth are damnable. Pretensions to gentility conceal a devouring rapacity. Waldo's failure to communicate has its counterpart in the failure to see in people's faces more than the cartoon features of a reprobate coarseness.

The Australian words—which report, for instance, the 'chattering of sods in the coral tree'—could appear exotic, rather than demotic, to the foreign reader conscious of an overworked exoticism elsewhere in the text. The strange words are a description of Australia: but, as in the Chatwin, they may also be a distancing agent, a means of getting away from the place. And the novel may be served by a pun which opens on the esoteric. If Arthur is missing some of his marbles—in the redneck, Sarsaparilla sense of the word—then he makes up for it by hoarding real marbles. The Solid Mandala is a glass marble with a knot inside it which acquires mystic properties by association with a symbol from the Yeatsian arcane, the Mandala, which means 'totality' and may be meant as a figure for this human involute, for the twins' togetherness.

This is a novel about solitaries which may also be a solitary's novel; the phobias which provide its subject-matter may also be its point. Arthur's incoherence dominates the book, but Waldo's enters in, though he is not approved of by the writer. Waldo is a writer too, who toils and tinkers with his lifelong drafts, one, perhaps, who could be expected to speak of totality. He burns his drafts eventually: but you might say that the novel is his monument. The novel punishes people, submits them to caricature, and in so doing submits in part to Waldo's fastidiousness, chilling disapprovals, and literary pretensions, whereby the novelist could well be punishing himself. But it has the power of a truthful and suffering account of the marriage of Waldo and Arthur. This account enables the reader to believe, from time to time, in the abominations of the Australia which surrounds the brothers as they cuddle up in bed.

In 1978, four years before Bruce Chatwin's twins book, a twins book by Martin Amis appeared. *Success* is an orphan delirium, and the first of three fictions, of a series of turmoils, in which orphan and double meet. Terry is 'well aware of the full corniness of my status (orphan of underprivilege, changeling of panic and disgust)'. In corny traditional fashion, he is at once a 'singular' fellow—at the start, singularly outcast and uncouth—and a plural, Siamesed to a dandy foster-brother, Gregory, whose contributions to the narrative are like those of some student of Nabokov's *Lolita*. Both dote on, and unite to destroy, Gregory's sister, whose suicide attempts evoke from the brothers patterns of response which help us to identify differences within what we quite often take to be a symbiosis. A sister of Terry's had also been destroyed, at an earlier time: their respective family backgrounds are otherwise very different, and can even seem to be employed in order to explain the differences between two different people. Nevertheless, it survives, the sense of a single life. Both youths steal. Both are lookers-up at the London sky—Martin Amis's skyscapes, interesting and beautiful, are among the common features of this series of fictions. Both keep falling down, towards the status of the tramps who roam the streets. The novel is a malicious comedy of orphan malice and adolescent trauma. These heartless sufferers are for the most part rivals, and their competing diaries focus, again in traditional style, on the capture and simulation of success—success with girls, and in the working world. For all his poor start, Terry is the likelier lad: he manages to grow up and leave home, while Gregory goes drooping back. The world of madness has never been far away. 'There's a lot of it about' in Gregory's family. 'My stuff', alleges Terry, 'all comes from without.'[7]

Martin Amis is the latest of Anglo-America's dualistic artists. He is a copiously expressive and inventive user of words, and the re-user of a standard language. 'Confession', 'consideration', 'queer', 'flying' fly past in *Other People*, published in 1981, which visits a small plagiarism on Bellow's *Victim* in affirming a concern with 'the lost, the ruined, the broken, the effaced'. The names of the characters are equally allusive: Mary Lamb is also Amy Hide, and is attended by an ambiguous Prince. The novel opens with Mary's awakening to a strange world. She has forgotten who she is, and her ensuing experiences are themselves dream-like. She explores her environment—at times, in the wide-eyed, 'alien' manner of the 'Martian' poets of recent years—and we eventually gather that before her awakening 'she had got bored, met the man, gone bad; she had been cruel to her mother and father, and to many others; the man had nearly killed her . . .'. 'Lost time' is of the essence; psychic duplication is engineered by this amnesia. Mary gazes into her mirror, thinking of that other, that contrary Mary, alias Amy Hide, her precursor: 'Perhaps every girl was really two girls . . . As she turned away from the mirror she saw the ghost of a smile from the knowing genius that lived behind the glass. The image flickered: there was chaos in there somewhere.' The bad girl of the past is now good, but is pursued by the policeman, or social worker, Prince, who may be her protector, but who can also wear the face of her old abductor, the very man with whom she had gone bad.[8]

This pursuit wears the face of a generic mystification and theatricality: the orphan delirium or madman's diary can always be made to appear stranger than strange. The genre includes Hermann Hesse's novel of 1927, *Steppenwolf*, which makes the most of itself in these respects. It speaks up, in a carnival spirit, and yet solemnly and self-consciously, for a bohemian artiness and for a related conception of madness; and it speaks up for multiplicity, saying that adversary duality, the twofold self, is an outmoded fiction—a thousand souls are liberated in the novel's reclaimed recluse. *Other People* defiantly conveys that every girl is really two girls; it is no celebration of insanity, and its obscurities may be considered a necessary element. But there are obfuscations somewhere in there too, which look like a way of flying the generic, the Gothic flag, and like a deference paid to Mary's discovery that 'most people were mad,' and that women 'went a little mad for five days every month', and to the authorial advice that 'the most confident men and women you know—they haven't got confidence. No one has. Everyone has fear instead. (Unless they have that third thing, which men call madness.)'[9] Mary herself, however, can be considered pleasantly sane.

The third of these novels by Martin Amis came out in 1984, swarming with street words, vogue words, and with the words of romance. *Money* is an obscene orphan delirium, that of the guttersnipe film-maker John Self, who shuttles in continuous escape between London and New York, and is ripped off by a tempter, a money-man. The movie they are making is a family romance in which Self's own orphan-oedipal predicament is mirrored. One of the most brilliant strokes in the annals of the genre is delivered when the narrator, Self, takes up with a serious-minded, not to say disapproving writer by the name of Martin Amis, who rewrites his movie, and narrowly beats him at chess. (The symbiotes play chess together in *Success*—and the same game has been attributed to the Deacon Brodie who awaited execution in the solitude of the Tolbooth jail in Edinburgh.) After his victory, 'Martin Amis' offers poor Self what comes across as an authorial apology for making him up and putting him through this turmoil.

The reader is plunged into a momentous, aerial, ethereal, lunar, pre-menstrual, manic, antic, frantic 'panting present',[10] of ups and downs, fights and flights and gutters. Here is an antinomian duality which is also an emetic, diuretic, onanistic duality. Here is a narcissist who is never done playing with himself, and not only at chess: in the light of this performance the uniqueness of William Sharp/Fiona Macleod pales. Onan is an orphan, and there are two of him. Masturbation, no less than suicide, is a dualistic proof, and both proofs are furnished in the course of Self's self-exposure.

The duality of the novel can be further characterized in terms of its way with women. Kingsley Amis—Martin Amis's father—has suggested in his time,[11] unequivocally enough, that

Women are really much nicer than men:
No wonder we like them,

but has been thought to have withdrawn the suggestion in his recent fictions. And now his son has joined this debate about the strangeness of women—attractive women in particular. The heroine of *Other People* feels that women go a little mad once a month. 'Women are more civilised,' reflects the hero of *Money*,[12] a ferocious consumer of pornography who treats them as sex objects. Father and son have seemed to punish an excessive or delirious machismo, and yet they have been charged with misogyny. Arguments break out as to whether or not these writers really like them.

'The world wavers,' the novel reports. 'People are doubling.'[13] The doubling in the novel itself is both intricate and strategic, ranging as it does from alter egos to double-takes and double-pates (there's a scalper's keen interest in hairstyles, 'rugs'). Duality drops a tear when the Selves, if that is what they are, the narrator and Martin Amis, watch the Royal Wedding of Prince Charles and Lady Di on television, and accuse each other of being moved. In New York, the disgusting Anglo-American Mid-Atlantic Self makes friends with sensitive sky-blue-blooded Martina Twain (*sic*), who points him towards a better life, subjects him to opera and evening dress, waters her plants, and serves as a sort of bridge between Self and the sobersides Martin Amis, over there in London reading and writing for all he is worth: Martina lends support, in other words, to the impression that the two males are sharers of a life. Reading is an activity in relation to which Self is something of a remedial case, and Martina has him trying his hand. After a while he finds he no longer *likes* what he wants: a version of Ovid's dualistic *deteriora sequor*—of that famous self-disapproval—which can be read as a sign of grace, and of change.

So Onan lets up and learns to read fancy books, and to write one. Onan and double meet. As usual in the literature of such conjunctions, the excluded is seen to escape, and in this work the escapes would appear to be from troubles and fiascos in which a first exclusion is repeated or remembered: we gather that John Self has a family which is anxious to exclude him (his mother is dead and his father proves false) and from which he is anxious to escape. At all events, he is a self-proclaimed 'escape artist' who can execute a 'full escape posture'. He strives upwards, with the help of aeroplanes: 'Away! I thought, as we climbed through the air with the greatest of ease.' 'Away' is Keats's word, and this may even be Keats's exclamation mark. Allusion and parody are a dimension of the book's duality. Self 'moves like a ghost' as if to pour one of his countless drinks—the stride alluded to here ('strides' means trousers in the street talk of the novel) is that of the ravishing Tarquin in *Macbeth*; and he then supposes himself in hell. Film is called a 'delirium' and people are 'paranoid': this, too, is allusive. The novel utters, as *Other People* does, a refrain of the present book, when it observes that even the most confident are afraid: and 'confidence' is another time-honoured term. Brash John Self attempts suicide. This confidence-man comes to regard confidence as a 'psychopathic state'. Nervousness is best. The novel carries and declares a range of co-ordinate fictions, including Melville's novel, and precipitates the arguments and debates of traditional duality into the panting present tense. It updates such concerns as 'possession' and puts a view of this, and of the superstitions of the past, to which many people would now assent:

> these tribes of spacefaced conquered would brood about God, Hell, the Father of Lies, the fate of the spirit, with the soul imagined as an inner being, a moistly smiling angel in a pink nightie, or a grimacing goblin, all V-signs, bad rug and handjobs. But now the invader is a graph shadow swathed in spools and print-outs, and he wears an alien face.
>
> I sometimes think I am controlled by someone. Some space invader is invading my inner space, some fucking joker. But he's not from out there. He's from in here.[14]

Parody and allusion, then, are compounded by affinity. The later Bellow is evident in the novel, as are the terrors of Mailer and Mickey Spillane. Like Bellow, Amis likes to write about change, metamorphosis, what he calls 'turnaround'. The problems raised by his novel are problems familiar to the reader of the literature of its affinities, which has witnessed a turnaround from the condition of the novel to the condition of the poem, and a new kind of subordination to the author of the other people he creates. This novel bears a relation to its author which makes it difficult for it to end. And indeed it is not altogether easy to say where it begins: some of the phobias which attack the Self sensorium—that of the disappearing penis, and of the borrowing of smelly second-hand clothes—are borrowed from the orphans in *Success*. Self is that rare bird, the dipsomaniac masturbator, and he is a man who can barely read who has written a fancy book which quotes from Keats and Shakespeare. He is a man who confesses what can appear to be less intelligible to himself than it is to that other man whose name is on the title-page—and to whom, at the time of Self's suicide attempt, there is a bewildering, or obfuscating, direct allusion, an allusion which operates quite independently of the presence in the novel of a 'Martin Amis'. We may conclude that Self is not a person but a part, a burlesqued proclivity, a preposterous Jonsonian humour, a bundle of at times incongruous—as distinct, we may feel, from dualistically inconsistent—bad habits. If he is the expression of some ulterior self-disapproval or disavowal, what are its scale and proportions? Where does it end? It is as if these bad habits are being made endlessly delightful, by an unending author. With such fictions, it is sometimes possible to sense that only the one man is on show, to doubt the authenticity of those characters who trail no shadow of a Siamese connection with the author. But this is not to doubt the authenticity of the show itself, or its appeal to *semblables*, to a paranoid orphan readership.

It is also possible to doubt whether this is a book about money. John Self coins it and blues it, but other things matter more. Nevertheless *Money* is its title, and in the autumn of 1984 a book entitled *Rich* is due to be published by the poet Craig Raine, who will be treated by some, and not for the first time, as Martin Amis's Martian Twain. Such coincidences or designs belong to a semaphore whereby these same *semblables* communicate. It signals the existence of a community of strangers. And on this occasion it signals that 'Martian' and 'alien' and 'orphan' are collusive terms. There exist a literature and an environment in which the individual who feels himself invaded, from without or from within, is perceived as an invader. Here once more are the orphan and the double.

Onan, as it happens, is an aspect of the psychic duplication exhibited in Vladimir Nabokov's novel *Despair*, which Martin

Amis greatly admires, and which is sure to have affected his own (dualistic) practices. Here once again duality occasions the self-referring text—and the work of self-reference was to be prolonged by the accidents of the novel's publishing history: it was written in Russian in 1932, translated into English by the author, then re-translated by him in 1965 for the edition which I have in mind. The narrator is a supercilious failing businessman, deceived by his wife. He is also a writer. And he discovers his double in the sorry guise of a tramp. Hermann 'steals' from the tramp in the dead of night, while enlisting him in an elaborate act of theft—an insurance fraud—which can appear to constitute the text of the novel. Presently he shoots him, according to plan, and goes on to impersonate him. The theft and the text miscarry in unison: hence Hermann's despair. Duplication is seen to be related to difference of class, and socialism to prefigure a world of clones. At the same time, the novel is stocked with material drawn from the literature of the past—with mirrors, portraits, talk of magnetism, of nerves, and of monsters. It refers, not only to itself, but to dualistic precedents which the connoisseur is expected to know. It refers to Hesse, and (superciliously) to Dostoevsky; in referring to noses, it refers to Gogol; and Hermann's last orphan ordeal, when he and his diary are pursued to a country refuge inhabited by simple folk, is symmetrical in mood and circumstance with a late stage in Hogg's novel of many years before—with the closing entries of Robert Wringhim's diary. Prominent there among the last words recorded by the suicide in his mania and misery, and dated 18 September 1712, is the word 'despair'. There is reason to think that Nabokov's novel remembers Hogg's, and this may be evidence—which is often unforthcoming in *Despair*—that its elegant author not only resembles but pities his monster.

XXI. ARE YOU DISTRAINING ME?

There can be no satisfying short description of what doubles are, or of what they have become in shedding some part of their supernatural origins, as harbingers of evil and death, and growing into an element of individual psychology and a domestic feature. But it is time to repeat that they have often been about running away, and revenge, when these pursuits are enjoined and desired and prevented, when they are left to the imagination. One self does what the other self can't. One self is meek while the other is fierce. One self stays while the other runs away. These are meanings which can be discovered as we patrol the secret passages of the literature of duality, and they can also be discovered in folklore. Doubles may appear to come from outside, as a form of possession, or from inside, as a form of projection. Doubles are both, and we see them as both when, as we sometimes do, we see them as devils or as dolls (the English language approximates these three words, though its etymology separates them). The rule of contraries, which is another name for the ambience of the double, with its constant inversions and reversals, lays down that if one self steals another may be stolen from, that the theft from a community which has been attributed to offenders in this book may also constitute a violation of the offender. Within these complications must surely lie an attempt to disclaim responsibility for events and crises which are internal to the individual but in which his environment will always seem to take part.

Very many other things, very many other orders of thing, can be said with reference to duality. This book has said that it directs, at a form of theft, a simultaneous praise and blame, that in playing with his dolls an author is playing with his doubles, and that a favourite doll has been the orphan and his opposite. The orphan author hides and seeks and soars. Duality is departure and return. It is theft and restitution. It is megalomania and magnanimity. It is weakness, illness, and illusion, and it is the advantages they confer. It is divided and diffusive, hostile and hospitable. Duality is suicide, and masturbation. It is bisexuality, and dual nationality. It courts and contemplates uncertainty, vacancy, doubt, dizziness, and arrest. It is the behaviour and capacity of an author, and it is the theory which explains him. It is the Eliot who encountered dissociation, and it is the Empson who encountered ambiguity.

From Empson's ambiguity we do not have to travel far to reach the practice of Derridean Deconstruction, with its interest in uncertainty, in the 'boundlessness' of context that can be envisaged for human discourse. Intention, reconciliation, and the determined meaning, are distrusted. What if the meaning of meaning 'is infinite implication? the unchecked referral from signifier to signifier? If its force is a certain pure and infinite equivocalness . . .'? Literature is here seen as 'protean' and 'strange', as a locus for otherness, for opposing forces and logics. Romanticism and Modernism are seen as one, and a sense of the second as a demystification of the first is itself demystified.[1] Deconstruction can be approached, as Empson can, through the heritage of romantic duality—which has taken effect once more at the level of theory. The scepticism of Derrida in France, and of adherents in Britain and America, has addressed itself to the language of literature, which is taken as a paradigm of language use, and as part of an oceanic textuality. The claim is that literature has acknowledged itself boundless and bottomless, unfathomably contradictory, and that it may be studied by means of the dualistic categories of Renaissance rhetoric, with its oxymorons and metonymies. Under Deconstruction, uncertainty is called by grammarians' names. But it is no different from an uncertainty that can be met with in nineteenth-century literature. We are free, I think, to say that the doubt and difficulty of the past are recalled in today's aporias and vertigos, that Deconstruction is an entertainment of duality. At the same time, it is clear that it is also intent on ending it—on finishing with the double and with the dominion of opposites. Derrida is an enchanter. He has been heard to talk familiarly, on television, about ghosts. But he is also their exorcist.

The nineteenth-century past is present in the explanation which has been offered in support of a feminism allied to Deconstruction: 'Male sexuality denies and resists otherness, while bisexuality is an acceptance of otherness within the self, as is writing.' And it is present in the confessional claim by a female writer to which this explanation refers: 'To man it is much more difficult to let oneself be traversed by the other; writing is the passage, entrance, exit, sojourn in me of the other that I am and am not.'[2] This last claim is eloquent, but, in relation to the romantic heritage, distinctly sectarian. Nineteenth-century duality does not depose that male sexuality, or the male imagination, is any less hospitable in this respect than its female counterpart. It can also cause us to doubt the difference between the two sexualities.

In saying as it does that strangeness steals, the romantic literature which is devoted to the concept and project of the double and several self expresses both a fear and a need of others. It serves the premise of a social instinct, and the imagination of a social reality which requires participation and survival. But it is strong, too, in its gestures of repudiation and departure. To belong to the world, to be dead to the world—'depart, yet live'—these are rival courses which impart, to this literature of human instability, many of its swerves and shifts, and many of its makeshifts, and which bear witness to the power of other people. The literature of instability has survived incorporation in the experiments of Modernism. It has indeed triumphed with the triumph of these experiments, as it has by virtue of an incorporation in the theories which have succeeded them. Dualistic works of art, moreover, continue to appear, and the new works have done little to deny or efface the old. Nabokov's *Despair* stands in conscious, knowing relation to the past, as we have seen; another work, some ten years later, reveals a different kind of dependency.

In Albert Camus's novel *The Outsider* (*L'Etranger*), published in France in 1942, the queer fellow Meursault takes up with a rudimentary double, kills on his behalf and is put on trial. Camus rather cryptically remarked that he intended the picture of someone who refuses to lie, to play society's game: 'not a waif, but a man who is poor and naked', 'the only Christ we deserved'.[3] For some of the novel's first readers, the issue seems to have been the unreality of a bourgeois ethos, and the absurdity of things in general. And we do indeed find in the book what can be called a dualistic absurdity: 'Either way one was for it,' 'To stay, or to make a move—it came to much the same,' 'there was no way out.'[4] The outsider, who is nevertheless a submissive office-worker, is followed about by other outsiders in the shape, dimly perceived, stranger than any Meursault, of Algeria's Arabs, one of whom he shoots. In colonial Algeria, no trial of a white man on such a charge would have gone the way this one does, ending with the prospect of a decapitation. This is the romantic trial which is murmured in the hero's name. What Meursault is being tried for is the offence of not having loved his mother or mourned her death; he had seldom gone to see her, in her old people's home.

The novel has in it Dostoevsky's mysteriously aligned crime and punishment, and those of Kafka, whom Camus was reading at the time. It takes the old form of a convicted murderer's confession, and fills it with an antinomian existentialism. Camus is unlikely to have read the *Confessions* of James Hogg. Yet the two works have much in common; and Camus—Spanish, Alsatian, Algerian, and French—shared with Hogg the strange compound of a socially divided identity, and something of the same relationship to a metropolis. In 1944, in 'provincial' Algiers, André Gide blessed Hogg's book, which it seemed that no Englishman or American there then knew, and went on to write an influential preface for the London Cresset Library edition. In his *Journal* Gide recorded: '*un des plus extraordinaires livres* I ever read . . . *Se peut-il qu'il n'ait pas encore été traduit? et, si traduit, qu'on ne le connaisse si peu? Je voudrais le faire lire à Roger, à Mauriac, à Breton, à Green, à quantité d'autres.*'[5]

There has never been a time, since the Romantic period, when duality has been exempt from condemnation. But in most literate cultures now a dualistic practice can be considered unimpaired, undeterred, and even routine. As in earlier times, there are human beings at large in the world—beyond the purview of a detaining psychiatry—in whose conduct the tradition speaks. I shall close this book with reflections on two autobiographies and an early death. Each of these three lives is a dualistic text, and each is that of an orphan, though two of these people, wrapped in the glamour of a brilliant abrasiveness, may have gone undetected as such. They are all of uncertain nationality, and are artists and entertainers, and there appears to me to be more to this than accident. Let us say that they are brought to the page, as exemplary, with some assistance from the magic of coincidence. The first two belong to the category of friends of the author, and the death of the third came while I was completing this book.

Poet, critic, and wit, superstar and Anglo-Australian strange case, Clive James is a living example who is still alive and kicking. The nature of the case includes precocity, and his *Unreliable Memoirs* was precociously published in 1980. While keeping you aware of what he has since become in journalism and in show business, Clive James climbs back into his shorts and re-enacts the experience of being an outsiderish boy just outside Sydney, hardly a stone's throw—and he threw a large number of stones—from Botany Bay, where the English outcasts of a previous time were disembarked. The Kid from Kogarah, the cape-whisking Flash of Lightning, and other aliases, ride again. The memoirs end when the days of his youth end—with graduation from Sydney University and a fairly prompt departure for the fresh fields of England on board a creaking ship. Its timbers were shivered by the love-making of passengers and crew, from which, as he passed into exile, Clive James was excluded.

His book is like other memoirs of modern times in assuming that while fiction may be treated as a form of autobiography, autobiography may be practised as a form of fiction. The preface calls it 'a figment got up to sound like truth'. The spirit of his early life may be here; the letter is not. The reader is left to work out for himself what processes of elision, deletion, and addition this may have inspired, and to ask whether they may be meant to still the cries, down under, of the offended. 'Nothing I have said is factual,' he concludes, 'except the bits that sound like fiction.'[6] The reader isn't always able to tell which bits are which, but he may feel that the conclusion itself sounds fictional, and there's a fiction in the preface which is easy enough to identify: 'I had an absurdly carefree upbringing.' On the contrary, the book is full of grief and fear, as well as fun, and Kogarah is no unqualified improvement on Patrick White's Sydney suburb of Sarsaparilla. Australia's insects , to a mandible, are on the hunt for Clive James. Each chapter is a chapter of accidents. 'Death, & Poverty, & Shame, & Pain'—the list is that of the philosopher Hume—are all here. And so are some other 'Calamities of Life' which Hume for one would have been unwilling to commit to print.[7]

In turning his memoirs into fiction, while explaining that he has done his best 'to tell the truth about what it was like', James has also turned them into romance. He speaks of a 'confessional urge', and he parades his 'failings'. This is his romantic clean breast. He knows that the confessional bad light in which so many autobiographers bathe themselves is suspect, and the preface refers to Santayana's opinion of Rousseau's *Confessions*: according to Santayana, he points out, Rousseau's book demonstrates, 'in equal measure, candour and ignorance of self'. But he later announces that his own character 'consists mainly of defects', and the literary provenance of his own book is, in part, Rousseauesque. Powered by the humour with which he learnt to defend his forlornness, the self-portrait is a success. At the same time, it is, in a sense, the portrait of a failure. The James who steps forward is solitary, bereaved, badly-behaved; not very far away there can nevertheless be seen an alarmed and cherishing mother.

The book belongs to a tradition in which candour can go with ignorance of self, but can also go with the cultivation of self, with the possession of more than one self, with aliases and impersonations, and with zeals and games and ploys not essentially different from those to which James has elsewhere, if I haven't misunderstood him, applied a name from the romantic heritage—*Einfühlung*, empathy, by which he meant 'the intellectual love for the objects of experience'.[8] To the extent that it entails a capacity to be engrossed, taken out of yourself in contemplation, and at one with the objects of that contemplation, this last quality, or faculty, of mind might be thought to bear some resemblance to the condition known to other romantics as negative capability. Love does seem to enter into it, but this is not the love that friends feel for one another. *Einfühlung* is a quality which can sometimes inhibit personal or social relations, and impede the self-knowledge which derives from a knowledge of other people. It is a state in which there can appear to be both an assertion and a suspension of self, and which, in purporting to escape from personality, will sometimes appear chimerical. We don't always know where we are with this empathy and openness. In James's case, the state used to be associated with an addiction to the cartoon and feature films of the Forties.

In many cases, as I've implied, it is associated with a certain innocence or indifference concerning the other people that there are in the world, with the possible exception of a passionately-favoured few, and it is true that the other people of this self-portrait are scarcely ever portrayed except swiftly and impressionistically. They are objects of experience in the sense that they are rarely there for what they are in themselves. They are collected, rather as his cartoon films were collected, and indeed they tend to be presented in the manner of a cartoon. The collector's confessional self and sensorium are what chiefly matter. This is not to deny that the animation of James's acquaintance makes a great show, that his other people are shrewdly and vividly described, and that he can also be shrewd, and genuinely forthcoming, about his own distressed and defective character. He is not yet, he writes at the age of 40, 'sufficiently at peace with himself'.

Tersely but unequivocally, the book conveys that his character was formed by bereavement. His main bereavement was the loss of his father, who was captured by the Japanese during the war, and killed in an air crash while being repatriated. The book takes as an epigraph the grieving of Andromache in the *Iliad*: 'Husband, you are gone so young from life, and leave me in your home a widow. Our child is still but a little fellow, child of ill-fated parents, you and me. How can he grow up to manhood?' And Clive James writes: 'I have never ceased to feel orphaned.' This rings both true and traditional. And what he goes on to say is traditional too: 'nor have I ever felt less than lucky.'[9] The romantic orphan has often had to face the consequences of his pride and cheek, chutzpah and hubris: but he has also been entitled to a touch of magic, to lucky breaks and a charmed life. Eager and ambitious from the first, unfazed by his disasters, Clive has done at least as well as Cinderella. Those tunnels he used to dig in the back-garden are very much in character—at once an escape, a fiasco, and a famous feat.

A second loss which he sustained may have represented an imagination of the first: he speaks of 'the kind of brother I would have liked to have, and I suppose miss even now'. His mother's life was gravely wounded by her husband's death, and it drew the two survivors together. She is characterized in terms of her proximity to the author, while becoming, on such terms, a leading presence in the book: boastfully pleased with her bright, impressionable, exhibitionist boy, delicately skilled at coping with the troubles that befell him. When he proposed to run away, the threat was dealt with by the preparation of peanut-butter sandwiches and pyjamas. It's no joke being an orphan's mother. And it's no joke being a joker's mother.

Ernest Mossner's life of David Hume relates that the young philosopher was said to have been in a drawing-room when a dreadful smell broke out, and was blamed on the dog. But then Hume was heard to say: 'Oh do not hurt the Beast. It is not Pod, it is Me!'[10] The story places the owner-up, the truth-teller, in a good light. It reports the kind of accident which might have figured in a chapter by James, whose bad smells are firmly placed in the light which so often shines in autobiography, and which is both bad and good. Most of the cares commemorated in his chapters are more or less shameful. Throughout Clive James's 'It is Me!' there are worries about his private parts, which are awarded a momentous publicity: the shocks to which they were heir are enough to suggest a further precedent for the book in *Tristram Shandy*. It was inevitable that his parts should eventually encounter the barbed-wire fence of the rude song, and this duly happens, at a youth camp in the bush. Other calamities approximate quite closely to the David Hume disgrace, which is very much the kind of thing which most people, and most traditions, have kept secret:

> Next day when I answered my name at the morning assembly roll-call, the headmistress said, 'Ah yes, that's the little boy who ran away from his mother.' Thanks a lot, witch. I kacked my pants on the spot.

One secret deserves another. The next paragraph proceeds:

> The whole secret of kacking your pants, incidentally, is to produce a rock-solid blob which will slide down your leg in one piece and can be rolled away into hiding at the point of the toe. That way, your moment of shame can be kept to the proportions of a strictly local disaster. But if you let go with anything soft, it takes two teachers to clean you up and the whole affair attracts nation-wide publicity. You get people interviewing you.[11]

The Jamesian art of excretion is offered to a readership which is bound to have something of its own to bring to the subject, while perhaps needing a bit of instruction. But the passage is not so much instruction as expression: these words are a way of communicating the enormity of the occasion, the dimensions of an ordeal.

Clive James lost very little time in getting his act together, in developing into the type of 'all-round entertainer' who would one day be eligible, and available, for interview. The boy who kacked his pants went on to become an accomplished petomane—not so much an owner-up as a virtuoso. Here, too, he has a secret to impart: 'The whole secret of raising a laugh with a fart in class is to make it sound as if it is punctuating, or commenting upon, what the teacher is saying.' It seems that as soon as he could stand he began to seek immunity by being funny, that he caused laughter in order to avoid being laughed at. Such self-defence is a sizeable part of what the book chooses to commemorate: but then the book itself is, without intermission, humorous and entertaining, an extension of his act. We hardly need to be told that his early fears and uncertainties are still with him. Show business proved hard work at times, and brought its own calamities and consequences:

> I cultivated a knack of exaggeration. Lying outrageously, I inflated rumour and hearsay into saga and legend. The price of fame was small but decisive. I had to incur the accusation of being a bull-artist—a charge that any Australian male of any age wants to avoid. But I wanted notoriety more. Rapidly I acquired it. From a small circle of listeners in class, I progressed to a large circle of listeners in the playground. Bigger boys came to mock and stayed to listen. Adapted from a recently seen film, my story of the Okinawa kamikazes lasted an entire lunchtime and drew an audience which, if it had not come equipped with its own sandwiches, would have had to be fed with loaves and fishes.

He goes on: 'Gradually even the most scornful among my listeners came to accept that what Jamesie said wasn't *meant* to be true—only entertaining. If it wasn't that, key figures drifted away, and soon everyone else was gone along with them, leaving me alone with my uneaten sandwiches.'[12]

He pictures himself, convincingly, as a boy who caused a good deal of pain but who shrank from consciously inflicting it. It is difficult, though, to be the kind of wit who specializes in satirical invective, like the later James, without causing, as well as feeling, pain. A dilemma opens up here which he does not confess but which can be inferred from his confession. You might say that the whole secret of human life is in this dilemma—one orphan biting another, like something out of Dante.

The book is full of bravuras and exaggerations, and, as it admits, lies of a sort. When the infant satirist is nearly drowned at the bottom of the garden, where his tunnels were to be located, we get the following legend or saga:

> Aunt Dot was attired in a pink corset but it didn't slow her down. She covered the ground like Marjorie Jackson, the girl who later became famous as the Lithgow Flash. The earth shook. I was going down for the third time but I can distinctly remember the moment she launched herself into the air, describing a parabolic trajectory which involved, at one point, a total eclipse of the sun. She landed in the trench beside me. Suddenly we were sitting together in the mud. All the water was outside on the lawn.[13]

This is no lie, but a manner of speaking, and of entertaining. It is a manner which extends widely into his critical writings, where I have no doubt that some of the mirthless bigger boys among his readers may disapprove of it as one in which it is impossible to tell the truth. James holds that humour can make sense, and that those without humour can't be trusted. His own critical writings make sense of the first half of that claim: their adversary humour is stronger than their lavish praise, and collaborates with his best arguments. At the same time, they have their element of risk, as his performances have always had, even the least frantic of these, and it can be said without severity (or humour) that the exhibitions and exaggerations of his criticism, like the 'unreliability' of his memoirs, are both a pleasure and a problem.

The suffering delinquent, the joker's wretched or hostile eye, smiling through his tears and staring through his smiles—these have long been features of a conventional wisdom in respect of the doubtful and dual orphan state. The convention persists, and the tough egg who has written this romantic book has seized on it. The Clive James Show is shown to have its roots in loneliness and desperation; a zest for the objects of experience serves to express a certain estrangement from the people around him. The book embodies an impulse to confess and an impulse to aspire, and it suggests an elaborate experience of exile. It is written from the standpoint of exile from Australia, in order to declare a longing for the country which he'd once dreamed of leaving, and which he now calls—it is his last word—'home'. Meanwhile this longing has to be seen as inseparable from the longing for a country of the past, and of the mind, and for his own irrecoverable, and at the time highly insecure, childhood.

Few British readers who are old enough to do so can have failed to recognize in this account of the Australia in which he grew up—for all its exotica, strange predators, surfs, heats, and Hollywood veneer—the same suburban semi-countryside, the same quarries and scrub, the same sprouting bungalows, as they remember from the outskirts of, say, Wolverhampton. For many people, in their early days at opposite ends of the British Empire, the late Thirties were a half-built house. They were a peer at the churning guts of a cement-mixer, a perching in rafters. a crouching in foundations, as in some chamber or passageway of the Great Pyramid. James's cigarettes, cigarette cards, cartoons, records, back-numbers of *Flight*, and tinkering with machines, were all experienced by growers-up in Britain too. His way with such objects is among the attractions of a book which is, as it had to be, both attractive and abrasive. Not all of the objects were lethal.

The second of the three people I have in mind is the jazz musician Sandy Brown, who died in 1975. I was a friend of his for many years, but I never learned that he was part Hindu, or that there were two of him, in the persons of Sandy Brown and Alastair Babb, until I read an autobiography written in hospital towards the end of his life, and published posthumously in a collection of writings entitled *The McJazz Manuscripts*. Here, too, is a set of unreliable memoirs. Sandy saw himself, with justice, as preoccupied with 'derision'; and in the course of a parody deriding some psychoanalyst, he once produced a version of the 'Cretan liar' paradox, a paradox which appeals to specialists in duality, saying that 'almost nothing I say or write is true.'[14] But there is much that I can vouch for in the memoirs. Was his multiplicity true?

We both went to the Royal High School of Edinburgh, with Sandy slightly older and already a notorious Mephistophelean playground presence before I got to the Temple of Theseus. Built in the 1820s as a further monument lavished on the city's

Classical New Town, the school was a copy of the Athenian edifice of that name, and is now, very sadly, a school no longer, but a government property. Its glooms, colonnades, and fine proportions were not unwelcoming: an impressive building, but pre-Victorian in the sense that it was scaled to accommodate human behaviour rather than overwhelm or sneer at it. Ankle-breaking steep staircases—no warm welcome, I admit—seemed, in taking you down to the school's nether regions, to descend into the nineteenth century. In the classrooms were roaring fires, large enough for suttee or the stake. I remember the hearth of Room Three, with one boy inadvertently toasting a standing penis which had slipped out of his shorts in the heat of the moment—as if to poke the past, or to salute the embers and old flames of the Athens of the North.

The boys wore black jackets and caps which displayed the school badge, a white castle, with a motto on a scroll: *Musis respublica floret.* A civic place, with a trust in the muses, the High School has now been subjected to a civic betrayal. But Sandy would have nothing to do with these sables and insignia. He wore what I remember as a yellow bow-tie, and what he remembered as a brown velvet bow-tie: whatever it was, it hung out, and fell about, in a very mocking way. He was bald, and bold, and bad. And he was a jazz musician. At the Royal High, 'musical' was a word which described those who belonged to the choir and orchestra, which performed to applause in spotless white on the platforms of concert halls, and were drilled and fretted over by a red-haired elderly Englishman (the name, Mellalieu, was euphony itself, and comprised, he said, all the vowels used in vocal music). In that world, Sandy was an outcast and an outlaw—as he had already recognized himself to be in the world of Willowbrae Avenue, where he lived with his mother. Sandy was late for school, comical, hostile, friendly, formidable. I was a swot, less late for school, and we could not be pally. But I was keenly conscious of him, and perhaps I was to be conscious that it was Sandy, rather than the swots and concert artistes, who was in touch with the muses. And in the playground there were others like him in that respect—such boys as Al Fairweather and Stan Greig. The Royal High helped to make the British jazz of the Forties and Fifties the most flourishing in Europe. And yet at the school itself jazz was an extra-curricular activity rated low and dirty by the authorities. Education is a wonderful thing.

For a number of years after we left school we met only once or twice, in the thick of jazz-band balls, where he had come to blow his clarinet. Then, in London, we became pals. I edited the *Listener* for a time, and he used to write for it about jazz, leading, meanwhile, two lives—that of a musician and that of an acoustician-architect. In the second capacity he worked as a BBC employee, before quitting to start his own firm, and as a BBC employee he must by some have been found awkward and intransigent. His jazz pieces, which form part of the posthumous collection of his writings, would tax the Corporation with a failure to take jazz seriously, and with a policy which imposed the destruction of important tapes. These pieces came full of character, and of knots and congestions. They bore the stamp of the talent and wit that never deserted him, and of an excellent pride. It was very like him to answer as he did when asked in a BBC Television interview whether he'd prefer to be an eminent acoustician or the world's best jazz clarinettist: 'Excuse my arrogance but do you really believe that I'm *not* the latter?'[15] His pieces were the pieces of the man who made that reply.

The combativeness of his articles may possibly have been affected by the resentments of a jazz musician whose standing, and hearing, had been attacked by the explosive arrival, in the Sixties, of pop music and the groups—of all that jazz which was not his jazz. Ironically, he was to design its auditoria, and the acoustician in him counted the decibels of the new sounds, and the cost in eardrums. But I'm sure he never doubted that his own music had kept its virtue. There were times when an evening of that music among his friends was like a gathering of brave spirits, a blessed remnant, surrounded by their fit audience though few. But they had gathered to play and listen, not to complain and commiserate.

In the year of Sandy's death I published a book, *Cockburn's Millennium*. Cockburn, lawyer and autobiographer, author of the *Memorials of his Time*, was an Edinburgh man, and a High School man, and in writing about him I became interested in my present theme. It was no secret to me, though I had always felt a little sceptical on the matter, that Scotsmen were thought to have been more than usually exercised by the theme of double identity, and to have been responsible for some of the most memorable treatments of it, from Hogg's *Confessions* to R.D. Laing's *The Divided Self* of 1960. I didn't want it to be thought that Cockburn was a split personality or a subscriber to the Gothic account of human nature: but he was a rebel, or half-rebel, who could employ and at times invite the vocabulary of duality, so that I felt it might be worth trying to say a little, in the book, about the mutinous mutability of Scotsmen. Common sense knows for a fact that doubles are a dream—as if dreams and fictions could never be expressive or instructive. While I was writing the book, I used to wonder what it could mean to feel divided, and to claim the sanction of the literature of duality. At that same time the politician John Stonehouse could be heard to claim that in his own case an established personality had been supplanted by another, and that in order to lead a new life he had pretended he had died. But then many might be suspicious of that claim. I had known what it was to experience contradictory desires, but the self I was conscious of—for all that I could be conscious of it—had always seemed the same. I had always felt myself sole and undivided—*e pluribus unum*, like the United States of America. It was at this point that Sandy's memoir, 'Straightening Jazzers Out', arrived to enlighten me. Here was someone who was both a real and an imaginary orphan. Here was a recent double life confessed in terms of autobiography rather than fiction. Here, one might hope, were contemporary duality's very words.

Confessions, fantasies and affectations of duality are largely restricted to the literature of the subject. But the literature of the subject may be reckoned to have brought a disposition to feel split, to affect to feel split, and to behave in Gothic ways. It may well have encouraged Mr Stonehouse to inform the House of Commons in 1975 that a 'parallel personality took over, separate and apart from the original man'. And it may equally well have encouraged the psychiatrist referred to in that statement to instruct Stonehouse to use this language, to speak of his 'psychiatric suicide'. The advent of this parallel personality, we were to think, caused Stonehouse to simulate a drowning in Miami, and to disappear. While writing my Cockburn book, I came across a manuscript letter of his in which there's a discussion of an Edinburgh youth who, oppressed by the feats expected of him at the school Cockburn helped to found, Edinburgh Academy, feigned a drowning in the Danube, and disappeared. Seized by 'a sudden Germanising of the noddle', supposed Cockburn.[16] Was Stonehouse's noddle Germanized? Whether or not he was ever impressed by a reading of Hoffmann, Hogg, and Stevenson, it is hard to suppose him unaffected by the impact of the Gothic tradition, by the correspondence between its doctrine of duality and other less extravagant conceptions of the strain under which people live—specifically, in his own case, the strain of public and political life—and by the survival of that doctrine in the doctrines of some of our current psychologies. And I believe the same could be said of Sandy Brown, alias Alastair Babb.

Stonehouse's 'Confessions', entitled *Death of an Idealist*, came out in the same year as *Cockburn's Millennium*, 1975. His book is by no means forthcoming about a breakdown which common sense might propose was an alibi which assisted him to face the criminal charges which imprisoned him. Common sense might be wrong. But it may well be that neither his readers nor Stonehouse himself will ever be in a position to form a reliable judgment on the matter. *Death of an Idealist* does not allow one to guess how far he has controlled, and how far he has been controlled by, his impersonations and performances. It is very much a politician's book, as we can see when, during his troubles, Stonehouse feels the truth of the saying: 'I can deal with my enemies but heaven save me from my friends.' Cockburn once wrote: 'Enemies are easily managed, but wrong-headed friends are the very devil.'[17] Cockburn's statement is linked, in my book, to a quarrel between himself and his kin, but it is also the kind of thing that politicians say, and think. At the same time, the statement is like a précis of those Gothic tales where such friends are a way of talking about someone's capacity to prove his own worst enemy, in the days when heaven and hell were thought to care about plights of that sort. Cockburn has accidentally described what happens in Hogg's *Confessions*.

Sandy Brown needn't have read the nineteenth-century fictions of duality, if he did, in order to have been aware of the view that double lives were especially Scottish. He was once friendly, in a sceptical sort of way, with the Scotsman whose book *The Divided Self* is that of an expert in clinical duality, and who has since become known, and in certain quarters suspect, for his favourable view of madness, for his polemical concern with the self-protective powers which it has been felt to bring to bear in relation to family life. A mad synopsis of Sandy's, for his memoir, contains a Chapter Three which reads: 'Ronnie Laing, a famous mind doctor, diagnoses a problem and tries to kill me in order to save Brown. I point out his mistake and survive, but am suddenly taken drunk and assaulted by a loved one.'[18] How far Sandy's autobiography derives from an influential literature, how far it copies the fictions which it may be thought to corroborate, is unclear. How far it derives from, while also deriding, the popular duality promoted by these fictions is equally unclear. It is likely that it owes something to Laing, who owes something to Scotland, and to its literature. But this does not mean that we would do well to look in *The Divided Self*, which makes use of diagrams, for any diagram of Sandy's personality.

In *The Divided Self* Laing speaks of a true self and a false.[19] In the healthy human being—the beneficiary of a state of ontological security established early in life—there is no false self. But a true self may abdicate—delegate to a false self transactions with the outside world, and with the life of the body. In so doing, it becomes dead or gone, or may suffer splits of its own. It seems that the onus of coping with attackers and spies has been transferred to the false self, but that the false self denies the world it deals with—denies it in fantasies of omnipotence. Anything is possible. As a result, the false self is as vacant as the self that has invented it. In relation to others, the false self steals, and fears to be stolen from. The book explores strategies which are prefigured in Romanticism, and which cause the Pelican publisher to explain that this is a book about 'the outsider, estranged from himself and society'. We read about Peter, who took journeys and believed himself to be sent from God, and who enacted the fantasy 'of being anonymous, or incognito, or a stranger in a strange land'. We read that certain schizophrenics terminate in a condition of 'chaotic nonentity'—a condition which is linked to the books of the prophetic Blake —and that Shakespeare's Ophelia, 'latterly undoubtedly a schizophrenic', is one of these nonentities and not-theres:

> In her madness, there is no one there. She is not a person . . . Incomprehensible statements are said by nothing. She has already died.

It would appear from the discussion of Ophelia, and from much else, that the apologist for madness who was to emerge in Laing is no more than incipient in this early book. Yeats's *A Vision*, which has diagrams in it too, presents, as the Laing does, an interplay between subjectivity and objectivity. But Yeats's map of duality, and of the constituents of selfhood, differs from Laing's in lacking the constituent of ontological security, which produces the reflection that this is not a thing that Sandy could possibly be thought to have lacked. There was no false self. For all that his autobiography records a split, Sandy was sane. The autobiography suggests, moreover, that he was quite suspicious of the talk of dual personality that he had listened to in his time. And Laing himself may have been a little suspicious of some of it: at all events, we are led to believe that he lost interest in Sandy Brown on catching a glimpse of his two selves during a night of drink.

Sandy was an intelligent and hard-headed man who could feel himself double—to the extent of adopting the old confessional metaphor of the second self in order to evoke his experience of life. In order to make sense of what had become of him, lying in a hospital bed at the end of his days, he chose to be someone with two selves at least, one of whom was an orphan. These memoirs of his could not readily be broken down to form an item in the *Dictionary of National Biography*. A few early episodes are dwelt on to the exclusion of a very great deal. It is as if they were the matrix from which issued everything of importance that he ever was, though this would have to be called a false impression: the memoirs are family-free, for instance, as far as his wife and children are concerned. They open with a meditation on colours which have obsessed him, and this introduces a strain of phantasmagoria. For the purposes of his autobiography, family is parents. His upbringing in India is sketched: there are words about a father—of whom Sandy may have been very much the son—who cut himself off from the Raj by marrying a woman who was coloured. In that same environment Sandy suffers an ostracism and orphaning of his own. Then he is bereaved by his father's death, which shook him, launching, amid his fantasies, like a ship of death, the yellow submarine of a coffin. Masturbation and girls put his fantasies to brisk work—whereupon Onan breaks a leg and endures operations at the Edinburgh Royal Infirmary.

The operations are traumatic, conveying the sense of an agony of birth mingled with one of bereavement. The acid, threatening colours of before recur as the colours of birth, with the wave-machine at Portobello Pool directing an additional element of threat. Out of all this travail—born, bereaved, cast out, and of doubtful caste, operated on, threatened, sobbing, ejaculating—step an orphan lad, and a fellow who is two fellows: Alastair Babb and Sandy Brown, his real name scarcely less apt than his pseudonym. At one point, having mentioned Laing's 'book about The Divided Self', then being written, the memoirs observe: 'Sandy Brown had the unreal but supplementary Al Babb.' The first name of this supplementary self is sometimes Americanized in this way, but the self would appear to be called after the well-known oriental Ali Baba, with his forty thieves. Babb is said to be a half-caste, a 'dusky stevedore', and can play the part of the thuggish self that Clive James owns up to owning at times.[20] It is Babb who tends to come across as the managerial side of Sandy, as opposed to the side that took messages from the muses. A difference between art and business comes into it all somewhere. But I can only be tentative about the principle which governed the separation of his two selves, which governed his self-administered Siamesing (Cockburn's word, and Stonehouse's), and about the 'ligature' which bound these selves together. This strange operation, in which the Royal Infirmary played its involuntary part, can't be said to be carefully explained in Sandy's Memorials, though it is made to seem vividly authentic. The invented name, incidentally, may allude, not only to Ali Baba, but to the word 'alibi'.

Those who knew Sandy-Alastair might object that he wasn't *like* an orphan: no one could have been less plaintive. I agree. He was not like any Victorian orphan of the storm, on the wrong side of the window-pane in his nightie, while the thunder pealed loud and long. In point of appearance, he was not unlike that bald, coal-black-bearded Scots engineer who appeared to Conrad on the Furca Pass, and not unlike some fierce sailor—say, Captain Haddock of the Tintin books. In point of style, he was much more like a Captain Hook than a Peter Pan. Or, to return to the dramatis personae of Gothic duality, he was more of a princely tempter than like any of the outcasts tempted by such princes, though he was occasionally tempted and occasionally fell. It was like him to tempt me to give up football, on grounds of age: he told me that when he'd come to watch me play, as he'd stealthily done the previous weekend, he'd found that I was past it. You don't say that lightly to a Sunday footballer. The untouchable was uttering the unspeakable. The untouchable didn't seem to mind that Rodney Marsh of Queen's Park Rangers was quite old. Sandy rightly admired the brilliance of Marsh's individualism, his eccentric or orphan style.

He was both parts of the several pairs of opposites or opponents that could be detected in him. But this is not to say that these states were other than united. On the evidence of his autobiography, a second self now stands disclosed as an orphan; the document conveys that he wasn't half as fierce and sardonic as he seemed. Not only was he not deranged, however—he may not even have been especially divided. Nevertheless, the orphan in him seems to have mattered, and his autobiography sets out to say so—to expose the self that might not have been detected amid the activities of the outlaw, the acoustician, and the rest. We have his word for it—a word spoken partly in derision, spoken, too, in illness and perhaps from the standpoint of the mental vulnerability that can come with middle age—that his behaviour incorporated the fears of an outcast, bewildered by the country to which, leaving an unfriendly India, he had made his way, and which turned out to threaten him too, and would threaten his music.

On the face of it, his double life was that of a romantic, hairy jazzman, off to Ronnie Scott's or rattling in his van to places like Craigellachie, who was also a business executive with his auditoria in Iboland. But there was more to it than that: it seems to have amounted to a complex of double, or to several, lives. Duality is easily seen now as multiplicity. And to see it as that is to wonder who can be free of it—to wonder who isn't a *pluribus*, who isn't the polity of multifarious denizens that

Stevenson predicted. In a world where the subject has become a second nature, where Marilyn Monroe was able to declare that there were 700 Arthur Millers, the single life has looked meagre and insufficient. The Sandy who called himself by two names could behave as a victim who was also an outlaw or pirate. In other words, there was an isolation in him, never outgrown, which accompanied his being masterful, ambitious. His autobiography, as I've said, promises duality's very words. But these words could well be taken to mean that his two or several selves were hypothetical or figurative, and they do not allow one to know for certain whether he was, or considered himself, more divided than most people are. At the same time, they suggest that the hypothesis was believed, and experienced, that it could be experienced with the force of hallucination, and that it may be best described in the language of hallucination.

Among the symptoms of his condition was the way he had of making you feel both liked and disliked, of attacking his friends with ironies. In my own case, memories of school may have sharpened his ironies, and fetched him to the touchline. He could see in me the swot who played second fiddle in the royal, high, and raucous, school orchestra. This enabled him to discover that I couldn't play football.

The Englishman and the Scot have long served as one another's alter ego. Renaissance duality, in the person of Francis Bacon, said of the Scots that if they were at a disadvantage in respect of 'the external goods of fortune', nevertheless, 'for the goods of the mind and body, they are *alteri nos*, other ourselves.' They were the same, 'of one piece' with the English.[21] Then came the two-piece, adversary duality perceived and pursued in the modern world, and in Sandy's day Scotland and England could sometimes be seen as id and ego, the savage and the polite, the raw and the cooked. From such materials we might romantically suggest that the strange compound of a double life could be assembled: or we might choose to say, in the related language of psychoanalysis, that a complex could arise. Strange sounds could certainly be heard. The speech of the Anglo-Scot, and of the middle-class Scot, with its employment and alternation of two languages, Scots and posh English, could appear complicated, and indeed cooked. Sandy's autobiography is eloquent about the part played by language in his life. In India and afterwards, his father's isolation and death were referred to by the family in embarrassed words which seemed to be surrounded by inverted commas; and in Edinburgh at large, words were similarly self-punctuating. Double-tongued schoolboys displayed quaintness, and a precarious aplomb, a tendency to be pedantic, to talk about 'the latter', and a taste for jargon and the higher gibberish. Were these traits less pronounced among the one-tongued Southerners whose forbears Henry Cockburn had mocked and urged his children to emulate, in the expectation that that one tongue would conquer? The truth is that there were double tongues and different languages in the South too, and the same element of alternation and cuisine, and that if Scotland and England have become the one nation favoured by Francis Bacon, they are still a long way from making the one sound.

On a certain occasion in Sandy's youth the manager of Edinburgh's West End Café, where jazz was played, refused to let him in after closing-time. Out in the cold, Sandy inquired: 'Are you destraining me?'[22] The last brown-and-cream tram—with its little lurching alternative spiral staircases at either end, like the two parts of a double life—had long gone to Joppa or Corstorphine, at opposite ends of the town. There he was, lost in the dark and stormy night of Shandwick Place and Princes Street, frowned at by Binn's department store, cast out by the Caledonian Station: there was Caledonia's orphan, whose word for his own plight, 'distraining', was a practical, legal word signifying bankruptcy and the surrender of worldly goods, a word of doubtful application here, and of doubtful spelling, and yet the *mot juste*.

Words mattered to Sandy because he was a wit. Humour was his element, almost as much as music. His wit discharged itself, not so much in repartee and epigram, as in stories and fantasies, and in the letters he wrote. Once he was showing his mother-in-law the sights of London. They were riding in a bus, and the bus was moving along Fleet Street. 'And this,' said Sandy, calling attention to a recently excavated temple, 'is where they found the Roman remains.' Round-eyed, in the accents of Edinburgh, his mother-in-law cried: 'Tairrible!' Once, at the entrance to some BBC building, he asked permission to leave with the commissionaire the monstrous Martian sky-blue crash-helmet which he then wore. Sorry, it was more than the commissionaire's job was worth. Sandy explained that this man belonged to a class with which jazz musicians were familiar, and for which they had a name. Like many another janitor, custodian, and high official, he was a Job's Worth.

Sandy was not. He was the latter. And he was seldom sorry. His blue bonnet or helmet buzzed with verbal bees, with coinages and christenings. The disease that killed him bore the grim name of malignant hypertension. It could be a name for what happens to artists—to jazzmen, whose lives are often short. He used to point out that, after forty (a further reason for the Alastair Babb coinage?), he was living on borrowed or stolen time, statistically speaking. But when he gave the news of his illness he spoke humorously—and I failed to take in for a while that he was done for. He died a Roman death. He wouldn't go into intensive care after a heart attack: instead, he sat at home with a glass of whisky and waited for its successor while watching the Scotland–England rugby game, in which his native country generally plays the orphan's part and is robbed of a triumph. Once again, Scotland lost.

Clive James and Sandy Brown are two men in whose talent for derision orphan and double meet, in whom shows of hostility have been seen to come from and to conceal a victim. Underneath the shocking outlaw, the shorn lamb. These are lives which do something to explain the power of imaginative works whose characters are hung between the Devil and the deep blue sea, and in which the endurance of pain is its infliction. The third and last of the lives I am discussing is more eirenic: but there is derision, and aggression, here too, and it can be said that an intimate hostility took its revenge. I am referring to John Lennon, the pop star murdered by a crazy fan. After the murder Yoko Ono asked for a world silence in remembrance of her husband. 'The soul of Adonais, like a star' was to concentrate the thoughts and lift up the hearts of the many people who mourned him. The idea of such a silence seemed a good one for Lennon. The communion of absent friends at some appointed hour—or, as it has often been, of parted lovers, who arrange to watch the Moon together—is a romantic practice which goes back a thousand years, to the first novel, *The Tale of Genji*, and further still, and Lennon was a romantic artist, who helped to bring people together. In his departure can be seen the early death of a poet as this has long been known to the culture of romance.

Literary critics have been heard to suggest that romantic themes and mass culture—to both of which he gave himself—are bad things, and that they are in collusion with one another: that romance is what never was and never will be, and that mass culture promises to deliver it, or that romance stands in an antithetical, a wishful relation to what human beings do, and to their reasons for doing it. But Lennon's fate is far from proving that romance never makes anything happen, and cannot explain what does happen. I am writing here about the Lennon made public in his art and sayings. I am romanticizing him. I am not trying to psychoanalyse him. But then these two activities have been in collusion since psychoanalysis began. It was said that his inner life should be left alone in the tributes that were paid: but if the ideas which affected him, both in life and in death, and which are affirmed in his art, are to be left out of account, there might be very little to talk about except money and the chances of the profession, lucky breaks, bad scenes—'show business', as the saying goes. There was more to Lennon, and to his music, than that, but show business—in the sense of the profession itself—has been no better than literary criticism at recognizing it.

He was the kind of person who is the author and subject of much romantic literature. He was the kind of person, that is to say, who can readily be experienced as an orphan. And his life reveals what certain literary texts reveal: an encounter between the orphan and the double. Lennon, it turned out, was experienced as a double by a person whom he did not know, but who loved and hated him. Such are the hazards of stardom. If his death can be seen as an accident, it can also be seen, perhaps, in some bewildered way, as a kind of suicide.

He was deserted, to different degrees, by both parents, his mother was, it seems, to be killed in a car accident, and he was brought up by his Auntie Mimi. 'I always expect too much,' he was eventually to remark. 'I was always expecting my mother . . .'[23] He got married, but the marriage was dissolved when he met a managing Japanese woman, whom he would address as 'mother'. These circumstances form a basis for one of his best songs, the stark, raving 'Mother', to which the 'primal scream' attempted by the swinging psychoanalytic New Yorker may contribute, but which it doesn't spoil. The song is angry and inconsolable; it has action in it, and regression; it is pitched between raving and drowning, wanting to go and wanting to get back.

His programme was both to regain and to get rid of this mother, while engaging in a series of equivocal escapes. He escaped into stardom—in his case, if not in all cases, an equivocal and incongruous stardom—and into drugs, and to the foreign countries of America and of a Japanese wife. In the end, his escape collided with someone else's. The day came when 'he went off to the fatal encounter with his alter ego at the Dakota' in New York City: the language here is that of the *Newsweek* report of the murder,[24] and it is also the language of romantic duality. Mark Chapman was a former LSD tripper, programmatically married to a Japanese, capable of signing himself John Lennon and then of harshly revoking the signature: with a face as round as a lens of his hero's granny glasses, in which he could see his own reflection. A loner, apparently. Psychiatry has referred to the possibility that, seeing himself as Lennon, Chapman may at times have seen Lennon as an impostor. Meanwhile the *Newsweek* report refers to 'the wretched "fan" who killed' his star. But Chapman was a fan like lots of others, in that the Lennon identification appears to have held the promise of an escape from his troubles, while also arousing or attracting feelings of hostility.

The two of them were in one important respect alike. If Chapman was wretched, so was, so had to be, his hero. In the world in which we live, wretches are equivocal: they may be either sympathetic or hostile, or they may be both, and both these men, in their different ways, were both. One wretch speaking to another—this is the culture of romance. One wretch destroying another—the aggressions of the star-struck are as old as Orpheus, and they are now the Nine O'Clock News. The star as alter ego is someone who is exposed to injury, and a fan is someone who equivocates by adoring the star he may possibly attack. In another corner of the mass culture we inhabit, political leaders run the same risks as any star of stage and screen. Misery and mania are drawn to the excitements of star and leader worship, to which, at the same time, hardly anyone seems to be wholly immune.

The impulse to escape survived Lennon's attainment of a paradisal stardom, and it remained a big feature of his art, where it is mixed up in dualistic style with various opposites. He sang songs about mothers; about drugs, about being enskied by LSD; and about the love and peace preached by the protesting flower-children of the Sixties. In all this, to use an expression of his own, a 'double fantasy' is projected, causing us to be in doubt whether he is facing in the direction of other people or turning his back. How can a flower protest?

Something of these complications is evident in his song 'Imagine'. It proposes the idea of a take-off from the realities of life, but it does so ambivalently. It says that it's not difficult to imagine a world without a heaven and hell, and without countries and killing. But this is also to say that such a world, that the brotherhood of man, is imaginary, a dream, and that heaven and hell are realities, together with countries and killing. Here is a truth which can inspire, and inhibit, efforts to escape, and which had him taking drugs and running to America (to be safe from his fans, he said).

Dylan Thomas's early death resembles Lennon's. Each is the death of a poet as a romantic culture has dreamed it, believing that comets burn out, that talent dies young. Both deaths belong to a toll in which accident and suicide are often indistinguishable—and in which suicide gives proof of a universal twoship: two parents, two eyes, two minds, and two people in at the death. Thomas's verse spoke darkly about the return to a mother, and, quite plainly, about the lost paradise of Fern Hill. He came to look like a baby. He drank heavily, and is popularly supposed to have died of that. He went to America, and is popularly supposed to have died of that too. The departure for a foreign country, the choice of a foreign partner—when these are combined with an early death, a spell is cast.

To care about Lennon, it is not necessary to have warmed to the Beatles as flower-children, or to their friendship with the Maharishi—there can never have been any question of the Maharishi's dying young. Nor is it necessary to believe that 'all you need is love,' or to be won by Lennon's talk of revolution, of 'power to the people'. But it is possible to feel that he was able, on occasion, to bring even the least plausible part of this material to life. In the manner of some romantics, he was both indolent and indignant. And he had a good deal to be angry about, and idle about, when he lived in his native country. It is enough to mention Paisley and Powell, those dividers and excluders—each of them worth saying goodbye to. For a long time, romantic escapism has been practised and deplored. It might be said both that everybody escapes, at times, and that, since there's only the one world, nobody does. In Lennon's case, we have to reckon, not only with his own wretchedness, which can't have been worse than that of many, but with the wretchedness of the country he left to go to America, and with that of America, which worshipped him and tried to deport him. The attacks made on the Beatles ought not to be forgotten. The poet David Holbrook said that they were talentless, and that pop music, and the dancing that went with it, were 'a low form of masturbation'. This was in a letter to the *New Statesman*, the people's friend, where an article had been published saying that the Beatles were common, and their fans a low form of human being, the dregs of a mass culture.[25] The attacks were often to use a language identical to that of the abuse poured by the officialdom of Russia on the vile commercial ways of the West, and they were worthy of the later scene at Lenin Hills where the Soviet police broke up a gathering of fans who had met to share their grief at Lennon's death, and who were in a position to notice that the culture of romance, where lookalikes can kill and the loved one be laid to rest with a pun, may incur the enemies it imagines.

Those to whom strange things happen are not all stars. People are paranoid, and strange things happen even to the sceptical. I shall set down a last coincidence, to bring to an end a book which has been devoted to coincidence. During the week in which I finished writing it a stranger came to see me—in the person of someone barely known, only very faintly remembered from the past. But the books I had been reading made it possible for me to think of him as an old friend. He left behind him a dark threat, inscribed in a paperback on urban terrorism, and it turned out that he had taken to calling himself by the name of Miller.

NOTES

Publication sources are British, except where otherwise stated.

CHAPTER I

1. The text from which quotations are taken is that of *The Private Memoirs and Confessions of a Justified Sinner*, ed. John Carey (1969).

2. *Blackwood's Magazine* (May 1826), republished in the second volume of *The Modern Pythagorean* (2 vols., 1838), in which Macnish's tales were collected, with a memoir, by D. M. Moir. See *Cockburn's Millennium* by the present writer (1975), pp. 204–7.

3. See Chapter Five. An English translation by William Tooke (2 vols.) appeared in 1796, entitled *The Private History of Peregrinus Proteus the Philosopher*; quotations from *Peregrinus Proteus* are taken from Tooke. An abridged version was translated by John Elrington (1804) and entitled *Confessions in Elysium, or The Adventures of a Platonic Philosopher*. Elrington refers to Peregrine's 'Confessions' as 'the extraordinary adventures and eccentricities of a Fanatic': see *German Literature as Known in England* by V. Stockley (1929), p. 89. Hogg's *Confessions* was retitled—for an edition of 1837, two years after his death—*The Private Memoirs and Confessions of a Fanatic*.

4. 'Strange Letter of a Lunatic' (1830): *James Hogg: Selected Stories and Sketches*, ed. Douglas Mack (1982), p. 166.

5. *The Devil's Elixir*, translated by R. P. Gillies (2 vols., 1824), ii. 299, i. 138.

6. *Life of Scott* (10 vols., 2nd edn. 1839), ii. 169.

7. Muschet's *Confession*, pp. 12, 54–61. Manasseh was an idolatrous King of Judah who fell among wizards and familiar spirits. For his abominations the Lord threatened a retribution that would make both ears of the hearer 'tingle' (2 Kings 21:12). The Assyrians captured Manasseh 'among the thorns' and bore him to Babylon. Then, 'when he was in affliction, he besought the Lord his God' (2 Chronicles 33:11, 12). The Lord proved merciful, and his grace sufficient to bring even Manasseh to repentance and confession. The case was to be used as a pattern of justification by exponents of a Calvinistic piety. Muschet's *Confession* is discussed in Louis Simpson's *James Hogg: A Critical Study* (1962), pp. 190–2.

8. By Simpson, pp. 171–3.

9. *Westminster Review* (October 1824): cited by John Carey in an appendix to his 1969 edition, pp. 257–8.

10. *Cockburn's Millennium*, p. 200.

11. *Confessions*, p. 154.

12. See Chapter Seventeen.

13. *Confessions*, p. 204.

14. Ibid., p. xvii.

15. Ibid.: see in particular pp. 13, 86.

16. See Dwight Macdonald's *Parodies* (1961), pp. 83–92.

17. *Confessions*, pp. 115–16.
18. *Memoir of the Author's Life* and *Familiar Anecdotes of Sir Walter Scott* by James Hogg, ed. Douglas Mack (1972), p. 11.
19. Ibid., p. 101.
20. 'Pierre Menard, Author of the *Quixote*', translated by James Irby: from the collection *Labyrinths*, ed. Donald Yates and James Irby (Penguin edn., reprinted 1978), pp. 67–8.
21. *Memoir of the Author's Life*, p. 55.
22. *Confessions*, p. xiv.
23. *William Blackwood and his Sons* by Margaret Oliphant (3rd edn., 2 vols., 1897), i. 337.
24. *Labyrinths*, p. 102.
25. *Memoirs of the Author's Life*, p. 9. *Labyrinths*, p. 82.
26. *James Hogg* by Douglas Gifford (1976), p. 233.
27. *William Blackwood and his Sons*, i. 318.
28. Francis Jeffrey called the 'Intimations' Ode 'illegible and unintelligible' (*Edinburgh Review*, October 1807).
29. *James Hogg: Anecdotes of Sir W. Scott*, ed. Douglas Mack (1983), pp. 33, 2, 31. This volume presents a recently discovered first draft of the recollections of Scott, by Hogg, which were published during Hogg's lifetime.

CHAPTER II

1. *Villette* (reprinted 1967), p. 190.
2. See *On Deconstruction: Theory and Criticism after Structuralism* by Jonathan Culler (1983), pp. 142–4.
3. From 'Henry James: An Appreciation' (1905), collected in *Notes on Life and Letters* (1921), p. 18.
4. Bernard Crick: *London Review of Books* (7–20 October 1982).
5. *Collected Poems* (reprinted 1949), p. 177.
6. Henry Vaughan: 'The Retreat'.
7. *London Review of Books* (19 March–1 April 1981).
8. Jekyll opens his 'Full Statement of the Case' by saying that in his youth he had been both grave and gay: *The Strange Case of Dr Jekyll and Mr Hyde* (Everyman edn., with other tales, reprinted 1974), p. 48.
9. Act I, Scene ii: *Complete Works*, ed. W. J. Craig (reprinted 1954). All references to Shakespeare's text are based on this edition.
10. 'The Quiet House', from *The Farmer's Bride* (1916).
11. Sonnet 73 has 'Death's second self'.
12. From *Labyrinths*, pp. 282–3. James Irby is the translator of all quotations from Borges.
13. By Alastair Reid (*New York Review of Books*, 25 January 1979).
14. *Labyrinths*, pp. 154–6.
15. *Personality* (1947), p. 451.
16. *Labyrinths*, p. 285.
17. See *The Mirror and the Lamp* by M. H. Abrams (1953), p. 245.
18. *William Hazlitt: Selected Writings*, ed. Ronald Blythe (Penguin edn., 1970), p. 273. *The Complete Works of William Hazlitt*, ed. P. P. Howe (21 vols.), viii (1931), p. 42.

19. 'Sir Proteus' (1814): *Complete Works* (10 vols.), vi (1927), p. 284.
20. *Labyrinths*, pp. 132, 233.
21. *William Blackwood and his Sons*, i. 196.
22. *Dr Jekyll and Mr Hyde*, p. 49.
23. *Tristram Shandy* (Everyman edn., reprinted 1961), p. 53.

CHAPTER III

1. *The Diary of Anne Frank*, translated by B. M. Mooyaart-Doubleday, (paperback reprint, 1983), pp. 119–20.

2. *Locutions des Pierrots* (12), in *L'Invitation de Notre Dame la Lune* (Paris, 1886).

3. *The Family, Sex and Marriage in England 1500–1800* (1977), p. 72.

4. *Changing Taste in Eighteenth-Century Art and Literature*, ed. Robert Moore and Jean Hagstrum (William Andrews Clark Memorial Library, University of California, Los Angeles, 1972), pp. 47, 61. The quotations are from an essay by Hagstrum entitled '"Such, Such were the Joys": The Boyhood of the Man of Feeling'.

5. From an epigram of Cowper's: *Poetical Works* (2 vols., 1854), ii. 169. See *Shirley* (Everyman edn., reprinted 1970), p. 87.

6. Diary of George Combe: National Library of Scotland, MS 7429, ff. 44^{v}. The reference is owed to Dr Richard Ely. Cockburn died in 1854, and his words were reported by a daughter. There is a version of Henry James's last words in which he refers to death as the 'august stranger'.

7. *An Introduction to the Study of Man* by J. Z. Young (reprinted 1976), pp. 130–1.

8. *Doubles in Literary Psychology* by Ralph Tymms (1949), pp. 29, 54–64, 72, 77. This enterprising study treats the rise and vicissitudes of Continental duality, and lays stress on its 'semi-intuitive' anticipations of the unconscious mind of later psychology (pp. 106–7).

9. *Cockburn's Millennium*, p. 206. *A Strange Story* (reprinted in 1973 by Shambala, California, from an edition of 1892), p. 145.

10. *Cockburn's Millennium*, p. 212.

11. From the essay on 'Compensation' in his first collection of essays, published in 1841: see the *Portable Emerson*, ed. Carl Bode, with Malcolm Cowley (revised Penguin edn., 1981), p. 168.

12. *Shirley*, pp. 406–7, 234–9, 276.

13. Ibid., pp. 376, 396–8.

14. *Excellent Women* (Penguin edn., 1980), p. 125.

15. *Don Juan*, ed. T. G. Steffan, E. Steffan and W. W. Pratt (reissued 1982), pp. 554–7.

16. Ibid., p. 518: Canto 15, Stanza 87.

17. Canto 16, Stanzas 97, 98. See Note to Stanza 97, line 4 (p. 752).

CHAPTER IV

1. *Cockburn's Millennium*, pp. xii, xiii, 68–9.

2. *The Thief's Journal*, translated by Bernard Frechtman (Penguin edn., reprinted 1976), pp. 69, 102.

3. Unpublished: from a sequence entitled 'Mikrocosmos'.

4. *Stories and Episodes*, translated by H. T. Lowe-Porter (Everyman edn., reprinted 1947), pp. 60, 68.

5. From the 'Life of William Cowper' which prefaces the *Poetical Works* of 1854, i. viii.

6. *All's well that ends well*, II. i, III. ii.

7. *Merchant of Venice*, V. i.

8. By Antonio: IV. i. 386.

9. *Midsummer Night's Dream*, IV. i.

10. *Paradise Lost*, ed. John Carey and Alastair Fowler (1968): Book Five, ll. 86–92.

11. The anthology forms part of the James and Marie Louise Osborn collection, Yale University Library. A detailed account of the manuscript by the present writer, entitled 'Cockburn, Nature and Romance', appears in *Lord Cockburn: A Bicentenary Celebration*, ed. Alan Bell (1979).

12. From a letter included in *Memorials of the Life and Writings of the Rev. Robert Morehead*, edited by his son Charles Morehead (1875), p. 102.

13. *Poetical Works of William Wordsworth*, ed. Thomas Hutchinson (1928), p. 626.

14. *Poems and Extracts chosen by William Wordsworth for an Album presented to Lady Mary Lowther, Christmas, 1819.* A facsimile edition was published in 1905, with introductory material by J. Rogers Rees and Harold Littledale.

15. *The Prelude: A Parallel Text*, the 1805 and 1850 versions, ed. J. C. Maxwell (Penguin 1971), pp. 156–7.

16. Ibid., pp. 54–7, 160–1.

17. 'Autumn', *Poetical Works*, ed. J. Logie Robertson (1908), ll. 1304–54, ll. 963–6.

18. Ibid., ll. 672–4.

19. Ibid., 'Summer', ll. 1397–8.

20. *Life and Letters of Thomas Campbell* by William Beattie (3 vols., 1850), ii. 436.

21. *Life of Lord Jeffrey* by Henry Cockburn (2 vols., 1852), i. 112.

22. *Epistles, Odes, and Other Poems* (1806).

23. *Life of Lord Jeffrey*, i. 172. *Life and Letters of Thomas Campbell*, ii. 171. Jeffrey's admiration was compelled, in 1809, by Campbell's 'Gertrude of Wyoming'.

24. *Life and Letters of Thomas Campbell*, i. 454.

25. Ibid., i. 461, ii. 213, 145.

26. Ibid., i. 143.

27. Ibid., i. 218–20.

28. *Keats and Embarrassment* (1974), pp. 201–3.

29. Book Two, ll. 275–6. All quotations from Keats are based on the Buxton Forman edition of the *Poetical Works*, first published in 1908.

30. *Letters of John Keats*, selected by Robert Gittings (1970), p. 43.

31. Ibid., p. 157.

32. Ibid., p. 398.

33. From 'Tradition and the Individual Talent' (1917): *Selected Essays* (2nd edn., 1934), p. 21.

34. Ibid., pp. 270, 19.

35. *The Pleasures of Imagination*, Book One, ll. 374–6: *The Poetical Works of Mark Akenside*, ed. Alexander Dyce (1894).

36. *Stephen Hero*, ed. Theodore Spencer (paperback edn., 1944), p. 166.

CHAPTER V

1. *Bloomsbury: A House of Lions* (Philadelphia and New York, 1979): see pp. 49, 123, 158, 178, 252.

2. From the introductory epistle 'to the Ingenious Reader': *The Man in the Moone* (Scolar Press facsimile edn., 1971).

3. Translated by A. J. Morrison (1847), the passage appears in *The Modern Tradition: Backgrounds of Modern Literature*, ed. Richard Ellmann and Charles Feidelson Jr. (New York, 1965), pp. 738–9.

4. *Rameau's Nephew* and *D'Alembert's Dream*, translated by L. W. Tancock (Penguin edn., 1966), pp. 94, 108, 113.

5. See Chapter One, Note 3.

6. 1796 edition, ii. 15.

7. Ibid., i. 43–4.

8. *Collected Works of Edgar Allan Poe*, ed. Thomas Mabbott (3 vols., Cambridge, Massachusetts, 1969, 1978), i (*Poems*, 1969), p. 172.

9. *Northanger Abbey* (Signet Classics, New York, 1965), pp. 9–18, 211.

10. *The Heroine* (3 vols., 3rd edn., 1815), i. 182.

11. Ibid., i. 46–8.

12. Ibid., i. 147–8.

13. Ibid., i. 101–3, 121, ii. 153. For Carlyle's opinion of Keats see *Keats and Embarrassment*, p. 120.

14. *The Heroine*, i. 161, 158, iii. 156.

15. Ibid., i. 55, 79, 80.

16. Ibid., i. 155.

17. Ibid., ii. 93.

18. *The Confidence-Man* (New York, reprinted 1955), pp. 263–7.

19. Ibid., pp. 200, 252–3.

20. New York, 1954.

21. *The Confidence-Man* (1955 edn.), p. 228.

22. See Elizabeth Foster's Introduction to the 1954 edition, p. xxv. The friend was Evert Duyckinck.

23. *The Eccentric Design* (1959), p. 217.

24. 1955 edition, pp. 85–8.

25. Ibid., p. 150.

26. See 'Aristotle and Women' by Jonathan Barnes: *London Review of Books* (16–29 February 1984).

27. The expression belongs to Melville's draft: see 1954 edition, p. 375.

28. 1955 edition, p. 169.

29. *Molloy*, first published in French, was translated into English by Samuel Beckett and Patrick Bowles (paperback edn., 1966), pp. 123–4.

CHAPTER VI

1. Scott's opinion was expressed in the *Quarterly* (October 1815) and in his *Journal* entry for 14 March 1826 (1972 edn., p. 114); for Cockburn's words see *Cockburn's Millennium*, p. 52; Walpole's words are in the Preface to the second edition of *The Castle of Otranto*; Hawthorne's are in the Preface to *The House of the Seven Gables*.

2. Introduction to *Persuasion* (Penguin edn., reprinted 1973): see p. 17.

3. *Mansfield Park* (reprinted Cambridge, Massachusetts, 1965), p. 245.

4. *Emma* (Oxford University Press paperback edn., 1975), p. 363.

5. *Cockburn's Millennium*, pp. 32–4, 123.

6. See *Burke and Hare* by Owen Dudley Edwards (1980).

7. *Memorials of His Time* by Henry Cockburn (1974 edn., Chicago and London), p. 427.

8. *Blackwood's Magazine* (March 1829), vol. XXV, pp. 382–9.

9. *Burke and Hare*, p. 285–6.

10. *Philosophy of Sleep*, p. 96.

11. *Cockburn's Millennium*, p. 171.

12. *Life of Jeffrey*, i. 126–7.

13. *Life and Letters of Thomas Campbell*, ii. 29.

14. 18 September 1867. See Oscar Maurer: 'Anonymity v. Signature in Victorian Reviewing' (*University of Texas Studies in English*, June 1948).

15. *Walter Scott: The Great Unknown* by Edgar Johnson (2 vols., 1970), ii. 1008.

16. The preface is given in the Signet Classics *Waverley*, ed. Edgar Johnson (New York, 1964), pp. 21–3.

17. Waverley Novels Centenary Edition (1871), 25 vols., xix. 331–4.

18. *I can see your lips moving: The History and Art of Ventriloquism* by Valentine Vox (1981), p. 58.

19. In a letter to John Morritt of 28 July 1814.

20. Signet Classics edn., pp. 434, 565.

21. *Journal*, p. 635.

22. *Cockburn's Millennium*, p. 27. Byron's portrait of Brougham was omitted from the opening canto of *Don Juan* and is given in the notes to the edition of the poem reissued in 1982 (pp. 585–6).

23. 28 June 1974.

24. 'Anonymity: An Enquiry' (1925), reprinted in *Two Cheers for Democracy* (1951), pp. 92, 96.

CHAPTER VII

1. *Reflections on the Revolution in France* (Penguin edn., 1978), p. 191; and see Conor Cruise O'Brien's Introduction, pp. 22, 34–5.

2. Niall Rudd discusses the protean personality of Classical times in *Lines of Enquiry: Studies in Latin Poetry* (1976): see p. 161. The two sayings come respectively from Cicero's *De Amicitia* (65) and from his *De Officiis* (3, 1), where Cicero attributes the second saying to Scipio Africanus, conqueror of Hannibal at the battle of Zama.

3. *Caleb Williams* (New York, reprinted 1960), p. 130.
4. *Peter Schlemihl, the Shadowless Man*, with an Introduction by Joseph Jacobs (Allen and Unwin, undated, the text based on a translation of 1844), pp. 140–1.
5. *Tales and Stories by Hans Christian Andersen*, translated by Patricia Conroy and Sven Rossel (Seattle and London, 1980), pp. 141–53.
6. Ibid., p. 258.
7. See Chapter Three, p. 49, and Note 8.
8. *Melmoth the Wanderer*, ed. Douglas Grant (paperback ed., 1972), pp. 519, 183–225.
9. Ibid., pp. 330, 323, 373.
10. Ibid., p. 207.
11. V. V. Vinogradov (1929), quoted in *Dostoevsky: The Seeds of Revolt 1821–1849* by Joseph Frank (Princeton University Press, 1976), p. 298.
12. Ibid., p. 299.
13. The Penguin translation of *The Double* by Jessie Coulson (reprinted 1977), from which quotations are taken, bears the subtitle 'A Poem of St Petersburg'.
14. *The Double*, pp. 159–65.
15. Ibid., pp. 166–73.
16. 'The Magic Mirror: A Study of the Double in Two of Dostoevsky's Novels'—*The Double* and *The Brothers Karamazov*. The thesis was presented at Smith College, Massachusetts in 1955. See Chapter Sixteen, and see *Sylvia Plath: Method and Madness* by Edward Butscher (New York, 1976), pp. 158–9.
17. Translated by Constance Garnett (reprinted 1948).
18. *Dostoevsky1821–1881* by E. H. Carr (reprinted 1962): see pp. 35–6, 150–1, 198–205.
19. *The Devils*, translated by David Magarshack (Penguin edn. 1981), pp. 675, 684, 692.
20. The 'inward division' and 'mockery' are described in *The Insulted and Injured*, translated by Constance Garnett (reprinted 1947), p. 47. For Dostoevsky's Mephistopheles (Speshnev, a member of the Petrashevsky circle of 1848), see Joseph Frank's *Dostoevsky 1821–1849*, p. 270.
21. *The Devils*, p. 676.
22. Ibid., p. 702.
23. *The Diary of a Writer*, translated by Boris Brasol (New York, 1954), p. 932. For Dostoevsky's 'real monsters' see p. 146.
24. *The Devils*, p. 687.
25. See *Dostoevsky* by John Jones (1983, p. 255) for the negativeness and for a negative view of Stavrogin. 'Nothing' can come from him.
26. *The Insulted and Injured*, pp. 2, 11.
27. Ibid., pp. 48, 103, 159.
28. Ibid., pp. 252, 259, 267.
29. 'The Black Monk': *The Oxford Chekhov*, translated by Ronald Hingley, vii (*Stories 1893–1895*, 1978), Appendix II, p. 229.
30. Ibid., p. 39.
31. *Oxford Chekhov*, iv, Appendix I, pp. 238–40.
32. Ibid., p. 133.
33. Ibid., Appendix I. See Ronald Hingley's Introduction, pp. 3, 4.

34. Ibid., pp. 38–40.
35. Ibid., pp. 42–3.
36. Ibid., Introduction, p. 8.
37. *Lady with Lapdog, and Other Stories*, translated by David Magarshack (Penguin edn., reprinted 1971), pp. 279–80.
38. Ibid., pp. 278–9.
39. *Oxford Chekhov*, iv, Appendix IV, p. 252.

CHAPTER VIII

1. Quotations from 'William Wilson' are taken from Thomas Mabbott's *Collected Works of Edgar Allan Poe*, ii (*Tales and Sketches 1831–1842*, 1978). Quotations from 'Hans Pfaall' are from *Tales of Mystery and Imagination* by Poe (Odhams Press, undated). The present chapter derives from an article published in the *New York Review of Books* (28 June 1979).
2. *Collected Works*, ii. 473.
3. Ibid., p. 423–4.
4. Ibid., pp. 436–7, 427.
5. Contemplating the nature of the detective Dupin, the narrator of 'The Murders in the Rue Morgue' dwells on 'the old philosophy of the Bi-Part Soul' and on 'the fancy of a double Dupin—the creative and the resolvent': *Tales of Mystery and Imagination*, p. 126.
6. *The Tell-Tale Heart* (New York, 1978), p. 183.
7. The notes to 'The Castle of Indolence' in J. Logie Robertson's edition of Thomson's *Poetical Works* quote this expression, without attributing it (p. 307). It seems that Thomson's 'wretch', the 'eccentric solitaire', was Henry Welby, Esquire.
8. The rule of contraries solves 'everything in the way of paradox and impossibility': *Tales of Mystery and Imagination*, p. 509.
9. Poe's words provide an epigraph for *The Edgar Allan Poe Scrapbook*, ed. Peter Haining (New York, 1977). This is a Poe-pourri dedicated to the Gothic actor Vincent Price, and it includes an admiring account (pp. 80–1) by Dostoevsky, who stresses Poe's power of detail, as in 'Hans Pfaall', while observing that his fantasies seem terrestrial, 'strangely "material"', compared with Hoffmann's. 'Even his most unbounded imagination betrays the true American.'
10. For Poe's pledge see *Edgar Allan Poe* by David Sinclair (New Jersey, 1977), p. 182. For Gilfillan's condemnation see *The Tell-Tale Heart*, p. 168. For McGonagall's encomia see *Poetic Gems* (reprinted 1954), pp. 49–50, 7. In the 'Brief Autobiography' which prefaces this selection McGonagall (pp. 6–7) tells how, in 1877, he discovered that he was a poet: 'I seemed to feel as it were a strange kind of feeling stealing over me . . .' This unfortunate then had the 'bright idea' of delivering, as his first poem, an address to the Revd George Gilfillan.
11. *Edgar Allan Poe* by David Sinclair, p. 256.
12. Ibid., p. 208.
13. *The Confidence-Man* (1955 edn.), pp. 228–9.
14. *The Tell-Tale Heart*, p. 101.

15. *Edgar Allan Poe: A Study in Genius* (New York, 1926), pp. 192, 197.
16. Louisiana State University Press (Baton Rouge, 1977).
17. See Chapter Five and Notes 7 and 8.
18. *The Tell-Tale Heart*, p. 206.
19. *Tales of Mystery and Imagination*, pp. 265–7, 299.
20. Ibid., p. 274.
21. *The Tell-Tale Heart*, p. 138.
22. *Building Poe Biography*, pp. 138, 38.
23. *The Tell-Tale Heart*, Introduction, p. ix.

CHAPTER IX

1. Presented in *Keats: The Critical Heritage*, ed. G. M. Matthews (1971), pp. 386, 401, 410.
2. *Letters of John Keats*, p. 390.
3. The Langhorne expressions are from a passage in his poem 'The Justice of the Peace'—a passage which, according to Scott, once made Burns weep, in public.
4. G. M. Matthews in *Keats: The Critical Heritage*, p. 1.
5. *Wilfred Owen* by Jon Stallworthy (1974), pp. 57, 221, 235, 264.
6. *Poetical Works*: *The Seasons*, 'Summer', ll. 1714–16.
7. *The Life and Letters of John Keats* by Richard Monckton Milnes (1867 edn.), p. 333.
8. *Cockburn's Millennium*, p. 75.
9. *Melmoth*, pp. 31, 540.
10. Wordsworth's words are from a letter to Benjamin Haydon of 16 January 1820: *Keats: The Critical Heritage*, p. 44.
11. *The Keats Circle: Letters and Papers 1816–1878*, ed. Hyder Rollins (2 vols., Cambridge, Massachusetts, 1948), i. cxiv.
12. 1867 edn., p. 333.
13. Ibid., p. 11.
14. *Keats: The Critical Heritage*, p. 308.
15. See John Bayley's essay of 1962, 'Keats and Reality', and Ricks's *Keats and Embarrassment*.
16. *The Life of Charles Dickens* by John Forster (7th edn., 3 vols., 1872), i. 27–49.
17. *Little Dorrit* (Penguin edn., 1967), pp. 254–5.
18. Ibid., pp. 795, 255.
19. Ibid., p. 691.
20. Ibid., p. 191.
21. Ibid., pp. 286, 657.
22. Ibid., pp. 302–4.
23. *The Keats Circle*, i. 273.
24. *Little Dorrit*, pp. 797–8.
25. *Letters of John Keats*, p. 183.
26. *Bleak House* (Signet Classics, New York, 1964), p. 262.
27. Ibid., pp. 82–7.
28. Ibid., pp. 599, 833.

29. *Letters of John Keats*, p. 398.

30. *Edwin Drood* (reprinted 1931), Chapter Three, p. 23.

31. 'Wireless': *Traffics and Discoveries* (Pocket Edition, reprinted 1928), pp. 230–1.

32. 'The Finest Story in the World': *Many Inventions* (paperback edn., reprinted 1964).

33. *The Great War and Modern Memory* by Paul Fussell (1975), p. 105.

34. *Memoirs of a Fox-Hunting Man* (1928), pp. 9–13, 227. *Memoirs of an Infantry Officer* (1930), pp. 112, 115, 323.

35. *Abba, Abba* (1977), pp. 49–50.

CHAPTER X

1. From a letter of 8 November (cited *OED*).

2. *Our Mutual Friend* (Signet Classics, New York, 1964), p. 754.

3. For Mrs Oliphant's opinion, and for Jeffrey's, and for Aldous Huxley's treatment of the matter in *Vulgarity in Literature* (1930), see *Dickens and his Readers* by George Ford (1955), p. 61. For Leavis's opinion see *Dickens the Novelist* by F. R. and Q. D. Leavis (Penguin edn., reprinted 1980), p. 298.

4. *The Old Curiosity Shop* (Penguin edn., reprinted 1977), p. 654.

5. Ibid., p. 203.

6. Ibid., pp. 236–9.

7. Ibid., Notes, p. 686.

8. Ibid., p. 261.

9. Ibid., p. 300–1.

10. Ibid., pp. 504–5, 404.

11. *Our Mutual Friend*, p. 153.

12. Ibid., pp. 270, 315–6.

13. Ibid., pp. 664–7, 757.

14. The *Nation* (21 December 1865).

15. *The Life of Henry James* (Penguin edn., 2 vols., 1977), ii. 128, 344, 447, 564. For 'The Altar of the Dead' see *In the Cage, and Other Tales*, ed. Morton Zabel (1958), pp. 98, 129.

16. *The Great Tradition* (1948), p. 158.

17. *The Notebooks of Henry James*, ed. F. O. Matthiessen and Kenneth Murdock (paperback edn., New York, 1961), pp. 169–73.

18. *The Wings of the Dove* (Penguin edn., reprinted 1977), pp. 44, 363.

19. *Villette*, p. 118.

20. *The Wings of the Dove*, pp. 71–2.

21. Ibid., pp. 291–2.

22. *Freud: The Man and the Cause* by Ronald Clark (1980), p. 497.

23. *The Wings of the Dove*, pp. 49, 50, 85.

24. *The Life of Henry James*, ii. 448.

25. *The Wings of the Dove*, pp. 184, 337–8, 456.

26. Ibid., p. 425.

27. *The Spoils of Poynton* (Oxford paperback reprint, 1982): for James's remarks, expressed in a New York Edition Preface, see p. xlviii. See also pp. 120, 164.

28. Ibid.: see pp. 112, 115, 123, 136.
29. Ibid.: see pp. 50, 64, 166–7.

CHAPTER XI

1. *Dr Jekyll and Mr Hyde, and Other Tales*, p. 51. The discussion of Stevenson incorporates material published in the *New York Review of Books* (29 May 1975).
2. *The Letters of Robert Louis Stevenson*, ed. Sidney Colvin (5 vols., 1924), v. 168.
3. *Dr Jekyll and Mr Hyde, and Other Tales*, p. 193.
4. Ibid., pp. 48–55.
5. *Cockburn's Millennium*, p. 213.
6. *Deacon Brodie—Father to Jekyll and Hyde* by John Gibson (1977), p. 67.
7. Ibid., p. 55.
8. Forbes Bramble's book was published in 1975.
9. *Cockburn's Millennium*, p. 113.
10. *Deacon Brodie—Father to Jekyll and Hyde*, p. 66.
11. *Robert Louis Stevenson* by James Pope Hennessy (1974), p. 263.
12. Ibid., p. 13.
13. *William Sharp (Fiona Macleod). A Memoir compiled by his Wife Elizabeth A. Sharp* (1910).
14. *Yeats* by Frank Tuohy (1976), p. 55.
15. *The Scottish Novel: From Smollett to Spark* by Francis Hart (Cambridge, Massachusetts, 1978), pp. 340–7. Whitman's words are from his essay 'A Sun-Bath—Nakedness': *Complete Poetry and Collected Prose* ('Library of America' edn., New York, 1982), p. 807.
16. Mrs Sharp, pp. 5, 11, 52–3.
17. Ibid., pp. 227, 346.
18. Ibid., pp. 424, 278. An Edenic, druidic 1960s hippyism can be got from Sharp: see 'Wilfion and the Green Life' by Konrad Hopkins in *Twenty-Seven to One,* ed. Bradford Broughton (Clarkson College of Technology, USA, 1970).
19. Mrs Sharp, p. 108.
20. Ibid., pp. 305, 245.
21. *J. B. Yeats: Letters to his Son W. B. Yeats and Others, 1869–1922*, ed. Joseph Hone (new edn. 1983), p. 78.
22. See *Yeats: The Man and the Masks* by Richard Ellmann (reprinted with a new preface, 1979), pp. 29, 74, 211, 96.
23. From his essay on 'The Philosophy of Shelley's Poetry': *Yeats: Selected Criticism and Prose*, ed. A. Norman Jeffares (reprinted 1980), p. 79.
24. E. M. Forster's biographer, P. N. Furbank, has written: 'Yeats's notion of the anti-self or Mask, his theory that creativity is a matter of constructing a dream-identity antithetical to the natural self and the natural world, seems to me very profound and helpful—in fact, just true' (*London Review of Books,* 3–16 May 1984). Furbank thinks that the theory fits the case of Conrad, who constructed images of fidelity and endurance. But does it fit the case of Forster?

25. 'The Dream of Duncan Parrenness' appears in the collection *Life's Handicap* (paperback reprint, 1964), pp. 297–302.

26. *The Picture of Dorian Gray* (Penguin edn., reprinted 1973), pp. 194, 159.

27. Dan Jacobson relishes this description—which is drawn from the Monypenny and Buckle official biography—in 'Jew d'Esprit' (*London Review of Books*, 6–19 May 1982).

28. *Dorian Gray*, pp. 129, 65.

29. Ibid., pp. 67–8, 158, 85–6.

30. *Oscar Wilde* by H. Montgomery Hyde (new edn., Penguin, 1962), p. 235.

31. 'The Jolly Corner': see *In the Cage*, p. 324.

32. Ibid., p. 333.

33. Ibid., pp. 336, 340.

34. *The Sense of the Past* (2nd impression, 1917), p. 329.

35. Ibid., pp. 74, 86.

36. Ibid., p. 96.

37. Ibid., p. 103.

38. Ibid., p. 291.

39. *Selected Tales* by Henry James, ed. Peter Messent and Tom Paulin (Everyman edn., 1982), pp. 23–9, 39.

40. Ibid., p. 19.

41. 'The Great Good Place': see *In the Cage*, pp. 304, 313.

42. *Nineteenth Century* (November 1886), pp. 654–65.

43. *The Discovery of the Unconscious* by Henri Ellenberger (1970), pp. 314, 145–6.

44. *The Varieties of Religious Experience* by William James, ed. Martin Marty (Penguin American Library, 1982), pp. 513, 169. James's book appeared in 1902. The 'divided self' which is the subject of one of its chapters is identified with a variety of religious experience, that of the sick soul: but the characteristics awarded to a high degree of 'inconsistency' are those which had been awarded, in the fiction and speculation of the past, to a more general incidence of division. 'There are persons whose existence is little more than a series of zig-zags, as now one tendency and now another gets the upper hand. Their spirit wars with their flesh, they wish for incompatibles, wayward impulses interrupt their most deliberate plans, and their lives are one long drama of repentance and of effort to repair misdemeanours and mistakes.'

45. *Seven Types of Ambiguity* (revised edn., reprinted 1949), pp. vi, 192–226.

CHAPTER XII

1. *A Personal Record* (reprinted 1950), p. 122.
2. *Under Western Eyes* (paperback reprint, 1975), pp. 175–6.
3. *A Personal Record*, pp. 119, 111.
4. Ibid., pp. 35–44.
5. Ibid., pp. 92–5.
6. Ibid., p. 121.
7. *Lord Jim* (Collected Edition, reprinted 1948), pp. 213, 229.
8. Ibid., pp. 416, 334, 214–17.

9. *Joseph Conrad* by Jocelyn Baines (1960), pp. 271–6.
10. *Romance* (reprinted 1925), pp. 265, 417–18, 493, 433.
11. Ibid., pp. 455–6, 154. 'Heart of Darkness' (Collected Edition, reprinted 1948), p. 87.
12. *Victory* (reprinted 1943), p. 326.
13. 'The Secret Sharer' (reprinted, Bantam Classics, 1981), p. 172.
14. 'The Shadow-Line', in *Typhoon and Other Tales* (Signet Classics, New York, 1980): see pp. 366–77, 389–402, 416.
15. Ibid., pp. 417–26.
16. Ibid., p. 383.
17. Ibid., p. 443.
18. *The Outcast of the Islands* (Collected Edition, reprinted 1949), pp. 250, 129.
19. *Out of My System* (New York, 1975), p. 49.
20. 'Heart of Darkness', p. 141.
21. Ibid., pp. 113–19.
22. Ibid., pp. 114–43.
23. Ibid., p. 118.
24. *The Collected Letters of Joseph Conrad, 1861–1897* (1983), ed. Frederick Karl and Laurence Davies, p. 52. Conrad, in Africa, on his way to the Congo, calls himself (22 May 1890) a strange compound: 'What a concoction!' Employees of the company he has joined are called '*nevrosés*'—neurotics.
25. *Conrad in the Nineteenth Century* (1980), p. 239. For James's term 'preposterous' see p. 206.
26. *Out of My System*, pp. 56–7.
27. A reading expounded by Redmond O'Hanlon in *Joseph Conrad and Charles Darwin: The Influence of Scientific Thought on Conrad's Fiction* (1984).

CHAPTER XIII

1. This account of Edith Wharton's life and works owes much to R. W. B. Lewis's biography of 1975, *Edith Wharton* (Colophon edn., New York, 1977), and is based on a discussion, published in the *New York Review of Books* (23 February 1978), of Lewis's book and of Cynthia Wolff's *A Feast of Words: The Triumph of Edith Wharton* (New York, 1977).
2. See Lewis, Appendix C, pp. 544–8, and Wolff, pp. 300–5.
3. *The Age of Innocence* (reprinted 1966), pp. 291–2.
4. *Edith Wharton* by Blake Nevius (University of California Press, reprinted 1976), pp. 9–10.
5. *Portrait of Edith Wharton*, p. 186.
6. *A Backward Glance* by Edith Wharton (1934), p. 68.
7. Ibid., pp. 93, 70–3.
8. Ibid., p. 205. *The Reef* (reprinted New York, 1965), p. 95.
9. *Portrait of Edith Wharton*, pp. 57, 185, 21.
10. *Life of Henry James*, ii. 730.
11. *A Backward Glance*, pp. 285–6, 242–3.
12. Ibid., pp. 73, 127, 24.
13. *The Custom of the Country* (New York, reprinted 1956), p. 207.

14. Ibid., pp. 74–7.
15. Lewis, p. 187.
16. *The Age of Innocence*, p. 156.
17. Ibid., p. 225.
18. Ibid., pp. 205, 245, 263, 254.
19. *A Feast of Words*, p. 334.
20. *Ethan Frome* (New York, Scribner's edn., reprinted 1957), pp. 94, 161.
21. Lewis, Appendix A, p. 535.
22. *A Backward Glance*, p. 356.
23. *A Feast of Words*, pp. 293–5.
24. Ibid., p. 296.
25. *Portrait of Edith Wharton*, p. 143.
26. Lewis, p. 212.
27. *Portrait of Edith Wharton*, p. 221. Lewis, p. 327.

CHAPTER XIV

1. *Robert Frost* by Lawrance Thompson (3 vols., New York): i (1966), ii (1970), iii, with R. H. Winnick (1976). See iii. 10. The present chapter is based on a review of the biography which was published in the *New York Review of Books* (10 November 1977). Biographical references are taken from Thompson unless otherwise credited.
2. Ibid., i. 590.
3. Ibid., ii. 479, 347, 450.
4. Ibid., ii. 485, 694.
5. Ibid., ii. 270–9.
6. Ibid., iii. 234–5.
7. Lowell's sonnet, which remembers 'Robert Frost at midnight, the audience gone', appears in *Notebook* (1970), p. 122. Richard Poirier's book was published in New York in 1977.
8. 'To a Thinker in Office': see Thompson, ii. 427–8, 669.
9. Thompson, iii. 441.
10. 'Robert Frost: or, the Spiritual Drifter as Poet': *Robert Frost: A Collection of Critical Essays*, ed. James Cox (New Jersey, 1962), pp. 58–82.
11. Thompson, iii. 343.
12. Ibid., ii. 425, iii. 4.
13. *Robert Frost: The Work of Knowing*, p. 80.
14. Thompson, ii. 589.
15. *Huckleberry Finn* (Penguin edn., reprinted 1975), p. 332. The words are Tom Sawyer's, at the end of the novel; the prisoner is Jim.
16. 'An Equaliser': *The Poetry of Robert Frost*, ed. Edward Lathem (New York, 1969), p. 363. See Thompson, i. 98.
17. 'The Tuft of Flowers'.
18. Thompson, i. 594.
19. 'Build Soil—A Political Pastoral'.
20. *Robert Frost: The Work of Knowing*, pp. 73, 121.
21. Thompson, ii. 597.

CHAPTER XV

1. *Robert Lowell: A Biography* by Ian Hamilton (New York, 1982), pp. 298, 193. The book was discussed by the present writer in an article published in the *London Review of Books* (19 May–1 June 1983), and this chapter makes use of the article. The poems discussed appear in volumes published in Britain by Faber: *Poems 1938–1949* (1950—many of these poems, including 'The Quaker Graveyard in Nantucket' and 'Mr Edwards and the Spider', appeared in the collection *Lord Weary's Castle* (1968), published in America by Harcourt Brace Jovanovich), *Life Studies* (1959), which includes the poem 'Skunk Hour', *For the Union Dead* (1965), *Near the Ocean* (1967), *Notebook* (1970), *The Dolphin* (1973), *Day by Day* (1978), and *Robert Lowell's Poems: A Selection*, edited by Jonathan Raban (1974). The discussion of 'The Mills of the Kavanaughs' is based on the text published in the English magazine *Agenda* (Autumn 1980).

2. Hamilton, p. 355.

3. When discussing the poetry of Ivor Gurney in the *London Review of Books* (3–16 February 1983).

4. Hamilton, p. 85: from the transcript of a talk dated, approximately, 1960.

5. These poems—'Notice', 'Shifting Colours', 'Unwanted', 'Epilogue'—appear in *Day by Day*.

6. Hamilton, pp. 403–4.

7. From *Notebook*: see 'For Ann Adden: Coda', *Robert Lowell's Poems: A Selection*, p. 139.

8. Hamilton, pp. 257–8.

9. Ibid., p. 351.

10. Ibid., p. 404.

11. *Life Studies*, p. 35.

12. See Hamilton, p. 168, and the poem 'Man and Wife'.

13. Hamilton, p. 435.

14. 'Since 1939'.

15. Hamilton, p. 358.

16. 'Soft Wood'.

17. Hamilton, p. 132.

18. Ibid., p. 218.

19. Ibid., p. 382.

20. From *Notebook*: see 'The Charles River (3)', *Robert Lowell's Poems: A Selection*, p. 125.

21. 'My eyes have seen . . .' is the last line of the poem 'Dolphin'. 'Florence' is the poem that pities the monsters.

22. *London Review of Books* (17 May–6 June 1984).

23. 'Lancelot Andrewes', *Selected Essays*, p. 335.

24. Hamilton, pp. 99, 100.

25. *The Idiot* (translated by David Magarshack, Penguin edn., reprinted 1981), pp. 256–7.

CHAPTER XVI

1. The first of these books was published in 1975, and the second and third in 1976, in New York. They were discussed by the present writer in an

article in the *New York Review of Books* (24 June 1976) on which this chapter is based.

2. *Letters Home*, p. 60.
3. Ibid., p. 500.
4. Ibid., p. 290.
5. Ibid., pp. 105–7. Butscher, p. 70.
6. Butscher, pp. 13, 376.
7. *New Statesman* (7 December 1962).
8. *A Closer Look at Ariel* (1974), p. 57.
9. *Letters Home*, p. 284.
10. Butscher, pp. 197–8.
11. Kroll: see pp. 8, 12, 26–8, 32, 112.
12. Ibid., pp. 83–5, 114.
13. *Letters Home*, p. 113.
14. *A Closer Look at Ariel*, p. 59.

CHAPTER XVII

1. *The Discovery of the Unconscious*, pp. 124–6, 145–6, 171, 174.
2. *The Principles of Psychology* by William James (2 vols., 1910), i. 379.
3. Ibid., i. 399–400.
4. Ibid., i. 381–4. See Ellenberger, pp. 128–9.
5. *Principles of Psychology*, i. 391–3.
6. *Psychotherapy and Multiple Personality: Selected Essays* by Morton Prince, ed. Nathan Hale Jr. (Cambridge, Massachusetts, 1975): 'The Development and Genealogy of the Misses Beauchamp—A Preliminary Report of a Case of Multiple Personality', p. 151.
7. Ibid., 'The Problem of Personality', pp. 204, 210–11.
8. Ibid., p. 201.
9. By the editor of the volume: p. 10.
10. *Personality,* pp. 441–3.
11. Ibid., p. 451. Murphy's formulation is discussed in *Multiple Personality and the Disintegration of Literary Character: From Oliver Goldsmith to Sylvia Plath* by Jeremy Hawthorn (1983), p. 33.
12. Ibid., pp. 443, 448.
13. Ibid., p. 449.
14. The commendation is carried on the cover of the English edition (Penguin, reprinted 1977), from which quotations are taken.
15. *Sybil*, p. 102.
16. Ibid., pp. 311, 109.
17. Ibid., pp. 309, 310.
18. Ibid., p. 371.
19. Ibid., pp. 374, 395.
20. Ibid., pp. 387, 392.
21. Ibid., pp. 400, 414.
22. Ibid., pp. 341–2.
23. Ibid., pp. 99, 271.
24. Ibid., p. 289.

25. Ibid., p. 379.
26. Ibid., p. 400.
27. Ibid., pp. 108–9, 290.
28. Ibid., p. 411.
29. Ibid., p. 411. *Principles of Psychology,* i. 390.

CHAPTER XVIII

1. *The Adventurer* (New York, 1974): see pp. 13, 149, 154, 163–89, 236.
2. *Dylan Thomas* by Paul Ferris (New York, 1977), pp. 294–6.
3. *Humboldt's Gift* by Saul Bellow (Penguin edn., reprinted 1979), p. 12. *Ragtime* by E. L. Doctorow (1976), pp. 6–9, and see pp. 29, 165, 170, 96–8.
4. From the transcript of a programme broadcast by London Weekend Television. Excerpts appeared in the *London Review of Books* (6–19 May 1982).
5. *Dangling Man* (2nd edn., 1960): see pp. 30, 101, 127–54.
6. *The Victim* (reissued 1965), p. 25.
7. Ibid., pp. 11, 16, 45.
8. Ibid., pp. 264, 244.
9. Ibid., pp. 143, 151.
10. Ibid., pp. 200–1, 25, 219.
11. Ibid., pp. 119, 229.
12. Ibid., p. 256.
13. Ibid., p. 259, *Humboldt's Gift*, p. 18.
14. *Humboldt's Gift*, pp. 7, 20–31, 282.
15. The passage from *Augie March* is referred to in Tony Tanner's *City of Words* (reprinted 1976), where we read (pp. 70–1) that it is important for American heroes, as they sit around in their disguises, to know why they are dissembling, and that they have been 'tempted to abandon society altogether'. See also *Humboldt's Gift*, pp. 423–4.
16. *Humboldt's Gift*, pp. 66, 99, 10, 135, 12, 26.
17. Ibid., p. 216.
18. Ibid., p. 419.
19. Ibid., pp. 115, 236, 299.
20. See *City of Words*, p. 72.
21. 'Some Notes on Recent American Fiction': *The Novel Today*, ed. Malcolm Bradbury (1977), pp. 62, 68.
22. In the transcript mentioned in Note 4 Mr Bellow says: 'My intention in this book was to be hard, to abandon rhetorical flourishes and keep myself to direct statement. I don't think I've ever written a book with so many simple declarative sentences.'
23. *The Dean's December* (1982), p. 122.
24. Ibid., pp. 308, 261.
25. Ibid., pp. 307, 277.
26. Ibid., pp. 122, 290, 310–12.
27. *Fiction as Wisdom*, a collection of essays by Irvin Stock (Pennsylvania State University Press, 1980), contains one on Bellow, and the jacket of the book carries Bellow's comment: 'I thought it quite right about the Romanticism, the early Romanticism, of much that I have written.'

28. *An American Dream* (1965), pp. 15, 20.
29. Ibid., p. 51.
30. Ibid., p. 260.
31. *A Fire on the Moon* (paperback reprint, 1971), p. 429.
32. *Marilyn* (paperback reprint, New York, 1975), pp. 135, 21–2.
33. Ibid., pp. 28, 136–7.
34. *Cockburn's Millennium*, p. 86.
35. *Marilyn*, pp. 302–7.
36. Ibid., pp. 153, 338.
37. Ibid., p. 50.
38. *Of Women and their Elegance*, with photographs by Milton Greene (1981), pp. 28–9.
39. 'This sane and magnanimous book': *London Review of Books* (6 March 1980).
40. *The Executioner's Song* (paperback reprint, 1980), pp. 271, 324.
41. *Advertisements for Myself* (paperback reprint, 1972), pp. 273, 271.
42. *The Executioner's Song*, pp. 106, 305.
43. *The Times* (16 May 1981), *Sunday Times* (17 May 1981).
44. *In the Belly of the Beast: Letters from Prison* (New York, 1981), pp. x, xi, 128.
45. Ibid., p. 76.
46. Ibid., p. xvi; the *Times* (16 January 1982).
47. *The Times* (11 August 1981).
48. *In the Belly of the Beast*, p. xiv.
49. *The Executioner's Song*, pp. 305–6.
50. *In the Belly of the Beast,* p. 21.
51. Ibid., pp. 5, 133, 59, 122.
52. Ibid., p. 8.
53. Ibid., pp. 97, 165.

CHAPTER XIX

1. 'Song of Myself': *Complete Poetry and Collected Prose,* p. 202.
2. *The Ordeal of Mark Twain* by Van Wyck Brooks (paperback reprint, New York, 1955), p. 49.
3. See pp. 101–2 and see Chapter Five, Note 23.
4. *The Complex Fate*, p. 158.
5. *The Eccentric Design*, p. 289.
6. *The Complex Fate*, p. 17.
7. Ibid., pp. 153–4.
8. For the lines from 'Crossing Brooklyn Ferry', see *Leaves of Grass*: *Complete Poetry and Collected Prose*, p. 311. Marius Bewley's essay on Hogg's *Confessions* (*New Statesman*, 26 October 1962) calls attention to the 'representatively human quality in his criminal protagonist' and to the universality of the antinomian bias. The essay was occasioned by Louis Simpson's study of Hogg.
9. Quoted by Stephen Fender in 'The Prodigal in a Far Country Chawing of Husks: Mark Twain's Search for a Style in the West' (*Modern Language Review*, October 1976).

10. See Hannah Arendt's Introduction to the volume of essays by Walter Benjamin, *Illuminations* (New York, 1968), p. 46. For James's life of Hawthorne see Edmund Wilson's *The Shock of Recognition* (2nd edn., New York, 1955), pp. 436, 459.

11. *The Eccentric Design*, p. 18.

12. *Masks and Mirrors* (New York, 1970).

13. *Mr Clemens and Mark Twain* by Justin Kaplan (1967), pp. 153–4.

14. *Sincerity and Authenticity* (1972), pp. 39–42.

15. *The Eccentric Design*, pp. 202–4.

CHAPTER XX

1. *On the Black Hill*, p. 192. This chapter makes use of a review of the novel, by the present writer, which was published in the *London Review of Books* (21 October–3 November 1982).

2. Charles Lamb's words for their relationship, quoted in *Young Charles Lamb 1775–1802* by Winifred Courtney (paperback reprint, 1984), pp. 240–1.

3. *On the Black Hill*, pp. 244–5.

4. *The Viceroy of Ouidah* (paperback reprint, 1982), pp. 16, 14, 22–3.

5. *On the Black Hill*, pp. 118, 216–17.

6. *The Solid Mandala* was discussed by the present writer in a *New Statesman* review (27 May 1966), and some of that discussion is reproduced here.

7. *Success* (paperback edn., 1979), pp. 27, 96, 121.

8. *Other People* (paperback edn., 1982), pp. 70, 201, 34, 75.

9. Ibid., 144, 175, 90.

10. *Money*, p. 198.

11. In his poem 'A Bookshop Idyll'.

12. *Money*, p. 310.

13. Ibid., pp. 192, 65.

14. Ibid., pp. 368, 215, 92, 210, 214, 226–7, 367, 308–9.

CHAPTER XXI

1. See *On Deconstruction* by Jonathan Culler, pp. 128, 133, 182, 248.

2. Ibid., p. 173. The female writer is Hélène Cixous.

3. *Camus* by Conor Cruise O'Brien (1970), p. 20.

4. *The Outsider*, translated by Stuart Gilbert (Penguin edn., reprinted 1978), pp. 26, 62, 83.

5. *Journal 1942–1949* (Gallimard, Paris, 1950), p. 224. The entry is dated 5 July 1944, and its remarks concerning Hogg's novel are repeated at the start of Gide's Introduction to the Cresset Press edition (1947) of the *Confessions*. In this Introduction Gide's first acquaintance with the work is misdated 1924. The error may have been assisted by his reference to a 'recent edition' of the *Confessions*—T. Earle Welby's, presumably, which appeared in that year.

6. *Unreliable Memoirs*, p. 170. This chapter draws on a review of the book published in the *London Review of Books* (22 May–4 June 1980).

7. *The Life of David Hume* by Ernest Mossner (2nd edn., 1980), p. 65.
8. *At the Pillars of Hercules* by Clive James (1979), p. 224.
9. *Unreliable Memoirs*, p.170.
10. *Life of David Hume*, p. 65.
11. *Unreliable Memoirs*, pp. 28–9.
12. Ibid., pp. 102–3.
13. Ibid., p. 14.
14. *The McJazz Manuscripts* by Sandy Brown, ed. David Binns (1979), p. 15. A manuscript of the *Manuscripts* was seen by the present writer, who wrote about it in an article in the *New Review* (May 1976) which supplied material for this chapter.
15. Ibid., p. 14.
16. *Cockburn's Millennium*, p. xiv.
17. *Death of an Idealist* by John Stonehouse (1975), p. 57. *Cockburn's Millennium,* p. 39.
18. *The McJazz Manuscripts*, p. 12.
19. *The Divided Self* by R. D. Laing (Penguin edn., reprinted 1976): see pp. 128, 162, 195.
20. *The McJazz Manuscripts*, pp. 50, 24, 40.
21. The words come from a speech to the House of Commons of 17 February 1607, in which Bacon argued a case, consequential on the Union of the Crowns, for the naturalization of the Scots—to 'take out the marks of a foreigner': *The Letters and the Life of Francis Bacon* by James Spedding (7 vols.), iii (1868), pp. 314–15. Bacon adds that the Scotsman is foreign enough to seem like some 'fierce horse' which can give better service but is harder to manage.
22. *The McJazz Manuscripts*, pp. 28–9.
23. *Newsweek* (20 December 1980). The present discussion of John Lennon's death began as a tribute published at this time in the *London Review of Books* (22 January–4 February 1981).
24. Ibid.
25. *New Statesman* (28 February and 13 March 1964). The article was by Paul Johnson, who had seen these wretched fans on television: 'What a bottomless chasm of vacuity they reveal! The huge faces, bloated with cheap confectionery and smeared with chain-store make-up . . .'.

INDEX